URBAN
PLANNING and
SOCIAL POLICY

EDITED BY BERNARD J. FRIEDEN
AND ROBERT MORRIS

Urban Planning and Social Policy

BASIC BOOKS, INC., Publishers | New York | London

URBAN
PLANNING and
SOCIAL POLICY

EDITED BY Bernard J. Frieden
AND Robert Morris

© 1968 by Basic Books, Inc.
Library of Congress Catalog Card Number: 68–16874
Manufactured in the United States of America
74 75 76   10 9 8 7 6 5

TO ELAINE AND SARA

THE AUTHORS

Eveline M. Burns, an economist, is Professor at the Columbia University School of Social Work. She has been president of the National Conference of Social Welfare and vice-president of the American Economic Association. She has also been a member of numerous governmental commissions, including the Advisory Commission on Area Development and the Commission on Social Security for the Secretary of Health, Education, and Welfare; and a consultant for many federal agencies, including the Federal Reserve Board and the Treasury. Among her many publications are *Social Security and Public Policy; The American Social Security System; The British Unemployment Program;* and *Toward Social Security.* She is an honorary Fellow of the London School of Economics.

Robert A. Dahl is Professor of Political Science at Yale and author of *Who Governs? Democracy and Power in an American City; Politics, Economics, and Welfare* (with Charles E. Lindblom); and *Congress and Foreign Policy.*

Preston David is Director of the Department of Social and Community Services, New York City Housing Authority. He was formerly Associate Director of the Federation Employment and Guidance Service and of the Jewish Child Care Association, both of New York City.

Robert A. Dentler is Deputy Director of the Center for Urban Education in New York City and Associate Professor of Sociology and Education at Teachers College, Columbia University. He is the co-author of a number of books, including *The Politics of Urban Renewal; Politics and Social Life;* and *Big City Dropouts and Illiterates.*

Marc Fried is a psychologist who has written extensively on psychological and social problems associated with social change. He is Research Professor and Executive Director of the Institute of Human Sciences at Boston College. Formerly he was Research Director of the Center for Community Studies (Department of Psychiatry of Massachusetts General Hospital and the Harvard Medical School), studying the West End of Boston, a working-class community displaced by urban renewal.

Bernard J. Frieden is Associate Professor of City Planning at M.I.T. and a re-search member of the M.I.T.–Harvard Joint Center for Urban Studies. From 1962 to 1965 he was editor of the *Journal of the American Institute of Planners*. He has been a consultant to several federal agencies and served as a staff member of President Johnson's 1965 Task Force on Urban Affairs. His publications include *The Future of Old Neighborhoods* and a report for the Advisory Commission on Intergovernmental Relations, *Metropolitan America: Challenge to Federalism*.

Herbert J. Gans is Senior Research Sociologist at the Center for Urban Education in New York City and Adjunct Professor of Sociology and Education at Teachers College, Columbia University. He is the author of *The Urban Villagers: Group and Class in the Life of Italian-Americans; The Levittowners: Ways of Life and Politics in a New Suburban Community;* and the forthcoming *Mass Culture: An Analysis of High and Popular Culture in America*.

Eunice S. Grier is Director, Research Division, U. S. Commission on Civil Rights, and *George W. Grier* is with the Washington Center for Metropolitan Studies. Formerly he was Coordinator of Anti-Poverty and Social Welfare Programs, District of Columbia. Both have served widely as staff members and consultants to federal, state, and local governments and to private agencies concerned with housing, planning, and human relations. They are co-authors of two books: *Equality and Beyond* and *Privately Developed Interracial Housing*.

William G. Grigsby is Research Associate Professor of City Planning and Associate Professor of Finance at the University of Pennsylvania, where he is also associated with the Institute for Environmental Studies. He is the author of *Housing Markets and Public Policy* and co-author (with Chester Rapkin) of *Residential Renewal in the Urban Core* and *The Demand for Housing in Eastwick*.

David A. Grossman is Assistant Director of the New York City Bureau of the Budget. During the first two years of operations of the Office of Economic Opportunity, he was Director of its Program Management Division, Community Action Program. Formerly he was Director of the Community Development Branch, Urban Renewal Administration, which administered the Community Renewal Program.

Edgar M. Hoover is Professor of Economics and Director of the Center for Regional Economic Studies at the University of Pittsburgh. He has been Director of the Economic Study of the Pittsburgh Region, sponsored by the Pittsburgh Regional Planning Association, and previously participated in the New York Metropolitan Region Study while a Visiting Professor of Economics at Harvard. In addition to the three volumes of the Pittsburgh Region Study, his books include *Anatomy of a Metropolis* (co-author with Raymond Vernon); *Projection of a Metropolis* (with Barbara R. Berman and Benjamin Chinitz); *Population Growth and Economic Development in Low-Income Countries* (with Ansley J. Coale); and *The Location of Economic Activity*.

Avner Hovne is Economic Adviser to the Israeli Ministry of Labor. In addition to his work as an economist in several positions in the government of Israel, he has served as economic consultant to the Puerto Rico Planning Board, the International Labor Office in Geneva, and UNESCO. His publications include *Automation: Experiences Abroad and Recommendations for Israel* and *The Labor Force in Israel.*

Joan Levin is a sociologist who worked as research associate on the study of the West End of Boston, a working-class community displaced by urban renewal. She is now Assistant Research Professor at the Florence Heller Graduate School for Advanced Studies in Social Welfare, Brandeis University.

Peter Marris has been associated with the Institute of Community Studies, London, since 1955. He surveyed urban renewal in eleven American cities in 1961, and in 1964 he returned to the United States for a year to evaluate the "gray area" programs of the Ford Foundation. He has also studied slum clearance in Lagos, Nigeria, and is now working on a study of entrepreneurship and social change in Kenya. Among his books are *Family and Social Change in an African City; The Experience of Higher Education;* and, with Martin Rein, *Dilemmas of Social Reform: Poverty and Community Action in the United States.*

S. M. Miller is Professor of Sociology, Maxwell Graduate School, and Senior Research Associate, Youth Development Center, at Syracuse University. In 1965–1966 he was Visiting Professor of Education and Sociology at New York University. He is an Associate Editor of the *American Sociological Review* and has been a consultant to numerous social welfare and labor union organizations. Among his books are *Applied Sociology: Opportunities and Problems* (co-editor); *Max Weber: A Reader* (editor); and several forthcoming works: *Poverty and The Great Society* (with Martin Rein); *Education and Social Class* (with Frank Riessman); and *Social Mobility and Economic Development.*

Robert Morris is Professor of Social Planning at the Florence Heller Graduate School for Advanced Studies in Social Welfare, Brandeis University. He was Editor-in-Chief of the *Journal of Social Work* from 1962 to 1966 and a member of the editorial board of the *Encyclopedia of Social Work.* He is co-author (with Robert Binstock and Martin Rein) of *Feasible Planning for Social Change;* editor of *Centrally Planned Change: Prospects and Concepts;* and editor of *Trends and Issues in Jewish Social Welfare in the United States, 1899–1958.*

Richard C. Murray has conducted project studies for neighborhood community organizations and is the author of a forthcoming book on the subject.

Harvey S. Perloff is Director of Regional and Urban Studies at Resources for the Future, Inc., in Washington. Formerly Professor of Planning at the University of Chicago, Dr. Perloff has been an adviser on social and economic planning as well as urban development. He is the author of *Education for Planning: City, State, and Regional.*

Lee Rainwater, Professor of Sociology at Washington University, is currently directing a five-year study of social and community problems in the Pruitt-Igoe housing project of St. Louis and a two-year study of the poverty of white families in St. Louis. He is the author of *And the Poor Get Children* and *Family Design: Marital Sexuality, Family Size and Contraception* and co-author of *Workingman's Wife: Her Personality, Work and Life Styles* and *The Professional Scientist.*

Chester Rapkin is Professor of City Planning at Columbia University. Until recently he was Professor of City Planning and Professor of Finance at the University of Pennsylvania, where he also served as Chairman of the Urban Studies Group at the Institute for Environment Studies. In 1965 he was Staff Director of President Johnson's Task Force on Urban Affairs. He has been a consultant in housing and economics to many governmental agencies and private developers. Among his books are *Residential Renewal in the Urban Core* and *The Demand for Housing in Eastwick* (co-author of both with William G. Grigsby) and *Urban Traffic: A Function of Land Use* (with Robert B. Mitchell).

Everett W. Reimer is Consultant to the Secretary of Education, Commonwealth of Puerto Rico. Previously he was Social Development Advisor to the Coordinator, Alliance for Progress. As Executive Secretary of the Puerto Rico Committee on Human Resources from 1954 to 1961, he advised on methodological aspects of social planning.

Martin Rein is Associate Professor in the Department of Social Work and Social Research at Bryn Mawr College. He is also a lecturer in the Department of City Planning, University of Pennsylvania. Dr. Rein has been a consultant to many federal and private agencies and is co-author of *Feasible Planning for Social Change* and co-author (with Peter Marris) of *Dilemmas of Social Reform: Poverty and Community Action in the United States.*

Janet S. Reiner is a consultant and researcher in social planning who has worked with the Office of Economic Opportunity, American Friends Service Committee, and the Institute for Environmental Studies and the Fels Institute of the University of Pennsylvania.

Thomas A. Reiner is Associate Professor of Regional Science at the University of Pennsylvania and author of *The Place of the Ideal Community in Urban Planning.*

Bayard Rustin is a leading figure in the civil rights movement and organized the 1963 March on Washington. He is Executive Director of the A. Philip Randolph Institute.

Alvin L. Schorr is Deputy Assistant Secretary for Individual and Family Services in the Department of Health, Education, and Welfare. Since July 1966 he has been Editor-in-Chief of *Social Work.* Previously he was Deputy Chief, Research and Plans, with the Office of Economic Opportunity and a family-life specialist on the research staff of the Social Security Administration. He is the author of *Slums and Social Insecurity; Filial Responsibility in the Modern American Family; Social Security and Social Services in France;* and *Poor Kids: A Report on Children in Poverty.*

Thomas D. Sherrard is Professor of Urban Affairs and Director of the Urban Development Institute at the Calumet Campus of Purdue University, Hammond, Indiana.

Charles E. Silberman is a member of the Board of Editors of *Fortune* and author of *Crisis in Black and White*.

Robert M. Solow is Professor of Economics at M.I.T. He has served on the staff of President Kennedy's Council of Economic Advisors and is the author of numerous articles and books on economic theory, including *The Nature and Sources of Unemployment in the United States* and *Capital Theory and the Rate of Return*.

Edward V. Sparer is Legal Director of the Center on Social Welfare Policy and Law at the Columbia University School of Social Work. Formerly he served as Director of the Legal Services Unit at Mobilization for Youth in New York.

Melvin M. Webber is Professor of City Planning at the University of California, Berkeley. He is a former editor of the *Journal of the American Institute of Planners* and co-author of *Explorations into Urban Structure*.

James Q. Wilson is Associate Professor of Government and Member of the Faculty of the Graduate School of Public Administration at Harvard University. From 1963 to 1966 he was Director of the Joint Center for Urban Studies of M.I.T. and Harvard University. He is co-author (with Edward C. Banfield) of *City Politics* and author of *Negro Politics: The Search for Leadership* and *The Amateur Democrat: Club Politics in Three Cities*.

Eleanor P. Wolf, Associate Professor in the Department of Sociology and Anthropology at Wayne State University, has long been active as a professional intergroup-relations worker. She has written extensively on race relations and housing and was recently Co-Director of a series of studies of change and renewal sponsored by the Detroit Community Renewal Program.

Robert C. Wood is Under Secretary of Housing and Urban Development. Before his appointment to this post he was Professor of Political Science and Head of the Political Science Department at M.I.T. He has often served as an adviser to government and was Chairman of President Johnson's 1965 Task Force on Urban Affairs. Dr. Wood is the author of *Suburbia: Its People and Their Politics* and *1400 Governments*, a volume of the New York Metropolitan Region Study.

PREFACE

The initial conception of this volume arose out of a concern with the accumulation of special difficulties which cluster in and plague major cities. This accumulation of trouble threatens to undermine confidence that the urban environment can be controlled and shaped to satisfy the physical, economic, social, and esthetic needs of urban dwellers. This concern has been shared by many who have cried havoc, have produced elaborate plans, or have worried in private.

Several years ago we decided to try an unconventional way of understanding the modern city by linking the different concepts and methods of our two fields. We organized a joint seminar to explore the interplay between urban planning and social policy with the help of M.I.T. graduate students in city planning and Brandeis University graduate students in social welfare planning. The seminar has continued as a useful testing ground for expanding the concepts of city and social planning, and it has provided the basis for this book. For the opportunity to conduct this seminar we are grateful to our students and to the Massachusetts Institute of Technology and Brandeis University. Our colleagues have given steady encouragement, particularly Charles I. Schottland, Dean of the Florence Heller Graduate School for Advanced Studies in Social Welfare at Brandeis University. Professors Arnold Gurin and Robert Perlman of the Heller School also participated in teaching the seminar.

Professor Edward C. Banfield of Harvard University first suggested to us the need for a book which would bring together relevant contributions from the growing but scattered literature on urban social policy. Our greatest debt is to the authors who gave permission to reprint their work, for they have agreed to share the results of their varied experiences and their insights into many complex facets of urban life. Only by a pooling of such expert knowledge is it possible to construct a hopeful and coherent approach to the modern city. Their publishers were generous in permitting this re-use of their material.

The tempo of urban change is so rapid, and so pressing has been the demand to act, that several aspects of the subject demanded that original and specially commissioned articles be added. We are grateful to Marc Fried, Joan Levin, Martin Rein, Peter Marris, and David Grossman for contributing the unpublished results of research and of firsthand experience with innovative urban programs.

Many individuals shared in the unglamorous chores of editing and preparing manuscripts. Among them, Barbara Isaacson, Adeline Shumsker, Colene Abramson, and Cornelia Menger were especially helpful.

As always, our wives contributed fully, by releasing many claims on our time, by acute if informal criticism, and by patient forbearance.

BERNARD J. FRIEDEN
ROBERT MORRIS

January 1968

Contents

Part I APPROACHES TO SOCIAL PLANNING

Editors' Introduction

The subject of this volume is the conscious, willed effort to improve the conditions of life, and the opportunities for a good life, open to some 75 per cent of the American population now living in cities and towns. The terms in which such an inquiry is usually undertaken have become familiar with repetition: planning, urbanism, and social policy. They convey a sense of definition, however, which is more illusory than real, for each term is heavily weighted with subjective and personal values. Their use helps us clarify problems of the city, but they conceal those limitations of present technology which militate against mastering them.

Influences shaping the urban social condition

Variations in the character and composition of American cities are considerable and repeat, with differences in scale, the character of cities throughout recorded history. Nevertheless, certain conditions give to the modern city their special character and thus help to outline the nature of urban problems. The size of major urban areas has increased at an extraordinary rate during the past sixty years. By 1960, nearly 65 per cent of the American population lived in 212 standard metropolitan statistical areas, and this proportion is expected to increase to 75—and perhaps 85—per cent over the next thirty years. This growth has been a compound of flight from rural areas, a rising birth rate, and a declining infant mortality rate.[1] Such an inflow of population to urban centers has strained their capacity to house this population and to provide it with essential services.

At the same time, ethnic, racial, and economic differences have produced tensions that sharpen the internal redistribution of urban populations. City dwellers have moved at a very rapid rate from the city center to suburbs sprawling far into the former countryside, creating new political jurisdictions as they grow. Between 1950 and 1960, when the population of metropolitan areas increased in number by 24.6 per cent, the population of central cities rose only 1.5 per cent, holding 1950 municipal boundaries constant. By contrast, the numbers of suburban residents increased by 50 per cent. The very poor, the elderly, and the Negro dominate the city center. In several central cities the white population will soon be a minority. Cultural activities, services, education, and even employment are spread widely through a large urban area rather than concentrated in the city center. Technological and economic shifts are almost continuous, and a large part of the population is mobile both physically and economically. At the same time, a significant minority of the population does not share in the benefits of this mobility but remains caught in a cycle of poverty, inadequate education, and unsuitable housing.

The essays in this book describe some of the current approaches to the development of practical and workable ways to improve the conditions of urban living, however those are in the end defined, and thus to improve man's management of the urban environment which the twentieth century has produced. Two main approaches have been selected, that of the city planner and that of the social planner. These two disciplines have had concrete responsibilities in the past: they have supplied major guidelines for the shaping of urban policies; they have exposed critical issues; and they are becoming increasingly influential in the operation of governmental programs. Economic planning, which clearly affects city life, has been omitted because its main development has been at the national level dealing with the gross national product, gross income distribution, and economic cycles, although Perloff and Hovne treat, in later sections, of the convergence between economic and social planning. Certain public health activities might well have been included but their approach has been quite specialized.

The search for more comprehensive approaches to urban planning

The city planning and social planning approaches converge most clearly in the scope of action for which they call, in the comprehensiveness of their views, and in their common stress upon spreading urban benefits to all the population. The impulse toward comprehensiveness seems about to close a circle which started at the close of the nineteenth century when the conversion of the economy from an agricultural to an industrial base after the Civil War, and the inflow of European immigrants, combined to produce serious urban social problems which were strange to a pioneer nation. The citizens of that time, early builders of the social sciences (economics, sociology, and political science), and political leaders were drawn together in a search for ways to counter the noxious effects of rapid urban industrialization—an unskilled labor force drawn from agriculture and thrust unready into new city life, gross overcrowding, child labor, sweated and cottage labor in the city, concentrated poverty, growing crime and juvenile delinquency, deterioration of city areas and slums, cycles of depression alternating with great wealth accumulation by a few. Whether to relieve the misery of the poor, to improve the quality of the city, or simply to govern in a city of unruly forces—citizens and experts were drawn together to improve the life for all people in the city.[2]

Following World War I, these several groups drew apart as each began to develop its distinctive pattern of work. City planning, engaged directly with the governmental forces of the city, became technically proficient in zoning, land use, and traffic patterns. Social science, or at least sociology, became concerned with the evolution of general laws and abstract constructs about society which were, for the time being, quite removed from the daily reality of urban life. Even the Chicago school, with its concentration upon city and community, ended up with primary attention to description rather than prescription. And social welfare became more and more a profession and less a calling, giving its first attention to financial and psychological help for underprivileged individuals rather than to the social causes and remedies for the distress.

By 1960 the inadequacy of these more specialized approaches became well recognized. Webber, Morris, and Rein consider, each in his own way, the necessary interrelationship between several criteria: a decent modern environment includes not only physical comfort and work, but education, services, and social relationships which open opportunity for all; physical elements are not sufficient to establish the urban environment; and social measures are not powerful enough either; change which occurs by chance is not necessarily suitable for human needs. Thus, work and the economy, culture, patterns of behavior, physical environments, and the politics of decision-making become web of interacting forces.[3]

To this now recognized need for more comprehensive approaches city and social planning bring distinctive contributions. City planning has developed methods for shaping the physical environment and the spatial organization of activities in accord with social goals and changing standards. It has a capacity to analyze quantitative data such as population movements, economic resources, and land values; it has a familiarity with the mechanisms of municipal policy-making and with the legal control of urban development; and it has unique tools for depicting environmental and social relationships. However, it lacks an intimate connection with the diversity of human wants expressed in the reality of urban life, although it gropes toward an identity with human aspirations beyond those expressed by political power groups. Most significantly, city planners have come to recognize how inevitably the decisions about use of urban space shade into decisions about social policy: Who will live where? What will the future population of the city consist of? What influences people and groups to use urban space the way they do? For the city planner, the gap is too great between the kind of life most people seek and which is technically feasible—security, beauty, comfort, and stimulation combined—and the reality of congestion, squalor, ugliness, insecurity, and monotony in the modern city.

City planning is, by and large, conducted by departments of city government, responsible and accountable to elected officials. In recent years, the locus of such responsibility has broadened to include, in varying degrees, departments or commissions of city planning, urban renewal, housing, and transportation. To a very limited extent, non-governmental voluntary associations for regional planning have evolved but their role is, with few exceptions, educational.

By contrast, the American social welfare system is an imperfectly articulated network made up of over 100,000 independent agencies or associations, most of which are organized on a local or state basis although the largest are instrumentalities of the federal government. Policy-making is widely decentralized through the autonomous character of these agencies.

Functionally, the system contains separate types of agencies each developed empirically for dealing with a loosely defined general problem: children, families, the aged, the delinquent, the sick, and income maintenance. Each of these general areas is further broken down into an intricate analysis of specialized agencies and services. In the area of income maintenance, there are: the federally aided programs of aid to dependent families and children, aid for the aged, aid for the blind, aid for the totally disabled; the state programs of general relief, veterans' aid, workmen's compensation, and unemployment insurance; and the wholly federal programs of social security, permanent and total disability under social security, and veterans' benefits, to name only a few.

In the area of child welfare, there are separate voluntary agencies for placing dependent children, protecting neglected children, treating disturbed and predelinquent children, and caring for the sick or rehabilitating the handicapped. There are also state governmental agencies dealing with the same subjects. To these are added federally financed programs of social services, services to children in their own homes, treatment of handicapped children, and financial support through the social security act; the veterans' administration; and public relief (aid to dependent families and children).

The organizational varieties are further compounded by the religious or cultural origin of many voluntary services, which are organized primarily for Catholic, Protestant, or Jewish communities.

This network is very loosely coordinated or—more accurately—the units are kept in communication with each other by several hundred local and regional welfare or social planning councils. These have limited authority over agency policy, but do serve to keep the major components in touch with each other. Within the limitations of scant staff and budget, the councils conduct social studies and develop guides for the evolution of welfare services.

The social welfare system, which is in daily communication with the reality of individuals, their wants and difficulties, has seen mainly the pathological conditions and has been out of touch with circumstances on which the more successful majority thrives. It has been in touch with only one segment of political influence, that of middle-class, professional, voluntary leadership, which has so often produced champions of the community good in opposition to the pressure of other special interests. It has held firm to the unity of individual and social forces, although its techniques have been limited.

This loosely knit system accounts for an expenditure of some $50 billion annually for social insurance and welfare. If health and educational expenditures are taken into account, the total rises to over $100 billion. About 15 per cent of this total originates in private philanthropic sources. A manpower pool of nearly 120,000 social workers staffs the system, supported by an unknown number of aides and clerical and maintenance workers. Despite the dispersion of authority over 100,000 independent administrative units, the field is held together by common values, aims, and methods so that it constitutes a major, if cumbersome, means for dealing with urban problems.

It is natural that two such different but partly complementing groups should be again drawn together as each widens its perspectives and approaches the working boundaries of the other, thus renewing a liaison begun seventy-five years ago. The city planner thinks about jobs, job training, low- as well as middle-income housing, educational facilities, citizen groups and associations, race relations, and human resources; the social planner begins to consider the requirements of people regardless of income, the movement of urban populations, the reorganization of urban space, the housing of people. By the middle 1960's, as these authors make clear, this rapprochement is mainly a search for comprehensiveness in viewing or in perceiving urban difficulties which have long been present. Among these difficulties, the persistence of poverty for a large segment of the population and of racial discrimination have led to a national concern and public action. The war on poverty and the civil rights movement have been twin forces for a coalescence among various types of urban planning. The selection of these issues is justified not only by a scale of priorities and a sense of common justice; they have complex roots and demand broad-scale as well as comprehensive remedies, cutting across several disciplines. The road to "extended access to opportunity" and "jobs, minimum income, and decent environment for all" is reached by way of blighted areas, economically declining districts, and the income, leisure, and social dilemmas of the poor.

The evolution of technical resources

Achievement of such broad goals depends not only upon a way of viewing the situation, but upon the refinement of methods and techniques sufficient for the task. The papers presented here discuss the current state of technical evolution and the difficulty inherent in attempting to fashion social concepts into tangible and quantifiable terms which permit plan, projection, and measurement. The concept of a healthy neighborhood or environment, for example, needs to have its specific elements identified before methods can be developed which are more science than intuition. Fortunately, rule-of-thumb criteria are available about differing class patterns of living and about the distinctions between a disorganized and a well-integrated neighborhood community. Webber and Gans have each taken steps to formulate such concepts into operative terms, although exact techniques are still lacking. If the focus is displacement and new housing, how is community life maintained? If jobs are the center of attention, how can we reconcile housing patterns with the ever-widening geographical distribution of economic organization in which workers change jobs frequently, living close to work today and twenty or fifty miles away tomorrow? If adequate public facilities are the planning focus, how shall we balance the claims for centralized structures versus the desire for decentralization?

These papers also identify new and more important civic roles which planners have been given in urban life and which the demand for technical competence has increased. Cost-benefit analyses have helped improve the engineering and economic aspects of modern life, and these methods are now being adapted to social considerations as well.[4] Forecasting and prediction have been established in the physical and the economic world, and today planners for the city are trying to improve the predicting and forecasting techniques applied to social phenomena and human behavior.[5]

All such advances depend, in the end, upon access to resources and the philosophy which governs their distribution, and it is here that the relationship between economic and social planning becomes most clear. Webber treats of both the value and the factual foundations in his thesis of an expanding, wealth-developing society which uses its gain for desired social ends. This view is buttressed by the overall growth in the American economy. Between 1940 and 1961 the Gross National Product of the nation increased by 500 per cent, while the population increased by 40 per cent. Despite inequities in the distribution of this growth, the nation's economic capacity to carry out its plan seems clear.

However, technical advances in the service of a social ideal bring in their wake some concern about the risk of technocratic dictation in a democratic society. These issues are dealt with at many levels, but usually to justify the planner's new role; and, although the authors selected are optimistic about the political implications, the reservations of other writers are worth mentioning. Seeley, for one, believes that the partnership of planning and administrative experts with legislative policy-makers introduces a real weakening of the citizen function in making basic policy choices in a representative democracy; whereas the proponents of local community development and local initiative argue that no decisions and plans are worthwhile, regardless of their technical perfectibility, if the citizen directly affected does not make decisions at each step of the way.[6]

Whatever view one takes, that of the expert or of the citizen, the need to master quite complex technical processes, such as those just mentioned, is clear if the general aims are to be achieved by rational action.

Restructuring the jurisdictions for planning

The clarification of goals and the evolution of means for urban planning are taking place on a new scale, in which metropolitan areas, or regions, have replaced the city once defined by sharp geographical and political boundaries. Urban populations have spread into many conflicting jurisdictions, each of which plays some part in the creation of urban tension and is necessary for resolution. However, jurisdictional rivalries seriously impede both analysis and cooperative action; there is lacking either a dominant city core or a supervening state authority capable of introducing a coherent approach; social and class differences among sections of the metropolitan region are diverse, not cohering; resources are scarce and competition sharp; needs and resources are unevenly distributed. City planning departments and social planning agencies have evolved within the confines of the older city jurisdictions, and few have been able to extend their structure or their authority to encompass this new and wide canvass of urban life.[7]

Various approaches have been proposed but few are beyond the experimental testing stage. Supermetropolitan governments have been suggested to subordinate existing jurisdictions, but the latter have had too strong an appeal to separate interests of many groups which now constitute the present cities and suburbs. The Office of Economic Opportunity and the Department of Housing and Urban Development of the federal government have begun to introduce administrative devices by which the federal government can aid regions to cope with regional problems; and the Advisory Commission on Intergovernmental Relations has explored the subject in depth. But these can only be considered the initial steps to achieve the regional approach which most of these authors propose. In the meantime, their analyses of the situation constitute the framework against which the search continues.

Until new structures and forms of urban organization emerge, a great deal of planning effort is directed at introducing flexibility, cooperation, or change in the behavior of existing organizations and political entities which make up the structure of the modern city. Such efforts have had to confront the natural tendency for social organizations of all kinds toward the stasis which means resistance to change and to cooperation, unless self-interest is clearly served.[8] Reliance upon an untempered interplay of group interests has produced the persisting difficulties with which this volume opens; and earlier planning concepts or theories about organizational behavior proved insufficient to insure the kind of cooperation and flexibility which the times require. This has led to the deeper study of how organizations select their policies and how they can be encouraged to change. One result of this search is an enhancement in the role and influence of the executive branches of government, which constitute the usual employment base for urban planners.

If this assessment of the role of planning is accurate, then planners for the city will continue to move along the paths here outlined: from intuition and trial or error to a technically sophisticated methodology, yet infused with a continuity of social ethic and idealism which seeks the wider distribution of the good life made possible by science and technology.

NOTES

1. See Albert Rose, "Social Services in the Modern Metropolis," *Social Service Review*, XXXVII, No. 4 (December, 1963), 375–388, for a summary of these trends.
2. Robert H. Bremner, *From the Depths: The Discovery of Poverty* (New York: New York University Press, 1956); and Roy Lubove, *The Progressives and the Slums* (Pittsburgh: University of Pittsburgh Press, 1962).
3. See such diverse reports, among others, as: Harold Kaplan, *Urban Renewal Politics* (New York: Columbia University Press, 1963); and Martin Meyerson and Edward C. Banfield, *Politics, Planning, and the Public Interest* (Glencoe, Ill.: The Free Press, 1955).
4. Bertram M. Gross, "Toward a System of National Social Accounts," prepared for the American Academy of Arts and Sciences, Committee on Space Efforts and Society (June, 1964).
5. For prediction applied to social phenomena, see Bertrand de Jouvenal, *The Art of Conjecture* (New York: Basic Books, 1966); Daniel Bell, "Twelve Modes of Prediction," *Daedalus*, XCIII (1964), 846–847; and "Urban Development Models: New Tools for Planning," special issue of the *Journal of the American Institute of Planners*, XXXI (May, 1965).
6. See John Seeley, "Central Planning: Prologue to a Critique," in Robert Morris (ed.), *Centrally Planned Change*, (New York: National Association of Social Workers, 1965).
7. See Part VI, especially Frieden, Chapter 20, for a further treatment of possible approaches.
8. Robert Morris and Robert H. Binstock, *Feasible Planning for Social Change* (New York: Columbia University Press, 1966); and David Braybrooke and Charles E. Lindblom, *A Strategy of Decision* (New York: The Free Press, 1963).

1

Comprehensive Planning and Social Responsibility

MELVIN M. WEBBER

A time for re-examination

The period of postwar prosperity has launched what appears to be a golden age in city planning. Keynoters at professional meetings have been proclaiming the coming-of-age to ever-larger audiences of men who are themselves struck by their sudden popularity and by their marks on the city's skyline. Never before have we been accorded such status as we now enjoy; never have so many governmental and civic leaders been so openly dependent upon our counsel; never has the American city planning movement been in a position to influence the welfare of so many Americans so profoundly. And yet, never has the path of righteousness been less clearly marked out.

Dating from 1909, when the first National Conference on City Planning was called to consider the problems of population congestion, the city planning movement has been fueled by deep-rooted concerns for the conditions of urban life. The plight of the immigrant groups, crowding into the big-city tenements, provoked a wave of social reform in search of effective means for attacking poverty and for accelerating social mobility. A sense of crisis and personal mission marked those early beginnings of the city planning, housing, social welfare, public health, and the related helping professions; but by now, despite the persistence of immigrant poverty and despair, these have been considerably calmed. The natural course of professionalization has taken its toll, by turning many would-be missionaries into security-conscious bureaucrats. But, potentially more important than that, the processes of professionalization are also establishing the channels through which the findings of the social sciences are being fed into practice settings. One result of the expanding flow of knowledge is the transformation of many do-gooders into good-doers, as Meyerson once phrased it. Another result is the introduction of a crop of new doubts about our traditional approaches to human betterment.

For generations it had been generally understood that the physical environment was a major determinant of social behavior and a direct contributor to individuals' welfare. Having accepted professional responsibility for

From *Journal of the American Institute of Planners*, XXIX (November, 1963), 232–241. An earlier version was presented at the 1963 AIP Government Relations and Planning Policy Conference.

the physical environment, the city planner was thus accorded a key role as agent of human welfare: the clearly prescribed therapy for the various social pathologies was improvement of the physical setting. If only well-designed and well-sited houses, playgrounds, and community facilities could be substituted for the crowded and dilapidated housing and neighborhoods of the city's slums, then the incidence of crime, delinquency, narcotics addiction, alcoholism, broken homes, and mental illness would tumble. Acculturation of ethnic, racial, and other minority groups to the American, middle-class, urban ways-of-life but awaited their introduction to the American, middle-class, physical environment.

As the findings of systematic research into the relations between social-and-physical aspects of environments and social behavior have been accumulating, however, what were once stable pillars of understanding are melting down to folklore, heartfelt wishes, and, more typically, partial truths embedded within complex networks of causes. The simple one-to-one cause-and-effect links that once tied houses and neighborhoods to behavior and welfare are coming to be seen as but strands in highly complex webs that, in turn, are woven by the intricate and subtle relations that mark social, psychic, economic, and political systems. The simple clarity of the city planning profession's role is thus being dimmed by the clouds of complexity, diversity, and the resulting uncertainty that seem to be the inevitable consequences of scientific inquiry and of the deeper understanding that inquiry brings.

But simultaneously, while social scientists are questioning city planning's central doctrine of physical environmental determinism, other critics are decrying the powerful consequences that are alleged to follow in the wake of recent physical developments. On the one hand the suburban housing tracts are accused of spawning a generation of deprived children, who are being reared by neurotic, coffee-addicted mothers in a matriarchal society from which traffic-stressed fathers and most other dissimilar people are all but excluded. On the other hand, central city redevelopment is charged with dispossessing lower-income groups of their preferred habitats, inflicting psychic disturbance, and destroying their social communities. In turn, the design of the new high-rise housing is indicted for breeding a new, sterile, culturally disinherited species.

It is very appropriate, then, in the midst of these seemingly conflicting contentions, that we should again seek to re-examine our roles as agents in the service of the city's people. We may quite properly ask ourselves again, what are our purposes? In what ways can we, who hold such large responsibility for the physical city, so conduct our affairs as to affect positively the lives of its residents?

To extend access to opportunity

The city planner's responsibilities relate primarily to the physical and locational aspects of development within a local government's jurisdiction. Although this focus of attention derives in part from the idea of environmental determinism and in part from the belief that paramount values are intrinsic to the physical city, his activities have been directed to these features of the city for important instrumental reasons as well.

Local governments are charged with building certain large and costly public works which, once constructed, are likely to exert powerful and continuing influences upon locational choices made in the private sector of the urban economy. In turn, some of these choices may contribute to changes in the social-psychic-economic-political environments within which people live, and may therefore exert at least indirect influences upon their welfare. Decisions on these investments therefore demand the most deliberate efforts to improve rationality—to help assure (1) that the distribution of the benefits and the costs among the city's publics is consciously intended and democratically warranted, (2) that levels and priorities of investments are so staged as to induce the desired repercussions in the private markets, and (3) that public resources are used for those projects and programs promising the highest social payoffs.

Although it is true that we have overestimated the roles that buildings play in shaping social behavior, it is nonetheless also true that some aspects of the physical environment can bring appreciable direct benefits to the city's residents. Imaginative and carefully designed buildings, streets, and open spaces are in themselves direct rewards of an advanced society; and the visual qualities of the physical environment warrant considerably more attention than they have been receiving. The beautiful city remains a goal we have yet to achieve.

Decent, sanitary, and spacious housing is itself one of the salient attributes of the good life, and our effort to accomplish the Congressional objective of "a decent home and a suitable living environment for every American family" properly remains a high-priority goal to which our profession is dedicated. Similarly, the range of facilities that municipalities construct—as accommodations for the various health, education, recreation, and other human-service agencies—necessarily affects the qualities of the services rendered; and, as inseparable aspects of the services, these facilities can contribute to full lives for the beneficiaries.

But the locational arrangements of facilities and activities bear upon the qualities of urban living in more subtle ways, too. The urban settlement has always stood at the center of civilization—the place at which the largest varieties of goods, services, and ideas are produced and distributed, and, therefore, where the most, and the most diverse, human interaction occurs. Here is where the individual is able most readily to tap the accumulated riches of the culture. This is because bare physical distance works as a barrier to human interaction. As its unique and most important commodity, the city offers reduced distances between partners to a friendship, and between sellers and buyers, employers and employed, informers and informed, helpers and helped. Metropolitan areas have flourished in our age precisely because that type of spatial arrangement has expanded people's opportunities to find fruitful associations with others.

Having been assigned responsibility for guiding land-use patterns, we seek, then, to induce those patterns that will effectively increase accessibility to the diverse opportunities for productive social intercourse that are latent in an advanced civilization.

Recent improvements in transportation, combined with recent increases in incomes and other familiar changes, have made it possible for many families and firms to gain spacious quarters in the amiable outlying areas, while they simultaneously endeavor to maintain accessibility to expanding varieties of activities and sources of learning. In this time of rapid suburban development, we are striving, through further improvements in transportation and communication, to help these groups reconcile their new-found locational freedom with their growing capacities to pursue diverse interests with persons who are spatially removed.

Some classes of business and industrial establishments continue to depend upon the external economies offered by concentrated business districts, while the society as a whole continues to depend upon the flow of information and ideas that concentrated centers have traditionally fostered. With mounting sensitivity to these economic and cultural imperatives, we are trying to encourage the formation of new centers of various types and sizes and to redevelop and stabilize existing centers as the communication foci of a large-scale urban society.

For some segments of the lower-income populations, locational inaccessibility to employment opportunities, when compounded with skill deficiencies and with discriminatory practices, erects an additional handicap which acts to further depress earning capacities. Especially for Negroes seeking work in the suburbanizing manufacturing and wholesaling industries, exclusion from the suburban housing market couples with deficient outbound commuter service to make these growing job opportunities relatively inaccessible, while opportunities near their central-city homes are contracting. Thus, the spatial relationships of residences and employment places for the various classes of employees and jobs remain a central issue for the profession; here, improved land-use patterns and transportation systems can directly help to raise the levels of human welfare. Housing stocks in the lower and lower-middle price ranges need to be expanded in all parts of the metropolitan areas; the filtering process needs to be accelerated; the entire metropolitan housing market needs to be opened to those who are now excluded by reason of race, religion, or national origin; and transportation systems need to be developed that can serve all groups within the region.

But while physical accessibility is a necessary condition for realizing latent opportunities, it is not the sufficient condition. Differences in social status and race, shortage of job opportunities, inadequate education, low income, and personal inadequacy are likely to be far more serious obstructions to the social and economic mobility that leads to the rewards of the society. Especially for the 16 to 25 per cent of Americans who have yet to achieve a minimum acceptable standard of living, a multi-frontal attack on inaccessibility is necessary.

We face the prospect of continuing underemployment in some regions of the nation, and accelerated automation of industrial and clerical processes is eliminating many of the least-skilled jobs at the very time when the post-war babies are swelling the labor force. The chronic despair of so many central-city residents is accentuating their plight; for, when expectations for betterment are low, so too are aspirations. And thus, job shortages, sense of personal insufficiency, poor performance in school, deficient cognitive, occupational, and social skills, rejection by the larger society, and a range of other disabling conditions resonate upon each other in self-perpetuating waves.

America must demonstrate that cultural deprivation and the life of the slum need not be the permanent condition for any of her people. By opening new opportunities for learning new skills and for earning a better living, we can help those who are dependent upon outside supports to gain the self-respect and the dignity they have been denied. Especially for Negroes, Puerto Ricans, and Mexican-Americans, who are encountering the most numerous obstacles along the paths of social mobility, we must demonstrate that America's affluence can be as accessible as it was to the European immigrants who preceded them in our urban centers. Especially for them, the city must become the school for learning the means of earning the city's riches.

But it is not only the residents of slum and deteriorating areas whom we seek to serve. Our expanding aged populations, relieved of their roles as productive members of the society, must find new ways of contributing their skills and knowledge for the welfare of others and, more important, for recapturing their own sense of personal pride and dignity. The large-scale housing projects for the aged, removed from the lifestream of the larger community, are not likely to contribute to these ends. And so, we are searching for new housing arrangements and new social programs to help them remain active members of the communities in which they live. Similarly, the middle-class majority groups, although usually self-supporting, nonetheless require a wide variety of governmental services and facilities that will further expand their opportunities for self-improvement and for creative contributions to the welfare of the total community.

For all these groups, there are probably no more direct routes to human betterment than improvements in the educational systems and stimulation of the regional economies. No other public activities are likely to be more effective in equipping individuals for self-dependency and growth.

Although the locations of physical facilities for schools and economic activities are certainly of but secondary importance to their successes, they are nonetheless contributive. The physical planner does indeed have a significant role to play in pursuing the larger social purposes, but his greatest potential contribution will be realized only if he can accurately appraise the relative effectiveness of the various servicing and facilities-building programs in which he has a hand.

To integrate larger wholes

We are coming to comprehend the city as an extremely complex social system, only some aspects of which are expressed as physical buildings or as locational arrangements. As the parallel, we are coming to understand that each aspect lies in a reciprocal causal relation to all others, such that each is defined by, and has meaning only with respect to, its *relations* to all others.

As one result of this broadened conception of the city system, we can no longer speak of the physical city versus the social city or the economic city or the political city or the intellectual city. We can no longer dissociate a physical building, for example, from the social meanings that it carries for its users and viewers or from the social and economic functions of the activities that are conducted within it. If distinguishable at all, the distinction is that of constituent components, as with metals comprising an alloy.

With improved understanding of economic and social systems, the idea of "capital" is being extended beyond "things" to encompass the human, intellectual, and organizational resources as well. The skills and capacities of our populations, the accumulated knowledge and wisdom of the culture, and the ways in which we organize ourselves for the joint conduct of our affairs, all contribute to our productive capacities and wealth in ways that are inseparable from those of the physical equipment and natural resources we use.

Planning for the locational and physical aspects of our cities must therefore be conducted in concert with planning for all other programs that governmental and non-governmental agencies conduct. Public capital-improvement programs and budgets must allocate financial and other resources among all constructing and serving activities, in an effort to create the most effective programmatic mix of facilities and services of the various types.

As the minimum condition necessary to this task, each municipal agency should be expected to trace out the probable and significant consequences that its programs would have upon those aspects of the city that other agencies focus upon. In this way, each agency would be better informed about the likely conditions in the future and hence better able to make rational recommendations of its own. But mere exchange of good forecasts is not enough.

All proposed programs must be subjected to systematic valuation, if intelligent choices are to be made among them. The new sophistication developing in benefit-cost analysis is beginning to make it possible to appraise a heterogeneous array of proposals against a common set of criteria. Such a valuative method would permit comparisons of the relative social payoffs that might accrue from pursuing one bundle of policies versus another; for example, in assessing the likely returns from alternative social-welfare programs, alternative economic-development programs, and alternative public-works projects. Similarly, it would permit economic public investments to be made by identifying more effective and less costly program packages that might be substituted for less effective and more costly ones.

With improved capacities to forecast probable consequences and to assess probable payoffs, planners in the various governmental agencies should be more effective investment counsellors to their legislatures. Improved data systems will permit planners continuously to meter the states of affairs of the various population groups, the economy, the municipal fisc, the physical plant, and other aspects of the city. Improved theory, describing and explaining the processes of city life and city growth, will permit us more sensitively to identify those crucial points of public intervention that are appropriate to accomplishing specified objectives. The newly developing decision models—which rely upon the new data, the new theory, and, equally, upon the goal hypotheses of politicians and planners—are already permitting us to simulate what would happen *if* given policies were adopted, and thus to pretest the relative effectiveness of alternative courses of action in accomplishing stated ends.

But none of these is sufficient. Improving capacity for rationality must be joined with improving wisdom—there is no other name. It is *here* that the road forks, the one route leading to technocratic control by elites, the other to guided expansion of individual freedom. That map has often been misread to place the fork at junctions that are sometimes labeled "art" and "science" or sometimes as "intuition" and "reason." But we now know that those signposts are false, that he who would be planner must thereby be artist-scientist—no less than that the so-called artist is thereby rigorous analyst of the real world and that the so-called scientist is thereby imaginative and perceptive innovator. Whatever his professional affiliation, the governmental planner may boast that proud title only if he is at once insightful critic, informed analyst, and ingenious designer of action programs, in turn aimed by images of social betterment that are built of reason and wisdom.

There is cause for much optimism in all these respects. Now, for the first time in democratic society, we are acquiring the conceptual and the technical competence to undertake planning of comprehensive policies. Now that we are learning how to predict systematically the kinds, scales, and distributions of benefits and costs that various public programs generate, we can more effectively and more wisely integrate the programs of the various agencies into mutually reinforcing program bundles. Now, when so many thoughtful and creative minds are being turned to the big urban-policy issues, the rate of social invention is increasing. If it were possible to gain consensus on objectives, we would be more likely than ever before to succeed in our efforts to attain them.

Of course, ideal solutions to problems, full identification of probable consequences, and faultless evaluation of alternative actions are all patently impossible. We will always lack perfect knowledge; mature judgment will always be too scarce; and the limitations of human intellectual capacities will never permit adequate comprehension of the urban system's complexities. The best will always elude us; only the better can ever be found.

Even so, the better is seldom self-evident; for the city's many publics rarely hold mutually compatible objectives. Some students of urban politics have been describing the city as a jungle in which overlapping interest groups of all sorts compete avidly for favor and advantage in pursuing their separate ends. Because the rewards and penalties of the political game are so large, few are willing, voluntarily, to sacrifice personal gain for even the most studied and judicious image of a "public welfare." The recent spate of studies on decision-making in city councils reveals a persistent unwillingness of elected officials openly to confront hotly contested issues and a preference to deal with them covertly or to regard them as "technical matters" for professional staffs to decide.

In pursuit of their respective images of the public welfare and of democratic decision-making, the professionals in city hall have been seeking to change the rules of that political game. A major ploy in this effort is simply to supply better information and better analysis and then to open the information channels to public view; for with reduction of ignorance and secrecy goes a reduction in special advantage. Similarly, with public exposure of the probable social consequences of legislative actions, legislators are less likely to respond insensibly and less likely to retreat from political responsibility through the "technical matter" route. And, when confronted with fuller information of market conditions and governmental plans, the private investor is less dependent upon special advantage, for he will often find that his private interest really is compatible with the public interest.

Among the more powerful of the interest groups affecting governmental policies are the professional staffs within municipal government, who hold vested interests in their own brands of programs and projects. Each tends to see the road to social betterment through the biasing lenses of its own profession's filters, and each therefore competes with the others for the limited financial resources they must divide. Physical planners are no less guilty of this sort of professional partiality than are their colleagues in public health, education, law enforcement, or engineering. But there are many hopeful signs suggesting that this narrow perception is giving way to a more holistic view of the policy-making task.

Professional staffs are now working together with a commonality of interests that may be unprecedented. The current beginnings of local social planning councils and inter-agency coordinating committees reflect a growing search for the social consequences that really matter, and a growing recognition that the web of interdependencies inexorably unites them all. In some cities collaboration is already being supplanted by coordination, and in a few leading cities systematic integration of programs is being attempted. Despite the inevitable rigidities of municipal bureaucracy, some agencies *are* searching for higher-level optima to which their own programs might contribute.

Much more than local integration of plans will be necessary, however. Many state and federal programs operate as indirect, and frequently unintended, influences upon the choices and the opportunities that are opened to people in cities and metropolitan areas. The capital-gains provisions of the federal and state income-tax laws, the mortgage-insurance programs of the VA and the FHA, the Federal Reserve System's controls on rediscount rates, the changes in accessibility affected by transportation and communication facilities and rates, the federal water and power projects, the allocation of defense contracts, and numerous other actions of non-local governments modify locational market conditions to which individual firms and households respond. Although the effects of these indirect controls may be more difficult to predict, they are surely more influential in shaping urban-settlement and land-use patterns than are some of the more direct land-use controls.

The construction and grant programs of federal and state agencies—in education, health, transportation, housing, economic development, urban renewal, delinquency control, and related fields—still lack the integration that would permit common ends to be sought. The ideas of the workable program and the community renewal program need to be extended substantively, as ways of raising the quality standards for local planning and as further means of assuring that the many interacting local, state, and federal activities are effectively fitted together.

City planners are likely to be key members in the new partnerships among professionals and politicians at the several governmental levels. The planners have long occupied a uniquely important position in local government, having been the custodians of the holistic view and the utopian tradition. The profession's history has been distinguished by a restless concern for those intangible attributes of the city that are too easily neglected in the day-to-day concentration on short-run problems and partial solutions. The city planners who have earned our highest respect are those whose visions of betterment became epidemic in their communities, raising civic aspirations and forcing solutions of specific problems to be sought within the larger and longer-term policy frameworks they helped establish.

As men who have specialized in the general, the truly effective city planners have functioned as catalysts for synthesizing the developmental plans prepared by the more specialized groups in government. By bringing representatives of public and private agencies together, they have helped to create new amalgams that better reflect both the separate and the mutual goals of the various participants. Individual plans for components have thus been reframed to accord with criteria established by the plans for the next-larger systems of components that, in turn, conform to more comprehensive overviews of the future and of the community's objectives.

Thus, for example, community housing policy is now typically treated as an integral aspect of over-all community social-welfare and land-use policies. Highway and transit facilities, only recently regarded by the transportation engineers as devices for satisfying traffic demand, are now treated as both servers and shapers of the larger land-use and accessibility relationships. In urban renewal the focus of attention is being expanded from the decaying slum buildings to include the larger life environments of the disadvantaged occupants. In turn, this is leading to more enlightened programs in community development, to individualized approaches to human development, and to more humane procedures for family relocation.

In these and numerous other ways, the city planner's realistic idealism, his orientation to the whole city, and his focus upon future conditions have placed him in a position of intellectual leadership. With increasing numbers and varieties of skilled specialists now entering the city's employ, the city planner's outlook will become increasingly important, and his educational mission more difficult. But simultaneously, with improved understanding of the relationships among the various aspects of the city, rational integration will become increasingly possible.

Of course, we claim no monopoly on knowledge, foresight, or wisdom in the urban field. Many of the functions that city planners have traditionally performed are now being assumed by others who are better equipped to conduct specific studies, to lead specific programs, and to integrate them with others. In the presence of increasingly sophisticated theory and method, the planner's conventional reliance upon personal experience and private intuition is unlikely to be accepted as readily as it was in the past. Unless he can keep apace of the intellectual developments in urban theory and planning method, it is quite possible that his integrative roles will be largely assumed by some new group of planners, oriented to more comprehensive wholes, while the city planner becomes a specialist in land use, community facilities, and urban design. In this respect the future is indeterminate, but the profession has no jurisdictional claims to protect. We do stand prepared, though, to participate actively in these endeavors and to represent a human purpose and a holistic approach to the city's problems and opportunities which, we are persuaded, are most likely to increase the welfare of the people, who, as Henry Churchill succinctly put it, *are* the city.

To expand freedom in a pluralistic society

As the comprehensiveness of municipal planning expands and as operating programs become more effectively integrated, the sheer efficiency and inflexibility of it all may inadvertently reduce the range of some citizens' choices. Unlike unorganized or ineffective series of separate programs, the mutual reinforcements of an all-out, coordinated effort can build a rolling momentum, which, should it be poorly designed, might seriously hurt some people before the course of action could be redirected.

This could be especially troublesome for the minority racial and ethnic groups whose value systems and behavior differ greatly from those of the middle-class professionals who design the programs intended to help them. We, in the several welfare professions, have frequently assumed that our ways are best ways, that our aspirations are or should be their aspirations, that a neighborhood designed to suit us is just the type that would best suit them.

There is now a growing appreciation, though, that cultural diversity is an intrinsic characteristic of our society, and we are coming to accept this kind of pluralism as a societal goal deliberately to be pursued. As one of its paramount functions, then, planning in a democratic society is being seen as a process by which the community seeks to increase the individual's opportunities to choose for himself—including the freedom to consume the society's produce and the freedom to choose to be different.

During the course of our history, the nation has learned that we cannot rely upon either chance or unseen hands to assure widened choice and abundance for all. Expanding freedom requires deliberate governmental actions, designed both to extend and to restrict individuals' liberties, as the contextual circumstances demand. To the end of expanding freedom and increasing the nation's wealth, a variety of controls that restrict individuals' liberties have by now been firmly established in custom and in law. Among the more notable are the antitrust laws that seek to avoid the concentration of power in too few hands and to increase productivity; the regulations of the various public-utility commissions that establish prices and set rules of conduct; the pure food and drug laws that seek to protect consumers from the errors or the wiles of the industry; and the various municipal regulations designed to improve health and increase safety. Any restriction of liberties is of course fraught with hazard, for it is too easy either to invoke the doctrine of majority rule in usurping individual rights or to invoke the doctrine of individual rights in limiting majority freedom. A number of guiding principles are clear, however.

1. Certain regulations may be justified as means of forestalling *social costs,* that is, preventing one person from imposing hardships upon others without compensating them for their losses. If the spill-over effects of an individual's actions are likely to harm others, those actions may be prohibited, thus converting potential social costs into private costs to be borne by the actor. Or, if it is not possible to avoid the actions, he may be required to pay the persons who suffer the costs, again requiring that the actor bear the burden. (This is, of course, the prime justification for nuisance-control zoning, pollution-control legislation, and, indeed, the fundamental proposition underlying the police power.)

2. Some regulations and public programs find their justification in explicit political decisions to *redistribute income* among the populations. In matters of this kind the polity is sovereign; and income-redistribution decisions may be based upon purely moral grounds, so long as due process is respected. (Examples of income-redistributive measures are by now plentiful. They include public housing, public education, aid to dependent chil-

dren, recreational programs, and the property and income taxes that finance them.)

Each of these two circumstances involves transfers of costs, benefits, or prerogatives from some individuals to others, with governmental agencies serving as coercive brokers to the transactions. Total wealth of the community is not necessarily affected by these transfers. Other types of governmental activities, however, do seek to increase the total wealth.

3. Under special circumstances *all individuals profit by yielding certain of their rights* to a central authority, because the total returns to the community are thereby increased, and each person's share can be greater. This is in the nature of an economic game in which all players are winners. (Examples here include popular allegiance to a governmental system of legislatures, executives, and courts, whose stability is prerequisite to individual security and freedom; the universal acceptance of the traffic signal's authority, which assures time savings and greater safety to all; and the assignment to governments of exclusive production rights for the "collective goods," such as national defense and city streets that, by their very nature, are available to everybody if they are supplied at all.)

4. In a similar way, tax-supported *information services* serve to foster increased productivity by increasing opportunities for making more rational private decisions, by stabilizing investment expectations, and by raising aspiration levels concerning the community's development. (Examples are the federal censuses and the new state and metropolitan data-reporting systems that serve to inform all interested members of the community about the current states of affairs; and governmental declarations of intent, as expressed in city plans and budgets, that aid private persons and groups in their efforts to anticipate future conditions, and that may encourage them to conform to collective aims.)

Having been closely associated with zoning regulations and land-clearance procedures, we are well aware of the vices that can be committed under the general-welfare sanctions. These controls have too often dispossessed some individuals of their property rights in the name of majority benefits, and they have too often been used as instruments of political power to further the private ends of some groups at the expense of others. Zoning and redevelopment programs carry unavoidable income-redistribution features that make them particularly susceptible to favored application and make them extremely difficult to apply equitably. As one reflection, large-lot zoning and exacting building codes in suburban municipalities have recently been used as tools for social discrimination and as unnecessary constraints upon individual freedom. Some aspects of urban redevelopment programs have been similarly criticized for the hurts they have imposed upon groups they have displaced.

We would prefer that these and other controls be applied with greater restraint and with greater sensitivity to the question of who benefits and who sacrifices. To accomplish the larger society's purposes, we look to the gradual reduction of controls on individual choice when benefits cannot be explicitly demonstrated and warranted. To this end, we seek ordinance revisions favoring greater permissiveness and greater flexibility for individual actions.

Although we recognize the necessity to centralize certain kinds of decisions in governments, a major purpose in setting these decisions should be to expand the possibilities for decentralized decisions—to increase the number of options that are thereby opened to individual persons. Through explicitly goal-directed investments in public-service programs and in public works, governments can help expand the volume and the diversity of the society's produce and, in turn, can help increase individuals' capacities selectively to consume it.

The history of public education in America reveals a model for other governmental programs to emulate, for here the overriding purpose has been to give, rather than to take—to open, rather than to foreclose, choices. Those who have been successfully served by our public schools have been better equipped to support themselves and have been less dependent upon the social-welfare services than are their less fortunate neighbors. In turn, they are able to contribute to and then consume the growing varieties of goods, services, and ideas that prophesy the eventual elimination of poverty from the nation.

Since we are a long way from achieving equal opportunity, however, our plans must account for wide variations in degrees of freedom and in capacities to consume. Poverty and the deprivations of racial minority groups persist as the most pressing social issues confronting municipal governments. They call for an all-out reappraisal of programmatic priorities and for imaginative new programs aimed, above all, at increasing a sense of personal dignity and at fostering positive images of self and group.

Many of our present municipal programs are proving inadequate to this need. Lower-income families, who must budget larger proportions of their earnings for rent, are typically more eager to find cheap housing than they are in getting the modern housing facilities that middle-income families enjoy. Similarly, they must place higher priorities on developing low-cost transit service to employment places than they put on the amenities of open space and recreational facilities that others are seeking. Enforced relocation into higher-priced but superior housing is not likely to improve their standards of living if it requires reductions in the food budget. Declines in transit service, which may be tolerable for those who can afford automobiles, can be severely damaging for those who cannot.

Family- and youth-guidance services, occupational retraining programs, empathetic teachers and compatible school curricula, professionalization of low-skilled service jobs, inexpensive health services, the removal of racial bars, and increased employment opportunities are certain to be more immediately helpful to the city's underprivileged groups than are many of the community facilities that now absorb large proportions of municipal budgets. Although many of these activities do not fall within the city planner's areas of special competence, he is nonetheless a key agent in setting municipal-investment priorities; and he is thus in a position to guide municipal policies toward the issues that really matter.

Our purpose is to find those wealth-increasing approaches that will benefit *all* members of the society. Where such consummate returns are not possible, we seek to design those minimum controls that will avoid abuses by forestalling probabilities of individuals or groups harming others. Where income-redistribution effects are either unavoidable or publicly intended, we would have the gains go to those most in need of help. And when sacrifices must be made, especially when they must be made by those least able to sustain them, we would have them accompanied by commensurate payments.

City planning is moving through a period of rapid change—some have called it a revolution, so dramatic is the transformation likely to be. The major sign is a growing sophistication. The main prospect is a large increase in the profession's effectiveness. The chief stimulant has been the injection of a large body of theory and method that has been accumulating in the social and behavioral sciences over the decades and which, until recently, the profession had been largely immune to. Now, the problems of urbanization are attracting the attention of men from all the arts, humanities, and social sciences; and they are allying themselves with the urban-policy professions in what is fast becoming a saturation of talent into urban policy-making.

The infusion of new blood into the planning profession has brought with it a growing appreciation of the organizational complexities marking the societal systems that the city mirrors. Concomitantly, attention is being redirected from the form of the city to the processes that relate the interdependent aspects of the city one to the other. And, in turn, with improved understanding of how the city-system works, our capacities for effective intervention and willful change are improving rapidly. But effectiveness and will can come to nothing if they are not guided by wisdom. Worse, the damages wrought can be severe, the more because the levers of contemporary government sweep wide arcs.

The contemporary planners inherit a proud tradition of service, an egalitarian ethic, and a pragmatic orientation to betterment that are as old as the early social reform movements that spawned the profession. The caretaker of the idea of progress during the long years when it lay in disrepute in respectable quarters, the planner is now being wooed as the Cinderella of the urban ball. The resulting marriage of the social sciences and the planning profession holds out the promise that a new level of intelligence will be merged with noble purpose, in confronting the problems and the opportunities of the day. And then, the payoffs of this new partnership will come, if they are to come at all, in imaginative social inventions that will increase the city's riches, while distributing them to all the city's people.

2

Emerging Patterns in
Community Planning

ROBERT MORRIS AND MARTIN REIN

The field of community organization and community welfare planning is experiencing a renaissance of activity characterized by new ideas, questionings, criticisms, and mechanisms. An assessment of our theoretical framework for planning in social welfare is long overdue, and voices seeking it are heard with increasing persistence. The purpose here is to highlight some of the factors that account for this ferment and to identify the dilemmas and choices associated with a period of transition. The strategy of this attempt rests on the conviction that a theoretical framework must come as close as possible to describing social reality, and must strive to reduce the complexity of the problem by examining limited but focal aspects of planned change.

Present welfare planning structures and ways of thinking about welfare planning have been historically conditioned. Community organization emerged from a complex of voluntary social-welfare organizations whose primary commitment was to assist the individual in coping with his social reality. Their chief, although not exclusive, preference was to work with "the infected individual rather than to eliminate the infection from the environment." [1] Welfare planning was therefore based upon this approach to social problems. In addition, the voluntary agencies were reluctant to have government sponsor welfare services. This concern found expression in their preoccupation with the reduction of pauperism (the receipt of financial aid from governmental sources). It will be recalled that the Charity Organization Society bitterly opposed public pension schemes for widows and children lest such programs might come to be regarded as a right; and it favored a voluntary program designed to work with individuals.

In urban centers, where our planning structures flourish, an extraordinarily complex variety of organizations has developed over the decades to form the matrix for planning, with their irrationalities, contradictions, and overlappings providing the impetus for action.

In this scheme the importance of a local community deserves special comment. Voluntary agency planning flourished in the belief that local communities constitute the essential foundation of American society—local

From *Social Work Practice, 1963* (New York: Columbia University Press, for the National Conference on Social Welfare, 1963), pp. 155–176. Copyright © 1963, National Conference on Social Welfare, Columbus, Ohio.

communities which are reasonably stable and capable of being comprehended in their entirety by the citizens residing in them. Out of this view emerged welfare's concept of the total community.

This commitment to the locality was accompanied by conviction that local destinies could be locally controlled. National and nonlocal influences were certainly recognized, but they were considered secondary and controllable by local forces.

This local commitment required reconciliation between the realities of select leadership and the aspirations of democratic participation. Thus, welfare services and planning became recognizably controlled by an essentially elite leadership in each community, consisting at first of those well-established personalities who had developed over the years a sense of civic obligation and, appropriate for their time and background, a comprehensive view of their communities. Associated with the socially elite were an economic elite, often combined in the same families. Economic power in the nineteenth century was believed to be vested in local industry, under local control. These economic sinews became the foundation for the support of much of social welfare. It was only later recognized that this elite leadership was primarily white and Protestant, representing the early social stratification of American society.[2]

The leading citizens who controlled welfare nevertheless sought to make room for a widening democratic participation in the hope that other citizens would acquire the same values and the same broad, comprehensive view of the community. Differences of opinion and point of view were certainly recognized, but it was assumed that these differences would be overcome or resolved as more citizens acquired views not unlike those of their leaders. While in retrospect we can recognize that this total community view tended to reflect the dominant culture of the times, that is, the white-Protestant ethic of community leadership, that in no sense reduces the significance of this comprehensive aspiration.

Lest this schematic summation of historical origin seem too pat, regional differences can be early identified. Patterns of welfare planning varied discernibly as one moved from the Northeast sector of the country to the West and to the South.[3]

Other factors have contributed to the development of our present ways of thinking about welfare planning, and as a result of this past, our current thinking about planning is controlled by four aspects: a belief in a federated structure; a confidence in a rational utopia; a goal of reallocating, rearranging, or coordinating existing resources; and a professional strategy of consensus seeking.

1. *The dominant characteristic of our welfare planning is its federated character as typified by local welfare planning councils.*

Federation aims at representation of autonomous groups; hence it has responsibility but limited authority. Various subgroups are brought into cooperative participation through representatives, although not all groups in community life are necessarily represented, nor do all groups have equal power and influence. This structure serves as an arena in which change is discussed and argued by the various subgroups represented, but the federated structure itself remains primarily neutral. The structure is circumscribed by the interests of the groups that have assembled within its fold. The strength of the federation is dependent upon the willingness of constituent groups to relinquish their autonomy on occasion. The functioning of this structure is best characterized as a commitment to one view of democratic participation and is reflected in such statements as "to help diverse interests, recognize and respect difference, resolve conflict and achieve mutually satisfying community goals." [4]

Consistent with this view is the belief that the federated body can best serve as a neutral ground from which contending positions can be aired and as a battleground on which members can find ways of meeting the crises which they mutually experience. Such a structural commitment leads inevitably to an avoidance of conflict whenever possible and the seeking of action in the name of the "total community" only where overwhelming consensus can be secured from constituent members of the federation. [5]

These qualities of elitism and the shunning of controversy have been described by a trustee of a federated organization:

> Voluntary welfare administration is—and has been—essentially a gentleman's avocation. People who offer their experience and services to this work are generally from social, intellectual, and income levels well above the average. They have social consciences. They want to do something about conditions in the world around them. And they do. But, by nature, they are not inclined to take unpopular positions about things. They tend to work through reasonableness, thoughtful discussion and compromise. Controversy, in general, is avoided. Playing it safe is sometimes the preferable strategy when key community issues come up. [6]

2. *Federated structure is the organized expression of a belief in rational utopianism.*

Much available community organization theory is utopian in that not only are its goals based on values, but the precepts designed to guide actions are also based upon these same values. The consequence is that guides for action are formulated from a theory of what the world ought to be and proceed as if the world *is* what it ought to be. Manser says that "we believe that communities as aggregations of individuals possess inherent capacity to change—to choose wisely in the management of their affairs, and the right and responsibility to determine how best to serve the health and welfare needs of their citizens." [7] Murray Ross, the most articulate spokesman of this emphasis on the interchangeability of ends and means, refers to the process of "community integration" wherein the primary goal of community organization is to advance the democratic process and strengthen a community's members' capacity to work together. [8] Thus the means become the end.

The existing philosophy for planning is furthermore utopian in that it equates services with goodness. The provision of more and more adequate services to meet a social problem is usually considered a social good, while decrease in services is considered to be a social evil. Social agencies are seen as primarily needs-meeting institutions. While this construction is sound, frequently, and perhaps unintentionally, it fails to take into consideration the agency as a social system which reflects the interest of diverse supporting community subgroups. Thus agencies must survive in the environment which supports them, and frequently their survival and growth dominate in decisions about action alternatives. The fact that agencies can become ends in themselves, have power in their own right, and can become instruments of vested interests is often overlooked. When this tendency is recognized it is viewed in a moral light and not as a normal phenomenon of human social organization which requires appropriate theory as to handling.

Finally, community organization theory is utopian in that it sees a community as essentially unstratified and not representative of various and often conflicting subgroups. The inherent good nature of man should enable him to act in good faith for the good of the total community when certain good impulses are liberated in him. Conflicts in vested interest as integral facets of the relationship between man and his environment are largely omitted in this view.

Current theory is rational as well as utopian in that it is based upon a conviction that, if communities have enough knowledge, have gathered enough facts, and are forcefully confronted with certain problems, they will act appropriately to solve them. Ignorance and faulty communication are considered to be prime obstacles to desirable action. "Once the violations of this doctrine became inescapably visible to everyone, community members felt obligated to take action against the discrimination in their midst and the moral position of those who openly defended the discrimination became clearly untenable." [9]

This view further assumes not only that knowledge will lead to action, but also that it will lead to rational action. A given set of facts can lead to only one logical conclusion, and this conclusion will be accepted by decision-makers and others in positions of influence once they understand the underlying facts. Alternatives for action which do not stem from such a single-track rational process are seldom taken into account—methods of negotiation, bargaining, and coalition are seldom stressed.

3. *Federated bodies in the past have devoted most of their energies to problems which grew out of distribution and redistribution of resources among agencies, clients, personnel functions, and funds.*

Other forms of change and community action have been acknowledged as desirable by federated bodies, but all frank examinations of their operations have concluded that a predominance of their energy has been directed to this redistributive or coordinative function. The federated agency is primarily concerned with the network of health and welfare agencies which constitute its domain. This network consists mainly of direct-service agencies, with the various components interdependent upon each other; their shifts in the goals or operations of any one agency will affect the capacity of others to achieve their ends.[10] For example, if a child-care agency ceases to be a legally protecting organization and becomes a therapeutic agency, this immediately affects the demands made upon other community services and an accommodation must be arranged.[11] Similarly, the distribution of resources is affected by whether these resources are in a state of equilibrium, expansion, or contraction. Thus, when financial resources are primarily derived from voluntary philanthropy and these funds are increasing in volume, certain types of coordination may take place; when funds from the same source are restricted or contracting, other consequences result, and become the chief interest of the coordinating agency.

While planning is essentially coordinative, change efforts are attempted, but they are largely initiated because of crises and disequilibria in the resource bases of agencies (such as a drop in united fund income) or because of overwhelming, uncontrollable demands upon stable resources (caused, perhaps, by a sharp rise in unemployment). Because of the origin of these federated bodies, the changes they attempt to make in response to crisis seldom involve basic alterations in the conditions of the surrounding society which may be responsible for the crisis. Instead, the federated body concentrates necessarily upon changes within its own network of welfare agencies. At one extreme are mergers in the interest of efficiency. At the other extreme are efforts to coordinate activities in instances where the autonomy of agencies is largely unaffected. Further changes may, over a substantial period of time, lead to the emergence of new resources and new services, but these seldom involve an attack upon the causes of social problems in the society.

Thus federated bodies are able, in the main, to focus upon a limited band of problems that are important to the types of agencies which have been brought together in federation. Whether such bodies have, in fact, dealt more substantively with changes going beyond this limited arena remains for further study and proof.

4. *The strategy of choice developed out of this past history has been one of consensus seeking.*

Community planning, education, and practice have concentrated upon those techniques which will help divergent interest groups to search for a common denominator for joint action. Since the viability of the federated body depends upon almost complete agreement, the dissenting organization carries a degree of influence disproportionate to its contribution to the solution of the social problem with which it deals. Thus it becomes clear that decisions frequently must be reached through informal channels so that the federation is not divided into factions by premature and divisive action. Formal voting oftentimes is simply the expression of a general consensus previously reached. Chairmanship is developed to a fine art to avoid calling an issue to a vote unless there are clear indications of widespread preagreement. Similarly, goals are frequently couched in broad and ambiguous terms to avoid a concentration of conflict. Proper decisions for action are those which avoid resentment of major participants in the federation and sustain the stable affiliation of many subgroups.

These four basic characteristics which emerged from the historical antecedents described above served that history in many significant ways. A stable community with a comprehensive community view necessarily requires a mechanism for assembling diverse interests in order to assure their loyalty and a set of procedures and strategies directed primarily to achieving the comprehensiveness of view and the rationalization of resources which its over-all pattern requires.

The situation in which planning today takes place is materially different from that we have described. American communities and American life are no longer stable, nor is there any substantial indication that stability will be either desirable or achievable in the foreseeable future. Instead, we are experiencing an unprecedented explosion in population and an extraordinary mobility of people back and forth across the face of the nation as economic, political, and social waves of the mid-twentieth century require. Only 5 per cent of our people die in the community of their birth. Thus southern California, the Southwest, and the South are expanding by an increment of a thousand families a day, while other parts of the country are losing population at an equally rapid rate. The great exodus of Negro families from the South to the North constitutes one of the great migrations in all history and has changed the character of our urban centers. Annually, one in four American families makes a major move of residence. Not only are new communities growing, but old ones are either expanding or contracting so rapidly that stability can hardly be expected. More significantly, a flow of population means that the goal of an encompassing comprehensive view of any community is both difficult to achieve and certainly difficult to extend to masses of the population in any generation.

The economic character of American communities has changed. Today, with only a few exceptions, industries which exert a great economic influence on community life are locally sited but nonlocally controlled. Moreover, they are administered by a new managerial class which, in turn, is extraordinarily mobile. One of the substantial foundations for welfare control and policy-making is thus removed from the local community to regional or national centers.

There has further been the remarkable growth of public health and welfare organizations with a preponderant responsibility for services, both as regards the numbers of people served and the volume of funds expended. While voluntary associations remain vigorous, they are no longer paramount. These public programs are to a large extent sustained and generated by nonlocal resources derived from federal and, to a lesser extent, state levels of public authority. Another essential for welfare planning is thus located outside the local community, representing a major shift in the conception of the community to be served by welfare planning structures.

Minority groups have assumed a new position of influence in our urban centers (and since welfare planning has flourished in urban centers, these people become our major interest); for in most urban areas nonwhites constitute 25 to 30 per cent of the population. This proportion is likely to grow, and these groups are already grossly underrepresented in our health and welfare planning structures.[12]

As a result of these four changes, our community life has become infinitely more complex than the one out of which our present welfare thinking was derived. More than 75 per cent of our people reside in metropolitan areas in the new megalopolis. Many autonomous, strongly organized special-interest groups live side by side, but independently and uncontrolled, either in the core city or in its suburbs. These groups are rooted in the primary forces of modern industrial life. National economic interests, ethnic groups, trade unions, and others are now added to the traditionally voluntary, and essentially elite, sectarian and religiously rooted welfare influences of the past. There is as yet no sure indication that these powerful basic influences can be brought together intimately in a voluntary structure, although they are contained effectively by our basic governmental and political processes of local, state, and national government.

The new community is full of strife, conflict, uncertainty, and anxiety. At the same time, there can be discerned the recurrent strain of many quite old-fashioned problems. Juvenile delinquency, poverty, dependency, family disorganization, poor housing, disease, and mental illness are all still with us. However, their origin, their scope, and their understanding have all been substantially altered. There is wider acceptance of the view that the etiology of many social problems is rooted as much in social conditions as in the individual. Many would argue that social conditions are a fundamental cause, and even those who are committed to individual adjustment to the environment recognize that the unhealthy environment must be treated as much as the ill individual.[13]

The great scientific and technical achievements of the twentieth century altered the character but have not significantly reduced the prevalence of physical and mental ill-health, delinquency, poverty, poor housing, and the other social problems with which we have always been concerned. Even if there has been no increase in the incidence of these social difficulties, their firm persistence has been disturbing. We have attempted to deal with them by *ad hoc* legislation, by the development of extensive public welfare programs, and by an elaboration of therapeutic skills directed to the individual. None of these developments seems to have made sufficiently deep inroads to satisfy either social workers, health workers, or the citizens. The result has been a renewed search for ways of dealing more effectively with these problems.

The ferment has not been solely one of intellectual and scientific pursuit. The impetus to develop new, specialized service organizations is a well-known phenomenon. The growth of specialized health agencies since World War II is too well known to require elaboration.

The discovery that social problems persist has troubled us because we had been lulled into complacency by welfare expansion and by overconfidence in the tempo of our great technical achievements. Advances in the medical sciences have only brought us to a confrontation of even more intractable chronic diseases for which we have no medical solution and for which we need a combination of social and medical approaches. Appropriate care of the large volume of long-term illness requires a great expansion of manpower and of physical resources. Important discoveries in psychiatry have not noticeably diminished the incidence of mental illness, although they have permitted us to consider new methods of treatment. Unfortunately, the treatment of mental illness outside institutional walls encounters the gross hazards provided by the new environment just described. The handling of delinquency and all forms of antisocial deviant behavior, such as illegitimacy, drug addiction, and so on, must be dealt with in a community in which multiple standards exist side by side without synthesis or apparent coherence. Poor housing cannot be resolved solely by the construction of new buildings because these new structures must somehow be related to the racial relationships which characterize our urban centers. Solutions through public assistance and vast public programs are not sufficient in themselves because they fail to take into account the enlarged aspirations of diverse social and economic groups, the raised plateau of expectation about what is a minimum standard for social existence.

These problems, or the new understanding about the dimensions of old problems, along with the new centers of influence in community life, have not been adequately articulated with the previously developed welfare planning structures for health and welfare. As a result, old planning structures have been increasingly criticized, and both new structures and new approaches to welfare planning are increasingly being experimented with.

The new forms for planning and the new planning practices can be reviewed by comparison with the federated structure, the rational utopian view, the goal of coordination, and the strategy of consensus which characterized our past.

These new forms can also be understood in light of the changed community circumstances which we have just been discussing. If our past history led naturally and logically to the development of a certain approach to planning, it may be equally true that the new community life will lead equally to its own appropriate forms of planning.

What are these new approaches to planning? They are the new urban planning agencies, the mobilizations for youth, the community mental health centers, the public health department, the new rehabilitation concepts in public welfare. A comparison between these approaches and those of the traditional community-wide welfare planning council has been blurred because each of them uses the term "comprehensive community planning" with equal ease.

In some fifteen or twenty major cities urban renewal planning has stimulated the development of new organizations committed to the human and social aspects of urban renewal. These organizations are rooted in the necessities for the actual rebuilding of our core cities. They are equally committed to a comprehensive view of the needs of the human beings who are affected by this renewal. As a result, they turn to the schools, the family welfare agencies, the settlement houses, the hospitals, and seek to engage all of them in program development directly associated with the problems of family relocation and physical rebuilding.

Community mental health centers are committed to the development of positive mental health and adequate care of the mentally ill. They seek to encompass in this effort our schools, our family welfare agencies, our settlement houses, our general hospitals, and our mental hospitals. In similar fashion, our youth development efforts, best characterized by Mobilization for Youth in New York City, are concerned with juvenile delinquency and the lack of opportunity for deprived youth. They seek to involve the school system, family welfare agencies, public welfare agencies, settlement houses, industry, and labor unions in the problems of youth opportunity as a major attack on delinquency.

Public welfare agencies are attacking the problem of dependency with a broadened concept of rehabilitation. They seek to engage the interest of schools, family welfare agencies, settlement houses, rehabilitation centers, hospitals, and industry with the view of overcoming the conditions which lead to dependency and opening up opportunities for families now on public assistance.

What we see is that a number of key social problems—mental and physical illness, deviant behavior or delinquency, financial dependency, and poor housing—are each viewed as a central organizing theme for comprehensive community planning. Each subject identifies a community of agencies and interests demanding its own action. Each grouping has the character of a community and each of them is approaching the same resources for its purposes.

This proliferation of planning centers has been decried and has met with harsh criticism on the grounds that it destroys the essential unity of comprehensive community planning. What critics of this evolution have not taken into account is the generating source for these multiple developments, namely, the changed community. The stable community has been replaced by a community of great complexity with many special interests. Each of these special interests is sufficiently complex in itself to justify a perception of itself as a community with many subelements. The fact that these specialized communities are paralleled by other specialized communities is a matter of no great concern to any of them because the requirements of their own community demand all their energies. Thus one interpretation would be that the total community concept has been paralleled by, if not eclipsed by, the rise of multiple special communities. These new welfare planning approaches are characterized by the following elements: they are partisan rather than federated; their influences are derived from nonlocal rather than local sources; they are likely to be public rather than voluntary; they are concerned with political skills more than they are with consensus-forming skills; and their goal is change in the community structure rather than coordination of available resources.

The new planning structures are essentially partisan in character. Their policy-making leadership consists primarily of like-minded persons with a definite image of the change they seek to promote and the objectives toward which they are striving. They seek to modify their environment so that it becomes consistent with their aims and objectives. Cooperation is desired, but primarily around their focal concerns. This contrasts with the federated approach in which the federated planning organization seldom if ever seeks to impose its image upon its cooperating organizations.

The base for much of the specialized interest planning is found outside the local community. The origin of stimulation of ideas is mainly located outside the local community—in the Ford Foundation, the national health agencies, the Federal Urban Renewal Program, the President's Committee on Juvenile Delinquency and Youth Crime, and the Hill-Burton Hospital Construction Program, to mention but a few. At the same time, funds are gathered (from local citizens, it is true) at national centers, especially through taxation, and redirected into local communities through national channels, such as the United States Department of Health, Education, and Welfare, the Housing and Home Finance Agency, and others. These channels are often fixed by congressional action which governs the funding of new programs.

The magnitude of change envisioned by some of the new planning organizations is so great that it has not yet been grasped by voluntary welfare agencies. As a result, public and governmental structures are either the centers for this planning or they become the dominant partners. Public health departments or state rehabilitation commissions are likely to be the generating source of planning in the field of physical health; state departments of mental hygiene, community health clinics, and community mental health boards, in the field of mental health; the Department of Public Welfare, in the field of dependency; the mayor's office or an urban renewal agency or department of public housing, in urban renewal.

Where the initiative is not vested chiefly in public programs, new organizations are created which bring public and voluntary organizations together into a new alignment, illustrated by agencies established to deal with the social consequence of urban renewal—Action for Community Development, in Boston; Community Progress, Inc., in New Haven; Philadelphia's Council for Community Advancement. Public organizations and city government are likely to be the principal partners in these new organizations. Thus the redevelopment authority, the schools, and the health or mental health departments enlarge their functions and assume responsibilities for community-wide planning (albeit along the axis of their special interest) previously considered the domain of the comprehensive voluntary welfare council.

The goals of the new planning organizations can also be contrasted with those of past planning bodies. They are concerned with new ways in which to alter the environment out of which social problems emerge. They are thus engaged in the pursuit of defined objectives, the achievement of which can be measured. They are less satisfied with coordination of available resources and seek in some more fundamental fashion to change the conditions which give rise to these problems. They seek to develop and enlarge rather than to integrate. Thus the problems of delinquency are attacked through the schools and employers. The schools provide a base for reaching all youth and their function is enlarged to provide, not only minimum education, but also appropriate educational facilities for all youth commensurate with the requirements of the society into which they are going to move. The schools may even become centers for much broadened character-building activities since they are more widely based than were settlement houses.

The approach is not primarily one of motivating youth to desire a better life (an approach based upon the assumption that the problem rests within the individual), but rather one of opening up jobs in industry, on the assumption that the problem lies in the character of economic opportunity available. In the field of mental health, the community clinics are not exclusively concerned with assisting mentally ill individuals to adapt to the harsh realities of a competitive world; they turn to the development of supporting attitudes on the part of large segments of the community or to a major improvement in community receptivity of the mentally ill or handicapped. As part of the planning stimulated by the United States Department of Health, Education, and Welfare, the federal government is now employing workers who have a history of mental illness, a significant departure from previous policies.

In the health field there is no longer satisfaction with motivating individual patients through health education to seek medical care. Attention is now being directed to the organization of medical care to assure comprehensive and continuing health services. Many of the deficiencies in our health picture are viewed as inherent in the way in which we have organized the use of physicians, social workers, nurses, and so on, rather than as due to lack of information on the part of patients, necessitating devices to motivate potential consumers to use health services. The current assumption calls for unification of home care services, expansion of social insurances and group practices, and development of inclusive outpatient services; the former assumption demanded guidance, therapy, and education of the individual.

As is common with any form of social innovation, new problems are encountered as we seek to resolve old ones. It is perhaps readily evident that in the new situation, unclear and changing as it is, two problems can now be identified. The several planning approaches, each organized around a special interest, are necessarily in competition for limited funds and personnel. There is no definite allocation of funds and other resources for a balanced plan of action.

There is also in any community competition for the interest and help of citizens. The mental health organizations, the health agencies, the youth organizations, the urban renewal groups, are all endeavoring to attract the wholehearted interest of supporting citizens. The schools seek to develop parent-teacher associations with enlarged responsibilities; urban renewal agencies want to develop local block organizations; welfare councils try to organize neighborhood planning councils; settlement houses encourage the formation of tenant groups. In the abstract, it would appear that each of these organizations is appealing to the same citizen reservoir. In fact, they may be appealing to different citizen constituencies, but this remains to be determined by further analysis and study. It is not yet clear whether the central pool of community leadership with a comprehensive community view survives today and is the object of search by each of these special interest planning groups, or whether there are fragmented leadership centers, each attracted to one of the special groups mentioned above.

The present situation is still too new and too fluid to permit any final conclusions. However, one trite issue is clearly presented. Shall we strive for a new reintegration of these multiple planning centers into a comprehensive community planning organization consistent with our past tradition? Or shall we accept the existence over an indefinite period of time of multiple planning centers which must be in parallel competition? The first approach has been forecast by Zimbalist and Pippert;[14] the second has been developed most lucidly by Banfield and Dahl.[15]

Since our communities are now not only more complex, but also include a greater diversity of powerful influences and special interests, the question may reasonably be asked whether a reintegration into comprehensive community approaches can take place at any level other than government—or within government at any level other than regional, state, or federal. If we seriously believe that reintegration can take place within the voluntary concepts of the past, we need to visualize a voluntary association capable of embracing the powerful economic, ethnic, and sectarian interests which dominate in our urban centers. It is unclear whether any community can delegate so much authority and influence to any voluntary organization based upon past patterns. If this is to be the route followed, new voluntary structures not now envisioned will have to be fashioned.

This position is not widely promoted today. Commenting on the exhaustion of nineteenth-century ideology by 1950, Bell observes that "few 'classic' liberals insist that the state should play no role in the economy, and few serious conservatives, at least in England and on the continent, believe that the welfare state is 'the road to serfdom.' " [16]

If the development of such potentially reintegrative planning is to center within our basic democratic governmental framework, we are also confronted with new and complex problems. Social problems will not defer to existing political boundaries. The need for regional planning and for embracing larger and larger units of government presents us with an ideological dilemma. Social workers favor self-determination and the control by the local citizen of his own destiny, while the increasing importance of state and federal intervention to constrain local choices is apparent. The nonlocal center where resources for planning and service are abundant has become the chief locus for social innovation. Yet fiscal partnership between the locality and these larger units of government of necessity limits the autonomy of a local community.

The issue of centralized planning—an increasing reality in social work practice—will need to be squarely faced if we are to free ourselves from our ideological distortions of social reality. We have seen the growth of planning responsibilities in public health, public welfare, and urban renewal organizations. Much of this development to date has been located in executive departments, and our sense of community comprehensiveness has frequently been outraged because we have observed that the competition between public departments is frequently as sharp and severe as that which once characterized relationships between voluntary agencies.

This has necessarily raised the question of whether there is any provision in our political framework for coping with this type of competition—a mechanism comparable to the voluntary welfare council in its dealing with voluntary agency competitiveness. It can be suggested that a mechanism does exist in our political environment, namely, the central executive office of government found at all levels. In several municipalities the mayor's office has begun to assume the kind of integrative responsibility over executive departments which has traditionally been carried by voluntary welfare councils over voluntary agencies. In these communities the mayor has brought together his commissioner of welfare, commissioner of health, and director of housing or urban renewal and in his own cabinet sought to integrate their approaches to fundamental social problems in the municipality. This integration has been challenged as being essentially unstable or dictatorial. It is argued with equal vigor that the basis for our democratic process permits the total citizenry of every jurisdiction to exercise its wishes by frequent elections; the acts of the mayor or of the executive officer in pooling the efforts of his own executive department heads are therefore subject to the constant review of the electorate. It is possible that the conception of the voluntary welfare council, representative of the public interest, has sufficient vitality to be extended to government.

Similarly, there has been in recent years an attempt to use the governor's office to bring about an integration of executive departments at the state level. California has brought together for more effective planning the departments of public health, mental health, and public welfare. In Pennsylvania, there has recently been advanced a proposal for a council on human resources to encompass these interests in the executive branch. In some less populous states, departments of public welfare and health have already been merged into one executive branch. In certain very populous states, such as New York, the governor's office has established interdepartmental committees with strong staffing responsible directly to the governor.

At the federal level, this development is not so clearly discernible, although the organization of the Department of Health, Education, and Welfare itself a few years ago was a major step in the attempt to bring together the executive interests in public health, mental health, welfare, and education in one manageable administrative unit. This trend may not continue, for there has been persistent talk of a separate cabinet post for health, which would suggest the strength of counterinfluences which derive from the special interests previously discussed.

It is also possible to envision a continuation of the present competitive situation between various centers for planning with each one focused on a special interest. Political scientists frequently seem to agree that the essence of democracy is the freest competition between special interests. In this view, special interests are neither evil nor undesirable but are the best assurance that the great variety of human needs will be ultimately served by the fullest expression of differences free to compete with each other. This theory has been advanced by authors as diverse as Sills, Banfield, Dahl, and Truman.[17]

The period in which we are living is obviously difficult and exciting. The outcome is uncertain, and there is ample room to argue for either of the preceding approaches. However, whichever we choose, one consequence for professional practice in community organization seems inevitable. Social work's concern with community planning needs to develop skills, not only in the traditional enabling processes, but equally in the political processes, in an understanding of conflict, and in negotiation, bargaining, and diverse strategies which can be utilized to reconcile differences.

Political knowledge and skill to achieve one's ends have often been considered by social workers to be unprofessional. We have somehow believed that strong advocacy of a particular point of view and the development of techniques to achieve those ends violate our professional commitment to the democratic process. We have generally ignored the fact that other professions, such as the law, have been built largely around the adversary principle, which assumes a conflict of interest. Professional expression is guided by ethical and legal limits in the promotion of the client interests.

The question for us is whether our commitment to professional neutrality and noninvolvement is to continue to sustain our professional practice. If it is, it can be predicted that our contribution to modern life will lie largely in the coordinative realm—coordinative among organizations that share common interests. The requirements of the new community demand skill in advocating special points of view and in living with other professionals who advocate competing points of view. Thus social workers may be concerned with planning in health, youth development, or housing and each worker may be a respected member of the profession. Each may seek to engage the support, interest, or collaboration of the other. Each may succeed or fail in varying degrees and still be professionally reliable.

On the other hand, if we choose to seek a new level of reintegration so that we can recapture the over-all community view, we cannot avoid the development of political skills which are essential to bring together into agreement the competing interest groups which characterize the public scene. It is our view that this reintegration will probably take place at the public level in a form consistent with our heritage of political democracy. If this integration does take place at the governmental level, it will have certain similarities to the integration at the welfare council level in that consensus will have to be developed among a variety of interests, and this will then draw upon the community organization skills with which we have become so familiar. In one sense, we will be concerned with coordination and consensus simply on a wider field, and it could be argued that our practice will not differ much from that of the past.

However, this type of integration will differ substantially from the one we have known in one significant respect. The voluntary welfare councils have succeeded because they have concentrated on bringing together groups of leaders, trustees, and organizations with a largely common foundation of interest and association. The voluntary council has been able to screen out those likely to produce major conflict divisiveness, and to concentrate attention upon those who accept the standards and patterns expected by the voluntary council.[18] However, if we are to have community planning in the executive branch of government, the dynamism of our political processes makes it impossible to be so self-limiting. Therefore, the new forms of planning will of necessity have to deal with potentially and actually conflicting areas of interest in each community. The challenge which will be placed upon community organizers then will be how to deal with openly conflicting interests and how to bring them together in a general community approach. This type of conflict handling will call upon the skills and knowledge of all the social sciences—sociology and psychology, with which we are familiar, political science and political economy, with which we are unfamiliar.

NOTES

1. Barbara Wooton, *Social Science and Social Pathology* (New York: Macmillan, 1959), p. 329. Note that this preference refers to the early agencies of social work in the United States, not to the later emerging professional organizations.
2. Paul A. Miller *et al., Community Health Action: A Study of Community Contrast* (East Lansing, Mich.: Michigan State College Press, 1953).
3. Sanford Kravitz, "Sources of Leadership Input for Social Welfare Planning" (unpublished doctoral dissertation, Brandeis University, 1963).
4. Violet M. Sieder, "Current Developments and Problems in Changing American Communities—an Over-all View of Community Organization," Workshop on Community Organization and Community Development, Brandeis University, 1960.
5. Robert Morris, "Basic Factors in Planning for the Coordination of Health Services," Part I, *American Journal of Public Health,* LIII (1963), 248–259; Part II, *ibid.,* pp. 462–472.
6. Harry T. Seeley, "The Challenge of Social Change to Community Welfare Councils," Citizens Conference on Community Planning, Indianapolis, 1963.
7. Gordon Manser, "A Critical Look at Community Planning," *Social Work,* V, No. 2 (1960), 35.
8. Murray Ross, *Community Organization: Theory and Principles* (New York: Harper, 1955).

9. Ronald Lippitt, Jeanne Watson, and Bruce Westley, *The Dynamics of Planned Change* (New York: Harcourt, Brace and World, 1958), p. 45.

10. Sol Levine and Paul E. White, "Exchange as a Conceptual Framework for the Study of Interorganizational Relationships," *Administrative Science Quarterly,* V (1961), 583–601.

11. Martin Rein and Robert Weiss, "An Analysis of the Network of Community Agencies Providing Child Protective Services in Massachusetts" (Brandeis University, 1962; mimeographed).

12. The NAACP bitterly attacked the Philadelphia Council for Community Advancement, a new community welfare planning organization financed by the Ford Foundation and the President's Committee on Juvenile Delinquency, for its failure to include sufficient Negroes in key leadership positions. Such disputes are now commonplace.

13. Richard A. Cloward, "Social Problems, Social Definitions and Social Opportunities," prepared for the Regional Institute on Juvenile Delinquency and Social Forces, 1963.

14. Sidney E. Zimbalist and Walter W. Pippert, "The New Level of Integration in Community Welfare Services," *Social Work,* V, No. 2 (1960), 29–34.

15. Edward C. Banfield, *Political Influence* (New York: The Free Press, 1961); Robert A. Dahl and C. E. Lindblum, *Politics, Economics and Welfare* (New York: Harper, 1957).

16. Daniel Bell, *The End of Ideology* (New York: Collier Books, 1961), p. 402.

17. Banfield, *op. cit.;* Dahl, *op. cit.;* David Truman, *The Governmental Process* (New York: Knopf, 1951); and David M. Sills, *The Volunteers: Means and Ends in a Natural Organization* (Glencoe, Ill.: The Free Press, 1957).

18. See Martin Rein, "Organization for Social Innovation" (Columbus, Ohio: National Conference on Social Welfare, 1963).

3

Social and Physical Planning for the Elimination of Urban Poverty

HERBERT J. GANS

I

City planning has traditionally sought community betterment through so-called *physical* methods, such as the creation of efficient land-use and transportation schemes, the sorting out of diverse types of land use, and the renewal of technologically obsolescent areas and buildings to achieve functional, as well as esthetically desirable, arrangements of structures and spaces. This chapter deals with a new planning concept which places greater emphasis on economic and social methods of improving community life. In some places it is called human renewal; in others, community development; in yet others, social planning. Although none of the names is quite appropriate, the programs to which they refer are of crucial importance to the future of the city, for they seek to do away with—or at least to decimate—urban poverty and the deprivation that accompanies it. If these programs succeed, they are likely to have a lasting impact on city planning and on the other professions concerned with planning for community welfare.

The fight against poverty is not new, of course, and, in fact, the elimination of urban deprivation was one of the goals of the founders of modern city planning. The planning movement itself developed partly in reaction to the conditions under which the European immigrants who came to American cities in the mid-nineteenth century had to live. The reduction of their squalor was one of Frederick Law Olmsted's goals when he proposed the building of city parks so that the poor—as well as the rich—might have a substitute rural landscape in which to relax from urban life. It motivated the Boston civic leaders who first built playgrounds in the slums of that city, and the founders of the settlement house movement, notably Jane Addams, who argued strongly for city planning. It also sparked the efforts of those who build model tenements to improve the housing conditions of the poor. And Ebenezer Howard had this goal in mind when he proposed to depopulate the London slums through Garden Cities.

Most of these planning efforts were not aimed directly at the reduction of

From *Washington University Law Quarterly*, No. 1 (February, 1963), pp. 2–18. An earlier version was presented at the 1962 Conference of the American Institute of Planners and appears in American Institute of Planners, *Proceedings of the 1962 Conference* (Washington, D.C.: The Institute, 1963), pp. 176–190.

poverty and deprivation, but sought to use land planning, housing codes, and occasionally zoning to eliminate slums and reduce densities in the tightly packed tenement neighborhoods. The apotheosis of this approach—slum clearance—followed upon the arrival of the newest wave of poor immigrants: the Southern Negroes, Puerto Ricans, and Mexicans who came to the city during World War II and in the postwar era. After a decade of noting the effects of the federal slum clearance program, however, some observers became concerned because, while this method was eliminating slums, it was not contributing significantly to the improvement of the slum dwellers' living conditions.

In many cases, the reduction in the already short supply of low-cost housing brought about by slum clearance, together with faulty or nonexistent relocation planning, sent slum dwellers into adjacent slums or forced them to overcrowd declining areas elsewhere. But even where slum clearance was accompanied by adequate relocation programs, the housing of poor people in decent low-cost dwellings did not solve other—and equally pressing—problems, such as poverty, unemployment, illiteracy, alcoholism, and mental illness. Nor could rehousing alone do away with crime, delinquency, prostitution, and other deviant behavior. In short, it became clear that such physical changes as urban renewal, good housing, and modern project planning were simply not enough to improve the lives of the poverty-stricken.

As a result, planners and "housers" began to look for non-physical planning approaches.[1] In this process, they made contact with other professions that are concerned with the low-income population, for example, social workers. Working in tandem with them and others, they have developed new programs, bearing the various names indicated above. Most often they have been referred to as social planning, a term that had been coined by social workers to describe the coordination of individual social agency programs carried out by such central planning and budgeting agencies as the United Fund.[2]

Although the term has already received considerable attention in city planning circles, I prefer to use another term. Insofar as the programs seek to aid low-income people to change their fortunes and their ways of living, they are attempts to guide them toward the social and economic mobility that more fortunate people have achieved on their own. For this reason, the programs might best be described as planning for *guided mobility*.

Such programs are now under way in many American cities. Some are designed as programs in juvenile delinquency prevention, which have come into being under the aegis of the President's Committee on Juvenile Delinquency and work mainly with young people.[3] Others are oriented toward low-income people of all ages, and since planners have been most active in these, the rest of the chapter will deal primarily with such programs.[4] Although most of the programs are just getting started, some over-all similarities between them are apparent. Needless to say, any generalizations about them are preliminary, for the programs are likely to change as they progress from initial formulation to actual implementation.

The guided mobility plans and proposals which I have examined have four major programmatic emphases: (1) to develop new methods of education for children from low-income and culturally deprived homes, so as to reduce functional illiteracy, school dropouts, and learning disabilities which prevent such children from competing in the modern job market in adulthood; (2) to reduce unemployment by new forms of job training among the young, by the retraining of adults, and by the creation of new jobs in the community; (3) to encourage self-help on an individual and group basis through community organization methods that stimulate neighborhood participation; and (4) to extend the amount and quality of social services to the low-income population. Within this last group are traditional casework services, new experiments for giving professional help to the hard-to-reach, multi-problem family, and the provision of modern facilities and programs of public recreation, public health, and community center activities.

The educational phase of guided mobility includes programs such as Higher Horizons, which attempt to draw bright children from the culturally restrictive context of low-income environments and to offer them the academic and cultural opportunities available to bright middle-class children. There are also programs to help average and backward youngsters, using remedial reading and other devices to guide them during the early school years, so that they will develop the skills and motivations to stay in school until high school graduation. The occupational phase of the plans includes job programs which will employ young people in useful community projects and in quasi-apprentice programs in private industry, as well as various vocational training and retraining programs for young and old alike. Meanwhile, added effort is scheduled to attract new industries, and thus to bring new jobs to the community.

The extension of social services and the community-organization phase of the programs use decentralization as a means of reaching the high proportion of low-income people who usually abstain from community contact. The provision of social services to the hard-to-reach will be attempted by bringing programs to the neighborhood level, with neighborhood directors to supervise the process. In addition, the social agencies plan to coordinate their services, so that individual agencies working with the same individual or family know what the other is doing, and duplication and contradictions can be avoided. More neighborhood facilities will also be established, including community schools, public health clinics, and recreation centers, sometimes grouped in a "services center," so that people will be encouraged to come there when they need help.

The decentralizing of community organization activities is intended to create a sense of neighborhood and an interest in neighborhood self-help. Community organizers will work in the neighborhood for this purpose, and will try to involve "natural leaders" living in the area, who can act as a bridge between the professionals, the city, and the neighborhood population.

This is a very general description of the programs. In actuality, each community has a somewhat distinctive approach, or a different emphasis in the selection of programs, depending partly on the lineup of sponsoring agencies. But some city planners who have become interested in guided mobility programs are still preoccupied—and sometimes too much so—with traditional physical planning approaches, notably two: the realization of a neighborhood scheme—originally devised by Clarence Perry[5]—consisting of a small, clearly bounded residential area, built up at low density, with auto and pedestrian traffic carefully separated, considerable open space, and with a combination elementary school and neighborhood meeting place in its center; and the provision, both in such neighborhoods and in the larger community, of a standard array of public facilities for recreation, health, education, culture, and other community services.

The concern with neighborhood is of course traditional in city planning, and even the new challenge of finding non-physical ways of helping the low-income group has not diverted the planner from it. In some cities, guided mobility plans are thus almost appendages to physical planning programs, based on the traditional belief that the rebuilding of the city into a series of separate neighborhoods to encourage a small-townish middle-class form of family life is a proper solution even for poverty. Elsewhere, the program may be an appendage of urban renewal activities, the main intent still being the upgrading of the physical neighborhoods. Thus, guided mobility is used partly to organize the neighborhood into undertaking—or helping the city with—this task. But in most cases, the neighborhood emphasis is based on a genuine concern that one of the causes of urban deprivation is to be found in the poor quality of neighborhood life.

The provision of public facilities is also a traditional planning emphasis, dating back to the days when the planner was an ally of the reformers who were fighting for the establishment of these facilities. Out of this has come the belief that public facilities are crucial agencies in people's lives, that up-to date facilities and programs will encourage intensive use of them, and that this in turn will help significantly in achieving the aims of guided mobility planning.

Despite the intensity of the planner's belief in neighborhood and public facility use, there is no evidence that these two planning concepts are as important to low-income people as they are to planners. Consequently, it is fair to ask whether such concepts are as crucial to the elimination of urban poverty and deprivation as is signified by their appearance in some guided mobility plans. The answer to this question requires a brief discussion of the nature of the contemporary urban poverty.

II

The low-income population may be divided into two major segments, which sociologists call the *working class* and the *lower class*.[6] The former consists of semiskilled and skilled blue-collar workers, who hold steady jobs, and are thus able to live under stable, if not affluent, conditions. Their way of life differs in many respects from those of the middle class; for example, in the greater role of relatives in sociability and mutual aid, in the lesser concern for self-improvement and education, and in their lack of interest in the good address, cultivation, and the kinds of status that are important to middle-class people. Although their ways are culturally different from the dominant middle-class norms, these are not pathological, for rates of crime, mental illness, and other social ills are not significantly higher than in the middle class. This population, therefore, has little need for guided mobility programs.

The lower class, on the other hand, consists of people who perform the unskilled labor and service functions in the society. Many of them lack stable jobs. They are often unemployed, or forced to move from one temporary—and underpaid—job to another. Partly because of occupational instability, their lives are beset with social and emotional instability as well, and it is among them that one finds the majority of the emotional problems and social evils that are associated with the low-income population.[7]

In past generations, the American economy had considerable need for unskilled labor, and the European immigrants who performed it were able to achieve enough occupational stability to raise themselves, or their children, to working-class or even middle-class ways of living. Today, however, the need for unskilled labor is constantly decreasing, and will soon be minimal. Consequently, the Negro, Puerto Rican, and Mexican newcomers who now constitute most of the American lower class find it very difficult to improve their condition.[8]

Guided mobility planning is essentially an attempt to help them solve their problems and to aid them in changing their lives. This makes it necessary to find out what causes their problems, what they themselves are striving for, and how they can be helped to achieve their strivings.

The nature of the problem is not difficult to identify. For economic reasons, and for reasons of race as well, the contemporary lower class is frustrated—if not barred—from opportunities to hold well-paid, stable jobs, to receive a decent education, to live in good housing, or to get access to a whole series of choices and privileges that the white middle class takes for granted.

In addition, some lower-class people lack the motivations and skills needed to participate in contemporary society, and, more important, to accept the opportunities, if and when they become available. Moreover, the apathy, despair, and rejection which result from lack of access to crucial opportunities help bring about the aforementioned social and emotional difficulties.

There are a number of reasons for these reactions.[9] When men are long unemployed or underemployed, they feel useless, and eventually become marginal members of their family. This has many consequences. They may desert their families, and turn to self-destructive behavior in despair. If male instability is widespread, the woman becomes the dominant member of the family, and she may live with a number of men in the hope of finding a stable mate.The result is a family type which Walter Miller calls female-based, which is marked by free unions, illegitimate children, and what middle-class people consider to be broken homes.[10] Boys who grow up in such families may be deprived of needed male models, and are likely to inherit some of the feelings of uselessness and despair they see in their fathers. In addition, the children must learn at an early age how to survive in a society in which crisis is an everyday occurrence, and where violence and struggle are ever-present. Thus, they may learn how to defend themselves against enemies and how to coexist with an alcoholic parent, but they do not learn how to read, how to concentrate on their studies, or how to relate to the teacher.[11] Those that do must defend their deviant behavior—and it is deviant in the lower class—against their peers, who, like peers in all other groups, demand that they conform to the dominant mode of adaptation. Also, many children grow up in households burdened with mental illness, and this scars their own emotional and social growth. Out of such conditions develops a lower-class culture with a set of behavior patterns which is useful for the struggle to survive in a lower-class milieu, but which makes it almost impossible to participate in the larger society. And since the larger society rejects the lower-class individual for such behavior, he can often develop self-respect and dignity only by rejecting the larger society. He blames it for his difficulties—and with much justification—but in this process rejects many of its values as well, becoming apathetic, cynical, and hostile even toward those that seek to help him.

This overly brief analysis is at present mostly hypothetical, for we do not yet know exactly what it is that creates the lower-class way of life. We know that the nature of family relationships, the influence of peers, the kind of home training, the adaptive characteristics of lower-class culture, the high prevalence of mental illness, and the need to cope with one crisis after another are all important factors, but we do not yet know exactly which factors are most important, how they operate to create the way of life that they do, and how they are related to the lack of opportunities that bring them about.

Similarly, we know that lower-class people are striving to change their condition, but we do not know exactly for what they are striving. It is clear that they want stable jobs and higher incomes, and there is considerable evidence of an almost magical belief in education and high occupational aspirations for the children, especially among Negroes.[12] The lack of opportunity and the constant occurrence of crises frustrate most of these aspirations before they can be implemented, but they do exist, especially among the women. On the other hand, the failure of settlement houses, social workers, and other helping agencies to reach the majority of the lower-class population suggests that these people either cannot or do not want to accept the middle-class values which these professionals preach and which are built into the welfare activities they carry out. Such programs attract the small minority desirous of or ready for middle-class life, but they repel the rest. A number of social scientists suggest that what lower-class people are striving for is the stable, family-centered life of working-class culture, and at least one delinquency prevention program is based on such an assumption.[13]

These observations about the nature of lower-class life have many implications for guided mobility planning. As a result of the sparsity of knowledge, much research, experiment, and evaluation of experience will be necessary in order to learn what kinds of programs will be successful. It is clear that the most urgent need is to open up presently restricted opportunities, especially in the occupational sphere. The guided mobility programs which stress creation of new jobs, attack on racial discrimination, education, and occupational training as highest-priority items are thus on the right track. Even so, new ways of bringing industry and jobs to the community must be found, for conventional programs have not been sufficiently productive. Then ways of channeling lower-class people into new jobs and keeping them at work, even if their initial performance is not so good as that of other people or of labor-saving machines, must be invented. Racial barriers will also have to come down more quickly, especially in those spheres of life and activity most important to lower-class people, so that they can begin to feel that they have some stake in society. This too is easier said than done.

Not only is desegregation difficult to implement, but the most successful programs so far have benefited middle-class nonwhites more than their less fortunate fellows. For lower-class people, access to jobs, unions, and decent low-cost housing is most important, as is the assurance of fair treatment from the police, the courts, from city hall, storeowners, and helping agencies. The integration of high-priced suburban housing, expensive restaurants, or concert halls is for *them* of much less immediate significance.

Also, methods of encouraging motivations and skills and of maintaining aspirations in the face of frustration must be found. If the matriarchal lower-class family is at fault, ways of providing boys with paternal substitutes must be developed. Where the entire lower-class milieu is destructive, children may have to be removed from it, especially in their formative years. Treatments for mental illness, alcoholism, and narcotics addiction that will be effective among lower-class people have to be discovered, and the causes of these ills isolated so that prevention programs may be set up. Schools must be created which can involve lower-class children. This means that they must teach the skills needed in a middle-class society yet without the middle-class symbols and other trappings that frighten or repel the lower-class student.[14] Finally, it is necessary to develop urban renewal or other housing programs that will make livable dwellings available to the low-income population, within its price range, and located near enough to its places of employment so as not to require unreasonable amounts of travel time and expenditures.

These program requirements demand some radical changes in our ways of doing things. For example, if lower-class people are to find employment, there will need to be economic enterprises not geared solely to profit and to cost reduction, but also to the social profits of integrating the unemployed. In short, eventually we shall have to give up the pretense that nineteenth-century free-enterprise ideology can cope with twentieth-century realities, and learn to replan some economic institutions to help the low-income population, just as we are now redesigning public education to teach this population's children. Likewise, if lower-class people are to become part of the larger society, there must be changes in the way the police, the courts, and political structures treat them. To cite just one instance, lower-class people must be represented more adequately in local party politics, and their needs and demands must receive more adequate hearing at city hall than has heretofore been the case. Similarly, the professions that now seek to help lower-class people will have to be altered so as to be more responsive to how lower-class people define their needs, and this may mean the replacement of some professionals by skilled nonprofessionals who are more capable of achieving rapport with lower-class clients. Also, urban renewal policy must concern itself less with "blight" removal, or with the use of new construction to solve the city's tax problems, and more with improvement of the housing conditions of the slum dwellers. Changes such as these, which require redistribution of power, income, and privileges, and the alteration of established social roles, are immensely difficult to bring about. Even so, they are necessary if urban poverty and deprivation are to be eliminated.[15]

III

Proper guided mobility planning must be based on methods that will achieve the intended goal. If the hypotheses about the causes of urban deprivation are correct, the basic components of guided mobility planning must be able to affect the economy, the political and social structures that shore up poverty and racial—as well as class—discrimination, the foci of lower-class culture that frustrate the response to opportunities, notably the family, the peer group, and the milieu in which children grow up, and the helping agencies that now have difficulty in reaching lower-class people, especially the school. Any programs which lack these components, and cannot bring about changes in the position of the lower-class population vis-à-vis the institutions named, are unlikely to contribute significantly to the aim of guided mobility.[16]

The list of basic components does not include the two that have been especially emphasized by planners: the belief in neighborhood and the importance of public facilities. This omission is not accidental, for I do not believe that these two concepts are of high priority. Indeed, it is possible that they may divert guided mobility programs from the direction they ought to take.

By focusing programs on neighborhoods as spatial units, planners are naturally drawn to what is most visible in them, the land uses, buildings, and major institutions, and their attention is diverted from what is hardest to see, the people—and social conditions—with problems. It should be clear from the foregoing analysis that the program must concentrate on the people and on the social and economic forces which foster their deprivation, rather than on neighborhood conditions which are themselves consequences of these forces.

Moreover, too much concern with neighborhoods may cause the programs to seek out the wrong people: the working-class segment of the low-income population rather than the lower-class one. This may happen for two reasons. First, the planner often finds it difficult to distinguish between areas occupied by working-class people and those occupied by lower-class people, mainly because his concept of standard housing blinds him to differences between low-rent areas, usually occupied predominantly by the former, and slums, which house the latter.[17] Also, working- and lower-class people sometimes live together in the same planning area, especially if they are nonwhite, and a neighborhood focus makes it difficult to reach one without the other. This is undesirable because—as I noted earlier—the working-class population does not need guided mobility, whereas the lower-class population needs it so badly that all resources ought to be allocated to it.

Even so, these drawbacks would not be serious if neighborhood planning could achieve the aims of guided mobility. But this is not the case, mainly because people's lives are not significantly influenced by the physical neighborhood. The important aspects of life take place within the family and the peer group and on the job, and the neighborhood does not seem to affect these greatly. Moreover, although middle- and working-class people do sometimes participate in neighborhood activities, this is not true of lower-class people.[18] Not only do they shy away from organizational participation generally, but because of their great transience they do not spend much time in any one area. More important, since life is a constant struggle for survival and an endless series of crises, lower-class people are often suspicious of their neighbors, and even more so of the landlord, the store owner, the police, and the local politician. They harbor similar feelings toward most other neighborhood institutions and local public facilities.

Thus, the lower-class population's involvement in the neighborhood is at best neutral, and more often negative. Yet even if it were more positive, the components of neighborhood planning and the provision of the entire range of modern public facilities can contribute relatively little to solving the problems which concern lower-class people the most. To a poverty-stricken family, the separation of car and pedestrian traffic, or the availability of park and playground within walking distance, are not very crucial; their needs are much more basic.

This is not to reject the desirability of such planning concepts, but only to say that, given the present condition of lower-class life, they are of fairly low priority. The location and equipment of the school are much less important than the presence of the kinds of teachers who can communicate with lower-class children, and a conventional public health facility is much less vital than an agency that can really help a mother deserted by her husband, or a person who must cope with mentally ill family members.

The standard neighborhood-and-facilities planning package cannot even contribute significantly to the improvement of the lower-class milieu. The significant components of this milieu are other people, rather than environmental features, and until these other people are socially and economically secure enough to trust each other, the milieu is not likely to improve sufficiently to prevent the perpetuation of past deprivations on the young growing up within it.

In short, it seems clear that the kind of neighborhood scheme sought through traditional planning and zoning methods cannot be implemented among lower-class people until the basic components of guided mobility programs have been effectuated. A stable, peaceful neighborhood in which there is positive feeling between neighbors assumes that people have good housing, the kind of job that frees them from worrying about where the next meal or rent money will come from, the solution of basic problems so that the landlord, the policeman, or the bill collector are no longer threatening, and the relief from recurring crises so that they can begin to pay some attention to the world outside the household. Similarly, only when people feel themselves to be part of the larger society, and when they have learned the skills needed to survive in it, will they be able to take part in school or community center activities, or to develop the ability to communicate with the staff of a health clinic. In short, the programs which the neighborhood planner proposes cannot come about until more basic problems have been solved; they are consequences of the elimination of urban poverty rather than devices for it.

Neighborhood planning is necessary, of course, but what is needed is of a social and political type which supports the community, state, and federal programs for the elimination of poverty. Thus, the methods required to help the low-income population develop the skills and attitudes prerequisite to survival in a modern society must reach into the neighborhood and the street in order to recruit people who do not, for one reason or another, come by themselves into public facilities established for such programs. Also, local political activity must be stimulated so that low-income people can use the one power they have—that of numbers and votes—to make their wishes heard at city hall and in Washington. This differs considerably from the need for "citizen participation" often called for by planners and community organization experts; that has usually been defined as citizen consideration of—and consent to—professionally developed programs, or civic activity which is decidedly non-political. The kind of local citizen participation that is needed is quite political, however, and since its aim must be to change the political status quo, it is unlikely that community organizers, who are after all employees of the existing political institution or of establishment-dominated welfare agencies, will be able to encourage such activity even if they are personally willing to do so. Hopefully, enlightened civic leaders and politicians will eventually realize that the low-income population must be more adequately represented in the political process, but in all likelihood they will resist any change in the existing political alignments until they have no other choice. Thus, the initiative for local political activity must come from the areas in which low-income people live. But whoever the initiating agencies may be, these are the types of neighborhood planning that are required to do something about urban poverty.

IV

The incompatibility of traditional city planning aims and the basic components of guided mobility programming is not to be blamed on one or another set of planners, nor indeed is it a cause for blame at all. Rather, it stems from the history and nature of modern city planning, and from the basic assumptions in its approach. The description of two of these assumptions will also shed some light on the relationship between social and physical planning and their roles in the improvement of cities.

The first of these assumptions is the belief in the ability of change in the physical environment to bring about social change. Planners have traditionally acted on the assumption that the ordering of land uses, and improvements in the setting and design of buildings, highways, and other physical features of the community would result in far-reaching improvements in the lives of those affected. The validity of this assumption has been seriously questioned in recent years, and indeed, the rise of what has been called social planning is one expression of this questioning.[19]

But the traditional city planning approach can also be described in another way, as being *method-oriented*. By this I mean that it has developed a repertoire of methods and techniques which has become professionally accepted, and which distinguishes planning from other service-giving professions. As a result, the planner concerns himself largely with improvements in these methods. In this process, however, he loses sight of the goals which his methods are intended to achieve, or the problems they are to solve. Thus, he does not ask whether the methods achieve these goals, or whether they achieve *any* goals.

This concern with method is not limited to the planning profession; it can be found in all professions. The attempt to maintain and improve existing methods is useful if the goals are traditional ones, or if the profession deals only with routine problems. But it does not work so well when new goals are sought, and when new problems arise. As I have already noted, improvements in neighborhood planning cannot contribute significantly to the new problems of the city, or to the new goal of eliminating urban poverty.

What is needed instead is a *goal-oriented* or problem-oriented approach, which begins, not with methods, but with the problems to be solved or the goals to be achieved. Once these are defined and agreed upon, the methods needed to achieve them can be determined through the use of professional insight, research, and experiment until the right methods, i.e., those which will solve the problem or realize the goal, are found.[20] This approach was used in the foregoing pages, in which I questioned the usefulness of traditional planning methods and proposed instead programs to cope with the problems of the lower-class population—and their causes—as well as programs which would lead toward the goals this population was seeking for itself.

This approach is more difficult to implement than a method-oriented one, because it does not respect accepted methods—unless they work—and because it rejects the claims of professional traditions or professional expertise that are not supported by empirical evidence. It may require new methods and new approaches, and thus can wreak havoc with the established way of doing things. However much the goal-oriented approach may upset the profession in the short run, in the long run it improves its efficiency and thus its expertise and status, because its methods are likely to be much more successful, thus reducing the risk of professional failure. In an effort as pioneering and difficult as guided mobility planning, a problem- and goal-oriented approach is therefore absolutely essential.

The conception of method-oriented and goal-oriented planning can also aid our understanding of the relationship between physical and social planning. In the professional discussions of this relationship, the subject has frequently been posed as social planning *versus* physical planning. Although it is not difficult to understand why the subject has been framed in this competitive way, the resulting dichotomy between social and physical planning is neither meaningful nor desirable. There are several reasons for rejecting this dichotomy.

First, social planning is said to deal with the human elements in the planning process. When planners talk of the human side of renewal, or of the human factors in planning, they are suggesting by implication that physical planning is inhuman, that in its concern with land use, site design, the redevelopment of cleared land, and the city tax base it has no concern for the needs of human beings. I would not blame physical planners for objecting to this implication, and am surprised that they have not done so.

But even if this implication is inaccurate, the dichotomy has led to another, even more unfortunate implication, which has some truth to it. Every planning activity, like any other form of social change, creates net benefits for some people, and net costs for others. These may be nonmaterial as well as material. Whether intentionally or not, physical planning has tended to provide greater benefits to those who already have considerable economic resources or political power, be they redevelopers or tenants who profit from a luxury housing scheme, central business district retailers who gain, or expect to gain, from the ever-increasing number of plans to "revive downtown," or the large taxpayers who are helped most when planning's main aim is to increase municipal revenues. The interest in social planning is a direct result of this distribution of benefits, for it seeks to help the people who are forced to pay net costs in the physical planning process. Too often, these are poor people, for example, residents of a renewal or highway project who suffer when adequate relocation housing is lacking. Needless to say, this political bifurcation, in which physical planning benefits the well-to-do, and social planning the less fortunate ones, is not a desirable state of affairs either for the community or for planning.

Finally, in actual everyday usage, the dichotomy refers to skills possessed by different types of planners. Physical planning is that set of methods which uses the traditional skills of the city planner and zoning official; social planning, that set favored by sociologically trained planners, by social workers, and by other professionals concerned with welfare aims. Yet if the planning activities of each are examined more closely, it becomes evident that the terms social and physical are inaccurate labels. Zoning is considered a physical planning method, but an ordinance which determines who is to live with whom, and who is to work next to whom is as much social—as well as economic and political—as it is physical. So is a transportation scheme which decides who will find it easy to get in and out of the city, and who will find it difficult. Conversely, social planners who urge the construction of more low-rent housing, or argue for scattered units rather than projects, are proposing physical schemes even while they are ostensibly doing social planning. Since all planning activities affect people, they are inevitably social, and the dichotomy between physical and social methods turns out to be meaningless. Moreover, in actual planning practice, no problem can be solved by any one method, or any one skill. In most instances a whole variety of techniques are needed to achieve the goal.

The social-physical dichotomy is a logical consequence of viewing planning as method-oriented, because when methods are most important, there is apt to be competition between the people who are skilled in one method rather than another. All successful professions want to apply the methods they know best, for this permits them to maintain their power and social position most easily.

If planning is conceived as goal-oriented, however, goals become most important and methods are subordinated to the goal. In such a planning process, in which a large number of different methods are used in an integrated fashion, any single method loses its magical aura. Moreover, no goal can be defined so narrowly that it is only physical or only social. In a goal-oriented approach, then, there can be no social or physical planning. There is only *planning,* an approach which agrees upon the best goals and then finds the best methods to achieve them.

This way of defining planning has a number of implications for the future of the professions concerned with planning matters, as well as for the improvement of cities. If professionals continue to emphasize traditional method when and where it is not applicable, they can easily lose their usefulness and their professional prerogative for participating in programs of community betterment.

But it is not only the methods which must be reconsidered. Even the goals which are built into these methods are turning out to be less important today. The neighborhood concept has received little support from the clients of planning; the same is true of the planner's insistence on a reduction in the journey to work, which has not been accepted by the journeying populace. Also, in an age of automation and increasing unemployment, the need for economic growth, even if it is disorderly, is becoming more vital than the ordering of growth and the planner's desire for stability. It is, of course, still important to have efficient transportation schemes and to locate noxious industry away from residences, but there is less noxious industry than ever before and, for those who are affluent, the inefficiency of the automobile seems to matter little, especially if it is politically feasible to subsidize the costs of going to work by car. And even the concern with land use per se is becoming less significant. In a technology of bulldozers and rapid transportation, the qualities of the natural environment and the location of land are less important—or rather, more easily dealt with by human intervention—and increasingly, land can be used for many alternatives. The question of what is the best use, given topography and location, is thus less important than who will benefit from one use as compared to another, and who will have to pay costs, and how the public interest is affected.

In short, so-called physical planning questions are receding in importance, and socioeconomic and political ones are becoming more relevant. This, of course, is why the issue of social and physical planning has been discussed as social versus physical. In the long run, however, it seems clear that the future of city planning lies less in the reliance upon land-use plans than in the development of a range of methods that will guarantee the improvement of those aspects of community life that are most in need of improvement.

V

One of the most important tasks in the improvement of cities is the elimination of urban poverty, and of the deprivations of lower-class life. Poverty is fundamentally responsible for the slums we have been unable to eradicate by attacking the buildings, and for the deprivations which ultimately bring about the familiar list of social evils. Moreover, poverty and deprivation are what make cities so ugly and depressing, and they hasten the flight of more fortunate people into the suburbs. And this in turn contributes to economic decline, the difficulties of financing municipal services, political conflict, corruption, and many of the other problems of the contemporary city.

I would not want to argue that all of the city's problems can be laid at the doorstep of poverty. There are technological changes that affect its economic health, and result in the obsolescence of industrial areas and street patterns. There are political rigidities that inhibit its relations with its hinterland. And the desire of most families to raise their children in low-density surroundings suggests that suburbia is not produced solely by the flight from the city, and would exist without urban poverty. Even so, many of the suburbanites have come to hate the city because of the poverty they see there, and this in turn helps to create the hostility between city and suburb and the political conflict that frustrates schemes for metropolitan solutions.

If planners are genuinely concerned with the improvement of cities, the fight against poverty becomes a planning problem, and one that needs to be given higher priority than it has heretofore received. A beginning is being made in the guided mobility programs that are now in operation, but a much greater effort is needed, both on the local and the federal scene, before these programs can achieve their aim. If such efforts are not made, all other schemes for improving the city will surely fail.

NOTES

1. Another impetus came from the fact that several cities scheduled urban renewal projects in their skid-row areas, and programs to "rehabilitate" its residents were developed as part of the relocation plan.
2. The term has also been applied to plans which attempt to outline social—that is, non-physical—goals for the entire society, a procedure that would be more aptly called *societal* planning.
3. Of these, the leading program is New York's Mobilization for Youth. This is described in Mobilization for Youth, Inc., "A Proposal for the Prevention and Control of Delinquency by Expanding Opportunities" (New York, December, 1961, mimeographed).
4. Examples of the many such plans are: Action for Boston Community Development, "A Proposal for a Community Development Program in Boston" (Boston, Dec. 1961, mimeographed); Action Housing, Inc., ". . . Urban Extension in Pittsburgh Area" (Pittsburgh, September, 1961, mimeographed); City of Oakland, "Proposal for a Program of Community Development" (Oakland, Calif., June and December, 1961, mimeographed); Community Progress, Inc., "Opening Opportunities: New Haven's Comprehensive Program for Community Progress" (New Haven, April, 1962, mimeographed); and Department of City Planning, "A Plan for the Woodlawn Community: Social Planning Factors" (Chicago, January, 1962, mimeographed). My comments about the plans below are based on a number of published and unpublished documents which I have examined, as well as on discussions about existing and proposed plans in which I have participated in several cities. My description of these plans is, in sociological terminology, an ideal type, and does not fit exactly any one of the plans now in existence.
5. Clarence A. Perry, "The Neighborhood Unit," *Regional Survey of New York and Its Environs* (New York: Committee on Regional Plan of New York and Its Environs, 1929), VII, 22–140.
6. Herbert J. Gans, *The Urban Villagers* (Glencoe, Ill.: The Free Press, 1962), Ch. 11. See also S. M. Miller and Frank Riessman, "The Working Class Subculture: A New View," *Social Problems*, IX (1961), 86–97. The nature and extent of urban poverty are described in Michael Harrington, *The Other America* (New York: Macmillan, 1962), Chs. 2, 4, 5, 7, 8.
7. An excellent brief description of lower-class culture may be found in Walter B. Miller, "Lower Class Culture as a Generating Milieu of Gang Delinquency," *Journal of Social Issues*, XIV (1958), 5–19. The everyday life of the lower class is pictured in Oscar Lewis, *Five Families* (New York: Basic Books, 1959), and *The Children of Sanchez* (New York: Random House, 1961). Although Lewis' books deal with the lower class of Mexico City, his portrait applies, with some exceptions, to American cities as well.
8. For an analysis of the occupational history of the European immigrants and the more recent immigrants, see Oscar Handlin, *The Newcomers* (New York: Anchor Books, 1962).
9. For a more detailed analysis, see Gans, *The Urban Villagers*, Ch. 12, and Institute for Urban Studies, *Social Planning: A New Role for Sociology* (Philadelphia,

1962, mimeographed). See also Mobilization for Youth, Inc., *op. cit.,* and Walter B. Miller, *op. cit.*

10. Walter B. Miller, *op. cit.* This family type is particularly widespread in the Negro lower class, in which it originated during slavery.

11. The educational and other problems of the lower-class child are described in more detail in Patricia C. Sexton, *Education and Income* (New York: Viking, 1961); and Frank Riessman, *The Culturally Deprived Child* (New York: Harper, 1962).

12. For the most recent example of this finding, see R. Kleiner, S. Parker, and H. Taylor, "Social Status and Aspirations in Philadelphia's Negro Population" (Philadelphia: Commission on Human Relations, June, 1962, mimeographed).

13. Mobilization for Youth, Inc., *op. cit.*

14. See Sexton, *op. cit.,* and Riessman, *op. cit.*

15. For other programmatic statements, see Peter Marris, "A Report on Urban Renewal in the United States," and Leonard J. Duhl, "Planning and Poverty," in Leonard J. Duhl (ed.), *The Urban Condition* (New York: Basic Books, 1963), pp. 113–134, and 295–304, respectively. See also Harrington, *op. cit.*

16. For a more detailed critical analysis of current guided mobility plans, see Gans, *Social Planning.*

17. Herbert J. Gans, "The Human Implications of Current Redevelopment and Relocation Planning," *Journal of the American Institute of Planners,* XXIV (1959), 15–25, or *Urban Villagers,* Ch. 14.

18. Generally speaking, middle-class people participate in formal neighborhood organizations to a much greater extent than other classes, although their social life often takes place outside the neighborhood. Working-class people are less likely to participate in formal organizations, but most of their social activities take place close to home. For a discussion of working-class attitudes toward the neighborhood, see Marc Fried and Peggy Gleicher, "Some Sources of Residential Satisfaction in an Urban 'Slum,' " *Journal of the American Institute of Planners,* XXVII (1961), 305–315.

19. See, for example, Irving Rosow, "The Social Effects of the Physical Environment," *Journal of the American Institute of Planners,* XXVII (1961), 127–133.

20. This approach is currently receiving considerable attention in planning literature. My discussion is based on an initial formulation by Martin Meyerson, and is treated in more detail in studies conducted by him, John Dyckman, and this writer which are now being prepared for publication. For a summary statement of this approach, see Paul Davidoff and Thomas Reiner, "A Choice Theory of Planning," *Journal of the American Institute of Planners,* XXVIII (1962), 103–115.

Part II HOUSING AND URBAN RENEWAL

Editors' Introduction

The persistence of slums in American cities has stimulated a long series of programs and policies aimed at improving housing conditions. Unlike other areas of urban policy, where the goals of public action have not been stated directly, housing policy has been based on an explicit objective. The national objective, according to the Housing Act of 1949, is "the realization as soon as feasible of the goal of a decent home and a suitable living environment for every American family."

This goal seems clear enough, until one questions the meaning of "decent" and "suitable." Who is to define what constitutes decent housing and a suitable environment, and what are the criteria? In practice, the housing objectives sought by both federal and local agencies have been defined almost exclusively in physical and economic terms. Programs to provide housing have been concerned with securing minimum standards of space, utility service, and physical condition, and with keeping costs to a reasonable level. Programs to remove slum housing have been similarly concerned with the physical characteristics of structures: dilapidation, lack of plumbing and heating, inadequacies of size or layout. To the extent that these programs have considered the living environment outside the house, they have similarly tended to define a suitable environment in terms of minimum physical standards: exterior space, protection from noise and traffic hazards, access to schools and playgrounds.

Physical standards for housing are useful in many ways. They furnish guidelines for designing individual programs; they serve as benchmarks for measuring progress toward the national goal; and they reflect a measure of agreement on the minimum housing conditions appropriate for our society.

At best, however, these standards are incomplete. They fail to consider the full range of values and needs that people hope to satisfy by their choice of housing. At worst, a narrow concern with the provision of physically adequate shelter can shade easily into programs that frustrate other goals. Urban renewal projects, for example, have often decided the fate of old residential areas solely on the basis of their physical condition. In some cases, the clearance of blighted buildings has become an end in itself, with little regard for social values destroyed in the process. In public housing, too, policies governed unduly by physical criteria have led to housing projects that are clean and well heated, but unacceptable to many low-income families who object to "project living."

The national goal needs a broader definition. Evaluation of recent experience has shed new light on the complex needs and the values of the people who live in slums. Housing is an important element in self-perception, conveying status connotations both to the outside world and to the resident. Housing that conveys an image of institutional care may be as destructive of self-esteem as housing that proclaims neglect and poverty. Other social values are bound up with the freedom to use and adapt housing space as a means of personal expression and to satisfy individual needs. Status factors and the desire for personal expression both have significant implications for housing design and management. The neighborhood location of housing is another critical factor, for many values relate to the surrounding community more than to the house itself. A familiar and satisfying environment, with nearby friends and relatives, supportive local institutions, and specialized activities adapted to the character of the population, often means more to people than the physical standards of their housing.

The current effort to link physical and social planning more closely arises in large measure from a new understanding of the social dimensions of housing and urban renewal. In this section, articles by Marc Fried and Joan Levin and by Lee Rainwater present the findings of recent research into the significance of housing and the social environment for low-income groups. Lee Rainwater focuses attention on personal security as a neglected factor among the special housing needs and perceptions of lower- and working-class families. Marc Fried and Joan Levin interpret the social functions of slum communities, stressing their positive role in helping people adapt to urban life. Fried and Levin argue that public policy has been misdirected toward the annihilation of slum areas without providing adequate replacements for their social functions.

By comparison with urban renewal, public housing has had a clearer mandate to improve housing conditions for low-income groups. Rehousing the people who live in slums has been the goal of a few renewal projects, but many others have aimed at rejuvenating the downtown shopping district or promoting industrial development. To many proponents of renewal, serving the needs of the poor is only an incidental objective; some contend that renewal programs are obligated only to give the poor fair treatment while taking over their homes for other purposes. But public housing has as its major responsibility providing decent housing for poor people. Despite the continuing need for public housing, confirmed by long waiting lists for admission to projects in most big cities, there has been increasing dissatisfaction with this program. Outside observers have been criticizing the impersonality and ugliness of large projects as well as the chaotic living conditions that have become part of the public-housing image. More to the point, many low-income families in need of housing have been "voting with their feet" and choosing to live in substandard private housing rather than in a public project. Of the families displaced by urban renewal, about half have been eligible for public housing; yet only a third of these eligibles have actually moved to public housing. The article by Preston David calls attention to the many problems that beset people who live in public housing. David contends that public housing should do more than build a roof over poverty, and that housing authorities need to give equal attention to social planning for their clients.

Housing priorities

The recurring theme that social components need to be built into housing and renewal programs does not, of course, imply that these programs are entirely adequate in meeting their prior objective, decent physical accommodations. The task of reorienting housing and renewal policies to reflect the current state of social knowledge is one major challenge confronting urban planners and policy-makers, but not the only one. It is equally important to ensure that these programs are large enough to meet national housing needs and that they assign high priority to low-income groups, whose needs are greatest.

In terms of the measurable physical characteristics of housing, there has been steady progress toward the national housing goal since World War II, but much remains to be done. Between 1950 and 1960, the number of families living in substandard housing was reduced by more than one-third, both in the nation at large and within our metropolitan areas. In urban areas, this improvement did not result primarily from direct action under public housing or urban renewal, but came about mainly as an indirect consequence of the movement of millions of people from the central cities to the suburbs.

The movement of middle-income families to new houses in suburbia made possible substantial improvements in living conditions for those who remained in the older cities. Housing vacated by departing families did not remain vacant for long. Many small apartments were merged to form larger ones to accommodate formerly crowded families. Many large households, in which grown children lived together with their parents and other relatives, split up as people moved out to live in separate quarters. Crowding was reduced, not only within the dwelling units but also within formerly crowded neighborhoods where the population declined. In addition, much of the old housing was renovated. Dwellings that formerly lacked plumbing facilities or bathrooms, or needed other repairs, were put in sound condition.

Despite this impressive progress in upgrading substandard housing, some 8.5 million families were still living in substandard dwellings in 1960, and about two-fifths of these were in metropolitan areas. Further, a large number of families are living in housing that is standard in terms of Census classifications (in sound condition with all plumbing facilities) but that falls below the more rigorous conditions established by local housing codes. Others are living in housing that is standard but overcrowded; and the number of families forced to pay more than one-fifth of their income for housing has increased substantially since 1950.

Thus the national housing goal still calls for a very large scale of operation to meet the minimum physical shelter needs of the American people. The limited scale of present national programs can be gauged by comparing the figure of 8.5 million families in substandard housing in 1960 with the total production of low-income public housing from the 1930's to the present: thirty years of effort have produced some 600,000 housing units.

Alvin L. Schorr calls attention to the very limited funds that are allocated to subsidize the housing of poor people, particularly in comparison with the major but indirect subsidies supplied to house middle-income people. His proposals call first for an adequate level of spending to supply the needed volume of housing. Schorr's article suggests that urban and social planners need to find ways of developing the social components of housing programs, but that a retreat to small programs for the sake of increasing social sensitivity would be self-defeating. The task is to fashion programs and policies that incorporate social elements while increasing the scale of national effort.

Relocation

Urban housing problems have become more complicated recently with the rapid growth of public programs that demolish low-cost housing and displace large numbers of families. Chief among these are urban renewal and highway construction, which together will displace as many as 100,000 families a year in the decade ahead. Various aids are available to families displaced by public action, but these differ considerably from one program to another and one locality to another. Federal policy has moved toward equalizing relocation benefits among different displacement programs, but the disparities are still considerable. Meanwhile, relocation is seldom regarded as a high-priority function of local government, requiring continuing attention and advance planning.

The results of relocation to date are subject to some controversy, arising in part from the lack of consistent information on what has been happening to displaced families. The program that has paid most attention to relocation and has provided most information on it is urban renewal. Experience with renewal points up many of the problems of relocation planning—problems of priority, scale, timing, and sensitivity to the diverse needs of displaced families. Neither urban renewal nor the other displacing programs have given major emphasis to building subsidized housing for relocation purposes. Instead, the emphasis is on finding suitable vacancies from among the existing stock of housing and on compensating displaced people for property losses and certain other expenses.

The greatest obstacle to successful relocation is this dependence on vacancies in the private market. Even though the vacancy rate has been increasing in the core cities, housing that is in sound condition and available at low cost is still scarce. The basic problem of a continuing shortage of good low-income housing is further compounded by the need to find housing available to Negroes (who form a majority among urban renewal displacees), housing for large families, and housing suitable for the elderly— all while demolition programs reduce the available supply and throw large numbers of people on the market at once.

Thus the results of relocation surveys indicate grounds for continuing concern. Families relocated for urban renewal are generally forced to pay higher rents in their new housing, often amounting to an unreasonable share of their income. Many families have been shifted into deficient housing: local renewal-agency reports claim that more than 90 per cent of families that have been traced have moved into sound housing, but independent surveys have found higher proportions of displaced families in substandard housing and in other locations slated for clearance. The most comprehensive review of relocation studies, published in 1964, concludes that "on the whole relocation has made a disappointingly small contribution to the attainment of 'a decent home in a suitable living environment for every American family.' Given the premise that one of the cardinal aims of renewal and rehousing should be the improved housing welfare of those living in substandard conditions, it is questionable whether the limited and inconsistent gains reported in most studies represent an acceptable level of achievement." [1]

The article by Marc Fried and Joan Levin goes beyond considerations of cost and quality of relocation housing by focusing on the social and psychological impact of relocation. The problems that people face when they are uprooted from familiar surroundings may well be more severe than any direct costs resulting from price increases or physical shortcomings of their new housing. Improved relocation policy will call for attention to the social problems of adjustment as well as to the traditional concerns with housing quality and price, and improved procedures will have to lend themselves to application on a large scale consistent with the total volume of relocation need.

NOTE

1. Chester Hartman, "The Housing of Relocated Families," *Journal of the American Institute of Planners*, XXX (November, 1964), 266–286.

4

Some Social Functions of the Urban Slum

MARC FRIED AND JOAN LEVIN

The slum as focus of moral protest

For at least a century journalists and public health officials, architects and social service workers, aristocrats and revolutionaries have inveighed against the evils of the slum. All the lurid details of illicit sexuality, crime and gambling, alcoholism and drug addiction, moral debility, physical crowding, and filth have been described so frequently that the slum has appeared as the true Sodom and Gomorrah of the modern, industrial world. In characterizing the slum, such diverse attributes as poverty, poor housing, illiteracy, disease, and truancy are mingled indiscriminately with the evidence of social pathology. Thus, causal sequences have more often been confounded than clarified.

In this light, it is hardly surprising that the abolition of the slums has been a banner under which men of good will might rally in the expectation that only the public good could be served through the eradication of slum areas. Primary initial targets of reform, of badly needed efforts to eliminate intolerable housing conditions and inhuman standards of living, have been easily submerged in tidal waves of misguided moralism. Even George Bernard Shaw's socialist cynicism could perceive little more than charming malevolence in Doolittle's refusal to discard his slum surroundings, a view that Shaw captured in his term "the undeserving poor." The social functions of the slum, if they were ever appreciated, are readily ignored. Most attempts to eradicate slums, now as in the past, have evoked passionate opposition from the inhabitants, but this opposition has only rarely been viewed as a sign of the value and integrative potential of working-class communities.[1]

Jane Addams, the pioneer of the American settlement house movement who started Hull-House in Chicago, did perceive fragments of social organization in the willingness of many slum inhabitants to help one another in distress.[2] She was also sensitive to the positive value of maintaining familiar patterns of behavior among recent immigrants to facilitate the process of transition. However, the fact that so many slum dwellers were people of relatively recent foreign origin with strange cultural patterns and beliefs tended to obscure the important social relationships and indigenous social resources of the slum from many observers who firmly held the social ideals of upper-middle-class Americans. Many of these patterns were, in fact, adaptations and transpositions from rural, peasant life in foreign countries for newcomers to the industrial city. Not until late in the 1930's, when William F. Whyte decided to participate in the life of a streetcorner society, did the limitations and destructive oversimplifications of the "disorganized" conception of the slum become apparent.[3] With the growth of a larger body of work on slum communities and on working-class people, Whyte's observations and insights have been implemented and expanded to alter our understanding of these physically deteriorated areas. On the basis of a host of studies, it is now possible to develop a more general conception both of the value and of the limitations of slum life.

Many varieties of dilapidated residential areas have been readily assimilated to a unitary conception of the urban slum. Indeed, the failure to distinguish different kinds of areas of poor housing from one another is a major source of difficulty in clarifying the problem of poverty and of housing among low-status people.[4] One of the main impediments to understanding slum areas is the fact that the different kinds of slums do share some common physical attributes, are geographically contiguous to one another, and often draw upon people of similar cultural origin. The great wave of studies on the urban environment at the University of Chicago during the 1920's revealed some of the diversity of slum areas without clarifying the patterned differences. The deviant qualities of the slum most clearly distinguished these areas from stable, middle-class neighborhoods and thus attracted the attention of young investigators, reinforcing the pervasive image of the slum as the locus of all the ills of an urban, industrial civilization.

Robert Park, the godparent of these studies, fully perceived the place of such exotic issues as hobohemia, gangland, ghettos, delinquency, dance halls, and vice in the larger trends of urban development, migration from rural areas, and population change.[5] But, without this broad perspective, it is easy to conceive of all working-class slum life on the model of the most visible, notable, and notorious characteristics associated with slum areas. These qualities are likely to be most evident when rates of migration of low-status people exceed any possibility of their rapid and stable assimilation and temporarily exacerbate urban social problems.

The skid-row type of slum, in particular, has determined the popular conception of slums out of all proportion to the distribution of populations in different kinds of slum areas. *Yet, stable, family-based working-class slum areas include a population many times the size of the skid rows in any city. And stable, family-based working-class people, economically deprived but without extensive dependence on professional services and assistance, represent the vast majority of slum populations.* This is not to say that problems of urban slums and of urban slum populations do not command our attention. The critical issue is to appreciate the functional as well as the dysfunctional features of slums. Unless our attention is directed to the appropriate issues and is conceived in an accurate image of working-class populations and residential areas, our efforts at understanding or change are likely to be misdirected.

This is most evident in contemporary views of the massive current problem posed by Negro slums. That the needs of Negro slum populations are great vastly understates the issue. But the facts of extensive marital disruption, of widespread unemployment and underemployment, of high rates for many social and psychological problems, must not obscure the equally evident fact that these are the visible difficulties of a minority of the population. These are only crisis manifestations of the larger set of problems— problems of segregation, discrimination, migration, inadequate education and occupational opportunity, in brief, of social and residential ghettoization for potentially stable and effective working-class people—that present the core of the issue.

Indeed, another of the very important distinctions to be made among slum areas is that between the working-class slum and the ghetto. And the primary difference lies in the degree of freedom of choice, the inner comfort, and the external opportunity to select the housing and a residential area in which to live. As Park pointed out, Jews often remained in ethnic ghettos long after they moved out of residential slums.[6] In somewhat similar fashion, most Negro ghettos in the urban areas of the United States include some housing that is hardly slum housing, inhabited by middle-class and relatively high-income Negroes. The restriction to residential areas defined by ethnicity or color, whether due to the lack of external choice or of internal options, is a primary index of ghettoization although it often transcends economic limitations.[7] The many gross and subtle differences that may be induced by ghettoization are relatively unknown, apart from the likelihood of its impact on self-esteem. Nonetheless, one must distinguish the working-class slum as a residential and social phenomenon from the characteristics superimposed by ethnic segregation and discrimination.

Taking these differences in types of slums into account, however, we can observe the many similarities among slums. Widely dispersed working-class, family-based slum areas are strikingly alike in their histories, in the origin of their populations, in their forms of social organization, and in their dominant values and life styles. This is quite evident in a host of studies from various parts of the United States, England, Scotland, France, Holland, and even highly urbanized places in Africa and Latin America.[8] Important differences may appear when discriminatory segregation compels a large population group such as the former Jews of Warsaw or the Negroes in the United States into ghetto-like situations which cannot readily be modified by the usual processes of mobility and dispersion in the city. But, despite the inadequacy of the data, there are suggestions that the urban, Negro working-class slum may be more similar to familiar ethnic slums than superficial differences would imply.[9] Other differences among slums are evidently associated with the level of economic development of the country or region and, more generally, with standards of living and with rates of economic expansion. However, the similarities are great and point to functional consistency under varied social and economic conditions.

All the stable, working-class slums share some of the more ostensible, physical attributes of low-status areas: relatively poor housing, few physical amenities, excessive crowding in households and neighborhoods. These may range from the relatively high standards achieved in highly developed industrial areas to the miserable hovels of the nineteenth century or those of underdeveloped countries today. But the importance of slum areas for working-class populations persists in spite of these physical qualities. *Most strikingly, widespread commitment to the residential slum persists in spite of dissatisfaction with the narrower qualities of housing.* The reasons for this commitment emerge from a fuller understanding of the slum and its people. The slum can best be understood as a transitional community and a transitional way of life adapted to the personal and social needs of rural preindustrial populations confronted with the complexities of urban, industrial life. But the slum does have a history which, in turn, is closely related to its contemporary forms and functions.

Historical perspective on the slums

During the past few hundred years, two concomitant changes have taken place which have more drastically and more rapidly altered the face of the earth than any known changes in human history. The first was the exponential acceleration of technological and industrial growth. The second was the dramatic increase in population throughout the world. The phenomenon of the modern urban slum is a consequence of these changes, of the Industrial Revolution, of the population explosion which started in the eighteenth century, and of some of the correlated phenomena of industrial location and population movements. Certainly there were slums before this time, but they harbored the relatively small populations that had voluntarily migrated or had been involuntarily displaced from their rural tenures of land before there was adequate opportunity for craft, commercial, or industrial occupation. Whether or not they truly included only the destitute, the vagrant, the beggar, and the criminal, this is the impression which much of the literature reveals.[10] Employed workers generally lived in the households of their employers or masters or, in the case of larger enterprises, adjacent to their masters' homes. With the coming of the Industrial Revolution, a great many industrial and commercial jobs became available in urban areas. The simultaneous population expansion, and the demise of seigneurial responsibilities for the rural population, increased opportunity (and often necessity) for migration, and the greater difficulty of earning a living through local craft activities led to vast population movements in Western Europe which left a host of deserted villages in their wake.

Conditions of life in the newly created slums were almost beyond description. On this score, Handlin seems hardly to have exaggerated. He discusses the slums of Boston when the great Irish famines of the middle of the nineteenth century created an influx of destitute peasants.

Baths were unheard of; inside water was uncommon, and the apartments with their own water supply few indeed. Walls were damp, roofs leaked. Stairs were generally dilapidated, windows were often broken, and many buildings had not felt the hand of the repair man in ten or more years. Decay and slothfulness led directly to the prevalence of fires which involved great loss of life and much suffering.[11]

With respect to sewage, Handlin also reveals the horror of Boston slums:

No one was responsible for the care of the communal instruments, and as a result they were normally out of repair. Abominably foul and feculent, perpetually gushing over into the surrounding yards, they were mighty carriers of disease. To make matters worse, lack of direct access to the streets in court dwellings made the disposal of rubbish a burdensome problem, most easily solved by permitting it to decay at its leisure in the tiny yards, a process which converted the few feet between adjoining buildings into storehouses of accumulated filth.[12]

Housing conditions were unbelievably bad, poverty was widespread and extreme, and social chaos always seemed on the verge of erupting into major disorder. However, as Polanyi asserts,[13] the degree of suffering and disorganization at the height of the Industrial Revolution is not wholly explained either by work conditions or by low salaries. The disruption of several centuries of relative stability, brought to a focal point by the changes surrounding industrialization and by the influx into the cities of larger numbers of people than the most rapid urban expansion could encompass, appears to have been critical in creating the degradation of the working class so closely associated with the Industrial Revolution.

The historical source of the modern slum was the necessity for agglomerating a cheap labor force of unskilled and semiskilled workers near the expanding factories of the eighteenth and nineteenth centuries. Inexpensive public transportation did not develop until after the middle of the nineteenth century, so that housing for factory workers had to be adjacent to the factory itself.[14] The need for large masses of low-status workers was largely fulfilled by the migration of vast numbers of dispossessed agricultural workers from rural areas, a process that has continued throughout the last two hundred years. In some instances, as in the migration of the Irish and the Jews to the United States or of Southern rural Negroes to industrial cities, the situations from which they departed were so intolerable that the "pull" of opportunity was probably a less potent force than the "push" of discrimination and misery. But no matter what the reason or which country or area was the source of emigration, the greatest proportion of these migrants from rural to urban, industrial areas have become laborers, performing the work that few people voluntarily chose, living in areas that were readily available and accessible, and in which they were accepted.[15]

The Industrial Revolution and the factory system produced the social conditions which necessitated residential concentrations of low-skilled workers. Population growth and migrations into the cities actually created the high densities of working-class areas. But real estate exploitation and housing policies (or, more often, the absence of housing policies or fragmentary housing programs) gave rise to the specific conditions of inadequate housing that resulted in working-class slums. The cities of the nineteenth and early twentieth centuries were ill prepared to house the large numbers of workers who came to dwell in their recesses. This pressure for dwelling space eventually gave rise to the tenement, initially a philanthropic effort to improve the housing of workers, which miscarried in the striving for real estate profits. As Mumford points out, "The ground rents rose and the living quarters worsened." [16] With continued expansion of technology, industry, and urban areas, and with continued migration, the tenements and converted dwellings became the mark of declining areas.

To gain perspective on the functions of the slum, we must concern ourselves with many factors—not only with the qualities of housing and of social pathology which so frequently obtrude themselves and obscure other features of slum residence. There is little doubt that poor housing and higher rates of social pathology are associated with slum residence, but whether these are functions of residential location or of socioeconomic status remains an open question. Many efforts to implicate the slum as cause of social pathology have failed and, even in the sphere of physical health, there is evidence to suggest that socioeconomic status is more critical than slum residence.[17] On the other hand, there has been relatively little work on the effects of residential movement and rural-to-urban migration on medical and social pathology. The literature on migration and mental health would strongly suggest that large-scale social and cultural transitions as well as socioeconomic status may produce some of the apparent relationships between slums and pathology.[18]

Although there is little adequate evidence to support the view that slum housing has direct effects on medical, psychiatric, or social pathology, there is every reason to view the *housing* conditions in slums as a serious form of economic and social abuse. Indeed, among the several distinctions that are necessary for understanding the problem, one of the most important is to disjoin the image of slum housing from that of working-class residential areas. *Just as the working class has been subject to many forms of economic and social tyranny, those conditions which necessitated local housing for a mass of unskilled and uneducated working-class families have most often led to unscrupulous exploitation in housing.*[19] It is all the more telling that these poor conditions of housing have not vitiated the importance of the slum area as a meaningful and satisfying social environment.

The later phases of slum development in highly industrialized countries reveal a slow but inevitable reduction in congestion and an improvement in housing for urban workers. Paradoxically, the very factors that produce lower densities and improved housing in working-class slums are often viewed as indications of the decline of a slum area since this transition involves a decrease in population with larger out-migration than in-migration. However, in many of the underdeveloped countries of the world and, to some extent, under the pressure of new waves of migration from rural areas into industrialized cities, some of the earlier conditions of extremely high densities and extremely poor housing conditions become visible anew.[20] But the process of dispersion from slum areas continues for many reasons. Social and residential mobility among former slum dwellers, along with the extension of inexpensive transportation and public services into outlying areas, has encouraged the development of working-class and lower-middle-class suburbs for ever larger proportions of each succeeding generation.

Although there has been no dramatic equalization of incomes during the past few decades,[21] the standard of living for the population as a whole has risen, weighting the scales toward better housing. The process of dispersion of the white ethnic groups from the slums has continued over past decades[22] and, while discrimination appears to reduce the rate of such dispersion among Negroes, an equivalent process of increased movement out of the slums and out of ghettos appears to be slowly taking place in recent years.[23]

The United States may not have been the simple melting pot envisioned by popular conception, but it has seen a slow, gradual assimilation of varied populations to new cultural and social patterns.[24] And the very same slums that have seen the dispersion of one ethnic group have served as ports of entry for more recent migrants to the urban, industrial society. *The processes of urbanization and industrialization are mirrored in the succession of habitats and the progression of social statuses among the newcomers to this modern world as they accomplish the many-sided and complex adaptations of urban, industrial man.* The slums from which former migrants have moved remain as memoirs to the past of many different ethnic groups in American life.

This process is halting and sporadic, far from universal, difficult, and fraught with many varieties of insult and injustice, but it is a process that persists and, at each stage of passage, leaves room in the cycle for new incumbents. The old, tenemented slums with their alleyways, narrow streets, and small, densely crowded apartments have become a major target of urban renewal at the American midcentury, but continue to be the main entry points for this entire progression and the main ports of embarkation into acculturated, assimilated American-middle-class life. Technologically, these areas may be anachronisms. Morally, they belie any sense of justice in the adequacy of housing within an affluent society. Functionally, however, they are critical elements in the progression of rural population groups into contemporary life and, although one may dispense with their decayed and dilapidated housing conditions, one cannot ignore the significance of the slum as a residential area.

Traditional functions of urban slums

The slum has many social functions which vary, within limits, according to larger societal processes and to the population segment involved. Clearly, its most general social function is to serve as a local labor market for low-status workers. Indeed, one of the important developments in recent years has been the suburbanization of industry, which, in turn, has led to the expansion of working-class areas into suburban, single-family and small multiple-family residential locations. This appears to be a relevant trend, however, mainly for established semiskilled and skilled workers who have achieved a stable occupational adaptation and a long-term sense of security in the job. But the function of the high-density, central-city slum as a residential base for low-status workers without stable job expectations but within reach of many job possibilities remains a vital feature of the slum and is likely to persist for a long time.

The single most important function of the slum is as a transitional community, a social environment halfway between the preindustrial society of the rural worker and modern, industrial, urban society. This function provides an opportunity for gradual adaptation to the complex demands and expectations of an unfamiliar and challenging environment. The city has often been viewed as extremely heterogeneous and confusing. The relatively circumscribed and homogeneous character of the urban slum cushions the impact of the larger city. The slum provides a relatively stable and secure environment which can be relinquished as people achieve a greater sense of inner comfort and psychological freedom within the larger geographical and social environment of the city. In this way lower-class areas facilitate a gradual and selective movement out of the more limited and parochial atmosphere. These movements may take place initially around the necessities of work, of shopping, of schooling. Slowly they encompass a larger range of activities and engender a broader sense of the city as a meaningful geographical and social entity rather than as a strange and forbidding place.

In addition to the transitional function, the urban slum serves several other functions for different kinds of people. One of the more important of these is the function of the slum as a haven. Whether or not individuals living in family-based slums are occupationally and socially mobile, the slum serves as a port of entry and as a place which provides many links to the past. In this respect, the working-class slum provides an environment of relatively low pressure for social adaptation and change, a most important function in view of the inevitable demands for large and immediate adjustments to work and the job.[25]

The slum also houses a certain, but unknown, number of people who show few signs or little likelihood of any social mobility: the poverty-stricken, those with chronic difficulties in work, the lower-status aged, and the "disorganized" multiple-problem family. Some of these groups are undoubtedly transient and, both because of unpaid rents and because of unrealistic dreams of improvement, keep moving from one working-class slum to another. But others in this group, *in order to maintain whatever precarious balance they have achieved, require the sense of familiarity, of psychological security and of acceptance, that the slum community offers.*

The slum also serves as a haven for many of the people who are, temporarily or permanently, moving down the status scale. Although the exact frequency of downward mobility in our society is not known, it is evidently quite widespread.[26] And the working-class slum provides a residential (and often social) resource for many people who experience a loss of occupational status or of income due to difficulties in physical health, social adjustment, or emotional well-being. *The possibility of retreating to the encompassing security and peculiar inviolability of the slum allows for the kind of "psychosocial moratorium" that is sometimes essential in coping with complex demands for adaptation under conditions of stress and crisis.*

In sum, the slum serves different functions for several categories of inhabitants: those who are newcomers to an urban, industrial environment, those who are temporarily or permanently downwardly mobile, and those who are unable to achieve stability within the stresses of urban life. Despite this variety of functions, the long-term expansion of our economy has given particular significance to the transitional function associated with gradual social mobility. The slum is the locus of social "training" in bridging the contrast between former experiences in rural communities and the roles and expectations of the industrial world. The rural area is always extremely parochial, whether it be a Balkan peasant village, a Latin-American Indian farming community, a Southern Negro backwater, or a Midwestern cluster of stores two hours from Toledo. Its intense localism, limited horizons and goals, and profound traditionalism, and the halting and distorted intrusion of urbanism on rural village life have been extensively described.[27]

An impressive if almost certainly rose-colored description of the rural village appears in the monumental comparison of Poles in Poland and in America by Thomas and Znaniecki.[28] The Polish peasantry represented one extreme in the emphasis on communal life, in the central importance of the extended family, in the subordination of individualism to the collectivity, and in the rigid adherence to the customary and familiar. While other Eastern European peasant societies shared many of these characteristics, the earlier decline and more varied history of feudalism in the West made many incursions on these patterns among the peasantry of Western Europe. But patterns of social organization so well adapted to maintaining stability in the face of perpetual crisis and tragedy do not readily disappear. In many rural areas, even in industrial societies, the communalism has been fragmented but not destroyed, kin have been dispersed but not disbanded, custom and tradition struggle with the inevitable invasion of change but do not altogether succumb.

There is little doubt, from the many reports by immigrants and from the many studies of immigrant groups, that the initial impact of immigration is overwhelming.[29] It is difficult for anyone to move into a totally unfamiliar environment in which one knows neither the language, the places, the people, nor the characteristic patterns of expectation. For the immigrant from a peasant society, adapted to the stability and sameness of centuries, the change is enormous. There is all the unpredictability of the unfamiliar. But there is also a dramatic shift from an experience of living within well-charted physical and social bounds to a demand for coping with the ambiguity of an urban, industrial environment in an open society. It is hardly surprising, therefore, that the migrant retreats from urban ambiguity and complexity and almost invariably moves into the far more secluded and restricted realm of the working-class slum community.

For most lower-status migrants to the city, the working-class slum looks like an island of familiarity in the midst of a completely strange environment. Thomas and Znaniecki pointed out that the urban, working-class community contains many elements comparable to the peasant community. This is certainly true for the ethnic slums and, in more attenuated form, for most working-class districts. The greater visibility of people who reside there and the greater expressiveness and openness of gestures and words alone create important points of initial similarity. Considering the comparison of peasant village and urban, working-class slum, Gans has referred to the latter as an urban village and to its people as urban villagers.[30]

There is a widespread concern that such comparison of the peasant village and the working-class slum leads to an unwarranted romanticism. But, for all the important functional attributes of peasant communities, they provide little basis for such romanticism. Life in the peasant village has, more often than not, been hard and restrictive. Seen from a modern bias, nothing could be more damning than the inbred collectivities and conflict of peasant communities.[31] However, the very same orientation to tradition, authority, and group dominance that offers powerful resistance to social change and necessarily is malfunctional in confronting the challenge of an open society is a fundamental bulwark against chaos in peasant life. And to the extent that similar qualities of restricted opportunity, of deprivation, of discomfort with competition and change operate in working-class life, similar patterns of social organization in the urban slum provide some of the stability necessary for effective coping with the complexities of industrial society.

To speak of some of the attributes that make life meaningful and satisfying in the urban slum is a far cry from romanticism. Indeed, it represents an effort to disengage issues of fact from issues of value and to understand the context in which the urban slum exists and functions. It would seem rather to be an exercise of sociological romanticism to believe that all that is necessary to vitiate the functions of the slum is to provide a maximum of open, external opportunity for education, for occupation, for cultural achievement. That may be all that is necessary for many people who are prepared, by prior experience, for utilizing these goods and services, for experiencing a wide range of options as opportunity. *For most working-class people whose background lies in a relatively recent and confined rural past, individualism and options are more likely to be perceived as threat rather than as opportunity.*

The special characteristics of social-class positions in our society, as Louis Hartz has pointed out, devolve on a sense of achievement or failure rather than on a conception of a differentiated range of social classes.[32] Moreover, this view of omnipresent opportunity, of potentials for social mobility, and of a fundamentally egalitarian society has persisted despite vast and, in part, hereditary differences in income, in power, and in control. European societies more readily conceptualize the same issues in social-class terms derived from their feudal tradition, although the evidence points to few differences in rates of upward social mobility.[33] The American conception implies that working-class status must involve a diminished sense of self-esteem, a sense of failure that may be exacerbated by poverty. Thus, it is equally likely that another function of the working-class slum lies in the large and available reference group of peers who are of similar class position and who can modify the personal implications of failure to achieve in our society. In this view, the primary significance of the working-class slum does not inhere in its low rentals (and often these are not low for the accommodations offered); nor does it function primarily for the poor. Rather, it establishes a relatively homogeneous segment of society in a residential environment within which one can maintain a sense of place, of acceptance, and of self-esteem on grounds other than those of the larger society.

The characteristics of the family-oriented slum are of critical importance in providing a basis for coping with the immediate community and with the larger society. *The concentration of activities and relationships within a single area produces a geographical and social localism, a primary and, at times, exclusive concern with people and places within the compass of the neighborhood.*[34] It is an orientation quite similar to the world-view of the peasant or rural villager. The impact of the larger society is mitigated by the fact that the world outside is a world of strangers and, no matter how frequently working-class people have contact with people and places outside their immediate radius, the large majority continues to feel that they are in foreign territory.[35] This local orientation serves to intensify the sense of exclusive commitment to familiar places and familiar people, giving them greater importance and insuring a more integral sense of belonging some place, to some responsive group of people.

Beyond the apartment or house, the working-class residential slum is *home* for a great many people. This feeling about an area is in sharp contrast to middle-class conceptions of home as a house or as bounded by the walls of an apartment. Most frequently, the working-class inhabitant of a stable slum has lived there for a very long time. In the West End of Boston, 60 per cent of the population had lived there for more than ten years; similar results obtain in other communities reported.[36] While some of the people with whom the working-class slum resident most often associates may be relatives by blood or marriage, this is not so universal or important as the fact that he has known most of his friends forever and a day, *as if* they were kin. If most of your friends live nearby, if you meet them regularly on the street or in the shops or near the schoolyard, settlement house, corner, or bar, if you see them through your windows and hear them through the doors and walls, the dwelling unit extends into the street. Even the physical limits of a small and dark apartment are extended by the active use of windows, halls, doors, and adjacent areas. Qualities of housing in a more limited sense are certainly important to most working-class people, but the conception and salience of housing are different because the context of values, social relationships, and spatial orientations are different.[37]

Most working-class people are not primarily concerned with the *social* status of their housing and, in any case, their demands for housing are modest. But the working class has relatively few options in the choice of housing. Rental costs are certainly severe limitations to improved housing. Most important of all, however, is the fact that if one *wants* to live in a particular residential area, within a physical neighborhood which is conceived of as home, there is generally no alternative but to remain in the same apartment. Hartman has shown that there were widespread desires in one slum for housing improvements but that, because of the high degree of uniformity in size and quality of apartments and because of the strong desire to remain in the same residential area, people accepted their current situation.[38] They did make improvements in the way that was open to them, by cleaning, painting, repairing, and decorating their apartments, and thus the quality of the interiors was considerably higher than that of the buildings.

There are many factors which account for the feeling of commitment and sense of comfort in the working-class slum. In contrast to characteristic patterns in the middle class, those of the working class do not generally have as central a commitment to personal achievement in the occupational role or as exclusive an involvement with spouse and immediate family. Work is obviously a central focus in the adjustment of the low-status migrant to an industrial city. But the workingman works in order to live; he wants mainly decent pay, decent hours, a good boss, and pleasant relationships with a group of co-workers.[39] A long period of industrial experience and transition is required before either a sense of pleasure in occupational tasks or a true "work morality" can envelop occupational roles with the quality of highly significant life goals. Nor does the marital relationship in the working class typically have the intense interpersonal meaning and sense of intimacy which represent the ideal of middle-class marriage. Working-class marital patterns are generally embedded in a network of familial, kinship, or community relationships; for both husband and wife, companionship is a function of peers of the same sex, rather than of the spouse.[40] Thus, almost by default, it devolves upon the community to supply some of the sense of belonging, of social participation, of continuity, and of reciprocity in interpersonal relationships which neither work nor marriage sufficiently affords among the working class.

We have already indicated that social relationships in the working-class slum community have several striking characteristics: continuity of contact with the same people over long periods of time, spatial contiguity of residence, frequent interaction in a variety of circumstances, informality of contact in daily activities. These factors create a context within which extremely close, mutually dependent relationships develop among clusters of people. Mutual helpfulness in major and minor matters, automatic responsiveness to need, and omnipresent support and acceptance among the members of a peer group are taken for granted. A woman normally *expects* her friends to watch her children if she has to go away or to do her shopping for her if she cannot leave the house. A man may pay for a friend's drink without any expectation of immediate reciprocity; but, should he be out of money, he assumes his friend will buy his drinks without hesitation. Contact with the group of peers is likely to be maintained through different phases of the life cycle and to be only minimally modified by changes in membership or by internecine conflict. However, other types of social relationship are also widely manifest. For some people it is the general friendliness and warmth of people rather than specific intimacies which are important. For others it is a more confining and obligatory kinship group which plays a central role. But for those who feel they are a part of the area and the area a part of them—and this includes the majority of working-class slum residents—the sense of belonging among people who are visible and available is the crucial source of the powerful commitments which are so widely evident.[41]

Clearly, any attempt to regard the slum as only a residential habitat for the working class, as merely a locus of poor housing and low rent, or as mainly a harbor for many forms of social pathology, neglects its prime significance in rendering possible a meaningful life in a society which is oriented to different values and to different patterns of social relationship. It is only by virtue of the availability of such communities to incorporate immigrants from rural villages and from a preindustrial way of life, to allow them and their children to familiarize themselves with the varied and quite different demands of industrial society and slowly to accustom themselves to the opportunities provided by the urban milieu and by modern industry, that the process of adaptation can be relatively smooth and continuous. Certainly one may reject the pattern of competitive strivings and incessant mobility as values to be encouraged. Working-class community life, under the best conditions of modest but adequate housing and modest but sufficient income, appears to have many characteristics that are extremely satisfying to working-class people and might conceivably offer suggestions for improving the quality of urban life among higher-status people. But in a deeper sense, there is relatively little freedom of choice. Rewards for achievement in our society affect most directly and powerfully precisely those people who have already achieved the most effective adaptation to working-class community life.[42]

Despite the significance of the working-class slum for most working-class people, the explicit and implicit incentives to *social* mobility can hardly be ignored, once they have acclimated themselves to the complexities of urbanism and industrialism. And eventually social mobility leads to upward *residential* mobility. Social mobility within and without the working class is quite widespread in most highly industrialized countries.[43] But mobility processes, at best, are slow and rarely follow the familiar Horatio Alger pattern. Upward mobility consists mainly of single-step occupational changes within a single generation, and these often arise in the course of work, without any conscious and deliberate intention of moving up the social scale. Moreover, these mobility rates appear to be in fairly stable equilibrium with available opportunities which necessarily restrict the amount of upward social mobility that can occur.

In this light, the social function of the working-class slum community can be seen as a nodal point in a number of adaptive processes in modern society. In the first place, it provides an essential haven for the bewildered and anxious migrant from the rural village. At the same time, the pressures and rewards of an industrial civilization force their way into the working-class community with such clarity that some accommodation necessarily occurs. But the demands and opportunities of the larger society are also sufficiently threatening and anxiety-provoking, and the haven is sufficiently secure and attractive, to allow for selective accommodation according to the abilities, motivations, and goals of the individual. While this may impede a more rapid and a fuller grasp of the ultimate rewards of this society for some newcomers, it also prevents the tragedy of futile strivings and repeated crises for the majority.

Slums, social deprivation, and social policy

It is unfortunate that scientific questions that bear upon important human issues are easily confounded with questions of evaluation. Freud observed this more than fifty years ago in his efforts to place sexuality in the larger context of a system of human motivation. We may be struggling with a similar threat to conventional views in the many efforts to place man and his individuality within a larger context of social processes and to examine significant human experiences within a system of social patterns and institutions. *Such an effort does not imply the absence of evaluation so much as it necessitates other criteria for evaluation and a shift in emphasis from the evaluation of social problems to the assessment of processes that engender these social problems.*

In portraying the dominant pattern of working-class life in our society as a series of transitions from rural, preindustrial status to that of the manual worker living in the slum, to the selectively timed achievements that lead to social mobility and residential change, a number of considerations are implied that need further explanation. This approach can also be viewed as a romantic conception of the socioeconomic melting pot. To formulate the processes of mobility, however, carries no implication that the movement toward middle-class status is intrinsically desirable. Moreover, it is quite clear that these transitions in role and status generally involve a series of severe and often disastrous crises and struggles. Not only can we and should we modify and facilitate this process today in the face of the massive demand for change on the part of the vast, underprivileged Negro working-class population, but we could have and should have done something to make these transitions more humane for the large immigrant populations who underwent similar changes in previous decades. Finally, in view of the fact that the slum and other manifestations of working-class deprivation are merely the visible problems stemming from more deep-seated inadequacies in our society, we cannot assume that the continuing process of social and residential mobility will eventually eliminate either lower-class populations or lower-class slums. In fact, to the extent that we persist in focusing exclusively on the social symptoms, we will insure the continuity, in one form or another, of the underlying, system-bound injustice.

The future of the slum must necessarily be viewed in the light of potential changes in the social-class structure and in the various processes of technological and institutional development in our society. There is no evidence that the *community structure* of the urban slum has outlived its usefulness despite inexcusable conditions of housing. Quite apart from the special problems of massive population movements and segregation in the United States, many other highly industrialized countries continue to have high rates of in-migration of low-skilled laborers whose needs for housing, urban experience, and modern education create comparable situations.[44] Moreover, many of the developing countries appear to be struggling with similar conditions of widespread migration to the cities by uneducated, "preindustrial" populations whose needs for urban experience and industrial skills are great. These countries generally cannot provide even the minimal conditions of slum housing and sanitation.[45] The social functions of the urban slum remain viable despite the vagaries of economic change and public policy that may eventually result in decent housing even for that portion of the population who have not yet learned to utilize the resources and rewards of the society.

The massive development of working-class Negro slums and the marked ghettoization that has resulted, in part, from severe discrimination represent the most serious challenge to the conception of the slum as a transitional environment. Several factors are involved. Since discrimination operates toward all Negroes, free access to housing affects even Negroes who have achieved high levels of education, occupation, and income. Further, there is a widespread belief, not unfounded although based on inconclusive evidence, that Negro mobility and urban assimilation will not readily achieve the levels that have characterized changes in social-class position and in residential mobility of other ethnic groups. Finally, the urban Negro ghetto may not share some of the communal attributes of other working-class slums that have proved of such significance for stability during transitional stresses and crises.

Even if all of these factors are operative, major changes are occurring that are nonetheless likely to emphasize increasingly the transitional function of Negro working-class slums. Higher-status Negroes are gradually spearheading an increase of integrated housing,[46] which necessarily means leaving the lower-status ghetto behind. Increased opportunities for better education, for higher-status jobs, and for improved income may not be adequate to existing social needs, but they are occurring at a rate sufficient for us to envisage a continuing process of social mobility out of the Negro working-class ghetto. And there is increasing evidence to indicate that, although patterns of community and family cohesiveness in the Negro working class may be different from those with which we are most familiar in other ethnic groups that recently migrated from rural areas, there are important strengths and resources in the patterns of social organization of Negro working-class populations. All these considerations point up the fact that discrimination and ghettoization may modify the extent and significance of the transitional function that working-class slums perform, but its fundamental importance is clearly perceptible.

In discussing poverty, working-class status, social problems, and slum housing, several distinctions seem essential that have often been ignored. First, we must stress the vital importance of distinguishing the low-status person, minimally assimilated and unprepared for utilizing the full scale of opportunities of urban life, from the chronic and multiple-problem case. A conglomerate view of lower-status populations that confounds this distinction can be traced at least as far back as the Elizabethan Poor Laws.[47] Such indiscriminate treatment of all low-status people—the poor, the criminal, the beggar, and the insane—was characteristic in Europe during the seventeenth and eighteenth centuries.[48] In principle, these distinctions are widely recognized today and we no longer automatically assume the gamut of social problems for all low-status populations. Yet, in recognizing the real and widespread problems of underprivileged people, we are too easily inclined to regard these as typical when they hold only for a minority of any population group or as intrinsic to individuals although we grant them immunity from responsibility. *Our policies and programs are thus oriented to problem populations rather than to a fundamental re-evaluation of institutional patterns and situational crises that produce these problems.*

A second distinction, closely related to the first, is that between the family-based, working-class slum and other types of slum areas more closely approximating the skid-row model. In making this distinction, it is important to bear in mind that skid rows are also "functional" and that their elimination does not inevitably signify the disappearance of alcoholism, prostitution, drug addiction, or the host of other patterns of behavior they house. However, the family-based working-class slum must certainly be seen in its own right as a highly functional residential area which provides some of the stability and familiarity necessary for encouraging effective adjustment to the most critical requirements of industrial society. The fact that some of these slums are also residential ghettos and the fact that intolerable housing conditions are often widespread in these slums present reasonable foci for urban social policy. *But to confound the social problems we have created or have allowed to develop in working-class residential areas with the significant functions of these residential areas can only lead to perpetuating the difficulties from which we hope to escape.* The elimination of residential slum areas, whether by drastic demolition schemes or by other kinds of residential planning and rehabilitation that have a similar effect, is likely to result in new crises of group formation and of social identity when the greatest need is for the dependability and security of a community from which one can move out selectively.[49]

These considerations imply a distinction between slum housing and a residential slum area. Poor housing is unnecessary and inexcusable in an affluent society. But the communal life of family-based slum areas provides important socializing and security functions. In the face of the manifest and highly visible conditions of housing in the slums, public concern and public policy have more often been directed to their annihilation than to their improvement. Writing in the middle of the nineteenth century, James Hole perceived many of the problems with which we are familiar today. After discussing the rapid growth of towns, he notes:

> Rents of property, particularly in the central parts, rise enormously. The large private houses are transformed into offices, shops, and warehouses, whose occupants remove to suburban villas and terraces—miles of which spring up as if by magic. To these occupants, the change is almost an unmixed benefit. But with the poorer inhabitants the case is very different.[50]

Although Hole was an advocate of new housing schemes for the working class, he appreciated some of the impact of slum demolition:

> Public improvements which should ameliorate the condition of the poor are often one of their great afflictions. Their dwellings are razed to the ground to make way for more remunerative structures. Now and then a railway sweeps away scores or hundreds of small cottages . . . Though paying high rentals, the poor are not always a *desirable* class of tenants; for they are troublesome, uncertain, and changeable. Then the land in the immediate neighbourhood of towns, if eligible for a better class of houses, is often restricted by building conditions forbidding the erection of houses below a certain value. The town labourer . . . finds in the toil of the day quite enough physical exertion, without adding to it by a long walk to and from his home. That he may live as near his work as possible, he crowds with two or three families into one small house, or squeezes himself and family into a miserable cellar—dark, often damp, and always unhealthy—for which he pays a rent out of all proportion to the accommodation offered.[51]

The focus of urban renewal has only slowly moved from a primary concern with land values to increased concern with the housing of working-class people. With this gradual shift, there has been a perceptible change from total demolition to various forms of rehabilitation and efforts at improved, low-cost housing. While recent evidence is not yet available, there is every reason to believe that, despite the shift from drastic demolition schemes associated with urban renewal to modified demolition-rehabilitation, many housing programs will persist in undermining the social integrity and continuity of working-class residential areas.[52] But—as an aspect of urban policy—neither improved housing alone, nor the association of social services with housing improvements, nor even the modification of some of the worst ravages of poverty is sufficient to replace the social functions of the slum. There is no doubt that the old and dilapidated housing stock of any city requires consistent attention. As Frieden has pointed out, however, the selective demolition and continuous upgrading of dilapidated housing can offer most of the advantages of more massive and concerted renewal procedures without the disadvantages of closing off the residential and social base of working-class life.[53] *Unless we can envisage a more drastic change in our social-class structure than any current evidence allows, low-rent working-class residential communities will remain necessary resources in our society.*

At the very least, the large proportion of people living below minimal subsistence conditions in the midst of widespread affluence sets a realistic lower limit to our expectations regarding immediate changes in the necessity for low-status residential areas. The consensus among economists and sociologists who have studied economic status in recent years is that (a) there is still a great deal of poverty in the United States, with estimates varying roughly from 15 to 25 per cent of the population,[54] and (b) the proportion of those living below the subsistence level does not appear to be diminishing markedly.[55] For these people the relatively low rentals and the community resources of working-class residential areas appear essential. Unless there is a marked shift in social policy, however, it seems certain that many of these residential areas will involve dilapidated or otherwise inadequate housing. As several investigators have recently pointed out, even a rising standard of living is likely to be distributed inequitably, to the disadvantage of lower-status groups.[56] Nothing in our social policy, including the recent efforts to improve economic opportunities for the underprivileged, indicates that we are addressing ourselves to this overarching problem. Consequently, we can anticipate relatively little change in the numbers, the character, or the life experiences of those suffering from economic deprivation and from the social problems often associated with such deprivation. By the same token, we can anticipate little change in the functional necessity for residential slums.

Through a larger conception of urban and social planning, of course, it is possible to modify more effectively than in the past some of the disastrous consequences of widespread poverty and of deterioration of urban housing. Public housing, wholly inadequate to its initial purpose, could enlarge its scope through improved design, through greater freedom for imaginative site selection and use of materials, through more careful consideration of the needs and desires of working-class people, and through less restrictive administrative regulations. A variety of forms of housing assistance, including the subsidization of rents for low-income families living in private housing, could lead to more selective and progressive improvement in urban housing conditions for the poor. Moreover, our society has barely touched the potentialities of imaginative educative procedures and social services, informed by knowledge and understanding of working-class patterns and expectations, which might facilitate the process of adaptation to the demands and opportunities of the urban, industrial environment. Recent changes in urban renewal legislation, "gray areas" programs, and the activities of the Office of Economic Opportunity have all moved in this direction and have effected minor changes in traditional services. But, as we have indicated, these cannot be viewed only as temporary problems or as problems only for the poor. Without a more direct confrontation of the economics of housing, the orientation of social services, the conception of education, and the organization of work in our society, as these affect all social classes and all income levels, we can make only token and piecemeal improvements.

Improvements both in housing and in the standard of living can undoubtedly ameliorate the life situation of severely deprived groups. Both housing and income certainly have effects on many aspects of life and behavior. But housing, like income, is more frequently a *result* than a *cause* of other attributes of social-class position. Any reasonable social policy dedicated to the modification and diminution of poverty and social problems must include a wide variety of measures. Certainly, a preventive approach would initiate the process with a fundamental change in the economic climate. As Tobin points out:

> The fact is that the economy has not operated with reasonably full utilization of its manpower and plant capacity since 1957. Even now, after four and one-half years of uninterrupted expansion, the economy has not regained the ground lost in the recessions of 1958 and 1960.[57]

Indeed, there is every reason to believe that a tight labor market, with more jobs than job-seekers, would go far toward diminishing other problems such as discrimination, marital disruption, and the insecurity of the aged.[58] Yet we have been content to watch the extremely slow diminution in rates of unemployment without interceding in any major way, focusing all of our attention on such secondary features as upgrading skills, educational opportunities, and housing.

These secondary features have great potential only when they can be utilized within a constantly expanding framework of opportunities. Within our system of social stratification, levels of education and occupation and other forms of assimilation to industrial society have been the critical determinants of social-class status. To that extent, these status criteria entail a particular outcome in relative income and housing condition. Changes in opportunity which mitigate social-class differences can facilitate the solution of many problems of housing and slums in a fashion most effectively equilibrated with motivation toward social and residential mobility. In the absence of solutions to the structural basis of extreme inequities, improvements in residential housing and slum clearance are, at best, meager and tentative substitutes for realistic social policy. At worst, such superficial improvements are disarming, frequently harmful, and inevitably ephemeral architectural façades.

As long as large inequities in social position continue to pervade our society and a moderately large proportion of the population suffers the relative deprivation of low status and its consequences, stable working-class residential communities will continue to serve important social functions for the underprivileged. The historical function of the urban working-class slum persists in an environment that requires way stations to the personal, social, and economic goods of our society. The open society needs communities to serve these functions and not merely to provide low-rent housing for the poverty-stricken. Far from diminishing in importance, these social functions become more crucial as the rate or complexity of social change increases. This need can optimally be fulfilled in conditions of far better housing and less serious deprivation. But optimal fulfillment of the social functions of the working-class slum can be encouraged only if the working-class community is itself preserved rather than, in a narrow concern with physical housing and problem families, slowly eliminated.

NOTES

1. Walter Firey, *Land Use in Central Boston* (Cambridge: Harvard University Press, 1947); and James Hole, *Homes of the Working Classes* (London: Longmans, Green, 1866).
2. Jane Addams, *Twenty Years at Hull-House* (New York: Macmillan, 1911).
3. William Foote Whyte, "Social Organization in the Slums," *American Sociological Review*, VIII (1943), 34–39.
4. Herbert Gans, in *The Urban Villagers* (Glencoe, Ill.: The Free Press, 1962), suggested, on these grounds, that organized working-class residential areas be distinguished from slums. However, it would be equally reasonable to limit the term "slum" to areas with poor housing and to realize that poor housing may, but need not, be associated with social pathology.
5. Park reveals his profound understanding of these issues in his own studies as well as in his introductions to the published work of his students. See, for example: Nels Anderson, *The Hobo* (Chicago: Phoenix Books, 1963); Frederick M. Thrasher, *The Gang* (Chicago: Phoenix Books, 1927); Louis Wirth, *The Ghetto* (Chicago: Phoenix Books, 1928); Robert E. Park, *The Immigrant Press and Its Control* (New York: Harper, 1922); Robert E. Park and Herbert A. Miller, *Old World Traits Transplanted* (New York: Harper, 1921); and Robert E. Park, *Race and Culture* (New York: The Free Press of Glencoe, 1964).
6. Wirth, *op. cit.*
7. In *The Middle-Income Negro Family Faces Urban Renewal* (Waltham, Mass.: Brandeis University, 1964), Louis G. Watts *et al.* reveal the very powerful internal resistances to moving into integrated areas even when income and availability are not barriers.
8. For studies of diverse slum areas, see: Pierre Chombard de Lauwe, *La Vie quotidienne des familles ouvrières* (Paris: Centre Nationale de la Recherche Scientifique, 1956); Albert Cohen and Harold M. Hodges, "Characteristics of the Lower Blue-Collar Class," *Social Problems*, X (1963), 303–334; Thomas Ferguson and

Mary G. Pettigrew, "A Study of 388 Families Living in Old Slum Houses," *Glasgow Medical Journal*, XXXV (1954), 169–182; Gans, *op. cit.;* Richard Hoggart, *The Uses of Literacy* (Fairlawn, N.J.: Essential Books, 1957); Vera Hole, "Social Effects of Planned Rehousing," *Town Planning Review*, XXX (1959), 161–173; Genevieve Knupfer, "Portrait of the Underdog," *Public Opinion Quarterly*, XI (1947), 103–114; Peter Marris, *Family and Social Change in an African City* (London: Routledge & Kegan Paul, 1961); John W. McConnel, *The Evaluation of Social Classes* (Washington, D.C.: American Council on Public Affairs, 1942); S. M. Miller and Frank Riessman, "The Working Class Subculture: A New View," *Social Problems*, IX (1961), 86–97; J. M. Mogey, *Family and Neighborhood* (Oxford: Oxford University Press, 1956); O. A. and S. B. Hammond, *Social Structure and Personality in a City* (London: Routledge & Kegan Paul, 1954); Lee Rainwater, Richard P. Coleman, and Gerald Handel, *Workingman's Wife* (New York: Oceana Publishers, 1959); John R. Seeley, "The Slum, Its Nature, Use, and Users," *Journal of the American Institute of Planners*, XXV (1959), 7–14; Michael Young and Peter Willmott, *Family and Kinship in East London* (London: Routledge & Kegan Paul, 1957); Romuald Zaniewski, *L'Origine du prolétariat romain et contemporain* (Louvain: Éditions Nauwelaerts, 1957); and Ferdynand Zweig, *The British Worker* (Harmondsworth, Middlesex: Penguin Books, 1952).

9. In the absence of studies of Negro working-class communities in urban areas, the issue must remain one of conjecture. However, it seems likely that, before the vast and sudden migration of Southern Negroes to urban areas, working-class Negro residential areas were similar in their high degree of informal social organization and in the marked level of commitment to the area. Cf. Gilbert Osofsky, *Harlem: The Making of a Ghetto* (New York: Harper, 1966).

10. M. Dorothy George, in *London Life in the Eighteenth Century* (London: Kegan Paul, Trench, & Trubner, 1930), points out that London began to show signs of residential location by social-class groups during Elizabeth's reign but that, apart from small and notorious regions, the status differentiation of housing in London did not become highly developed until the eighteenth century.

11. Oscar Handlin, *Boston Immigrants* (rev. ed., Cambridge: Harvard University Press, 1941, 1959), p. 116.

12. *Ibid.*, p. 115.

13. Karl Polanyi, *The Great Transformation* (New York: Farrar and Rinehart, 1944).

14. Sam B. Warner, Jr., *Streetcar Suburbs* (Cambridge: Harvard University Press, 1962).

15. H. S. Bennett in *Life on the English Manor* (Cambridge: Cambridge University Press, 1937) suggests that the same pattern occurred during the Middle Ages.

16. Lewis Mumford, *The City in History* (New York: Harcourt, Brace, 1961).

17. Unfortunately, loose reasoning and inadequately controlled data are the rule in this area of inquiry. However, Alvin L. Schorr's dexterous bibliographic effort, *Slums and Social Insecurity* (Washington, D.C.: Government Printing Office, 1963), and the careful empirical study of Daniel Wilner *et al.*, *The Housing Environment and Family Life* (Baltimore: Johns Hopkins Press, 1962), both oriented to the expectation that poor housing would prove of considerable causal significance, provide little substantial support for this view. There is even some question whether the long-held view that housing density leads to increased rates of tuberculosis is not largely due to the contaminating effects of socioeconomic status; cf. G. E. Brett and B. Benjamin, "Housing and Tuberculosis in a Mass Radiographic Survey," *British Journal of Preventive and Social Medicine*, XI (1957), 7–9.

18. The literature on migration and mental health is very large, but some of the most recent studies, which include references to the earlier literature, are: Marc Fried, "Effects of Social Change on Mental Health," *American Journal of Orthopsychiatry*, XXXIV (1964), 3–28; Everett S. Lee, "Socio-Economic and Migration Differentials in Mental Diseases," *Milbank Memorial Fund Quarterly*, XLI (1963), 249–268; and H. B. M. Murphy, "Migration and the Major Mental Disorders," in Mildred Kantor (ed.), *Mobility and Mental Health* (Springfield, Ill.: Charles C Thomas, 1965). For an outline of the problem as it bears on

medical epidemiology, see John Cassell *et al.*, "Epidemiological Analysis of the Health Implications of Culture Change; A Conceptual Model," *Annals of the New York Academy of Sciences,* LXXXIV (1960), 938–949. The literature on migration and social problems is virtually nonexistent, but there is some evidence for the effects of rural-to-urban migration on unemployment; see Marc Fried, "The Role of Work in a Mobile Society," in Sam B. Warner (ed.), *Planning for a Nation of Cities* (Cambridge: M.I.T. Press, 1966).

19. Osofsky, *op. cit.,* in discussing the gradual transition of New York City's Harlem from a genteel upper-middle-class, white residential area to a predominantly Negro area, to a slum, points up the role of excessive rentals in the final degradation of the area. Although the largest proportion of real estate was owned by Negro landlords (often Negro churches), the rents were so high that Negro rentals varied from 33 to 40 per cent of income, compared to the approximately 20 per cent expected as a reasonable rental figure for white families. These excessive rentals, in turn, led to extreme crowding, doubling-up of families, and other forms of maintaining a large number of people within a minimum of space. By 1925, Harlem's Negro districts contained 336 people per acre, in contrast to the average (and extremely high) density of 223 people per acre for Manhattan as a whole.

20. In the United States, this is evidently the case in the repetition of slum housing conditions in the wake of the vast migration of Negroes to industrial areas out of the South since 1920. Similar problems appear to be arising again in other highly industrialized countries under equivalent, if not identical, conditions, as in England, Holland, France, and Israel.

21. Gabriel Kolko, *Wealth and Power in America* (New York: The Free Press of Glencoe, 1963); and Herman Miller, *Income of the American People* (New York: Wiley, 1955).

22. Stanley Lieberson, *Ethnic Patterns in American Cities* (New York: The Free Press of Glencoe, 1963).

23. See two publications by Karl and Alma Taeuber: "The Changing Character of the Negro Migration," *American Journal of Sociology,* LXX (1964), 429–441; and *Negroes in Cities* (Chicago: Aldine, 1965). Some of the appropriate comparisons and analyses of Negroes with white ethnic groups appear never to have been made. Thus, if we assume that the influx of rural Negroes to urban industrial areas during the period 1920–1960 is comparable to the influx of immigrants from Ireland, Poland, Russia, and Italy during the period 1870–1910, the dispersion from slum areas and the development of integrated housing should be compared for equivalent periods. Moreover, such comparisons must take account both of slum ghettoization and of the "middle-class" ghettoization which has been part of the process of residential movement for most ethnic groups in the course of adaptation to the urban industrial milieu.

24. Nathan Glazer and Daniel P. Moynihan, *Beyond the Melting Pot* (Cambridge: M.I.T. Press and Harvard University Press, 1963).

25. Fried, "The Role of Work in a Mobile Society."

26. Seymour Martin Lipset and Reinhard Bendix, *Social Mobility in Industrial Society* (Berkeley: University of California Press, 1959).

27. The literature on rural communities is so extensive that an adequate sample of its content and diversity would outrun our space here. Some important studies are: Conrad M. Arensberg, *The Irish Countryman* (New York: Macmillan, 1937); Edward C. Banfield (with the assistance of Laura Fasano Banfield), *The Moral Basis of a Backward Society* (Glencoe, Ill.: The Free Press, 1958); Theodore Bienenstock, "Social Life and Authority in the East European Jewish Shtetel Community," *Southwest Journal of Anthropology,* VI (1950), 238–253; George M. Foster, "What Is Folk Culture?" *American Anthropologist,* LV (1953), 159–173, and George M. Foster, *Traditional Cultures and the Impact of Technological Change* (New York: Harper, 1962); Frederick G. Friedmann, "The World of 'La Miseria,'" *Community Development Review,* September, 1958, No. 10, pp. 16–28; Oscar Lewis, *Tepoztlan* (New York: Holt, Rinehart and Winston, 1960); Robert Redfield, *The Folk Culture of Yucatan* (Chicago: University of Chicago Press, 1941), and *The Primitive World and Its Transformation* (Ithaca, N.Y.: Cornell University Press, 1953); Irwin T. Sanders, *Balkan Village*

(Lexington: University of Kentucky Press, 1949); W. I. Thomas and Florian Znaniecki, *The Polish Peasant in Europe and America* (New York: Dover Publications, 1918); Melvin Tumin, *Caste in a Peasant Society* (Princeton, N.J.: Princeton University Press, 1952); Erik Wolf, "Types of Latin American Peasantry," *American Anthropologist,* LVII (1955), 452–471; Laurence Wylie, *Village in the Vaucluse* (Cambridge: Harvard University Press, 1957).

28. *Op. cit.*

29. See Mary Antin, *The Promised Land* (Boston: Houghton Mifflin, 1912); Emily Greene Balch, *Our Slavic Fellow Citizens* (New York: Charities Publications Committee, 1910); Francis J. Brown and Joseph S. Roucek (eds.), *One America* (New York: Prentice-Hall, 1946); Maurice R. Davie, *World Immigration* (New York: Macmillan, 1936); Samuel N. Eisenstadt, *The Absorption of Immigrants* (London: Routledge & Kegan Paul, 1954); Robert Ernst, *Immigrant Life in New York City, 1826–1863* (New York: King's Crown Press, 1949); Oscar Handlin, *op. cit.,* and *Immigration as a Factor in American History* (Englewood Cliffs, N.J.: Prentice-Hall, 1959); Frank E. Jones, "A Sociological Perspective on Immigrant Adjustment," *Social Forces,* XXXV (1956), 39–47; Park and Miller, *op. cit.;* William C. Smith, *Americans in the Making* (New York: Appleton-Century, 1939); Everett V. Stonequist, *The Marginal Man: A Study of Personality and Cultural Conflict* (New York: Scribner's, 1937); Abraham A. Weinberg, *Migration and Belonging* (The Hague: Martinus Nijhoff, 1961); Louis Wirth, *The Problem of Minority Groups* (New York: Columbia University Press, 1945).

30. Gans, *op. cit.*

31. Banfield, *op. cit.*

32. Louis Hartz, *The Liberal Tradition in America* (New York: Harcourt, Brace, 1955).

33. Lipset and Bendix, *op. cit.*

34. Hoggart, *op. cit.*

35. Marc Fried and Peggy Gleicher, "Some Sources of Residential Satisfaction in an Urban Slum," *Journal of the American Institute of Planners,* XXVII (1961), 305–315.

36. The stability of slum residence revealed in empirical studies is in sharp contrast to a widespread conception of transience among slum inhabitants. While the evidence regarding Negro slum residence is not available in the same degree and while the extensive migrations within recent decades would necessarily modify any such finding, a similar pattern of stable residence appears to be developing. If the results of other studies can be extended, it is likely that such stability can be attributed to discrimination only to a small extent.

37. Fried and Gleicher, *op. cit.;* Chester Hartman, "Social Values and Housing Orientations," *Journal of Social Issues,* XIX (1963), 113–131.

38. Hartman, *op. cit.*

39. Most workingmen would like more than this; it is easy to overstate the limitations of working-class job aspirations. Nonetheless, expectations of job opportunities are sufficiently restricted, and the cultural life of working-class people stresses a sufficient number of alternative sources of satisfaction, to keep occupational aspirations at a fairly low level. Cf. Fried, "The Role of Work in a Mobile Society"; Eugene A. Friedmann *et al., The Meaning of Work and Retirement* (Chicago: University of Chicago Press, 1954); Nancy C. Morse and Robert S. Weiss, "The Function and Meaning of Work and the Job," *American Sociological Review,* XX (1955), 191–198.

40. Mirra Komarovsky (with the collaboration of Jane H. Phillips), *Blue-Collar Marriage* (New York: Random House, 1964).

41. Marc Fried, "Grieving for a Lost Home," in Leonard J. Duhl (ed.), *The Urban Condition* (New York: Basic Books, 1963).

42. Robert K. Merton, in *Social Theory and Social Structure* (New York: The Free Press, 1957), has referred to some of these adaptive changes and, particularly, their intergenerational effects as "anticipatory socialization." It is important, in utilizing this concept, to appreciate the fact that such anticipatory socialization need not be conscious nor need it involve any self-conscious striving for status or even for social rewards. It may include only a shift in conceptions of self and society, implying an incorporation of socially rewarding forms of motivation

and evaluation, which lead to *un*anticipated consequences in the form of status achievement.

43. Lipset and Bendix, *op. cit.*

44. G. Beijer, *Rural Migrants in Urban Settings* (The Hague: Martinus Nijhoff, 1963).

45. Egbert deVries, *Man in Rapid Social Change* (abridged edition; New York: Dutton, 1929).

46. Taeuber and Taeuber, *Negroes in Cities* (Chicago: Aldine, 1965).

47. In a society still dominated by a feudal conception of social relationships, the failure to discriminate between the vagrant and the low-status immigrant, the criminal and the indigent, the poverty-stricken, the emotionally disturbed, and the social deviant seemed justified by their common status as "masterless men." Moreover, the process of feudal demise led to an increasing number of landless and jobless men for whom there was no clear-cut jurisdiction and for whom there were only inadequate and decreasing welfare services. Elements of the problem were recognized quite early, as in Sir Thomas More's introduction to *Utopia* (New York: Dutton, 1935), originally published in 1518. But the eighteenth-century materials indicate a serious failure to link the several manifest issues to their underlying social causation: Sir Frederick Eden, *The State of the Poor* (abridged edition; New York: Dutton, 1929), originally published in 1797, and M. Dorothy George, *English Life in the Eighteenth Century* (London: The Sheldon Press, 1923), Distinctions between unwillingness to work and inability to work or unavailability of jobs were necessarily quite arbitrary and must have varied considerably from one local area to another, but they uniformly included only low-status people (George, *London Life in the Eighteenth Century*).

48. Michel Foucault, *Madness and Civilization* (New York: Pantheon Books, 1961).

49. As the data from one study (Fried, "Grieving for a Lost Home," previously cited) indicate, even those people living in a working-class slum whose sense of commitment to the residential area seems weakest may be most thoroughly dependent on their fragmentary ties for providing stability in the midst of a chaotic and problematic world.

50. James Hole, *op. cit.*

51. *Ibid.*, p. 4.

52. Chester Hartman, "The Housing of Relocated Families," *Journal of the American Institute of Planners*, XXX (1964), 266–286.

53. Bernard J. Frieden, *The Future of Old Neighborhoods* (Cambridge: M.I.T. Press, 1964).

54. Robert J. Lampman, *The Low Income Population and Economic Growth* (Washington, D.C.: United States Congress, Joint Economic Committee).

55. Kolko, *op. cit.;* Herman Miller, *op. cit.;* James N. Morgan *et al., Income and Welfare in the United States* (New York: McGraw-Hill, 1962).

56. Michael Harrington, *The Other America* (New York: Macmillan, 1962); Kolko, *op. cit.;* Herman Miller, *op. cit.;* Morgan *et al., op. cit.;* and Richard M. Titmuss, *Income Distribution and Social Change* (Toronto: University of Toronto Press, 1962).

57. James Tobin, "On Improving the Economic Status of the Negro," *Daedalus*, XCIV (1965), 878–898.

58. Daniel P. Moynihan's demonstration of the close and sequential association of increased rates of unemployment among Negro males and the number of female-based households in the subsequent year lends considerable weight to this view: "Employment, Income, and the Ordeal of the Negro Family," *Daedalus*, XCIV (1965), 745–770.

5

Fear and the House-as-Haven in the Lower Class

LEE RAINWATER

Men live in a world which presents them with many threats to their security as well as with opportunities for gratification of their needs. The cultures that men create represent ways of adapting to these threats to security as well as maximizing the opportunities for certain kinds of gratifications. Housing as an element of material culture has as its prime purpose the provision of shelter, which is protection from potentially damaging or unpleasant trauma or other stimuli. The most primitive level of evaluation of housing, therefore, has to do with the question of how adequately it shelters the individuals who abide in it from threats in their environment. Because the house is a refuge from noxious elements in the outside world, it serves people as a locale where they can regroup their energies for interaction with that outside world. There is in our culture a long history of the development of the house as a place of safety from both nonhuman and human threats, a history which culminates in guaranteeing the house, a man's castle, against unreasonable search and seizure. The house becomes the place of maximum exercise of individual autonomy, minimum conformity to the formal and complex rules of public demeanor. The house acquires a sacred character from its complex intertwining with the self and from the symbolic character it has as a representation of the family.[1]

These conceptions of the house are readily generalized to the area around it, to the neighborhood. This fact is most readily perceived in the romanticized views people have about suburban living.[2] The suburb, just as the village or the farm homestead, can be conceptualized as one large protecting and gratifying home. But the same can also be said of the city neighborhood, at least as a potentiality and as a wish, tenuously held in some situations, firmly established in others.[3] Indeed, the physical barriers between inside and outside are not maintained when people talk of their attitudes and desires with respect to housing. Rather, they talk of the outside as an inevitable extension of the inside and of the inside as deeply affected by what goes on immediately outside.

When, as in the middle class, the battle to make the home a safe place has long been won, the home then has more central to its definition other functions which have to do with self-expression and self-realization. There is an elaboration of both the material culture within the home and of inter-

From *Journal of the American Institute of Planners*, XXXII (January, 1966), 23–31.

personal relationships in the form of more complex rituals of behavior and more variegated kinds of interaction. Studies of the relationship between social-class status and both numbers of friends and acquaintances as well as kinds of entertaining in the home indicate that as social status increases the home becomes a locale for a wider range of interactions. Whether the ritualized behavior be the informality of the lower-middle-class family room, or the formality of the upper-middle-class cocktail party and buffet, the requisite housing standards of the middle class reflect a more complex and varied set of demands on the physical structure and its equipment.

The poverty and cultural milieu of the lower class make the prime concern that of the home as a place of security, and the accomplishment of this goal is generally a very tenuous and incomplete one. (I use the term "lower class" here to refer to the bottom 15 to 20 per cent of the population in terms of social status. This is the group characterized by unskilled occupations, a high frequency of unstable work histories, slum dwellings, and the like. I refer to the group of more stable blue-collar workers which in status stands just above this lower class as the "working class" to avoid the awkwardness of terms like "lower-lower" and "upper-lower" class.) In the established working class there is generally a somewhat greater degree of confidence in the house as providing shelter and security, although the hangovers of concern with a threatening lower-class environment often are still operating in the ways working-class people think about housing.[4]

In Table 5–1, I have summarized the main differences in three orientations toward housing standards that are characteristic of three different consumer groups within the lower and working classes. I will elaborate below on the attitudes of the first group, the slum dwellers, whose primary focus in housing standards seems to be on the house as a shelter from both external and internal threat.

Attitudes toward housing

As context for this, however, let us look briefly at some of the characteristics of two working-class groups. These observations come from a series of studies of the working class carried out by Social Research, Inc., over the past ten years. The studies have involved some 2,000 open-ended conversational interviews with working-class men and women dealing with various life-style areas from child rearing to religion, food habits to furniture preferences. In all of this work, the importance of the home and its location has appeared as a constant theme. These studies, while not based on nationally representative samples, have been carried out in such a way as to represent the geographical range of the country, including such cities as Seattle, Camden, Louisville, Chicago, Atlanta, as well as a balanced distribution of central city and suburban dwellers, apartment renters, and home owners. In these studies, one central focus concerned the feelings working-class people have about their present homes, their plans for changes in housing, their attitudes toward their neighborhoods, and the relation of these to personal

Table 5–1. Variations in Housing Standards within the Lower and Working Classes

Focus of Housing Standard	Core Consumer Group	Most Pressing Needs in Housing	
		Inside the House	Outside Environs
Shelter	Slum dwellers	Enough room Absence of noxious or dangerous elements	Absence of external threats Availability of minimum community services
Expressive elaboration	Traditional working class	Creating a pleasant, cozy home with major conveniences	Availability of a satisfying peer group society and a "respectable enough" neighborhood
All-American affluence	Modern working class	Elaboration of the above along the line of a more complex material culture	Construction of the all-American leisure style in terms of "outdoor living" "Good" community services

and familial goals. In addition, because the interviews were open-ended and conversational, much information of relevance to housing appeared in the context of other discussions because of the importance of housing to so many other areas of living.[5] In our studies and in those of Herbert J. Gans and others of Boston's West End, we find one type of working-class life style where families are content with much about their housing—even though it is "below standard" in the eyes of housing professionals—if the housing does provide security against the most blatant of threats.[6] This traditional working class is likely to want to economize on housing in order to have money available to pursue other interests and needs. There will be efforts at the maintenance of the house or apartment, but not much interest in improvement of housing level. Instead there is an effort to create a pleasant and cozy home, where housework can be carried out conveniently. Thus, families in this group tend to acquire a good many of the major appliances, to center their social life in the kitchen, to be relatively unconcerned with adding taste in furnishings to comfort. With respect to the immediate outside world the main emphasis is on a concern with the availability of a satisfying peer group life, with having neighbors who are similar, and with maintaining an easy access back and forth among people who are very well known. There is also a concern that the neighborhood be respectable enough—with respectability defined mainly in the negative, by the absence of "crumbs and bums." An emphasis on comfort and contentment ties together meanings having to do with both the inside and the outside.

Out of the increasing prosperity of the working class has grown a different orientation toward housing on the part of the second group which we can characterize as modern instead of traditional. Here there is a great emphasis on owning one's home rather than enriching a landlord. Along with the acquisition of a home and yard goes an elaboration of the inside of the house in such a way as not only to further develop the idea of a pleasant and cozy home, but also to add new elements with emphasis on having a nicely decorated living room or family room, a home which more closely approximates a standard of all-American affluence. Similarly there is a greater emphasis on maintenance of the yard outside and on the use of the yard as a place where both adults and children can relax and enjoy themselves. With this can come also the development of a more intense pattern of neighborhood socializing. In these suburbs the demand grows for good community services as opposed to simply adequate ones, so that there tends to be greater involvement in the schools than is the case with traditional working-class men and women. One of the dominant themes of the modern working-class life style is that of having arrived in the mainstream of American life, of no longer being simply "poor-but-honest" workers. It is in the service of this goal that we find these elaborations in the meaning of the house and its environs.

In both working-class groups, as the interior of the home more closely approximates notions of a decent standard, we find a decline in concerns expressed by inhabitants about sources of threat from within and a shift toward concerns about a threatening outside world—a desire to make the neighborhood secure against the incursions of lower-class people who might rob or perpetrate violence of one kind or another.

As we shift our focus from the stable working class to the lower class, the currently popular poor, we find a very different picture. In addition to the large and growing literature, I will draw on data from three studies of this group with which I have been involved. Two studies deal with family attitudes and family planning behavior on the part of lower-class, in contrast to working-class, couples. In these studies, based on some 450 intensive conversational interviews with men and women living in Chicago, Cincinnati, and Oklahoma City, housing was not a subject of direct inquiry. Nevertheless we gained considerable insight into the ways lower-class people think about their physical and social environment, and their anxieties, goals, and coping mechanisms that operate in connection with their housing arrangements.[7]

The third study, currently ongoing, involves a five-year investigation of social and community problems in the Pruitt-Igoe Project of St. Louis. This public housing project consists of 33 eleven-story buildings near downtown St. Louis. The project was opened in 1954, has 2,762 apartments, of which only some 2,000 are currently occupied, and has as tenants a very high proportion (over 50 per cent) of female-headed households on one kind or another of public assistance. Though originally integrated, the project is now all Negro. The project community is plagued by petty crimes, vandalism, much destruction of the physical plant, and a very bad reputation in both the Negro and white communities.[8] For the past two years a staff of ten research assistants has been carrying out participant observation and conversational interviewing among project residents. In order to obtain a comparative focus on problems of living in public housing, we have also interviewed in projects in Chicago (Stateway Gardens), New York (St. Nicholas), and San Francisco (Yerba Buena Plaza and Westside Courts). Many of the concrete examples which follow come from these interviews, since in the course of observation and interviewing with project tenants we have had the opportunity to learn a great deal about both their experiences in the projects and about the private slum housing in which they previously lived. While our interviews in St. Louis provide us with insight into what it is like to live in one of the most disorganized public housing communities in the United States, the interviews in the other cities provide the contrast of much more average public housing experiences.[9] Similarly, the retrospective accounts that respondents in different cities give of their previous private housing experience provides a wide sampling in the slum communities of four different cities.

In the lower class we find a great many very real threats to security, although these threats often do seem to be somewhat exaggerated by lower-class women. The threatening world of the lower class comes to be absorbed into a world view which generalizes the belief that the environment is threatening more than it is rewarding—that rewards reflect the infrequent working of good luck and that danger is endemic.[10] Any close acquaintance with the ongoing life of lower-class people impresses one with their anxious alienation from the larger world, from the middle class to be sure, but from the majority of their peers as well. Lower-class people often seem isolated and to have but tenuous participation in a community of known and valued peers. They are ever aware of the presence of strangers who tend to be seen as potentially dangerous. While they do seek to create a gratifying peer-group society, these groups tend to be unstable and readily fragmented. Even the heavy reliance on relatives as the core of a personal community does not do away with the dangers which others may bring. As Walter Miller has perceptively noted, "trouble" is one of the major focal concerns in the lower-class world view.[11] A home to which one could retreat from such an insecure world would be of great value, but our data indicate that for lower-class people such a home is not easy to come by. In part, this is due to the fact that one's own family members themselves often make trouble or bring it into the home, but even more important it is because it seems very difficult to create a home and an immediate environment that actually do shut out danger.[12]

Dangers in the environment

From our data it is possible to abstract a great many dangers that have some relation to housing and its location. The location or the immediate environment is as important as the house itself, since lower-class people are aware that life inside is much affected by the life just outside.

In Table 5–2, I have summarized the main kinds of danger which seem to be related to housing in one way or another. It is apparent that these dangers have two immediate sources, human and non-human, and that the consequences that are feared from these sources usually represent a complex amalgam of physical, interpersonal, and moral damage to the individual and his family. Let us look first at the various sources of danger and then at the overlapping consequences feared from these dangers.

There is nothing unfamiliar about the non-human sources of danger. They represent a sad catalogue of threats apparent in any journalist's account of slum living.[13] That we become used to the catalogue, however, should not obscure the fact that these dangers are very real to many lower-class families. Rats and other vermin are ever present companions in most big-city slums. From the sense of relief which residents in public housing often experience on this score, it is apparent that slum dwellers are not indifferent to the presence of rats in their homes. Poisons may be a danger, sometimes from lead-base paints used on surfaces which slum toddlers may chew. Fires in slum areas are not uncommon, and even in a supposedly well-designed public housing project children may repeatedly burn themselves on uncovered steampipe risers. In slums where the tenant supplies his own heating there is always the possibility of a very cold apartment because of no money, or, indeed, of freezing to death (as we were told by one respondent whose friend fell into an alcoholic sleep without turning on the heater). Insufficiently protected heights, as in one public housing project, may lead to deaths when children fall out of windows or adults fall down elevator shafts. Thin walls in the apartment may expose a family to more of its neighbor's goings-on than is comfortable to hear. Finally, the very cost of the dwelling itself can represent a danger in that it leaves too little money for other things needed to keep body and soul together.

That lower-class people grow up in a world like this and live in it does not mean that they are indifferent to it—nor that its toll is only that of possible physical damage in injury, illness, incapacity, or death. Because these potentialities and events are interpreted and take on symbolic significance, and because lower-class people make some efforts to cope with them, inevitably there are also effects on their interpersonal relationships and on their moral conceptions of themselves and their worlds.

The most obvious human source of danger has to do with the violence directed by others against oneself and one's possessions. Lower-class people are concerned with being assaulted, being damaged, being drawn into fights, being beaten, being raped. In public housing projects in particular, it is

Table 5–2.   A Taxonomy of Dangers in the Lower-Class Home and Environs: Each of These Can Involve Physical, Interpersonal, and Moral Consequences

Source of Danger

Non-human	Human
Rats and other vermin	Violence to self and possessions
Poisons	Assault
Fire and burning	Fighting and beating
Freezing and cold	Rape
Poor plumbing	Objects thrown or dropped
Dangerous electrical wiring	Stealing
Trash (broken glass, cans, etc.)	Verbal hostility, shaming, exploitation
Insufficiently protected heights	Own family
Other aspects of poorly designed	Neighbors
or deteriorated structures (e.g.,	Caretakers
thin walls).	Outsiders
Cost of dwelling	Attractive alternatives that wean
	oneself or valued others away
	from a stable life

always possible for juveniles to throw or drop things from windows which can hurt or kill, and if this pattern takes hold it is a constant source of potential danger. Similarly, people may rob anywhere—apartment, laundry room, corridor.

Aside from this kind of direct violence, there is the more pervasive, ever present potentiality for symbolic violence to the self and that which is identified with the self—by verbal hostility, the shaming and exploitation expressed by the others who make up one's world. A source of such violence, shaming, or exploitation may be within one's own family—from children, spouse, siblings, parents—and often is. It seems very likely that crowding tends to encourage such symbolic violence to the self but certainly crowding is not the only factor since we also find this kind of threat in uncrowded public housing quarters.[14] Most real and immediate to lower-class people, however, seems to be the potentiality for symbolic destructiveness by their neighbors. Lower-class people seem ever on guard toward their neighbors, even ones with whom they become well acquainted and would count as their friends. This suspiciousness is directed often at juveniles and young adults whom older people tend to regard as almost uncontrollable. It is important to note that while one may and does engage in this kind of behavior oneself, this is no guarantee that the individual does not fear and condemn the behavior when engaged in by others. For example, one woman whose family was evicted from a public housing project because her children were troublemakers thought, before she knew that her family was included among the twenty families thus evicted, that the evictions were a good thing because there were too many people around who cause trouble.

Symbolic violence on the part of caretakers (all those whose occupations bring them into contact with lower-class people as purveyors of some private or public service) seems also endemic in slum and public housing areas. Students of the interactions between caretakers and their lower-class clients have suggested that there is a great deal of punitiveness and shaming commonly expressed by the caretakers in an effort to control and direct the activities of their clients.[15]

The defense of the client is generally one of avoidance, or sullenness and feigned stupidity, when contact cannot be avoided. As David Caplovitz has shown so well, lower-class people are subjected to considerable exploitation by the commercial services with which they deal, and exploitation for money, sexual favors, and sadistic impulses is not unknown on the part of public servants either.[16]

Finally, outsiders present in two ways the dangers of symbolic violence as well as of physical violence. Using the anonymity of geographical mobility, outsiders may come into slum areas to con and exploit for their own ends and, by virtue of the attitudes they maintain toward slum dwellers or public housing residents, they may demean and derogate them. Here we would have to include also the mass media which can and do behave in irresponsibly punitive ways toward people who live in lower-class areas, a fact most dramatically illustrated in the customary treatment of the Pruitt-Igoe Project in St. Louis. From the point of view of the residents, the unusual interest shown in their world by a research team can also fit into this pattern.

Finally, the lower-class person's world contains many attractive alternatives to the pursuit of a stable life. He can fear for himself that he will be caught up in these attractive alternatives and thus damage his life chances, and he may fear even more that those whom he values, particularly in his family, will be seduced away from him. Thus, wives fear their husbands will be attracted to the life outside the family, husbands fear the same of their wives, and parents always fear that their children will somehow turn out badly. Again, the fact that you may yourself be involved in such seductive pursuits does not lessen the fear that these valued others will be won away while your back is turned. In short, both the push and the pull of the human world in which lower-class people live can be seen as a source of danger.

Having looked at the sources of danger, let us look at the consequences which lower-class people fear from these dangers. The physical consequences are fairly obvious in connection with the non-human threats and the threats of violence from others. They are real and they are ever present: One can become the victim of injury, incapacitation, illness, and death from both non-human and human sources. Even the physical consequences of the symbolic violence of hostility, shaming, and exploitation, to say nothing of seduction, can be great if they lead one to retaliate in a physical way and in turn be damaged. Similarly there are physical consequences to being caught up in alternatives such as participation in alcohol and drug subcultures.

There are three interrelated interpersonal consequences of living in a world characterized by these human and non-human sources of danger. The first relates to the need to form satisfying interpersonal relationships, the second to the need to exercise responsibility as a family member, and the third to the need to formulate an explanation for the unpleasant state of affairs in your world.

The consequences which endanger the need to maintain satisfying interpersonal relations flow primarily from the human sources of danger. That is, to the extent that the world seems made up of dangerous others, at a very basic level the choice of friends carries risks. There is always the possibility that a friend may turn out to be an enemy or that his friends will. The result is a generalized watchfulness and touchiness in interpersonal relationships. Because other individuals represent not only themselves but also their families, the matter is further complicated since interactions with, let us say, neighbors' children, can have repercussions on the relationship with the neighbor. Because there are human agents behind most of the non-human dangers, one's relationships with others—family members, neighbors, caretakers—are subject to potential disruptions because of those others' involvement in creating trash, throwing objects, causing fires, or carrying on within thin walls.

With respect to the exercise of responsibility, we find that parents feel they must bring their children safely through childhood in a world which both poses great physical and moral dangers, and which seeks constantly to seduce them into a way of life which the parent wishes them to avoid. Thus, childrearing becomes an anxious and uncertain process. Two of the most common results are a pervasive repressiveness in child discipline and training, and, when that seems to fail or is no longer possible, a fatalistic abdication of efforts to protect the children. From the child's point of view, because his parents are not able to protect him from many unpleasantnesses and even from himself, he loses faith in them and comes to regard them as persons of relatively little consequence.

The third area of effect on interpersonal relations has to do with the search for causes of the prevalence of threat and violence in their world. We have suggested that to lower-class people the major causes stem from the nature of their own peers. Thus, a great deal of blaming others goes on and reinforces the process of isolation, suspiciousness, and touchiness about blame and shaming. Similarly, landlords and tenants tend to develop patterns of mutual recrimination and blaming, making it very difficult for them to cooperate with each other in doing something about either the human or non-human sources of difficulty.

Finally, the consequences for conceptions of the moral order of one's world, of one's self, and of others, are very great. Although lower-class people may not adhere in action to many middle-class values about neatness, cleanliness, order, and proper decorum, it is apparent that they are often aware of their deviance, wishing that their world could be a nicer place, physically and socially. The presence of non-human threats conveys in devastating terms a sense that they live in an immoral and uncontrolled world. The physical evidence of trash, poor plumbing and the stink that goes with it, rats and other vermin, deepens their feeling of being moral outcasts. Their physical world is telling them they are inferior and bad just as effectively perhaps as do their human interactions. Their inability to control the depredation of rats, hot steam pipes, balky stoves, and poorly fused electrical circuits tells them that they are failures as autonomous individuals. The physical and social disorder of their world presents a constant temptation to give up or retaliate in kind. And when lower-class people try to do something about some of these dangers, they are generally exposed in their interactions with caretakers and outsiders to further moral punitiveness by being told that their troubles are their own fault.

Implications for housing design

It would be asking too much to insist that design per se can solve or even seriously mitigate these threats. On the other hand, it is obvious that almost all the non-human threats can be pretty well done away with where the resources are available to design decent housing for lower-class people. No matter what criticisms are made of public housing projects, there is no doubt that the structures themselves are infinitely preferable to slum housing. In our interviews in public housing projects we have found very few people who complain about design aspects of the insides of their apartments. Though they may not see their apartments as perfect, there is a dramatic drop in anxiety about non-human threats within. Similarly, reasonable foresight in the design of other elements can eliminate the threat of falling from windows or into elevator shafts, and can provide adequate outside toilet facilities for children at play. Money and a reasonable exercise of architectural skill go a long way toward providing lower-class families with the really safe place of retreat from the outside world that they desire.

There is no such straightforward design solution to the potentiality of human threat. However, to the extent that lower-class people do have a place they can go that is not so dangerous as the typical slum dwelling, there is at least the gain of a haven. Thus, at the cost perhaps of increased isolation, lower-class people in public housing sometimes place a great deal of value on privacy and on living a quiet life behind the locked doors of their apartments. When the apartment itself seems safe it allows the family to begin to elaborate a home to maximize coziness, comfortable enclosure, and lack of exposure. Where, as in St. Louis, the laundry rooms seem unsafe places, tenants tend to prefer to do their laundry in their homes, sacrificing the possibility of neighborly interactions to gain a greater sense of security of person and property.

Once the home can be seen as a relatively safe place, lower-class men and women express a desire to push out the boundaries of safety further into the larger world. There is the constantly expressed desire for a little bit of outside space that is one's own or at least semiprivate. Buildings that have galleries are much preferred by their tenants to those that have no such immediate access to the outside. Where, as in the New York public housing project we studied, it was possible to lock the outside doors of the buildings at night, tenants felt more secure.

A measured degree of publicness within buildings can also contribute to a greater sense of security. In buildings where there are several families whose doors open onto a common hallway there is a greater sense of the availability of help should trouble come than there is in buildings where only two or three apartments open onto a small hallway in a stairwell. While tenants do not necessarily develop close neighborly relations when more neighbors are available, they can develop a sense of making common cause in dealing with common problems. And they feel less at the mercy of gangs or individuals intent on doing them harm.

As with the most immediate outside, lower-class people express the desire to have their immediate neighborhood or the housing project grounds a more controlled and safe place. In public housing projects, for example, tenants want project police who function efficiently and quickly; they would like some play areas supervised so that children are not allowed to prey on each other; they want to be able to move about freely themselves and at the same time discourage outsiders who might come to exploit.

A real complication is that the very control which these desires imply can seem a threat to the lower-class resident. To the extent that caretakers seem to demand and damn more than they help, this cure to the problem of human threat seems worse than the disease. The crux of the caretaking task in connection with lower-class people is to provide and encourage security and order within the lower-class world without at the same time extracting from it a heavy price in self-esteem, dignity, and autonomy.

NOTES

1. Lord Raglan, *The Temple and the House* (London: Routledge & Kegan Paul, 1964).
2. Bennett M. Berger, *Working-Class Suburb* (Berkeley: University of California Press, 1960) and Herbert J. Gans, "Effect of the Move from the City to Suburb" in Leonard J. Duhl (ed.), *The Urban Condition* (New York: Basic Books, 1963).
3. Anselm L. Strauss, *Images of the American City* (New York: Free Press of Glencoe, 1961).
4. In this essay I am pulling together observations from a number of different studies. What I have to say about working-class attitudes toward housing comes primarily from studies of working-class life style carried out in collaboration with Richard Coleman, Gerald Handel, W. Lloyd Warner, and Burleigh Gardner. What I have to say about lower-class life comes from two more recent studies dealing with family life and family planning in the lower class and a study currently in progress of social life in a large public housing project in St. Louis (being conducted in collaboration with Alvin W. Gouldner and David J. Pittman).
5. These studies are reported in the following unpublished Social Research, Inc., reports: *Prosperity and Changing Working Class Life Style* (1960) and *Urban Working Class Identity and World View* (1965). The following publications are based on this series of studies: Lee Rainwater, Richard P. Coleman, and Gerald Handel, *Workingman's Wife: Her Personality, World and Life Style* (New York:

Oceana Publications, 1959); Gerald Handel and Lee Rainwater, "Persistence and Change in Working Class Life Style," and Lee Rainwater and Gerald Handel, "Changing Family Roles in the Working Class," both in Arthur B. Shostak and William Gomberg, *Blue-Collar World* (New York: Prentice-Hall, 1964).

6. Marc Fried, "Grieving for a Lost Home," and Edward J. Ryan, "Personal Identity in an Urban Slum," in Leonard J. Duhl (ed.), *The Urban Condition* (New York: Basic Books, 1963); and Herbert Gans, *Urban Villagers* (New York: The Free Press of Glencoe, 1962).

7. Lee Rainwater, *And the Poor Get Children* (Chicago: Quadrangle Books, 1960), and *Family Design: Marital Sexuality, Family Size and Family Planning* (Chicago: Aldine, 1964).

8. Nicholas J. Demerath, "St. Louis Public Housing Study Sets Off Community Development to Meet Social Needs," *Journal of Housing*, XIX (1962), 472–478.

9. See, D. M. Wilner *et al., The Housing Environment and Family Life* (Baltimore: Johns Hopkins University Press, 1962).

10. Allison Davis, *Social Class Influences on Learning* (Cambridge: Harvard University Press, 1948).

11. Walter Miller, "Lower Class Culture as a Generating Milieu of Gang Delinquency," in Marvin E. Wolfgang, Leonard Savitz, and Norman Johnson (eds.), *The Sociology of Crime and Delinquency* (New York: Wiley, 1962).

12. Alvin L. Schorr, *Slums and Social Insecurity* (Washington, D.C.: Department of Health, Education, and Welfare, 1963).

13. Michael Harrington, *The Other America* (New York: Macmillan, 1962).

14. Edward S. Deevey, "The Hare and the Haruspex: A Cautionary Tale," in Eric and Mary Josephson, *Man Alone* (New York: Dell Publishing Company, 1962).

15. A. B. Hollingshead and L. H. Rogler, "Attitudes toward Slums and Private Housing in Puerto Rico," in Leonard J. Duhl, *The Urban Condition* (New York: Basic Books, 1963).

16. David Caplovitz, *The Poor Pay More* (New York: Free Press of Glencoe, 1963).

6

The Human Dimension in Public Housing

PRESTON DAVID

Public housing, in a historical sense, is new. The program is little more than a quarter of a century old, yet in that brief period of time it has moved onto the public stage with great momentum and an influence that has yet to be fully measured. The critics of public housing—and its earnest advocates—could equally make use of additional documentation, and in the near future it would help if responsible social scientists were to evaluate—comprehensively—the full thrust and impact of government-subsidized housing upon the American community. Not the "public image," whatever that means. Not statistics on the number of substandard dwelling units in any given community. Not partial estimates of the degree to which crime has been increased or decreased in a specific project.

What is needed is a large-scale study to understand whether—and how—public housing is being properly integrated into the system of governmental helping services, what effect the building programs can or do have upon the larger programs of urban renewal, what relationships have been or can be developed between the projects and the surrounding neighborhoods, what the tenants themselves feel with regard to project living. A long list could be developed, and on it would be a fresh assessment of the role of local housing authorities in providing social and community services for low-income tenants. An evaluation of this kind is badly needed and long overdue. This paper does not attempt to provide the required analysis. It is subjective, it is the reaction of a relative newcomer to public housing, and it is frankly biased with regard to questions of human services.

Regulations are outdated

The thesis of this paper is that the community service programs of the New York City Housing Authority operate under state and federal regulations that apply, by and large, to a day that has long since passed. We are in a new era in which a changed urban environment and a changed urban population require new approaches. These do not exist currently and they are prevented from developing by a philosophy that is now outdated.

Overly simplified, the credo of the regulatory bodies states that (1) the responsibility of public housing is basically that of providing shelter and

From *Social Work*, IX (January, 1964), 29–37.

(2) the necessary "human" services should be found within the community. This viewpoint can—philosophically—be defended. Practically, however, it does not work and is not now operable in a way that can provide satisfaction for a series of persistent problems.

The dilemma grows from the original assumption that public housing was meant to deal primarily with slum clearance and the construction of decent living quarters. Given the problems such an assignment entailed, this limited view could never have been maintained. And whatever the movement was meant to be originally, the nature of the operation over the years has invested it with far broader responsibilities. Public housing today, with all its limitations, has become (almost despite itself) one of the great social welfare developments of the twentieth century—a major instrument of rescue that has removed, in New York City alone, hundreds of thousands of persons from conditions of absolute slum horror. Public housing has had responsibility thrust upon it for tenants who, by the very nature of their eligibility, are poverty stricken. The vast majority are self-sufficient, but many require additional support, and it is unsound reasoning to hope or to assume that adequate community programs will somehow be found elsewhere.

This, then, is the thesis of this paper, and the material to follow will deal with (1) descriptive background information, (2) a statement of the major problem and various subproblems, (3) a general commentary, and (4) a summary and series of recommendations. It is pertinent to note that the material in this paper deals with New York City. This does not always have relevance for the country at large, but as public housing advances nationally the principles drawn from the New York City experience may be of some value to other large urban areas. A few of the principles may indeed be helpful to middle-size or smaller communities.

Social and community services

The New York City Housing Authority (HA) is an operation of such massive consequence that it modifies the city. At the time this was written (November, 1963) the HA was administering 111 projects, and 60 more were either under construction or in planning. The tenancy numbers approximately 122,000 families (almost 500,000 persons) of which 78 per cent are low income and the remainder middle income.

To assist management in dealing with the vast human problems that exist in public housing, the HA has established a Department of Social and Community Services, currently organized through three operating divisions: Community Services, Social Services, and Tenant Organization. Other units in the department provide social planning, program evaluation, and consultation on the design of community space.

The *Community Services Division* is responsible for a broad program that includes community centers, day care centers for children of working mothers, centers for the aged, child health stations, libraries, elementary school annexes, health maintenance clinics, mental hygiene services, and related programs. Whenever possible, private or public agencies serve as sponsors of these facilities. Sponsorship is not a problem with the health services, day care centers for children, and centers for the elderly, as these are financed basically by the Departments of Health and Welfare. It is a major problem, however, for the recreation and community center programs. When sponsors cannot be found in these areas, the centers are operated by the HA directly in cooperation with a board of directors drawn from the tenants and civic leaders from the neighboring community.

This approach, unfortunately, seems to be the direction for the future. Sponsors are no longer available, and the HA finds it necessary to administer its own centers under limiting conditions. The regulations of the supervisory agencies allow only one or two group workers in each development, a restriction that makes it all but impossible to operate a community center properly. Under the circumstances, these are financially undernourished, inadequately staffed, and programmed at a minimal level. In short, they do not meet the needs of the tenants and it is valid to question whether they should, in fact, be open under such conditions.

The *Social Services Division* deals with families that present potential or actual problems in their adjustment to living in the developments. Its general functions are (1) assistance to the Tenant Review Board in providing a social assessment of families being considered for termination of tenancy, (2) consultation to managers and short-contact casework and referrals to social agencies for families who may be helped to avoid termination of tenancy, and (3) consultation to the Tenant Selection Division on families whose admission to public housing might be problematical.

Under the regulations of the supervisory agencies, the social service staff is prohibited from engaging in intensive casework treatment. Preventive and rehabilitative services are desperately needed before tenancy is terminated, but the service is restricted to referral to private resources. As with community services, the regulations covering function and allowable staff make it impossible to deal in a meaningful way with an overwhelming need for casework service.

The *Tenant Organization Division* is responsible, on a broad-scale basis, for attempting to develop project stability and an improved social environment. The HA believes that community strength develops best through voluntary citizen participation. Pride in neighborhood and a sense of adult responsibility, it is believed, will protect property and stimulate the development of many constructive community efforts. It is toward these self-help goals that the efforts and activities of this division are directed.

The division assists management in the stimulation and promotion of tenant organizations, prepares and disseminates "curricular" materials, promotes the development of credit unions, conducts leadership training sessions for tenants, and provides a speakers' bureau on a variety of homemaking subjects: consumer buying, home decoration, financial management, and other aspects of homecraft. These are desirable activities, but the allowable staff for so large an agency makes any form of coverage impossible. The program is a token effort in an area that demands great efforts.

Problems of the tenant population

With regard to the tenancy, it is necessary to recognize that a fundamental change has occurred in the ethnic composition of the city. From 1950 to 1960 the white population declined by approximately 837,000, while the nonwhite and Puerto Rican population rose by 727,000 (City Planning Commission figures). This sharp reversal involved not only a marked change in racial composition, but the replacement of middle-income families by low-income residents, and a consequent increased strain upon governmental services of many kinds. Necessarily, the population shift affected the demand for public housing and the need for improved community programs. In December 1962 42.7 per cent of HA apartments were occupied by whites, 39.8 per cent by Negroes, and 17.5 per cent by Puerto Ricans and others. These are over-all statistics, however, and the proportion of Negroes and Puerto Ricans is larger in low-income developments than in middle-income projects.

The euphemism "low income" should also be recognized as modern phraseology for an older and more descriptive word: "poverty." Low-income families cannot afford adequate housing in the private market. They require government rent subsidy and, even with such assistance, many lead crisis-ridden lives. In an age of affluence, the average annual income for families residing in low-income housing in New York City is $3,500. Large numbers of the aged subsist on annual incomes of $1,500 or less.

The tenant population numbers more than 25,000 persons above the age of 60, six or seven thousand of whom live alone. Approximately 16,000 families are "broken" (single-parent units). Eleven to 12 per cent of the families are registered with the Department of Welfare, although many more living below subsistence refuse to apply for public relief.

This is not to say that the entire tenant body can be characterized as difficult. Generally, the tenants lead decent, hard-working lives, pay their rent on time, are not troublesome to the HA, and do not cause dissension in project living. The great bulk of them are not considered problem families, and the best estimates indicate that only 3 per cent of the residents fall into this category.

Nevertheless, along with other underprivileged groups in the community, low-income tenancy is, in the main, a "burden" upon society. It is costly to various governmental services, and all possible efforts must be made to provide the opportunities through which this body may reach the mainstream of American life. Many of the tenants, unfortunately, are caught in a vise of difficulty: inadequate employment levels, educational achievement, income, cultural aspiration, and family structure—an imprisoning and self-perpetuating series of circumstances that dim any hope of breaking through to the surrounding abundant life. Many have migrated from rural areas or from other cultures and are unprepared for the problems of modern urban existence. They are overwhelmed by the indifference of the city dweller, the economic exploitation, the racial barriers, the unequal opportunity, and the complexity of the urban machine.

The original philosophy of providing buildings and hoping that community services would be provided "elsewhere" has proved—in New York City—unrealistic. Social problems become more visible under conditions of urban renewal, and the population of the core city has changed so markedly that the currently available range of services will simply not do the required job.

Within the overriding question of the degree to which the HA itself should provide such programs, there are a number of involved subproblems. These relate to (1) the HA's role regarding the service programs of outside (public and private) agencies, (2) questions concerning the amount of community space (the physical plant) the HA might be expected to provide, and (3) the extremely complicated issue of trying to coordinate a variety of governmental and voluntary services to lodge program responsibility adequately. The problem is, therefore, to determine what proportion of the total social service burden can reasonably be expected to be borne by public housing and what proportion of this belongs to and can be supported by the community.

Services of outside agencies

The problem of services of outside agencies can be stated simply. In New York City, the end of the line has been reached with respect to meaningful private agency support for necessary group work and recreation services. From time to time voluntary sponsors of community centers may be found, but by and large this approach has been exhausted. Faced with rising costs and strong competition for philanthropic contributions, the private agencies have severe fund limitations.

At issue here would also be the philosophic question as to whether a government body, with its vast needs, should properly expect private philanthropy to assume so major a role. The problem cannot be treated in this paper, except to point out that many voluntary centers are increasingly dependent upon public funds. In some instances, these agencies are primarily coordinating bodies, operating programs on funds or staff provided, largely, by various public agencies plus foundation grants and state or federal research and demonstration funds. The complexity of such arrangements does not provide a firm base for the HA's constantly expanding needs.

In negotiating with private sponsors for group work and recreation services, the HA offers to provide the physical structure, heat and light, basic equipment, expendable supplies, janitorial services, and limited professional staff. This is a large contribution, but even with these major inducements voluntary agencies are no longer available to administer new centers as they are built.

Government bureaus are also handicapped by financial limitations and are restricted, in addition, by the individual charges of their specific agencies. The Board of Education, for example, which operates a number of community centers in HA developments, relates basically to youth and not to adult concerns. The Youth Board (charged with problems of delinquency) is not geared to provide programs for the general population and its total age spectrum. The Department of Welfare, which supplies funds for children's and old-age centers, can make only limited casework services available and these are restricted to welfare clients, excluding a large number of HA tenants who are not on relief or who refuse to apply for public assistance despite marginal incomes. In the field of social services, the voluntary casework agencies have long waiting lists, are selective in their intake, and by and large have shown insufficient interest in the problems of truly underprivileged people.

In sum, the lack of financing and the gaps or restrictions in service provide little hope that the community agencies (public and private) can be expected to meet the increasing needs of a disadvantaged and growing public housing tenancy. And, if this is currently true, the situation will be worsened when the various tools of urban renewal have seriously begun to rebuild the huge remaining areas of slum and blight.

Provision of community space

With regard to space, there is an equal number of complicating problems. Regulations of the supervisory bodies allow community space on the basis of a square-foot formula related to the number of dwelling units. With five different age groups (pre-school, school age, teen-age, adult, and aged) requiring different types of facilities, it is quite difficult to provide enough space for the wide range of tenant needs. Limited as the facilities are, however, the community has begun to depend upon the HA as the construction agency for many kinds of social programs. For example, 75 per cent of the Department of Welfare day care centers, 39 per cent of the Department of Health child health stations, and equally high proportions of other kinds of community facilities are located in public housing. The building of new facilities by the HA has become a community expectation and a great burden, especially when the space is used heavily by the outside neighborhood.

The HA operates on a rough rule of thumb that at least 51 per cent of the persons served by community facilities should be project residents. This is not precise, of course, and varies throughout the developments. There is no question that the facilities should be available to the neighboring areas and to the larger community as an important method of integrating project and nonproject residents. This is not to say, however, that the HA must take care of the total building needs of the community. No one would seriously dispute this, yet once again the reality is at variance with a position that is philosophically correct. The HA is a builder, it is in continual expansion, and it produces a number of new community plants each year. As a consequence, the community simply assumes that it will increasingly supply the necessary physical facilities. Thus, with regard to the question of space as well as the question of program we are led back to the major problem: To what degree must the HA assume responsibility that belongs to the larger community?

Coordination and planning

The difficulty in providing adequate services for public housing tenants is complicated by the lack of a city-wide social planning mechanism. The major change in the physical condition of the city accomplished by the building program of the HA and other urban renewal efforts has not been accompanied by a parallel effort to deal comprehensively with social problems. The waves of migration, population shifts within the city, and changing complexion of various neighborhoods must be treated for what they are: problems in human adjustment. But an over-all plan for health and welfare services does not exist, nor is the structure available through which proposals might be evaluated and implemented to accommodate the changing city pattern.

As public housing advances, it is no longer possible to plan social services for the projects on a one-by-one basis. These must be related to the larger subcommunities that contiguous projects now form, and more particularly to the larger neighborhoods surrounding the developments. To do this takes the problem immediately into areas that are the concern of a variety of independent bodies in health, education, and welfare.

A number of interdepartmental instruments exist currently, but these do not treat with total social planning concerns. Efforts that have been made in this direction have been more successful with regard to *physical* planning and *urban* renewal than with *social* planning and *human* renewal. This is partially true because of the higher priorities assigned to the physical problems. Another reason may be that public housing has not as yet been fully meshed with the network of older governmental services.

Improving the image of public housing

The naïve assumptions of twenty-five years ago—that decent housing would eradicate social problems—have long since been discarded. The naïve assumptions of today—that public housing creates social probems—are equally unsound and, with proper interpretation, will hopefully be discarded as well.

Subsidized housing was created to clear slums and to provide shelter for poor people. Under these circumstances many severe problem situations have, of course, been taken into the developments. But to accuse housing of creating social problems is to accuse hospitals of causing illness, schools of breeding illiteracy, the police of fostering crime. These are ministering agents, programs to alleviate the difficulties that affect the city at large. The problems of juvenile delinquency, adult crime, and social disorder belong to the general unrest of our day. These difficulties exist on a city-wide basis and in every major urban center of the country.

These are basic problems far beyond the task or the remedy of public housing, no matter how beneficial safe and sanitary accommodations may be when compared with the horrible conditions they have replaced. The disastrous effects of racial discrimination, unequal opportunity, the employment inroads of automation, and related issues control the lives of low-income people and exclude them from the benefits of American life. These are transcending concerns that can be met only through a total national effort and through machinery that can effect basic alteration. More concerted action is essential not only for the tenant body itself, but for its effect on the larger community. To the extent that adequate service programs can be constructive and helpful, the HA contributes to the general health of the New York metropolitan area.

Harsh criticisms have been leveled against public housing for destroying old communities. In many respects these charges are correct. There has been a good deal of romantic nonsense and false nostalgia about the desirability of the old slum communities, but the fact is that no matter how inadequate these were, social fabric has been demolished and some forms of community life dissolved. In rebuilding new communities it is essential that a variety of techniques be devised through which tenants can learn to come together on common concerns. In this way "roots" can be established, "tradition" hurried, and new forms of community life organized.

It is of importance that the image of public housing be improved through enhanced human services. Even now, critics of housing make it difficult to find sites, and the search for new locations runs into the constant refrain that low-income housing is desirable—but elsewhere. The single greatest measure in building a more positive image of public housing will come from an improved program to deal responsibly with the human dimension.

Too little is known, unfortunately, of the assets the developments contain or of the many positive accomplishments the HA has already achieved. Despite its limitations, the HA has moved constantly toward socially desirable goals, a firm policy of stimulating tenant organization and leadership training, conscious efforts to develop an ethnically balanced tenancy, coordination with other urban renewal agencies to aid economic integration, specially devised health and welfare services for the aged, cooperation with social research bodies to understand more fully the nature and attitudes of the tenant body, and development of a network of community services programs. These are important undertakings, but they require expansion to realize the desired goals.

With regard to the problem of human renewal, we are only at the beginning. The climate in America today is one that will ultimately produce increasingly strong programs of assistance. Across the nation, in many different ways, this feeling is being expressed in the development of improved programs for medical care, aid to juvenile delinquents, vocational rehabilitation, services to the aged, facilities for the retarded and handicapped, and the like. Public housing itself belongs to this great national impulse of compassion.

The means of channeling this impulse and these programs into the housing projects has, however, been imperfectly achieved. The recent joining of the Department of Health, Education, and Welfare and the Housing and Home Finance Agency in a task force to provide social services in public housing is a step in the right direction. It is limited in the number of demonstration programs it is attempting, but this approach has clear logic on its side. It has, in addition, the important advantage that funds for such programs flow more easily through people-centered agencies than through housing (brick and mortar) operations. This obvious "marriage" was late in developing, but a start has been made and it is to be hoped that similar devices can be established at the levels of state and city government.

Much more work can be done to provide a wide range of vocational services. To the extent possible these should be found within the community; it is not recommended that the HA enter such spheres of work. It is nevertheless true that employment services and vocational counseling for school dropouts, rehabilitation of the handicapped, sheltered workshops for the elderly, small business consultation, and related services are of extreme value. Economic support and income maintenance are props so essential to family stability that they can materially reduce the incidence of domestic tension. Work provides status and dignity to the individual. It affords a place within society to troubled youngsters and to displaced oldsters alike. And, as economic problems are resolved, related difficulties can also be diminished materially. Programs of this kind and other supporting services can influence the behavioral climate of the projects.

For the HA programs, adequate staff is an absolute need. But no workable plan has yet been devised to staff community space in public housing properly. Large-scale resources have been developed, but this is an uneven and uncertain patchwork. Improvisation is no answer to demands that grow steadily.

Management staff, security employees, and custodial and maintenance workers are all provided. These are essential and there can be no quarrel with care for the physical plant. With growing awareness and growing responsibility for the human needs of the tenants, however, the means must be found to finance the necessary social welfare personnel on an ongoing basis.

Finally, with regard to the necessary social planning, it should be noted that the HA develops a large number of new social agencies in any one year and can become a "cutting edge" for neighborhood and community planning. It would be a mistake for the HA to assume a central role in such planning, but it can convene meetings of a variety of public and voluntary agencies and so focus on the larger problems that require comprehensive attention.

Summary and recommendations

If public housing is viewed primarily as shelter, it will be unable to realize its complete potential. If it is viewed as a broader effort—providing more fully for physical *and* human needs—it will be possible to deal with the interrelated problems of adequate social services, community space, and social planning.

There is no argument—in theory—with the philosophy that public housing should not assume responsibilities that belong to the community. Despite the logic of this position, however, the de facto situation is such that community services have not been forthcoming in the required degree and, in their absence, public housing itself has been diminished. This is not a situation that can be answered through unsupported logic; pragmatic answers are required.

An over-all social planning mechanism is urgently needed to coordinate and integrate the efforts of government agencies, citizen groups, voluntary agencies, and other responsible community organizations. In addition to the services provided by the community, a comprehensive and aggressive social welfare program is required to provide:

1. Enhanced preventive and rehabilitative services for the relatively small number of multiproblem families whose conduct causes difficulty to other tenants and to management.

2. Social group work and recreational programs for all age groups.

3. An expanded program of tenant organization and tenant education to identify and train leadership, aid in the development of constructive self-help organizations, and build cooperative community efforts.

Adequate community space must be provided in all new developments, even assuming that (1) waivers are required on the allowable square-foot formula and (2) sponsors are not immediately available to operate the centers. We live now with the mistakes of the past. Today's decisions will stand for fifty years or more, and a restricted approach can only produce future difficulty.

At the federal level, it is suggested that the HEW-HHFA task force move more urgently and more directly into programs that might provide continuing grants-in-aid. Demonstration and research programs are valuable but limited in the face of overwhelming and recognizable need. To achieve a new approach may require amended administrative regulation or new forms of legislation. Given the will, both are possible.

At the state level, it is suggested that a joint task force be established in the federal pattern. The range of agencies in health, education, welfare, youth services, and related bodies should begin—through formalized structure—to deal attentively with public housing concerns. Much of this currently exists, but not in the systematic and comprehensive manner the situation demands.

At the city level, it is suggested that additional funds be allocated for direct services, primarily in the areas of group work and recreation. The city now provides large-scale assistance in staffing the health stations, day nurseries, and old-age centers. Other than the centers operated by the Board of Education, however, this is not true for group work services, and it is in this area that the major problem exists.

In this regard, it would seem that the city and the HA might jointly weigh their respective contributions. The HA, in effect, has become the capital construction agency for many city services. If these have, indeed, saved city capital funds, would it not seem appropriate for the city to provide operating costs in those areas the HA cannot finance?

The recommendations at the city, state, and federal level should be the first steps to be explored. If these fail, however, or produce minimally, it is then recommended that the financing of social and community services—at the required level—be built into the annual subsidy mechanism, whereby the lending agencies fund the difference between the tenants' rents and the operating costs.

An approach of this kind departs from present policy and present practice. If we are to deal responsibly with the immediate and long-range needs of the vast tenant body, however, this reassessment is badly needed. The stakes are too high either to look the other way or hope that the problems will be solved by the "community." Public housing itself is at issue!

7

National Community and Housing Policy

ALVIN L. SCHORR

What are the nation's objectives in housing? To see every family housed? Congress said that sixteen years ago, and it is still unexceptionable. To wipe out poverty? The President and Congress have not quite run that banner up the masthead of the housing agency. Still, what they have said is firm enough, and perhaps we may assume that it applies to housing programs. To create and support a sense of community? That explicit objective is the platform for this essay.

As used here, "community" means that all one hundred and ninety million of us should feel that we have an assured and respectable place in the nation. It means that all the people in one elevated train or one bus or one public park should feel some sense of common bond. We may feel a special tie to other Poles or Presbyterians or Pennsylvanians, but we may not feel set apart from those who belong to other groups. We may not deliberately treat them badly, and we may not be oblivious to their serious problems. The closed-in face that does not see and the angry face that spits are problems to us. Even more serious problems are the self-hating, hopeless, or vengeful people who accept such judgments. Thus, the sense of national community has two aspects which are really one—a sense of identity as an American, which naturally concedes to others their sense of American identity.

The evidence that we lack such a sense of community is all about us. It was manifest in our surprise at the announcement that quite a large number of our people are poor. It is manifest in delinquency and addiction rates. It is at work every day in phenomena harder to count but not less terrible—marital or parental cruelty, defeat, and private desperation. The newspapers do not fail to cover this story in their own way, with detailed accounts of assault before onlookers who are horrified and passive. Here and there settlement houses and others have struggled to produce and preserve a sense of community. They have made one point: that such a struggle may conceivably be successful. But have they not also made another point: that it is

From *Social Service Review*, XXXIX (December, 1965), 433–443, by permission of The University of Chicago Press. Copyright © 1965 by the University of Chicago. This essay was prepared for presentation as an Elizabeth Wood Lecture at the School of Social Service Administration of the University of Chicago, March 9, 1965.

terribly difficult to maintain an island of community in a sea of seclusiveness, contempt, and hatred?

It is sometimes said that a sense of community is undermined in our country because we are industrial. The argument is familiar—we are detached from a sense of family, a sense of work, and a sense of place. But no European country has paid the same price. Community is eroded, it is said, by bureaucratic organization. Still, France, which is said to be the most bureaucratic country of all, requires citizens to aid one another and enforces the law. A sense of separation from others may have roots in Puritanism or the open frontier, but these are history. Nothing requires that each of our loyalties should contain an animosity—Forest Park against Hyde Park, poor against less poor, off-white against non-white. Nothing in our current situation bars us from a sense of identity with the main body of our society.

Yet clearly the problem flows from existing conditions. It is these conditions that we must change. This observation is often made in such a large and general context that it is not really possible to enter a detailed discussion of the changes that are necessary. However, this essay is limited to the question: What can housing policy do to create a sense of community? It deals with three major concerns: housing supply, segregation or stratification in residential patterns, and the citizenship role of poor people in relation to housing.

Housing supply

If we are to be one nation, those who have money and power must devote the resources required to produce housing for poor people. Complicated reasons may be advanced to account for our failure to provide adequate housing; it is easy to be drawn off into the esoteric realms of sociology or economics. But a simple fact lies at the core of the problem. We have never spent for housing of the poor a sum of money that begins to offset the disadvantage they suffer. Two pairs of numbers will establish the dimensions of the complaint they might make. In 1962, the federal government spent an estimated $820 million to subsidize housing for poor people. (The sum includes public housing, public assistance, and savings because of income-tax deductions.) In the same year, the federal government spent an estimated $2.9 billion to subsidize housing for those with middle incomes or more.[1] (The sum includes only savings from income-tax deductions.) That is, the federal government spent three and one-half times as much for those who were not poor as for those who were. That is very nearly the relative proportion of the poor and non-poor in the population, some might say that the federal government spends equally per capita for the rich and the poor. What majestically even-handed justice is reflected there!

These are not conventional and some will say not impeccable statistics. Public assistance, public housing, and income tax are not often combined.

There is no doubt, however, that they represent the consequential federal subsidies for housing. Only urban renewal is omitted—because it is impossible to divide the federal subsidy between business and residential purposes and to determine what portion of the latter would be for poor people. Loan guaranties are not included in these figures either. As they do not cost the government money, they are not regarded as subsidies. In any event, both omissions weight the estimates on the conservative side. Neither urban renewal nor mortgage guaranties conspicuously serve poor people. Finally, there is no doubt that an income-tax deduction is quite as effective a grant of money as a public assistance payment.

However, the pair of figures offered above does suffer from dealing with one hundred and forty-five million people who were not poor as if they benefited uniformly from federal subsidies. Closer examination shows that the subsidy is heaviest for the largest incomes. Therefore, a second, rather more refined pair of figures may be helpful. In 1962, the federal government spent $820 million to subsidize housing for poor people—roughly 20 per cent of the population. For the uppermost 20 per cent (with incomes over $9,000) the federal subsidy was $1.7 billion.[2] A family in the uppermost fifth got about twice as much, on the average, as a poor family.

The composite picture is as follows: The income-tax deduction is by far the government's largest direct subsidy for housing. It gives more to those who have more. The two programs that express the national conscience in housing—public assistance and public housing—together manage to raise poor families to per capita equality with the income-tax subsidy that goes to all the rest. No more than that! Indeed, in a way less than that, for the poorest fifth got half the subsidy that went to the wealthiest fifth. That will not build a sense of community; and it will not build the housing that is needed.

How is it that we do no more for the poor than for the rich? How is it that we think—unless we are faced with the figures—that we are pouring enormous amounts of money into housing for the poor? To begin with, we are chronically afflicted with an impediment to vision called "slum clearance." Eighty years ago a British Royal Commission for Inquiring into the Housing of the Working Classes[3] observed, with dismay, that poor people rarely benefited when land was cleared and model houses erected. Somehow or other, the issue of providing enough dwellings for *all* people fades from the mind when attention is focused on rebuilding streets and neighborhoods. When the total supply remains inadequate, despite conspicuous new working-class districts, it is naturally the poorest who do without. As Octavia Hill pointed out, the Royal Commission was relearning a lesson that should have been learned thirty years earlier. Again in the 1930's the British failed to do the job with slum clearance. Just in the past decade they have solemnly restudied the same text.

The situation in the United States is no better. From the Housing Act of

1937 until now, despite everything that experience might teach us, Americans have looked to slum clearance and its metamorphoses—urban renewal and community renewal—to provide housing for poor people. Urban renewal has a responsibility to the poor people whose lives it alters. Judging from the record, it has not taken this responsibility with sufficient seriousness. But the tools given to urban renewal are suited, if anything, to producing a city beautiful or a city prosperous. Although the tools are or must be made adequate to housing dislocated families, they can do little at best for all the others. Urban renewal deals with land which, even when subsidized, is expensive. Therefore it is likely to be regarded as an achievement when it provides housing for families with incomes of $5,000 or $6,000. Despite the current emphasis upon city-wide planning, the great sums of money are funneled into one project area or another. This purview is too narrow and the process moves too slowly to produce dwellings by the hundreds of thousands.

To turn to the record, from the Housing Act of 1949 to the end of 1963 about one hundred thousand new and rehabilitated units have been completed. If all of them had gone to poor people they would have made a very small contribution indeed to solving our national problem. Here the problem is encountered in a single statistic. One must avoid being hypnotized by the striking symbols we see rising in every city. One must keep in mind their magnitude in relation to the magnitude of the problem. Preoccupation with slum clearance, to the exclusion of all else, is a historically proven method of failing poor people to the tune of a rousing campaign song.

Another device by which those who are interested delude themselves is research and demonstration. Some issues are researchable, and some are not. For example, the President has proposed a direct housing subsidy to poor people. The idea has been tested out on occasion, with some success and some difficulty. But it is necessary to ask whether any project is a genuine test of what would happen if we embarked on a new national program of this sort. The whole housing market would be transformed, and crucial activities, such as construction and code enforcement, might change character. Apart from what can and cannot be studied, there is a time for study and a time to act. The national poverty program illustrates both points. First, although some attempts have been made to evaluate the concept of the community-action program, obviously nothing that preceded the actual program carried the same sense of national priority or seriousness. One may doubt how relevant the findings would have been. Second, in fact the poverty program was launched when the country was ready and before the results of evaluation studies were in. The poverty program is in itself a multibillion-dollar experiment, and why not?

It is not necessary to labor this point. Properly used, study and demonstration may avoid mistakes and lead to action. But demonstration-grantism should not substitute for action when its time has come. For those moments when it may be appropriate, we may turn to one of W. H. Auden's ten commandments for men of action:

> . . . Thou shalt not sit
> With statisticians nor commit
> A social science.[4]

If we are to avoid diversions, what alternatives are open? First, public housing is open. The problems and prospects of public housing are well understood, as well as the new directions in which it should move. If we assume a progressive direction, public housing is a vehicle for substantial increase of dwellings open to poor people. Second, a direct housing subsidy to poor people offers the possibility of dealing directly with large numbers.[5] Still, a direct housing subsidy might do little to improve the supply of housing. If more homes were not built the subsidy would, in the end, bring poor families little benefit. Therefore, third, the new low-interest-rate program of the Federal Housing Administration might receive the financing necessary for rapid expansion. Although only three years old, the program has already produced as many units as urban renewal. However, this program carries no federal subsidy and is, indeed, not intended to deal with the poorest families. Therefore, fourth, the urban renewal principle of direct cash subsidy for the production of housing might be extended to poor people.

These four possibilities may make clear the kinds of concepts that are relevant to producing enough housing for poor people. Obviously, more space and details are required to propose a program. The country is spending $2.1 billion less on the housing of poor people than on the rest of us. If we are to achieve a sense of community, we might begin by spending equally.

Residential patterns

It is probably not necessary to document the observation that Americans tend to live in single-class neighborhoods. Apparently, however, we have been a little too willing to assume a universal tendency to lock into the centers of our cities those who are poor, Negro, poorly educated, and poorly housed. It now appears that this is an accurate profile only of our largest metropolitan areas and those in the Northeast. In many of the metropolitan areas of the South and the West, the classic picture is reversed: poverty and deprivation are characteristics of the suburbs.[6] Thus, our cities do not provide consensus on preferred locations. There is consensus only on classifying and separating people somehow, and inside each town and county we are sorted out into neighborhoods of specified income, or specified color, or specified religion, or specified combination of all of these.

The forces that produce residential separation are all too familiar. The family cycle plays a role. People with children feel the pull of the suburbs; others may not be so charmed. Racial segregation plays a role, historically at least. A city council or housing authority can, of course, assist racial segregation without excess guilt by locating low-cost dwellings in renewal areas or yielding too readily to opposition in higher-cost areas. Local and state tax structures play a role that is often overlooked. Officials become adept at calculating the increase in property tax that is necessary to provide services to a housing development of specified size, income, and family composition. Eventually, they avoid tax increases by zoning actions to prevent developments that would make increases necessary. The Commission on Intergovernmental Relations has called this practice "fiscal zoning." [7] Banks, builders, and real estate brokers, in pursuit of nothing more odious than a secure profit, combine to assure the pure poverty of one neighborhood and the pure wealth of another. Evidently, successful businessmen have misjudged the effect on real estate values when Negroes move into white neighborhoods.[8] It is difficult to know whether they are just as wrong about the outcome if $12,000 houses take their places next to $20,000 houses.

We have constructed a tight myth that feeds from the forces just named and feeds back to strengthen them. The myth is simple: If someone with less money or any other characteristic both exotic and inferior moves next door, then one is not safe in his bed, his children are not safe in school, and his mortgage is endangered. The myth is wrapped around an irony, as myths so often are. We have created poor neighborhoods in all our cities, neighborhoods in which people are afraid to live. Not only the people outside are afraid; those who live in the neighborhoods are afraid. They are afraid of being assaulted; they are afraid of being shamed; they are afraid of being exploited—by one another and by functionaries of various sorts.[9] From these neighborhoods springs the violence that makes us afraid to walk the streets of our own cities. We created this problem by the myth, and now the problem justifies the myth.

The myth is now possibly the portion of this syndrome that is most resistant to change. Therefore, it may be worth pausing to see how it is dealt with by those who should understand it best. Social scientists have been struggling for some two decades against the conviction that stratification is inevitable. On the whole, academics that they are, their impulses have been toward heterogeneity or democratic mixture. But they had to concede that people try to stratify themselves. Their studies have seemed to show that difference leads to conflict. Conversely, the evidence has seemed clear that people feel satisfaction when they are like one another.[10] Reformers such as Paul Goodman and Catherine Bauer have scorned such notions, but their wit was more telling than their bibliographies. The situation has been awkward. At this juncture there appears a solution (also put forward in England in the last few years) that will permit us to have and eat our cake at once.

It is reported that the developers of Columbia, a new town proposed to lie between Washington and Baltimore, have taken counsel with social scientists. One might applaud the determination and vision of those who would plan a new town. But their consultants have not served them as well as they deserve. The town will have room for a variety of economic classes, from those with moderate income upward, but each class in its own section.

Slogans for such a town may come to mind: "Integrated but equal!" "Democratic but not extreme!" The proposal is reminiscent of the timid experiments in desegregation that followed World War II. Each building in a development was segregated, some for Negroes and some for whites, and so the total development was regarded as integrated. These strained compromises have vanished.

The problem which all these studies and earnest ideas fail to recognize is that they are conducted inside the myth. The operating principle may be stated in a Gertrude Stein-ism: If like must like like, like likes like. What else! The nub of the problem is to take hold of the myth and call it a lie, loudly enough so that people do not feel bound. The prospects, if that takes place, are not unpromising. Studies have shown that Negroes and whites get along fine as neighbors—a small breach in the like-likes-like principle where once it was thought strongest. Studies have shown that people redefine likeness when they wish to, focusing on common interests rather than on color, on children in school rather than on precise level of income.[11] And city-planning literature brims with the advantages that would develop: Employers and employees would be able to find one another. Commuting would be reduced. Neighborhoods would not empty during the day and fill up at night or vice versa. The greatest advantage of all, of course, and the central point, is that so much xenophobia might be dissolved.

The myth is used to justify all the rest, but more material advantages are also involved. Change requires that several forces be altered. It is hardly necessary to make proposals about racial segregation. Obviously, ending it is part of the problem that must be pursued by citizens, city councils, housing authorities, and all the rest. Neither is it necessary to discuss how schools must be improved. If we take the steps we should, families are less likely to think that they must take their children to the suburbs. The financing structure of local government must be altered. In the first place, officials should be educated to calculate the marginal costs of additional services. That is to say, they should appreciate the situations when average costs will decline with additional families. Beyond this, however, expenses of local governments must be shared so that low-income families will not be seen as a threat. Anything that increases the amount of state or federal aid to localities is likely to have this effect, but it is possible to act directly. For example, a subsidy may be paid for a specified period to a locality in which a dislocated family finds housing. The subsidy would be calculated to cover the cost of public services during an adjustment period—say, five years. Moreover, banks and builders must be educated to the desirability of mixed development. The government can itself set an example by scattering public housing and mixing public housing with moderate-income FHA dwellings.

We shall not, in the end, erase family preferences. That is far from what is intended. We need only to melt down the rigid conduits through which personal preferences now flow. Then we shall have more diversity, more freedom, and more sense of unity.

The citizenship role of poor people

The terms "citizen participation" or, more recently, "indigenous leadership," are used variously. One meaning of these terms is simple—that poor people who are touched by a public decision (a housing decision, in particular) have techniques and a measure of power which they exercise to influence the decision in what they regard as their own interests. It is peculiarly difficult to discuss the matter at this particular moment. Everyone approves of indigenous leadership, but never has more lip service been proffered to so little reality. Citizen participation has never been a conspicuous success in housing programs, even though it is a legal requirement. Accounts of genuine, lasting success by indigenous leaders are hard to come by. It goes without saying that this generalization does not "put down" but rather adds luster to the few successful efforts that are known.

It may be useful to begin by uncovering the high cards that are stacked against successful indigenous leadership. First, cynicism about the fruits of one's own activity is taught to poor people by the facts of everyday life. Second, poverty-stricken people who were once better off introduce a distinct ideological strain. In views they are conservative and in mood optimistic and grateful, despite their come-down. These attitudes may serve their conviction that they retain or will regain their earlier status, but, as Harold Wilensky observes, they also "function to reduce working-class solidarity and social criticism from below." [12] Third, analogy of the efforts that the poor might make to trade-union or civil rights movements overlooks a difference in sense of identity. Negroes and industrial workers possess a status which, in general, seems permanent and which they may regard as desirable. A poor person whose aspiration is awakened can only wish to become something other than poor. No sense of identity is present around which people can organize.

Fourth, the professional workers who set out to stimulate indigenous leadership inevitably have other motives, which are not necessarily blameworthy. Professional workers are sensitive to secondary consequences of achieving their ends such as having an important neighborhood program lose favor and funds. They may understand better than the residents of a neighborhood the larger ends that will be served—by clearance, for example.

Finally, when poor people do assert themselves, they are likely to threaten established interests and pay a penalty. The public attacks on Mobilization for Youth may have been a case in point. One issue was apparently that Mobilization for Youth gave promise of successfully advancing the independent interests of poor people.[13] Not only did it teach poor people to picket schools, but it also provided them counsel to go to court as plaintiff against municipal agencies. It is hard to know, from the outside at any rate, whether Mobilization for Youth won this point. In any event, professional workers all over the country will have read the message of the savage attacks and learned to interpret with more delicacy the next clarion calls to citizen action.

The obstacles are not listed in order to say that indigenous participation should be abandoned. They are listed because it is important to understand that it is difficult to achieve. It is intolerable to talk as if citizens have only to pack a luncheon and embark on an Independence Day picnic. There are two major reasons why indigenous leadership should be promoted. It is being said of late that the sense of being helpless is the crucial psychological experience of poverty.[14] Each time a man is moved against his will or without his will confirms a pattern of living that keeps him poor. If one is attempting to alter some of the elements of a lifetime of poverty (poor education and training, for example), it will be wise to alter as many of the components as he can reach. With a critical combination of elements the human spirit takes off against all odds. The nation seeks to provide the maximum opportunity for take-off.

From the point of view of the professional worker or community agency, indigenous participation must be sought for another reason. Agencies know much less about how to deal with poor people than they need to know. An inevitable bureaucratic process "enfeebles" the response to direct client need or wish.[15] With the increase in what is called "good" government, it becomes harder to get anything at all done, whether good or bad.[16] It may seem glib to suggest that agencies accept the built-in motive force and corrective to their ways of working that indigenous leadership would assert. Boiled down to people and daily activities, such acceptance means that agencies should not fight with all the weapons at their command when the ignorant and ungrateful go over their heads or suggest that they do not know what they are doing. Yet it may be that our professional, technocratic, and political systems must find room for such concepts or grind to a halt.

A reasonable assessment of human capacities and bureaucratic tendencies must raise doubts about whether a housing authority can consistently promote independent citizen activities. Other important and sound considerations govern the authority. Although it may set out with the purest vision of democracy, matters may look different as unattractive personalities emerge and time schedules fall behind. Perhaps, therefore, urban renewal funds should be given in unrestricted block grants, not subject to housing authority control. In particular, the grants might be made to various housing associations and settlement houses and, when they are available, to universities that have been experimenting with urban extension. Much of the money will doubtless be used wastefully, but this is not a field in which anyone knows how to achieve high efficiency.

In summary, there are two major reasons why citizenship participation must be built into housing policy, despite uncertainty of success and all the difficulty. One reason has to do with its function for poor people; the other has to do with avoiding ossification of our system of governing and serving ourselves. Each, in a different dimension, is a method of promoting communication between the haves and the have-nots, between those who are served and those who serve. To the degree that we achieve these objectives, we move toward a sense of community.

Three elements of housing policy relate to a sense of national community. First, housing must be supplied in the quantity needed. If we are to be a single nation, we shall make a larger investment and divide it more justly. Second, no one would attempt to tell a family what sort of neighbors it must have. But history and public policy have conspired to produce just that result. It is widely thought that a family must seek to live among so many mirror images of itself. Because the myth exists, it does, in fact, have effect. We are now in a position to set the process going in the opposite direction. Third, we must pursue the tedious, seditious task of nourishing political sense and effectiveness even among the least of our people.

These significant elements of housing policy bear price tags, each in a different coinage. Housing supply costs money; that is, perhaps, easiest to calculate and dedicate. Mixed residential patterns will cost status. At least until we reorient ourselves, it will be harder to know that one is moving up or has arrived. Indigenous leadership will cost security. Poor people, if they influence decisions, will certainly move them in directions that are uncomfortable for others. Money, status, and security are a high price to pay for community; the high price may explain why we have permitted ourselves to get into difficulty.

Each of the three efforts can be and, indeed, usually is viewed independently. One might think an adequate housing supply important but mixed residential patterns visionary, unrealistic. Or one might think all efforts important but not in the magnitude that has been suggested. However, we must recognize that the hour is late. We must devote all the resources necessary to be one nation, or we shall be two or several. Whoever considers the consequences of inaction must think a sense of national community well worth its price.

Supplement

The estimates of the federal subsidy for housing were prepared as follows:[17]

The federal subsidy for public housing was $157 million in fiscal 1962. Assistance payments from federal funds for Aid to Families with Dependent Children, Old Age Assistance, Aid to the Blind, and Aid to the Permanently and Totally Disabled in fiscal year 1962 totaled $2.2 billion. It is arbitrarily assumed that 25 per cent of this, or $552 million, was spent for housing.

Non-business real estate tax deductions from income tax totaled $263 million by those with less than $3,000 income and $4.8 billion by those with more income in calendar 1962. Non-business deductions for interest by those with less than $3,000 amounted to $273 million and by those with more to $10 billion in calendar 1962. Interest attributable to home mortgages is calculated at two-thirds of the total, on the basis of a small sample study by the Treasury Department.

In the first pair of figures, actual tax savings are calculated at 25 per cent of the deductions, on the basis of a sample study by the Treasury Department. In the second pair of figures, tax savings for the uppermost 20 per cent of the population (incomes over $9,000) are calculated at 25 per cent of allowable deductions up to income of $15,000, at 30 per cent between $15,000 and $20,000, and so forth, up to 90 per cent at $200,000 income and over. Calculations of actual tax savings in income tax are at 1962 rates. For 1964 or 1965, actual savings would be a smaller percentage, but the total of deductions would be higher.

More than half of the income-tax returns took a standard deduction rather than itemizing deductions. Although the standard deduction was, in intent, an average of deductions that might be itemized, it is not in its effect a subsidy for housing or any special item. That is, its advantage accrues to the taxpayer regardless of what he spends on housing. Therefore, no estimate was made of the saving from standard deductions. (The advantage for those who buy homes tends to lie in itemizing deductions; those who buy homes tend to have moderate incomes or more. Therefore, it is likely that inclusion of the savings from standard deductions in the estimates would reduce the imbalance between the uppermost 20 per cent and all the remainder. The poor, who would not be paying tax in any case, would not benefit from standard deductions either. Therefore, inclusion of the savings from standard deductions in the estimate would increase the imbalance between the lowest 20 per cent and all the remainder.)

The federal subsidy for urban renewal in fiscal 1962 was about $160 million, but is not included in the calculation of the federal subsidy, for reasons given in the text.

NOTES

1. A brief supplement at the end of this essay provides the reasoning on which these estimates were based.
2. See the supplement for the basis of these calculations.
3. Great Britain, Royal Commission for Inquiring into the Housing of the Working Classes, *First Report* (London, 1885).
4. "Under Which Lyre—A Reactionary Tract for the Times," *Nones* (New York: Random House, 1951). Copyright 1946 by W. H. Auden. Quoted by permission of Random House, Inc.
5. The magnitude of programs is our main point. The housing subsidy proposal presented to Congress in 1965 carried a first-year cost of $50 million—3 per cent of the $1.7 billion subsidy that goes to the uppermost 20 per cent of the population. As passed by Congress in July, 1965, first-year cost was $30 million, rising to $150 million in the fourth year.
6. Advisory Commission on Intergovernmental Relations, *Metropolitan Social and*

Economic Disparities: Implications for Intergovernmental Relations in Central Cities and Suburbs (Washington, D.C., 1965).

7. *Ibid.*

8. Davis McEntire, *Residence and Race* (Berkeley and Los Angeles: University of California Press, 1960).

9. Lee Rainwater, "Fear and the House-as-Haven in the Lower Class," Chapter 5, this book.

10. Gordon Campleman, "Some Sociological Aspects of Mixed-Class Neighborhood Planning," *Sociological Review*, XLIII, No. 10 (1951), 191–200; Leon Festinger, Stanley Schachter, and Kurt Back, *Social Pressures in Informal Groups* (New York: Harper, 1950); William H. Form, "Stratification in Low and Middle Income Housing Areas," *Journal of Social Issues*, VII, Nos. 1–2 (1951), 109–131; Herbert J. Gans, "Planning and Social Life: Friendship and Neighbor Relations in Suburban Communities," *Journal of the American Institute of Planners*, XXVII (1961), 134–140.

11. Gans, *op. cit.*

12. Harold L. Wilensky and Hugh Edwards, "The Skidder," *American Sociological Review*, XXIV (1959), 215–231.

13. For a summary of developments before MFY and the city arrived at agreement, see Herbert Krosney, "Mobilization for Youth: Feuding over Poverty," *The Nation*, December 14, 1964.

14. For example, see Dan W. Dodson, "Power as a Dimension of Education," *The City Church*, XIV (1963).

15. Harold L. Wilensky, "The Professionalization of Everyone?" *American Journal of Sociology*, LXX (1964), 137–158.

16. James Q. Wilson, "An Overview of Theories of Planned Change," in Robert Morris (ed.), *Centrally Planned Change* (New York: National Association of Social Workers, 1964).

17. See United States Department of Health, Education, and Welfare, Social Security Administration, Bureau of Family Services, *Trend Report* (Washington, D.C., December, 1962); United States Treasury Department, Internal Revenue Service, *Statistics of Income . . . 1962, Preliminary, Individual Income Tax Returns for 1962* (Washington, D.C., 1963); and unpublished studies by the Treasury Department.

Part III RACIAL BIAS AND SEGREGATION

Editors' Introduction

The question of where Negroes can find places to live in American cities is a continuing source of conflict, for whatever racial patterns may exist at any time are subject to constant pressure. The rapid growth of Negro population in urban areas makes it imperative for Negroes to obtain more housing. Between 1950 and 1960, the nonwhite population grew from 9 million to 13.2 million in metropolitan areas, with more than 80 per cent of this increase occurring in the central cities. Living space for this growing population comes almost entirely from older housing formerly occupied by white people. Only a small proportion of Negroes who need housing manage to buy or rent new housing, or move into newly built public housing. According to Census surveys, almost a million metropolitan housing units went from white to nonwhite occupancy between 1950 and 1959; fewer than 100,000 went from nonwhite to white occupancy during the same period. Thus in 1959, as many as 30 per cent of all nonwhite families in metropolitan areas were living in housing where white families had lived in 1950.

Housing turnover is the basic process by which Negroes find places to live in the cities. This is the same process by which low-income groups, regardless of race, improve their housing once they are in the cities. As a result of the great middle-income move from central cities to suburbs since World War II, a large supply of vacant housing was left behind to facilitate this turnover process. Moving into vacant housing, however, often means moving from one neighborhood to another. Families that are able to move freely throughout the city have the best prospects for securing decent housing. Because of discrimination in the sale or rental of housing, and because of resistance to Negro entry into white neighborhoods, Negroes suffer from special disabilities in the competition for good used housing. Despite the general improvement in urban housing in recent years, they remain concentrated in substandard and overcrowded housing. The following table indicates the gains of the 1950's for both Negroes and whites, but also makes clear the continuing disparities:

Characteristics of occupied urban housing units		1950	1960
White:	Sound condition with all plumbing facilities	82%	86%
	With fewer than 1.01 persons per room	88%	92%
Non-white:	Sound condition with all plumbing facilities	40%	54%
	With fewer than 1.01 persons per room	70%	75%

Source: U.S. Housing and Home Finance Agency, *Our Nonwhite Population and Its Housing* (Washington, D.C., July, 1963), p. 86.

In part, these differences reflect the relatively low incomes of Negroes compared with whites, but income differentials are not the sole explanation. When Negro and white families at the same income levels are compared— even in the middle-income bracket of $7,000–$10,000 per year—a substantially greater proportion of nonwhites live in substandard housing. Nor is this simply a matter of Negroes spending less than whites in the same income bracket: for the same rent and even at high rent levels, a far greater proportion of nonwhites live in substandard conditions.

Negroes are the victims of a discriminatory housing market, as the articles in this section demonstrate. Eunice and George Grier review the elements of both public and private housing policy that operate to restrict housing opportunities for Negroes. Housing policies of the private sector are essentially those of financial institutions, builders, and real estate brokers. These same groups have been highly influential in determining the policies of public programs in housing. Together, these policies operate to frustrate the national housing goal. Negroes compete for their housing in a restricted market where good homes are scarce and where the limited housing supply leads to inflated prices for whatever is available.

Poor housing conditions are not the only reason for concern about racial bias in the housing market. Residential restrictions imposed on Negroes have led to a high degree of racial segregation, which compounds the disadvantages confronting Negroes. Segregation often serves as a basis for other forms of discrimination, particularly in the provision of public services that are supplied on a neighborhood basis. De facto school segregation is a prime example of inequality in a vital public service, and a direct outcome of segregated neighborhoods. Much civil rights activity has focused upon school desegregation, and a number of techniques have been developed to attack it.

Robert A. Dentler's essay reviews the various approaches that have been used or proposed, as well as the many impediments to effective school desegregation. Yet Dentler concludes that such methods as redistricting and bussing of students are effective solutions mainly in the smaller communities. In the big cities, desegregation efforts run up against the stubborn facts of massive residential segregation, with Negroes concentrated in large areas of the city and almost totally excluded from other sections. In addition, the big cities as a whole are the victims of segregation practiced at the metropolitan level. While the suburbs of large metropolitan areas in the North exclude all but a handful of Negroes, the central-city population is becoming increasingly Negro and public school enrollment still more so. The Griers predict that before 1980 Baltimore, New Orleans, Cleveland, Detroit, Philadelphia, and St. Louis will join Washington as cities with Negro majorities.

Other consequences of racial segregation are less direct than segregated schools. Negroes in central city ghettos are at a disadvantage in terms of access to the growing number of jobs located at suburban industrial centers. They tend to be out of touch with the suburban job market and thus fail to find out about openings; and low-income workers without cars have to organize car pools or make other cumbersome arrangements to commute to the outlying plants. Residential segregation has much to do with poor communication between whites and Negroes and with the maintenance of stereotypes of both races. Thus the social and physical isolation of a neighborhood such as Watts makes it possible for the larger community to ignore its complaints while they build to the breaking point. More basically, the maintenance of segregated neighborhoods has come to symbolize the inferior position of Negroes in the American city.

Desegregation strategies

In the long run, solutions to this web of related problems will call for a greater degree of residential integration, in the central cities and in the suburbs. Both governmental and private activities have developed to combat segregation in housing. Governmental approaches have involved federal action to prohibit discrimination in the sale or rental of federally aided housing, and a number of state and local laws to prohibit discrimination in private housing. The coverage of existing laws and federal policies together is far from complete, and enforcement is difficult. Private groups have played a major role in stimulating government action, and they have also worked directly at the local level. Citizen groups and private developers have sponsored a number of housing developments planned for racially mixed occupancy from the outset. Neighborhood associations have worked to prevent panic selling and to stabilize areas of racial transition. More than a thousand local fair-housing organizations have been established to find homes for Negro families in white neighborhoods on an individual basis.

There has been some tendency to regard the public and private approaches as separate fields of concern, but in many ways they are mutually supporting. Civil rights organizations, for example, have been able to test whether real estate brokers comply with state laws against discrimination and to furnish public agencies with the evidence they need to enforce the laws. Several new federal-aid housing programs rely heavily on private non-profit groups to sponsor developments that will supply low-cost housing on an open-occupancy basis. Since public as well as private channels are needed to counter the long-standing patterns of segregation, planning should overlap both sectors. Government measures can strengthen the work of private groups by providing a supporting context of law and public policy, while private groups can often operate best in local situations.

Effective planning of private and public action requires a detailed understanding of the process of racial change in urban areas. This process has been the subject of much casual observation but little systematic research. The notion of a tipping-point—a certain proportion of Negro population that brings about the rapid flight of all white residents—has been widely accepted and even used as a basis for managing public and private housing developments. In this section, Eleanor Wolf reports on research in two areas of Detroit that casts serious doubt on the validity or usefulness of the tipping-point concept. The decision whether to remain in a racially mixed area depends on many factors, and cannot be predicted solely on the basis of racial composition.

Chester Rapkin and William Grigsby have studied neighborhood racial change by analyzing the complex operation of the real estate market in several areas of Philadelphia. The excerpt from their study included in this section makes it clear that neighborhood change reflects the interaction of many market factors, and does not correspond directly with the extent of prejudice among whites or even with discrimination in the sale of housing. A number of white families were attracted to buy housing in areas that Negroes had already entered, despite the fact that many were unhappy to have Negroes nearby. If integrated neighborhoods are to be maintained, the level of white demand for housing is critical, but this demand can evidently be influenced by such factors as the price of housing and the attractiveness of the neighborhood. The findings of this Philadelphia study imply that public policy can promote neighborhood integration by its indirect influence on the housing market.

The major problems of race and housing will not be solved by even the most sensitive planning of integrated neighborhoods, however. Segregation is tied closely to the shortage of low-income housing. Until there is a serious national commitment to supply this housing, neighborhood integration efforts will involve small numbers of Negroes, mainly those in middle-income brackets, while massive segregation continues for the Negro poor. Eunice and George Grier provide a broad overview of the dimensions of segregation and the very limited impact of present measures to counteract it. They call attention, as well, to the racial implications of private and public action that will influence the future distribution of people in metropolitan areas. They point out the failure of a recent metropolitan plan for Washington, D.C., to consider racial patterns in planning for future urban growth, leading to the likelihood of an extension of segregation into future suburban development. Similarly, they question current concepts of building new towns at the fringe of metropolitan areas. A number of private new towns are now under construction, and federal support for new community development may soon be forthcoming. The Griers point out the potential of such communities for aiding in desegregation, but they criticize present examples for their failure to come to grips with racial problems. In reviewing present policies and proposing new strategies, the Griers anticipate the discussion of guidelines for social policy which appears in the final section of this book.

8

Equality and Beyond:
Housing Segregation in the Great Society

EUNICE AND GEORGE GRIER

Riots, racial protests, and rising waves of crime and violence in Los Angeles and other cities across the nation have focused attention upon a problem unique to America—and one which, if not dealt with decisively and soon, can wreak wholesale destruction upon the objectives of the "Great Society." The point at issue is the increasing dominance of Negro ghettos, with all their human problems, at the heart of the nation's metropolitan areas. While racial segregation is by no means new to this country, in recent years it has assumed new dimensions. And the long-smoldering difficulties and disillusionments of a suppressed Negro population have simultaneously taken on new and frightening forms of expression.

The newly emergent pattern of segregation is as simple to describe as it is ominous in its implications. Since the end of World War II, Negroes have rapidly been replacing whites as the dominant population of our greatest cities. Meanwhile, the vast new suburbs growing up around these same urban centers—sharing most of the same problems and feeding upon a common economic base, but separated from the cities politically—have become the residence of an almost exclusively white population. Too many of the suburbanites disavow any concern or responsibility for the cities they have left behind.[1]

Yet the ghettos will not be ignored. To the degree that human problems —economic, social, educational, health—are concentrated in the ghetto, they become self-reinforcing. Exploitation flourishes, since "captive" markets can be forced to pay exorbitant prices for inferior merchandise and services, and continuing Negro population growth presses inexorably upon an inadequate and overage supply of housing. Discouragement and bitterness are the natural expressions. As the Negro ghettos have grown in size, these symptoms of the deeper disease have sometimes reached epidemic proportions.

Unless drastic measures are taken, the ghettos and their problems will continue to grow. They contain within themselves the seeds of their own further expansion. The present urban non-white concentrations result only in part from the recent migration of Negroes out of Southern rural areas. They are also the product of natural increase (the excess of births over

From *Daedalus*, the Journal of the American Academy of Arts and Sciences, XCV (Winter, 1966), 77–106.

deaths) among populations already in residence. As a result, even if migration were to cease tomorrow, the ghettos would continue to grow. During the next few years, this trend will be rapid as the postwar "baby boom" reaches maturity and has its own offspring. With this expansion are likely to come greater pressures of people upon available space, and probably more damaging racial explosions.

Today there are very few major cities where Negroes do not constitute a significantly greater proportion than the roughly one-tenth they average across the nation as a whole. In virtually every city they are increasing rapidly. During the 1950's alone, Negro populations increased in New York City by 46 per cent; in Philadelphia by 41 per cent; in Washington, D. C., by 47 per cent; in Los Angeles by 96 per cent.[2]

One consequence of this growth pattern is that Washington has become the first important city to have a Negro majority. But it almost certainly is not the last. Baltimore and New Orleans are likely to join Washington by 1970 at the latest; Cleveland, Detroit, Philadelphia, and St. Louis, before 1980.

Insight into both the nature and the causes of racial change in America's urban areas can be gained from the example of Washington, D.C. Since 1920, the metropolitan population of Washington (encompassing both the central city and its suburbs in neighboring Maryland and Virginia) has grown more than threefold, from less than 600,000 to over two million. Meanwhile, the proportion of Negroes in that population has remained essentially constant at roughly one-fourth of the total. In other words, Negroes have both migrated to and multiplied within *metropolitan* Washington at roughly the same over-all rate as whites.

Yet within the central city of Washington, D.C. (which now contains only about one-third of the total metropolitan population) Negroes have increased from one-fourth of the total to well over one-half, since virtually all the Negro increase has gone to the city. At the same time, the proportion of Negroes in the suburbs has declined from 25 to only 6 per cent as an almost exclusively white outflux has overwhelmed long-existing suburban Negro enclaves.[3]

Rapid Negro increases have been almost universal in cities of large and medium population alike. But in proportional terms, the change has often been greater in the middle-sized cities. Syracuse, Rochester, New Haven, San Diego, and Forth Worth all saw their Negro populations approximately double during the 1950's. Thus these cities can no longer look with smug superiority upon a few urban giants marked by the blight and disorder of Negro ghettos. By the same token, Rochester, New York, and Springfield, Massachusetts, recently achieved the headlines through racial disturbances.

Not all the predominantly Negro portions of today's cities are decaying, crime-ridden, potentially explosive slums, however. The movement of white families to the suburbs has recently opened up a number of highly desirable living areas for the small minority of Negroes who can afford them. Some of the finest residential sections of cities like Washington and Philadelphia—

once predominantly white—now are interracial or heavily Negro. Their physical character and general flavor have changed little. Imposing stone and brick homes still stand on immaculately maintained lawns. Only the color of the occupants is different.

Yet these too are *Negro* neighborhoods, and—like the sprawling all-white subdivisions surrounding the cities or like the less desirable central districts where most Negroes are allowed to live—they betoken the growing segregation which is splitting our metropolitan areas into two huge enclaves, each the territory of a single race. Their continued social and physical stability, furthermore, is threatened by many of the same pressures of population increase and exploitation which beset the Negro slums. Segregation itself may not be new, but never before has it manifested itself on such a giant and destructive scale.

The growth of residential segregation

How did this change occur so swiftly and so massively? Discrimination and prejudice are certainly among the causes, but they are not the only ones. America cannot escape responsibility for the many decades in which the rights of its Negro citizens were denied. Nonetheless, the present situation cannot be fully understood, nor can solutions to its perplexing aspects be found, without recognizing that it was produced and is maintained in significant part by forces that are both broader than and different from racial discrimination.

The background to all that has happened lies in certain facts concerning the rapid urbanization of America's people—facts racially neutral in themselves, but having profound racial effects. As the nation has grown more populous, its inhabitants have located increasingly within metropolitan centers. A century ago Americans numbered 31 million, about one-fifth of whom lived in urban areas. By 1920 the total population had risen to 106 million, and the urban proportion had grown to one-half—a ninefold jump in absolute numbers (from about 6 million to 54 million) in only sixty years.

After World War II, population growth accelerated sharply. The largest ten-year increase in the nation's history took place between 1950 and 1960. During that decade 28 million new citizens were added, a total nearly equal to the entire population of a century ago. About 85 per cent of this increase occurred within 212 metropolitan areas, making about two-thirds of the nation's people urban today.

In addition to increase through births and immigration during these fruitful years, the cities gained also from large-scale population movements from the center of the country toward its boundaries (especially to the seacoasts and Great Lakes region) and from the South to the North. These streams of people, most experts agree, were both "pulled" toward the cities by job opportunities and other urban attractions (especially in the coastal areas) and "pushed" out of the rural areas by shrinking labor needs, especially in the depressed portions of the agricultural South. Negroes and whites shared in the migration—Negroes to a somewhat, but not drastically, greater degree in proportion to their share of the total population.

Migration to the cities helps explain why, after World War II, the nation turned to its suburbs in order to satisfy housing needs which had been accumulating during almost two decades of economic depression and world conflict. The previous growth of the cities had used up most of the land suitable for development within their boundaries. Yet the people had to be housed somewhere, and swiftly. The easiest place, requiring no costly and time-consuming demolition of existing buildings, was the suburbs.

How should the suburbs be developed? In answering this question, certain key public policy decisions—involving racial implications which were probably neither foreseen nor intended—joined with private actions to help produce the present situation. Primary among these was the critical decision to allow the private-enterprise system to meet the housing shortage on its own terms. Most of the government mechanisms mobilized to aid in the task, especially the mortgage guarantee provisions of the Federal Housing Administration and the Veterans Administration, served to support and encourage the efforts of private enterprise.[4]

Such a decision was completely in accord with America's social philosophy and economic structure. And, in light of the inherent dynamism of the private-enterprise system, it is not surprising that the home-building industry was able to provide usable physical shelter. Indeed, this success can be counted as one of the major achievements of a nation which has never been satisfied with small accomplishments. Almost every year following World War II more than one million dwelling units were constructed and occupied, a figure which is double the rate at which new families were formed. And, despite rapid population growth during the fifties, the 1960 Census showed that Americans were far better housed than ever before. Overcrowding and "doubling up" (two or more families in one dwelling) had been considerably reduced. So had dilapidated and otherwise substandard housing. To a greater or lesser degree, the entire population benefited from this widespread improvement—even Negroes, though they continued to be less adequately housed than whites.[5]

Nonetheless, the decision to let private enterprise satisfy the housing need carried with it unfortunate consequences for future residential patterns. It meant that the great majority of the new postwar suburban housing was built for those who could afford to pay the full economic price. Thus the basic mechanisms of the private enterprise system, successful as they were in meeting over-all housing needs, selectively operated to reinforce existing trends which concentrated low-income families in the cities. At the same time, they encouraged the centrifugal movement of those who were more wealthy to the outskirts of the cities.

Most Negro families were among those with low incomes, the result of generations of discrimination in employment and education. Quite apart from direct racial discrimination, in which the private housing industry also indulged whenever it felt necessary, economics posed a giant barrier to the free dispersal of the growing Negro populations. The findings of a market analysis conducted by Chester Rapkin and others at the University of Pennsylvania's Institute for Urban Studies at the peak of the postwar housing boom in the mid-1950's were quite typical. At that time, only 0.5 per cent of all dwellings costing $12,000 or more in Philadelphia had been purchased by Negroes—a fact which the authors laid mainly to economic incapacity. This was about the minimum cost of a modest new house in Philadelphia's suburbs.[6]

But this is only part of the story. Federal policies and practices in housing reinforced and increased the separation between the "Negro" cities and the white suburbs. In part, this was intentional. From 1935 to 1950—a period in which about 15 million new dwellings were constructed—the power of the national government was explicitly used to prevent integrated housing. Federal policies were based upon the premise that economic and social stability could best be achieved through keeping neighborhood populations as homogeneous as possible. Thus, the *Underwriting Manual* of the Federal Housing Administration (oldest and largest of the federal housing agencies, established by the Housing Act of 1934) warned that "if a neighborhood is to retain stability, it is necessary that properties shall continue to be occupied by the same social and racial group." It advised appraisers to lower their valuation of properties in mixed neighborhoods, "often to the point of rejection." FHA actually drove out of business some developers who insisted upon open policies.[7]

More recently, a number of studies by competent real-estate economists have thrown serious doubt upon the thesis that Negro entry lowers property values. Laurenti, in his thorough analysis entitled *Property Values and Race,* found that prices *rose* in 44 per cent of those areas which Negroes entered, were unchanged in another 41 per cent, and declined in only 15 per cent. These were long-term trends, and they were measured *relative* to trends in carefully matched neighborhoods which remained all white—thus obviating any possibly misleading effects of generally rising prices.[8]

Surveying the literature, Laurenti noted similar results from other studies in various cities extending back as far as 1930. But erroneous though the allegation of non-white destruction of property values may have been, it nonetheless provided "justification" for widespread discriminatory practices, as well as active encouragement of private discrimination, by agencies of the federal government during a period of critical importance in determining present residential patterns.

However, discrimination per se was only a small factor in the impact of federal policies and practices upon racial patterns during this crucial period. Much more important were more basic aspects of the structure and functioning of federal housing programs. Three major programs have dominated the field. The largest and most significant has been the Federal Housing Administration's mortgage insurance program, with its post-World War

II counterpart for veterans, the Veterans Administration's loan guarantee program. Both granted their benefits chiefly to the "modal" family recently embarked upon married life, with children already born or on the way, and willing to commit itself to the responsibilities of home ownership with a mortgage. For such families, down-payment requirements were minimal, repayment periods lengthy, and credit restrictions lenient. A certain minimum of present earnings and good prospects for future income were paramount, as well as some evidence of faithful repayment of past obligations. Households which did not fit these criteria—smaller families, older couples, single persons, people with low or precarious earnings, families who sought dwellings for rent rather than for sale, even families dependent upon the wife's employment for an adequate income—all were required to satisfy their needs chiefly through the older housing left vacant by people moving to new homes in the suburbs.

Prominent among those left behind, of course, were Negroes. The federal programs permitted them to "inherit" the cities, along with an assortment of whites who did not meet the conditions for access to the new suburbs: the old, the poor, the physically and mentally handicapped, the single and divorced, together with some persons of wealth and influence who preferred the convenience of living in the central city. The significance of the housing programs for residential patterns, however, lay also in their tendency to pull young and upwardly mobile white families away from the cities and out toward the suburbs.

It may be that a large number of these families, given free choice, would have preferred to remain within the cities, close to work and to older relatives. But the FHA and VA programs generally did not provide nearly so liberal terms on the mortgages of older homes in the cities. Down payments were usually larger; repayment periods shorter; monthly payments higher. For most young families, therefore, the suburbs were the only practical areas in which to solve their housing needs. In this way, the FHA and VA programs, essentially independent of any direct racial bias in their decisions on applications, enhanced the tendency toward white dominance in the suburbs.

The second of the federal government's major housing programs is subsidized low-income public housing, administered by the Public Housing Administration through local housing authorities. Its criteria for admission are based upon *maximum* rather than minimum income levels. Under these conditions relatively small numbers of whites can qualify because their earnings exceed the required standard. In many areas, even where conscious efforts are made to attract an interracial clientele, the great majority of residents are Negro. In further contrast to the FHA and VA programs, most public housing projects have been constructed in the central cities rather than in the suburbs—since one of their objectives is to reduce the incidence of blighted housing.

The differences between the two programs thus reinforce each other in their effects upon patterns of residence. While the FHA and VA have helped promote white dominance in the suburbs, public housing has helped enhance Negro dominance in the cities.

The third of the major federal housing programs is urban renewal. Established by the Housing Act of 1949, its chief goal is to combat physical decay in the central cities. In a sense, urban renewal has worked against FHA and VA programs, since, among other things, it attempts to draw back to the cities the more prosperous of the families who have left it. Until recently, the renewal program has usually cleared off blighted sections and replaced them with housing units priced in the middle- to upper-income brackets. Most often, as might be expected, the occupants of the site before renewal have been low-income members of a racial minority. They have been displaced by housing which, for economic reasons alone, was available mainly to whites and to very few Negroes. Some civil rights groups therefore have dubbed urban renewal "Negro removal." [9]

Renewal agencies are required by law to relocate displaced families into "decent, safe, and sanitary" housing. Relocation procedures have recently received a great deal of criticism throughout the nation. Whether or not all of it is valid, it is an undeniable fact that most relocatees move only a short distance from their former homes. One study found, for example, that two-thirds of them relocated within a radius of twelve city blocks. As a result, displaced low-income minorities ring the renewal site.

Sometimes this movement appears to set off a chain reaction. Whites in the neighborhoods to which the displacees move take up residence elsewhere—as do some of the more secure Negroes. The ultimate effect too often is to touch off spreading waves of racial change, which in the end only produce a broader extension of segregated living patterns. Thus, if the FHA, VA, and public housing programs have helped produce metropolitan areas which increasingly resemble black bulls'-eyes with white outer rings, urban renewal has too often created small white or largely white areas in the center of the bulls'-eyes—simultaneously causing the black ghettos to expand outward even further.

Combined with rapid population growth in the metropolitan areas, the interacting effects of federal policies and practices in the postwar era did much to produce the present segregated patterns. But they were not the only factors. Clear discrimination by private individuals and groups—including the mortgage, real-estate, and home-building industries—has also played its part. The activities of the "blockbuster" provide a good focus for examining the way this works.

The *modus operandi* of the blockbuster is to turn over whole blocks of homes from white to Negro occupancy—the quicker the better for his own profits, if not for neighborhood stability. Once one Negro family has entered a block, the speculator preys on the racial fears and prejudices of the whites in order to purchase their homes at prices as low as possible—often considerably below fair market value. He then plays upon the pent-up housing needs of Negroes and resells the same houses at prices often well *above* their value in a free market situation. Often he makes a profit of several thousand dollars within a period of a few days. Studies have indicated that skillful blockbusters frequently double their investments in a brief interval. They can do this only because tight residential restrictions have "dammed up" the Negro need for housing to such a point that its sudden release can change the racial composition of a neighborhood within a matter of weeks or months. Apart from the damage done to both sellers and buyers and to the structure of the neighborhoods themselves, blockbusters have a far wider negative impact. By funneling Negro housing demand into limited sections of the city (usually around the edges of the Negro slums, since these neighborhoods are easier to throw into panic), the blockbusters relieve much of the pressure which might otherwise have encouraged the dispersion of Negroes throughout the metropolitan areas.[10]

Technically speaking, blockbusters represent an unscrupulous minority of the real-estate industry—"outlaws" in a moral if not a legal sense. However, their activities would not prove profitable if racial restrictions on place of residence were not accepted and enforced by the large majority of builders, brokers, and lenders, backed by the supporting opinion of large segments of the white public.

By retraining the Negro market and permitting its housing needs to be satisfied only on a waiting-list basis, "reputable" members of the banking and housing industries have helped perpetuate the conditions under which their less-scrupulous colleagues can flourish. For reasons they consider entirely justifiable, they guard assiduously against the entry of Negroes into white areas. In recent testimony before the Commissioners of the District of Columbia, the president of the Mortgage Bankers Association of Metropolitan Washington stated bluntly that "applications from minority groups are not generally considered in areas that are not recognized as being racially mixed." A study by the Chicago Commission on Human Relations found that such a policy was pursued by almost all lending sources in that city. Voluminous evidence from both social research surveys and testimony before legislative and executive bodies indicates that the same is true of most real-estate boards in cities throughout the country.

Supporting this activity is the subjective equivalent of the ostensibly objective economic argument that underlay federal housing policy for years: the belief in neighborhood homogeneity—that is, neighborhood exclusiveness. The general attitude of much of the public (or the most vocal) has been that neighborhoods were better off when the people within them all belonged to the same broad socioeconomic groups and had the same ethnic or racial origins. In practice, of course, this commitment to neighborhood homogeneity has tended to exclude individuals who fell below a certain status level, not those who were above it. The latter, however, usually have "excluded" themselves in neighborhoods restricted to occupants of their own status.

After 1948, when the Supreme Court ruled that racial and religious covenants were unenforceable in the courts, minority groups began to find it somewhat less difficult to obtain access to neighborhoods on the basis of financial status and preference. Still, neighborhood exclusiveness remained a commonly accepted value, widely enforced by the real-estate, home-building, and lending industries. It served as the final factor in the constellation which created the nation's new patterns of residential segregation.

The shape of the future

The future shape of metropolitan areas, in racial terms, is outlined clearly in population statistics. The growth of segregated patterns has attained a momentum that now tends to be self-sustaining. Most of the young white families who will provide the future increase in white population have moved outside the city limits. In Washington, D.C., for example, half of the remaining white population (children included) are over the age of forty. Even among the young adults, a disproportionate number are single.[11]

On the other hand, the central cities continue to be the place of residence of Negroes of all ages, including the young couples and teenagers approaching maturity who provide the potential for future population growth. Left to themselves, these population patterns can have no other effect than to swell the ghettos and further exacerbate the color dichotomy between cities and suburbs.

What steps would be necessary to halt or reverse these trends? The magnitude of the effort required is suggested by statistics computed by George Schermer for the Philadelphia metropolitan area. Schermer has estimated that merely to prevent the current areas of Negro concentration from expanding further would require an annual outflux of 6,000 Negro households. To *reverse* the trend and to disperse the Negro population evenly throughout the metropolis by the year 2000 would require the entry of 9,700 Negro households *annually* into currently white districts and the counter-movement of 3,700 white families into areas now Negro. No comparable shift of populations is presently occurring in Philadelphia or in any other metropolis. And, each year that the ghettos continue to expand, these figures grow progressively larger.[12]

The costs of segregation

Today's wide-scale patterns of segregation and the prospect of their further expansion have several extremely important consequences for the nation as a whole. One of the most dramatic of the current ramifications is the fact that the problems long associated with the Negro ghetto because of generations of discrimination—educational deficiencies, high rates of illness and social disorders, low employment rates, and predominantly low incomes even among those who are employed—all press with increasing force upon the cities as the ghettos continue to grow. At the same time, the financial and leadership resources of the cities have been severely depleted by the middle-class white movement to the suburbs. As a separate political entity, the city has, with growing force, been deprived by the expanding rings of suburbia of the resources it needs to set its house in order.

The newly emergent residential patterns have thus transformed segregation from a parochial concern largely confined to the South (though posing a moral dilemma for the entire nation) into the hardest kind of practical economic problem affecting all the urban centers of America.[13]

But the problem no longer stops at the city line. Today, segregation increasingly threatens the rational planning and development of entire metropolitan areas—a consequence of profound significance in light of continued population growth and the scarcity of urban land, which make it essential that future generations be housed in a less haphazard fashion.

In recent years choice land on the periphery of the larger cities has been devoured at a ferocious rate. In metropolitan Philadelphia, for example, while the population of the "urbanized" or heavily built up area grew by 24 per cent during the 1950's, its geographic spread doubled. This reckless consumption of land cannot continue much longer. Municipalities are already grappling in various ways with the challenge of making more efficient use of the land which is still within feasible commuting distance. The aim of their plans is to keep the metropolitan areas fit places in which to live, with a satisfactory balance of the various elements that together constitute an adequate human environment: homes, commercial and cultural centers, adequate transit facilities, industries, parks, and other necessities and amenities.

In metropolitan Washington, regional planning agencies recently devised a "Plan for the Year 2000." This plan is essentially a general set of principles for meeting the needs of a population that is expected to grow to more than twice its present size before the end of the century. The plan suggests that future growth be channeled along six radial "corridors" extending outward in star fashion from the central city. Highways and transit lines would run alongside the corridors; centers of commerce and various service areas would be located at appropriate intervals. To preserve as much as possible of the green countryside, parks and open recreation areas would be placed between the corridors.

The plan, however, fails to take into account one vital consideration: the effect of race. If the movement of the city's population continues in its present directions, three of the planned corridors will be heavily Negro. They will have their central origins in neighborhoods which currently are Negro and which already are expanding outward in the directions proposed by the plan. The other three corridors will be almost exclusively white, since they originate in the only white residential areas that remain within the city. Thus segregation will be extended for an indefinite period into the new suburbs. If, on the other hand, Negro expansion is cut off along the three corridors which are presently "open," the future population growth will be forced back into the city, thereby intensifying dangerous pressures which already exist.[14]

Still another instance of the way racial segregation thwarts planning can be found in the emerging new towns which, in some parts of the country, at least, may soon begin to offer an alternative to the previous norm of suburban sprawl. These new communities—of which Reston, Virginia, and Columbia, Maryland, both already underway, are two important examples—will be planned and built from the outset as complete urban complexes, with a full panoply of shopping, employment, and recreational facilities. The most comprehensive of the new towns will also contain a wide selection of housing, ranging from bachelor apartments to large single houses, so that the residents will be able to satisfy their changing needs without moving from the community. Over-all population densities in these new communities will be considerably higher than in the dormitory suburbs of the recent past. Yet, through imaginative planning, they can offer their residents an even greater sense of spaciousness and privacy.

Already popular in Europe and Great Britain, the new town concept offers important advantages over the formlessness that characterizes America's postwar suburban development—advantages that accrue not merely to the residents of the towns but to the entire nation. The new towns offer a way of comfortably accommodating population growth while conserving irreplaceable green space. The proliferation of multi-million-dollar superhighways can be slowed down. Pollution of the air by exhaust fumes will be reduced. Speedy, economical mass transit systems, now virtually unfeasible in many areas because of the low density and wide geographic spread of suburban growth, will become practical once more. There will even be substantial savings in taxes for municipal services, as well as in utility and commuting costs.

But the new towns, despite the hopeful prospect they represent, also confront the ever-present specter of race. To be successful in realizing their diversified goals, the towns will require a large number of service workers—including manual laborers, domestics, custodians, and sales people, to mention only a few categories. Today, the only significant reservoir of labor available for many of these occupations is the Negro population. Furthermore, civil rights laws now require equal access by all citizens to employment opportunities. Yet, in most instances, the new towns will be located too far from the central cities for easy and economical commuting. Thus, in all likelihood, the workers will have to be housed in the towns themselves.

But on what basis? Will the new towns contain, from the outset, pre-planned ghettos? If not, how is integration to be accomplished, given the differential income levels of the people involved and the many problems connected with providing low-cost housing under private auspices? Even if this last obstacle is overcome—as might be possible if Congress implements new and imaginative forms of governmental aid and subsidy—will white Americans long conditioned with the encouragement of their own government to rigid spatial separation, not only of races but of economic groups, accept any other arrangement?

If, on the other hand, the new towns do not offer accommodations to families of low income, what will happen as they draw away more and more of the cities' remaining affluent residents, while providing no comparable outlet for their growing low-income populations? Will vast new towns then be planned especially for the low-income populations, thus extending patterns of racial segregation upon a scale even now unknown? Or will the cities merely be expected to absorb the population increase indefinitely?

Within some cities, the low-income housing needs are already reaching crisis proportions. In Washington, D.C., for example, public attention has recently been focused on the problem through widespread civic protests. With virtually no vacant land remaining, and with a population which has grown since 1960 both in total numbers and in the proportion of low-income Negroes, Washington now faces a perplexing dilemma indeed. Virtually every improvement of any magnitude in its physical structure, whether publicly or privately sponsored, further reduces an already inadequate low-income housing supply.

Development of expressways to relieve traffic congestion has been threatened as a result. Even code enforcement aimed at improving housing conditions is endangered because it often results in evicting poor families with no place else to live. Yet private construction, stimulated by Washington's booming economy and unhampered by considerations that often affect public action, is proceeding apace. Almost all centrally located homes which are privately renewed for occupancy by middle-class families, and many of the sumptuous new apartment houses and office buildings as well, gain their valuable land by removing additional units from the low-income housing supply. Some Washington observers are wondering how much longer this process can continue without triggering racial outbreaks similar to those which have already disfigured other major cities.

The complex issues which surround land development, both present and future, constitute only one of the concerns made increasingly problematical by the city-suburban racial split. Paradoxically, it presents obstacles also to current major attempts to aid minority groups in escaping from poverty and deprivation.

A good case in point is the multiple efforts to upgrade Northern public schools in a state of de facto segregation. For the most part, these schools are desegregated in principle, but because of surrounding residential patterns have become segregated in practice. A considerable amount of this segregation, it should be realized, occurred during the fifties as a direct result of population shifts. At the time of the Supreme Court decision barring school segregation, Washington, D.C., which is located among the border states, had a completely segregated educational system. Once the decision was announced, the city immediately desegregated. Yet only a decade later, because of intervening population shifts, the school system once again is almost entirely segregated. "Resegregation" is the term some concerned local citizens have coined for this disturbing phenomenon.

De facto segregation tends to create poor, inadequately serviced schools. The concentration of culturally disadvantaged Negro children makes it difficult to provide the intensive programs they need to reach an equal footing with their white contemporaries. In racially mixed schools, their deficiencies are leavened through contact with children more fortunate in background and home environment. One attempted solution has been to bus Negro children to better schools which are underutilized and for the most part are predominantly white. But this approach has met with strenuous resistance from many of the parents (including some Negroes) whose children attend the better schools. Some officials fear that continued bussing in the face of such protests would cause even more middle-class whites to leave the cities and thus make the situation even worse in the long run.[15]

The whole problem is exacerbated by the fact that most heavily Negro schools are located in the older and more depressed neighborhoods of the city. Both the schools and their surroundings are often in physical and social decay. Thus, in addition to everything else, it becomes difficult to attract or keep good teachers.

But the nation quite rightly, although belatedly, has committed itself to providing equal educational opportunities for all its citizens. In the face of de facto segregation, it is now trying to meet that commitment by a huge complex of experimental programs costing millions of dollars. If the programs are successful, their extension to all those who need them will ultimately mean the spending of many more billions. But aside from the question of money, the nation currently confronts the much more difficult question of whether the programs can in fact work, given the complex of environmental obstacles which exist.

Most of the dilemmas and problems posed by residential segregation in the United States are brought into focus by the current war against poverty. Can poverty among Negroes ever be eliminated while rigid segregation increases within the metropolitan centers? On the other hand, can the metropolitan areas ever be desegregated as long as the majority of Negroes remain poor? As segregation continues to grow and Negroes reach numerical predominance in more and more urban centers, will not the cities which house the majority of the nation's industrial and commercial life find themselves less and less able to cope with their problems, financially and in every other way? What then will be the answer for the metropolitan complexes where two-thirds of America's population currently reside and where as much as 85 per cent of the nation may live by the year 2000?

Aside from these large and basic questions of public policy and social change, residential segregation causes havoc on a more personal and individual level. And the personal damage is not to Negroes alone. Many of the neighborhoods newly entered by Negroes since World War II have been occupied by middle-aged and retired white families who often look upon their current homes as being their last—and whose emotional attachment to both house and neighborhood is based upon ties of familiarity and friendship built up over many years. These occupants feel deeply threatened by the entrance of a Negro family. The result often is mental stress, misery, and loneliness, as well as a sense of overwhelming personal loss at being "forced" to leave a home and neighborhood one had grown to love.[16]

The effects of precipitate change are particularly sad in ethnic neighborhoods where much of the community's life has centered around a house of worship and where neighbors often include kinfolk as well as friends. In such cases, the change is harmful not only to individual families but to institutions and social organizations that can rarely survive transfer to another location. Constant change is normal, of course, and neighborhood institutions should adapt constructively to it and help their members to adjust. Nevertheless, many institutions are unprepared, and the rapidity of racial change often gives them little opportunity to catch up with their responsibilities.

In all these ways, then, residential segregation is or has become central to major domestic problems of the nation. There is no way to determine the ultimate sum of its costs. It ranges into so many areas that it may accurately be designated the key question of our national life in the 1960's.

The upsurge of civic concern

Over the past decade and a half, as the situation has worsened, the significance of residential segregation has steadily been pushing itself into the forefront of the national consciousness. As public comprehension has grown, one response has been a groundswell of concern and action on both public and private levels. This development cannot be overvalued. It is a change of almost revolutionary proportions, a change that has been accomplished not through violence or political disorder but through the constitutional mechanisms of the government and through the exercise of individual freedoms that form the basis of American society. Yet, this counteraction, despite its importance, is in itself presently insufficient for the task at hand. The best way to indicate both the limitations of the current activity and the general direction in which the country must now move is to outline the various ways in which mounting public concern has expressed itself.

Between 1950 and today, the federal government has completely reversed its racial policy, moving from official sanction of segregation to a Presidential order that prohibits discrimination in any housing receiving federal assistance. The first official impetus for this change came in 1948, when the Supreme Court ruled that restrictive racial covenants were legally unenforceable. At first the Federal Housing Administration declared that the decision was inapplicable to its operation. Finally, late in 1949, it removed the model covenant and all references to neighborhood homogeneity from its manual and declared that after February 1950 it no longer would insure mortgages having restrictive covenants. The Veterans Administration and the Urban Renewal Administration both issued similar statements.

Further changes ensued. By 1960, they included the following: both the FHA and VA had ruled that the insured property they acquired (usually under foreclosure proceedings) would be made available to all buyers or renters, regardless of race, creed, or color; the administrative head of the FHA had instructed local offices to take "active steps to encourage the development of demonstrations in open occupancy projects in suitably located key areas"; both the FHA and VA had signed a series of formal agreements of cooperation with state and local agencies responsible for enforcing laws and ordinances against housing discrimination; the government had dropped a system of racial quotas in housing built for persons displaced by urban renewal; and it also had banned discrimination in a special loan program to assist the elderly in their housing needs.

These regulations and directives clearly represent a large stride forward from the directly discriminatory policies pursued before 1950. Yet their practical effect on the rigid patterns of segregation that had developed over the years was very small. In 1962, federal reports revealed that nearly 80 per cent of all public housing projects receiving a federal subsidy were occupied by only one race. Segregated projects were located as far north as Scranton, Pennsylvania, and Plattsburgh, New York—and, as might be expected, in practically every locality in the South. The vast majority of new suburban housing backed by FHA and VA mortgage guarantees was occupied exclusively by white families. A scattering of developments built on urban renewal sites were made available to both Negroes and whites; but they were limited mainly to the largest cities of the North and West and generally priced at or close to luxury levels. Where integration existed, it was largely the result of state and local laws rather than national directives. Only seldom, however, were these laws adequately enforced.[17]

Nonetheless, by 1962, partly because of the ineffectiveness of previous changes, it had become clear that the broad problems of discrimination and segregation were too interwoven to be solved with piecemeal changes in federal policy. The first step toward a more comprehensive approach came on November 20, 1962, when the late President Kennedy issued an Executive Order barring discrimination in all housing receiving federal aid after that date. At the end of April 1964, it was estimated that 932,000 units of housing had come under the directives of the Order. In June 1964, it was estimated that between 12 and 20 per cent of all new residential construction was covered.

But the segregation that had developed in previous years still remained. Charles Abrams summed up both the limitations and the value of the Executive Order shortly after it was issued in the following way:

> The Executive Order will . . . touch only a small fraction of the housing market. If any real gains are to be made, its coverage must be widened or more individual state laws laboriously sought. The President's Order is no more than a small first federal step toward breaking the bottleneck in housing discrimination.
>
> Nevertheless, its importance cannot be discounted. First steps in civil rights legislation have often led to second steps when the will to move ahead has been present.[18]

The federal government has also made special, though limited, efforts to mitigate the unintended racial effects of its housing programs. Housing legislation gave the FHA, in cooperation with the Federal National Mortgage

Association, the right to issue insured loans from government funds at below-market interest rates for housing to be occupied by families with incomes too low to acquire new homes in the private market. This indirect form of subsidy was intended in part to reach a larger number of Negro families. Urban renewal programs have begun to pay more attention to relocation procedures and to stress rehabilitation of existing dwellings rather than total clearance. In some cities, Community Renewal Programs aided with federal funds are attempting to develop comprehensive plans for housing all groups in the population. In the public housing program, where Negroes predominate, federal action has paradoxically been least decisive. Still, many local authorities have tried to promote racial balance in their projects, and some have been experimenting with various types of nonproject housing scattered throughout the community.

But the fundamental orientations of the federal programs remain today —as do the deeply entrenched consequences of their operation throughout the peak years of the post-World War II housing boom. It will take more than piecemeal efforts to shatter such a solid foundation for the continued growth of segregated living patterns.

While the federal government was moving toward its policy of nondiscrimination in housing, many states and municipalities were moving in the same direction—and, in recent years, at a more rapid pace. Prior to 1954, only a few of the states in the North and Midwest had legislation which barred discrimination in any segment of their housing supply. The laws usually covered only low-rent public housing and, occasionally, units receiving such special forms of assistance as tax exemptions or write-downs on land costs.

As of mid-1965, however, sixteen states and the District of Columbia had barred discrimination in a substantial portion of their private housing supply. At the 1960 Census these states together contained about 80 million people, or 44 per cent of the total population. Thus nearly half the citizens of the United States are now living in communities whose public policy is clearly opposed to deliberate segregation on the basis of race—even in housing built under private auspices. President Kennedy's Executive Order of 1962 therefore was basically an extension on the federal level of a principle already gaining widespread acceptance in states and localities across the nation.

However, mere nondiscrimination cannot by itself overcome the problem of segregation. It will take vigorous positive efforts on the part of government and private citizens to halt, let alone reverse, trends now so firmly entrenched.

Contributors to change

Changes in public policy can usually be attributed to the determined efforts of a small minority of citizens who recognize a need and work tirelessly to bring it to public attention. In no case has this been more true than with residential segregation. Led by the National Committee against Discrimination in Housing—a small and meagerly financed organization which grew out of the first successful campaigns for housing laws in New York—religious, civic, and labor groups in many parts of the country have spearheaded similar campaigns in their own states and cities. The resulting laws have provided a foundation upon which other types of private effort could build.

A second important variety of private effort toward housing desegregation is the intentional development of new housing on an open-occupancy basis. Beginning in 1937 with a small Quaker-sponsored project in southwestern Pennsylvania, the spontaneous development of nondiscriminatory housing by private groups got under way in earnest following World War II. Despite concerted opposition by the federal government, many local governments, and most segments of the real-estate industry, a 1956 survey found that some fifty new interracial communities had been produced by private efforts up to that time. Some of them had been inspired by civic and social service organizations to foster racial equality, but a number had been constructed by businessmen for profit. Today, such developments are estimated to number in the high hundreds or even the thousands.[19]

In a third approach, "grass-roots" organizations in many cities across the country have sought to stabilize the occupancy of their own neighborhoods following the entry of Negroes. In numerous instances they have accomplished what many once thought impossible—quelling panic, avoiding possible violence, maintaining sound neighborhood conditions, even bringing new white residents into areas where formerly the prognosis had been for complete transition to all-Negro occupancy.[20]

Finally, in the suburbs of a number of cities, concerned white residents have banded together to help open their own neighborhoods to Negro families able to pay the price. The first of these "fair housing committees," established in Syracuse, New York, in the mid-1950's, was sponsored by the local Quaker Meeting. Religious influence of various denominations remains strong in many of the later organizations, now estimated to number more than one thousand.[21]

These private efforts represent one of the most encouraging examples of the inherent strength of American democracy and its capacity for change. They have helped shatter many racial myths, have opened new housing opportunities for Negroes in areas not previously open to them, and have done much through practical demonstration to alter the attitudes of the white majority toward the prospect of Negro neighbors.

But in the face of population forces, they can have little effect in destroying racial segregation. The point was passed some years ago where either legal bars against discrimination or the best-intentioned of meagerly financed "grass-roots" endeavors could accomplish the task. If Americans wish not only to create truly equal opportunity for all, but also to solve the many domestic problems which stem from inequality and the artificial separation of the races, they must now be prepared to move beyond mere nondiscrimination and good will—in a sense, beyond equality—into an area of positive and aggressive efforts to undo the damage already done. It will require a massive national effort, calling upon the full resources of both the public and private sectors.

The task and the methods

That the country possesses the fundamental resources it needs to solve the problem is fortunately clear. What is required is less the creation of new mechanisms than the effective harnessing and, where necessary, the reorientation, of those which already exist. Otherwise it will be impossible to meet the goal of rendering segregated housing patterns ineffective as an obstacle to the objectives of the "Great Society."

This aim, it must be stressed, need not be sought through methods which run counter to the basic tenets of American democracy. For example, it need not be attempted through forced redistribution of population. Force is not only intolerable, but unnecessary. The normal mobility of the American people is so great (about half of all households moved during the latter half of the 1950's alone) that redistribution can be achieved through the operation of free choice—if sufficient resources are applied to make socially desirable patterns of residence as attractive to the public as socially undesirable ones have been in the past.

Nor is it necessary to attempt a rigidly planned dispersal of Negro households. The aim, rather, should be to achieve complete freedom of choice in place of residence without respect to racial barriers. Within this framework of unconstrained choice, some substantial concentrations of Negro families would doubtless persist, just as Jews have remained in certain neighborhoods even after obstacles to their residing elsewhere have largely been eliminated. But the present monolithic character of the Negro ghettos, their inexorable growth, and the social evils they encourage would be broken.

The following are some specific measures which would help achieve the goal. The list is not all-inclusive; doubtless many readers will think of others which would be of value:

A central federal agency possessing the competence to plan comprehensively for all phases of urban development and the authority to translate plans into effective action. This agency must have the power to draw together federal operations in such diverse areas as housing, urban renewal, highways, transportation, and community facilities and to guide them toward a set of common objectives. The newly created Department of Housing and Urban Development can be such an instrument—if it can overcome the handicap of its origin in the Housing and Home Finance Agency, a loosely knit combination of essentially independent agencies, and achieve better coordination of individually powerful organizations than has the similarly amalgamated Department of Health, Education, and Welfare. This will not be easy.

A total strategy for desegregation. The segregation problem is too complex to be solved without a total approach which recognized all the manifold forces which brought it to its present magnitude and threaten to enlarge it further. This approach must take maximum strategic advantage of all available resources and knowledge. It must be adaptable to varying local conditions and flexible enough to permit changes as "feedback" from early applications dictates. But it must be directed always to a clear and unwavering set of goals.

Broadened federal incentives for effective action by local governments and private entrepreneurs. Incentive programs have proved one of the most acceptable means of applying governmental leverage in a democratic system, for they do not involve compulsion and do not infringe upon freedom of choice. In housing, for example, incentives have promoted urban renewal (through grants to local authorities to clear slum land for redevelopment) and the construction of specific types of housing (through liberal mortgage insurance). Incentives must now be used to encourage comprehensive planning and action toward social goals. For example, suitable incentives can encourage private builders to construct balanced communities serving all population groups, can attract and assist low-income minority families to move to such communities, can stimulate existing neighborhoods to self-renewal and racial stabilization, can encourage local governments to attack segregation in the comprehensive manner it requires by cooperation throughout the metropolitan areas.

Imaginative new forms of subsidy for low-income families. Traditionally, housing subsidies have been available almost exclusively for units built by local nonprofit authorities—chiefly in the form of multi-unit public "projects," which stood apart from their surroundings and amassed the social ills associated with poverty in much the same fashion as did older and less solidly constructed ghettos. More recently, various localities have experimented with methods for widening the range of choice and location in subsidized housing. The Housing Act of 1965 contains provisions which can make subsidies a much more valuable tool in combatting segregation. But their operation toward this end cannot be left to chance; it will require vigorous and imaginative guidance.

Comprehensive measures to increase minority incomes. Any measure which increases the purchasing power of racial minorities will bring a corresponding reduction in the critically important economic barriers to desegregation. Minimum wage floors must be raised; present ones are actually below the level defined by the federal government as "poverty." Federal resources must be directed toward expanding the number of jobs available, particularly for those of limited education. The most important need of the minority poor is for decent jobs at decent pay. Economic measures can and should be tied to housing. For example, low-income minority persons should be trained for the specific kinds of jobs which will be made available in the new, comprehensively planned communities on the outskirts of metropolitan areas. Housing should be planned for them close to these new job opportunities. Similarly, relocation from urban renewal areas should be coupled with a range of services, including training and assistance in finding employment, to help assure that displaced families improve not only their housing conditions but their economic situation as well.

Intensive efforts to improve the attractiveness of central cities. To date, urban renewal, in its efforts to draw middle- and upper-income families back to the urban cores, has focused mainly upon the physical aspects of decay. It is increasingly obvious that social renewal is required also—that many of the economically more capable families, Negro as well as white and especially those with children, will not be persuaded to return to the central areas until they are assured of protection from the social pathology of the ghetto. City schools, for example, must be drastically improved; yet there is growing evidence that this will require not merely replacement of individual buildings and teaching staffs but also comprehensive restructuring of entire school systems. Crime and violence are among the greatest deterrents to affluent families who prefer to live in central areas, and the cities will be at a disadvantage until they prove that they can control both the chronically lawless and those driven to crime by frustration and economic need.

Vigorous enforcement of antidiscrimination laws and affirmative measures to promote equal opportunity. As noted earlier, antidiscrimination laws in themselves are unable to solve a problem which stems from much broader causes. But, if vigorously enforced, they can prove a most important weapon in the arsenal of measures against segregation. Further, as many of the more effective law-enforcement agencies already recognize, it is not sufficient merely to remain passive and wait for a minority conditioned by generations of segregation to recognize and claim its newly guaranteed rights. Affirmative measures are necessary to promote awareness of the law both among those it protects and those who offend against it.

Expanded support for "grass-roots" citizen efforts. While the efforts of spontaneous, citizen-led groups have had impressive success in helping change attitudes, practices, and laws across the nation, these groups have been severely handicapped by their meager resources. A few have been fortunate enough to receive substantial support, usually from local foundations. Where funds have permitted hiring full-time staff, the increase in effectiveness has often been dramatic. Compared to the many millions spent annually by philanthropic organizations on problems of comparable or even lesser importance, the few thousands devoted to housing segregation have been infinitesimal. This is still another way in which available resources must be redirected if the problem is to be solved.

A national educational campaign. For the first time in American history, the majority of the white public appears aware that discrimination and segregation defeat the goals of democracy. But it is a long step forward from this recognition to a vigorous and affirmative effort equal to the need. This will require a type and degree of comprehension and commitment, by majority and minority peoples alike, which are still far from achievement.

National consensus is most readily achieved through full information about the problem and stimulation of public debate on the means of solution. A full-scale campaign to arouse and inform the American people must begin immediately if public understanding and support are to reach the necessary levels before segregation grows so much larger that it appears insoluble to many. The turning point may well come with the 1970 Census. If some tangible progress has not been made—or at least a plan of action proposed—before its statistics appear, discouragement may rule.

The core of organized citizen support necessary to mount such a campaign already exists—in such national organizations as the American Friends Service Committee, the Anti-Defamation League of B'nai B'rith, and the National Committee Against Discrimination in Housing and in the hundreds of citizen fair-housing groups across the country. But their efforts must be focused, coordinated, and, above all, adequately financed. And they must be brought into the context of related activities such as urban planning and the war on poverty.

The task of eliminating segregation rests ultimately with the American people as a whole—led, as in every major struggle in their history, by a small group of devoted citizens. If they do not succeed, the result will almost certainly be the continued spread of Negro ghettos; large-scale physical blight generated by population pressures and exploitation; economic loss to many citizens of both races; persistent social disorder; and spreading racial tensions which strike at the very foundations of a free and democratic society. The choice is not merely between segregation and desegregation, but between wholesale destruction of property and human values and the continued growth and security of American society itself.

NOTES

Note: Contents of this essay were basically prepared prior to employment of Mr. George W. Grier by the Government of the District of Columbia and Mrs. Eunice S. Grier by the United States Commission on Civil Rights. The opinions expressed by the authors are, therefore, not necessarily reflective of the views of either the Government of the District of Columbia or the United States Commission on Civil Rights.

1. There is a vast literature on the implications for local government of the divergence between population patterns and political boundaries in today's metropolitan areas. For an overview of governmental efforts to cope with the resulting problems, see Roscoe C. Martin, *Metropolis in Transition: Local Government Adaptation to Changing Urban Needs* (Washington, D.C.: Housing and Home Finance Agency, 1963). This study contains an extensive bibliography. An early and prescient discussion of the racial implications of metropolitan population shifts will be found in Morton Grodzins, *The Metropolitan Area as a Racial Problem* (Pittsburgh: University of Pittsburgh Press, 1958). While Grodzins' prescriptions for solution sometimes seem a bit naïve in retrospect, his dramatic presentation of the problem has been amply confirmed by later knowledge. A provocative discussion of the suburbanites' viewpoint toward metropolitan-area-wide cooperation toward solution of urban problems will be found in Charles R. Adrian, "Metropology: Folklore and Field Research," *Public Administration Review*, XXI, No. 3 (Summer 1961), 148–157.

2. Unless otherwise indicated, these and all other statistics which deal with population and housing characteristics are drawn from the United States Censuses of Population and Housing, which can be found in any well-stocked public library. These censuses, taken at the beginning of every decade, are the nation's most valuable storehouse of data on many social and economic problems.

3. For a detailed discussion of recent population shifts and their bearing on racial patterns of residence, see George and Eunice Grier, "Obstacles to Desegregation in America's Urban Areas," *Race,* The Journal of the Institute of Race Relations, London, VI, No. 1 (July 1964), 3–17. The topic has received intensive treatment by local scholars in a number of major cities. See, for example: Mildred Zander and Harold Goldblatt, *Trends in the Concentration and Dispersion of White and Non-White Residents of New York City, 1950–1960,* New York City Commission on Human Rights, Research Report No. 14, November 1962. Also: D. J. Bogue and D. P. Dandekar, *Population Trends and Prospects for the Chicago–Northwestern Indiana Consolidated Metropolitan Area: 1960 to 1990,* Population Research and Training Center, University of Chicago, March 1962.

4. The indirect racial effects of federal housing policies are discussed in Bertram Weissbourd, *Segregation, Subsidies and Megalopolis* (Santa Barbara, Calif.: Center for the Study of Democratic Institutions, 1964). Also, in more detail, in an unpublished paper by Eunice and George Grier, "Federal Powers in Housing Affecting Race Relations," prepared for the Potomac Institute and the Washington Center for Metropolitan Studies in September 1962.

5. *Our Non-White Population and Its Housing: The Changes between 1950 and 1960* (Washington, D.C.: Housing and Home Finance Agency, 1963).

6. Chester Rapkin and William G. Grigsby, *The Demand for Housing in Eastwick,* prepared under contract for the Redevelopment Agency of the City of Philadelphia by the Institute for Urban Studies, University of Pennsylvania, Philadelphia, 1960.

7. The federal role in enforcing housing discrimination is documented in Charles Abrams, *Forbidden Neighbors* (New York: Harper, 1955). Also in Eunice and George Grier, *Privately Developed Interracial Housing* (Berkeley, Calif.: University of California Press, 1960). The later volume contains, in Chapter VIII, detailed case histories of two post-World War II developments intended for interracial occupancy which were driven to financial ruin by FHA opposition despite powerful private support.

8. Luigi Laurenti, *Property Values and Race* (Berkeley, Calif., 1960).

9. The impact of race upon urban renewal, and vice versa, has been touched upon in many places. Among them: Robert C. Weaver, "Class, Race and Urban Renewal," *Land Economics,* XXXVI, No. 3 (August, 1960), 235–251. Also L. K. Northwood, "The Threat and Potential of Urban Renewal," *Journal of Intergroup Relations,* II, No. 2 (Spring, 1961), 101–114; and Mel J. Ravitz, "Effects of Urban Renewal on Community Racial Patterns," *Journal of Social Issues,* XIII, No. 4 (1957), 38–49. For an optimistic view on the consequences of renewal for displaced families, see *The Housing of Relocated Families,* a summary of a Bureau of the Census survey of families recently displaced from urban renewal sites, published by the Housing and Home Finance Agency, Washington, D.C., in March 1965. The "pro-renewal" viewpoint is also presented in *New Patterns in Urban Housing,* Experience Report 104, published by the U.S. Conference of Mayors, Community Relations Service, Washington, D.C., May 15, 1965.

10. Probably the most thorough and telling analysis of the economics involved in racial turnover mediated by real-estate speculators was published by the Chicago Commission on Human Relations, a municipal agency, in 1962. In a single block which had changed from all-white to virtually all-Negro, with heavy involvement by speculators, the differential between the price paid by the speculator and that paid by the Negro buyer upon purchase under an installment contract ranged from 35 to 115 per cent, with an average of 73 per cent. The installment contract itself is a financing device which yields higher-than-average returns to the entrepreneur, so the profiteering only began with the sale. For a graphic description of the activities of these speculators, see Norris Vitchek (as told to Alfred Balk), "Confessions of a Blockbuster," *Saturday Evening Post,* July 14, 1962.

11. Eunice S. Grier, *Understanding Washington's Changing Population* (Washington, D.C.: Washington Center for Metropolitan Studies, 1961).

12. George Schermer, "Desegregation: A Community Design," *ADA News,* published by the Philadelphia Chapter of Americans for Democratic Action, July 1960. (Statistics somewhat revised by the author in light of subsequent information.)

13. Municipal governments must now confront the problem of race in many of their decisions. For an overview of local governmental action *vis-à-vis* race as of the early 1960's accompanied by a good bibliography, see "The City Government and Minority Groups," *Management Information Service,* International City Managers Association, Report No. 229, February, 1963. This report can be obtained from the Potomac Institute of Washington, D.C., which participated in its preparation. See also many of the publications of the U.S. Commission on Civil Rights dealing with local practices in housing, employment, and so forth. But the extent to which racial considerations now affect local decisions in many subject areas is only scantily documented.

14. The relationship of racial factors to the Washington metropolitan plan is discussed in George B. Nesbitt and Marian P. Yankauer, "The Potential for Equal Housing Opportunity in the Nation's Capital," *Journal of Intergroup Relations,* IV, No. 1 (Winter, 1962–1963), 73–97.

15. The problem of de facto educational segregation and the civic conflict it often creates has been widely discussed in the public print. The *New York Times Index* is an especially useful source. For more scholarly treatments, see Max Wolff (ed.), "Toward Integration of Northern Schools," special issue of the *Journal of Educational Sociology,* February 1963. Also, "Public School Segregation and Integration in the North," special issue of the *Journal of Intergroup Relations,* November 1963. A provocative view on the feasibility of desegregation will be found in James B. Conant, *Slums and Suburbs* (New York: McGraw-Hill, 1961).

16. The pain caused to long-time residents of ethnic neighborhoods by forced relocation in connection with urban renewal has been documented in Marc Fried, "Grieving for a Lost Home," in Leonard J. Duhl (ed.), *The Urban Condition* (New York: Basic Books, 1963). No doubt much the same kind of agony is caused when long-established white residents feel "forced" to give up their homes in changing neighborhoods.

17. The most complete and reliable source of up-to-date information on the status of housing antidiscrimination laws and ordinances throughout the nation is *Trends in Housing,* published bi-monthly by the National Committee against Discrimination in Housing, 323 Lexington Avenue, New York, N. Y. 10016. A comprehensive analysis of action at all governmental levels up to the period just before the Federal Executive Order of 1962 will be found in Margaret Fisher and Frances Levenson, *Federal, State and Local Action Affecting Race and Housing,* National Association of Intergroup Relations Officials, September 1962. The texts of state and local laws as of the end of 1961 are summarized in *State Statutes and Local Ordinances Prohibiting Discrimination in Housing and Urban Renewal Operations,* published by the Housing and Home Finance Agency, Washington, D.C., December 1961.

18. Charles Abrams, "The Housing Order and Its Limits," *Commentary* (January 1963). For another discussion of some of the limitations of the Order, as well as a legal rationale for its extension, see Martin E. Sloane and Monroe H. Freedman, "The Executive Order on Housing: The Constitutional Basis for What It Fails To Do," *Howard Law Journal,* IX (Winter, 1963), 1–19.

19. A nationwide study which examined the experiences of some fifty private housing developments open from the outset to interracial occupancy is reported in Eunice and George Grier, *Privately Developed Interracial Housing, op. cit.* A more recent but less comprehensive compilation of experience, which leads nonetheless to many of the same conclusions, is found in *Equal Opportunity in Housing—A Series of Case Studies* (Washington, D.C.: Housing and Home Finance Agency, June 1964).

20. The experiences of various neighborhoods with efforts to achieve racial stabilization have been discussed in the public print, oftentimes in local newspapers. Among the more valuable studies on this topic is Eleanor Leacock, Martin Deutsch, and Joshua A. Fishman, *Toward Integration in Suburban Housing:*

The Bridgeview Study (New York: Anti-Defamation League of B'nai B'rith, 1964).
21. An excellent presentation of techniques which have been found useful in efforts to promote open housing opportunities in neighborhoods formerly closed to Negroes is contained in Margaret Fisher and Charlotte Meacham, *Fair Housing Handbook,* published jointly by the National Committee Against Discrimination in Housing and the American Friends Service Committee, 1964. See also various issues of *Trends in Housing.*

9

The Tipping-Point in Racially Changing Neighborhoods

ELEANOR P. WOLF

Observers and students of racial transition in Northern urban neighborhoods have for some time been interested in the impact of *numbers* upon the maintenance of integration. There has been much discussion and speculation concerning the operation of a hypothetical "tipping-point" beyond which racially integrated housing situations cannot be sustained. In this essay I want, first, to attempt to explore the meaning of the term *tipping-point,* and, second, to examine data from a racially changing neighborhood in Detroit to see if some empirical evidence for the operation of a tipping-point can be detected in this instance.

The tipping-point concept

In his distinguished study, *The Metropolitan Area as a Racial Problem,* Morton Grodzins describes the "tipping mechanism" as follows:

> The process by which whites of the central cities leave areas of Negro in-migration can be understood as one in the social-psychology of "tipping a neighborhood." The variations are numerous, but the theme is universal. Some white residents will not accept Negroes as neighbors under any conditions. But others, sometimes willingly as a badge of liberality, sometimes with trepidation, will not move if a relatively small number of Negroes move into the same neighborhood, the same block, or the same apartment building. *Once the proportion of nonwhites exceeds the limits of the neighborhood's tolerance for interracial living (this is the "tip-point"), the whites move out.* The proportions of Negroes who will be accepted before the tip-point is reached varies from city to city and from neighborhood to neighborhood.[1]

A similar meaning is imputed to the concept by Oscar Cohen, veteran professional in intergroup relations, in his article on benign quotas:

> Although the movement of whites out of the area may proceed at varying rates of speed, *a "tipping-point" is soon reached which sets off a wholesale flight of whites.* It is not too long before the community becomes predominantly Negro.[2] [My emphasis.]

From *Journal of the American Institute of Planners,* XXIX (August, 1963), 217–222.

Later, in support of his general argument that *numbers* of minority-group members are a crucial factor in integration, Cohen cites poll data from the American Institute of Public Opinion of March 1959:

When asked "Would you, yourself, have any objection to sending your children to a school where a few of the children are colored?", 92% of Northern white parents said they would have no objection. When asked, "Would you have any objection to sending your child to a school where half of the children are colored?" 63% of Northern white parents had no objection. But "more than half" . . . brought the proportion of Northern white parents having no objection down to 35%.[3]

Hans Spiegel introduces the tip-point concept in his discussion of the problem of maintaining integration in public housing:

One of the most difficult problems that public housing authorities face in the effort to desegregate their buildings is that, when the proportion of Negroes to whites in housing units approaches the 50–50 ratio, many of these units become predominantly or all-Negro. . . . Is 30% Negro representation the *"tipping-point,"* a figure that seems to be suggested by two housing experts as the upper limit? [4]

Spiegel is here referring to Banfield and Meyerson, who report that:

The experience of the [Chicago Housing] Authority suggested, as we have indicated, that if there were more than about one-third Negroes in an otherwise white project, the whites would leave until the project eventually became almost all Negro.[5]

Meyerson and Banfield go on to quote the chairman of the Chicago Housing Authority:

. . . . "I knew what had happened in those projects that were supposed to be 50–50; the whites had never moved in and so they had become all-Negro projects. I saw that Cabrini was successful with 30 per cent Negroes. I figured that more than 30 per cent wouldn't work but between 10 and 30 would work all right. More than 30 would *tip it over.*" [6] [My emphasis.]

Eunice and George Grier discuss this problem under the heading "The 'Scare Point' Hypothesis." It is their view that its more appropriate application is to "some older neighborhoods into which nonwhites have entered," rather than to new planned housing developments. They quote John Mc-Dermott (staff member of the Philadelphia Commission on Human Relations) as follows: "In Philadelphia at least, and in my judgment, when the minority proportion gets as high as from 30%–40% in a given block, the situation becomes shaky and stability is threatened." [7]

Recently the concept has found its way into non-professional journals. *The Reporter* article, "The Tipping-Point in Village Creek," describes the attempts of some Negro and white residents in a presumably integrated community to prevent a Negro family from buying a home on a block which already had nine Negro-occupied dwellings. In his discussion, the author states:

What the community fears is a *phenomenon sociologists call the "tipping point"* [my emphasis]—a percentage of nonwhites that gives a neighborhood the appearance of a Negro rather than an integrated section so that whites will not move in. . . . Where this pattern operates 'integration' often turns out to be merely a period of transition while a neighborhood changes its color . . . the present residents are convinced that if Village Creek is to fulfill its purpose and survive as an integrated community, it must keep from being *tipped*.[8]

These examples of the use of the term *tip-point* (by no means an exhaustive listing) will suffice to show that the concept includes a number of diverse ideas. It may refer to:

1. What might be called the *preference point*. This is a verbal expression, usually secured on a poll or during an interview, in which individuals indicate their willingness to participate in some kind of social situation with varying proportions of out-group members.

2. What might be called the *leaving point* in a housing situation. This is probably the most common way in which the term is used. This "point," however, refers to overt action and may have little to do with a "preference point." We found it to be markedly affected by market conditions. Even the *wish-to-leave* point (as distinguished from the point at which a house is actually sold and the family departs) is affected by a number of factors other than the number of Negroes present in a neighborhood or block.

3. What might be called the *willingness-to-enter* point of whites. Here again a number of factors are involved; for example, must the newly entering white households buy into the area, or can they make the lesser investment of renters?

In addition, as I will attempt to show later, the concept of a tip-point has rather different meaning for housing situations where there is a policy of controlled admissions as compared to those where no such controls exist.

The tipping-point in Russel Woods

The application of the concept to a specific neighborhood situation presents certain problems. What would be the evidence that the tip-point had been reached; that is, how would it manifest itself? If the tip-point is that racial proportion after which white households *move out* of the neighborhood (following the definition of Grodzins and others cited above) then one would expect to see, at that time, a marked acceleration in the rate of racial transition. It is difficult to find such a point in the set of figures shown in Table 9–1.

These data reveal a rather steady rate of change toward Negro occupancy. When did the neighborhood "tip"? From one point of view one might contend that this point occurred soon after Negro invasion began. In 1955, during the first round of interviewing, although only one or two Negro families had moved in, we found considerable concern and disturbance in this neighborhood; approximately half the respondents indicated

Table 9–1. *Racial Transition in Russel Woods*, 1955–1961

| | Per Cent of Dwellings Occupied | |
Year	by Whites	by Negroes
1955	100	0
1957	78	22
1959	50	50
1961	26	74

Note: Percentages have been rounded. In each set of figures a few vacant dwelling units have been ignored and the percentages are for *all occupied units* in the sample of 232 out of a universe of approximately 670.

that they expected the area "to change racially." By 1957, although the area was but slightly more than 20 per cent Negro-occupied, the remaining white households were, for the most part, so convinced of its future composition that fewer than 15 per cent would "advise a friend to buy here." [9] The prevailing assessment of the neighborhood was a projection into the future based on past experience as well as an estimate of presently-existing *trends.* For example, white demand for homes in Russel Woods declined markedly before a single Negro family had moved in, apparently in part because of racial change in surrounding areas. One might contend that the tip-point (in the sense of white willingness-to-enter) had already been reached at that time. Unfortunately, there is insufficient information on year-by-year rates of racial transition in various kinds of neighborhoods. It is entirely possible that our case is unrepresentative.

It would appear that the basic difficulty in the use of the tipping-point concept as it refers to white exodus from (or entrance into) a racially changing neighborhood is that individual decisions to leave or enter tend to be based on *one's estimation of what the situation will be in the future,* rather than upon the actual proportions of Negro households in the area at any particular moment. Human decision-making is characteristically oriented to the future and is based upon some kind of calculation of what the future will be. This is particularly evident in decisions which, like selling one's home, represent the largest single financial transaction in the affairs of most households, and which tend to be regarded as a fairly permanent choice. Such transactions stimulate individuals to attempt to assess the fairly distant future.

This basis for decision is illustrated by the contrasting definitions of the racial situation revealed in responses of the residents of a new housing redevelopment area in Detroit, Lafayette Park, as compared with the reactions of Russel Woods residents.[10] Lafayette Park is a high-cost housing development which, at the time of our study, had somewhat under 10 per cent non-white occupancy, with considerable vacancies in its low-rise units, then for sale. Yet there were few expressions of concern about the future racial composition of the project. Some respondents volunteered the opinion that "because of the cost, not many Negroes can move here." A few reported that they had heard informally or "through the grapevine" that a policy of controlled admission would be instituted in the highly unlikely situation that large numbers of Negro families applied. (We do not know if this rumor was well or ill founded; we know of no public statement to this effect.) By contrast, in the first round of interviewing in Russel Woods (in 1955) although only one or two Negro families—out of about 700 households—had moved in, there was, as I have indicated, considerable concern and much fear and apprehension about the future.

Russel Woods is now 75 per cent Negro-occupied. The remaining white households are a hard core of non-mobile families, plus some white renters who come and go. Approximately 70 per cent are over forty-five years of age and only one-third have school-age children. We have kept these remaining white families under "sociological surveillance" for almost seven years now and we do not find that their attitudes toward Negroes are more enlightened, or their "preference point" (in terms of numbers of Negroes) any different from that of their former neighbors who have long since departed.

Perhaps the tip-point concept is most applicable to housing situations where there is some kind of controlled-admissions policy. The term then comes closer in meaning to "tolerance level" or acceptance level. In many instances, public housing projects have tended to become predominantly Negro-occupied not because of the operation of a tipping-point but because if the administration policy is color-blind the majority of eligible families are Negroes. If bi-racial occupancy is a desired goal, a policy of controlled admission may be more influential than the precise percentage at which the ratio of whites and Negroes is established, within certain limits, of course.

The concept of a tipping-point in established neighborhoods as the moment when there exists that proportion of Negro families after which whites move out and "new" white households will not enter presents problems in its application. There undoubtedly are preferred proportions of minority-group members in various kinds of interracial settings, including housing. But individual decisions concerning when it is desirable to buy or sell in racially changing neighborhoods appear to be influenced by a number of factors of which the preferred level for certain proportions of Negro neighbors is but one. A more serious obstacle in the use of the tip-point concept is that these residential decisions, especially when home ownership is involved, appear to be oriented rather far into the future and may not reflect at all the existing proportions of nonwhites in the area.

Housing market factors in racial transition

Rates of racial transition are influenced by a number of factors which affect both the propensity-to-leave of white families already resident in a given neighborhood, and the willingness-to-enter of new white households.[11] These two sets of influences, furthermore, affect each other, since the observed behavior of the "old" white residents (are they fleeing?) affects the decisions of white families who are considering entrance—while the willingness of white newcomers to enter likewise has an impact on the residential decisions of those already there. Both these groups are in turn influenced by their assessment, present and *future,* of Negro demand for housing in the area. This demand is in itself the outcome of a number of forces: how many Negro buyers have the means to purchase housing in a particular price range, as compared with the supply of alternative homes available to them in other parts of the community? It is apparent, too, that for housing in a given area, white demand is markedly affected by the presence or absence of alternative housing opportunities. The availability of attractive housing in all-white suburbs or other restricted areas is a powerful force working toward rapid racial transition; it prevents the dispersion of Negroes while offering an escape hatch for whites who have the means to buy in such areas.[12]

Recent research has indicated a number of other factors which appear to influence the demand for housing and therefore have an important bearing upon patterns of racial transition:

1. *The amount and kind of real-estate activity.* While there is a tendency in some circles to make the real-estate agent a scapegoat as the "cause" of racial transitions, it is reasonable to infer that the use of scare tactics to promote the exodus of whites does hasten the transition process. So does the practice of promoting sales mainly among Negroes once a neighborhood is "invaded." [13]

2. *Special advantages (or disadvantages) of the area and its dwellings affect demand.* Location, transportation facilities, price and type of housing, and physical features are all involved.[14] The reputation of schools serving the neighborhood appears to be of prime importance. Often a neighborhood has declined in attractiveness to white households considerably in advance of Negro invasion, although frequently this is because of a calculation that such entrance is impending.

3. *Proximity to existing Negro neighborhoods.* There is general agreement in the literature that such proximity suggests that the newly entered area will experience heavy in-movement by Negroes.[15] It is interesting to note, however, that mere physical proximity to dense Negro settlement does not in itself create this expectation. The Lafayette Park redevelopment area, for example, is luxury housing set down in the midst of Negro slums, but it is obvious to all that this surrounding territory cannot possibly supply potential candidates for the costly enclave. Its proximity does not, therefore, create any fear of inundation. However, in the usual case where the newly entered area is on the edge of existing concentrations, there is evidence that Negro demand is greater than for more remote neighborhoods. Not only is there less fear of resistance and rejection, but there is an element of self-segregation arising from the wish to live with other Negroes.[16]

4. *Community organization and action.* A number of neighborhoods throughout the country, beginning with the Hyde Park–Kenwood area in Chicago, have developed vigorous programs of citizen action to discourage exodus, guard neighborhood and school standards, and promote the area

among potential white buyers. Although it is difficult to evaluate their impact upon racial transition, researchers generally agree that such activity tends to slow the process by increasing white demand.[17]

5. *Amount of rental property.* A number of studies have noted that the presence of rental property contributes to racial stabilization, since, as noted above, many white households may be willing to rent although unwilling to buy in a neighborhood with an uncertain future.[18]

Other factors which have been viewed as influencing transition rates are the socioeconomic characteristics of the incoming population[19] and the way in which it is spatially distributed within the area. Rapkin and Grigsby find that, contrary to popular belief, clustering of Negro families within an invaded area may be more favorable to the maintenance of integration than scattering, because of the reluctance of many white households to live next door to Negroes.[20] Finally, the characteristics of the white population must be considered. There is some suggestion, for example, that Jewish households, because of their mobility and tendency to self-segregation, may tend to regroup themselves in another area quite speedily once their neighborhood is entered.[21]

It will be noted that no mention has been made of variations in the level of racial prejudice as a factor which is influential in determining the rate of racial transition. Most research now seems to suggest that, if there are significant differences in these attitudes in various Northern urban neighborhoods, they are overshadowed or offset by other factors. For example, the relatively tolerant neighborhood is likely to be one where Negroes feel relatively secure and safe; Negro demand for housing may be great in such an area. In such an area, whites would not feel very powerful sanctions against selling to Negroes—again, a factor which would tend to increase the in-movement of Negro households. But these effects could scarcely be considered an outcome of intense racial prejudice, although they hasten the transition process.

Most important of all factors are those related to the supply of and demand for housing. Preliminary findings from a study of a Northwest Detroit area reveal that although the attitudes and values of the residents, as well as many of their socioeconomic characteristics, are quite similar to those in the Russel Woods area referred to above, racial transition has thus far proceeded very slowly.[22] The first Negro family entered, apparently unnoticed, in 1959. A second was known to have entered in the summer of 1960. Two years later the area was not more than 1 per cent Negro-occupied. Unfavorable economic conditions in Detroit, a good supply of housing available to middle-class Negroes in a number of desirable neighborhoods, and the fact that much of the previously pent-up demand for housing for such households had already been satisfied, appear to be the chief reasons for the slow transition thus far.

NOTES

1. Morton Grodzins, *The Metropolitan Area as a Racial Problem* (Pittsburgh: University of Pittsburgh Press, 1958), p. 6.
2. Oscar Cohen, "The Case for Benign Quotas in Housing," *Phylon,* XXI (1960), p. 21.
3. *Ibid.,* p. 24.
4. Hans Spiegel, "Tenants' Intergroup Attitudes in a Public Housing Project with Declining White Population," *Phylon,* XXI (1960), p. 30.
5. Martin Meyerson and Edward C. Banfield, *Politics, Planning and the Public Interest* (Glencoe, Ill.: The Free Press, 1955), p. 135.
6. *Ibid.*
7. Eunice and George Grier, *Privately Developed Interracial Housing* (Berkeley: University of California Press, 1960), p. 60.
8. Donald Pfarrer, "The Tipping Point in Village Creek," *The Reporter,* February 1, 1962, p. 34.
9. Eleanor P. Wolf, "Racial Transition in a Middle-Class Area," *Journal of Intergroup Relations,* I (Summer, 1960), pp. 75–81.
10. Mel J. Ravitz and Eleanor Wolf, "Lafayette Park Research Project" (unpublished, January, 1961).
11. For a comprehensive analysis of the entire subject see Chester Rapkin and William G. Grigsby, *The Demand for Housing in Racially Mixed Areas* (Berkeley: University of California Press, 1960). On pp. 17–19, the authors consider the differences between decisions to *depart* and decisions to *enter* a changing neighborhood.
12. See Chapter 10, pp. 160–161, this book; Eleanor Caplan and Eleanor P. Wolf, "Factors Affecting Racial Change in Two Middle-Income Housing Areas," *Phylon,* XXI (Fall, 1960), p. 228.
13. See p. 159, this book; Commission on Race and Housing, *Where Shall We Live?* (Berkeley: University of California Press, 1958), p. 25. See also Eleanor Wolf, "The Invasion-Succession Sequence as a Self-Fulfilling Prophecy," *Journal of Social Issues,* XIII (1957), 7–20.
14. Robert C. Weaver, "Integration in Public and Private Housing," *The Annals,* CCCIV (March, 1956), p. 92; Rapkin and Grigsby, *op. cit.,* p. 116; Caplan and Wolf, *op. cit.,* pp. 228–230.
15. Weaver, *op. cit.,* p. 91; Commission on Race and Housing, *op. cit.,* p. 15; Caplan and Wolf, *op. cit.,* p. 229; and Rapkin and Grigsby, *op. cit.,* pp. 114–115.
16. See p. 160, this book.
17. Marvin Sussman, "The Role of Neighborhood Associations in Private Housing for Racial Minorities," *Journal of Social Issues,* XIII (1957), 31–37. See also Rapkin and Grigsby, *op. cit.,* p. 135; and Eleanor Wolf, "Racial Transition in a Middle-Class Area," *Journal of Intergroup Relations,* I (Summer, 1960), 79–80.
18. Rapkin and Grigsby, *op. cit.,* p. 54.
19. Caplan and Wolf, *op. cit.,* p. 229; Rapkin and Grigsby, *op. cit.,* pp. 129–130.
20. *Ibid.,* p. 55.
21. Caplan and Wolf, *op. cit.,* p. 231.
22. This is a research project currently being conducted by the author under a grant awarded by the Graduate Division, Wayne State University, in 1962.

10

The Prospect for
Stable Interracial Neighborhoods

CHESTER RAPKIN AND
WILLIAM GRIGSBY

The past decade has witnessed the racial transition of many neighborhoods in Philadelphia. This process has been stimulated by a rapid increase in the numbers and income of the nonwhite population, buttressed by a virtual absence of newly constructed houses available to Negroes anywhere in the metropolitan area. The most logical areas to undergo racial change, prejudices considered, were on the periphery of established nonwhite sections where a point of contact had been established, and change, since it was expected, was usually not strongly resisted. Thus, in the study areas, transition was the natural extension of existing Negro neighborhoods.

The expansion of these mixed communities has, however, not been without pattern. For transition to begin in a new block or neighborhood, a portion of the supply must be made available to Negroes by white homeowners, and this usually requires a soul-searching decision. In the study areas, sales that opened blocks or neighborhoods were frequently made by professional traders and other absentee owners, who presumably were subject to less community pressure than were owner-occupants. Generally speaking, however, the initial sales were made by ordinary homeowners who did not explore the possibility of selling to Negroes until it became evident that white buyers willing to pay a satisfactory price could not be found.

The contraction of white purchases was related to some extent to the proximity of Negroes themselves. As the border of the Negro community moved closer and closer to a given street front, white buyers were harder to find. Owners who had to move from the area may have preferred to sell to white families, but were unable to do so. The threat of Negro entry was, however, not the only deterrent to white acquisitions. After the postwar housing shortage had eased and new housing became readily available in the suburbs, the study areas with their old and obsolescent homes were no longer attractive to a substantial sector of the white market. Initially, in fact, the age and quality of the houses may have been the most important factor limiting white demand and thus promoting Negro entry.

Negro entry into white blocks was also encouraged by the absence of violence directed toward nonwhite purchasers, a response that has accom-

From Chester Rapkin and William Grigsby, *The Demand for Housing in Racially Mixed Areas* (Berkeley: University of California Press, 1960), pp. 114–121.

panied Negro residential expansion in most sections of the city. The vigorous action of the Philadelphia Commission on Human Relations which has stopped many potential disturbances in their nascent stages may have been a principal deterrent to violence in some areas, but it is also true that exceedingly few Negroes entered neighborhoods in which the danger signs were clear. In the study areas, there were few reported instances of hostile action toward first Negro entrants, who, by and large, reported a reasonably friendly attitude on the part of white residents. This is not to suggest that there was no opposition to Negro entry, but that there were very few ugly incidents.

The mixed area housing market

The housing market in the study areas did not differ materially from the markets in other sections of the city. The white families who purchased homes were very much like other homeowners in the areas and similar to home purchasers in the rest of Philadelphia. The majority by far were couples with children. They earned moderate incomes and engaged in a wide variety of occupations. These purchasers were not motivated by a drive to symbolize racial democracy and, in fact, many of them were not pleased by the presence of Negroes in their neighborhood.

As far as the structure of prices and home financing is concerned, Negroes and whites paid approximately the same prices for comparable houses; the usual institutional sources of mortgage funds were available to finance the purchases; and mortgage terms were extremely liberal by any standard. Equally important, the entry of Negroes was not accompanied by price declines; on the contrary, there were substantial increases in home values.

It is not unfair to say that families were attracted to the areas for commonplace reasons. First and foremost, the families sought a home in the lower price and quality levels, and although such dwellings were available in other sections of the city, the choice was somewhat limited. Their selection, however, was not made on the basis of house price alone, but was influenced also by specific advantages of the areas, such as nearness or ready access to place of employment, good transportation service, and proximity to a variety of shopping facilities. In addition, many of the purchasers were attracted by existing concentrations of persons of similar religion or national heritage. In view of these positive factors the white buyers evidently felt that the presence of Negroes was an insufficient reason to avoid the areas.

We have found that the nature of neighborhood change is by no means one-directional. The widely held view that no white will ever purchase in an area once it is entered by a Negro is in need of serious reconsideration. This is an important conclusion, but it would indeed be premature to use it as the basis for a firm generalization regarding the future of housing demand in mixed areas. Although almost five hundred white families bought homes in the mixed areas, they comprised only one-fourth of the total purchasers. Moreover, white purchases declined as the relative proportion of resident Negro population increased, and few were to be found even in sections in which the proportion of non-whites was low. But perhaps the most important reservation of all is the fact that the number of white purchasers was not sufficient to keep the population in these areas from becoming increasingly nonwhite.

Patterns of transition

The rate of racial change varied widely from neighborhood to neighborhood and even from block to block. On several street fronts, each containing as many as fifty to sixty homes, virtually the entire inventory changed from white to Negro ownership in less than three years. In other blocks, transition was much slower, with a fair proportion of white families remaining in residence five or more years after Negro entry. In the relatively expensive West Mount Airy section of Germantown, and in the low-price Tasker area of South Philadelphia, racial change with one or two short-lived exceptions proceeded at an extremely moderate rate, whereas transition in most of the Strawberry Mansion and West Philadelphia areas was quite rapid.

The variations in the rate of transition are not, as commonly thought, simply a measure of differences in the intensity and extent of prejudice and discrimination. Rather, differences in rates are due to variations in all the factors which affect the level of white demand, the level of Negro demand, the number and race of families who wish to sell their homes, and the interaction of these three variables. Indeed, the factors which control these variables not only fix the rate of transition, but also determine whether it will occur at all.

Rapid transition in the study areas was the product of numerous influences: liberal mortgage terms, sustained Negro demand, a substantial supply of old houses of fair quality and moderate value, rising prices, considerable activity by professional real estate operators, and ready availability of high-quality housing for whites in other sections of the city and in the suburbs. Although these factors tend to explain the fairly rapid change in two of the study areas, they do not explain the pockets of slow transition in some sections within these areas. These sections contain a larger proportion of rental units, a greater amount of land in commercial use, higher-priced homes, and parochial schools where the percentage of nonwhite students was relatively low at the time of the study.

Rapid transition in other neighborhoods in the city appeared to stem from factors identical or similar to those in West Philadelphia and Strawberry Mansion. By comparison, slow transition in other neighborhoods was associated with a moderately large percentage of low-quality housing for which financing was difficult to obtain, or of expensive homes which most Negro families could not afford. Prices in these areas either were stable or rose at a slower pace than in the areas of rapid transition. White demand dropped as sharply in the neighborhoods of slow change as in the sections where the racial transformation was more rapid. In the neighborhoods of both slow and rapid change, absentee sellers, most of whom were in the market for the short run, appeared to have facilitated the transition process.

There are a number of additional factors which appeared to be vital in determining the rate of transition, even though data were lacking to demonstrate their importance. Foremost among these were expectations. The predictions of white families concerning the eventual racial mix of a neighborhood and their apprehensions regarding the possibility of inundation may be more significant than any other factor in determining the level of white demand. Yet it is largely the level of white demand that determines the eventual racial mix. Also of consequence are the demographic characteristics of the resident and in-migrant populations, the racial composition of the schools, activities of community organizations, the policies and practices of market intermediaries, and the spatial distribution of the Negro residences in the mixed area. Depending on the interaction of these and the other variables discussed above, transition may be fast or slow or may not occur at all; there may be transition without discrimination or discrimination without transition.

The future of residential areas

Taking the developments described in this study, together with more general information relating to the city as a whole, what speculations may be ventured regarding the future racial composition of Philadelphia's residential areas? Does the evidence indicate that all areas in the city and suburbs will eventually become mixed, or do the data suggest a continuation of the segregated patterns of the past?

The study by itself reveals conflicting tendencies, the net effects of which cannot be evaluated without considering a number of additional factors. On the one hand, Negroes were able to purchase homes not only on equal terms with whites, but more importantly, in areas which until very recently had been closed to them. This was true not only in the areas chosen for study but in many other sections of the city as well. In addition, a significant number of white families continued to purchase homes in areas which were mixed or showed indications of becoming mixed in the immediate future. These facts considered by themselves would support the conclusion that the Negro population will gradually be dispersed throughout a large number of residential areas in the city, and while some whites will tend to leave these areas, others will stay, and still others will move in. Thus, stable mixed areas would become the typical pattern.

The contrary tendencies, however, must also be examined. Although many whites living in predominantly white sections of mixed areas had no objections to or even awareness of the small percentage of Negroes nearby, when this percentage was exceeded and the trend in sales indicated that the proportion of Negroes would continue to increase, many white residents chose to move to other areas. At the same time, the number of whites who purchased in the areas fell very sharply. Although the data are by no means conclusive, they suggest that the threshold is rather low, perhaps much lower than the proportion of Negroes in the population of the city. Thus, although a hard core of whites might remain and a few more move to the area for a variety of reasons, the prospect is that the proportion of Negroes in such areas will gradually increase. If this is the typical case, it implies a pattern of predominantly Negro communities interspersed throughout the city.

A number of additional factors are crucial in determining whether a pattern of concentration or dispersion will, in fact, emerge. Although new areas will become available to Negroes, some will be entered more readily than others, and there will undoubtedly be a tendency for nonwhites to purchase in areas that already have been entered. In the areas investigated in this study, the spread of Negro population occurred basically on the edges of existing concentrations despite the fact that some larger jumps were observed.

The tendency to move to areas in which Negroes are already in residence is due in part to the desire to obtain satisfactory housing without the risk of rebuff and in part to a positive desire to live in an area in which there is an appreciable number of other Negroes. This phenomenon has been observed among other ethnic groups such as Jews and Italians who attach considerable value to the comfort and ease of communication with people of like culture and heritage. As the housing shortage for Negroes eases, nonwhites may lack the incentive to pioneer their way into new areas. Thus, although segregation may disappear, congregation may not.

A continuation of the present nonwhite nodes is to be expected on other grounds as well. Although rising incomes and increased market freedom may enable many nonwhite families to leave the ghettos, the racial composition of existing Negro communities will remain unchanged, for it is not likely that white families can be attracted to them. Such an occurrence would be counter to virtually all past experience and cannot be expected until urban renewal programs materially alter existing nonwhite residential areas.

But what about the fringe areas? Will there be bands of stable mixed neighborhoods extending for miles around nonwhite nodes or will the mixed peripheral zones separating Negro and white areas be narrowly restricted? Again we must go somewhat beyond the findings of the study and examine other relevant factors. Many whites who wish to move from mixed neighborhoods may be prevented from doing so because equivalent houses are not available in acceptable all-white areas at prices they can afford to pay. Their housing alternatives will be closely related to the relative size of Negro demand. Although Negroes comprise one-quarter of the total population in Philadelphia, they constitute more than one-third of the group with incomes less than $4,000 and only 10 per cent of those with incomes in excess of $6,000. Thus, Negro-white competition for housing will be concentrated to a large extent in price ranges below the minimum for new construction. Demand from these groups, therefore, will be limited to moderate-priced units in the existing stock.

Consequently, many whites in the lower-middle-income groups who might prefer to move from mixed areas will have a diminishing number of all-white neighborhoods available to them and, as a result, rapid change in neighborhood composition will be inhibited. Moreover, if pending legislation is enacted requiring home builders, and perhaps owners of existing housing and real estate brokers as well, to pursue a policy of nondiscrimination, the incentive for whites to move from existing mixed areas may be greatly reduced as alternative opportunities disappear. Thus, stable mixed areas may emerge as a general pattern in those sections of the city in which moderately priced homes are located. In higher-income areas, where the proportion of Negro demanders is very small, there will be a greater likelihood that a white family will be able to purchase a home in an all-white area. Even if some Negroes in this income bracket do not choose to live among non-whites, this sector of the housing market will be almost entirely white.

Of all the factors that will determine the ultimate racial composition of our urban areas, perhaps attitudes are most important. It has been noted that many whites did not think of themselves as living in mixed areas even though they knew there were Negroes only a block away. This may well be a precursor to a more pervasive change in attitude. There is little doubt that both whites and Negroes have improved their view of each other over the past decades and that the present trend in the direction of social and economic equality for Negroes will continue unabated. With widening educational opportunities and opening of new occupational lines, differences between whites and nonwhites will diminish. As this time approaches, perhaps men will be more and more inclined to choose their neighbors on the basis of their essential worth and not according to the color of their skin.

11

Barriers to
Northern School Desegregation

ROBERT A. DENTLER

The current scene

Northern public schools, from kindergarten to the graduate level, have been racially segregated on an extensive scale since the Reconstruction. Statistics have been collected by communities and states only since the Brown decision in 1954, but these show that *hundreds* of elementary and secondary schools in the Northeast and the Midwest have student bodies composed of more than 90 per cent Negroes.

The racial census released by the New York Education Department in 1962 is typical. Twenty elementary schools outside of New York City had over 90 per cent Negro pupils; forty-six had more than 50 per cent. A total of 103 was 31 per cent or more Negro.[1] And this was true in a state in which the proportion of Negroes within the total population of all but a few communities is less than 15 per cent!

In the largest survey of school segregation in the North to date,[2] 200 public school systems were studied. These were in towns spread across nineteen states, which included 75 per cent of the Negro population in the North. Some 1,141 schools were listed as having nonwhite enrollments of 60 per cent or more. About 60 per cent of these segregated schools were clustered in six of the larger cities: New York City, Chicago, Philadelphia, Detroit, Cleveland, and Los Angeles. Most of the others were located in other large central cities or in neighboring suburbs. School segregation is thus so pronounced in certain cities in the North that if public schools are placed on a scale from all-white pupils to all-Negro, the great majority of them will cluster at the far extremes. Mixed student bodies are very uncommon.

However, as the New Jersey Supreme Court noted in June 1965, a public school need not be all or even 80 per cent Negro in order to be racially segregated. A school is racially segregated if the ratio of Negro to white students is substantially in excess of the ratio common to the community as a whole.[3] This definition applies to a school that is 50 per cent Negro in a community where Negroes comprise 20 per cent of the total population. It also includes a school that is 95 per cent white in the same community.

Minority segregated public schools in the North tend quite uniformly to

From *Daedalus*, the Journal of the American Academy of Arts and Sciences, XCV (Winter, 1966), 45–63.

have poorer facilities, less qualified staff, and inferior programs of instruction than majority segregated schools.[4] Even when differences in facilities are eliminated, minority segregation impedes both teaching and learning. Attendance at a minority segregated public school tends to reinforce the damage already experienced by children maturing in a milieu drenched with discriminatory stimuli. Indeed, attendance at a racially segregated public school is probably harmful whether the segregation is minority or majority. The isolation experienced by students in all-white schools stimulates ignorance, fear, and prejudice, just as it confirms the self-belief in inferiority among students in all-Negro schools.[5]

Protests were lodged by Negro groups against school segregation in the North on many occasions between 1917 and 1954. But the Brown decision brought awareness among educational decision-makers to a new focal point.[6] Only in the last decade have the gravity and scope of the problem been identified, solutions advanced, and resistance to change mobilized.

We are presently in the eye of a Northern storm of community conflict. The issue has been joined; it has become a one-sided question with but one set of social facts, all of which indicate that Negro racial segregation in schools is bad, and most that white segregation is bad, too. It has become a matter which *must* be dealt with if racial and cultural cleavages are to be resolved and if social inclusiveness within cultural pluralism is to be achieved. Moreover, the elimination of school segregation has, like all serious modern social problems, become an issue illuminated by an awareness of attendant *costs:* If school desegregation is to be achieved, public education, its political context, and its fiscal support must be changed too, in ways that are demanding, even harsh.

The pace of racial integration in Northern schools has been equivalent to that of integration in Southern schools, although the Southern pace quickened enormously with the incentive of federal aid in 1965. Most cities and suburbs in the six Northern states with a Negro population of 5 per cent or more contain at least one minority segregated school. Five to ten of these have been eliminated each year since 1960, while new ones crop up to replace them as populations redistribute. If no new rate of change develops, the North will exhibit deep and extensive racial segregation in its urban schools as late as the middle of the next century.

The smaller communities

There is little point in talking about Northern school segregation as a uniform condition. More than two-thirds of all the racially segregated public schools in the North are located in ten of the largest cities. There, population density, the hardening of ghetto boundaries, the class structure, and political organization, all militate powerfully against school desegregation. These must be distinguished from the hundreds of smaller urban communities where desegregation is not only as desirable but more feasible.

The communities in the North where school desegregation has been agreed upon and sometimes implemented effectively are all smaller cities and suburbs. Berkeley, California, is one.[7] There, the Board of Education authorized a citizens' committee to recommend approaches to the problem of segregation as early as 1958. The committee was established after pressure from the Berkeley chapter of the NAACP. It made several good suggestions, none of which was implemented effectively, however, for several years.

But in 1962, the Berkeley Superintendent, responding to pressure from CORE and to growing convictions about the educational undesirability of school segregation, secured his board's authorization of another citizens' committee. This group worked for nearly a year. It defined de facto school segregation as extant in any public school whose white to non-white ratio "varies significantly from the same ratio of the District as a whole." With this yardstick, the committee found that three elementary schools, one junior high school, and the high school were not segregated, while sixteen schools were.

The committee asserted that this condition was bad, blamed it on the concept of neighborhood schools and on housing patterns, and proposed ten programs for its elimination. These included redistricting, pairing of some schools, open enrollment, a program of curricular improvement, and the strengthening of services and facilities. Some of these potentially transformative proposals were implemented, including positive, fairly radical changes in the composition of junior high schools. Indicative of the mood of the community is the fact that, in 1964, two members of the Berkeley school board were re-elected in a recall election.

White Plains, New York, offers a comparable illustration and, as an Eastern community, is more relevant to the problem of Northern school segregation than is Berkeley.[8] The Board of Education and the Superintendent of Schools in White Plains were aware of "racial imbalance" in their system as early as 1961; they had instituted special services in the one elementary school which was roughly two-thirds Negro, and they had made a few minor adjustments as early as 1962. Beyond a concern with compensatory education and related services, however, there was little professional readiness to define school segregation as salient.

Two forces converged to change this. The Negro leadership of White Plains and the officers of the New York State Education Department in Albany exerted persuasive pressure. The leadership threatened political action, and the state officials offered assistance, advice, and a flow of information showing how school segregation (always referred to in communications as "racial imbalance") impaired public education. The Superintendent and his Board then began carefully planned but prompt, unanimous action to desegregate. They acted during 1964, the same year in which the Superintendent became convinced that "racial imbalance" was a blight on the level of professional performance of his administration and teaching staff. Had this redefinition not occurred, it is unlikely that change would have taken place.

Other small cities have desegregated their public schools during the last five years in response to similar political and educational administrative pressures, or for different yet functionally equivalent reasons. Englewood, New Jersey, and New Rochelle, New York, for example, desegregated under court orders. Other towns have desegregated for essentially social reasons, such as population change, special real-estate conditions, or cultural values. Greenburgh, New York, is a case in point. There, in one of four districts, school integration began early and has become a source of social pride.

From participation in several school desegregation programs in smaller Northern communities, I would speculate that there are some rather uniform conditions under which desegregation becomes *possible* politically and educationally. Negroes must protest in a visible, unequivocal manner. This protest must resonate positively with some segment of the white population which already commands the attention of local schoolmen or board members.

Of equal importance is a clear, sufficiently intense stimulus from state or other extra-local authorities. Little change has occurred in Pennsylvania and Illinois, where many smaller cities maintain segregated schools because of weak state education agencies. It also seems plain from case experiences that a community must be free from a very highly *stratified* class structure grounded substantially in religious or racial groupings. The prospect of too severe a change in the foundations of the local structure of social rewards is relatively certain to prevent school desegregation.

Illustrating barriers in smaller cities

We can best depict these conditions and connect them with impediments to change within the school systems themselves through details from a case study of a smaller city on the Northeastern seaboard which moved to the edge of school integration but then drew back and renewed its efforts to preserve its historic ghetto. We shall call the community "Little City."

Interviews documented the belief that the status quo system of race relations persists in Little City, that the system is old and durable, and that most Negroes as well as whites in the community subscribe to and reinforce it, in spite of its disadvantages.

This status quo is common to hundreds of established, thriving Northern communities. Under it, Negroes are tolerated by whites and there is cooperation as long as the minorities accept the confines of what is a partial caste system. Whites assume that Negroes "prefer" to live in the Bilbo Area Ghetto (although a few families are sprinkled elsewhere in other low-income blocks). They also presume that Negroes will share unequally in the resources and services of the community, but that few Little City Negroes will ever aspire to upper-level occupational positions. They will instead aspire toward, and then be employed in, service and lower semiskilled jobs.

There are, in other words, *niches* for Negroes in the residential, resource, and job structures of the community. The value of the niches to Negroes is dual. They supply more opportunities than are available in some other localities, and they are equal to those available to a small proportion of low-income whites within Little City. Historically, the status quo has been maintained because Negroes have fared better in Little City than they have reason to expect they might fare elsewhere. In exchange, they have maintained polite civil relations.

This pattern has been challenged in Little City within the last few years. Nearly all Little City parents are aware of this challenge. A majority, regardless of race, try to suppress this awareness by attributing it to the work of CORE or other "outside troublemakers." The attempt fails, however, for the same parents have internalized the message from the nation at large that a fundamental change in race relations is taking place.

All of the imagery of school segregation among parents concentrates upon the Bilbo Street School and neighborhood, in spite of the zoning change and the fraction of Negroes located in other neighborhoods. Generally, most parents think of Bilbo as having a sound enough physical plant and as *equal* to all other Little City schools in quality of services. Some combine the two ideas and think of the Bilbo School as slightly superior to some other schools. A few Bilbo parents and a smaller minority of others say openly that the Bilbo School staff is inferior and, more significantly, that Negro children are less well educated than whites within the Bilbo School. Most Little City parents favor current school zones and desire *no change* in the future. They view the neighborhood schools as the best of all possible arrangements; they believe that revising the neighborhood concept would reduce Negro progress and produce added evils such as traffic hazards.

A few parents advance the idea that minor additional zoning changes and some "open enrollment" would be appropriate for Little City. About 20 per cent of the tax-paying parents *favor* more change than this. Another 20 per cent would resist greater change with vigor, particularly if the concept of the neighborhood school, upon which the residential structure of the town is grounded, were altered drastically.

White parents in Little City, in the main, do not know what would be gained through school desegregation. In view of the saturation coverage of this question through the mass media, this suggests that they do not want to know. Most parents emphasize that Little City neighborhood schools at present all offer the same quality of education, that they use the same books, and teach the same subjects. As one white father commented, "What difference would it make if 'they' sat next to a white child? How will they learn more that way?"

A majority of Little City parents believe, according to one of them, that "There is no racial problem in Little City. Whatever trouble has developed has come from four or five hotheads who have turned this supposed problem into a political football." A Negro mother confirmed this interpretation: "I grew up in Little City and I have several children in school here and the schools give equal opportunity for all." A Negro couple followed this remark with the statement: "There is no racial issue here at all. If some people feel that there is, they are wrong or mistaken."

It is therefore not surprising that most parents see *no need* to search for desegregation. This indifference cuts two ways, however. At least half of the parents are vocally disposed to accept the Superintendent's and the Board's definitions of what is needed. They are tolerant of authority; they prefer clearly stated, authoritatively designed changes. They *trust* those in control of the public schools, and this trust extends into the area of race relations.

If the Board and the Superintendent announce that specific changes— short of radical revision of the neighborhood concept—are necessary, a majority of the parents would accept this definition of the situation at face value. Moreover, most parents believe that such changes are the province of the Board and the staff—that expert and authoritative leadership is requisite to decisions on problems of school segregation.

There are many ways in which segregation and any attempted resolution of it can touch off older social, economic, and religious tensions latent in the social organization of Little City. Neighborhood residents are aware of minute differences between localities; a sharply stratified class structure exists and will undergo stresses with changing racial balances.

In view of the nature and depth of these attitudes, planning for school integration and implementing even part of the plan must depend upon an exceptional convergence of counterforces. Little City, for instance, began to plan for integration because the State Commissioner of Education pressed for such action, because a secure, long-established local superintendent saw the value of desegregation as one part of a program of educational reconstruction, and because civil rights groups mustered an effective protest. These pressures were checked, however, by the death of the superintendent, by simultaneous changes in the composition of the school board, and through the failure of the civil rights supporters to sustain their protest over a two-year period. In other words, the requisite conditions for surmounting an entrenched partial caste system, even in a single public institution such as education, are so elaborate as to be undone at any turn of events. The attitude structure of the public, Negro as well as white, is an enduring impediment, whether active or passive. In Little City, the views of teachers and other school officers were neither felt nor defined as relevant to the issue.

Fortunately, in the process of persuasion which leads smaller urban communities to decide to integrate public schools, the more salient conditions sometimes compensate for one another. Thus, a highly stratified local population with group interests invested deeply in maintaining school segregation may be moved nonetheless by firm sanctions from a state commissioner or superintendent. In New York State, for example, the present position of the Court of Appeals is that

The Board of Regents, under authority of section 207 of the Education Law, has declared racially imbalanced schools to be educationally inadequate. The commissioner, under sections 301 and 305 of the Education Law, has implemented this policy by directing local boards to take steps to eliminate racial imbalance. These decisions are final, absent a showing of pure arbitrariness. . . . Disagreement with the sociological, psychological and educational assumptions relied on by the commissioner cannot be evaluated by this court. Such arguments can only be heard in the Legislature, which has endowed the commissioner with an all but absolute power, or by the Board of Regents, who are elected by the Legislature and make public policy in the field of education.[9]

Differently weighted influences, then, can combine to induce desegregation of public schools. There is a ceiling on how much any one influence fostering desegregation can compensate for resistances. Even court orders and sanctions from state superintendents are insufficient if no other factors are aligned in support of local change.

Perhaps most important in smaller communities is the fact that technical solutions are available in abundance. Small districts can be merged, zones changed, buses introduced, or schools paired. Old buildings can be revised in use, and new ones can be introduced to provide extra degrees of freedom. Several reasonable courses of action toward school integration are ordinarily apparent.

Moreover, in smaller communities, a board's decision to integrate can be communicated to parents clearly and quickly, in combination with programs of social preparation and civic as well as school staff planning. A touch of ingenuity, or merely the adoption of successful features of neighboring systems, also enables smaller communities to make school desegregation a time for improving educational programs in general—for upgrading the quality of instruction or staff or facilities. This prospect and stories of success in integration are gradually becoming commonplace in the professional journals and newsletters of teachers and schoolmen, so the trend should quicken over the next few years.

The big cities

An improved rate of change in school integration in the smaller communities contributes little to the acceleration of desegregation in the great central cities of the North. While the suburb of Englewood, New Jersey, eliminates a single segregated school and, over a period of a decade, evolves better school services as a result, neighboring New York City will continue to be burdened with hundreds of highly segregated public schools.

There are technical solutions to minority school segregation in the great cities, but they are few in number and generally drastic in effect upon both the clientele and the practitioners. Rezoning, district reorganization, pairing, free transfer, and open enrollment are valuable devices, but to have any effect upon the problem as a whole, these schemes must be applied in a system-wide and combined fashion.[10] No one mechanism among these, and no combination of devices applied in some but not all sublocalities, will result in any significant change. Technical solutions attempted in pilot fashion thus far have failed or have proved ungeneralizable, because of population density in the big city ghettos and because of traffic congestion.

Several partially adequate technical solutions have been proposed for each of the larger Northern cities. The simplest of these is rationally planned assignment of pupils. Philip Hauser and others demonstrated in their report on the Chicago public schools that, if pupils were assigned to schools in terms of proximity and with full but not excessive utilization of seating capacities, many all-white public schools which are underutilized in that city would be desegregated, and many mainly Negro schools which are now overcrowded would be integrated and thinned out.[11] Rational use of seating capacity would probably reduce the level of school segregation within any one city by no more than 15 to 20 per cent. But, compared with a condition of no change, that is progress.

A second solution entails revising the building programs of city systems so that the sites of all new and renovated structures are chosen with a view toward integration. This means a moratorium on the construction of schools *inside* burgeoning ghettos. Students would be transported in increasing numbers to schools located outside their neighborhoods. A third solution combines revision of building plans with the reorganization and combination of existing schools through pairing and complexes. In complexes, a series of neighboring schools engages in staff and student interchange.[12]

The two most promising technical solutions are also the most radical. One is the concept of the education park.[13] Here, big city systems would abandon neighborhood schools (or use them for very different purposes, such as community centers) and erect consolidated facilities housing from 5,000 to 20,000 students. Such a campus-style institution would be located to draw its students from a very wide residential base, one broad enough, perhaps, to surmount long-term changes in class and ethnic settlements. A second, related idea is to *merge* mainly white suburban school districts with increasingly Negro inner-city districts. District mergers could be achieved by state authorities and could break through ancient patterns of residential restriction.

These proposals imply enormous transformations in the character of public schools. Under contemporary urban conditions, use tends to follow facility. That is to say, if a new kind of physical plant is erected, whether a park, a parking lot, or a new type of school building, enthusiastic users tend to follow. The programs of instruction within an education park, moreover, based as they would be upon new resources of centralized administration and greater staff specialization and flexibility of deployment, would be a major innovation.

For a time, critics of school segregation in the big cities believed the situation to be fairly hopeless. Imaginable solutions like those mentioned above were viewed as infeasible both politically and fiscally. As discontent with urban public schools deepens, and as federal and state aid prospects grow, radical solutions to segregation which have major implications for quality of instruction begin to intrigue critics, specialists, and policy-makers alike.

Not all modes of desegregation contribute to improvement in the quality of public education, nor are technical solutions, by themselves, sufficient to stimulate either integration or excellence of program. If these qualifications are kept in mind, however, it becomes apparent that durable, system-wide excellence in big city schools cannot be attained without integration, and that integration can serve not only the ideal of justice, but also the urgent goal of better public instruction.

Sources of resistance in big cities

Our view is thus that valuable technical solutions have been proposed and that fiscal resources for using them are becoming available. The political dialogue about school segregation rages in the big cities against the background of possibilities. Yet, little or no integration of public schools is taking place. After ten years of talk and five years of visible struggle, only Detroit among the six largest and educationally most segregated central cities of the North has made some progress. New York City, Chicago, and Philadelphia, among other major cities, are more severely segregated today than they were in 1954.

Partly, this is the direct outcome of the continuing northward migration of Negro families and the reciprocal flight of whites to the suburbs. Still, the evidence of virtual inactivity among city school boards (or rather the evidence of *no effort* save experiments with open enrollment, rezoning, and a handful of pairings) calls for more than a demographic interpretation.

We must look to the social and cultural bases of Northern big-city life to understand why so little change has occurred. In the case of school segregation, especially, we must take into account the political context and the cultural milieu of urban public education. For example, in the great cities, any force toward desegregation is effectively countered by organized opposition. Big-city school superintendents, however, get paid more, have better protective clauses in their contracts, command a greater power base, and receive clearer indications of the educational damages resulting from segregation. If a superintendent of a big city did define school segregation openly as a *major* educational issue, change toward integration would occur. Opposition can be squelched with counteropposition.

Consider Chicago, where the role of the Superintendent, Benjamin C. Willis, illustrates the big-city pattern. Superintendent Willis announced in 1963 that he considered proposals for altering neighborhood school boundaries in order to provide free choice to Negroes, or for transferring white students into mainly Negro schools, to be "ominous." [14] He informed his Board of Education that, in his judgment, the manipulation of attendance and assignment procedures might prove disastrous *educationally*. Radical tensions could increase as a result, he believed, and more white families might move out of the city and into the suburbs.

Plans to desegregate had been accumulating in Chicago since 1960. These were submerged in litigation, direct and occasionally even violent political action, the intervention by invitation and strategic intrusion of social scientists and educational experts from the universities and the nation at large, and upheavals within the Board and the Office of the Superintendent itself.

There emerged from this a characteristic Northern urban pattern. On August 28, 1963, the Chicago Board of Education resolved that some schools in the system were all-Negro in student composition, and that such "separation" might interfere with learning. The Board then appointed a distinguished Advisory Panel, including Philip Hauser, then Chairman of the Department of Sociology at the University of Chicago, and Sterling McMurrin, former United States Commissioner of Education. They directed the Panel to suggest remedies.

The gap between Superintendent Willis and his own Board is suggested by one event at the same August meeting. The Board accepted Superintendent Willis's proposal to allow those pupils in the top 5 per cent of the city's high-school students to transfer to another high school—*if* their present school had no honors program. Even this petty proposal stimulated intense public reaction. After massive white picketing, and after negotiation and review, the parents of several transfer applicants filed suit in the local Superior Court, requesting the judge to issue a writ of mandamus against Superintendent Willis on the ground that he had withheld the certification of transfer. The Appellate Court upheld the order. In reply, Willis resigned in protest over the Court decision in order to show the irreconcilable difference between his Board and himself, for the Board had directed him to transfer the students.

Two days after Superintendent Willis resigned, the Illinois Chairman of the North Central Association of Colleges and Secondary Schools warned the Chicago Board of Education that the city's high schools might lose their accreditation if he ever found that the Board had infringed on the Superintendent's administrative prerogatives. And two days after this warning arrived, the Board voted to refuse Superintendent Willis's resignation. Later, the Board voted to reconsider its previous order directing Willis to transfer students. Willis then withdrew his resignation.

The Advisory Panel on Integration made its recommendations in the early spring of 1964, after weeks of picketing, boycotting of stores as well as schools, and swirling controversy over this issue. Minor parts of the Panel's proposals were adopted by the Board in the fall, but by 1965 there was no indication that any important recommendations would be adopted. The report was *not* endorsed by the Superintendent.

A policy stand on school desegregation has not cost a single Northern big-city superintendent his job. Superintendent Willis has been attacked politically for four years for his opposition to desegregation, yet these attacks have done little more than tarnish his professional and public image. New York City Superintendent Calvin Gross did *not* lose his job because of his stand on this issue.

More important is the fact that no Northern big-city superintendent has committed himself emphatically to the pursuit of school desegregation. The barriers to school desegregation in large Northern cities will remain a subject of moot speculation until at least one such superintendent does take a strong, positive position and allows others to observe the consequences. The policy recommendations of city school superintendents are more than influential. They are profoundly indicative of changes in school practice, even where they are not determinative.

Sufficient conditions for inaction

There is probably one condition which is sufficient to maintain inaction on big-city school segregation in the North: If preservation of the status quo on this question helps to preserve the present distribution of power in the community, the status quo will in all probability be maintained, while the dialogue about segregation continues. Public officials, including superintendents, do not take unnecessary risks. They do not press for significant social changes if the effects upon their own access to authority are not predictable and promising.

There may be no change, then, because the ability of the city superintendent and his board to act on any question of general interest in the community is limited by the risks that the central political agency, usually the office of the mayor, is disposed to take. "In order for anything to be done under public auspices, the elaborate decentralization of authority . . . must somehow be overcome or set aside. The widely diffused right to act *must* be replaced by a unified ability to act." [15]

In the case of school segregation, the "unified ability to act" depends upon relations among the superintendent, his board, and the political power structure of the community as a whole. No one of these elements will jeopardize another intentionally, although a mayor or a city council often transfers responsibility for this problem to the board of education in lieu of agreeing to act in unity.

Trivial institutional impediments

Teachers and principals play a minor role in the policies of school segregation and desegregation. They are vital to the success of any program of desegregation, for their attitudes and practices either reinforce a positive integrative trend and make an educational opportunity out of it or undermine the worth of any effort.

But their role in the decision process itself is minor. The segregation issue is a general political one, and most school functionaries are disbarred from participation in it except under crisis conditions. Crises include incidents where Negro protest groups have managed to unite with teachers' unions for specific pickets and boycotts; but these are very rare. Moreover, it is seldom obvious in the negotiation of conflicts exactly how the teachers' and principals' own interests are involved. When these are touched upon, substantial mobilization occurs, as with all other urban interest groups.

Junior-high-school principals in New York City, for example, were *not* asked for their opinions about desegregation nor did they place themselves in the dialogue. But when a State Advisory Committee recommended in 1964 that segregated junior high schools should be abolished and the grade structure of all junior highs revised, the stake of the principals was defined. Their current arrangements threatened, these lower-line officers organized and communicated their opposition to change. When the Superintendent made no response, the principals undertook a strong newspaper advertising campaign opposing reorganization.

Headquarters staffs often impede desegregation efforts in less direct ways. The administrative staff officials responsible for planning transportation, pupil assignment, and even renovation and new construction of plants, all make hundreds of technical decisions each year which impede or foster revision of the status quo.

Change is costly, not only in money but in demands upon skill. School planners resist alterations in population estimation procedures they have grown accustomed to over the decades "merely" because ethnicity and changes in the distribution of minorities have not customarily been considered in detail. If a program of school desegregation involves administrative decentralization, then accountants, other business officers, and related staff workers must make socially costly adjustments that range from changing daily work procedures to changing one's place of work itself.

No values, and no pressures, dominant in the white majority community reward any readiness to change among staff members. The municipal educational bureaucracy, in short, responds much like any other institutionalized establishment. In the case of staff impediments, however, incomplete information, unimaginative assessments of feasibility, and an inability to innovate discourage desegregation more effectively than does the organized opposition of principals.

These resistances to change are trivial in their over-all contribution to the fate of the segregation question both because lower echelons do not have that much influence in policy decisions and because educators themselves are perplexed by competing messages and by a steady change in the salience of the issue *within* their profession. The National Education Association, the teachers' unions, the United States Office of Education, and some of the teacher-training institutions are now at work, through officers in charge of integration or "equal opportunity," emphasizing the importance of the question and the urgency of resolution. On this issue, these agencies work somewhat like the National Council of Churches in its limited bearing upon local Protestant congregations: There is a low ceiling upon the national association's influence.

Prospects for Northern school desegregation

My argument has been that Northern school desegregation is not difficult to accomplish in smaller cities and suburbs. Where the school superintendents of such communities have allied themselves with state authority and have responded to the protest from their Negro clientele, desegregation has been proven politically safe as well as technically feasible. Moreover, the educational outcomes of most of the efforts to date have been highly encouraging to professionals. News of the revitalization and improvement of staff morale and daily practices within such changing systems is being exchanged constantly at educational conventions and through the professional media.

The major part of the problem centers in a dozen of the largest central cities. In these, very little movement toward desegregation has occurred. The political risks continue to be too high, and the rewards within the educational establishment have not been worth the effort.

The seasonal campaigns of the civil rights and Negro protest groups have become strategic, though insufficient as a political force. These campaigns are strategic insofar as they maintain the level of priority on the segregation question and even, on occasion, heighten it. They are insufficient—even with annual improvements such as better publicity, broader constituency, and tighter alignment with other interest groups—because the big cities are too divisive and counter-protest is too readily available.

Moreover, school policy-makers know that very few citizens, Negro or white, are as intensely concerned with the educational question as they are with contending issues of housing, crime, and employment. Finally, there is not apt to be enough unity of leadership among Negro groups and politicians to allow for a much greater focus of effort on the school issue than has been achieved to date.

Nevertheless, some big Northern cities are likely to desegregate their public schools when their fiscal dilemmas intensify. Northern-style school segregation is expensive. In the big cities, school funds have been poured into the erection of expensive new plants to accommodate students in the burgeoning residential ghettos.[16] Funds that would once have been used to improve all-white schools in the developing or most desirable real-estate areas must now be diverted. The new ghetto schools that result, moreover, offer little political reward. They are not appreciated because they reinforce the ghetto and because the immediate electorate is a captive constituency that is apathetic about education. In white suburbs, a Negro ghetto school depresses real-estate values in its neighborhood. It is a standing advertisement *against* the educational magnetism to technical and professional workers seeking an alternative to city school facilities. It is often a sign of decadence and commercial deterioration to most whites.[17]

In the big cities, the issue has unraveled the sleeve of public education as a whole. For state and local policy-makers, and for chief administrators, school desegregation has great potential significance for the merger of school districts, the progressive consolidation of schools, the revision of grade structures, and whole programs of instruction. The issue also stimulates questions about the quality and equal distribution of facilities, the rights of substitute teachers, the assignment of teachers to one school versus another, and the *stability* of a career in neighborhood-school teaching in general. The dialogue in professional circles, particularly in Northern teacher-training institutions and among education reporters, even penetrates to the question of the *viability* of public education as it is now operated. The alternative most often imagined is one in which the public school system of the big city becomes a semicustodial institution serving the clientele of the welfare department, and where the advantaged white majority has elected either the suburbs or the private schools of the city.

The thesis is that, if public education cannot evolve toward its historic goal of *universality,* it cannot be maintained in its present form as a general municipal service. Much more than the question of racial segregation is involved in this conversation, but no other issue exposes the total dilemma so dramatically.

The most likely future response of educators to the problem of Northern school segregation will be to make important changes, but to make them only in the wake of the current period of identification of the problem, exploration of its implications, and political negotiation. The United States Office of Education's survey of the state of equality of opportunity in American schools, to be conducted under a directive in the 1964 Civil Rights Act, should have influence in this regard. The position of ancillary institutions, from the National Education Association to the Parent Teachers Associations, has just begun to become firm, let alone articulate.

When the question is somewhat commonly stated, and when the problem is extensively and authoritatively identified, some change toward desegregation that is more than random, or more substantial than token, will be achieved. In public school circles, this change will be noted first in the increasingly more open espousal of "racial balance" by Northern superintendents. Superintendents in many communities will acknowledge, through their conventions, journals, and professional associations in particular, that a "balanced system" is being defined as an educationally desirable system. "Racial balance" will come to be viewed as "essential" to quality. As the image becomes rewarding, superintendents will pursue it as their own *if* minority pressures are sustained and if majority resistance dwindles even slightly.

The ability to advance desegregation depends mainly on state authority and on board and community politics. No social scientist expects a school superintendent to become a culture hero rather than an administrator of a municipal service. But the option to champion desegregation each year becomes less dangerous for superintendents. We should come to a time soon when only the very largest cities of the North, and only a few unaspiring little communities, will still operate segregated schools. The gatekeeper for the institution will be the superintendent.

NOTES

1. *The New York Times* (July 31, 1962), p. 1.
2. Data reported by Herman Long, from survey conducted by the National Association of Intergroup Relations Officials, in *New York State Commissioner's Conference on Race and Education,* State Education Department (Albany, N.Y., 1964).
3. New York State Bar Association, *Racial Balance in the Public Schools: The Current Status of Federal and New York Law* (Albany, N.Y.: October 20, 1964), pp. 1–7. For a technical analysis, see Robert A. Dentler *et al., The Educational Complex Study Project* (Institute of Urban Studies, Teachers College, Columbia University, and New York City Board of Education, 1965; mimeographed).
4. For a good research summary see the Report of the Advisory Committee on Racial Imbalance and Education, *Because It Is Right—Educationally* (Springfield, Mass.: April, 1965), pp. 77–86.
5. Robert A. Dentler, Bernard Mackler, and M. Elleen Warshaur (eds.), *The Urban R's* (New York: Praeger, 1967).
6. New York State Bar Association, *op. cit.,* pp. 1–7.
7. Adapted from "Chronicle" in *Integrated Education,* X, XI, XII (December, 1964–January, 1965).
8. The author was State Consultant to White Plains in the planning of school desegregation there.
9. *The New York Law Journal* (July 26, 1965), "Court of Appeals," matter of *Michael Vetere* v. *James E. Allen.*
10. State Advisory Committee Report (Allen Report), *Desegregating the Schools of New York City* (Albany: May, 1964).
11. See *Report to the Board of Education City of Chicago* by the *Advisory Panel on Integration of the Public Schools* (Chicago: March 31, 1964).
12. *The Educational Complex Study Project, op. cit.*
13. Nathan Jacobsen (ed.), *An Exploration of the Education Park Concept* (New York City Board of Education Arden House Conference, 1964).
14. Marcia Lane Vespa, "Chicago Regional School Plans," *Integrated Education,* I, No. 5 (October–November, 1963), 25.
15. Edward Banfield and James Q. Wilson, *City Politics* (Cambridge: Harvard University Press, 1963), p. 104.
16. For example, the City Commission on Human Rights found that in New York City 45 per cent of the 1964–1965 school budget went toward the planning and construction of minority segregated schools. See City Commission on Human Rights, *Study of the Effect of the 1964–1970 School Building Program on Segregation in New York City's Public Schools* (New York, 1964). Also, the Advisory Panel on Integration of the Public Schools in Chicago found that most of the 243 new schools and additions in Chicago from January, 1951, to December, 1963, were constructed in Negro areas.
17. This is particularly true where an older but contained little Negro ghetto "suddenly" swells with new arrivals. This was the pattern in Englewood, New Jersey, and New Rochelle, New York.

Part IV CITIZEN ORGANIZATION AND PARTICIPATION

Editors' Introduction

Planning for urban areas necessarily takes place in the center of civic and political decision-making. Whatever the structure and process may be for governing the city, these are engaged in choosing alternative approaches to the allocation of resources, the distribution of the burden of taxation, and the balance to be struck among competing interests. The nature of the urban complex, with its multiple forces and types of organization, and with its massive concentration of diverse ethnic, social, and religious groups, demands an equally complex system for decision-making which will somehow reflect the wants and needs and interests of such groups. However, the people who inhabit the city and its suburbs do not possess equal influence in this complex process, and the result has been that some, especially the economically underprivileged, have been least effective in making their needs felt and in securing action relevant to their interests. For this reason, if for no other, planning has had to give substantial attention to the various processes by which citizens take part in shaping the design of their environment. While Parts I, II, and III have addressed themselves to the "how" of planning and the "what" of social policy, Part IV is concerned with matters of value—the "why" and "for whom" of planning.

The negative and positive influences of urban groups

The participation of the poor or less privileged is an especially sensitive and critical aspect of the general subject, for it throws into high relief the essential conflicts and contradictions which confront those who govern in the city. All groups turn, at some point, to the legal, financial, and moral authority of government to help them meet their needs; this is true for the businessman, the religious group, the neighborhood association, and the professions. Urban space is scarce and costly and there is competition among those who seek the space for industry, commerce, transport, or housing. Individual resources are often inadequate to provide housing plus public services (such as sewers, water, power, sanitation), and there is competition over the distribution of inadequate municipal funds. Ethnic and social groups display a generalized form of clannishness and one group resists the intrusion of others, meaning the free movement in a limited urban space, a resistance shown at its ugliest in the restrictions on housing opportunity for Negroes. In this competition, the poor usually have limited power for positive action, although their numbers frequently permit them to exercise a veto over the plans controlled or initiated by others. Planners have thus been interested in means for improving the participation of citizens from all economic and social classes for both principled and selfish reasons; out of a conviction that all groups should be afforded an equal voice in the framing of their environment; and also to minimize the risk of unexpected negative upset of professionally drawn plans through civic action at the polls.

This subject has usually been approached in one of four ways: (1) Political theory and social science have considered the general principles and processes of governing. (2) At the action level, reform seeks to redress the grievances of special groups, either through advocacy of these group needs or through organization of the poor into a more effective political voice. (3) Organizations and governmental departments have developed a science of administration which considers, among other things, the relation of any formal organization to its constituents. (4) And in recent years professional groups interested in crime and in mental health have come to believe that the alienation of the poor from the vital centers of urban life accounts for the growing rates of deviance—which can be overcome, as a therapeutic measure, by the involvement of such groups in city affairs.

The missing voices of the poor

Systematic attention to such questions has produced numerous hypotheses and some efforts to test their validity, but much analysis remains a composite of theoretical speculation, hypothesis, limited observation, and insufficient systematic study. These approaches have been effective at describing the nature of the process which excludes some groups and favors others, but they are less successful in outlining why this has occurred. Least convincing have been those analyses which have asserted that the fact of participation by the poor, in itself, will significantly alter the conditions deplored, as for example the belief that civic participation in itself leads to a reduction in deviant behavior. What remains thoroughly convincing in all analyses is the simple fact that the modern city provides inadequately for the basic needs of the poor, in housing, education, public services; and that the poor have very limited means with which to press these needs. The belief is shaken that the interplay of special interests alone will assure equity and that the appeal to the "general civic good" is powerful enough to assure that equity.

During the early 1960's a popular explanation for this state of affairs was built out of the hypothesis that there is a culture of poverty; that urban conditions contributed to an apathy and cultural deprivation among the poor which produced a self-perpetuating cycle of poverty. Although the urban condition is blamed for some of this situation, much of the proposed remedial course of action has been based upon the behavior of the poor, rather than upon the environmental conditions. One stream of sociological studies indicates that those who live in poverty take less part in the organizational life of their community, have a narrower range of interests outside of their family affairs, are preoccupied with the business of keeping alive, have less confidence that individuals can influence the course of their lives, and are more superstitious. They provide culturally deprived environments for their children who, as a consequence, do not progress suitably in the school system in competition with children from more comfortable homes.[1] These factors lead the children into blind-alley positions which provide minimum incomes and which leave them most vulnerable to changes in the labor market. This line of analysis has led to programs to enrich cultural opportunity for children in poor families, to special educational programs, to efforts to engage the poor in community activities to improve the conditions of their lives by self-help, and to special vocational training incentives. These efforts assume that social difficulties such as the above can be overcome by re-education and re-orientating the acts of individuals.

An alternate analysis locates the center of difficulty in the social situation itself, in discrimination against minorities, in lack of work opportunity, in poorly distributed educational facilities. Such approaches can point to the counter-evidence against a concept of apathy: the poor simply live a different community life than do the other social classes; when work or study opportunity is made available the demand is overwhelming from the very groups assumed to be apathetic; and the poor are explicitly excluded from many decision-making processes.[2] The remedy, under this analysis, as represented by Silberman, accepts the reality and value of conflict among special-interest groups. Those who are poor have distinctive wants and needs which are not fulfilled by the social and economic framework organized by more affluent groups. The solution lies in the organization of political power by the poor themselves, so that they can force attention to their views at any planning or decision-making center. To this end, almost any means are suitable: appeals to the conscience of others, direct action, exercising a nuisance value through protests. This approach assumes that the poor have the capacity for action and self-realization, but have been denied the means by imperfections in the situation in which they live.

Methods for increasing citizen participation

Systematic evidence to support both approaches exists; and it may be found that the source of the contradictions lies in imperfect definitions of the groups under consideration. Low income, poverty, and working class are not sufficiently exact terms with which to identify group characteristics, and thus to assess the nature of their difficulties. Some of the poor are very hard-working and upward aspiring; others are hard-working and content with a modest life; and still others who work may be quite apathetic or passive.[3]

Other more basic difficulties can be identified, which require attention before the issues of citizen organization can be treated in any comprehensive fashion. The "culture of poverty" approach is closely identified with community development activities first tried out in economically underdeveloped countries. Major attention is given to motivation and technical education of people at the simplest, "grass roots" level of social organization. It is assumed that if people are motivated, and will apply basic intelligence to the solution of their living problems, they will make progress. However, the problems of the modern city are embedded in very complex relationships which reach upward to the national and international scene and which require appropriately complex mechanisms for their management. Insufficient attention has yet been given by those who work at the neighborhood level to just how the transition will be made from the simple to the complex levels. How will the simply perceived and expressed wants of the poor at the neighborhood level be fitted into the intricate political and economic processes of the state?

The second approach, that of political action, has not yet resolved just how to make the transition from negative protest to positive action. Political and protest organizations have proven effective in calling attention to inequity and have often succeeded in halting action which does not conform to minority-group interests.[4] They have been less successful in devising constructive solutions for the problems of the cities which rise above a simple negative veto of someone else's plans. Once the disadvantaged have made a place for themselves at any negotiating or planning table, what will they contribute to the plans? What kind of technical competence will they have to develop or acquire?

A third approach concentrates upon the potential for altering existing social institutions and on the understanding of institutional change so that basic organization can become more responsive to the contemporary problems of the city. While Silberman looks at the political forces made up of human beings, Sherrard, Murray, and Wilson look at the institutions of the church and of municipal government to see how they may be altered, in response either to external pressures or to internal tensions. It is too soon to assess what institutional changes, if any, will result, but the fact of ferment and experimentation in organizational life is clear. The unlikely alliance between churches and the Industrial Areas Foundation of Alinsky, discussed by Sherrard and Murray, is one manifestation; the new quasi-public organizations described by Wilson are another. The latter represent a major national experiment in social policy, being embedded in legislation for housing, urban renewal, the war on poverty, and the attack on juvenile delinquency, to mention but a few. These steps represent efforts to break the crust of traditional behavior and to form wider and broader combinations of forces: church and nonchurch forces may coalesce; or the federal government and local government may forge new patterns of association unthought of only twenty years ago.

Such institutional changes will be studied with care in the next few years to ascertain whether or not they can resolve some of the most serious urban dilemmas. In such a perspective, Dahl and Wilson propose opposing views of optimism and mild skepticism. The multi-centered power distribution described by Dahl is one which seems capable of absorbing additional power centers which are activated as their vital interests are touched. On the other hand, Wilson points out that, the wider the participation of heterogeneous groups in urban decision-making, the less likely is the possibility for any agreement on action at all. As more conflicting interests confront each other with equal vigor, the more difficult it becomes to locate a common foundation and the easier it becomes for one group to veto the acts of others. This risk is seen best in the controversy over open housing for Negroes, in which white neighborhoods commonly act to block any change in the direction of reduced segregation when their own properties are affected. The possibility that wide participation may be antithetical to libertarian actions to solve serious social problems is disturbing, but it may be a necessary step on the road to more realistic citizen organization in the future.

Affluence and corporate organization as inhibitors of change

Two further issues are dealt with only indirectly by the authors in this section. As our society has become more affluent, and as the proportion of the population which shares in an expanding national economy rises to 60 per cent, 70 per cent, 80 per cent, it becomes proportionately more difficult to sustain a continuous interest of the majority in the needs of that declining majority who do not benefit. The majority develop a vested interest in the current state of affairs which underpins its own comfort, and changes in that state of affairs become increasingly uncomfortable. It becomes easier to attribute failure and distress to individual defect rather than to limitations and imperfections in the social or economic system; and as a result the poor are made the scapegoats for their own condition. This is already evident in the current economic debates about distribution or redistribution in the national income. A belief in personal deficiency is used to retain the present balance, while troublesome facts are ignored concerning the extent to which the poorer levels of the American society are now paying for their own services, due to distortion in the national tax system.[5]

Even more clear cut is the remaining issue, that of the citizen's relationship to the large bureaucracies which are required to operate the modern urban complex. The citizen depends almost completely for basic services upon large corporate or governmental bodies for transportation, employment, banking, merchandising, food supply, sanitation, housing, health, insurance, and so on. Perhaps the most widespread frustrations are those of the ordinary citizen who tries to secure attention to his individual requirements from a large bureaucracy, public or private, designed to deliver standard services only in a very large volume. The process is plagued by impersonality, an absence of personalizing relationships, and the mechanization or routinization of most processes so that they can be carried out by clerks without authority. Whatever action is taken about the citizens' voice in major urban policy-making, there will remain the need to confront these daily difficulties in matching large volume with high expectation and individual preference. How shall services be organized so that those which were once available only to a few can now be made usably available to the many? The new race is already on between exasperating decay in quality of service and the newer organizational means with which to reintroduce satisfying performance. The Ombudsman movement, which has spread to Sweden, England, Australia, and Israel among others, suggests one approach to this dilemma. In Part VI another American innovation is reported: the increased use of legal process to insure fair treatment for all citizens in the exercise of administrative discretion.[6] The concept of citizen participation has been widened from better representation of the minority in framing social policies to more effective and equitable execution of policies once they are adopted.

NOTES

1. See Norman Polansky, "Reaching Working Class Youth Leaders," *Social Work,* IV, No. 4 (October, 1959), 31–40; Edward J. Ryan, "Personal Identity in an Urban Slum," in Leonard J. Duhl (ed.), *The Urban Condition.* (New York: Basic Books, 1963); Alvin L. Schorr, *Slums and Social Insecurity* (Washington, D.C.: Government Printing Office, 1963).
2. See, among others, Arthur D. Shostak (ed.), *Blue Collar World: Studies of the American Worker* (New York: Prentice-Hall, 1964); Michael Harrington, *The Other America* (New York: Macmillan, 1963); and "The War on Poverty," Select Senate Sub-Committee on Poverty, Committee on Labor and Public Welfare, U.S. Senate (Washington, D.C.: Government Printing Office, 1964).
3. See S. M. Miller, "The American Lower Classes," Chapter 16, this book, and S. M. Miller and Martin Rein, "Will the War on Poverty Change America?" *Trans-Action,* II, No. 5 (July/August, 1965).
4. There are numerous instances in which city plans for urban renewal or minority housing have been frustrated when the other groups directly affected have protested that their interests are ignored: low-income renters forced to move into higher-cost housing as a result of urban renewal; small-property owners forced to move by highway and slum clearance projects; white families confronted with Negro neighbors, etc. See, as one such example, E. Banfield and M. Meyerson, *Politics, Planning and the Public Interest* (Glencoe, Ill.: The Free Press, 1955); and numerous local reports of "fair housing committees."
5. See Herman Miller, "Trends in Incomes of Families and Persons in the United States, 1947–1960," Bureau of the Census, Technical Paper #8 (U.S. Department of Commerce, 1963). It appears that lower-income families, as a group, pay in taxes a sum more than sufficient to account for nearly all of the social and economic benefits they receive under various forms of social security.
6. See Edward V. Sparer, "The New Public Law: The Relation of Indigents to State Administration," Chapter 23, this book.

12

Up from Apathy: The Woodlawn Experiment

CHARLES E. SILBERMAN

In recent years a growing number of liberals—reflecting the wistful American notion that with enough money any problem can be solved—have been pushing for a federal "crash program" to remove the disabilities and deprivations that bar Negroes from full participation in American society. Yet expenditures for welfare assistance have been rising at a rapid rate in every large city, and without making a dent in the problem. Many of these expenditures, in fact, have either been wasted or have proved to be a positive disservice to the dependent poor. One need not agree with Julius Horwitz, the novelist who was once a welfare worker, that the whole system of public assistance is an "ugly, diseased social growth [that] must be removed from American life." But few can argue with the studied judgment of Professor S. M. Miller of Syracuse University that "welfare assistance in its present form tends to encourage dependence, withdrawal, diffused hostility, indifference, ennui." For there is mounting evidence that the present welfare system is self-perpetuating—that far from relieving dependency, it *encourages* dependency.

Nor does the answer lie in expanding the number of social workers, settlement houses, mental-health clinics, and the like. In New York City, the *Directory of Social and Health Agencies* runs to 721 pages: social work is one of the city's major industries. In the Harlem–Upper Manhattan area alone there are, according to a study by the Protestant Council of the City of New York, some 156 separate agencies serving an estimated 240,000 people—roughly 40 per cent of the total population of the area. Without question, there are gaps here and there in the services offered, and many existing services are grossly inadequate. But it seems clear that the solution to Harlem's problems does not lie in any extension of the present system.

What has gone wrong? First of all, social agencies and social workers have concentrated more on symptoms than on causes—and on symptoms seen and treated individually rather than in connection with other symptoms. This concern with symptoms has been a reflection, in good measure, of the social-work profession's preoccupation with case work and the study and treatment of individual maladjustment. Unlike the early sociologists,

From *Commentary*, XXXVII (May, 1964), 51–58. Copyright © 1964 by Random House, Inc. Another version of this article appears in *Crisis in Black and White*, by Charles E. Silberman, published by Random House.

many of whom were reformers, contemporary sociologists and social workers, as Lewis Coser points out, have focused their attention "predominantly upon problems of adjustment rather than upon conflict." Their goal, that is, has been to teach maladjusted individuals to adjust to society as it is, rather than to change those aspects of society that make the individuals what they are. Social workers in particular have religiously followed Freud when they should have been listening to Émile Durkheim. For the troubles of the slum arise far less from individual neurosis (though certainly there is plenty of that) than from an objective lack of opportunity, from a social system that denies dignity and status to the individual.

The obsession with case work and individual pathology has had another unfortunate effect: the great bulk of resources, both financial and professional, have been devoted to "multi-problem families," who not only make up a small proportion of the population of the slums, but who are also the people least likely to benefit from public assistance. The great majority of slum dwellers work hard for very little material reward; they try their best to raise themselves, and their children, out of the morass in which they have been caught. Their problem is not a lack of good intent, but simply that their best is not good enough. Accordingly, the anthropologist Thomas Gladwin has suggested that it might be useful to revive the old distinction between the "deserving" and the "undeserving" poor (those who are truly antisocial in their behavior, destroying other people's lives or property, trading in narcotics, etc.). The fact that the two groups live in the same neighborhood in much the same way reflects a common state rather than a common interest, and social welfare resources might be far more effective if directed at the deserving rather than the undeserving poor.

Ultimately, however, the failure of the enormous American social welfare effort stems from the same factor that has produced the political strain between Negroes and white liberals: the idea of doing things *for* Negroes instead of *with* them—an approach that destroys the dignity and arouses the hostility of the people who are supposed to be helped. A particularly candid expression of this patronizing frame of mind—"welfare colonialism," as some critics call it—is found in a report published two years ago by Raymond M. Hilliard, director of the Cook County (Chicago) Department of Public Aid. In proposing that those on relief be deprived of their benefits unless they go to school, the report asserts: "Society stands in the same relation to them as that of parent to child. . . . Just as the child is expected to attend classes, so also the 'child-adult' must be expected to meet his responsibility to the community. In short, 'social uplifting'—even if begun on the adult level—cannot expect to meet with success unless it is combined with a certain amount of 'social disciplining'—just as it is on the pre-adult level."

Small wonder, then, that these "child-adults" should hate the colonial administrators who come to "uplift" them through "social discipline," or that they try to sabotage the disciplinarians' program. One typical East Harlem adolescent put it as follows to Richard Hammer of the *New York Times Magazine:*

> Most of them are rat fink types. They act like they think we're not human. They think they've got all there is, and all they've got to do is to convert us to think and do what they think and do . . . Man, these jerks pop up in the morning with their little briefcases, and they cut out for their homes a hell of a way around 5 or 6 at night, and that's it. If you are ever nuts enough to go to one of them they hand you the old crap, "Now, son, you shouldn't feel that way."

In general, the social workers and administrators remain aliens in a world they cannot understand and frequently do not even see. There is a large "youth center" in Harlem, for example, which provides counseling to some five thousand adolescents a year. Unbeknownst to the staff, the center was also a major contact point for the sale of narcotics—a fact discovered with ease by the Negro interviewers of HARYOU (Harlem Youth Opportunities Unlimited Inc., a federally supported research and demonstration program) when they began talking to the neighborhood kids.

The alienation of the welfare worker from the life of his clients is reinforced by the policing role the system requires him to play. In New York City, whose public relief administration is perhaps the most enlightened and sympathetic in the country, welfare workers are called "investigators," which is indeed what they are: in New York, as almost everywhere else, the administration of welfare is mainly a matter of enforcing regulations. The result, as S. M. Miller puts it, is that "the poor, thought of as being ignorant, illiterate, and unimaginative, have developed a variety of ways of coping with the welfare worker." They become "welfare-wise," and so enforcement on the one side produces a "matching effort of evasion on the other."

To be sure, many welfare workers resist the role of "social disciplinarians." But whether they do or not, the system still undermines self-respect, increases dependency, and arouses hostility. Where the Negro is concerned, moreover, these failures are aggravated by an inability to grasp the most basic fact about behavior in the Negro slums. The slowness of "acculturation" among Negro slumdwellers is caused less by ignorance or apathy than by an ingrained resistance to what Negroes call "going along with Mr. Charlie's program"—and to go along with Mr. Charlie's program is to betray your race. To compound matters, public officials, civic leaders, and foundation executives frequently draw up and publicize new programs for the downtrodden Negroes without bothering to consult those who are to be "uplifted." In city after city, Negro leaders have taken to telling their putative benefactors that they refuse to be planned for as though they were "children" or "guinea pigs in sociological experiments."

What all this means is that Negroes, like every other group, can be helped in only one way: by giving them the means with which to help themselves. In the last analysis, the rejection by Negroes of the conventional offers of help—the resentment they show—springs less from injustice per se than from their sense of inadequacy and impotence. White philanthropy, white liberalism, white sympathy and support, no less than white bigotry and discrimination, have had the effect of preventing Negroes from standing on their own feet, from "exercising their full manhood rights," to use W. E. B. DuBois's phrase. What Negroes need more than anything else is to be treated like men—and to believe in their hearts that they *are* men, men who can stand on their own feet and control their own destinies. Consequently, Negroes will not be able to climb out of their slums *en masse* until they can act in their own behalf—until they are in a position to make or to influence the decisions that affect them—until, in a word, they acquire power.

But can this be done? Can Negroes be mobilized in the face of the apathy and anomie of the Negro slum? The answer, quite simply, is that it *has* been done—in the Chicago slum of Woodlawn. Created in 1960, The Woodlawn Organization is a federation of some eighty-five or ninety groups, including thirteen churches (virtually all those with any influence in the community), three businessmen's associations, and an assortment of block clubs, neighborhood associations, and social groups of one kind or another; all told, the organizations represented in TWO have a membership of about 30,000. As the first broadly representative organization to be created in a Negro neighborhood, TWO is probably the most significant social experiment going on among Negroes in America today.

The existence of any coherent organization in Woodlawn would seem to be a complete anomaly. An oblong slum directly to the south of the University of Chicago campus, it contains between 80,000 and 150,000 people, depending on how the area is defined. Until the 1930's, Woodlawn was part of the university community—a desirable residential area with broad shady streets, excellent transportation facilities, and a respectable admixture of private homes and apartment houses. The decline of the neighborhood began during the Great Depression, and accelerated during the postwar rush to the suburbs. Around 1950, Negroes from the neighboring Black Belt started moving in, and the trickle soon turned into a torrent as Woodlawn became the "port-of-entry" for Negroes migrating to Chicago from the South. Within a decade, Woodlawn had become a virtually all-Negro slum. Today, nearly 25 per cent of the area's residents receive some form of welfare. They also pay an average of eighty-four dollars a month in rent— more than ten dollars above the city average—for an average housing unit of 2.2 rooms. There is a flourishing traffic in gambling, narcotics, and prostitution. The commercial business district is active but declining, with large numbers of vacant stores. In short, Woodlawn is precisely the sort of crowded, decaying, anomic neighborhood which social workers and urban planners assume can never help itself.

Yet Woodlawn *is* helping itself: it is taking concerted action toward a variety of goals. The impetus for The Woodlawn Organization came from three Protestant ministers and a Catholic priest, who had "worn out the seats of several good pairs of trousers attending an uncountable number of meetings held to 'do something about Woodlawn.' " After investigating various approaches to community organization, the clergymen "took the plunge," as two of them put it, and invited Saul D. Alinsky, executive director of the Industrial Areas Foundation, to help organize the Woodlawn community.

A sociologist and criminologist by training, Alinsky is a specialist in creating mass organizations that enable "the so-called 'little man' [to] gather into his hands the power he needs to make and shape his life." In the late 1930's, he was a leading force in the creation of Chicago's Back-of-the-Yards Neighborhood Council, which turned the stockyards area into one of the most desirable working-class neighborhoods in the city. Subsequently he established the Industrial Areas Foundation, a non-profit organization which has by now been called in by some forty-four groups across the country.

Though George N. Shuster is president of IAF and other notable figures from labor, management, politics, and religious affairs sit on its board of directors, Alinsky himself is nothing if not controversial. At various times, Alinsky (who is Jewish) has been attacked as a Communist, as a fascist, as a dupe of the Catholic Church and the mastermind of a Catholic conspiracy, as a racist, as a segregationist, and as an integrationist whose aim is to "mongrelize" Chicago. Certainly no one in recent memory has had as great an impact as Alinsky on the city of Chicago; and no one in the United States has proposed a program of action better calculated to rescue slum dwellers—Negroes or whites—from poverty and degradation. For Alinsky is that rarity in American life, a superlative organizer, strategist, and tactician who is also a social philosopher.

Alinsky really believes that the helpless, the poor, the badly educated can solve their own problems if given the chance and the means—that they have the right to decide how their lives should be run and what services they require. "I don't believe that democracy can survive, except as a formality," he has written, "if the ordinary citizen's part is limited to voting—if he is incapable of initiative and unable to influence the political, social, and economic structures surrounding him."

However, the individual can influence these structures in his own behalf only if he has power. As Alinsky sees it, there are two sources of power: money and people. Since the residents of Woodlawn and similar areas do not have money, their only source of power is themselves—and the only way they can draw on that power is by organizing. "The only reason people have ever banded together," Alinsky baldly states, "and the only reason they ever will, is the fact that organization gives them the power to satisfy their desires or to realize their needs. There never has been any other reason. . . . Even when we talk of a community lifting itself by its bootstraps, we are talking of power. It takes a great deal of power to lift oneself by one's own bootstraps." Needless to say, this kind of frankness offends a good many people who regard any open discussion of power as somehow lacking in taste.

Most efforts at organizing slum neighborhoods fail, Alinsky argues, not because of the nature of the community but because of the objectives and methods of the planners. The conventional appeal to the interests of home-owners in conserving property values, for instance, is useless in a community like Woodlawn, and even "civil rights" is too abstract. "The daily lives of Woodlawn people," an early Alinsky memo suggested, "leave them with little energy or enthusiasm for realizing principles from which they them-selves will derive little practical benefit. They know that with their educa-tional and economic handicaps they will be exceptions indeed if they can struggle into a middle-class neighborhood or a white-collar job." Instead of the conventional middle-class incentives, then, Alinsky uses the traditional appeal of trade-union organization: that is, to the self-interest of the local residents and to their resentment and distrust of the outside world. And following union practice, he seeks out and develops a local leadership to embody and direct this appeal.

But just as no factory could ever be organized without pressure and guid-ance from the outside, so no slum can be organized without a good deal of outside assistance. The mean and difficult job of building the organization must be handled by professionals who know how to deal with the apathy of the slum and who can find a way of bringing its disparate fragments to-gether into a working whole, for more often than not, the indigenous lead-ers of the slum area are out of touch with one another, and only very rarely do they possess the skills to set up a large organization and keep it running.

At the same time, however, the Industrial Areas Foundation is out to make the local community self-sufficient: Alinsky will not enter a commu-nity until he is assured that a workable cross-section of the population wants him, and he invariably insists that the community itself, no matter how poor, take over full responsibility for financing the new organization within a period of three years. Alinsky has a standard way of dramatizing the importance of financial independence. There is usually a convention at which the new group formally approves the constitution which has finally been hammered out. Alinsky will take a copy of the document, look at it briefly, and then flick it to the floor. "This constitution doesn't mean a damned thing. As long as the IAF organizers are on my payroll they'll do what I damn well tell them to do and not what it says on any paper like that." After a shocked silence, someone in the audience will inevitably pro-test: "I thought you were on our side!" "I am," Alinsky answers back. "But think of the number of people who've come down here telling you the same thing, and how many turned out to be two-timing, double-crossing s.o.b.'s. Why should you trust me? The only way you can be sure that the aims in that constitution are carried out is to get the organizers off my payroll and onto your payroll. Then *you* can tell them what to do, and if they don't do it, you can fire them and get someone who will."

The actual work of creating The Woodlawn Organization began in the spring and summer of 1960, eighteen months after the four ministers had called on Alinsky for help. A formal request to IAF now came from the Greater Woodlawn Pastors Alliance, supported by most other groups of any significance in the community, and subsidized by grants from the Catholic Archdiocese of Chicago, the Presbyterian church of Chicago, and the Schwarzhaupt Foundation.

How do you begin organizing an area like Woodlawn? Nicholas von Hoffman, chief organizer at the time for the IAF, says with studied casualness, "I found myself at the corner of 63rd and Kimbark and I looked around." What he was looking for were grievances—the basic agent in the Alinsky process of community organization. It didn't take much looking or listening to discover that a major source of complaints was the cheating and exploitation suffered in some of the neighborhood stores. In Woodlawn, as in most low-income areas, credit-purchasing is a pervasive trap. According to Dr. Leber, there were instances of customers being charged interest rates as high as 200 per cent; second-hand merchandise was sold as new; and prices bordered on outright piracy—for example, a six-dollar diamond chip in a gaudy ring setting would be sold for two hundred and fifty dollars, with a "Certificate of Guarantee" attesting that it was a real diamond. Other merchants also took whatever advantage they could of their ignorant customers: thus, food stores regularly gave short weight, overcharged, and in a few cases even rigged their cash register to produce false totals.

Before very long, enough such complaints had piled up to create an issue —one, moreover, on which the legitimate businessmen in the area could unite with the consumers. TWO promptly set up a committee of prominent members of the Businessmen's Association, several ministers, and some of the indigenous leaders of the Woodlawn area. (A leader, in Alinsky's definition, is anyone with a following—anyone, be he bookie, barber, minister, or businessman, to whom residents turn for help.) Together they worked out a Code of Business Ethics covering credit practices, pricing, and advertising. To implement the Code, TWO set up a Board of Arbitration made up of four representatives from the Businessmen's Association and four from consumer groups, with an impartial chairman from outside the community.

The next stage was to publicize the Code and the new organization. To these ends, a big parade was staged in which nearly one thousand people, singing and carrying signs, marched through the Woodlawn business section; the demonstration created enough of a stir to make the front pages of most of the Chicago newspapers. The following Saturday, a registered scale and an adding machine were set up at a nearby Catholic church. Shoppers from the suspected markets brought their packages directly to the church, with the result that false weights and false totals were exposed, and most of the offending merchants agreed to comply with the "Square Deal" code. Those who did not were harassed by leaflets distributed throughout the community. Within a few weeks, the "Square Deal" campaign had succeeded in eliminating a considerable amount of exploitation and chicanery.

More importantly, it had made the residents of Woodlawn aware that the new organization indeed existed and that it *could* improve some of the circumstances of their lives.

Moving quickly to harness the enthusiasm they had aroused, the IAF staff next began to organize rent strikes. A tenants' group was formed wherever a substantial majority of tenants could be persuaded to act together against building code violations—broken windows, defective plumbing work, creaky staircases, inadequate heat, vermin, etc. In each case the owner was given a period of time to make repairs; if it ran out before action had been taken, TWO called a rent strike: rents were withheld from the landlord and deposited in escrow in a special bank account. If a landlord still remained recalcitrant, groups of pickets were dispatched to his own home, where they marched with placards that read: "Your Neighbor is a Slum Lord." The picketing provided an outlet for anger and also gave the Woodlawn residents concerned a rare opportunity to use their color in an affirmative way. For as soon as the Negro pickets appeared in a white suburban block, the landlord would be deluged with phone calls from angry neighbors demanding that he do something to call the pickets off. In response to such pressure, some landlords agreed within a matter of hours to make repairs.

Another early focus for action was overcrowded and segregated schools. When William G. Caples, president of the Board of Education, refused to meet with TWO to discuss their complaints—he denounced the organization as "the lunatic fringe"—a delegation of eighteen Protestant and Catholic pastors staged a sit-in at the executive offices of Inland Steel, where Caples was vice-president in charge of public relations; other TWO members circled the building carrying placards denouncing Caples as a segregationist. (Caples resigned from the Board of Education the following month "because of the pressure of company business.") When the Superintendent of Schools, Benjamin Willis, denied that overcrowding could be relieved by transferring Negro students to all-white schools, TWO sent "truth squads" of mothers into neighboring white schools to photograph empty and half-empty classrooms. TWO members also staged a "death watch" at Board of Education meetings, which they attended in long black capes to symbolize their "mourning" over the plight of their children.

Such programs and tactics soon provoked denunciations of Alinsky as an agitator who dealt in hate and incited conflict. "The fact that a community may be stirred and organized by 'sharpening dormant hostilities' and 'rubbing raw the sores of discontent' is not new," said Julian Levi, in quoting from a TWO memorandum. "The technique has been proved in practice in the assembling of lynch mobs." Levi is executive director of the South East Chicago Commission and the key figure in the vast urban renewal activities of the University of Chicago, which once had plans of its own for Woodlawn. Specifically, Levi objected to a TWO leaflet naming a local food store and warning people to "watch out" for short weights, spoiled food, and short changing. "If this is what this merchant is really doing," Levi argued, "he should be punished by the court—but with all the safeguards the law provides. This is not the way people should be taught to protect themselves." They should be taught instead, Levi said, to register complaints about spoiled food with the Department of Health, about short weights with the Department of Weights and Measures, and about short change with the Police Department. Levi similarly objected to the tactic of rent strikes. If landlords were violating the building code, TWO should have brought action through the Building Department, following the practice of his South East Chicago Commission, instead of taking the law into its own hands.

But slumdwellers have been complaining to the Building Department and to other city agencies for years, usually to no avail. The reason the South East Chicago Commission has been able to get rapid action on its complaints from the Building Department or any other city agency is that it has political "clout": the Commission is the urban renewal arm of the University of Chicago, whose trustees include some of the most influential businessmen and politicians in the city.[1] Alinsky and TWO do not have these discreet but powerful influences at their disposal and perforce must rely upon more overt pressures. Levi's criticism, moreover, misses the further point that Alinsky's tactics are designed to serve other purposes besides the exerting of pressure. In TWO the most urgent need was not to persuade the local entrepreneurs to change their ways, but to convince the local population that it could solve some of its own problems through organized action.

The basic characteristic of the Negro slum—and the basic problem in organizing it—is that its "life style" is one of apathy. No organization can be created unless this apathy is overcome, but the slum residents will not be stirred until they see evidence that they *can* change things for the better. This reluctance to act contains a deep element of fear as well as hopelessness, for it is simply not true that the very poor have nothing to lose; in some respects, they have more to lose in their struggles with prevailing authority than the middle class does. They face the danger of having a relief check taken away, of being fired from an unskilled patronage job, of having a son on probation remanded to jail—and these are only a few of the reprisals that a politically powerful bureaucracy can impose. Indeed, one of the differences between lower-class Negro communities and middle-class white ones is that while the latter clamor for more protection *by* the police, the former frequently need protection *from* the police. Residents of a place like Woodlawn are often treated brutally and illegally by the police, and it is obvious that the traffic in narcotics, gambling, and prostitution that flourishes in most Negro slums could not go on without the active cooperation of the local police.

The net effect is that a community like Woodlawn seethes with inarticulate resentments and with muffled, dormant hostilities. The slumdwellers are incapable of acting, or even of joining, until these resentments and hostilities are brought to the surface and seen as problems, i.e., conditions they can do something about. Thus Alinsky calmly admits to the charge of being an agitator. "The community organizer," he writes, "digs into a morass of resignation, hopelessness, and despair and works with the local people in articulating (or 'rubbing raw') their resentments." His job is to "agitate to the point of conflict," to formulate grievances and persuade the people to speak out, to hope, and to move—in short, to develop and harness the power needed to change the prevailing patterns.

Agitation in itself, however, is not sufficient. To use the language of war (for that is what TWO is conducting), the only way to build an army from scratch is by winning a few victories. But how do you gain a victory before you have an army? The only method is guerrilla warfare: to avoid major battles and to concentrate on hit-and-run tactics designed to gain the small but measurable triumphs that can create a sense of solidarity and élan.

Once guerrilla warfare begins, the best organizing help of all comes from "the enemy"—the established institutions which feel threatened by the new organization. Thus, what really welded the Woodlawn community together was the University of Chicago's announcement on July 19, 1960, that it planned to extend its "South Campus" in Woodlawn by annexing a strip of land a block wide and a mile long. Woodlawn residents had no particular attachment to this strip, in which University buildings extended into a dreary amalgam of warehouses, tenements, and empty lots. But they suspected that annexation was the prelude to clearing a large part of Wood-lawn itself for middle- and upper-income apartment and town houses. There was ample basis for these fears: the huge urban renewal projects which the University was sponsoring in the Hyde Park–Kenwood district to the north had in fact been designed in good measure to remove Negroes along with "crime" and "blight." [2] Unless they acted quickly to establish the principle that no plan should be adopted for Woodlawn without active participation by Woodlawn residents in the planning process itself, the Negro community might wake up one morning to find bulldozers in every front yard. According to Rossi and Dentler, "the characteristic mode of action of the University and of the South East Chicago Commission, was to develop plans quickly, announce proposals in general terms, and then ob-tain quick approval through political leverage downtown." Almost immedi-ately and quite loudly, TWO therefore demanded that the city defer ap-proval until university and city-planning officials had met with TWO and negotiated a long-term plan for Woodlawn. Otherwise, the organization warned, its members would lie down in front of the bulldozers and wrecking equipment. Some three hundred TWO members crowded into a City Plan-ning Commission hearing and succeeded in blocking the quick approval the University had expected.

The Negro tenants and homeowners were not the only ones who were alarmed by the University's announcement. Having seen many of the small businessmen in the Hyde Park–Kenwood area flattened by the urban re-newal program, the Woodlawn merchants also became apprehensive; con-versations with University and city officials only increased their apprehensions. According to a local restaurant owner, Julian Levi told a meeting of the Woodlawn Businessmen's Association that "we could either accept the plan and help it or sit back and watch it go through." Philip Doyle, head of the Chicago Land Clearance Commission, was even less reassuring. "He said that the biggest investment he would advise us to make in our business was one coat of paint." The businessmen voted unanimously to join TWO.

It was not long before a full-scale battle was in progress, and as the velvet glove of the University began to wear thin against the serious opposition of TWO, its iron fist became quite visible. In February of 1961, for example, the University's Public Relations Director, together with Julian Levi and another PR man, called on several Chicago dailies to warn them against the "evil forces" of Alinsky, the Industrial Areas Foundation, the Catholic Church, and TWO. They brought with them a dossier on Alinsky and his foundation; the main item was a copy of the Industrial Area Foundation's income tax return—which the University happened to have in its possession—listing various Catholic groups as IAF's principal source of financial support for that year.[3]

The Chicago newspapers balked at running any articles based on the University's dossier, but eventually a piece was published in the student paper *The Maroon,* after being copyrighted under the name of the writer— a rare procedure which guaranteed the University immunity against a possible suit for libel. Under a banner headline reading "Church Supports 'Hate Group,' " the article led off by announcing that the IAF had "received over $56,000 last year from the Chicago Catholic Bishop and the National Conference of Catholic Charities . . . . [and also] received approximately $43,000 from the two Catholic groups in 1958." The article went on to quote Rev. Walter Kloetzli, a Lutheran minister, to the effect that the Catholic-IAF-TWO "conspiracy" was designed to keep Negroes locked up within Woodlawn in order to preserve the all-white parishes to the southwest and southeast. What was omitted from the article was any mention of the fact that Kloetzli's charges had been raised two years before at a meeting of some thirty Presbyterian, Lutheran, and Catholic representatives, and that Alinsky had answered the charges to the satisfaction of virtually everyone present. For this reason and others, Joseph Sittler, the distinguished Lutheran theologian and a faculty member of the University, charged that the publication of the article had been "irresponsible." Sittler also noted that on matters of integration in Chicago, the Catholic Church had been guided by "a wise and charitable policy." [4]

In any event, the truth is that The Woodlawn Organization, far from being a Papist conspiracy, represents one of the most meaningful examples of Protestant-Catholic amity and cooperation to be found anywhere in the United States—an amity that extends from the fellowship among local church members and leaders to the close collaboration between the Archdiocese, the Chicago Presbytery, and the Church Federation of Chicago. Indeed, TWO's involvement of church leaders of various denominations in direct social action to improve the Negro's lot may prove to be its most enduring contribution. In Kansas City, Missouri, for example, Presbyterians, Catholics, Episcopalians, and Jews are collaborating in an attempt to develop a program resembling that of TWO, while Catholics, Presbyterians, and Lutherans are doing the same in Gary, Indiana.

The controversy over the South Campus plan has been revealing in another respect. Federal legislation now requires as a condition of aid local citizen participation in the formulation of renewal plans, but the Woodlawn experience indicates that "participation" means something very different to planners and social scientists from what it means to the citizens being planned for. To the former, the requirement of "citizen participation" is satisfied by giving the local residents a chance to air their views *after* the plans have been drawn, not before; planning, in this view, is a matter for experts, and "participation" is really thought of as acquiescence.

Certainly the Chicago planners showed no eagerness to engage the Woodlawn residents in any active role. In March 1962 the City Commission presented a comprehensive plan for Woodlawn which included a huge program of urban renewal clearance, conservation, and rehabilitation; a massive investigation of illiteracy, ill health, crime, and unemployment; and a pilot attack on these problems to be financed by government and foundation grants. When asked if the planning committee had been guided by opinions from the community, the committee's coordinating consultant replied that "There is nobody to speak for the community. A community does not exist in Woodlawn." Philip Hauser, a University of Chicago sociologist and another consultant, remarked that "the people there have only one common bond, opposition to the University of Chicago," and added gratuitously, "this is a community that reads nothing."

The two consultants were quickly disabused of these views. In conjunction with the Woodlawn Businessmen's Association, TWO employed its own firm of city planners to analyze the City Commission's plan and present alternate proposals. Besides issuing a detailed critique of the commission's urban renewal plan for Woodlawn, TWO affirmed the principle that "self-determination applies in the field of social welfare. Therefore the best programs are the ones that we develop, pay for, and direct ourselves. . . . Our aim is to lessen burdens in practical ways, but in ways that also guarantee we will keep our personal and community independence. We go on record as unqualifiedly opposing all notions of 'social planning' by either government or private groups. We will not be planned for as though we were children." This radical assertion of independence did not please the planners. "Some of their resolutions against welfare are singularly unfortunate," Philip Hauser was moved to say. "What would they do without welfare?" Other of his colleagues regarded the resolutions as "revolutionary" and even "subversive"—much to the bemusement of the Negroes of Woodlawn. "They've been calling us 'welfare chiselers' and 'dependent' and everything else," said one TWO member. "Now they distrust us for trying things for ourselves."

The University of Chicago sociologists and the professional planners may have resisted the message, but the Chicago politicians did not. Mayor Richard Daley brought the reluctant Chancellor of the University to his office to meet with TWO representatives. Eventually negotiators from both sides agreed on a compromise which called for construction of low-income housing on vacant land *before* any existing buildings were torn down. Thus, for the first time in the history of urban renewal, people displaced by demolition will have new homes waiting for them in the same neighborhood. Instead of the usual wholesale replacement of lower-class housing by "middle-income" units, Woodlawn will be renewed in stages. Only houses beyond salvage will be torn down, and units to be rehabilitated will be repaired without evicting tenants. City officials also agreed to give TWO majority representation on the citizens' planning committee that will draw up further plans and supervise their execution, and Mayor Daley asked Dr. Blakely, one of the founders of TWO, to serve as chairman of the committee.

Forcing the University of Chicago and the city planners to take account of the community and its own desires is not the only victory TWO has won. As a result of TWO drives, double shifts have been eliminated and over-crowding has been substantially reduced in Woodlawn's public schools; a number of Chicago firms have been persuaded to open up jobs for Negroes; and several local block organizations have been stimulated into cleaning up and maintaining their neighborhoods, as well as into pressuring landlords to repair buildings. TWO's attacks on "the silent six" Negro aldermen of the city, moreover, have driven them into a position of militancy, thereby changing the whole complexion of Chicago politics.

But what finally makes The Woodlawn Organization so significant is not so much what it is doing *for* its members as what it is doing *to* them. When the first group from the community—forty-six busloads—went to City Hall to register, Alinsky commented that the chief point "was their own reaction. Many were weeping; others were saying, 'They're paying attention to us.' 'They're recognizing that we're people.'" Eighteen months later, an active member observed, "City Hall used to be a forbidden place, but we've made so many trips there and seen so many people that it's beginning to feel like a neighborhood store." Other members say similar things: "We've lost our fear of standing up and expressing ourselves." "We don't have to go hat in hand, begging, any more."

Besides giving its members a new sense of dignity and worth, The Wood-lawn Organization has given a good many people a sense of direction and purpose and an inner discipline that have enabled them to overcome the disorganization of the Negro slum. As one TWO officer remarked, "The organization has given me a real sense of accomplishing something—the only time in my life I've had that feeling." Like so many of Woodlawn's Negroes, he had once wasted an enormous amount of time and energy be-cause of personal inefficiency—a factor that originally made the work of Alinsky's organizers far more difficult than it had been in any white slum. Even such an apparently simple matter as rounding up half a dozen people to hand out leaflets involved a major effort: those selected would turn up at different times, the leaflets would be lost or misplaced, or the volunteers would grow bored and give up. From month to month, however, the members learned to take orders, to carry out a task and follow through on it; bit by bit they began to learn to give orders themselves, to organize a rent strike or a rally, to talk on their feet and debate an issue at a meeting and to handle opposition. And as the discipline of the organization continues to impose itself on their own lives, it slowly transforms the individuals within it as well as the community they inhabit.

It would be fatuous to pretend that Woodlawn has become a model community; it remains a slum, and it is largely sunk in poverty and crime. However, it is a slum with hope—one that is developing the means of raising itself "by its own bootstraps." "We've learned to live together and act as a community," a TWO activist says—and adds, "Two years ago I didn't know a soul." Most of the problems that make Woodlawn what it is—high unemployment, lack of education, family disorganization, poor health—cannot be solved by a community organization alone. Enormous resources must still be poured into Woodlawn in the form of compensatory education, job retraining, advice on child rearing, and preventive medicine. But experience in every city in the nation has also demonstrated that any paternalistic program imposed from above will be resisted and resented as "welfare colonialism." The greatest contribution of an organization like TWO is its most subtle: it gives the slum residents the sense of dignity that makes it possible for them to accept help. For help now comes not as charity but as a response to their own initiative and power; *they* have decided what services they need and want. Hence social programs which the community, in the past, would have contemptuously ignored as one more instance of "Mr. Charlie's brainwashing" are now eagerly sought after. Recent negotiations between TWO and the University of Chicago produced a nursery school program designed to reverse the effects of "cultural deprivation," while cooperation between TWO and a team of psychiatrists has led to the setting up of some promising experiments in group therapy. And so, throughout this once completely depressed and deprived area, a new sense of energy and possibility is at work, and a new conception of social welfare has begun to take form in America.

NOTES

1. In *The Politics of Urban Renewal* (New York: The Free Press, 1962), a study of the University's urban renewal program in the Hyde Park–Kenwood area, Peter H. Rossi and Robert A. Dentler note that the influence of the Administration and trustees enabled Levi to represent "the most powerful community interests in demanding protection from the Chicago Department of Buildings and the Mayor's Housing and Redevelopment Coordinator. Pressure on real-estate speculators was also channeled through the University's strong connections with the business community. Banks and insurance companies were warned that their funds were in jeopardy when invested as mortages on illegally converted property

in the area. Insurance companies were persuaded to suspend policies written on badly maintained properties."

2. Rossi and Dentler provide convincing documentation of this fact. For example: in answer to the question of "why the University did not consider expansion to the east (which seemed more plausible than expansion elsewhere in Hyde Park), a respondent high in the University administration replied that the area to the east contained 'our people' . . . Whether one liked it or not, neighborhood conservation and renewal meant the preservation of Hyde Park–Kenwood as a primarily *white* middle-class residential neighborhood." (Italics theirs.)

3. The same income-tax return was included in a dossier which the University sent to me in the fall of 1961, via a reporter, in the hope of dissuading me from writing about TWO in an article I was then preparing for *Fortune*. When I asked the reporter what the income-tax return was supposed to demonstrate other than support of the IAF by the Catholic Church, he replied that Catholic support was in itself enough to discredit the IAF and TWO.

4. The Chicago Archdiocese, in fact, has been one of the most outspoken advocates of integration in the city. Monsignor John Egan of the Cardinal's Committee on Conservation and Urban Renewal led the protest against the controversial Hyde Park–Kenwood urban renewal program, arguing that the plan would destroy a great deal of adequate housing occupied largely by Negroes, most of whom would be unable to afford the new apartments and houses that were to be erected.

13

The Church and
Neighborhood Community Organization

THOMAS D. SHERRARD AND
RICHARD C. MURRAY

Compelled by obedience to its Lord, the church has gone out into the life of people and discovered that it can become an architect rather than a victim of the city. By sharing in the life of its neighborhood, the church has been shown a path which leads to the renewal of community life and the renewal of the church itself. . . . Because [participation in community organization] has made the church's faith relevant and immediately applicable, involvement in community has resulted in growth in the faith for numerous laymen and ministers. . . . Churchmen involved have declared, "Now the church is getting down to business; at last I know what it is to serve God. . . ." [1]

This is only one of many recent statements from churchmen and church groups. The present upsurge of interest and activity on the part of the churches is most heartening—even if it is startling. Only a few years ago it was the rare priest, minister, or rabbi who could find the time to become deeply involved in community organization. The extent of this interest, the reasons for it, the methods being employed, and the results being achieved are, of course, of great interest to those social workers engaged or interested in community organization practice. There are, in addition, important implications for the entire welfare system and professional social work as a whole—not to mention political ramifications. If social work remains aloof from the major currents and conflicts of our time, it risks being forever behind.

Not only does this trend of church involvement represent a large-scale readjustment of a major institutional force in our society, it also has been undertaken with a militancy that is unprecedented in recent times. It has been accompanied by sharp criticism of the social welfare establishment and social workers in general. "Red Feather bosses" and "welfare colonialism" have become popular expressions, which reflect—or may presage—less publicized shifts in national church organization budget allocations

From *Social Work*, X (July, 1965), 3–14. This essay is based on studies undertaken as part of a project, under a grant from the President's Committee on Juvenile Delinquency and Youth Crime, to develop curricula in community organization for universities and professional schools, especially Schools of Social Work.

from social service departments to departments concerned with urban policy, politics, civil rights, and community organization.[2]

The churches have always engaged in charitable activities. Throughout the ages they have fed the hungry, clothed the naked, taught the ignorant, cared for the sick, and provided solace and counsel for the troubled. These activities have been expressions of Christian love, services provided to the faithful or designed to reach new converts. Dedication to community organization as a fulfillment of good works is new.

In recent years, however, many of these church social service activities have become increasingly professionalized, run by social workers and co-opted by government; from the standpoint of the clergy, they are impersonalized, secularized, and distant from the church organization, even when they have retained their religious support. They have not provided the kind of bridge required by the churchmen who are anxious to reach alienated, inner-city populations in a meaningful way. Therefore, as an alternative, the churches have recently begun to encourage, sponsor, and in many instances finance with substantial sums of money secular organizations of people with the frank objective of effecting social and political change.

It is hard to assess the extent of these developments with certainty, but in many large Northern cities—in Chicago, New York, Detroit, Cleveland, Rochester, Syracuse, Buffalo, Kansas City, and elsewhere—large-scale community organization activities sponsored by church groups are either under way or contemplated. In these and many other cities, related activities sponsored by urban church groups, city missionary societies, councils of churches, as well as by individual inner-city churches and the home missions departments of several denominations, are going on at an accelerated pace. In few instances are they being carried on in cooperation with social welfare institutions, and in even fewer instances are they manned by social work personnel. The reasons for the widening gap between these institutional forces with so much in common deserves serious attention.

Why the trend?

The dynamics of the trend toward community organization by the churches—which has engaged labor unions and student groups as well—are difficult to analyze. There are many forces loose in the land that have contributed to it. Most immediate is the civil rights movement and the profound impact it has had upon all American religious bodies. Even though in the beginning most institutional churches responded hesitantly or with grave misgivings to the stirrings of protest against racism, at present church involvement and commitment to civil rights and related causes are widespread. Undoubtedly there still exists among many clergymen a sense of guilt and impatience over the fact that "mainline" churches, and especially their active laity, remain vehicles for maintaining middle-class values, prejudices, and privileges. Community organization provides the means for both bypassing the conservative and involving the timid church members.

Many of the younger clergy particularly have experienced a sense of guilt and frustration after exposure to the realities of brutal injustice against minorities and other lower-class groups, and it is this that has been transformed into a profound discontent and impatience with their own churches. Many of the men coming out of the seminaries have turned away from the parish ministry and are looking for other institutional forms through which to carry out their mission. They have found their way to the expanding and experimenting urban church departments, the home missions departments of the various denominations, or councils of churches.

In a time of profound social change and doubt such as the present—epitomized in the civil rights movement but manifested also in direct action by students on the nation's college campuses and in large-scale peace movements—redefinition of leadership within institutions is to be expected. Established leadership searches for new symbols, slogans, and programs to retain shifting allegiances; new leadership comes to the front as unusual opportunities present themselves to attract followers.

Another factor has been the role of the government and the politician. In response to this social unrest, the first half of the current decade has witnessed unusual activity by government after the quiet of the late fifties. The present climate of crisis makes it politically feasible and necessary for government to move ahead on many fronts. The attack on the problem of delinquency has become a community campaign and a national effort; longstanding economic and social disparities have become dramatized in the national War on Poverty; such diverse issues as population control, capital punishment, exploitation of migrant workers, water and air pollution, and conservation have come alive again. Because they depend on personal commitment, voter enthusiasm, and dedicated volunteer activity and involvement, political organizations must either try to rise to the spirit of the times or find attractive substitutes if party loyalty and voter enthusiasm are to be maintained.

It is not always so clearly seen that religious organizations have a corresponding dependence for their continuing vitality on the active involvement of a broad constituency in secular affairs. Since the Reformation, centuries of a conservative or other-worldly disregard for social and political events (punctuated by occasional nonconformist religious movements) have ill-prepared mid-twentieth-century Americans for the current shifts by religious institutions in response to the internal crises and other generalized threats to Western European society.

High membership but low influence

Clergymen are further troubled by an apparent paradox. Church membership—especially in the suburbs—has been growing to the point where it is at an all-time high, and churches are sharing in the general affluence. At the same time, they sense a diminution of effective religious influence in our society. In fact, it may be precisely these opportunities they see in the social movement atmosphere that make them impatient. Instead, as urban transition has taken place, they have become conscious of the inability of established churches to maintain effective relationships with the rapidly growing, alienated, low-income populations of the inner-cities or assume moral leadership on acute social issues.

The liberal theological spokesmen and the young emerging church leadership have clearly perceived that in order to maintain or to recapture a position of influence for the churches in the midst of present-day social movements, religious bodies must provide vigorous leadership in the fight for social justice. In a very real sense, the churches are engaged in a competition for the loyalties, the commitment, and the engagement of the residents of the large Northern urban centers, particularly the inner-city residents of deprived neighborhoods, Negro and white. In some instances, this may take the form of interchurch rivalry. Often it seems to take the form of aggressive ecumenicism and solidarity against certain local secular forces. It is expressed as a war on City Hall, on petty corruption or economic abuse (such as in Chicago, Cleveland, and Detroit), and in the seeking of support from federal or state government in battles for social issues.

The declining numbers of parishioners and the declining strength of the inner-city churches in the face of population shifts have strongly motivated these churches, both Protestant and Catholic, to look to a broader constituency. They attempt to build a platform or construct an arena, based on the neighborhood, in which the influence of the church can be more effectively applied.

One explanation for these phenomena in the inner-city churches has been in terms of economic losses of real estate owned by both Protestants and Catholics, particularly the ethnic Catholic parishes, their churches, schools, and social services. The same problem has already faced universities, hospitals, and other institutions, both commercial and nonprofit, which have had to make the difficult choice of whether to flee to more felicitous surroundings or to face urban deterioration. When the latter choice has been elected, often the institution has become the focal point around which local forces have become mobilized, often with the help of urban renewal and other governmental aids to arrest urban blight and to spur redevelopment. No doubt this same dynamic is at work in the case of the churches, and in many instances the problem is heightened and the choice narrowed by the flight to the suburbs at great distance of entire congregations. But for those churches that have a commitment, not only to a potentially mobile congregation but also to a geographic parish, the problem is intensified.

Crisis in the church

Closer examination suggests that such economic determinants are only contributing factors. The commitment of these new voices among the clergy appears to go much deeper than mere economic consideration or sentimental attachment to a geographic area and traditional buildings. In fact, in only a few instances—Chicago for example—has strong church organization tied to strong community organization been able to withstand the forces of urban deterioration and racial succession. One such example is in the Back-of-the-Yards neighborhood, which was tightly organized during the 1930's and has remained so ever since, successfully resisting the breakup of first- and second-generation Catholic parishes.

Urban missionary activities are, of course, nothing new in the history of organized religion, although often frowned on and ignored, or at the most grudgingly supported by the church establishment. Whether Nonconformist, Methodist, Evangelical, Christian Socialist, the Social Gospel Movement, Labour Chapels, or the Salvation Army, each in its time reached out to the poor and the dispossessed. They went outside the buildings, formalities, and conventions of the established churches and into the streets, the slums, the saloons, or brought new services to the poor with only a minimum of religious rituals. The National Council of Churches of Christ in America has had its home missions department and most denominations have a similar department, but it is perhaps a measure of the deep alienation of modern urban low-income population from established churches that the clergy of the inner-city have been unable to establish a truly productive relationship to slum populations through older mission methods. Instead, they have launched into what is in fact organized political and social reform as a basis for establishing rapport. These clergy have set out to prove the "relevance of the church" by creating a new earthly society.

There is, however, a still deeper crisis within churches over what it is these institutions and their clergy actually should do and should be. The moral crises of the two world wars, threats of atomic destruction, and the postwar rise of Eastern European and Asian Communist nations and non-Christian developing countries have severely shaken the security of the Christian churches—just as it has shaken the general security of America in ways that have yet to be appreciated. The ecumenical movement and reforms in the Catholic church testify that these currents of change are truly different in quality and quantity from previous pressures in recent centuries.

Thus, when urban clergymen in apparent desperation throw their energies into community organization, civil rights, and urban politics, seemingly in disregard of their traditional duties and goals, something more is afoot than a few men attempting to get their churches out of debt or seeking to enhance their careers. These men are searching for a new meaning of "church" in urban society. For many of them, the traditional role of church pastor has lost its meaning.

Nor should this be looked on as a "rump" movement within the churches that will soon pass away. The movement is now being supported at the highest levels in the larger church administrative bodies. Large sums of money have been allocated for this organizational activity, even in the face of obvious political risks. Churchmen are looking to community organization as a means of capturing leadership in one of the most significant social movements of the day as the Social Gospel movement supported labor unions fifty years ago.

It is fairly obvious that use of the Catholic and Protestant churches as instruments of social change presents problems to clergy who were trained in the use of a somewhat different technology. They have looked for technical assistance and have found willing help from the Industrial Areas Foundation, which has been providing organizational assistance in Chicago for the past half dozen years. The IAF is now moving with the encouragement of the National Council of Churches and the national offices of several of the denominations to other Northern cities to do likewise.

Saul Alinsky

The authors have been observing informally during the last six years, and more systematically during the last two, the activities of these church-sponsored community organizations in Chicago. As in all Northern urban centers, there are many community organizations sponsored, or participated in, by churches, as well as organizations sponsored by foundations, social agencies, and business groups. However, the concern in this discussion is with those organized under church sponsorship, with the help of organizers from the IAF under the direction of Saul Alinsky, a familiar figure on the community organization scene since the mid-thirties, when the already-mentioned Back-of-the-Yards Council was formed under Catholic auspices. He and his organization were subsequently active in a number of places across the country, but achieved no great claim on public attention until they joined forces with the urban church movement already described.[3]

There are four such organizations (including the Back-of-the-Yards) in the city of Chicago. They operate in different parts of the city in different types of communities, with widely differing populations, and therefore differ correspondingly in many important respects. However, in addition to the fact that their instigation and major support have been derived from the Catholic church (and in two cases also from Presbyterian churches), they have other important characteristics in common.

Organizational characteristics

Alinsky's organizations primarily seek to impose a monopoly of control over limited areas in the city—either neighborhoods, groups of contiguous neighborhoods, or community areas, as they are often called in Chicago. They differ from more conventional or traditional community organizations in that this attempt to gain monopolistic control over affairs in the area takes precedence over the development of social services. It appears to take priority also over other common goals, such as improved housing, sanitation, law enforcement, and education. These latter matters, however, often constitute the subject matter for mounting campaigns for developing interests and providing an agenda for action, in order to attain the primary objective of organizational control. In this sense, then, they may be said to have basically political objectives.

The organizations are like labor unions in trying to maintain their status as sole bargaining agents. Typically they represent themselves as spokesmen for all the citizenry and all the interests in the area. They purport to speak for the citizen, the parent, the voter, the businessman, the taxpayer, the tenant, the homeowner, and—in order to do so with any degree of reality—they must necessarily dispute the legitimacy of any other group wishing to represent either "the people" or significant interests in the community. When internal conflicts exist, they tend to represent the more powerful in order to maximize their strength.

These are organizations of organizations, built from the top down with a core of committed local clergy at the center. Other groups, such as local businessmen's organizations, PTA's, service groups, block clubs, and so on, are added as rapidly as they can be attracted, coopted, overcome, or digested. As might be expected, this behavior has brought them into conflict with other agencies and organizations.

Another characteristic of Alinsky's organizations is their ready recourse to direct action techniques, such as picketing, rent strikes, demonstrations, sit-ins, and the like, but these direct action methods no longer guarantee certain results. Civil rightists, students, teachers, political activists of all hues, and many other groups have taken to the streets also to achieve their goals. Even the students and faculty of the art school at the local art museum in Chicago hit the streets with placards recently to air obscure differences with their patrons. But a half-dozen years ago these methods were profoundly disconcerting to the Establishment, helped to delineate issues, and guaranteed a wealth of publicity, which is an indispensable commodity for organizations of this sort. Now, however, an inflation in direct action has occurred. What fifty pickets could accomplish in front of City Hall now takes five hundred, and it still may not be effective. After two massive school boycotts and large-scale school demonstrations, smaller local organizations are hard put to find impressive means to register dissatisfaction with schools as easily as The Woodlawn Organization (TWO, the IAF's only Negro community organization) did with a partial boycott of a single school in 1962. Direct action against private individuals such as landlords continues to be effective.

A somewhat related characteristic is the use of conflict as organizational cement. The creation of conflict situations is quite openly espoused as the best means of gaining public attention, attracting adherents, and overcoming the existing apathy of the residents of lower-class communities. Scapegoats are carefully chosen for their availability and vulnerability, and causes for complaint chosen for ready comprehensibility, mass appeal, and potential for dramatic exploitation.

It follows, then, that organizations which depend primarily on a turnout of demonstrations, pickets, and other signs of irate mass support in order to expose, threaten to expose, or compel others to act require a continuous stance of militancy and righteous anger that can readily be directed at those who hesitate to comply. The rationale for this goes beyond the efficacy of coercion and compulsion. It is perhaps assumed that this stance of righteous anger attracts and holds certain kinds of people who seem to require more compelling and intensive involvement than they get by attending meetings and engaging in community problem-solving. A militant stance of this sort may also encourage the timid who have legitimate complaints and have suffered and been exploited to come forward and air their grievances. It is also assumed that aggression is a natural way for people who have been oppressed, mistreated, exploited, or neglected to respond to those who have misused them, and that this mode of organization will, therefore, overcome apathy and sustain participation among those who would not otherwise be willing to expend their energies on any social enterprise.

This activity may indeed be therapeutic, if by acting out and giving vent to their hostilities these deprived individuals and groups attain subsequently a more stable and realistic relationship to their institutional environment. However, unless there is accompanying change in their environment such activity may disrupt and further prevent the participants from making a new social adjustment. Any "therapy" must, above all, be realistic and honest at the same time that it raises aspiration and motivation—admittedly a difficult balance to achieve. It is yet to be proved that conflict organization is indeed therapeutic.

Finally, and perhaps most important of all, is what appears in these organizations to be an almost paranoid preoccupation with power. It follows, of course, that if one is to carry out successfully a strategy of conflict and to attempt to coerce and compel others, one has to move from a position of power. There is constant talk of "naked" power, even of "revolutionary" power, and every organizational move is designed primarily to enhance the power of the organization and its bargaining position. The argument is a clear and simple one, that the residents of low-income neighborhoods (most residents of the city for that matter, but particularly lower socioeconomic groups) suffer from a pervasive sense of powerlessness, which in large part accounts for civic apathy. This, in turn, accounts for the persistence of conditions that prevail in the slums of the large cities—bad housing, lack of medical care, delinquency, crime, drug addiction, segregation and discrimination, inadequate education, and related conditions associated with poverty.

There is also the assumption that the "power structure"—or to use the more all-embracing and currently popular term, "the Establishment" (which presumably includes all those who in some way gain, or think they do, from maintenance of the status quo)—opposes substantial social reform. Nor will the Establishment permit any concessions, it is maintained, except those that are forced by the exercise of power. The only recourse for the people is to establish "power-based mass organizations" designed to wrest concessions from the powers-that-be. This envisions a perpetual contest of the weak against the strong as the essence of democracy.

Some time ago, Alinsky addressed the annual meeting of the Association of Community Councils in Chicago. Among many provocative and challenging remarks were what he identified as three principles, or "propositions," that presumably contain the kernel of his thinking about community organization. Based on observations of his current actions and utterances, there seems to be no reason to assume that he has substantially altered his position during the last eight years.

> I would like to state my first proposition: *The first function of community organization is community disorganization.* Disorganization of the accepted circumstances and the status quo of the arrangements under which they live—these circumstances and arrangements must be disorganized if they are to be displaced with changing patterns, providing the opportunities and means for citizen participation. All change means disorganization of the old and organization of the new. . . .
>
> This brings us to the second proposition: *The character of the means or tools through which change can be effected must be clearly understood by the people at all times—it is power through organization.* . . . No individual or organization can negotiate without the power to compel negotiation. . . . This in essence is the function of the community organizer. Anything otherwise is wishful non-thinking. To attempt to operate on good will rather than on a power basis would be to attempt something which the world has not yet experienced.
>
> This brings us to our third proposition: *Prevailing arrangements, or power patterns, can only be altered by power.* Here it is important that we pause and examine the words which are being used in this discussion. This is a prime issue if we are to achieve any understanding of points of view. It was obvious earlier in this presentation that such terms as "agitation," "to rub raw the resentments," "to stir up dissatisfaction and discontent," "create conflict"—that these were harsh words, grating and jarring on many ears, which prefer phrases such as "stimulating citizen participation." This is a critical point where our tongues trap our minds.[4]

Appeal to the clergy

Such hard-hitting, off-the-cuff remarks, coupled with a gift for polemics, have endeared Alinsky to the urban clergy.[5] This is exciting stuff, heady talk—phrases such as "naked power," "revolution," "guerilla warfare" are bandied about freely. The impression is given by Alinsky and his workers that "gut" issues are being dealt with, that the participants are at last coming to grips with some of the central social issues of our times. Here finally is the relevant church, the meaningful mission! At long last in the smoke-filled room of the storefront organizational headquarters, exciting, behind-the-scenes decisions are made and political manipulations managed. At last the young clergy are in the thick of battle, exerting their influence on the course of events. At mass meetings the pastors on the platform give public evidence of their commitment to the cause. In the conflict atmosphere of Alinsky's organizations they can give full vent to their sense of frustration over the church's failure in the past to provide adequate leadership to the social movements of the day.

One may well speculate why these noisy and seemingly radical activities in the inner-city have not attracted more attention from the conservative sectors of the sponsoring churches, and why some strong counteraction has not developed within church circles. The communication gap between the city and the suburbs may be just another measure of the alienation in our society, what William Wheaton referred to as the "two cultures"—the affluent and the deprived.[6] It may be that many of the suburban laity are unaware of what is going on in the inner-city, and feel so remote that they do not even care. However, the suburban clergy cannot be wholly unaware.

Curiously enough, there also may be a certain kind of quiet satisfaction in the suburbs in the fact that the target of much of the protest and the challenge of these militant organizations is City Hall. Even though, as in Chicago, big business has by and large made its peace, at least temporarily, with the Democratic political machine, there is widespread contempt and distaste in the suburbs for the machine politics of the inner-city, which is associated with sin, graft, corruption, crime, and squalor. Viewed in this light, these new community organizations may in some respects be the successors to the middle-class civic reform movements, whose supporters are now commuters rather than voters in the city. There may well be a tacit agreement to let the political pot boil and even encourage the gadflies. But though they may be annoying to the Democratic office holders and city administrators, there is little evidence of the building of an effective political structure—in Chicago at any rate—that can challenge the machine in the near future.

One of the young analysts from the New Left has described these organizations as devoid of ideology and maintains that the claims to radicalism and all the "revolutionary" talk simply satisfy some angry people but fail to come to grips with basic issues.

> Alinsky is an independent operator who gets his money from private institutions, particularly the Catholic and Presbyterian churches. Alinsky eschews ideology and program, seeking only to develop lower-class protest movements which he has faith will evolve their own program (as if in some mystical way lower-class people will gain the technical and ideological means to fathom the larger implications of specific city policies which currently affect them). But despite his contempt for official agencies, Alinsky remains an organizer from the top. . . .
>
> Despite the fact that he employs mass power to win limited objectives, Alinsky seems to have no over-all philosophy of political power, nor does he espouse the need for alternative politics to achieve broader social change. . . .
>
> He is true to the American pragmatic tradition which exalts action and denies the practical value of theory. With these perspectives, Alinsky-organized movements are bound to lead to frustration because they cannot transcend the immediate object of oppression toward an understanding of the larger economic and political forces which lie behind the grievance.[7]

Arthur Hillman, a long-time observer of the IAF, suggests a parallel with the Goldwater movement—"protest without a program." [8] Perhaps what is in the making is a potential conservative alliance against the so-called liberal establishment.

Evaluating the Chicago experience

Making any objective evaluation of the success of these organizations is difficult. What are to be the criteria for measurement? If success is to be rated by high visibility, local notoriety, nationwide newspaper and periodical coverage, reluctant attention paid by local officials, and respectful attention by federal officials and congressmen, then these organizations, particularly The Woodlawn Organization (TWO), have been very successful.

Without any doubt the hostile and aggressive stance of the organization stalled for three years the expansion of the University of Chicago through the use of urban renewal legislation and dissuaded the city from attempting to develop the large-scale federally financed anti-juvenile delinquency program in the neighborhood that was later unsuccessfully begun on the Near North Side. If one regards urban renewal as "Negro removal," and if one considers "welfare colonialism" to be a major threat, then these results can be viewed as positives rather than negatives.

Another criterion of success might be the successful involvement of people and the development of leadership. This, too, is difficult to assess because there are many levels and qualities of "involvement." The value and significance of involvement must be defined in terms of purposes and results. TWO can turn out several hundred or more people for large public meetings occasionally, and probably attains a higher level of continuous participation than most other organizations of this kind. Anyone who has worked in such communities knows how difficult it is to keep participation at a high level. Thus, because of their high visibility, both inside and outside the community, IAF organizations in Chicago and especially TWO can be considered quite successful.

However, the claim to have reached the most deprived segment of the community would be most difficult to support. [9] To what extent the large mass of residents really feel represented, are even aware of or affected by the existence and activities of these organizations is moot and could only be assessed, if at all, with an elaborate research effort. Only then could claims for the therapeutic effect of conflict organization be judged.

These church-sponsored organizations have introduced a number of persons into political and city-wide prominence but they have not become city-wide leaders. Organizational preoccupation with local self-interest and hostility toward city-wide institutions severely limits their municipal leadership potential while continuing the behind-the-scenes control more suggestive of leadership management than leadership development.

But to refer to these organizational activities in Chicago as "community development" programs, as many of their supporters have done, raises serious questions.[10] Community development, particularly as practiced in the developing countries overseas, has been judged by some critics to be one of the most significant social inventions of our time. A cherished objective of community workers has been to find out whether these methods and techniques can be adapted to conditions in industrialized Western countries.

The criteria for community development have become fairly well established in the literature.[11] The most important component is, of course, significant involvement and local direction at the grass roots. As has often been noted, however, there is another and equally important criterion for such programs—they must be more than mere local bootstrap self-help operations. They must be carried on in the context of over-all national—or, at the very least, regional—social planning, with the economic, social, and political developmental goals spelled out and clearly understood at all levels. This is not just an academic or doctrinaire distinction. It may actually determine the difference between solid accomplishment and mere organizational thrashing about. There is some evidence of the latter in Chicago.

It is perhaps understandable, because of church sponsorship, that the activities of these four organizations in Chicago have tended to be somewhat parochial. Instead of finding ways to relate themselves effectively to governmental or even to large voluntary planning units, they have in most instances adopted an aggressively hostile and even contemptuous stance toward them, making cooperation in planning extremely difficult, if not impossible.

In this connection one additional aspect of the TWO program should perhaps be mentioned. It was, of course, the neighboring University of Chicago that bore the full brunt of aggressively hostile, organizational attention at the outset. The University, as an awkward Leviathan playing its role in urban renewal and institutional expansion, was chosen as the organizational scapegoat—a characteristic technique of IAF organizations. "If you could bite the University so it would howl, if it would deign to take angry notice of you, then you had it made," is the colorful way one organizer put it.

With a demonstration of forbearance, a group of the University faculty explored, negotiated with TWO, and finally persuaded the United States Department of Labor, through the federal manpower program, to give a substantial demonstration manpower training grant to the organization.[12] Although there is a research and evaluation provision in the grant, results of the project are not yet available at this writing. Preliminary information available to the writers indicates that the project results rank above average among similar training experiments. The existence of this project and similar concessions suggests improved relations with the University of Chicago in the future. However, sensitive public officials may not be so forgiving, especially if they have been bitterly, and in part unfairly, attacked on both local and national platforms.

Social work and social change

It would be unwise for the profession to dismiss these organizational activities as emanations of a disaffection and frustration, or to assume that the movement will soon dissipate itself. The serious intentions of leaders in high church circles are unquestionable, and the strength and potency of this movement and its enduring effects should not be underestimated.

> Church leadership, clerical and lay, needs to be trained in new and radical methods of initiating action and in guiding low status groups based on developing indigenous leadership; helping people identify their own concerns; developing mutual associations varied in form to help people help themselves; and encouraging participation in the larger community.[13]

Many social workers could also subscribe wholeheartedly to this statement, but to what extent can the social work profession demonstrate that it has of late been devoting major resources to effect large-scale social change in lower-class communities? To what extent has social work been receptive to radical ideas, much less to actively developing radical new methods? In recent years the profession has not been notably successful in helping and guiding low status groups. As one of the authors noted last year:

> We are obviously at our weakest when facing the need for basic changes in the societal system in lower-class communities. Numerous efforts to apply the same time-tested techniques in such situations have been notably less than successful. Obviously some differential approaches are in order.[14]

It becomes increasingly evident that not only are new approaches required, but also a new commitment, a rededication to some of the basic purposes and values of social work.

As Bremner has pointed out, social work had its roots in and drew its earliest inspiration from organized religion. In many respects religion and social work have maintained these connections over the years, although estrangements and tensions have occurred from time to time, some serious and some not so serious. Social work gained its original impetus, not from the churches as a whole, but from movements within the church designed, as Bremner quotes, to counteract

> the tendency of organized Protestantism to seek "comfort and ease in the society of the rich." He [the Reverend Rainsford] charged that as a result of indifference to the urban working class, the Protestant churches had lost the initiative in the years between 1830 and 1890.[15]

This is not unlike many of the complaints and warnings being sounded by some of the clergy today.

It must also be recognized, however, that any new cooperation with the churches cannot be based on nineteenth-century concepts of charity and service to the poor. They must be compatible with bold desires to change conditions that produce poverty and deprivation in the urban slums.

While the government—a secular force—is now, and will increasingly become, the major protagonist with which the social work profession must deal, organized religion will continue to have a stake in social affairs. They are potential allies. This objective might help to reduce the distance between the staid stance of social workers and the much more socially and politically involved role of the clergy.

The institutionalization and the transformation of the civil rights movement into more political channels will create problems for both social workers and churchmen as they accommodate themselves more to changing institutions and less to changing hearts of men caught up in active social movements. They may then be able and willing to join together again to intercede for the weak and forgotten individuals who are unable to keep up with the swift current of social forces, and to break down antiquated barriers that freed those forces.

NOTES

1. Robert Christ, "The Local Church in a Community Organization" (New York: Board of National Missions, United Presbyterian Church in the U.S.A., 1965; mimeographed), pp. 10 and 14.
2. For more extended discussion of the churches and their role in community organization in urban areas, see *The City Church*, XIV No. 4 (September–October, 1963), which is devoted to church social action and community organization in Chicago; Colin W. Williams, *Where in the World* (New York: National Council of Churches, 1963), Ch. 4; Gayraud S. Wilmore, *The Secular Relevance of the Church* (Philadelphia: Westminster Press, 1962), Ch. 4; Lyle E. Schaller, *Conflict, Reconciliation and Community Organization,* manuscript in preparation, 1965; Dan W. Dodson, "Power as a Dimension of Education," *Journal of Educational Sociology,* XXXV, No. 5 (November, 1961), 203–215; Wayne A. R. Leys, "Machiavelli in Modern Dress," *Christian Century,* LXXVI, No. 45 (November, 1959), pp. 1308–1309; Editorial, "Justice and Beyond Justice," *Christian Century,* LXXXII, No. 8 (February, 1965). *Social Action,* XXXI, No. 6 (February, 1965), entitled "Strategy for Community Change," is a full issue devoted to community organization in relation to the churches, with articles by Robert N. Davidson, William Biddle, and Dan W. Dodson.
3. For discussion of the IAF and its method by the staff and various observers and critics, both pro and con, see Saul D. Alinsky, *Reveille for Radicals* (Chicago: University of Chicago Press, 1945); Alinsky, "The Urban Immigrant," in T. T. McAvoy (ed.), *Roman Catholicsm and the American Way of Life* (Notre Dame, Ind.: University of Notre Dame Press, 1960); Alinsky, "Citizen Participation and Community Organization in Planning and Urban Renewal," address to National Association of Housing and Redevelopment Officials (Chicago, January 1962); Nicholas von Hoffman, "Reorganization in the Casbah," *Social Progress,* LII, No. 6 (April, 1962); V. B. Blakely and C. T. Leber, Jr., "Woodlawn Begins to Flex Its Muscles," *Presbyterian Life* (September 15, 1962), pp. 12–15, 41–42; Charles E. Silberman, *Crisis in Black and White* (New York: Random House, 1964), Ch. 10 (this is essentially the same as "Up from Apathy—The Woodlawn Experiment," *Commentary,* XXXVII, No. 5 [May, 1964]); Stephen C. Rose, "Saul Alinsky and His Critics," *Christianity and Crisis* (July 20, 1964). See in *Christian Century:* Editorials in the issues of May 12 and June 7, 1961, July 18 and August 22, 1962; E. C. Parker, "How Chelsea Was Torn Apart" (February 3, 1960), p. 130; Letters to Editor, February 12 and April 7, 1965. See also Walter Kloetzli, *The Church and the Urban Challenge* (Philadelphia:

Muhlenberg Press, 1961), Ch. 4; Harold E. Fey, "The Industrial Areas Foundation: An Interpretation" (Chicago: National Lutheran Council, 1964; mimeographed); Philip Hauser, "Conflict vs. Consensus," *Chicago Sun-Times,* December 13, 1964, Sect. II, pp. 1–3.

4. Saul Alinsky, "From Citizen Apathy to Participation." Paper presented at the Association of Community Councils of Chicago, October 1957, pp. 4 and 6. (Mimeographed.)

5. See, for instance, Dolores McCahill, "Controversy Necessary Ministers Told," *Chicago Sun-Times,* September 29, 1964.

6. William L. C. Wheaton, "The Two Cultures and the Urban Revolution." Paper presented at the National Conference on Urban Life (Washington, D.C., March, 1962, mimeographed.)

7. Stanley Aronovitz, "Poverty, Politics and Community Organization," *Studies on the Left,* IV, No. 3 (Summer 1964), 104.

8. Arthur Hillman. Memorandum, January 15, 1965, and Letters to Editor, December 28, 1964. See also Alvin L. Schorr, "The New Radicals Manqués," *Social Work,* IX, No. 4 (October, 1964), 113.

9. To refer to these as "mass organizations," as is constantly done by IAF supporters, is an exaggeration. Nicholas von Hoffman, the principal organizer in Woodlawn for the IAF, wrote recently, after he had left the organization: "It is an organization of perhaps two per cent of the people. Those who talk about organizing 'all the people,' or 'the masses,' or 'the great majority of the people,' are talking unrealizable balderdash." "Finding and Making Leaders" (Ann Arbor, Mich.: Students for Democratic Society, 1964), p. 9.

10. John C. Bennett, "The Church and Power Conflicts," *Christianity and Crisis,* (March 22, 1965).

11. For example, see Lloyd Ohlin, "Urban Community Development," paper presented at the Conference on Socially Handicapped Families, UNESCO (Paris, February, 1964, mimeographed) pp. 15 and 16; Arthur Dunham, "Some Principles of Community Development," *International Review of Community Development,* No. 11 (Columbia: Department of Community Development, University of Missouri, 1963); Thomas D. Sherrard, "Community Organization and Community Development, Similarities and Differences," *The Report of the United States Committee to the Eleventh International Conference of Social Work, 1962* (reprinted in *Community Development Review,* AID, Department of State, 1962).

12. It should be noted that the manpower program was financed through a direct contract with the federal government and that local officials had no part in its negotiation. The writers have the distinct impression that even state officials were either carefully neutral or very cool to the whole idea.

13. "The Churches and Persistent Pockets of Poverty in the U.S.A.," *Town and Country Church* (1963). Report of a Joint Consultation of the Division of Home Missions and the Division of Christian Life and Work (National Council of Churches, January, 1962).

14. Thomas D. Sherrard, "Planned Community Change," *Social Welfare Forum* (New York: Columbia University Press, 1964), pp. 107–109.

15. Robert H. Bremner, *From the Depths* (New York: New York University Press, 1964), p. 57.

14

Planning and Politics: Citizen Participation in Urban Renewal

JAMES Q. WILSON

Few national programs affecting our cities have begun under such favorable auspices as urban renewal. Although public housing was from the very first a bitterly controversial policy, redevelopment and renewal by contrast were widely accepted by both Democratic and Republican administrations and had the backing of both liberals and conservatives, labor and business, planners and mayors. Yet today, almost fourteen years after urban redevelopment was inaugurated as Title I of the Housing Act of 1949, the program is beset with controversy and, what is even more dismaying to its supporters, lagging far behind its construction goals.

Although there are nearly 944 federally approved slum clearance and urban renewal projects scheduled for over 520 different communities, only a little more than half have proceeded to the point where the cities are authorized to begin assembling and clearing land. And most important, of all the projects authorized, only 65 have been completed.[1] In New York, the city which has been the most active in renewal programs of all kinds, all the publicly supported projects undertaken over the last quarter-century cover less than 1 per cent of the city's surface.[2] Further, most of the projects completed can be found in or near the central business districts of cities rather than in residential areas, and they have often involved clearing, not slums, but deteriorating commercial and industrial structures.

Some of the reasons for the relatively slight accomplishments of urban renewal are not hard to find. Federally sponsored projects such as renewal require dealing successfully with almost endless amounts of red tape; it has taken a long time for city governments and private developers to acquire the knowledge and experience required for this. Furthermore, even though the federal government pays most of the cost of assembling and clearing the land in which a project is planned, it is not always easy to find a private developer to whom the land can be sold.

An additional reason for slow progress in urban renewal is racial. Blighted areas are often Negro areas. The political and social problems involved in relocating Negroes in other areas of the city are often sufficiently formidable to make opposition to the renewal program as a whole very powerful.

From *Journal of the American Institute of Planners*, XXIX (November, 1963), 242–249.

But the most important reason for controversy and slow progress is the mounting disagreement over the methods and even the objectives of urban renewal. The coalition among liberals, planners, mayors, businessmen, and real estate interests which originally made renewal politically so irresistible has begun to fall apart. Liberals, who still see the rehabilitation of the central city as a prime goal for government, have begun to have doubts, particularly about redevelopment that involves wholesale clearance by bulldozers. They are disturbed by charges from many Negro leaders—whom liberals are accustomed to regard as their natural allies—that liberals have aided and abetted a program which under the guise of slum clearance is really a program of Negro clearance. They have been disturbed and even angered by the elimination of whole neighborhoods, like the Italian West End of Boston; by the reduction in the supply of low-cost housing to make way for high-cost housing built with federal subsidies; and by what they take to be the inhuman, insensitive, and unrealistic designs of some city planners. Jane Jacob's book, *The Death and Life of Great American Cities,* is expressive of one powerful segment of opinion in this regard.[3] The liberals are everywhere demanding that redevelopment (that is, wholesale clearance) be abandoned in favor of rehabilitation—conserving as many existing structures as possible.

Mayors and other city officials in some cities (although not yet in all) have seen in these debates a sign that a program which began as "good politics" has turned into something which at best is difficult politics. When it seemed possible that a vigorous and ambitious mayor could place himself at the head of an alliance of liberals, planners, businessmen, and newspapers on behalf of restoring the central city, urban renewal became a top-priority civic objective. An initial burst of enthusiasm greeted renewal in almost every city where the idea was broached. But after the first few projects were undertaken, the hidden political costs began to become evident. Voters who did not like being called slum-dwellers and who liked even less being forced out of their old neighborhoods began to complain. As the enthusiasm of the civic boosters began to wane, many mayors began to wonder whether they were going to be left alone on the firing line to answer for projects which the boosters had pushed them into in the first place.

What in many ways is the most interesting aspect of the controversy surrounding urban renewal is not the breakup of this coalition, however, but the growing resistance of neighborhoods to clearance and renewal programs. The growth of neighborhood resistance to urban renewal has been gradual and cumulative. Many of the earliest redevelopment projects were completed with little organized opposition. Somehow, however, people have learned from the experience of others, and today, in cities which have been engaged in renewal for several years, the planners often find prospective renewal areas ready and waiting for them, organized to the teeth. In Chicago, for example, the Lake Meadows redevelopment project met with relatively little organized indigenous opposition (although considerable opposition from forces outside the area). The Hyde Park–Kenwood project, undertaken a few years later, was greeted with considerably more opposition. Today, plans for the Woodlawn and Near West Side areas have been met with impassioned opposition from many of the residents of the neighborhoods involved. Similarly, the West End project in Boston had relatively little difficulty in dealing with people in the area; the project planned for Charlestown, begun some time later, has been—at least for the time being—stopped dead in its tracks by organized neighborhood opposition. Today, according to Robert C. Weaver, Administrator of the Housing and Home Finance Agency, "in nearly every major city in the country and many small cities there are heated debates over urban renewal projects that are under way or under consideration." [4]

Mr. Weaver might well be concerned over these debates, for federal policy requires local citizen participation in the formulation of local renewal plans before federal money can be spent on them. As he himself stressed on another occasion, "We mean [by citizen participation] not just a passive acceptance of what is being done, but the active utilization of local leadership and organization which can profitably assist in the community's efforts." [5]

Local citizen participation on a city-wide basis is usually not difficult to obtain. "Civic leaders" representing various groups and interests in the community can always be assembled for such purposes. But getting the participation, much less the acquiescence, of citizens in the renewal neighborhood is something else again. Although federal law does not require participation at this level, the increased vigor of neighborhood opposition has made such participation expedient if not essential—particularly with the new emphasis on rehabilitation and self-help.

The Hyde Park–Kenwood experience

The fullest account we have of such participation is that found in the book, *The Politics of Urban Renewal,* by Peter H. Rossi and Robert A. Dentler. This study dealt with one neighborhood—Hyde Park–Kenwood in Chicago—which in many ways is remarkable if not unique. The site of the University of Chicago, it is heavily populated with University professors and business and professional people, all possessing an inordinate amount of education, experience, and skills, and all having a strong commitment to the community. From 1949 on, these people were organized into the Hyde Park–Kenwood Community Conference, a neighborhood group with a professional staff, dedicated to conserving the area against blight. Actual planning for the area was not, of course, done by this organization—that was beyond its resources—but by the planning staff of the University of Chicago and by various city agencies.

The Community Conference took a deep and continuing interest in the $30,000,000 urban renewal plan for the area and meticulously examined and discussed every part of it. Local and federal authorities judged the Conference to be an excellent example of genuine grass roots participation in a major renewal effort. After the plan was finally approved by the Chicago City Council, it commanded widespread (although not unanimous) citizen acceptance, even though about 20 per cent of the buildings in the community were to be torn down.

In evaluating the work of this local citizens group, Rossi and Dentler conclude that the Hyde Park–Kenwood Community Conference played two important roles. First, it stimulated public awareness of the necessity and practicability of change and gave people confidence that something could be done to save their neighborhood. Second, the Conference managed to create a climate of opinion in which the actual planning was done, and, although it is impossible to tell exactly what impact this climate had on the planners, it is likely that the general mood of the community as articulated by the neighborhood organization influenced at least the most general goals that were embodied in the final plan.

But it is also important to note what the Conference did not do. According to this study, the organization did not play a crucial part in influencing the specific details of the plan. Instead, it created broad popular acceptance for a plan which was not entirely in keeping with it own objectives. Rossi and Dentler conclude that the "maximum role to be played by a citizen-participation movement in urban renewal is primarily a passive one." [6]

Considering what I have said about the rising opposition of local neighborhoods to urban renewal, the acquiescence of this grass-roots organization seems to require explanation. In the narrowest terms, this support was due to the fact that the Hyde Park–Kenwood Community Conference represented that part of a very heterogeneous community which would ultimately benefit from renewal. The upper-middle-class professors, housewives, and business and professional men (both white and Negro) that made up the bulk of the Conference were mostly people who were going to remain in the community and whose peace, security, cultural life, and property values would probably be enhanced by a successful renewal plan. The persons who were to be moved out of the community and whose apartments and homes were to be torn down were usually lower-income Negroes who, with very few exceptions, were not part of the Community Conference.

But this narrow explanation in terms of self-interest is only partly true, for if low-income Negroes were not directly represented on the Conference they were often represented vicariously—at least in the eyes of the Conference members. Time and again the Conference, or leading members of it, pressed the city to provide middle- and low-income public housing in the renewal area in part to accommodate persons who would be displaced by demolition. The Conference was firmly committed to the idea of a multiracial community; some of its members were committed in addition to the idea of a multiclass community.

I would argue that this broader consideration was equally as important as the narrower one in explaining the positive and constructive role of the Conference. The organization was made up to a large degree of persons who attached a high value to community-wide and neighborhood-wide goals, even (in some cases) when attaining those goals entailed a sacrifice in personal, material satisfactions. They are people who partake to an extraordinary extent of what Edward C. Banfield and I have called the "community-regarding" or "public-regarding" political ethos.[7] This ethos, which is most likely to be found among citizens who rank high in income, education, or both, is based on an enlarged view of the community and a sense of obligation toward it. People who display it are likely to have a propensity for looking at and making policy for the community "as a whole" and to have a high sense of personal efficacy, a long time-perspective, a general familiarity with and confidence in city-wide institutions, and a cosmopolitan orientation toward life. In addition, they are likely to possess a disproportionate share of organizational skills and resources.

It is just these attributes, of course, which make such people most likely to participate effectively in organizations whose function—whatever their ostensible purpose—is to create a sense of community and of community confidence and to win consent for community-wide plans. They are, in short, precisely those attributes which are likely to produce "citizen participation in urban renewal" that planners and community organizers will consider "positive and constructive"—this is, participation which will influence some of the general goals of renewal and modify a few of its details, but allow renewal to proceed.

Social differences in citizen participation

Most neighborhoods which planners consider in need of renewal are not, however, like Hyde Park–Kenwood in Chicago and are not heavily populated with citizens like the ones who organized the Hyde Park–Kenwood Community Conference. Most renewal areas are likely to be low-income, often Negro sections, many of whose inhabitants are the opposite in almost every respect from the cosmopolitan elite of Hyde Park–Kenwood. Such people are more likely to have a limited time-perspective, a greater difficulty in abstracting from concrete experience, an unfamiliarity with and lack of confidence in city-wide institutions, a preoccupation with the personal and the immediate, and few (if any) attachments to organizations of any kind, with the possible exception of churches.[8] Lacking experience in and the skills for participation in organized endeavors, they are likely to have a low sense of personal efficacy in organizational situations. By necessity as well as by inclination, such people are likely to have what one might call a "private-regarding" rather than a "public-regarding" political ethos. They are intimately bound up in the day-to-day struggle to sustain themselves and their families.

Such people are usually the objects rather than the subjects of civic action: they are acted upon by others, but rarely do they themselves initiate action. As a result, they often develop a keen sense of the difference between "we" and "they"—"they" being outside, city-wide civic and political forces which seek to police them, vote them, and redevelop them. It is quite natural that the "they" are often regarded with suspicion.

Although such people are not likely spontaneously to form organizations to define and carry out long-range very general civic tasks, it is wrong to assume that they are not likely to organize—or to allow themselves to be organized—for any purpose. The important thing is not that they are unorganizable, but that they can be organized only under special circumstances and for special purposes. Except for organizations which are in some sense extensions of the family and the church, lower-income neighborhoods are more likely to produce collective action in response to threats (real or imagined) than to create opportunities. Because of the private-regarding nature of their attachment to the community, they are likely to collaborate when each person can see a danger to him or to his family in some proposed change; collective action is a way, not of defining and implementing some broad program for the benefit of all, but of giving force to individual objections by adding them together in a collective protest.

The view which a neighborhood is likely to take of urban renewal, then, is in great part a product of its class composition. Upper- and upper-middle-class people are more likely to think in terms of general plans, the neighborhood or community as a whole, and long-term benefits (even when they might involve immediate costs to themselves); lower- and lower-middle-class people are more likely to see such matters in terms of specific threats and short-term costs. These differences account in great measure for some of the frustrations of the planners, redevelopers, and community organizers who are involved in urban renewal. Whereas it is relatively easy to obtain consent to renewal plans when people are thinking in terms of general goals and community-wide benefits, it is much harder—often impossible—when people see the same set of facts in terms of possible threats and costs.

This interpretation of lower-class behavior applies in its full force only in the extreme case, of course. There are many stable working-class neighborhoods where indigenous leadership can be developed and involved in urban renewal programs on a "constructive" basis. The Back-of-the-Yards area of Chicago is an example of one neighborhood of blue-collar families with strong local leadership. But many potential renewal areas, particularly in Negro sections, do not even qualify as "stable working class." Half of all urban Negro families had an income of less than $3,000 a year in 1960. Thus, although the contrast I draw between middle-class and lower-class with respect to their attachment to neighborhood and community is deliberately extreme, it must be remembered that urban renewal is a policy intended in great part to apply to "extreme" areas.

Community organization strategies

Among community organizers, two radically different strategies have been evolved to produce citizen participation under such circumstances. One recognizes the special character of depressed lower-income neighborhoods and seeks to capitalize on it. The most prominent and controversial exponent of this approach is Saul D. Alinsky, executive director of the Industrial Areas Foundation of Chicago. He has created in a lower-income, heavily Negro area near the University of Chicago an organization (The Woodlawn Organization) built in large part upon the residents' fears of urban renewal. According to a recent account, "Alinsky eschews the usual appeals to homeowners' interests in conserving property values or to a general neighborhood spirit or civic pride—appeals, in his view, that apply only to middle-class neighborhoods." Instead, he "appeals to the self-interest of the local residents and to their resentment and distrust of the outside world." [9] If residents do not have what I have called a "public-regarding" ethos, Alinsky is perfectly willing to appeal to their "private-regarding" ethos and to capitalize on the fact that collective action among such people is possible only when each person fears some threat to his own interests.

By stimulating and focussing such fears, an organization is created which can then compel other organizations—such as the sponsors of an urban renewal project—to bargain with it. Often the only terms on which such negotiations are acceptable to the neighborhood organization are terms unacceptable to the sponsors of renewal, for they require the drastic modification or even abandonment of the renewal plan. When an organization is built out of accumulated fears and grievances rather than out of community attachments, the cost is usually the tearing up of any plans that call for really fundamental changes in the landscape. On the other hand, such an organization may be very effective in winning special concessions from City Hall to remedy specific neighborhood problems.

Many, probably most, planners and community organization specialists reject Alinsky's tactics. To them, his methods produce and even exacerbate conflict rather than prevent it, alienate the neighborhood from the city as a whole rather than bring it into the normal pattern of civic action, and place a premium on power rather than on a cooperative search for the common good.

The alternative strategy of most community organizers is to stimulate the creation of neighborhood organizations which will define "positive" goals for their areas in collaboration with the relevant city agencies and in accord with the time schedule which binds most renewal efforts. In Boston, for example, efforts have been made to stimulate the formation of neighborhood associations which will provide citizen participation in (and citizen consent to) the plans of the Boston Redevelopment Authority (BRA). So far this strategy has had some success, but only in those areas where rehabilitation rather than clearance is to be the principal renewal tactic. In one Negro area, Washington Park–Roxbury, a middle-class Negro organization was given a BRA contract to help organize the neighborhood to discuss renewal plans calling for rehabilitation, spot clearance, and the construction of some lower-middle-income housing. The plans were approved. In Charlestown, an old Irish neighborhood, the original proposals of the BRA were rejected by a citizens' organization created by Action for Boston Community Development (ABCD), a city-wide welfare agency financed in part by the Ford Foundation. The BRA decided to modify the plans and dispense with the services of ABCD; the final plan, developed after protracted discussions between BRA planners and Charlestown residents, emphasized rehabilitation and was approved. In a third area, North Harvard–Allston, the BRA decided to rely on wholesale clearance and redevelopment; there, no effort was made to obtain citizen participation and the plan was approved by the city council without the consent of the neighborhood.

Implications for renewal programs

If one's goal is urban renewal on any really large scale in our cities, the implications of these observations are disturbing. The higher the level of indigenous organization in a lower-class neighborhood, the poorer the prospects for renewal in that area.

To say that the prospects are poorer does not, of course, mean that renewal will never occur with the consent of strong indigenous organizations in lower-class areas. But the difficulty is substantially increased, and a protracted, subtle, and assiduous wooing of neighborhood sentiment must first take place.[10] Perhaps this explains why, at least until very recently, most local urban renewal directors made no effort to encourage citizen participation except on a city-wide basis—with little or no representation from the affected neighborhood.[11]

In short, while the devotion of some planners today to the concept of "planning with people"—that is, citizen participation in neighborhood rehabilitation—may be an improvement over old-style urban redevelopment which ignored or took little account of neighborhood interests, the enthusiasm with which the new doctrine is being advocated blurs many important problems. The most important of these is that "planning with people" assumes on the part of the people involved a willingness and a capacity to engage in a collaborative search for the common good. The willingness is obviously almost never present when the persons involved will be severely penalized by having their homes and neighborhoods destroyed through wholesale clearance. Nor will that willingness be present when "rehabilitation" means, as it sometimes does, that the residents must at their own expense bring their homes up to standards deemed satisfactory to the renewal agency or have their homes taken from them. But what is less obvious is that it may not be present, even when such clearance is not envisaged, because of important class differences in the capacity to organize for community-wide goals. This means that middle-class persons who are beneficiaries of rehabilitation will be planned with; lower-class persons who are disadvantaged by rehabilitation are likely to be planned *without*.

The fact that some people will be hurt by renewal does not, of course, mean that there should be no renewal. There are scarcely any public policies which do not impose costs on someone. What it does mean is that planners might more frankly take such costs into account, weighing them against the benefits renewal may confer on individuals and the community. There is little except obfuscation to be gained from attempting to maintain, as the slogan "planning with people" implies, that urban renewal and perfect democracy are and always should be compatible; that not only can the city be revitalized, it can be revitalized with the consent of all concerned.

If we decide to try to obtain the consent of those neighborhoods selected for renewal, we had better prepare ourselves for a drastic re-evaluation of the potential impact of that program. Adjusting the goals of renewal to the demands of the lower classes means, among other things, substantially reducing the prospects for assembling sufficiently large tracts of cleared land to make feasible the construction of dwelling units attractive to the middle-class suburbanite whom the city is anxious to woo back into its taxing jurisdiction. This, in turn, means that the central city may have to abandon the goal of recolonizing itself with a tax-paying, culture-loving, free-spending middle class and be content instead with serving as a slightly dilapidated way-station in which lower-income and minority groups find shelter and a minimal level of public services while working toward the day when they, too, can move out to a better life. That, of course, is in great part the function that at least the older central cities of this country have always performed, and until we run out of lower classes (a day unfortunately far in the future), that may be the function they must continue to perform.

Political effects

Not only does the question of citizen participation in urban renewal have important implications for the goals of planning and even for one's conception of the function of the central city; it also goes to the heart of a fundamental problem in the urban political process. Resolving this issue is not simply a problem in planning priorities, but in addition a problem in electoral politics.

American mayors today are faced with the problem of governing cities in which to a great extent the traditional sources of political power have been dispersed or eliminated. The old-style political machine is gone except in a very few big cities. Party organization generally is weak. Mayors must still assemble the power to govern but they can rarely do so today by relying on loyal party lieutenants who occupy the lesser city offices and who sit on the council. Instead, the mayor must try to piece together that power out of the support he can receive from city-wide interests, such as newspapers, civic associations, business organizations, and labor unions. Support from such sources, valuable as it is, does not always carry with it the assurance that the support of the rank-and-file voter will also be forthcoming. Average citizens have a way of not sharing (or sometimes not even knowing about) the enthusiasms of the top civic leadership.

To insure against this possibility, many "new-style" mayors are trying to build up new neighborhood associations and enter into relationships with old ones in order to provide themselves with a way of reaching the average voter and of commanding his support. In Boston, for example, it is an open secret that Mayor John Collins is hoping that the support and attention he has given various neighborhood associations will be reciprocated, on election day, by the support of their members for him.

To the extent that these neighborhood associations are courted by mayors, they attempt to extract in return concessions on matters of city policy (such as street sweeping, garbage collection, or playground maintenance) which affect their areas. They see themselves as instruments for adapting the programs of an impersonal city bureaucracy to the various and often conflicting needs of neighborhoods. In a sense, they perform (for entirely different reasons, of course) the same function which the political machine once performed.

The neighborhood civic association is widely regarded as not only a new mechanism for representing citizen wants to the city bureaucracy, but a means of ending the political "alienation" of those citizens. Much has been written of late to suggest that a large and perhaps growing number of people are "alienated" from the American political process, but particularly from the political process in their communities. In Boston,[12] Cambridge,[13] Detroit,[14] Nashville,[15] upstate New York,[16] and various other places where studies have been made, the voters—usually (though not always) those with little income or education—feel, we are told, estranged from and even threatened by the political life of their cities. To the extent that this alienation exists (and the studies are not very precise on this), the neighborhood civic association is seen as an important way of giving the citizen a meaningful and satisfactory relationship with his community—a way, in short, of ending his "alienation."[17]

It is not yet clear, however, whether such neighborhood groups will provide a means whereby citizens overcome their "alienation" or whether they will simply provide a forum in which citizens can give expression to it. These groups, after all, are usually concerned about neighborhood, not city-wide, problems, and the member's attachment is often at most only to his immediate family and neighbors, not to the community as a whole. Neighborhood associations seek many goals in their dealings with City Hall. Generally speaking, however, they want higher levels of community services but they oppose extensive physical changes in their areas, as would be caused by highway construction or urban renewal programs.

For city-wide officials, such as mayors and planners, the crucial problem is how to make attention to these neighborhood demands compatible with city-wide programs, almost all of which will, to some extent, impose hardships on some neighborhoods. The old-style political leaders who were bosses of city machines were not faced to the same degree with this problem. Whenever they could, they avoided the conflict between neighborhood and city by not proposing any extensive programs designed to appeal to city-wide interests. When such programs were politically unavoidable, they resolved the inevitable conflict by "buying off" their neighborhood opponents. The bosses used the jobs, favors, and patronage which they controlled to enforce their wills on neighborhood political leaders and to compensate the neighborhood voters for their distress.

Today's mayor can neither avoid proposing large programs to satisfy city-wide interests nor can he buy off the neighborhood opponents of such projects. Under these circumstances, the mayor must move cautiously between the twin evils of doing so little as to disappoint community-regarding voters and doing so much as to antagonize private-regarding voters.

Citizen participation in urban renewal, then, is not simply (or even most importantly) a way of winning popular consent for controversial programs. It is part and parcel of a more fundamental reorganization of American local politics. It is another illustration—if one more is needed—of how deeply embedded in politics the planning process is.

NOTES

1. Housing and Home Finance Agency, *Housing Statistics: Annual Data,* April 1962, p. 76.
2. See Raymond Vernon, *The Myth and Reality of Our Urban Problems* (Cambridge: Joint Center for Urban Studies of MIT and Harvard, 1962), p. 40.
3. See also, as an example of liberal objections to renewal, Staughton Lynd, "Urban Renewal—for Whom?", *Commentary,* January 1961, pp. 34–45. The consequences of urban renewal for the underprivileged in American cities are discussed in Peter Marris, "The Social Implications of Urban Redevelopment," *Journal of the American Institute of Planners,* XXVIII (August, 1962), 180–186.
4. Quoted in *St. Louis Post-Dispatch,* February 27, 1963.
5. From an address to the 50th Anniversary Meeting of the Family Service Association of America, New York City, November 13, 1961.
6. Peter H. Rossi and Robert A. Dentler, *The Politics of Urban Renewal—The Chicago Findings* (New York: The Free Press of Glencoe, 1961), p. 287.
7. Edward C. Banfield and James Q. Wilson, *City Politics* (Cambridge: Harvard University Press, 1963), especially Ch. 16.
8. Cf. Seymour Martin Lipset, *Political Man* (Garden City, N.Y.: Doubleday, 1960), Ch. 4, and Robert Agger *et al.,* "Political Cynicism: Measurement and Meaning," *Journal of Politics,* XXIII (August, 1961), 477–506. See also the vivid account of the culture of a lower-income Italian section of Boston in Herbert J. Gans, *The Urban Villagers* (New York: The Free Press, 1963).
9. Charles E. Silberman, "The City and the Negro," *Fortune,* LXV (March, 1962), 88–91. See also Saul D. Alinsky, "Citizen Participation and Community Organization in Planning and Urban Renewal," address before the Chicago chapter of the National Association of Housing and Redevelopment Officials, January 29, 1962.
10. See the account in Alfred G. Rosenberg, "Baltimore's Harlem Park Finds 'Self-Help' Citizen Participation Is Successful," *Journal of Housing,* XVIII (May, 1961), 204–209. The initial reaction in the neighborhood to a renewal plan was

bitter and got worse for three years. Patient community organization managed to overcome some of this resistance after much effort.

11. See the survey reported in Gerda Lewis, "Citizen Participation in Urban Renewal Survey," *Journal of Housing,* XVI (March, 1959), 80–87. Questionnaires returned by about half the local renewal directors in the 91 cities which had approved "workable programs" as of July 31, 1956, showed that "the residents of project areas . . . seem to be relatively uninvolved in urban renewal"; representation from these areas on citizens' committees dealing with renewal was "almost totally absent."

12. Murray B. Levin, *The Alienated Voter* (New York: Holt, Rinehart & Winston, 1960), pp. 58–75. See also Murray B. Levin and Murray Eden, "Political Strategy for the Alienated Voter," *Public Opinion Quarterly,* XXVI (Spring, 1962), 47–63.

13. See William A. Gamson, "The Fluoridation Dialogue: Is It an Ideological Conflict?", *Public Opinion Quarterly* XXV (Winter, 1961), 526–537, and Arnold Simmel, "A Signpost for Research on Fluoridation Conflicts: The Concept of Relative Deprivation," *Journal of Social Issues,* XVII (1961), 26–36.

14. Arthur Kornhauser, *Attitudes of People toward Detroit* (Detroit: Wayne University Press, 1952), p. 28.

15. E. L. McDill and J. C. Ridley, "Status, Anomie, Political Alienation and Political Participation," *American Journal of Sociology,* LXVIII (September, 1962), 205–213.

16. Wayne E. Thompson and John E. Horton, "Political Alienation as a Force in Political Action," *Social Forces,* XXXVIII (March, 1960), 190–195 and Horton and Thompson, "Powerlessness and Political Negativism: A Study of Defeated Local Referendums," *American Journal of Sociology,* LXVII (March, 1962), 485–93.

17. Cf. William C. Loring, Jr., Frank L. Sweetser, and Charles F. Ernst, *Community Organization for Citizen Participation in Urban Renewal* (Boston: Massachusetts Department of Commerce, 1957), pp. 232–238.

15

The Analysis of Influence in Local Communities

ROBERT A. DAHL

I want to suggest a limited and fragmentary framework in which to locate the search for answers to those ancient questions: Who governs? How? Why? By "governing" I mean making decisions, and—to narrow the field of inquiry even more—I propose to restrict my attention to decisions made by "political" officials. Thus the question becomes: Who mainly influences political decisions, how, and why? [1]

This question, I hasten to point out, needs to be distinguished from two others: Who participates in decisions, how, why? And who benefits or suffers from decisions, in what ways? I will not try to deal with these two questions except indirectly.

Thus the central question may seem to be a very narrow one, indeed. But for all that, it is an important one for many reasons: Because people are curious and seek answers to it; because our evaluation of the worthwhileness of an order depends, in part (not wholly), on our answer; because government plays a special and critical role in life; and because many different answers have been suggested, all of them applicable in varying degrees to almost any city—and yet these answers are conflicting and contradictory. Moreover, insofar as the answers are actually false, they lead to unrealistic expectations of how a political system can operate. In some cases, as when reality turns out to be very different from the myth, they even lead to disillusion and cynicism.

Some of the most important answers that might be given to our question are:

1. That the system is democratic. There is much debate about what this means, but American beliefs about democracy seem to prescribe such things as: equality of influence over decisions; rational comparison of alternatives—rational "shopping"; high rate of participation by citizens; extensive information; debate and discussion of alternatives by citizens; and decisions mainly by means of elections.

2. That *party competition* and electoral participation insure popular control over public policy.

3. That policy is set by the activities of interest or *pressure groups*.

From Charles Adrian (ed.), *Social Science and Community Action* (East Lansing: Michigan State University Institute for Community Development and Services, 1960), pp. 25–42.

4. That mass democracy prevails. That is, leaders of a mass of anomic individuals dominate politics by catering to mass tastes, thus satisfying the mass, and using this mass base to establish hegemony over the system. There are no social ties, no intervening social layers.

5. That an *elite rules* in its own interests—usually an economic elite.

6. That a "prince" or *political manipulator* rules in his own interests.

There is, I think, a good deal of truth in all of these views, at least as they apply to the communities with which I am familiar. But they also contain much that is false and misleading.

Now, the question I have posed seems simple; yet it is actually rather complex. I want to show *why* it is complex, and *how,* despite its complexity, we can sensibly seek to answer it.

What the question means

Any investigation of society must begin somewhere, and some things must be taken for granted. We cannot define terms endlessly.

Some readers might, for example, dislike the word "decisions."

A decision is a set of actions related to and including the choice of one alternative rather than another. For a variety of reasons, the choices made by government officials and enforced by the means available to them are important to many people. We want to know who determines these choices.

But if we were to look at any *particular* choice, the problem would be unmanageable: we would have nothing more than a unique event. Consequently we have to look at some *collection* of choices that seem to have something in common. Any collection of choices of this kind I shall call a "scope," or, to avoid repetitiveness, an area, category, subject, etc.

A has influence over B with respect to B's activities of a given scope to the extent that A can bring about a change in B's actions. One measure of A's influence might be the magnitude of the change in probabilities that B will perform an act within the scope, contingent on some action by A. Individuals who have greater than average influence over a given scope are "leaders." Thus with respect to their students, teachers are usually but not always leaders; with respect to party nominations, politicians with considerable patronage are generally leaders, etc.

What we want to explain are certain aspects or properties of some political system. These are: (1) the *distribution* of influence; (2) the *patterns* of influence; (3) the extent of *conflict* and *cohesiveness* among the influential; and (4) *changes* in the system.

Before we can explain these, we first have to specify as precisely as possible what we mean by these terms and what the situation is in the particular community. Let me begin, therefore, by trying to clarify what we might mean by these terms.

The distribution of influence

It is possible to think of influence as being distributed to individuals in a political system. By a distribution I mean an array displaying how many people, or what proportions, have how much influence over decisions of a given scope. Thus a distribution is along two dimensions: the amount of influence and the number of people. It is easy to think of influence as distributed *equally* to *everyone* in the order; and at a slightly more complex level, Aristotle's famous classification of political orders rests partly on the idea of a distribution. But there are many possible distributions (in fact, an infinite number), so that the matter can become inordinately complex. There are, however, some rough ways of breaking down the various distributions to bring them within the compass of the human mind. That is what I shall do here.

One easy way (as with Aristotle) is to break down distributions by the relative *size* of the group that prevails on decisions: If the group that prevails is small, say less than 10 per cent of the adults, we might call this "elite" rule; if of moderate size, as 11–50 per cent, "minority" rule; if 51–100 per cent, "majority" rule.

But how "dominant" are the "rulers"? In the extreme case, suppose that the leaders regularly prevail over *opposition* from some or all of the people not in the leader group. Then the first system might be called a dictatorship, the second an oligarchy, the third a democracy. But how shall we classify these orders if the "leaders" can easily prevail whenever non-leaders are indifferent, but *cannot* do so when the non-leaders are opposed to them? These various possibilities are set out schematically in Table 15–1.

Table 15–1.

Size of ruling group	Does this ruling group prevail if some or all those outside the group are:		Type of Order
	Opposed?	*Indifferent?*	
1. Elite (> 0% < 10%)	yes	yes	1. a. Dictatorship
	no	yes	b. ?.
2. Minority (> 10% < 50%)	yes	yes	2. a. Oligarchy
	no	yes	b. ?.
3. Majority (> 50% < 100%)	yes	yes	3. a. Democracy
	no	yes	b. ?.

I have, you will notice, ruled out the case where a group does not prevail even when all others are indifferent, for if it could not prevail in such a case it would be unlikely to prevail when others were opposed: i.e., it would never prevail, and hence such a group would hardly be "leaders" in the sense defined above. (I have also excluded the case of perfectly equal division: where there are two groups of exactly 50 per cent—because this case is thorny, and irrelevant to our main concern here. Finally, I do not include complete consensus, where the "ruling" group includes 100 per cent of the citizens—because it raises no problems at all.)

Now it is obvious that if most people in a political order were indifferent on all issues, there could never be a majority and therefore the order would fall under the "elite" or "minority" heading. But if *sometimes* the "non-leaders" were not indifferent, we would need to know what happens when some or all of these non-leaders oppose the elite or minority. If, in these cases, the elite or minority should always win, then the order might be classified unambiguously (by our definitions) as dictatorship or minority rule. But if the elite or minority should sometimes lose, then the order must be, *some of the time,* a "democracy."

In the real world, political systems do in fact undergo transformations in their orders. In particular, what are usually called "democracies" are systems in which small elites or larger minorities determine outcomes most of the time; but sometimes they do not. And these exceptions are quite critical, for they comprise some of the restraints or limits under which the leaders operate. We need to learn how to think about a particular political system as if it might consist of many different political orders, varying not only over time but as to what is actually being decided. It is reasonable to suppose that political systems will undergo changes in the character of the political order from time to time, as a result of elections or changes in the social and economic structure. But it is also reasonable to suppose that the political order that deals with one kind of matter—say education—might be quite different from the political order that deals with another subject.

Although the distribution of influence is itself a matter of great interest, generally we also want to know something about patterns of influence. And it is obvious, I think, that unless we do pay strict attention to patterns, our capacity for understanding the differences among political systems will be distinctly limited. For example, suppose there are two political systems, in both of which we discover that in every scope of activity a small number of individuals have a very great deal of influence and most individuals have none. Yet upon further inquiry we might find that in one system the same individuals control decisions in all scopes, while in the other the tiny elite that runs things in one scope is entirely different from the elite who runs things in another scope. Whether or not the second political system exists in the real world is an empirical matter and not a question of definitions; so it is important to make sure that our theoretical apparatus will compel us to distinguish the two cases and not to overlook the differences if they should happen to occur.

Thus the problem of *patterns* arises because: (1) *Distributions* may vary from one scope to another: in education, say, the dominant group may be relatively small, whereas in elections it may be relatively large. (2) *Individual positions* may vary from one scope to another; e.g., individuals who are leaders in one kind of activity may not be leaders in another. (3) *Social* positions may vary. That is, the individuals may not only be different persons, but they may come from different strata of the society—those who influence urban redevelopment might be successful businessmen, while those who influence educational standards in the public schools might be mainly professional educators. These different arrangements of distributions and individuals are what I mean by patterns.

Unfortunately, the number of possible patterns is almost infinitely large. This can be shown if we assume only five people in a political system, and if we assume that we rank each of these individuals according to their influence over two different activities. If we exclude the possibility that two or more individuals might be equal in influence, there would be 120 possible orderings for just one field of activity. Consequently there would be 120^2 possible patterns for both fields—i.e., over 14,000. With 100 people, the numbers are truly astronomical. Consequently one must reduce the possibilities to a few simple patterns.

Consider two different areas of decision-making, say public education and urban redevelopment. Suppose we classify all the active participants in each of these areas according to whether their influence is high, medium, or low. (See Table 15–2.)

Table 15–2.

		Relative influence: participants in urban redevelopment		
		high	*medium*	*low*
Relative influence: participants in educational policies	*High*	Hh	Hm	Hl
	Medium	Mh	Mm	Ml
	Low	Lh	Lm	Ll

Now it is possible that all the cells in such a table would be empty; that is, there would simply be no participants in either area who participated in the other. This in itself would reveal a most interesting pattern, one of highly specialized and independent decision-making.

Assuming now that the two sets of participants do in fact overlap, then the number of possible patterns of influence is still unmanageably large. (If we were to make the convenient assumption that the members of one class in urban redevelopment, say the "highs" or top leaders, would turn up in one and only one class in educational policies, say in the "low" group, and conversely, then the three urban redevelopment groups could be distributed in the three educational policy groups in 27 different ways. Since the educational policy groups could in turn be distributed in 27 different ways in urban redevelopment, the possible number of patterns even under these somewhat simplified assumptions would be 27 x 27.) On the basis of common sense and experience, however, it is possible to single out some patterns of unusual interest and significance:

1. *Parallel hierarchies:* among those who participate in both kinds of activity, those high in the one are high in the other, those medium in the one

are medium in the other, and those low in the one are low in the other. (That is, all the cells are empty except Hh, Mm, and Ll.)

2. *Any pattern of dual leadership:* among all those who participate in both kinds of activity, those who are highly influential in urban redevelopment are also highly influential in educational policy, and conversely. (That is, any case where Hh is not empty and Hm, Hl, Mh, and Lh are empty.)

3. *Any pattern of overlapping leadership:* any case where some individuals who are influential in urban redevelopment are influential in educational policy and some people who are influential on education are also influential on urban redevelopment. (That is, Hh is not empty.) You may notice that what I have called parallel hierarchies represents a special case of dual leadership, and dual leadership represents a special case of overlapping leadership.

4. *Any pattern of strictly nonoverlapping leadership:* any case where none of the individuals who are influential in the one area are influential in another. (That is, Hh is empty.)

5. *Any pattern of weak hierarchies:* where some individuals who are highly influential in one area are definitely of less influence in the other area. (That is, at least one of the cells, Hm, Hl, Mh, or Lh is not empty.)

So far I have spoken as if "leaders" were cohesive. Actually, their strategies may *conflict,* in the sense that the attempt of A to achieve his objectives works against the success of B's attempts to attain his objectives. If strategies do not conflict, they may be (1) *independent,* in the sense that A's strategy has no significant effect at all on the success of B's strategy; (2) *complementary,* in the sense that, though different, A's and B's strategies both increase the success of the other or (3) *identical,* in the sense that they adopt the same strategy. (Because of an easy confusion, identity might appear to permit conflict. A and B could adopt *equivalent* strategies, and these could conflict; but in the sense meant here, equivalent but conflicting strategies would *not* be identical.)

Finally, with respect to distribution, patterns, and cohesiveness, it would be useful to know whether there have been any significant changes over time.

How are these characteristics to be explained?

The characteristics I have been talking about are, in the language of statistics, the "dependent variables." The "independent variables," the factors we use to "explain" why the system is the way it is, and if it has changed, why it has changed, are (1) certain properties of the bases or sources of influence and (2) the extent to which these bases are exploited.

A base of influence (which I shall also feel quite free to call a source, a resource, foundation, origin, etc., to avoid tediousness) is anything an individual or group might use to influence another person in that particular political system. The possible number of bases is thus very large. As with the question of scope, what we wish to classify as bases is determined by the research problem at hand and our theoretical interests: that is, what we believe is significant. Thus in American cities, one would not be interested in noble birth as a base, but he might well be interested in social status.

It may be wise at this point to call attention to a familiar paradox of social research that one also faces in the study of influence. One might suppose that one could gain indefinitely in *precision* by narrowing the classes of bases and scopes. But if one pursued this method as far as possible, one would ultimately reach the limit at which every case was treated as distinct from every other. This would permit one to make simple descriptive statements about the particular case. Yet the paradox is that often one cannot say anything about influence in a particular instance—one can only determine it for numerous cases. In a case where, say, A's action x_1 is followed by B's action y_1, often one cannot know whether the two actions are related except by chance. And one is not much better off even if in a second instance A's not doing x_1 is followed by B's not doing y_1. Conversely the more cases one has to judge from, the greater the confidence one might feel he could place in a statement about influence relations. If out of a thousand cases where A does x_1, B follows with y_1 about 990 times, and in another thousand cases where A doesn't perform x_1, B follows with y_1 only about 100 times, it is reasonable to place considerable confidence in the statement that A can generally influence B to do y_1. One might conclude, therefore, that one could gain indefinitely in *confidence* by broadening the classes of bases and scopes, so that more and more cases (which otherwise might be treated as non-comparable) could be placed in a single class. But the ultimate limit to this method would be a general statement covering all cases. However, since social actions are rarely identical with respect to all their important aspects, the more cases we include the more diverse and disparate they will be, and therefore the less variation one succeeds in "explaining."

What one generally does in the face of this dilemma is to adopt a compromise position that seems to hold the promise of explaining the most with the fewest factors.[2]

The following list includes, I think, many if not most of the important bases that have been suggested by various writers to explain the operations of influence in American communities: (1) money and credit; (2) control over jobs; (3) control over the information of others; (4) social standing; (5) knowledge and expertness; (6) popularity, esteem, charisma; (7) legality, constitutionality, officiality; (8) ethnic solidarity; and (9) the right to vote. In each case, our question is: to what extent can we explain differences in influence by differences in access to this particular base?

But it is clear that mere possession of or easy access to a base does not necessarily result in influence; at best it gives only potential influence. Of two equally wealthy people, for example, one might be interested in spending his time and money collecting art treasures and the other collecting politicians. One individual, that is to say, may employ more of his base in securing influence than another. But in addition, one man may exploit his base *more efficiently:* i.e., the same expenditure of resources yields a higher payoff in influence. I assume, then, that for any given base, influence is a function of (1) access to it: i.e., how much of it one has to allocate, (2) the rate of exploitation, and (3) the efficiency of exploitation.

The aspects or properties of the bases we are interested in are:

1. The *number:* How many different bases are there? (It is reasonable for example to suppose that a system with just *one* base, say possession of land, would function differently from a system with many bases.)

2. *Distribution:* Just as with the distribution of influence, we want to know how access to the various resources is distributed to the people in the system. For example, are there a very few wealthy people and many poor; or are incomes distributed fairly evenly?

3. *Patterns* of allocation: Here, too, it is not enough to know merely the distribution with respect to a particular base or even the shape of the distributions for all bases. One also needs to know what the patterns are. For example, are individuals who have great wealth also those who have the most access to all the other resources? Or do some individuals without wealth have easy access to resources denied the wealthy? As before, one can simplify the incredible variety of patterns to cases where the individuals who have access to one base are different from those who have high access to other bases; where they are identical; and where they overlap but not completely.

4. *Dominance:* Is one base dominant over others, in the sense that if an individual has access to this resource, he can always employ it successfully to influence an individual with access to resource but not conversely? (E.g., Marx believed that ownership of the means of production was a dominant base of influence in capitalist societies; on all key decisions over all important scopes, owners could influence the actions of workers but workers could not influence the acts of owners.) Some bases, of course, may be neither dominant nor dominated.

5. *Complementarity:* What is the relation between A's supply of resources and B's? If A increases his resources does this mean that B's resources decrease? Or, conversely, does an increase in A's resources entail also an increase in B's? Or, does a change in A's resources have no effects on B's resources? Obviously these possibilities parallel those for influence activities: conflict, complementarity, independence. (There are, of course, many additional refinements one might propose.)

6. *Generality:* Some bases are highly specific to one area; one can use that particular resource to influence decisions only within the one scope. Other resources, however, can be used much more widely. Thus access to a special kind of technical knowledge, such as public school administration, might provide technicians with influence over school activities and not much else. But in the same community people with access to wealth could probably exploit it to increase their influence over a great number of different areas.

Some general propositions

Let me now suggest some hypotheses of a quite general sort. The ones I set down here are too broad to be of much direct utility in community studies; but they are, I think, useful as elements of a framework. In the next section I shall set out some more specific hypotheses that will, I hope, be more directly useful. All the hypotheses that follow should of course be understood to contain the qualifying expression "other things being equal." (Many of them would be nonsensical on their face without this assumption.)

1. For any given base, the more evenly access is distributed to the individuals in the system, the more evenly is influence distributed. (Statistically speaking, the narrower the dispersion around the mean of the distribution for the resource, the narrower the dispersion around the mean of influence.) The greatest likelihood of equality of influence therefore exists if there is equality of access to a base. Conversely the more that access to the base is concentrated, the greater is the concentration of influence.

2. Among individuals with equal access to a given base, individual influence will vary with the rate and efficiency with which the individual exploits the resource.

3. The greater the overlap among individuals who have access to bases, the greater is the concentration of influence.

4. The more one base dominates others, the less conflict there is among leaders.

5. The less conflict there is among leaders, the greater is the concentration of influence.

6. The rate of exploitation of a base is a function of motivation and effort.

7. The relative efficiency of exploitation is only partly determined by motivation and effort. Additional determinants are length of experience and a number of factors that are not well understood.

8. A change in one's level of influence is a function of changes in one's access to bases, one's rate of exploitation, and one's efficiency.

9. These changes are partly determined by motivation, effort, and length of experience.

10. Changes in the distribution of access to bases may be a result of: (a) *Exogenous factors:* wars, economic growth, migration, technological change, etc. These may, e.g., affect the distribution of access to property, income, social status, information. (b) *Internal factors:* with a given distribution of access to resources, a leader (partly because of motivation, effort, and experience) increases the rate of efficiency of exploitation of his own resources. This in turn enables him to increase his influence over certain scopes. By his influence over these scopes he in turn brings about a distribution of access to bases more favorable to himself. Thus he pyramids his resources. (Note that revolutions are explained in both ways.)

11. In popular systems of politics there are large amounts of unused and inefficiently used resources of influence.

12. Thus it is possible for any skillful leader to pyramid his resources.

13. By creating threats to the supply of resources available to others, successive pyramiding of resources by one leader or leadership group will generate conflicts.

14. In any system there is a threshold below which a leader pyramiding his resources can be stopped and some of his resources dissipated by the more intense or more efficient exploitation of the resources available to his opponents. Beyond this threshold the resources available to opponents will be so diminished that even the most intense and efficient exploitation will not suffice to stop or dissipate his resources.

15. But in stable systems of popular ("democratic") politics, pyramiding stops well below the threshold of danger because (a) the resources available at the outset to any leader (or unified group of leaders) are limited by existing institutions that have a high degree of acceptance and legitimacy; (b) to pyramid his resources the leader must threaten to deprive others of some of their resources; (c) his actions therefore generate their opposition; and (d) in opposing him, they can employ resources that have hitherto been unused or inefficiently used.

The existence of slack in the system

To "explain" a political system we need to know more than the sources of influence available in the system. As I have already indicated, we also need to know how fully and how efficiently these resources are exploited.

Now in this respect totalitarian systems and those to which the vague label "liberal" might be applied furnish some interesting contrasts. And the contrast is perhaps even sharper with American urban communities. In totalitarian systems, access to resources of influence is distributed in a highly unequal way; in addition the individuals with the greatest access, the leaders, employ their resources fully and efficiently virtually to the limit of present knowledge; and even though most people have only limited access to resources of influence, they exploit these meager resources to the full. Thus the whole system is one with few untapped reservoirs of available influence; there is no slack in the system. And except for the effects of such outside factors as war and death or long run structural changes that elude the control of the leaders, the system tends to settle on an "equilibrium" where one and only one distribution of influence is consistent with the distribution of access to resources. Significant short run changes in distribution of influence are thus extremely difficult.

What is striking about "liberal" systems and particularly many urban communities is, by contrast, the appearance of great slack in the use of resources of influence. Very few people seem to exploit their resources to the limit in order to influence political officials; and even political officials often have resources available to them which they do not fully use. But precisely because of the existence of these slack resources, a great many significant, abrupt, short run changes in the distribution of influence can be brought about; for whenever someone in the community begins to exploit his available and hitherto unused resources much more fully and efficiently than before, he gains markedly in influence. As I have already suggested, in some cases it is possible in this way for a leader to pyramid his influence. By using his resources fully and efficiently, he gains in influence; he then uses his increased influence to allocate resources to himself; he then gains more influence with which to improve his access to resources, etc. But in doing so, he usually generates opposition sooner or later, and the process generally stops far short of the point where everyone is exploiting his influence to the full.

Now if this is a fair description of liberal systems (and it is almost certainly a correct description of some urban communities), the question immediately arises: Why so? Why the slack in the system? Why isn't everyone straining at the leash?

There seem to be several reasons. In the first place, from the perspective of the citizen of a liberal order, there are many better ways to use one's resources than to gain influence over political officials; indeed, I think one might go so far as to say, to gain influence over other individuals, though one would need to qualify this broader statement in many ways. Since the use of the term "resources" of influence suggests an economic process, one might carry the parallel further by putting what I have just said in the language of the economist; in liberal systems the "opportunity costs" of exploiting one's resources to influence political officials are relatively high.

Although there are some quite straightforward explanations for these high "opportunity costs," explanations I shall come to in a moment, it is at least plausible that a part of the explanation lies in beliefs widely endorsed in liberal societies which stress the essentially immoral quality of "power" by people over other people. These norms seem to be both specific and general: They specifically single out power over others as evil except under certain particular conditions, and unlimited power over others as always evil; and the specific view reflects a general morality in which self-indulgence and lack of self-restraint are frowned on. In the United States, certainly, a number of different institutions, including the family and schools, stress the propriety of maintaining a rough equality of influence in one's relations with one another; often the norms even seem to place heavy stress on avoiding influence entirely.

These are pretty speculative views, but not, I think, unimportant or irrelevant. If they are correct, then we would expect to find some evidence of anxiety or guilt traceable to the violation of these norms among people who do in fact exert great power over others. Alternatively, we might find that powerful leaders are considerably below average in the extent to which the norms have actually been internalized: that they are, compared with the rest of the population, deviants. But because the norms of any society as complex as ours are inconsistent at many points, we might also find that powerful leaders have internalized other norms—for example, norms stressing private rights or public responsibilities.

There are, however, several obvious and direct explanations for the fact that individuals prefer to use a large part of their resources for purposes other than influencing political officials. And these two explanations apply with particular strength to American urban communities. First, many and quite probably most of the rewards that are important to people are allocated mainly by mechanisms other than government. If a state legislature were seriously debating the possibility of requiring all children to be placed in community-run nurseries for the first ten years of their lives, to be seen by their parents only during visiting hours, a great many citizens would leave no stone unturned until the legislation was defeated; many parents would, no doubt, bankrupt themselves, or even commit violence, to prevent passage of the bill. But the example is absurd precisely because we cannot imagine such a legislative debate, given our present norms; we can imagine it (in a free political system) only if a large part of the population had reached a point where they no longer felt it important to keep their families intact.

Now if many important rewards are allocated by mechanisms other than government, then the "opportunity cost" of exploiting one's resources to gain influence over governmental decisions is relatively high, since (to continue the economic metaphor) these same resources can be more profitably employed elsewhere. To be sure, to speak of "opportunity costs" does not tell us much; for it is only another way of saying that to participate in politics isn't very satisfying for most people, that people enjoy doing other things. But it also suggests that we need to explain this fact by looking for alternative sources of satisfaction that are greater, from the viewpoint of the average person.

The second reason why individuals might prefer to use a large part of their resources for purposes other than influencing political officials is (to use the economic metaphor once again) that increasing utilization of any *particular* resource to influence political outcomes results in diminishing returns. Indeed, at some point, further use of the resource will probably decrease one's chances of a favorable outcome. In many communities, this is probably true of money, for example. Enough money to cover the minimal costs of a "standard" campaign is essential to a candidate, and the returns from it are, relatively, very high. But to put on twice as expensive a campaign as the standard requires probably will not have twice the effect. And to spend three or five times as much might even begin to lose votes for the candidate.

The fact that influence resources suffer from diminishing returns means that "opportunity costs" rise; i.e., individuals might reasonably prefer to use a large part of their resources for purposes other than gaining influence.

Consequently, there will be slack in the system—resources available whenever the opportunity costs decline. And the opportunity costs may decline if new opportunities of rewards from governmental decisions open up, or if new threats and dangers appear.

Now it is because of diminishing returns that a large amount of a single resource of influence is likely to be less useful than smaller amounts of several resources. If one has access to different resources, he can use one to the point of diminishing returns and then switch to another. Thus after the costs of a "standard" campaign are covered, the returns may be far less from the expenditure of more money than from a single dramatic proposal by the candidate, a gentle squeeze on patronage, and indications of strong support in the right quarters.

Wherever resources are distributed unevenly, as is almost everywhere the case, a third reason for not employing one's resources if they are slender is that the likelihood of securing a favorable action may seem so very low as to be an unwarranted risk. If resources suffer from diminishing returns, they may also have a lower threshold below which utilization may be futile or even damaging. Thus it is doubtful whether a contribution of ten cents to a campaign would ordinarily induce a strong feeling of benevolence and gratitude on the part of the candidate. True, individuals can pool their slender resources; but even to do this much generally requires organization and skills that many individuals feel they do not have. Indeed, even where the gains might be substantial, to organize a group may, as in the extreme case of the scattered stockholders of a large company, require greater resources than any one individual has at his disposal. Nearly every adult in an American community has at least one resource at his disposal: his vote. Yet for any particular individual the argument is logically unassailable that except in the most unusual circumstance where his preferred candidate ties for first place or loses by one vote, *his* vote won't count and thus his private decision not to go to the polls will not, if he keeps the decision to himself, influence the outcome. (Such a paragon of rationality might, if he wanted competitive democratic politics to survive, also argue without inconsistency that he would nonetheless support efforts to indoctrinate everyone, including himself, in the virtues of voting.) Thus in many cases where the joint action might be effective if it could only be arranged, the individual will see his own contribution as having so little effect on the probability of a favorable outcome or on the magnitude of his own share in the outcome that the risk entailed in using his resources is quite unjustified.

Variations among individuals and systems

It is, I think, a fact of common experience in many urban communities that most people do not exploit their resources very fully to gain influence over government. But it is equally true that *some* individuals do. How can we explain this? To begin with, the more slack there is, the easier (cheaper, in our metaphor) it becomes for anyone who might wish to do so. But this does not explain why, in a system with many unused opportunities for influencing officials, only a few people do seize these opportunities.

I cannot provide an answer here, at least not in any profound sense. I do not need to remind you of the vast and rapidly growing body of studies dealing in many different ways with the problem of political participation.[3] The only point I wish to stress is the abstract one (which falls just short, I believe, of being tautological) that the few who do participate must feel themselves (or expect) to be more rewarded by their political activity than by some alternative use of their time, effort, and other resources. A's willingness to use some resources in the hope of gaining influence, and B's unwillingness to do so, can thus be explained if A and B have different access to resources. For example, A and B may both feel that it is very important for them to contribute $100 to a particular campaign; but if A is rich and B is poor, A will almost certainly do so but B may not. Or, the difference may arise because A and B do not evaluate the rewards in the same way even though they may have the same access to resources. This may be because of "objective" differences in the effects of government action, as when a highway department seeks to condemn A's property but not B's, or when A is a contractor who does business with the city and B is an artist; or because of "subjective" differences in tastes, values, predispositions, and information.

No way of classifying the effects of governmental activity is a priori better than any other, but the following is, I think, a useful list. An individual's estimate of what he stands to gain from trying to influence official actions will depend on what he perceives as the net benefits or loss resulting from official action to: (1) his level of services: the magnitude, efficiency, and costs of public services performed for him or groups important to him; (2) his material interests: the present and future size of his income and wealth, via government jobs, contracts, taxes, zoning, etc.; (3) his power; the power he has over others; his effectiveness in getting what he wants; the amount of coercion, restraint, and regulation applied by or to him; (4) his self-esteem; (5) his social esteem: status, position, social class; and (6) his solidarity: libidinous gratifications, loyalties, sense of belonging, love, identification with a charismatic figure, etc.

Sometimes politics is interpreted as predominantly concerned with one or the other kind of public reward. Often, as with middle class reformers, it is seen as operating *in fact* with one set of rewards (e.g., material interests or power) when it *ought* to be operating with another (e.g., level of services). But probably in most urban communities, and indeed in most political systems, all six kinds of rewards, and many others as well, are important.

There can be, however, great variations among systems because:

1. The extent to which rewards are actually dependent on the actions of public officials varies from one particular system to another, and, within any system, from one time to another.

2. The allocations, though dependent on the actions of public officials, may be mostly dependent on the acts of elected politicians, or they may be highly institutionalized in bureaucracies. To the extent that allocations become highly bureaucratized, changes in elected officials, or in any officials at all, may result in only negligible changes in allocations.

3. The extent to which allocations are made through "public" commitments (public discussion, open hearings, legal actions aboveboard, etc.) or "private deals" can vary.

4. The importance attributed to variations in allocations by public authority varies greatly from one individual to another.

A proposal for a model: Hobbes inverted

Let me now attempt to draw the various points of this essay together by suggesting, in a loose and not very rigorous fashion, a kind of model of the operation of influence that seems to me to fit a great many urban communities much better than the alternatives usually proposed, although it certainly will not fit all communities.

I shall begin by making the following assumptions about the *characteristics of influence* over local governmental decisions. As to the distribution of *influence,* there is indeed rule by minorities but the minorities triumph over massive indifference rather than outright opposition. In each area of decisions, then, a rather small group of people substantially determines the outcome; but they meet with almost no opposition, either latent or manifest; in fact they are more likely to find opposition among themselves than opposition between themselves and other segments of the community. Moreover, outside of these small groups, and even to a large extent within them, most people do not by any means seize all the opportunities they have to influence decisions.

As to *patterns,* the community is multi-centered rather than single-centered. Although the proportion of the community that significantly influences the outcomes of decisions is ordinarily quite small, no *one* group of leaders coordinates all decisions. On the contrary, different groups of leaders control different kinds of decisions, with only limited overlap among the various groups.

As to *cohesiveness and conflict,* the strategies of the influential groups of leaders are to a high degree independent or conflicting. Identical strategies are almost unknown and complimentary strategies throughout the leadership are rare, although frequently a small band or team will adopt complimentary strategies against a rival band.

As to the nature and direction of change, the decline of the old-fashioned boss and the growing complexity and subtlety of the lines of social, economic, and occupational cleavage in the community are probably increasing the segmental aspects the processes for making decisions. If a single center strengthens its influence over other centers, the chances are that leaders in this center consist of elected officials rather than "private" or unofficial leaders. Over-all coordination by covert groups is increasingly difficult and unlikely.

These characteristics of the community are in turn explained in large part (although not necessarily altogether) by certain aspects of the *bases of influence* in the community.

First, in the *distribution of resources* of influence, not one alone, or even a small number, but a relatively large number of different kinds of resources can be used to influence official actions, including money, chiefly in the form of (overt and covert) campaign contributions, expertness, organization, friendship, prestige, publicity, legality, constitutionality, the right to vote, and many others. Except for the right to vote, access to these resources is, however, unevenly distributed throughout the community; for any given resource, a few people have access to a great deal and many people have access to relatively modest amounts.

Second, as to *patterns,* while the set of individuals who have extensive access to one resource overlaps to some extent with sets who have access to other resources, the overlap is very far from complete. For example, the set of wealthy individuals overlaps heavily with the set of individuals of high social status; but neither set overlaps extensively with the set of individuals enjoying great popularity and affection in the community, nor with those who have the highest access to the technical knowledge and expertness on which many decisions are based.

Third, no one base of influence is *dominant* over all others, though money probably has the greatest *generality* in its effectiveness.

Fourth, for most people the gains of exploiting what resources they have for gaining influence over officials are seen as relatively low (compared with what might be expected from using these resources for other purposes) because of widespread taboos about power, because the most valued rewards are allocated mainly by systems other than governments, and because the effects from using resources of influence are limited by a lower threshold and diminishing marginal returns at the top.

Fifth, and partly because of the fourth factor, there are typically many slack resources in the system. Most people see no gain and considerable loss from exploiting their resources to the full in order to influence officials.

Sixth, a person with a variety of bases of influence is much more likely to have a high degree of influence over several different areas of policy than a person with only one or two sources of influence.

Seventh, leaders sometimes pyramid their resources by using the influence available to them from one resource to increase their supply of resources.

Eighth, since resources are scarce, attempts to pyramid influence resources generate conflicts with individuals who sooner or later see their own resources declining (if only relatively) and hence their capacity to influence officials, now or in the future, as diminishing. To these individuals, it now is relatively more profitable to exploit their resources to reduce the growing influence of the rising leader. Typically, a modest increase in the level of efficiency of their exploitations is sufficient to bring the process to a halt and even to dissipate the newly gained power of the rising leader.

NOTES

1. Cf. Harold D. Lasswell and A. Kaplan, *Power and Society: A Framework for Political Inquiry* (New Haven: Yale University Press, 1950), Chs. 4 and 5, and Robert A. Dahl, "The Concept of Power," *Behavioral Science* (July, 1957), 201–215.
2. The statistically minded reader will recognize that what I have said is easily translated into the language of statistical inference.
3. The most comprehensive of these is R. E. Lane, *Political Life, Why People Get Involved in Politics* (Glencoe, Ill.: The Free Press, 1959).

Part V URBAN POVERTY

Editors' Introduction

Poverty, however defined, has been a recognizable and recognized condition in all of recorded history, but urban poverty in the twentieth century is surrounded by new circumstances. Urban poverty needs to be distinguished from its rural or agricultural counterpart, where the sense of community, personal ties, and a common destiny against nature introduce social supports which are easily discernible. By contrast, the city has usually sacrificed these in favor of the promise of greater variety, stimulation, and of higher material well-being. The city has not only attracted people from rural communities, but it has imposed on them a less personalized and more highly organized set of protections against economic insecurity.

A companion change is the rapidly rising level of expectation in which the measure of man's condition is no longer simple survival, subsistence, and shelter. Improvements in methods of food production and in the technologies of goods production have made it possible, at least in the Western industrialized nations, to assure a much higher level of material existence for a much larger part of the population than ever before. These material gains are seen most dramatically in the conditions of urban life, although they are not necessarily accompanied by esthetic, moral, or cultural gains.[1]

The relief of the poor has always been of some public concern. It was recorded in the Old Testament injunctions to leave gleanings of the fields for the poor, and in Joseph's advice to Egyptian kings for combating food shortages through a form of an ever-normal granary. In Rome, the public authority and wealthy families together were responsible for leisure and for food for the urban poor (the "bread and circuses" of Imperial Rome). And the Medieval and Renaissance Church developed an elaborate system of religious relief institutions. Much of the earlier effort was premised on a major distance separating the few rich from the majority poor, and on a rationale for relief limited mainly to ethical or moral arguments and political fear of violent reaction or revolt.

In more recent times action on behalf of the poor has also been generated by a conviction that a reduction of poverty is a positive public policy, with gains to the functioning of the economy as well as to an easy conscience and political stability. This shift in justification seems to have evolved as national wars of the nineteenth and twentieth centuries became dependent on the active support of the entire population of a nation, not just on the professional soldiers and elite rulers.[2] Whatever the causal connection, it has become the aim of much public and political policy to reduce the size of urban poverty through extension of opportunity to the bulk of the population and through some redistribution of gains in national production.

This enlargement of public responsibility, attached to an enlargement of expectation, has introduced new problems into any discussion of urban poverty: (1) Who are the poor in fact? This question includes the more technical question of how to define the line between those who require collective social attention in a social policy (be it for political, economic, or ethical reasons) and those whose fate can be left to the free working out of the economic market system. (2) However defined, what are the causes of poverty—do they lie in personal deficiency or in defects in the economic structure? (3) How useful or effective are our existing institutions for coping with these problems?

Discussion of this subject has been obscured by much semantic confusion. Stereotyped images about the poor (as the shiftless malingerers) have competed with one-dimensional descriptions based on family income. Orshansky has developed a technique for measurement which introduces a more objective framework.[3] Nutritional science can assign value to various diets, the cost of which can be computed for families of varying sizes. An "economy" food plan for a family of four, translated into dollar costs, was derived. Companion studies have indicated that urban families spend, on the average, one-third of their income for food. These elements suggest that families of four whose income is *less* than three times the cost of the economy food plan can be considered in poverty, since they are unable to secure even minimum nutrition for themselves.

By applying this improved measure to census data, the poverty profile emerges with some clarity.

1. From this viewpoint, 34.6 million Americans can be classified as being in poverty. The aggregate income of this group, including transfer and public assistance payments, is only 60 per cent of the amount required for their basic requirements.

2. Children under 18 years of age constitute one-half of this impoverished group, a total of 15.6 million minor children. Only 3.1 million of this group received public assistance through aid for dependent children. Families in which the mother is the head of the family (due to death or absence of a father) are especially vulnerable; 46 per cent of all such female-headed families are poor compared with 21 per cent of all families.

3. Fourteen per cent of the identified poor are aged; 40 per cent of all lone aged men and 60 per cent of aged women living alone fall below the poverty line.

4. A large proportion of the poor are families in which the male head of

the family works full time. Seventy-three per cent of the nonwhite male heads of poor families were employed full time at the time of study; and 42 per cent had worked full time for a full year. Among poor white families, the comparable figures are 56 per cent currently at work and 33 per cent working full time year round.

The poverty in urban areas can be contrasted with that in rural areas in several ways. The unfavorable economic status of the South, much of it still rural, is a major factor; and half of all the nation's poor (and seven-tenths of the nonwhite poor) live in a Southern state. In other sections of the country, rural poverty primarily affects elderly white families. The proportion of white aged is higher than elsewhere and the proportion of these aged who are poor is also higher.

In the central city, poverty erodes the lives of both white and nonwhite families, but two out of five nonwhite poor live in urban centers while only one in four white poor live there. But the white aged also concentrate so heavily in the central city that, in sheer volume, a fourth more white than nonwhite poor are found there.

Urban poverty is also a matter of sharp contrast between the relative affluence of the suburb and the decay of the core city. In aggregate and oversimplified terms, the core city has a high proportion of vulnerable urban families: Negroes, the aged, and children living in female-headed households. These are likely to be poor families by any definition. The suburbs have relatively fewer of these vulnerable populations so that economic segregation is especially noticeable.

Average income is higher in urban than in rural areas, but differences in cost of living and the differences in population—noted above—still produce the concentrations of the poor in the city.

With such a profile at hand, it is possible to consider alternative policies and interventions for urban planning.

Miller begins an admittedly incomplete effort to assess the extent to which all such groupings are more or less stable, self-perpetuating, and therefore unresponsive to chance. He faces the possibility that psychological or cultural patterns, as much as economic ones, may play some part in reduced income. However, he seeks to regroup the data on the poor in some manner which will combine both their objective economic circumstances and their inner or life-style patterns of responding to their situation. His terms "stable, strained, coping, and unstable" poor are useful in breaking up the stereotyping which has attached to the commonly used terms "lower class" and "working class," so long considered adequate shorthand descriptions of the poor as a class. Such concepts are useful for analysis but less so for programming, for they remain largely subjective in content. A stable or an unstable family can be described in such a manner as to be real and recognizable, but the constituents of instability vary for each observer; and the criteria are not suitable for mass application. One evidence of this difficulty is seen in the extent to which application depends upon a specific economic context. The family which is today strained or coping or unstable often proves to be quite capable of managing its affairs in a different context, as in wartime or economic boom. Then many families, only recently considered part of the hard core of the poor and maladjusted, hold jobs and function without undue strain.[4]

A further difficulty lies in the fact that some of these concepts seem more relevant to the short-term poor—for example, those temporarily out of work—while others are apt for those who are discriminated against by the market economy for long periods of time—the permanently disabled, the aged, and racial minorities. Especially in urban areas these groupings, as well as all other classifications, are densely intermingled with one another spatially. All groups may be found living in certain districts; and many with similar characteristics are found living in areas populated by the economically secure. This physical mingling of all groups in the modern city makes it not only difficult to identify one group from another, but it makes difficult the selective application of one policy in lieu of another in any operational sense.

The refinement and specification of policy in relation to specific groups marks a valuable step ahead in creating the scientific foundation for urban planning, but it cannot be said to simplify the remedial programs required. Simple, unidimensional approaches to avoid problems are longed for by policy-makers and there is the temptation to view one remedy as "sovereign." The difficulties of time and space just mentioned lead to the conclusion that all the strategies proposed by Miller will undoubtedly have to be applied simultaneously in any urban area chosen for testing. The experiences of the Office of Economic Opportunity, especially through its community action projects, indicate that each urban area has significant numbers of the poor who require direct economic change through jobs and training, direct services such as home helps and personal guidance, and changes in the urban environment through recreation areas, housing improvements, public facilities, etc.

Nonetheless, the combination of economic and sociological analysis which Orshansky and Miller bring to bear goes far to lay foundations for more refined and effective policies in the future.

The Solow and Hoover essays taken together explore some of the economic components of poverty. Although none of them challenges the basic health of the economic system, with its blend of private initiative and governmental intervention, they all agree that changes in the nature of the American economy have much to do with the emergence of the contemporary forms of poverty which has been described. It is not automation alone which causes unemployment (although it clearly plays a part in some industries). Taken in conjunction with a large increase of the population, with some 26 million new young workers entering the labor force during the 1960's, unexpected strains are placed upon the capacity of the economy to provide suitable employment for all who can work. The demand for higher vocational and technical skill increases. This is countered by moves to protect the rights of established adult employees who have proven their capacity through seniority; to this is added the pressure of new additions to the labor force.

The tension between employer and union efforts to stabilize work and the pressure of new additions to the labor force helps us visualize possible social-policy alternatives. If automation is seen as a stabilizing influence for older skilled workers, then intervention may be necessary to provide longer and better training to new workers and to retraining displaced older ones. New jobs and work opportunities can also be planned in the human-services sector—health, education, and welfare. If the pressure of population is taken as the point of departure, intervention can be in the direction of earlier retirement, and the creation of new noneconomic activity for older (though not necessarily aged) workers.

Much of this choice depends upon national economic policy, which lies beyond the scope of this volume. However, the national context is a necessary backdrop against which urban planners act. The continuing debate over the economic impact of technological change (automation) inevitably links national policy with urban programs. If automation is seen as a short-term hazard, then the shrinkage of opportunity for some citizens can be countered by reinvigorated vocational and industrial training, increasing the equality of access to jobs for minority groups, and support of geographic relocation of redundant workers.[5] If the change is seen as radical and fundamental, then the basic concepts of work and leisure are upset. For analysts such as Robert Theobald,[6] so much can be produced by so few workers that large numbers will be pushed into poverty unless leisure and its uses are socially legitimized and are economically supported. Facilities for leisure, education, and cultural development are called for by this analysis of trends.

Both interpretations of economic trends propose familiar remedies and must deal with human priorities. Should work opportunities be organized to favor the young, with earlier displacement of the adult worker, or should the entry of the young into work be further delayed? Should women be encouraged or discouraged from entering the labor force, and at what age—as youths or as mature adults after their children have been reared? To whom should leisure (with income) be assured, be it for study, creative expression, self-development, or sloth? And to whom shall preference be given in access to available occupations?

Analysts who turn their attention from the technology of automation to the general functioning of the economy are likely to argue, as does Solow, that economic and fiscal policies are at hand to correct any difficulties introduced by new automating technologies. Solow proposes fiscal tools to keep growth in production and the potential for growth (provided for by improved technology) in reasonable balance in order that all in the work force can be suitably employed. This approach puts in perspective the relationship of social to economic approaches, and especially the questions of value to be served. For example, if science increases potential economic growth, to what social group will the growth be applied? What shall be the goods produced? Does the new product to be stimulated require labor-intensive or capital-intensive methods? Human and social services are as yet labor-intensive, and large numbers of workers can be employed for understaffed sectors of health, education, and urban living. To act on this simple analysis requires attention to political processes, for many of these new careers are outside the private initiative and profit-making sector of the economy today.

Enlargement of this social sector for employment is culturally and politically unpopular. Of equal significance is the fact that some employments are not highly valued either in money or prestige and status. It is more and more difficult to recruit street cleaners, teachers, nurses, orderlies, waiters and dish washers, and household help. As a result there is a tendency to mechanize many of these functions as well.

Such considerations open up a new area for planning. It is now necessary to match the national and urban economic policy with a social policy which will increase the share of the GNP directed to now undervalued tasks. New political and cultural tools are needed to make such a shift feasible. In the end, automation and employment may not be antithetical, but it is necessary to consider whether their mutual adjustments are self-balancing and self-correcting or whether some intervention is necessary. If the answer is yes, what form should that intervention take? If technology is not the cause of unemployment, inadequate public policy may be; and public policy in service sectors lacks definite tools and clear guides.

The Pittsburgh study described by Hoover presents an effort to grapple with economic policies at an urban level, while setting the action within the context of national forces and trends. Its values seem to lie in two features: the stress on a metropolitan regional perspective and the recognition that major elements of the urban evolution, such as migration and unemployment, may respond to rational economic action. The three economic approaches discussed imply, although they do not specify, a single vital element in urban planning for poverty: the need to change certain secondary institutions of society. Industry must be modernized, in the Pittsburgh report; vocational training programs, which are extensive, need to shift from training for nonexistent jobs (e.g., in agriculture) to training for the newly growing work sectors; and legislators need to be moved to support relevant and informed governmental action, to close the gap between potential and actuality in economic performance.[7] The economic policies proposed all assure continuous growth and change in urban society.

The Pittsburgh data also suggest that planners need not be limited by municipal political fragmentation on one hand (with its economic weakness) and the fear of national dictation on the other hand. Metropolitan regions, between these extremes, contain more adequate economic and social resources than do municipalities, perhaps sufficient to be entrusted with major economic and social planning judgments. What is lacking is a political framework within which such judgments can be made and acted upon.

When we return to either the social or social welfare approach to poverty, its confusing content and emergency character become paramount points of departure. Burns points out that economic solutions are not complete; she evaluates the evidence that, for many of the poor, jobs are no answer to their poverty. Social value emerges as a vital aspect of planning. Mothers rearing small children should not be forced to work at the expense of their mothering; low pay is a product of the economic system and its skewed incentives and it is not due only to the lesser native ability of some workers. Work is no answer for those disabled by sickness, injury, and age.

While analysis of each current remedy can be concise and sharp, the suggested improvements in remedy still present serious contradictions. Measures to bridge short-term interruptions of income are well understood, but social and emotional attitudes seem to militate against widespread development. The average levels of unemployment insurance are still submarginal, and there is limited coverage for income loss due to illness. Prejudices about working mothers who are separated from their husbands keep such women in the awkward position of having to care for their children and also being expected to work as if they were single. Levels of relief allowances continue to be inhumanly inadequate because of state and local reluctance to provide support, although the futility of giving inadequate support as an approach to poverty was identified as early as 1904 by Solomon Lowenstein.[8] The proposal for children's allowances faces the hazard that political and economic opposition will keep them too low to affect the poverty group to any significant extent.

All financial assistance remedies need to overcome at least two general difficulties: cost and standardization. The attempt to reduce the indignity of the means test by some more general provision, such as a demogrant allowance,[9] or the negative income tax, or a pension benefit, becomes costly if widely applied and easily available. This is increased by the fact that many persons who do not require the economic aid by any strict measure of poverty become entitled to it. This widens the base of support in one direction, but also opens the program up to attack from another direction as being wasteful of tax money.[10] At the same time, no general category of assistance has yet been devised which can anticipate all the variations in human distress and need. A general grant which is suitable for a healthy, able-bodied retired couple, or for a mother with two healthy children, becomes wholly insufficient in case of illness or disability, be it physical or psychological.

The conclusion seems to be that a social judgment must be made between the advantages of a general or average grant for income supplement which is suitable for most but which injures some, and an individually administered needs-determining system in which administration discretion intrudes into personal lives of several million persons so that eligibility and investigation become inflated and overcomplicated.

The task for social planning is undoubtedly to reconstruct a pattern of income assistance which will recombine the equalizing and freeing concept of averaged grants for income support with some means for individualized supplementation where requested by individuals and families. The steps in this direction are made nearly impossible by the division of responsibility between federal, state, and local units of government. Adjustments of this kind can seldom be made at the urban level, although major state programs in Colorado and Pennsylvania have been able to introduce some variations.[11]

Social welfare approaches to urban poverty have recently uncovered two new dimensions of poverty. There is, first, the widespread reluctance of citizens to use many forms of social assistance. Morgan and others[12] have documented how small a proportion of persons suffering from any serious financial, social, or physical problem ever seek organized help. This is sometimes due to the repelling nature of many eligibility procedures; sometimes it is due to ignorance or fear; it may even be due to reluctance to change one's life pattern. Since this reluctance is also found among the physically ill who delay seeking medical care, the difficulty is pervasive among all economic classes. Urban planning must therefore consider steps to assure better utilization of services as well as simply to provide space and budget for them. It is possible that attractive and dignified public offices for social and health services would do much to improve utilization. Certainly, the construction of large, anonymous structures far removed from the living neighborhood, each one made unattractive and demeaning through crowding and inconvenience, contributes much to this difficulty.

More significant is a new appreciation of the fact that social welfare agencies themselves are steps on the economic ladder and assets for employment of the poor. The common belief that the poor can help themselves has been given an urban foundation in the experiences of Community Research Associates, Minneapolis, of Mobilization for Youth, New York, and the 1965–1967 projects of the Office of Economic Opportunity, which point to ways in which the poor can be employed. The enlargement of the health and social welfare functions in the modern city constitutes an employment and career resource. However, the appealing nature of this idea should not be exaggerated, as the Orshansky and Burns analyses make clear that this solution is open to only some of the new poor. Illness, age, care for children and lack of skill are realities, and a large proportion of the poor can never find a solution in work as it is now structured.

NOTES

1. Regardless of objective evidences, this change is perceived to be real by farm workers in all parts of the world who are ready to give up the benefits of a farming life, assumed to exist in the minds of urban romanticists, in favor of urban congestion and squalor. Despite difficulty, the hope for improvement seems more real in the city than in the country.

2. See Richard Titmuss, *Essays on the Welfare State* (New Haven: Yale University Press, 1959); Gunnar Myrdal, *Beyond the Welfare State* (New Haven: Yale University Press, 1960).

3. Mollie Orshansky, "Counting the Poor: Another Look at the Poverty Profile," *Social Security Bulletin*, XXVIII (January, 1965), 3–29.

4. During World War II, the employment and labor market data in both the United States and United Kingdom confirmed this explanation.

5. See Arnold Weber, "The Rich and the Poor: Employment in an Age of Automation," *Social Service Review,* XXXVII, No. 3 (September, 1963), 249–262.

6. Robert Theobald, "Free Men and Free Markets," in *Technology and the American Economy,* National Commission on Technology, Automation and Economic Progress (Washington, D.C.: Government Printing Office, 1966).

7. It has not been popular to consider the advantages of stabilizing, rather than growth, policies; although the debate over family planning deals with one major dynamic of growth-population increase. Would a stable city (in a stable nation) assure more personal happiness, equal material comfort and as much intellectual vigor? Fewer social problems? At the moment, urban planners deal with constant change in populations, economy, work patterns and the like, at a tempo for which man's history gives little precedent.

8. Solomon Lowenstein, "Adequacy of Relief," in *Proceedings, National Conference of Jewish Charities* (New York, 1904).

9. An allowance paid to a demographically determined sector or segment of the population—the aged or children.

10. Alvin L. Schorr, "Alternatives in Income Maintenance," *Social Work* XI, No. 3 (July, 1966), 22–29.

11. In Colorado there is a pension program for the aged; and in Pennsylvania the rehabilitation program in public welfare has raised both relief grants and human services for training. During 1966 the New York City Department of Welfare announced plans to simplify the administrative tasks of relief-giving, using a simple affidavit of need.

12. Joseph N. Morgan, Mertin H. David, Wilbur J. Cohen, and Harvey E. Brazer, *Income and Welfare in the United States* (New York: McGraw-Hill, 1962).

16

The American Lower Classes:
A Typological Approach

S. M. MILLER

In recent years, increasing attention has been directed to "the lower class" —those existing at the economic and social margins of society. The current concern with the limited economic prospects of dropouts,[1] the discussions of "hard-core" and "multiproblem" families,[2] the casualties of the welfare state,[3] the analysis of the numbers living below the "poverty line" in America,[4] and the conditions of the "submerged fifth" in Britain[5]—all reflect the growing awareness of the "underprivileged" in presumably affluent welfare societies of high industrialization.

Much confusion exists in these discussions. Those concerned with psychological and social dislocations (disorganization is the commonly used word) tend to understress the importance of economic pressures, and those interested in economic deprivation frequently discount the role of social and psychological problems in preventing people from coping with their difficulties. Who is or is not "lower class" is a moot point, as different axes of demarcation are utilized. As I have explained elsewhere, I prefer to use such terms as the *new working class* rather than the *lower class*. Because most of the literature is couched in terms of the *lower class,* I use this term here despite my objections to it.

A way of classifying a population is a way of thinking about them. A frequent practice is to classify as "lower class" [6] the large number of people who are members of households where the breadwinner is not involved in some kind of white-collar (that is, middle-class) occupation. This category is then considered to have high homogeneity and is treated as though it constituted a group with great centrality of attitudinal and behavioral patterns. This orientation has probably led to much of the confusion and conflict in discussions of the characteristics of those at the lower end of the social structure. For example, the inconsistent child-rearing results may be due to the variations from study to study in those who are sampled as members of "the lower class."

It is becoming more common, although not a consistent practice, to mark off distinctions within the manual category. Frank Riessman and I [7] have argued that a working class of skilled and semiskilled regular workers should be distinguished from unskilled, irregular workers who might be

From *Social Research,* XXXI (Spring, 1964), 1–22.

called "lower class." Preferably, the latter group might be called by less invidious terms like "the unskilled," "marginal workers," or "underprivileged workers," restricting the latter term of Allison Davis to a narrow scope.[8] But even where a distinction is made between the "working class" and the "lower class," the criteria of classification are frequently obscure or conflicting.

Two approaches, not always clearly noted, are employed in defining the "lower class." One approach emphasizes the definition of groups in terms of "class" characteristics, especially economic role or income. The other employs "cultural" or "status" criteria, such as style of life. The Hollingshead index—occupation, education, place of residence—is in the tradition of the first approach.[9] Walter Miller's discussion[10] of "the lower class subculture" is along the lines of the second. Social workers' discussions of "the lower-class client" and the "multiproblem family" almost always employ style-of-life indicators.

The two approaches intertwine but seem to make independent contributions to elucidating the characteristics of the "lower class" or the poor. Consequently, I have brought them together in an effort to move away from a broadly and vaguely defined "lower class" into a specification of types of lower-class individuals. The effort is to utilize class and status variables in categorizing a population. The combination of the two produces problems, but the current shifting between the two sets of dimensions in discussing groupings and issues: Walter Miller's "lower class" [11] is not Lee Rainwater's.[12]

Obviously, other dimensions, like education and region, should also be employed. Class and status dimensions should be more carefully marked off than in the following discussion. Unfortunately, the material to do an adequate job is lacking. The purpose here is to show one way of approaching the problem of differentiation within the poor. The intent is to direct more attention to the recognition of variations among the poor.

The class criterion

The advantage of using an economic indicator in defining the lower class is that such an indicator specifies a political-economic category to which legislation and other remedial programs could be devoted. Emphasis on style-of-life indicators can be confusing, because the meaning of an attitude or behavior or what it leads to can be quite different for the rich, for the middling well-off, for those "getting by," and for the poor. The same behavior may have different roots and consequences in varying milieus.

On the other hand, the class or occupational criterion is not so clear cut as it appears. Some unskilled workers have stable, fairly well-paid jobs and are, thus, not a pressing social or economic problem. (This is particularly true where the unskilled worker is employed in a unionized, mass-production factory.) Many semiskilled and fewer skilled workers suffer some degree of irregularity of employment, especially owing to seasonal factors. Another problem is that a considerable number of poor families (35 per cent to 50 per cent) have no member in the labor force.[13]

Consequently, I would suggest that an income criterion is more useful today than an occupational criterion in the definition of the lower class. The recent analyses of poverty in the United States can be employed for this purpose.[14] They show remarkable agreement, despite their different procedures, in estimating that from one-quarter to one-fifth of the United States population lives below the poverty line. The level of income defining poverty varies, depending upon family size, composition, age, region, and type of community. For our purposes, we can ignore these complexities and put the poverty line at $4,000 family income, following Keyserling. It is this population which, if we want to use the term, could be called "lower class" or "low income" or "the poor."

The advantage of utilizing the economic criterion, and particularly the income definition, is that it specifies a socioeconomic category toward which policy can be directed. For example, Morgan reports,[15] following Lampman's earlier lead, that 10 billion dollars would bring all spending units now below the poverty line to an income level above poverty. Questions of the distribution of income and of social services can be pinpointed, then, in terms of how they affect this particular population.

Obviously, income levels and sources of income vary considerably among the "low-income" population. Keyserling distinguishes between the very poor, the poor, and a higher income group who suffer what he terms "deprivation" but not outright poverty. What income level is used affects deeply the characteristics of the poor. Lampman uses lower income limits than does Keyserling or Morgan. Consequently, he describes a poor population with 50 per cent of the heads of households out of the labor market; while the others, using a higher income level to define poverty, report only 35 per cent of the heads of households as out of the labor market. We do not have data, but it is reasonable to deduce that a higher percentage of Lampman's poor are on welfare than is true of Morgan's or Keyserling's.

Clearly different income cutoff points shape the characteristics of those of "low income." The lower the income level used, the more economically and socially different are the poor.

Definitions of poverty and the poor are not technical problems but social and ideological issues. The low-income are not basically a "welfare poor." Only one-fifth of Morgan's poor receive welfare assistance. The social scientists and social-service specialists who write of the "welfare poor" are discussing only a slice of the poor; those concerned with "hard-core" and "multiproblem families" are, in turn, analyzing only a very thin wedge of this small slice.

The income criterion has several components: the level of income, the stability or regularity of income, and the source of income (employment or welfare). A number of observers believe that it makes a difference, holding income constant, whether a family is supported by welfare or not. The knowledge to make a fine classification of these components is lacking. I have resorted, therefore, to combining them into one indicator of economic security (roughly combining income and stability), and then dichotomizing this indicator into the two simple dimensions of high (security) and low (insecurity). Lumping together these components and dichotomizing them are inadequate.[16] But we cannot at present describe each of the cells of what should be an eight-fold or sixteen-fold table. I think, however, that the cells of a four-fold table can be usefully discussed. This capsulated table should rapidly be expanded as we acquire more knowledge and understanding.

The style-of-life criterion

The style-of-life variable also offers difficulties. It refers, at least, to attitudes and behavior in the areas of family relationships and consumption patterns. A major difficulty is that the content of the "lower-class style of life" is debatable. Further, evaluative judgments (as implied in the concepts of "family disorganization," "social disorganization," and "family instability") are invariably involved. As yet, it is not possible to formulate a clear-cut classification which avoids cultural biases and still enables us to render a judgment about the impact of life style on individuals. For example, does the absence of a permanent male figure mean that the family is inevitably "unstable" and that children are necessarily psychologically deformed by living in such a family? Assessments such as these are difficult to make because much of our knowledge and theorizing about fatherless families are based on middle-class situations.

I employ the notion of "familial stability/instability," a dichotomization of style of life, to summarize a variety of elements. Familial stability patterns are characterized by families coping with their problems—the children are being fed, although not necessarily on a schedule; the family meets its obligations, so that it is not forced to keep on the move; children are not getting into much more trouble than other children of the neighborhood. These are not satisfactory indicators; they are, at best, suggestive of the kind of behavior which is characteristic of stability among the "low-income." The aim is to be able to describe the degrees of effectiveness of different styles of life in handling the same environment. Our vocabulary is inadequate for this task.

The two approaches can be welded together by cross-tabulating the two dimensions of the two variables of economic security and familial stability in a 2 by 2 table (see Table 16–1.)

Table 16–1. Types of Economic Security and Familial Stability

| | | | Familial | |
			Stability	Instability
			+	−
Economic	Security	+	++(1)	+−(2)
	Insecurity	−	−+(3)	−−(4)

Cell 1 is referred to as *the stable poor;* cell 2, *the strained;* cell 3, *the copers,* and cell 4, *the unstable.*

To some extent, life-cycle stages may be involved here, as some young people escape from cell 4 via cell 2 or cell 3 to cell 1, a more stable pattern, and beyond. Or families may drop with age from cell 1 to cell 3, where they have lowered economic security but maintain family stability.

Each of the cells contains many variants. Although I believe that the four types are an improvement over analysis in terms of *"the* lower class," it is important to recognize that each type has many variations. One difference, of course, is whether the family is stationary in its particular pattern or moving to greater or less security-stability. *My general orientation is to emphasize flux rather than assuming a permanent position in a pattern.*

The stable poor

Cell 1 (*the stable poor*) is characterized by stability economically and familially. This cell points to the regularly employed, low-skill, stable-poor families.

Farm, rural nonfarm, and small-town persons undoubtedly make up the bulk of the stable poor, since they are the majority of the American poor: a recalculation of Morgan's data suggests that only 30 per cent of the poor live in metropolitan areas. The majority of all the poor and of the stable poor are white rural Southern populations. In addition, the nonurban poor are probably represented in this cell to a greater extent than they are among all the poor. Aged persons are also overrepresented and constitute a large part of the downwardly mobile poor, since most of them were better off at earlier points in their lives. Left-over third-generation immigrant populations in large cities are probably underrepresented.[17]

A number of Negro families are of the stable poor. They have higher social status in the Negro community than their economic counterparts have in the white community because of the general scaling down of incomes and occupational levels of Negroes in the United States. For reasons discussed below, Negroes and other discriminated groups are probably becoming more important politically, as well as in relative size, among the urban stable poor.

The children of cell 1 families are most likely of all the children of the poor to be educationally and occupationally mobile. Cell 1 might be the "takeoff" cell—the phase necessary before many can really make a big advance. But this is a dangerous metaphor, for obviously many youth from families in more difficult circumstances are able to make considerable gains.

The stable poor, then, are a varied group; one component, the aged, has a poor economic future, except to the extent that Social Security and old-age payments improve, and a declining future as an intact family unit.

The strained

Cell 2 (*the strained*) portrays a secure economic pattern but an unstable family one. This might be a life-cycle problem; that is, at certain points, the families of low-wage, unskilled workers are likely to exhibit unstable patterns. Examples might be "wild" younger workers or alcoholic older workers who disturb family functioning. Or the pattern could manifest the beginning of a move into cell 4, as a low-income family finds increasing difficulty in maintaining its economic security because of family and personal problems or the economic situation. Obviously, the two possibilities may be closely connected.

Movement may be viewed intergenerationally as well as in terms of life-cycle patterns. Many of the offspring of strained families "may fail to match the economic security of their parents" and experience intergenerational skidding.[18]

Strained familial relations may not, however, result in skidding. In earlier periods, immigrant groups faced considerable internal strain arising from the conflict between the younger and older generations in the course of acculturation. Nonetheless, the second generation generally improved its economic circumstances. The instability of today's strained families is regarded as more "pathological" than that of the immigrant populations, although some social-work accounts of families at the turn of the century differ little from current reports of "poor family functioning." The current stress is on fighting and drinking among parents, illicit sexual relations of parents, and neglect or brutality toward the children. Whether the economically secure and familially unstable are characterized by these patterns is not clear. If they are not, then the offspring of the strained family may not be as much prey to skidding. Further, not all children of deeply conflicted or hostile families are inevitably unable to maintain or improve their economic position.

I have looked at cell 2 as a transitional condition. This view may be misleading: many families persist with a low but steady income and a great deal of internal strain.

The copers

The copers of cell 3 manifest economic insecurity and familial stability—families and individuals having a rough time economically but managing to keep themselves relatively intact. This group probably increases considerably during extensive layoffs. Probably a considerable number of Negroes are in this group, and their children are more likely to be mobile than are those living in cell 2-type situations.

This cell probably contains a disproportionate number of families which have been downwardly mobile. Both Morgan[19] and I[20] have shown the sizable number of sons of nonmanual workers who end up in manual (and sometimes low-income) positions. In Great Britain, 40 per cent of those born in nonmanual families move into manual occupations. Many of these downwardly mobile are probably more likely to retain a stable family style than others in the same economic predicament. As in many other situations, however, a minority of the downwardly mobile may manifest extreme familial instability, which would place them in cell 4. Limited data suggest that children of downwardly mobile families have a better chance of rising occupationally than children of families which have been at this low level for some generations.

The unstable

In cell 4, *the unstable* have neither economic nor personal stability. It is this group which is probably most generally called "the lower class," and Jerome Cohen has suggested to me that the term *lower class* might be usefully restricted to this group. Because this recommendation is unlikely to be consistently utilized by social workers, economists, sociologists, political scientists, and others interested in low-income populations, I have not adopted it, preferring to focus attention on the varied segments of the low-income population. Within the unstable group there are degrees of stability and strain—*not every family is a "hard-core case" or has a "multi-agency problem."* Nor do we have sufficient longtitudinal data to assert that, once in cell 4, always in cell 4. It may be that families and individuals occasionally manifest both economic and personal instability, then overcome these problems for a while. Later they may again suffer from illness, unemployment, emotional upset, or familial instability.

In some ways, it is as important to note that cell 4 is a very varied grouping as it is to distinguish cell 4 from the other three cells that make up the "lower class." Cell 4 comprises partially urbanized Negroes new to the North and to cities, remaining slum residents of ethnic groups which have largely moved out of the slums, long-term (intergenerational) poor white families, and the *déclassé* of Marx. Also included are the physically handicapped and the aged who have dropped through the class structure. *The low-income class generally—and the unstable in particular—is a category of unskilled, irregular workers, broken and large families, and a residual bin of the aged, physically handicapped, and mentally disturbed.*

In some cases, such social characteristics as discrimination and recent rurality (resulting in unfamiliarity with urban problems and the lack of skills needed for dealing with them) handicap the low-income groups. These groups—Negroes and former mountaineer whites—would have the worst problems. Perhaps they would also have the greatest potential because elimination of their social limitations would lead to substantial change. Their handicaps are less self-inflicted and less self-sustaining. This may not be as true for mountaineer whites as for Negroes. In addition to people who drop into the poverty class along the life- and physical-cycle, the whites in the lower class who have no sound social reason for being there are most likely to be intractable to change.

Hylan Lewis[21] has suggested the categories of *clinical, preclinical,* and *subclinical* to delineate patterns among the poor. I would substitute the word *chronic* for *clinical.* The *chronics* refer to the long-term dependents, part of whom would be the "hard-core"; the *prechronics* would be a high-risk group which is moving toward a chronic situation but have not yet become chronically dependent. The *subchronics* are those who have many characteristics of dependence but who also have a greater ability to cope with their problems.[22]

A number of forces can lead individuals into chronic dependence. *"Lower-class" life is crisis-life constantly trying to make do with string where rope is needed.* Anything can break the string. Illness is one of the most important—"Got a job but I got sick and lost it"; "We managed until the baby got sick." The great incidence of physical afflictions among the poor—frequently unknown to the victim—is obvious to any casual observer. Particularly striking are the poor teeth of many. The tendency of lower-class people to somaticize their emotional difficulties may be influenced by the omnipresence of illness.

Familial and personal instability may be the sources as well as the consequences of difficulties. Although some frequent concomitants of low-income life, such as matrifocality, do not inevitably produce grave difficulties in family life, they frequently do. Alcoholism, an inability to handle aggression, or hostility or dependence—one's own or that of another toward one—can deeply disturb family functioning. A variety of direct personal aid may be necessary.

Sophistication along these lines of analysis has frequently tended to denigrate the importance of structural factors in producing "personal inadequacies," "social disabilities," "familial instability." The work of Raymond Smith[23] and Edith Clarke[24] strongly suggests that illegitimacy is related to economic conditions—the better the economic conditions among the "lower-class" Negroes of the Caribbean, the lower the rate of illegitimacy. Kunstadter[25] similarly argues that matrifocality as a "lower-class" trait is related to a particular set of economic characteristics.

Prolonged unemployment, irregular employment, and low income are important forces leading to a chronic pattern. Low-paid and irregularly employed individuals do not develop an image of the world as something predictable and as something with which they are able to cope. Control or directing of events appears (and frequently is) an unattainable achievement. When they suffer long-term unemployment they are less likely than other unemployed, who have had the experience of fairly regular employment, to maintain a personal stability. (Maslow[26] has argued that those who have had a stable past are more able to manage in disastrous circumstances than those who have had considerable prior deprivation.) A high-employment economy has relatively fewer "hard-core" cases than a low-employment economy. The American community studies suggest that the "lower class" is smaller in numbers in times of prosperity than in periods of depression. Peter Townsend in an informal lecture recently declared that during the 1930's in England it was believed that 500,000 to 1,000,000 of those not working were "unemployable." In 1940, with the pressures of the war, it was discovered that only 100,000 were really unemployables. Structural change would be of great importance in reducing dependence.

Strategies

Three basic policies are possible: (1) direct economic change, such as providing better employment, or directly raising incomes through the provision of a national minimum level of income; (2) direct services, such as casework activities to strengthen the ego-functioning of the individual, or family assistance through homemaker help; (3) indirect change by affecting the climate—social, psychological, or political—of the neighborhoods in which the poor live.

What would lead one type of low-income population in a given direction would not work at all for another type. A panacea does not work because there is no one thing which will have a pervasive impact in all cases if changed. What is dynamic for one type may be insignificant for others.

I find the concept of elasticity useful here.[27] It points to the extent of change resulting from the input of additional services or income. Some types of the poor have high income elasticity—a little change in income produces a big change in behavior; other types may have low income elasticity but high education elasticity or high casework elasticity. Still other types will respond rapidly and deeply to new housing, to a steady job, to counseling, or to a package of such ingredients rather than to, say, casework. The concept of elasticity introduces frontally the issues of variable remedies for different types. The issues of costs, substitution, and choice of different services or resources are made vivid by the notion of elasticity and productivity (the return per unit of expenditure).

The stable—those in cell 1—would be immediately helped if their incomes were raised so that they would come closer to the American standard of life. Unionization of their industries (especially in service trades and occupations), shifts from low-productivity land and industries to highly productive industries, and occupational retraining would be important. In some situations, individuals have to be prepared for retraining (where, for example, the level of literacy is low) or aided in moving to new localities where opportunities are greater. They may need help in adjusting to new urban conditions, but this adjustment would probably not be very difficult where jobs and housing are adequate. The stable poor, in short, would have a high income elasticity, rapidly improving and adjusting to increases in their income.

The inadequacy of social services and payments in the United States forces many into cell 1. Improving and extending Social Security, which keeps many in penury and does not help a substantial number in noncovered occupations and industries, would move many from cells 2, 3, and 4 into cell 1 and lead many of the stable poor into the main society. Harrington[28] and Titmuss[29] have pointed out that social services in the United States and Britain do not seem to be benefiting the poor as much as the middle-income population. Obviously, changes in social policy are necessary here.

Some of the strained of cell 2 might require some casework help in improving family conditions and operations, but other approaches might be effective. If they live in a locality that manifests high rates of disturbances, they might be helped by being moved to new areas. For some, an improvement in economic conditions may be necessary in order to get deeper family changes. Undoubtedly, a number are not sensitive to income changes or to neighborhood climate change, and for these sustained casework help would be necessary.

Familial instability may be a carryover from an earlier period when the family suffered from economic insecurity; the family has not caught up with its economic improvements. But, as Seymour S. Bellin and Jerome Cohen have pointed out, in some families where economic conditions have improved after a long period of economic deprivation and family difficulties, withdrawing the stress of economic insecurity may be insufficient. The toll of the stress frequently must be overcome. Special help may be necessary to bring about familial changes of great importance. Of importance would be the adaptation of social agencies to enable them to meet the requirements of these families at the time of need and to provide aid in ways which fit the outlook of these families.

The copers of cell 3, who maintain family stability in the face of grave economic difficulties, obviously need economic aid. Many of them would be helped by improvement in welfare payments and practices; others, where there is a working head of household, would be advanced by regularization of work and/or by shifting to more remunerative fields. The needs of the stable and the copers would seem to be similar. Improvement in the economic dimension would push more of the copers into the mobility possibilities of the stable poor of cell 1 and beyond.

Cell 4, containing the unstable, is the most discussed grouping of the poor today. Many, if not most, are on welfare allotments; women head many of the family units. A general improvement in economic conditions would not have much economic impact on the unstable, because they are largely out of the labor force and out of the economy. It is widely believed that unstable families do not have a high income elasticity, but the evidence is not strong. Specific programs aimed at this group would be important. Present-day welfare services are insufficient, since they have largely been budgetary and policing activities. Concentration on improving the educational achievement of the youth of these families would be more important, perhaps, than a diffuse effort to achieve better family functioning.[30] A number of interesting and aggressive casework services have been offered; their degree of long-term success is unclear. A variety of direct services may be effective with some of these families—including continuous homemaking and babysitting services, provision of nurseries, all-day schools, and consumer-buying protection.

It may be that a less direct approach would be effective. It would involve trying to mobilize politically the communities in which the unstable live with the more stable poor so as to provide greater feelings of strength and control. The anticipated but side effect would be the improving of family conditions. A general change in a low-income community, precipitated perhaps by the mobile, the strained, and the copers, may spread to affect the unstable of the community. The social-actionists, of whom Saul Alinsky is the best known, utilize this implicit strategy.

In all of the strategies, it is necessary to be clear about who exactly is the target population. This is frequently determined on the basis of the numbers involved, although there is always the delicate choice between helping a lot of people a little and helping a few people a lot. The second step is to discover what works with whom. There is probably nothing that will help all "lower-class" people in one move, although, as suggested above, a steady, meaningful, well-paid job as a general base of action should not be underestimated. A decent level of living for all as the minimal responsibility of an affluent society, no matter what people do around this level, may be an important point to maintain in a period when government welfare payments are under criticism. But there are some things that will help certain types. We have to find the right things for the right groups at the right time.

Political action

The poor are not rapidly declining; income and wealth inequality appear to be increasing in recent years; the incomes of Negroes are no longer advancing relative to those of whites; pension and assistance schemes are maintaining many in poverty rather than providing a "Welfare State" standard. The decline in the number of poor between 1927 and 1957 was due, Lampman contends, to general economic advance rather than to a redistribution of income and wealth in favor of the poor. Improvements in social services and a decrease in inequality would require a shift in the allocation of national product toward improving the relative position of the bottom 20 per cent.

These issues are political ones. They will be affected by the possibility that the present American poor may prove to be more politically active than is usually true of the poor. If this happens, it will be because a large slice of the urban poor is made up of Negroes, who have ethnic as well as economic forces moving them. Samuel Lubell [31] has argued that Negroes in large cities will furnish a new base for Democratic ward machines. They are becoming more and more politically active and demanding. This self-organization is not only important in getting changes from the government, but is also serving to change "lower-class" Negro communities from within.

Local leaders are developing, and the orientation of many community agencies to provide leadership and direction to "lower-class" communities will become increasingly ineffective. The conservative orientation of gaining change and social advance through a harmonious arrangement with local power forces is being superseded by disadvantaged groups themselves actively pressuring for the kinds of changes—in housing, in schools, and the like—that they believe to be important.

In the course of these pressures, it is likely that the *desegregation issue will emerge as a social-class issue* affecting all "lower-class" persons, and not only as a racial issue affecting Negroes alone. Mexican-Americans and Puerto Ricans, who with Negroes increasingly make the poor of the large metropolis a "colored poor," are increasingly moving into the stable and coping patterns and beginning to develop political effectiveness. Poverty may not be treated as a racial issue affecting only Negroes. Even *where Negroes operate alone, the impact of their demands will affect all the poor as they achieve better schools, better housing, better jobs, and better social services.*

Cause and consequence

A good deal of the tone of discussions of the "lower class," even by sociologists, has a negative quality. On the other hand, a few seem to have a romantic feeling about the "lower class," particularly their juvenile delinquents, and see them as rebels against the horrors of middle-class, conformist America. The former view suffers from the assumption that they have little potential for change; the latter, that there is nothing better in present-day America to which they can change.

Among other things, the glorification theme ignores, as Riessman has pointed out, the impact on the "lower class" of its limited education.[32] The negative view frequently confuses, as Keyserling has noted, cause and consequence. The personal instability of many "lower-class" persons may be a consequence of economic instability as well as a cause of it. The chain of cause and effect over time frequently becomes blurred. Where is there an effective way of cutting into the chain so that change will occur? This becomes the issue. My feeling is that structural forces have been under-played recently as a mode of change, as "the culture of poverty" has been over-stressed.[33]

The negative view has the danger of not seeing positive elements in "lower-class" life. By ignoring these elements, social policies can frequently worsen them. For example, in an exciting study of a Puerto Rican slum, Helen Icken Safa has reported the community and familial solidarity of the residents of a slum barrio. When families were moved into public housing, community ties were weakened. The project social workers centered on the wife. The husband's role and responsibility in the family and community diminished.[34]

It is perhaps a "heuristic" fallacy, as Frank Riessman has said, to believe that "lower-class" people are willing and capable of positive change. This is not always true, but if professionals and social reformers lack confidence in the poor, little can be accomplished in the social services or in political action. One might fail with this optimism—as we frequently do—but without it, it is doubtful if anything can be moved. Frequently, disenchantment and cynicism capture accurately a slice of life. They are also immobilizing, for they ignore the constructive and energizing role of hope.[35]

Conclusion

A clearly defined "lower class" does not exist—it is a varied, changing group, as Peter Townsend has noted:

> A misconception is that in a relatively prosperous society most individuals have the capacity to meet any contingency in life. Only a poor and handicapped minority need special protection or help. This ignores the infinite diversities and changing conditions to be found in any population. Men gain or fall in status and living standards; at one stage of their life their dependencies are minimal, at others unduly numerous; sometimes they need exceptional help to achieve qualifications and skills held to be desirable by society; and at all times they are susceptible to the vicissitudes of prolonged ill health, disability, redundancy of unemployment, and bereavement, which they are usually powerless to control or even reasonably anticipate. Unanticipated adversity is not the peculiar experience of one section of the working class.[36]

In England, Dahrendorf contends,[37] the unskilled category is a temporary position—individuals at various stages of the life cycle may drop into it, but for only a comparatively few is it a permanent position. In the United States, this is not so true, and if caste pressures grow, it will be even less true.

The changing economy of America is producing new property relations; at the same time, it is producing new working classes and lower classes.[38] The analysis of data and the development of our concepts have not kept up with the increasing differentiation within these populations. Many pressures and counter-pressures exist in any stratum. Despite a modal pattern, considerable variety in values and behavior occurs. Because cross-pressures affect the "lower class" to a considerable extent,[39] we should look for *types* of behavior patterns even among people apparently very similar in objective characteristics. Those at the social bottom see only a vague and ill-defined "them" up there, whereas those above believe that those below are rather similar. But the tops know how much differentiation within the top actually takes place; the bottoms are aware of much more differentiation than are the outsiders looking in. In particular, what has been taken as typical of the most unstable bottom group has been generalized to apply to all who are poor or who are manual workers.

The label "the lower class" increasingly distorts complicated reality. We must begin to demarcate more sharply types of poor people if we are to understand and interpret behavior and circumstance and to develop appropriate social policies. Evaluations of commentators are frequently masked as description. *Ways of coping with hard reality are interpreted as normatively prescribed whereas frequently they are actually weakly dissanctioned behavior.*

The resurgence of interest in the poor augurs well for a rethinking of the new kind of poverty in the "welfare state" which is unlike the mass unemployment of the 1930's or the grinding poverty of the employed workers of the nineteenh century. Our "received wisdom" should be superseded by new categories and concepts. New wine is being poured into old conceptual bottles, and the specialness of the new is being lost.

NOTES

1. Cf. Patricia Cayo Sexton, *Education and Income: Inequalities in Our Public Schools* (New York: Viking, 1961), pp. 10ff. S. M. Miller, Carolyn Comings, and Betty Saleem, *The School Dropout Problem—Syracuse* (Albany: New York State Division for Youth and the Syracuse University Youth Development Center, 1963). Herman P. Miller points out that the disadvantage of not having a college diploma grew from 1939 to 1958. See his "Money Value of an Education," *Occupational Outlook Quarterly* (September, 1961), p. 4.
2. Janet E. Weinandy, *Families under Stress* (Syracuse: Syracuse University Youth Development Center, 1962).
3. Audrey Harvey, *Casualties of the Welfare State,* Fabian Tract 321 (London: Fabian Society, 1959).
4. Michael Harrington, *The Other America: Poverty in the United States* (New York: Macmillan, 1962): Conference on Economic Progress, *Poverty and Deprivation in the United States* (Washington, D.C.: Conference on Economic Progress, 1961) (the main author of this analysis is Leon Keyserling and it is known as the "Keyserling Report"); Gabriel Kolko, *Wealth and Power in the United States* (New York: Praeger, 1962); Robert J. Lampman, "The Low Income Population and Economic Growth," Study Paper No. 12, Joint Economic Committee, Congress of the United States, December 16, 1959 (Washington, D.C.: Government Printing Office, 1959); James N. Morgan *et al., Income and Welfare in the United States* (New York: McGraw-Hill, 1962). These books are reviewed in S. M. Miller, "Poverty and Inequality in America: Implications for the Social Services," *Child Welfare,* XLII (November, 1963), 442–445 (republished in the Syracuse University Youth Development Center Reprint Series).
5. Brian Abel-Smith, "Whose Welfare State?", in Norman MacKenzie (ed.), *Conviction* (London: MacGibbon and Kee, 1957).
6. "The terms 'lower class' and 'middle class' are used here to refer to systems of behavior and concerns rather than groups defined in conventional economic terms." William C. Kvaraceus and Walter B. Miller, *Delinquent Behavior: Culture and the Individual* (Washington, D.C.: National Education Association, 1959), p. 62.
7. S. M. Miller and Frank Riessman, "The Working-Class Subculture: A New View," *Social Problems,* IX (Summer, 1961), 86–97.
8. Allison Davis, "The Motivation of the Underprivileged Worker," in William Foote Whyte (ed.), *Industry and Society* (New York: McGraw-Hill, 1946), pp. 84–106.
9. August B. Hollingshead and Fredrick C. Redlich, *Social Class and Mental Illness: A Community Study* (New York: Wiley, 1958), pp. 387–397.
10. Walter B. Miller, "Lower Class Culture as a Generating Milieu of Gang Delinquency," *Journal of Social Issues,* XIV, No. 3 (1958), 6, footnote 3. In his pene-

trating analysis, Miller notes the existence of "subtypes of lower class culture" but does not pursue this point. While his emphasis is on cultural characteristics such as "female-based" household and "serial monogamy" mating patterns, he elsewhere employs educational, occupational, and income variables to define the lower class. See his "Implications of Urban Lower-Class Culture for Social Work," *Social Service Review*, XXXIII (September, 1959), 229ff. His major stress is on cultural or status characteristics as defining the lower-class culture.

11. *Ibid.*

12. Lee Rainwater assisted by Karol Kane Weinstein, *And the Poor Get Children* (Chicago: Quadrangle Books, 1960). See also the distinctions made within the lower-lower class by Martin Loeb, "Social Class and the American Social System," *Social Work*, VI (April, 1961), 16.

13. Keyserling, *op. cit.;* Lampman, *op. cit.*

14. See footnote 4.

15. Morgan, *op. cit.,* p. 3.

16. Not all families receiving welfare assistance should automatically be classified in the economically insecure category. For the aged, perhaps, welfare assistance does not constitute a lack of security. In general, however, the fact of welfare assistance would put a family in the economically insecure category.

17. Richard Cloward and Lloyd Ohlin, *Delinquency and Opportunity* (New York: The Free Press of Glencoe, 1960).

18. Dennis Wrong, in a personal communication, has influenced this and the following paragraph. "Skidding" is discussed in Harold Wilensky and Hugh Edwards, "The Skidder: Ideological Adjustments of Downward Mobile Workers," *American Sociological Review*, XXIV (April, 1959), 215–231.

19. Morgan, *op. cit.*

20. S. M. Miller, "Comparative Social Mobility," *Current Sociology*, IX, No. 1 (1960), 1–89.

21. Hylan Lewis, "Child Rearing among Low Income Families" (Washington Center for Metropolitan Studies, June 8, 1961). This paper and others by Lewis are among the most stimulating on the problems of low-income patterns. Also see Hyman Rodman, "The Lower-Class Value Stretch," *Social Forces*, XLII (December, 1963), pp. 205–215.

22. I have used the terms *dependent* and *dependence* here for want of a sharper term; I find the concept of dependence murky and frequently used to cover a variety of conditions which a writer does not like.

23. Raymond T. Smith, *The Negro Family in British Guiana* (London: Routledge & Kegan Paul, 1956).

24. Edith Clarke, *My Mother Who Fathered Me* (New York: Humanities Press, 1957).

25. Peter Kunstadter, "A Survey of the Consanguine and Matrifocal Family," *American Anthropologist*, LXV (February, 1963), 56–66.

26. A. H. Maslow, *Motivation and Personality* (New York: Harper, 1954), pp. 80–106.

27. Carlsson has reintroduced the concept of elasticity into sociological thinking. See Gosta Carlsson. "Ökonomische Ungleichheit und Lebenschanchen," *Kölner Zeitschrift für Soziologie*, V (1961), 189–199.

28. Harrington, *op. cit.*

29. Richard Titmuss, *Essays on "The Welfare State"* (London: George Allen & Unwin, 1958), Ch. 2, "The Social Division of Welfare," in *Income Distribution and Social Change* (Toronto: University of Toronto Press, 1962). Although Titmuss is a seminal thinker in analyzing changes in the social structure of the modern society, he has been almost completely ignored by American sociologists.

30. Cf. S. M. Miller, "Poverty and Inequality in America," *op. cit.*

31. In his syndicated column which appeared in the *Syracuse Herald-Journal* (November 14, 1961).

32. Frank Riessman, *The Culturally Deprived Child* (New York: Harper, 1962).

33. Harrington seems frequently to write and speak as though all low-income persons are bound in an immutable chain of apathy and ineffectiveness, characteristics of "the culture of poverty." He has obviously extended this term beyond the intent of Oscar Lewis, who introduced it in his *Five Families* (New York: Basic Books,

1959), and in *The Children of Sanchez* (New York: Random House, 1961). Warren O. Hagstrom has countered this view in his "The Power of the Poor" (Syracuse University Youth Development Center, 1963).

34. Helen Icken Safa, *From Shanty Town to Public Housing* (Syracuse University Youth Development Center, 1962). The peculiar stresses of public housing life may be functional equivalents of the economic conditions of matrifocality discussed by Kunstadter.

35. Cf. S. M. Miller and Frank Riessman, "Working Class Authoritarianism: A Critique of Lipset," *British Journal of Sociology*, XII (September, 1961), pp. 263–276.

36. Peter Townsend, "Freedom and Equality," *New Statesman*, LXI, No. 1570 (April 14, 1961), 574.

37. Ralf Dahrendorf, "Unskilled Labour in British Industry," unpublished Ph.D. thesis in sociology, London School of Economics, 1956, pp. 429–430.

38. S. M. Miller, "Poverty, Race and Politics," in Irving Louis Horowitz (ed.), *The New Sociology: Essays on Social Values and Social Theory in Honor of C. Wright Mills* (New York: Oxford University Press, 1964).

39. See Miller and Riessman, "The Working-Class Subculture," and Hylan Lewis, *op. cit.*

17

Technology and Unemployment

ROBERT M. SOLOW

Whenever there is both rapid technological change and high unemployment the two will inevitably be connected in people's minds. So it is not surprising that technological unemployment was a live subject during the depression of the 1930's, nor that the debate has now revived. The discussion thirty years ago was inconclusive, partly because there were more urgent things to worry about and partly because economists did not then have a workable theory of income and employment as a whole. They have now. Curiously, the current discussion seems to take place mainly outside of professional economics. That may be because economists feel there are no longer any very important intellectual issues at stake. If that is so, it may be worth stating what the agreed position is.

First, however, one should have an idea of the orders of magnitude involved: how fast is technology changing? After all, an analysis that will perfectly well cover moderate rates of technological progress and moderate increases in the rate may not apply nearly so well if there are catastrophic changes in the role of labor in production. Fortunately this is a fairly straightforward question. Its answer does not depend on what fraction of all the scientists who have ever lived are now alive, or on the number of computers produced and installed last year, or on the existence of an oil refinery with nobody in it, or on any such exotic facts. Any major change in the quantitative relation between output and employment must show up in the conventional productivity statistics. Here productivity means nothing but the value of output per manhour, corrected for price changes. It goes up whenever labor requirements for a unit of final output go down, and by the same percentage. There are productivity statistics for certain industries, for manufacturing as a whole, and for even broader aggregates. It doesn't matter much which aggregate is selected. What such figures show is easily summarized.

For the private economy as a whole, the average annual increase in output per manhour between 1909 and 1964 was 2.4 per cent. But if we divide that long period at the end of World War II, it turns out that the increase was faster after 1947 than before. From 1909 to 1947 productivity rose by 2 per cent a year on the average, while from 1947 to 1964 it rose by 3.2 per cent a year. Moreover, from 1961 to 1964, productivity rose by 3.4 per cent a year.

I said that this was a fairly straightforward question: only *fairly* straight-

From *The Public Interest*, No. 1 (Fall, 1965), pp. 17–26.

forward because it is not easy to interpret changes in productivity extending over just a few years. Recessions and recoveries have their own productivity patterns and there are erratic fluctuations besides. The 1961–1964 rise, part of a long upswing, is especially suspicious. Still, it is hard to mistake what the figures are trying to say. There was a definite acceleration of the productivity trend about the time of the war. (The biggest year-to-year increase came in 1949–1950 for reasons not hard to understand.) There may even have been a slight further acceleration after 1961. It is too early to say, and in any case the amount involved is small.

This rough statistical indication is enough. It does not suggest the immediate disappearance of the job as an institution. But what does it say about the possibility of slower, less dramatic technological unemployment, if only a million or so at a time? Popular writing suggests that there are two schools of thought. One claims point-blank that automation necessarily— or at least in fact—"creates more jobs than it destroys." From this it would seem to follow that, if technological progress went at any slower pace than it now does, there would necessarily be more unemployment than there now is. The other school claims that automation necessarily—or at least in fact —destroys more jobs than it creates. So that if technological progress went at any faster pace than it now does, or only just as fast, severe unemployment would be inevitable.

Which school is right? I think the economist's answer has to be that both are wrong or, to be more precise, both are irrelevant. They have simply missed the point. Perhaps the question "Does automation create or destroy more jobs?" is answerable *in principle;* perhaps it is not. What is perfectly clear is that the question is simply unanswerable *in fact.* I doubt that anyone could make a good estimate of the net number of jobs created or destroyed merely by the invention of the zipper or of sliced bread. It would be a fantastically more complicated job to discover the net effect of *all* technological progress in any single year on employment. No one can possibly know; so no one has the right to speak confidently.

The Great Automation Question, as I have phrased it, is not only unanswerable, it is the wrong question. The important point is that, to a pretty good first approximation, *the total volume of employment in the United States today is simply not determined by the rate of technological progress.* Both theory and common observation tell us that a modern mixed economy can, by proper and active use of fiscal and monetary policy weapons, have full employment for *any* plausible rate of technological change within a range that is easily wide enough to cover the American experience.

The European experience

Consider, for example, the West German economy. Output per manhour has been increasing considerably faster there than in the United States— about 6 per cent a year since 1950, and 5 per cent a year since 1955. While the American *level* of productivity is unsurpassed anywhere, the economy of West Germany has certainly been no less technologically dynamic than our own in the past fifteen years. Yet for some time the German unemployment rate has been below 1 per cent of the labor force (compared with 5–7 per cent here) and there have been seven to ten unfilled vacant jobs for every unemployed person. What is even more striking is that this technologically advanced and advancing economy seems to have an insatiable appetite for unskilled labor. Having exhausted the domestic supply, it goes to Italy, Spain, Portugal, Greece, and Turkey to recruit workers who have only minimal education and can surely neither read, write, nor even speak German. One has the impression that even an American teen-ager could find employment in a German factory. Of course there are many special things that might be said about the recent history of the German economy, from the need for postwar reconstruction to the now-ended flow of refugees from the East. But they do not affect the point at issue.

Or take an example on the other side, Great Britain. Her productivity has grown a bit more slowly than ours. The conventional belief is that the British economy offers more resistance to technological progress than most others. The British economy has also had all sorts of other troubles—but the maintenance of high employment has not been one of them. The unemployment rate in Britain is now about 1½ per cent. There is even some discussion as to whether the economy might not function a bit more efficiently and smoothly with a slightly higher unemployment rate, say 2 per cent.

Polar examples like these give a strong hint that no simple yea-saying or nay-saying can be the right answer to the question about the likelihood of technological unemployment. The right answer is more complicated and goes something like this: At any one time, we can hope to identify something we can call the capacity output of the economy as a whole. (Sometimes it is called "potential" or "full employment" output; the idea is the same.) This is at best a rough-and-ready concept. Under stress an economy can produce more than its capacity for quite a while, so capacity output is not a rigid upper limit. Moreover, a modern economy can produce a wide variety of "mixes" of goods and services, heavily weighted with military hardware, or automobiles, or machinery, or food and fiber, or personal services, according to circumstances. When the economy as a whole is operating at or near its capacity, there may be some industries straining their plant and equipment to the limit while others have quite a bit of slack. Nevertheless, under normal circumstances the output mix changes slowly. We can know what we mean by capacity output and, subject to some error, we can measure it. (In the first quarter of 1965, the country produced a Gross National Product of about $649 billion, annual rate; the Council of Economic Advisers estimated that capacity output was about $25 billion higher.)

The productive capacity of an economy grows fairly smoothly—not with perfect regularity, of course, but fairly smoothly. The growth of productive capacity is determined by an array of basic underlying factors: the growth of the labor force in numbers; changes in the health, education, training, and other qualities of those who work and manage; changes in the number of hours they wish to work; the exhaustion and discovery of natural resources; the accumulation of capital in the form of buildings, machinery, and inventories; and the advance of scientific, engineering, and technological knowledge and its application to production. This is one of the important ways in which the level of technology enters our problem. If the rate of technological progress accelerates or decelerates, then the growth of capacity is likely to speed up or slow down with it. The different factors are not entirely independent of one another: new knowledge may require better-trained or differently trained people or wholly new plant and equipment for its successful application. It is also possible for changes in one of the underlying trends to be offset by changes in another, coincidentally or consciously engineered. In any case, they are likely to move with some smoothness, and their net resultant—capacity output—even more so.

The actual output produced by the economy fluctuates more raggedly around the trend of capacity, sometimes above it, sometimes—more often, in the case of the United States—below it. When production presses hard against capacity, it is capacity limitations that keep it from going higher. In all other cases, what governs the current level of output is the *demand* for goods and services. Demand is exercised by the interlocked spending decisions of all the final purchasers in the economy: consumers, business firms, all levels of government, and the foreigners who buy our exports. Technological developments play a part here too, among many other determinants of spending decisions. Changes in military technology may cause governments to spend more—or less; the invention of new commodities and new ways to produce old ones may induce industry to invest in new facilities and consumers to shift their purchases (and perhaps to change the total amount). Of course there are other reasons why the flow of consumption, investment, and government expenditures may vary. So long as capacity pressure is not too strong, bottlenecks not too pervasive, when total demand rises, total output will rise to match it; when total demand falls, total output will fall with it. This doesn't happen instantaneously; inventories provide one buffer. But it happens.

The picture, then, is of a fairly smoothly rising trend of capacity, propelled by some rather deep-seated forces. Moving around it is a much more volatile, unsteady curve of current output, driven by whatever governs aggregate expenditures, including economic policy decisions. Current output cannot be far above capacity for long, but it can drag along below for years at a time. During the first half of this century, the trend of capacity output in the United States seems to have risen on the average at about 3 per cent a year. From the end of the Korean War until very recently the rate of growth of capacity was more like 3.5 per cent a year; and the best evidence seems to be that the current and immediately prospective growth rate of capacity will be in the neighborhood of 4 per cent a year, possibly a bit lower now, possibly a bit higher later. The postwar acceleration was mainly a result of the speedup in productivity already mentioned. The current acceleration may draw a little something from a further speedup in productivity, but its main source is the arrival at working age of the first postwar babies.

The triumph of economics over fable

Now, the crucial fact is that when output is rising faster than capacity the unemployment rate tends to fall; when output is rising more slowly than capacity—even though it is rising, mind you—the unemployment rate tends to get bigger, and if output rises at about the same rate as capacity, so that the percentage gap between them stays constant, then the unemployment rate stays pretty nearly constant. It is a fairly safe generalization about the past ten years that when aggregate output has risen at about 3.5 per cent a year between any two points in time, just about enough new jobs have appeared to occupy the increment to the labor force, with nothing left over to reduce unemployment. The tax cut of 1964 is a kind of landmark in American economic policy, the triumph of Economics over Fable. I like to think that it was helped along by the sheer cogency of the arguments for it. But any realist has to give a lot of credit to the fact that, from the middle of 1962 to the middle of 1963, with the economy rising and setting "new records" every quarter, the unemployment rate stuck at about 5.6 per cent of the labor force and stubbornly refused to go anywhere, especially not down. Be thankful for small favors; but note also that during that time the GNP corrected for price changes rose only by a little more than 3 per cent. The gap between output and capacity was not narrowing: unemployment was not reduced. If it turns out to be right that the growth of capacity during the next few years will be nearer 4 per cent annually, then it will take a 4 per cent increase in demand every year to hold the unemployment rate constant; what was good enough to keep unemployment level in 1963 may by 1967 not be adequate to stem slowly rising unemployment.

Closer study of the facts suggests a more powerful generalization. On the average, an extra 1 per cent growth of real (i.e., price-corrected) GNP in any year has been associated with a reduction in the unemployment rate of roughly one-third of a percentage point. Or, what is the same thing, to get the unemployment rate to fall by one full point from one year to the next requires that real output (real demand) increase by about 3 per cent *over and above the increase in capacity*. To see how this works, consider the behavior of the economy since the tax cut.

From the middle of 1963 to the middle of 1964, real GNP gained 5 per cent. "Capacity GNP" probably went up by something less than 4 per cent. The rule of thumb I have mentioned (which sometimes goes under the name of Okun's Law) would predict a drop in the unemployment rate of something like .4 of a percentage point. In fact, the unemployment rate did go down, by .5 of a point, from 5.7 per cent to 5.2 per cent. In the half-year from the third quarter of 1964 to the first quarter of 1965 real GNP gained almost 2.5 per cent; this is more than one-half of 1 per cent over and above the rise in capacity. It should, therefore, have reduced the unemployment rate by some .2 per cent. The unemployment rate actually fell from 5.1 per cent to 4.8 per cent.

In all honesty I cannot leave the impression that the national economy ticks over like a bit of clockwork, predictable from a few simple rules of thumb. I have picked out a few instances in which the pat relation between output, growth, and unemployment worked just fine. It is not always so. The relation itself is compounded of the effects of changes in demand on hours worked, on the number of people seeking employment, on the short-run ups and downs of productivity itself. Each of these connections has some slippage; none is precise; there are lags sometimes before the expected response occurs. Moreover, something must depend on what mix of goods and services happens to be demanded. A billion dollars of services probably provides more employment than a billion dollars of goods, a billion dollars of missiles perhaps less than a billion dollars of aircraft. And yet, it's not at all a bad rule of thumb. If I had to predict what would happen to unemployment during the next year I would certainly begin by trying to estimate what is going to happen to the gap between capacity output and aggregate demand.

What does all this have to do with the question of technological unemployment?

Suppose that a surge of technological progress takes place, whether you call it automation or something less ominous-sounding. Productivity will begin to rise at a faster pace than it used to. So will the trend line of capacity output. If the demand for goods and services continues to grow only at its old rate, the gap between demand and capacity will get wider. In other words, if the increase in capacity is not matched by an increase in demand, the result will be an increase in unemployment. (All this, mind you, while new records are being set regularly and columnists assure us that the economy is "booming.") You can call this unemployment technological, if you like, but it is not different from ordinary unemployment. The way to get rid of it is to make sure that demand rises in step with the economy's capacity to produce.

I have already mentioned that changes in technology also have an effect on demand. New commodities, new materials, major cost reductions cannot fail to leave a mark on the way in which the public spends its income. (The "public" here includes businesses and governments as well as individual families.) It is possible that any particular burst of technological progress will carry along with it the extra demand necessary to keep extra unemployment from appearing. It is also possible that it will not. It is even possible that a series of innovations should generate a bigger increment to demand than to capacity, and therefore a net reduction in unemployment. The trouble is that nobody can say in advance which will actually be the case. Indeed, as I have suggested, nobody may be able to tell after the fact which has been the case. One can, of course, say whether unemployment has gone up or gone down. But there are many other influences on employment.

Faster growth of the labor force, for example, can also push up the capacity trend; it can also have effects on demand. Except under the best of circumstances, it may prove impossible to identify the particular effects of technical progress and separate them from the effects of other forces.

The moral of this analysis is that such an identification doesn't much matter. Unemployment above the "frictional" level occurs, usually, because total dollar demand fails to keep pace with productive capacity. Whether or not an acceleration of technological progress happens to be among the causes is not all-important. The remedy in any case is to keep total demand moving in step with capacity. And this, governments in the mixed economy do have the fiscal and monetary policies to insure—if they will use these powers.

So, as the examples of Germany and Britain confirm, it is possible to have full employment with slow technical progress and full employment with fast technical progress. *But it does not happen automatically.* It requires conscious policy to manage the volume of demand and keep it going at approximately the right pace. (Do not be misled, in this connection, by the case of Germany. The Federal Republic talks the best game of laissez faire in the world. At the same time it does dozens of things each one of which would be instantly denounced in the United States as creeping socialism.)

In the modern mixed economy there is no shortage of instrumentalities for operating on aggregate demand: monetary and credit policy, changes in taxation, adjustments in transfer payments—such as unemployment compensation, family allowances, and social security benefits—and, finally, the direct purchases of goods and services by the government. Since each of these instruments must serve other purposes as well, it may not always be clear exactly what is the best policy. That is what the discussion ought to be about, rather than mere anecdote about the wonders and horrors of modern technology.

The fine structure of unemployment

This analysis of the interrelations among technological progress, output, and employment is, as I have said, a first approximation, though a usable one. A second approximation would have to take account of the fact that each of these global concepts has a fine structure. The main new implication is that a period of rapid change is likely to be accompanied by much displacement of labor. Even if the total volume of unemployment is held unchanged, its composition may shift noticeably. This calls for additional policy measures designed to speed and cushion the necessary transitions.

Technological progress, whether it takes the form of new products or "automation," can be more or less labor-saving in its effects. And, however labor-saving it is, it can fall more or less heavily on the availability of skilled jobs or unskilled jobs, manual or white-collar jobs, manufacturing or service jobs, jobs for uneducated or jobs for highly educated workers. Any innovation has direct and indirect effects on employment, some of which are very complicated. New products and new methods of production require new machinery, new materials, new locations, and perhaps still other changes in economic activity. It is well to realize that *almost nothing is known about the full labor-saving effects of major innovations,* nor even whether "automation" is more or less labor-saving than earlier changes in technology, nor even whether it causes any consistent change in the general level of skill needed in production. There is always a small supply of anecdotes, but anecdote is a poor sort of evidence, given the universal tendency to tell the same anecdote more than once.

The second of our global quantities—output—also has a structure. I have already mentioned that shifts in demand between goods and services, and among various kinds of goods, may change the basic relations connecting total output and total employment. This is because the different things that families, firms, and governments buy contain different amounts of labor, and especially different amounts of labor of different types and from different places. The shift in defense procurement from aircraft to missiles may well have meant less employment per dollar of spending; it has certainly meant more employment for the sort of people who are at work in the electronics industry in the places where the electronics industry has settled, and less work for the occupations more at home in the making of airframes and engines in the places where that industry has been most concentrated. A similar story could be told about the replacement of natural by synthetic fibers and, above all, about the shift from agriculture to industry.

I remember that in 1961 one often heard the opinion that the shift from goods to services was accelerating, and that the demand for durable goods, in particular, was essentially saturated. The burden of the argument was that the blue-collar occupations and the traditional industrial cities—Detroit especially—were finished, would not respond to general economic expansion. The prescription was for salvage operations rather than fiscal and monetary stimulation. Well, as it happens, the expansion that began early in 1961 has been to an unusual extent concentrated in the goods-producing industries, especially in the durable-goods industries, most especially in the automobile industry. One result has been that employment has risen (and unemployment has fallen) relatively more rapidly in blue-collar than in white-collar occupations, more in manufacturing than in the service industries, and more among the unskilled and semi-skilled than among others. I do not conclude from this experience that white-collar occupations and service industries have had it; I conclude only that people ought to stifle the tendency, in matters they do not understand, to project the last six months into an irreversible trend.

As this discussion indicates, and as everyone must realize anyway, there is also a fine structure to unemployment. Everyone in the labor force does not have the same probability of becoming or staying unemployed. Unemployment rates differ according to age, sex, color, education, skill, occupation, place, and industry of attachment. The differences are far from trivial: in the first quarter of this year less than 3 per cent of white men 20 years old and older were unemployed, but more than 30 per cent of Negro girls between 14 and 19 years old were unemployed. The character of unemployment as a social problem depends critically on the composition of the unemployed. It is one kind of situation when unemployment is concentrated, as it now is, among the young; it would be a different, but perhaps even more serious, situation if the same amount of unemployment were concentrated among heads of families with long-standing attachment to the labor force. An economist will wish to separate the two questions: How much unemployment is there? Who has to bear it? I myself would not want to push the difference between these questions too far; but it is important to push the difference far enough. Otherwise confusion arises.

If, in fact, we are in for a period of comparatively rapid productivity increase in white-collar and service jobs, then some of the traditional unemployment *differentials* may shift. Whether they do so will depend on the speed with which the supply of different categories of labor adjusts to the demand. One cannot draw any simple conclusions about *total* employment in this way.

The Arizona fallacy

I have argued that the main determinant of the total amount of unemployment is the size of the gap between the economy's aggregate capacity to produce things and the aggregate purchasing power the economy is willing to devote to buying them. When it comes to the composition of unemployment, the important things to talk about are the particular nature of technological progress, the fine structure of demand, the path by which the present situation has been reached (I shall mention why in a moment), and perhaps the forces that govern the relative wages of different categories of labor.

That is a subject to itself. I want to make only a negative point, directly related to the Great Automation Question. It is all too easy to fall into a fallacy which goes like this. Many of the unemployed are uneducated and unskilled, and many of the uneducated and unskilled are unemployed. It must follow that the source of our high unemployment has to be something which strikes particularly at the unskilled and uneducated. What can that be but the tendency for automation to render the unskilled and uneducated unemployable? It is not often realized that the logic of this argument is about on a par with the logic that observes a relatively high incidence of deaths from tuberculosis in Arizona and concludes that the Arizona climate must be a powerful cause of tuberculosis.

It does seem true that, with the present state of the arts and the present wage structure, the skilled, the educated, the middle-aged and the permanently established are, generally speaking, more "desirable" employees than others. This suggests that in any substantial period of tranquility employers may succeed in exchanging their undesirable workers for more desirable ones. It does not at all deny that a sustained increase in output would induce them to absorb the "undesirable" workers. You do not have to be a high school graduate to sell soap in a department store. But so long as high school graduates can be had, they will be hired first; the dropouts will go to the end of the line, and remain unemployed. This sort of explanation is especially plausible in the circumstances we now face.

The American economy has sidled along with excessive but not catastrophic unemployment for almost ten years. There has been no deep recession, so there have not been extensive layoffs. With labor markets slack and new jobs hard to find, the number of voluntary quits and job changes has also stayed fairly low. When unemployment is generated by inadequate growth rates rather than by recession, labor turnover may thus be relatively slow. The natural result is that unemployment is disproportionately heavy among newcomers to the labor force, both young people just out of school and older women seeking work after raising children. This mechanism, together with the relative "desirability" of the better educated and with discrimination against Negroes, seems capable of explaining the observed distribution of unemployment. It gets a little more confirmation with each month that the current upswing lasts. The "imminent" skill shortages fail to appear; the hard core slowly melts; nearly all categories of unemployment dwindle, employment increases most rapidly among those groups with the highest unemployment rates. And if, as many observers fear, by the end of the year the growth of aggregate output slows down to about the growth of capacity and the unemployment rate stops falling, I shall take that as further confirmation, the hard way.

18

Challenge of the Future

EDGAR M. HOOVER

The possibilities for deflection of past trends of regional development are obviously so manifold, and in most cases so dependent upon the extent and success of constructive improvement efforts within the Pittsburgh Region, that a quantitative forecast of just what *will* happen would be delusive and (if taken seriously) actually harmful. The useful role of projections in a study like this is merely to establish, for guidance to planners and policy-makers, the range within which they can assume their actions (as well as other factors beyond their control) may influence the outcome. And this modest aim is in fact subordinate to the more fundamental identification of determining factors and relationships which represents the bulk of the Study's effort.[1]

Within those limitations of purpose and feasibility we have developed some projections of growth and structural change in the Region and its component parts.[2]

Our projections indicate that the over-all employment problem of the Region will remain at best as the overriding concern for many years and that it may even become worse.[3] It has to be approached, then, on a long-range basis; and corrective actions which might not have any real impact for several years cannot reasonably be dismissed on that score.

In view of the deep-seated character of the Region's economic malad-justment, as manifest in the fact that it has been gradually more and more evident for at least forty years, even "holding the line" with current rates of unemployment and net out-migration would represent a substantial accomplishment, not to be assured without major continuing effort. Since the end of World War II, the "Pittsburgh Renaissance" has been launched and has brought major accomplishments in downtown and industrial urban renewal, smoke control, river pollution abatement, expressway construction, and some vigorous industrial promotion and planning effort. Though the impact of these efforts is of course a continuing one, the Region's economic performance in the postwar period would unquestionably have been much less adequate in the absence of those policies and actions. Yet that performance was unsatisfactory. This suggests that not merely continued but greatly in-

From Pittsburgh Regional Planning Association, *Region with a Future* (Pittsburgh: University of Pittsburgh Press, 1963), pp. 227–289. This study was financed through a grant from the Ford Foundation and matching funds from the Commonwealth of Pennsylvania through the Regional Industrial Development Corporation of South-western Pennsylvania. The author of this section of the report, Dr. Edgar M. Hoover, directed the over-all study.

tensified improvement effort will be required to make a real bite on the chronic unemployment problem over the long run. So far, the Region has not fully demonstrated that it can "hold the line."

To say this is by no means to deprecate the achievement thus far. For the sake of perspective, we can compare the recent employment record of the Pittsburgh Region with that of a few other important Pennsylvania metropolitan areas which have roughly similar problems arising from intensive industrial specialization in coal and steel. As Table 18–1 shows, the Pittsburgh Region's recent record has stood up rather well in comparison with that of the Johnstown, Scranton, and Wilkes-Barre-Hazleton areas.

A further comparison may also be of interest. The Boston metropolitan area is another which has gone through some decades of progressive retardation of economic growth because of earlier specialization in non-growth industries combined with a loss of competitive position relative to other areas in the industries it had. In quite recent years, the Boston area has shown strong signs of revival involving the development of a first-rank research and development complex with emphasis on electronics, large-scale redevelopment of obsolete areas particularly in the central city, and some relatively bold attacks on the mass transit problem. In growth terms, Boston and Pittsburgh have for some decades kept each other company at the bottom of the list of the nation's major metropolises. Despite great

Table 18–1. Changes in Population and Employment, 1950–1960, in Pennsylvania SMSA's Highly Specialized in Coal and Steel.

Standard Metropolitan Statistical Area	Employment in coal mining and primary iron and steel industries as percentage of total SMSA employment, 1950	Percentage change, 1950 to 1960, in	
		Population	Employment
Pittsburgh	21.2	+ 8.7	+ 2.9
Johnstown	38.6	− 3.6	− 8.4
Scranton	13.4	− 8.9	− 9.3
Wilkes-Barre, Hazleton	23.5	−11.5	−12.2

Source: U. S. *Census of Population,* 1950 and 1960.

differences in past and present industrial structure, the areas have many points of similarity; and in terms of promising future directions of structural change and growth, Boston's breakthrough may provide some quite relevant guide lines for Pittsburgh's. Nevertheless, in spite of the impressive transformation of its economy, the Boston area manifested substantial net out-migration during the decade of the 1950's; about 3.6 per cent of the population, as compared with 4.7 per cent in the Pittsburgh Standard Metropolitan Statistical Area.

What can be done and how?

We have sought to provide an improved base of information and insight about the Region upon which planners and policy-makers could operate. The Study itself was not intended to frame a program. It is in order, however, to conclude this report of findings with some observations basic to the larger regional enterprise which does embrace both research and policy formulation. These observations have to do with objectives and criteria for constructive action.

UNEMPLOYMENT AND OUT-MIGRATION

When employment opportunities do not expand fast enough to keep pace with the natural increase of population in an area, this is normally manifest both in heavy chronic unemployment and in net outward migration. In other words, some but not all of the redundant manpower supply is drawn away. Thus the Pittsburgh Region has for some time been characterized by both high unemployment rates and a substantial outward balance of migration. For at least a decade or two into the future, and quite possibly much longer, we must reckon with the probability that the increments to the labor force through natural increase will continue to exceed additional employment opportunity; and presumably this will be reflected in some combination of unemployment and out-migration. Just how much of a role each will play will depend upon labor mobility, on qualitative "mix" of the Region's employment opportunity, and to some extent on policy decisions that may encourage or discourage mobility as such. It is relevant to consider, then, how the welfare of the Region's people may be affected by a substitution of out-migration for unemployment or the reverse. We cannot assume that it is a matter of indifference which of these two forms the adjustment to a deficiency of employment opportunity will take.

The adverse regional effects of chronic unemployment are painfully obvious. There is not only the direct loss of output and income, but a public assistance burden upon the employed members of the community and, quite possibly most important of all, the social problem stemming from frustration and demoralization of the chronically unemployed groups. The social, if not the economic, problem is particularly serious and dangerous when the dearth of job prospects for the most disadvantaged groups leads young people approaching the age of labor-force entry to drop out of school, and accept casual unskilled work or resign themselves to a lifetime prospect of aimless idleness or underemployment. These are problems even in many prosperous parts of the country today, heightened by reduced needs for unskilled labor and by discrimination against minority groups. They are naturally particularly acute in areas of over-all chronic unemployment.

By comparison, the implications of out-migration are far less clear cut. The migrants themselves, of course, have the expectation of bettering their condition and prospects. There is an adverse "moral" effect on the community they leave. Rare is the American community that welcomes the idea of a decline or a net outflow of population. This psychological effect cannot be ignored, even though in large part it is based simply on an anachronistic "pioneer" tradition that population growth is the key to well-being —a notion long discredited in most other well-populated parts of the world.

There is also some shadow of substance in the argument that if people remain in a community, even without employment, they will still in some degree help to support the business of local merchants, landlords, and other providers of consumer needs. That one sector of the business community may well have some stake in discouraging out-migration. But from the standpoint of the community or region as a whole, there is a net local benefit only if the incomes of the unemployed derive from outside sources (for example, federal or state assistance) more than balance the costs that the community or region incurs in assistance and provision of facilities and services. Retired millionaires are clearly an economic asset for Palm Beach; this does not mean that permanently unemployed miners are an economic asset for Uniontown.

For some types of areas, the fact that migration is selective introduces a further consideration. If the younger and more capable and skilled people predominate among those who leave the area, the remaining population will develop a relatively aged and inferior labor force as a result. This truism is, however, scarcely relevant to the question of the relative merits, for a large industrial region, of having manpower surplus manifest in out-migration as against chronic unemployment. Regardless of its qualities, a labor force is useful only if used. The types of worker who can be productively employed in the Region are not, in general, the ones who have occasion to look elsewhere.

All in all, then, it seems clearly to the Region's interest (as well as to the interest of the individuals directly involved) that any given amount of excess of manpower supply over jobs should result to a greater extent in out-migration and to a lesser extent in chronic unemployment. This is an evaluation essentially in economic terms, upon which any relevant consideration of other social factors can of course be superimposed so long as we do not lose sight of the economic implications.

This has two broad implications for policy guidance. First, that the Region stands to gain rather than to lose from any reduction in present informational, financial, or institutional (e.g., seniority) hindrances to labor mobility. Second, that the rate of population growth in itself is one of the poorest possible criteria of success in the basic aim of making the Region a better place for its people to live and work. And even in that regard, we may well be more successful in achieving a larger rate of population growth if we focus our attention more on the question of how to create productive opportunities for workers and less on the number of people who leave or stay.

ADJUSTMENT AND ACTION

It might quite reasonably be concluded from even a superficial examination of the state of the Region that (1) more jobs are needed; (2) new industries should be attracted; (3) specifically, more metal-fabricating industries in the Region could absorb a greater fraction of the steel output; or (4) labor-management relations should be improved. It would be hard to quarrel with any of the above statements, but they are of little use because they run in terms of symptoms. They restate the problem but do not suggest how to solve it.

Direct attack on a symptom, even if we have some means of attacking it, may well do more harm than good if underlying causes are ignored. The discussion of emigration vs. chronic unemployment, in the previous section of this chapter, furnishes an illustration. In the light of that discussion, it is clear that simply trying to block out-migration by impeding mobility would serve no useful purpose and would probably be damaging.

UNDERLYING TRENDS

Basic forces shaping the Region's structure and growth can be objects of policy action, to the extent that they are amenable to action from within the Region. Where they are not (as will often be the case), regional policy can seek only to promote the best adjustment to foreseeable changes. For example, the upgrading of the regional labor pool is a growth lever which can be pulled from inside the Region; while the future trend of demand for steel pipe or flat glass is something to which the Region can only adjust.

To a considerable extent the Region's economic future is conditioned by certain broad national shifts in population, markets, and industry that affect all regions. The West has been growing faster than the East for a long time, and is likely to continue to do so for at least a few decades. The various parts of the country are tending to become more nearly alike, or at least less sharply different, in respect to population density, degree of industrialization, industrial structure, level of income, and characteristics of population. And within major urbanized regions an outward suburbanization of both residence and business continues. All these are basic trends, neither peculiar to nor originating within the Region. Policy in the Region, then, should not be directed toward either abetting or combatting these trends, but toward adjustment to them—meeting the problems they raise and exploiting the opportunities they create. The broad shifts of population and markets, largely to the west, coupled with the increasing importance of market access for industry location and the tendency for more and more parts of the country to achieve their own diversified industrial bases, has inevitably limited the role that this Region, or any other, can play as a supplier of staple goods to nationwide markets.

The quickening stream of technological change represents another set of "outside" influences that profoundly affect the Region, but cannot be significantly affected from inside the Region. Here again, the regional policy decisions can promote appropriate adjustment and utilization of new opportunities provided.

Rapid technological change means rapid obsolescence of physical facilities and skills alike. By that token it poses particularly serious adjustment problems to areas like the Pittsburgh Region which have especially large proportions of their physical and human resources committed in terms of earlier technical conditions. Old industrial facilities are in general more expensive to keep up to date by piecemeal modernization, and the same holds true of old community layouts, public service facilities, and housing. Very much the same is true of human resources as well—the adaptability of workers and of business firms to new tasks and opportunities is less when a high proportion of those workers and firms have been doing substantially the same thing for a long time and have acquired a large stake in the status quo, and when there is a relative dearth of new and young entrants to the labor force and the business community who are prepared to take up new and unfamiliar functions.

There are several reasons why these problems of readapting both physical and human resources to changing needs in a region are much less likely to solve themselves in future, and will call for more public planning and effort than in the past. One is the accelerated pace of technical change itself. A second is the fact that the amount of "investment" tied up in physical facilities and human capabilities is increasingly great, which makes readaptation and flexibility a greater challenge. A third reason, related to this last, is that higher technical standards narrow the range of types of work in which a person with no special skills at all can simply "learn by doing" or earn a living by manual labor. A fourth reason has to do specifically with interregional competition and will be explored below.

When we look at the major factors that have determined the choice of location for specific industries in former times and those determining such choices today, what stands out most clearly is the diminished constraint of "natural" physical factors of location and the increased leeway that this provides for "man-made" regional advantages or disadvantages and thus by implication for conscious regional influence. This is nowhere more clear than in the case of the Pittsburgh Region. A century and a half ago, Pittsburgh's geographic advantages in terms of position and natural transport routes were such that it would have been difficult to prevent the rise of one of America's principal commercial and industrial centers. In the latter nineteenth century, it would scarcely have been possible to prevent Pittsburgh from becoming one of the world's greatest centers of iron and steel production. The glass and coal-chemical industries, similarly, became important parts of the Region's industrial foundation on the basis of strategic advantages of access or materials provided by nature.

Nowadays, however—as has been documented over and over again in this Study's findings—such factors of strategic transport advantage or availability of materials, fuels, and energy exert far less of a constraint. They apply to a smaller proportion of industrial activities, and the interregional differentials are narrower.

A similar change has occurred in regard to choice of location within the Region, reflecting vastly improved and more flexible intraregional transport and communication as well as an extended commuting range for workers. A vastly broader selection of sites is available for most types of industry except those requiring very large tracts or riverside sites.

Industry in general is increasingly footloose in its choice of location, in the sense of greater emancipation from nature's constraints. In some other respects as well, there has been a narrowing of regional differentials of advantage with implied greater latitude of choice. Capital, enterprise, and business know-how are transferred far more readily from one region to another in response to shifting opportunities. And there has been on balance a trend toward interregional equalization of wages and (probably) labor costs which tends to reduce the pressure upon employers to search for cut-rate labor market areas.

To a greater and greater extent, as a result, a region's success in holding and attracting employment is determined by other locational considerations. most of which can be influenced from within the region.

This radical change in the role of location factors poses for the Pittsburgh Region both its biggest economic problems and its biggest hope for the future. Most of the Region's loss of preeminence in its old industrial specialties is traceable to the emasculation of once-commanding advantages over other areas in transportation, fuel and energy supply, and business capital and enterprise. But the new kinds of advantage that will be decisive in the latter twentieth century are within the Region's capability to generate on its own initiative. People rather than physical geography will play the leading part in shaping the Region's future.

LINES OF ACTION

Flexibility, modernity, and receptiveness to change are the keynotes of policy here. And this is something that can be accomplished in and by the Region itself. It could not possibly be accomplished, in fact, in any other way. In respect to physical facilities, much of the action indicated comes under the general head of urban renewal. In respect to manpower resources, the central task is an educational one. The labor resources of the Region can be made adaptable to a radically new and continually changing set of demands and opportunities by (1) raising the standard of basic education, (2) providing improved and broader technical training for new entrants to the labor force, and (3) making it more possible for those already in the labor force to retool their abilities. The traditional notion of just one initial period of education in an individual's lifetime, which equips him to "follow his trade" from then on, is coming to be recognized as obsolete. During one person's working life of half a century, the kinds of work to be done in our society change out of all recognition. Today's teen-ager will have to acquire new skills, or whole new sets of skills, several times before he retires, if he is to maintain status and income as a productive member of society.

Massive effort involving physical replanning and renewal of structures, and upgrading of the readiness of the regional labor force, are thus certainly essential parts of any acceptable solution of the Region's economic problems. Certain further specific types of action can be identified too.

For example, an important part of the task of making the Region more attractive to new business enterprises or expansions is assistance in finding and acquiring suitable sites with adequate arrangements for public services, and—in the case of new and small firms—assistance in getting venture capital participation. In this area of action, the Regional Industrial Development Corporation and some other organizations within the Region are increasingly active. For the most effective stimulus to new types of industry in the Region, more effective ways have to be found for linking research and development activity to actual innovation within the Region and the securing of government contracts. Such organization for technological "spin-off" obviously requires more than just the corporate research laboratories and the pure-research facilities that have so far constituted the Region's main research assets. In this undertaking, the Region's universities obviously play a crucial role. For the more effective utilization of manpower resources, improved regional and interregional information flow on jobs and worker availability is needed.

Last, but by no means least, is a whole field of action involving improvement of the Region's attractiveness as a place to live and work. Age and the traditional industrial complexion of the Region, to say nothing of the largely outdated image of grime and obsolescence, are handicaps to be overcome in this regard. The Pittsburgh Renaissance has already made impressive strides, and some further bold plans already beginning to be implemented in the downtown and Oakland areas and elsewhere give bright promise. Higher living standards, more leisure, and greater population mobility make it increasingly important for any community to provide a far higher level of convenience, sightliness, public services, recreation and cultural and educational opportunity than was ever before the case, and this trend will continue.

For the Pittsburgh Region, the importance of improvement in this field is particularly great. The reason is that the Pittsburgh Region's future depends to such a major extent upon retaining and attracting highly qualified and professional and technical people and business enterprisers, who are in demand everywhere and who command a high standard of residential amenity and cultural and professional opportunities.

Such are the areas within which it would seem that specific programs of action can most clearly work to cope with the challenges identified in this Study. To achieve a better record than in the past will call for large investment of money and effort, and the assumption of risks inevitably associated with any investment that aims at a real breakthrough. It cannot be accomplished without a radically new degree of coordinated public and private action. What is involved here is a regional revitalization project for which there is no precedent among American urbanized areas.

NOTES

1. The Pittsburgh Regional Planning Association sponsored and suggested an exhaustive study of its Region, designed to bring together economic, demographic land use, construction, and social trends as a basis for future planning decisions. A large staff produced a series of reports, synthesized into a regional development plan.
2. Pittsburgh Regional Planning Association, *Region with a Future* (Pittsburgh: University of Pittsburgh Press, 1963), Chs. 6 and 7.
3. *Ibid.*, Ch. 6.

19

Where Welfare Falls Short

EVELINE M. BURNS

I find it helpful to break down the "war on poverty" into five major strategies:

1. There is first the approach which emphasizes lack of jobs or of capacity to hold jobs as the major cause of poverty.

2. There is the approach which stresses "loss or interruption of income" as the important problem.

3. There is the approach which places emphasis on the dire effects of heavy, irregularly occurring, but widespread charges on incomes, even when incomes are not interrupted.

4. There is what I would call the income-deficiency approach which, unlike those previously mentioned, stresses the need to assure some minimum income for all, regardless of the cause of the deficiency.

5. Finally, there is the approach which holds that it is not enough to insure that people have jobs or some form of socially provided income, but insists that certain types of social services must be made widely available if poverty is to be finally eradicated.

The employment approach

This is the approach underlying recent social policies. On the one hand, an increase in the number of jobs is sought through efforts to raise the general level of employment by tax cuts and other measures, through attacks on structural or geographically localized unemployment by such programs as Area Redevelopment or the Appalachia plan, and through special work programs for the young or accelerated public works for the unemployed in general. On the other hand, efforts are made to improve the employability of potential workers through training programs under Area Redevelopment, the Manpower Training and Development Act, and the community work and training programs for public assistance recipients under the Social Security Act. More recently these have been supplemented by a bewildering array of education, training, and human reclamation projects under the Economic Opportunity Act. The diagnosis is clear: elimination of poverty is a matter of creating more jobs and equipping people to fill them.

All of these programs are useful and worthwhile, in varying degrees. But

From *The Public Interest*, No. 1 (Fall, 1965), pp. 82–95. This article was first presented as a lecture at the Faculty Seminar on Poverty at the Institute of Government and Public Affairs, University of California, Los Angeles.

a closer look at the composition of the poverty population raises serious doubts as to the extent to which many of the poor would be able to benefit from full employment and an enhancement of employability. Mollie Orshansky's estimates, which are undoubtedly the best as yet available, yield a figure of 34.6 million people in poverty in 1963.[1] Of this group, 5.2 million were persons 65 or over. It seems unlikely that many of these older people will be helped out of poverty by full employment, retraining, or even basic education.

In addition, a sizable number of family heads and unrelated individuals were ill or disabled. Of those who either did not work at all, or who worked only part of the year, illness or disability was given as the reason by 18 per cent of the male family heads, 14 per cent of the female heads, 24 per cent of the male, and 17 per cent of the female unrelated individuals.[2]

A third important component of the poverty population is the 2 million families (including 5.7 million children) where the head *was* in full-time employment throughout 1963. To these must be added another half-million unrelated individuals who were also fully employed. For these groups there would seem to be two roads out of poverty. One is higher-paying jobs rather than more jobs; and to the extent that such persons might need further education or training to equip them to hold better-paying jobs, the wisdom of so largely concentrating training and retraining on the *un*employed might be questioned. The other is, for those with standard wages but unduly large families, some form of income subsidy (a topic to which I shall return below).

A fourth group among the poverty population likely to be little assisted by the full-employment approach comprises the families with children headed by a woman; these families numbered 1,570,000 and included 4,540,000 children. Although we do not have detailed knowledge of the characteristics of the total group (we do know that about 160,000 of them are employed), we possess some information about those—over half—who are supported by the Aid to Families with Dependent Children program.[3] As a group, the mothers in these families, in addition to being burdened with the care of children, are poorly educated; to the extent they have worked, they have been in unskilled, low-paying employment; they are disproportionately non-whites.[4] Even if their educational and health deficiencies were corrected, few of these women would be able to take advantage of broadened employment opportunities in the absence of adequate social provision for day-care centers or homemaker services to care for their children.

For all these poor people—and they form a clear majority of the total poor—remedial action must be sought outside the full-employment approach.

The interruption-of-income approach

THE AVAILABILITY OF PROTECTION

A concern about loss or interruption of income has been the most pronounced feature of American social policy in the last thirty years. And like most other countries, we have envisaged the problem as one of identifying specific risks to continuity of income and providing special programs for each identified risk. This policy entails certain consequences.

First, if it is to be successful, once a risk is identified, all persons subject to it must be covered by some appropriate program. This we have not done. Even our program of old age, survivors, and disability benefits under Social Security excludes about 10 per cent of all workers (although pending legislation may significantly reduce this proportion). Workmen's compensation and unemployment insurance cover only about four employees out of five. Temporary disability insurance exists only for railroad workers and for about four out of five other workers in four states.[5]

Second, all forms of interruption or loss of income must be identified and provided for. This we have not done. Typically, unemployment lasting more than 26 weeks has not been accepted as a risk for which specific provision should be made. Only a handful of states provide for extended benefits beyond this period. Only twice in our history, when persistent unemployment became a national scandal, was federal action invoked to facilitate payment of extended benefits, and on the first occasion only 22 states took advantage of the federal offer. Less than 20 states have availed themselves of the possibility of extending Aid to Families with Dependent Children to cover families where the father is not absent from the home but is unemployed, and only about 60,000 families currently receive income from this program. From the point of view of assuring income to the long-period unemployed, the country is indeed less adequately equipped with special programs than it was in the mid-thirties!

Only reluctantly have we come to recognize another risk to income security—namely, family break-up for causes other than the death of the breadwinner. Over the years, the number of recipients of Aid to Families with Dependent Children has steadily grown, despite the existence of survivors' benefits under Social Security, which today assures some income to about nine out of ten families when the breadwinner dies.[6] This growth (over 4 million persons are currently on the AFDC rolls) has been accompanied by a change in the composition of the case load. No longer corresponding to the earlier image of the "blameless" mother (usually a white widow) left alone to care for her children, the present AFDC population consists to an ever-increasing degree of women who are legally separated or divorced, who are deserted, or who are unwed mothers. Discovery of the prevalence of this risk to continuity of family income has not been accompanied by efforts to devise a program which would appropriately meet the needs of the group affected. Rather the reaction has been, in all too many states, to restrict access to the only existing program, AFDC, and to deny aid to families where the mother is held to be having illicit relations with a man, or to have produced illegitimate children, or who for other, often specious reasons, is held not to be providing a "suitable home." [7] Even where aid is given, its amount (as I shall later indicate) is typically lower than that received by other assistance recipients (e.g., the blind).

But it is perhaps the third requirement of the "risk approach" that we have so dismally failed to meet in this country. This is that even with the most skillful diagnosis of causes, and with the most careful drafting of eligibility requirements, not all cases of income loss can be fitted into the available "risk boxes." It has therefore always been held that an essential complement to this kind of attack on the problem of income discontinuity is the creation of a residual assistance program for which the sole eligibility requirements would be need *regardless of cause*. This we have not done. In some states or parts of states, general assistance to all intents and purposes does not exist. Elsewhere, access to general assistance is limited by residence requirements, by refusal to give assistance to families in which there is an employable member, or in which it is held that relatives are able to support the applicant (whether or not such support is, in fact, forthcoming), or by sheer lack of funds to provide aid to clearly eligible people.

LEVELS OF INCOME ASSURED

Determination that one is eligible for benefits or payments from one or more of our current income-maintenance programs is no assurance that one will thereafter be living above the poverty line. The most liberal payments are in general found in the social insurance programs; yet two-thirds of our retired couples receive less than $158 a month, the average for an aged couple being $130. And widows receive only 82.5 per cent of their spouses' single benefit.

Among disabled married workers who are 50–64 years of age, and who are supported by the Social Security program, median income from all sources (including the government benefit and earnings of spouses) in 1960 was $3,290—but one in five of the units had an income of less than $2,000 a year. The unmarried disabled beneficiaries' median income was only $1,260, and nearly a third of this group had income of less than $1,000.[8]

The inadequacies of unemployment insurance benefits are notorious. Average weekly benefits have declined from 42 per cent of average weekly earnings in 1938 to about 35 per cent in recent years. The depressive effect of the legal benefit maximums is most felt by the family head, whose earnings tend to be higher than those of single beneficiaries and secondary wage-earners. By reference to an absolute poverty standard, 35 per cent of 1963–1964 earnings may more nearly raise beneficiaries above the poverty level than the 42 per cent paid in the low wage years of 1938—on this, I know of no evidence. But it must be recalled that the adequacy of unemployment benefits must be judged in relation to the period of time for which benefits are payable. If a worker is unemployed only 15 weeks, he can supplement his unemployment insurance with savings or he can defer certain expenditures; if he is unemployed for 39 weeks or more, these possibilities begin to disappear.

Few people can realize how shockingly low are the payments received by the 7.5 to 8 million people who at any given time are supported by public assistance—for if they did, they would surely do something about the situation. In principle, these payments represent the difference between the amount of the applicant's own resources (and usually those of any legally responsible relatives) and the cost of the minimum basic needs as set by the state. These crucial standards of needs and their costs are in most cases below, and often far below, the poverty level. In January 1963, the monthly cost standard of basic needs for an aged couple fell below the Orshansky poverty level ($154.58) *in 33 states,* the median standard for the nation being $145.10 a month.

The showing in the AFDC program was even more miserable. This program, it may be recalled, is the source of income for over 4 million people; and while only four children in every hundred are supported by it at any given time, due to turnover, it has been estimated that one-sixth of all children have received AFDC at some time.[9] For a family of four headed by a woman, the Orshansky poverty standard would require a monthly income of $259.60. Only three states set their minimum budgets at, or above, this level. For the country as a whole, the median AFDC standard of basic needs for a family of this size was $202.95: in several states it was around $150 a month.

But only 19 states actually make payments sufficient to bring all eligible AFDC families up to their own excessively modest minimum standards! The others set dollar maximums to the payments to any one family, regardless of its size or needs—or, for financial reasons, pay only a percentage of the sum that elaborate investigation has shown to be needed. The reductions are often considerable. The highest monthly amount payable to a four-person family headed by a woman is less than 50 per cent of the total cost standard for basic needs (as defined by the state) in 9 states: it is less than 60 per cent in 13 states.

It thus should not surprise us that, in late 1961, the average AFDC family of about four persons had income (including assistance and all other sources) of approximately $140 a month, and in *no* state did the total income of such families average as much as $2,400 a year.[10] Yet the SSA poverty standard would call for $3,115.

NEEDED IMPROVEMENTS IN INCOME-MAINTENANCE PROGRAMS

It is convenient to discuss separately the social insurance and the social assistance programs. In social insurance, the obvious first essential is to broaden coverage, so as nearly as possible to include 100 per cent of those exposed to the defined risk. For old age, permanent disability, and loss of a breadwinner we are within sight of that goal. For short-period unemployment and occupational disability, there would seem to be no good administrative or other reason for the exclusion of workers in small firms or agriculture, though admittedly domestic employment coverage in unemployment insurance would create some awkward administrative problems in connection with the provisions relating to voluntary leaving, the payment of prevailing wages, and discharge for good cause.

The unlikelihood that all the states will follow the example of the four that have enacted temporary disability insurance (the last law was enacted in 1950) suggests the inevitability of federal action if this risk to continuity of income is ever to be adequately provided for. In fact, a very small change in the wording of the Social Security Act would accomplish this. It would merely involve dropping the word "permanent" and eliminating the qualification that disability must be "expected to continue indefinitely or to result in death."

More difficult problems are presented by the effort to insure at least a poverty level of living to all recipients of social insurance. For our social insurance programs are all wage-related in principle, and typically aim to replace only a fraction of previous earnings. To the low-paid worker, especially if, when employed, his income was below the poverty level, such a fraction will be far from adequate. Yet to provide even a poverty level will result in giving him more as a benefit than he was previously earning! [11]

But the wage-related character of our social insurance programs presents a further obstacle to using this instrument to assure all beneficiaries at least a poverty standard of living. For such a system has to maintain differentials. Indeed, to many people, including organized labor, its most important objective is thought to be insuring retirement incomes considerably above the poverty minimum to the majority of workers who normally earn much above poverty wages. As a result, increases in benefits at the lower end of the scale are invariably accompanied by increases at the upper end. But this may lead to earmarking an altogether disproportionate share of available funds to support of the disabled, the survivors, and above all the aged.[12]

An important feature of our social insurance programs, which tends to make it difficult to use them to assure every beneficiary an income at least equal to the poverty level, lies in the method of financing we have adopted: specifically, our decision that all costs must be met by wage and payroll taxpayers, now and in perpetuity. These include costs attributable to the heavy weighting of the insurance formula in favor of those with the lowest average monthly earnings, and to the increased benefits created when money increases are given to the already retired as well as the benefits given to people with very short periods of coverage. In consequence, workers in the higher earnings brackets receive a benefit that is much smaller in proportion to their previous earnings than do the low-paid workers. As we progressively raise the taxable earnings limit, we may expect more and more resistance from the higher paid, who may well come to find that, for the additional social security taxes they pay, they could do better for themselves by using the money to buy commercial insurance.

It is for these reasons that I believe we are unlikely to assure all the disabled and the aged and the survivors of wage-earners an income at least equal to the poverty standard through the mechanism of our self-contained social insurance system. I suspect, if this is our minimum aim, that we shall have to follow the example of Canada and Sweden (and, in effect, Great Britain) and provide for some form of a "demogrant" for these people—i.e., a uniform payment to certain categories of persons identified only by demographic (usually age) characteristics. If it is desired to provide income in excess of this sum to the higher paid workers, it would be possible to provide for a compulsory wage-related system on top of the demogrant—i.e., a double-decker system such as has been adopted in Great Britain and Sweden and is currently proposed in Canada.

The problems encountered in the effort to increase public assistance payments are different. For here, decisions as to the character of the programs rests with the states and, in many cases, with the localities. Hence two problems are faced. How to make it possible for states and localities with limited resources to meet higher standards if they wish to do so? And how to persuade the states and localities to wish to do so?

The grant-in-aid device has been used to meet the first problem, but it has been only partially effective. There is no federal aid for general assistance.[13] Moreover, the formula for the federally aided categories contains only a relatively small element of variability and the major effect of grants-in-aid has been to put more and more federal money into the program for rich and poor states alike. Finally, the federal government sets a bad example by discriminating against children—the matchable maximum being only $30 per recipient for AFDC, as against $70 for the blind and disabled, and $85 for the aged.

Changes in state policies have been hard to achieve. Federal standards, to be met as a condition of receipt of federal aid, have indeed transformed much of public assistance since 1935. But on one vital aspect of public assistance, the definition of the minimum standard of living to be assured (and conversely the criteria of need that govern eligibility), the Social Security Act has been silent. The states are not even required by the federal government to meet their own (often very low) basic budgetary standards for all eligible people. And in one respect federal leadership until recently has perpetuated one of the very worst features of public assistance, namely, the excessively detailed determination of budgetary needs, and the degrading necessity for the client, given the exiguous nature of the basic budget, to have to beg for and justify every item of expense not covered by the budget. More recently, federal leadership has been urging simplification of this process. But even so, it is not wholly certain that there is full recognition of the limits to what can be achieved in the way of simplification, without major policy changes.

Unusual drains upon family income

At least two kinds of unusually heavy and often unpredictable drains on income have been identified by most developed countries as causing poverty, and have been the focus of specific social programs—namely, the costs of medical care and the costs of child-rearing.

So much has been written about the uneven incidence of medical costs, and their frequently devastating effects on family security, especially for the aged who have little opportunity to replenish their savings, that it should be unnecessary to repeat the well-known facts.[14] The plight of children who are members of relatively large families is, however, less generally recognized.[15] The influence of family size on poverty is indicated by the fact that of the almost 15 million children falling below the Social Security Administration's poverty line, no less than 9 million were members of families with four or more children—and of this group 6.6 million (or over two-thirds) were in families headed *by a male*. Children in families with three or more children accounted for almost 12 million out of the 15 million; of these, two-thirds were in families headed by a male. And it is important to recall that 5.7 million of the children in poverty were members of families in which the breadwinner was regularly employed throughout the previous year.

In both cases, social policy in this country has so far recognized the problem only through the income-tax structure. Deductions or exemptions up to a certain amount are granted for medical expenses and for dependents. But this approach to the problem has two serious disadvantages. It confers the largest benefits on those who need assistance least, namely, those in the higher marginal tax brackets.[16] And many of those whose income deficiencies are greatest, are least able to benefit from the exemptions or deductions, for their incomes are so low that they fall far below the sum of the exemptions and deductions they could legally claim.

Recently, suggestions have been made for a limited "negative income tax" which would involve paying to such families the *tax value* (usually at the first-bracket rate) of the exemptions and deductions they are unable to claim. But even this policy would serve only to reduce the income deficiency of the large family by a fraction. It is, in effect, merely a very modest income-conditioned family allowance.

The most usual way in which other countries have attacked the poverty-causing effect of size of family has been through some system of children's allowances.[17] An allowance is payable either in respect of all children or of children in excess of some given number, regardless of the income of the parents. In a few countries, the system is a true demogrant, all children below a certain age being eligible. In the remainder, the payment is tied to coverage under a social insurance program or to the fact of employment. In the former case the cost is usually borne out of general revenues: in the latter, it is covered by social insurance contributions. In general, with the notable exception of France, the payments are modest in amount, and aim to supplement family income, rather than to provide for the full cost of rearing a family.

Medical costs are very generally covered by some form of compulsory health insurance or, in a few countries of which Great Britain is most noteworthy, by a free national health service.[18] The important point is that the income-security system in such cases is not expected to cover these unpredictable and unevenly distributed costs.

The income-deficiency approach

Given on the one hand a concern about poverty and on the other the difficulties of assuring some basic minimum to all through the classical social insurance and public assistance systems, it is not surprising that increasing attention has been paid in recent years to more comprehensive systems that would assure some desired minimum income to all, regardless of the cause of the income deficiency.

Two such proposals have recently received considerable publicity. The first is the so-called Negative Income Tax approach, recently popularized by Professor Milton Friedman and Mr. Robert Theobald, but familiar as an idea to students of social security and income distribution for many years. The second is the Social Dividend or Guaranteed Income proposal, long a familiar concept in socialist literature but made academically respectable through the writings of Lady Rhys Williams, Professor Peacock, and others.

The Negative Income Tax proposal has taken various forms. Some would have a Presidential Commission define annually a minimum income, others would take the sum of personal exemptions and the standard deduction in the income tax as defining the minimum sum which society deems necessary to insure the basic essentials of living and would provide that above this level individuals pay taxes while below it they receive payments ("negative taxes") equal to their income deficiency.[19]

The negative income tax, based as it would presumably be on declarations of anticipated income, would involve awkward administrative problems when realized incomes fell below those anticipated because of unemployment or sickness or whatever. Quite apart from questions of the level of payments, as compared to those available under current unemployment or disability insurance or workmen's compensation systems, it is doubtful whether even on grounds of administrative simplicity the Negative Tax would have much to commend it, at least for short-period or occasional interruptions of income. The administrative problems would, however, be much less serious if the system were confined to the long-period risks.

In the last analysis, the Negative Income Tax is merely a device for replacing a highly personalized and offensively administered test of need with one that is more impersonal and which, being already applied to all income receivers in their capacity as taxpayers, is accepted as carrying with it no stigma. As such, it is a real step forward. But it would still leave the population divided into two obvious groups, those who are "poor" enough to qualify for the negative tax and the rest. Some people would still be differentiated from others on the basis of economic status.

The universal payment or guarantee, on the other hand, would have the advantage of treating all people equally.[20] The question of the level of the guarantee would be of interest to all: it would not merely be a question of what was suitable for the "poor." It would eliminate the necessity of any eligibility test based on economic status, and avoid the awkward policy issue of what is and what is not "income" for Negative Income Tax purposes. It would escape the administrative difficulties associated with either the assurance of income to persons whose incomes in any one year prove to be less than estimated in the initial income declaration, or of collecting repayments in the event that actual income proves to be greater than estimated.

It is for these reasons that if we should ever contemplate a shift away from the present complicated structure of social security programs, with their different and often offensive or arbitrary eligibility conditions and their varying benefit levels, I hope we shall move toward the demogrant rather than some version of the Negative Income Tax. There are obvious limits to how fast we might move in this direction: the idea of the universal minimum, though increasingly accepted in theory and in some practices, is still far from universally approved, especially when minority groups are in question. In so heterogeneous a country as ours, with the per capita income of the poorest states only half that of the richest, any national minimum would probably be, initially at least, very low. It would therefore not obviate the need for supplementary measures. Yet there would seem no good reason why we could not, even now, adopt the policy for the aged and the permanently disabled and even perhaps for survivors. And we could at least make a beginning for children, with a modest children's allowance.

Several major questions are raised by both the Negative Income Tax and the Guaranteed Minimum (either in its universal form or as limited to certain population groups such as the aged and disabled or children). First is the question of expense. Orshansky has estimated that the income deficiency (relative to the Social Security Administration's poverty standard) of the 34.6 million persons in poverty was approximately $11.5 billion. Presumably all these individuals and families would be eligible for Negative Income payments of varying amounts. In fact, however, the total payments might be higher than $12 billion if knowledge of the availability of the Negative Tax payments were to reduce the incentive to work of some of those now earning, a consideration to which I return below. And this sum would, of course, *be additional* to whatever is contributed from tax funds by way of public assistance ($4.7 billion in 1963) and by way of the social insurance and veterans' administrations to members of the group, both of which probably form a substantial part of the $17.3 billion of income received by the 34.6 million poor.

Payment of a demogrant or universal minimum to all the aged, assuming a payment of $75 a month per person, would have cost $15.8 billion in

1963 and would rise to some $17.5 billion by 1975 with the growth in the aged population.[21] From this sum it would be proper to deduct much of the expenditure on current programs for the aged (approximately $12 billion) to arrive at the cost of supporting the aged at this level. Presumably, also, the additional tax exemption now granted to the aged (costing around $400 million in revenue) would also be abolished.

A children's allowance, even at the modest rate of $20 a month payable to the nation's 66 million children, would involve $15.8 billion annually and would rise sharply with the growing child population.[22] But from this one would have to deduct the revenue lost because of income-tax exemptions for child dependents.

The costs of these three income deficiency programs are indeed considerable in absolute terms. They loom less frightening when compared with other public expenditure items in 1963, such as national defense ($53.4 billion) or health, education, and welfare, including veterans' programs ($360.0 billion), and are only about the same as was spent on agriculture and commerce ($12.5) [23] What is even more important, however, is the probable future trend of our Gross National Product and the yield of federal revenues. It has been estimated that over the next ten years, at a growth rate of 3½ to 4 per cent a year, GNP by 1975 will rise to $950 billion and, if no changes are made in tax rates and structures, federal revenues would rise to $180 billion or $58 billion above present levels.[24] In terms of very broad social policy, the issue would seem to be how far we *wish* to use our growing affluence to assure minimum income to the poorest, how far we wish to use it for other needed items of government expenditure (such as health or education), and how far we use it to increase the income of the more comfortably off, through tax cuts. *But it is a matter of choice of how to spend, not of capacity to afford.*

One consideration would, of course, be the economic—as against social —effects of continuing present relatively high tax rates. Here we have little in the way of hard data to support conclusions either way. The stimulating effect of the tax cut last year would seem to suggest that taxes in general are already at a level that is depressive of growth. But it might well be the fact that, at *any* given level of taxation, a tax cut would stimulate at least a temporary business upsurge. On the other hand, despite the sharp increases in the tax-take over the last thirty years, the economy has in general forged ahead. With the possible exception of the impact of the corporation tax on the supply of investible funds for new or growing enterprises, there seems little solid evidence that current tax levels either seriously impede the desire to invest or dangerously reduce the supply of investible funds, although there are indications that they have influenced the kinds of investments people make.[25]

Serious concern has also been expressed about the effect of a significant negative income tax or a selective or general income guarantee on the supply of effort. To the extent that such payments go to the aged or to the disabled, this consideration is probably of minor significance. The same is probably true for the families headed by women. (I cannot refrain from commenting at this point that some of our alleged social policy dilemmas arise from our unwillingness to recognize that the work of keeping house and child rearing is an economic function which ought to be given a money valuation and entered in our calculations of G.N.P.)

But the problem may arise for individuals in the "employable" age groups, for it can be argued that up to the level of the guarantee there would be no incentive to earn. Friedman has endeavored to meet this difficulty by providing for the payment of only a fraction of the income deficiency. But unless the fraction yields a sum that is sufficient for minimum security (a figure that could be assured only if the dividing line between taxpayers and tax-receivers is set relatively high) his proposal will not obviate the need for other public measures to provide minimum security. And if the fraction does yield a significant payment to the man with zero income, the problem of incentive is not eliminated. It is perhaps no accident that Friedman's illustrations appear to envisage very small negative income taxes.[26]

Another approach is that used by New Zealand's and Australia's income-conditioned programs which, like our earned income Social Security retirement test, permit the recipient of the standard-minimum-guaranteed-income to retain other income up to some specified amount. Professor Schwartz and Mr. Theobald adopt this solution, although the latter's illustration would permit the recipient to retain only a very small percentage of his income from investments, work, or savings.[27]

The more revolutionary proposal for the payment of a Social Dividend or universal demogrant to all, regardless of means, would avoid the type of discouragement to initiative found in the simpler forms of the negative income tax, namely that (as is now usually the case in our public assistance programs) every dollar earned merely serves to reduce by one dollar the publicly provided income. Above the guarantee the worthwhileness of earning would of course depend upon the structure of income tax rates. The additional revenues needed to finance the guarantee would presumably necessitate pretty heavy rates all along the income scale, but it seems likely that it would still be possible to offer some inducement to increase incomes above the guarantee. But like the negative income tax, it too would still mean that the individual who was content to live upon the guarantee would be under no pressure to participate in production. Lady Rhys Williams proposed to meet this problem by requiring employable persons to be willing to accept suitable work as an additional eligibility condition.

There is, however, no escaping the fact that, if some incentive system is to be built into our income-deficiency programs, sizable additions to the cost of the program must be expected.[28] This cost would take the form both of making more people eligible for some negative tax payments and also reducing revenues because of an increase in the income level below which no tax would be payable.[29]

In the meantime we should note that we really know very little about incentive to work.[30] It is obviously different in a country like the United

States, where the general level of productivity would permit the offering of a significant differential between a poverty-level guarantee and the income from working (even after payment of taxes) and where we are so richly endowed with want-creating institutions, than it would be in a poorer country where advertising is less developed. Note, too, that our inferences or assumptions about the desire of the very poor to participate in production derive from observations of a group who have never, or seldom, known what it means to be able to look forward to the future with some past experience of a dependable and reasonably decent standard of living.[31] The real question seems to turn around the level of income that is customarily aspired to and the prospects of attaining it by additional work. The growing tendency of married women to work, the extent of moonlighting, and the complaints about "abuse" of unemployment insurance by workers who are not truly unemployed—all seem to suggest that in this country the image of the desirable and attainable income is high.[32]

Finally, questions are often raised, especially in regard to children's allowance programs, of the effect on population. Here again we have no satisfactory evidence. Given the relatively low level of the typical children's allowance, except in France, one would scarcely expect any effect. And even in France, where the family allowance is supplemented by a great variety of other special grants and subsidies to *familles nombreuses,* there is no conclusive evidence.[33] It is perhaps significant that in Canada, the original diminution in the amount of the allowance after the fifth child—in deference to fears of the effect of an allowance on the Quebec birth rate—was quietly dropped after the first few years. It seems likely that the factors which influence fertility and the birth rate are too numerous and varied to be taken into account when discussing children's allowances. Some would even hold that higher levels of assured income may even motivate families toward middle-class attitudes regarding control of family size.[34] More generally, it would seem to this writer that those who argue for a direct incentive relationship between the birth rate and the payment of a modest children's allowance (or for that matter a miserable $30 a month for an AFDC child) must grossly underestimate the physical discomfort and pain of a woman who carries and bears a child. For the majority it is no fun at all! To undergo this experience, a woman must either want children as such, or not know how not to have them.

The service approach to poverty

There remain for consideration other types of service (or provision for meeting a need in kind). Among them are the "service programs" envisaged in the 1962 Amendments to the Social Security Act. These are, of course, focused on the public assistance clientele, and include casework, community planning, group work, homemaker services, foster care and training for support or self-care. It is as yet too early to make any certain judgments as to the extent to which the states have availed themselves of the federal grant offer (a liberal 75 per cent) or of the effectiveness of the different types of services.[35] It can be admitted that for some of the poverty group personal support and individual counseling are necessary complements to efforts to improve health, education, and working skills. But neither should the limits to such assistance be underestimated.

First, it is doubtful whether many of these efforts are not doomed to failure because of the low level of living permitted by our current welfare allowances. Many would argue that social services are no substitute for an adequate standard of living and that more can be accomplished by raising relief payments than by spending twice the sum on skillful counsellors.

Secondly, full implementation of the 1962 Amendments will be a very expensive business: already there are serious bottlenecks of trained staff, and we do not know whether, on a hard benefit-cost analysis, the additional expenditure on these services will be economically worthwhile (though in human terms their effect may be very great, if incalculable).

Finally, a serious policy question is raised by the development and expansion of these services as an integral part of an attack on income deficiency or even income interruption. For many of the needs the social services aim to meet are not peculiar to the very poor. Access to birth control information and assistance in selecting and using appropriate methods is a generally felt need. Homemaker and day-care services are very widely needed, even by the middle classes. The mother left alone to bring up her children may often need advice and counsel even though she has no financial problems. So too may the estranged couple or the girl who has "got into trouble." It would be unfortunate if, in the area of very generally needed services such as these, we should, as we have already done to a sizable extent in health services, develop a dual series of services: one run by "the welfare" for the poor, and the other, under different auspices and at a higher level, for those who can afford to pay.

NOTES

1. Mollie Orshansky, "Counting the Poor: Another Look at the Poverty Profile," *Social Security Bulletin*, XXVIII, No. 1 (January, 1965), 3–29.
2. Orshansky (*ibid.*, p. 17) reported that most of the nonemployed men stated they were out of the labor force rather than unemployed.
3. In the fiscal year 1963 there was an average of 969,000 families including 2,933,000 children receiving AFDC, the average monthly payment per recipient being $31.75 including vendor payments for medical care. (*Welfare in Review, Statistical Supplement,* 1964, p. 3).
4. In late 1961 it was found that the mothers had 8.8 years of schooling in contrast to 12.1 years among women 20–54 in the general population—14 per cent had fewer than 5 years of schooling. Of the mothers who had ever worked, 75 per cent had been employed in domestic service or as other low-paid service or unskilled laborers or farm workers in contrast to less than 25 per cent of employed women in the general population in these occupations. Robert W. Mugge, "Education and AFDC," *Welfare in Review*, II, No. 1 (January, 1964), 1–14.
5. Workers covered by five temporary disability insurance laws incurred only 28

per cent of the nation's estimated wage loss due to disability in private industry in 1963. Alfred M. Skolnik and John W. Mitchell, "Income-Loss Protection against Short-Term Sickness, 1948–63, *Social Security Bulletin,* XXVIII, No. 1 (January, 1965), 30–37, 52–56.

6. At the end of 1964 approximately 470,000 widowed mothers and 1,870,000 survivor children were in receipt of OASI benefits. *Welfare in Review,* II, No. 11 (November, 1964), 34.

7. For the ways in which the "suitable home" clause has been utilized for restrictive purposes, see the forthcoming book by Winnifred Bell, *Aid to Dependent Children* (New York: Columbia University Press, 1965).

8. Social Security Administration, *The Disabled Worker under OASDI,* United States Department of Health, Education, and Research Report No. 6 (Washington, D.C.: Government Printing Office, October, 1961), p. 65. At the time the survey was undertaken, disabled workers under age 50 were not entitled to benefits although information was collected from a sample of younger disabled who had been allowed a wage freeze.

9. *Welfare in Review,* II, No. 3 (March, 1964), 16–17.

10. Gerald Kohn and Ellen J. Perkins, "Families Receiving AFDC: What Do They Have to Live On?" *Welfare in Review,* II, No. 10 (October, 1964), 7–15. See also Charles Lebaux, "Life on ADC: Budgets of Despair," *New University Thought,* IV, No. 3 (1963).

11. This was one of two considerations that led the Federal Advisory Council on Social Security to refrain from recommending an increase of more than 7 per cent to persons with low average monthly earnings. Advisory Council on Social Security, *The Status of the Social Security Program and Recommendations for Its Improvement* (Washington, D.C.: Government Printing Office), p. 60.

12. It is significant that relatively modest as were the proposals of the Federal Advisory Council for benefit increases (especially as they affected the lower paid) the additional cost, due largely to the increases awarded higher paid, was the equivalent of an increase of 1.15 per cent of payroll above the level cost of the current program (8.46 per cent of payroll). In contrast, the cost of the other liberalizations recommended (including benefits for disabled workers and extending child's benefits to age 22 if in school) amounted to only 0.4 per cent of payroll, while the cost of the proposed hospitalization program was estimated at 0.95 per cent. *Ibid.,* pp. 60 and 45–47.

13. In only 12 states does the state itself carry full financial responsibility. In 15 the localities pay between 50 and 96 per cent of the cost, and in 15 the locality carries the entire cost. When one considers the limited tax resources of the localities and the frequency with which high incidence of poverty coincides with low property values, the wisdom of thus financing our residual underpinning income security system becomes even more questionable. Consider, for instance, the problem of West Virginia where the localities carry 58.8 per cent of general relief costs (other than administrative costs which are paid by the state).

14. See, for instance, Leonore A. Epstein, "Income of the Aged in 1962: First Findings of the 1963 Survey of the Aged," *Social Security Bulletin,* XXVII, No. 3 (March, 1964), 3ff; Elizabeth A. Langford, "Medical Care Costs for the Aged: First Findings of the 1963 Survey of the Aged," *Social Security Bulletin,* XXVII, No. 7 (July, 1964), 3–8; Dorothy P. Rice, "Health Insurance Coverage of the Aged and Their Hospital Utilization in 1962: Findings of the 1963 Survey of the Aged," *Social Security Bulletin,* XXVII, No. 7 (July, 1964), 9–18. Additional data can be found in Hearings before the Committee on Ways and Means, Medical, Care for the Aged, House of Representatives, H.R. 3920, 88th Congress, First and Second Sessions, 1963–1964, especially Part I.

15. Until recently, Thomas J. Woofter, Jr., in the *Social Security Bulletin* (January, 1945), and James Vadakin, in *Family Allowances* (Miami: University of Miami Press, 1958), have been among the few drawing attention to the effect of family size on economic well-being.

16. It has been estimated that the ordinary exemptions at 1963 income levels and 1965 tax rates reduced revenues by $17.7 billions while the medical deductions reduced them by $1.16 billions (of which all but $220 millions was claimed by tax payers with incomes in excess of $5,000).

17. The 1961 edition of the Social Security Administration's *Social Security Programs Throughout the World* lists sixty countries with such systems.

18. For a summary of the characteristics of these programs see *ibid.* and Eveline M. Burns, "The Role of Government in the Health Services," *Bulletin of the New York Academy of Medicine*, XLI, No. 7 (July, 1965).

19. Edward L. Schwartz, "A Way to End the Means Test," *Social Work*, IX (July, 1964), 3–12, proposes the first method as an initial step and provides for annual cost of living adjustments and decennial adjustments to reflect rising productivity. Robert Theobald, *Free Men and Free Markets* (New York: Doubleday, 1965), suggests a level of $1,000 per adult and $600 per child to begin with.

20. Lady Rhys Williams' proposals are contained in her *Something to Look Forward To.* McDonald, 1943, and elsewhere. A discussion of this and related proposals will be found in Alan T. Peacock, *The Economics of National Insurance,* Ch. VII (London: Hodge, 1952). A brief discussion appears in Margaret S. Gordon, *The Economics of Welfare Politics,* Ch. VI (New York: Columbia University Press, 1963).

21. This figure would yield a couple a little less than the Social Security Administration poverty standard of $154.58. I have selected it to simplify the estimates and because it is the amount which, even now, Canada provides as a demogrant to all persons 70 or over.

22. In France, which has the most highly developed of all family allowance systems, the allowance in 1961 amounted to 5 per cent of the national income, almost 6 per cent of total resources available to families and 12 per cent of total wages and salaries.

23. Otto Eckstein, *Public Finance* (Englewood Cliffs, N. J.: Prentice-Hall, 1964), p. 5. I have taken only the federal expenditures as the Negative Income Tax would presumably be financed from federal funds.

24. A 4.75 per cent growth rate would yield corresponding figures, of $1050, $198 and $76 billions. A 5.5 per cent growth rate would yield $1110, $210 and $88 billions.

25. J. K. Butters, L. E. Thompson and L. L. Bollinger, *Effects of Taxation: Investments by Individuals* (Boston: Division of Research, Harvard Graduate School of Business Administration, 1953), concluded that the tax structure had "substantially reduced the capacity of upper bracket individuals to accumulate new investible funds, but that their remaining capacity is still very large" (p. 29). But the special provisions of the tax laws did tend to direct investments into either tax-exempt bonds of state and local governments, and life insurance policies or speculative common stocks held for capital gains, oil properties and real estate benefiting from liberal depreciation allowances.

26. Milton Friedman, *Capitalism and Freedom* (Chicago: University of Chicago Press, 1962), p. 192.

27. Schwartz proposes a Federally Guaranteed Minimum Income of $3000 per family of four with a "disregard" of 40 per cent of earnings up to $1000 and progressively smaller percentages of earnings up to $4000–$4500, above which no FGMI would be payable. Theobald proposes a guaranteed minimum of $3200 for a similar family with a disregard (or premium) of 10 per cent of private income up to an income ceiling of $9600.

28. It is estimated that removal of the OASDI retirement test, which above $1200 earnings a year is progressively discouraging to employment, would cost the system the equivalent of 1 per cent of payroll.

29. Schwartz (*op. cit.,* p. 9) has guessed that an incentive system that called for a tax free income up to $4500 might involve a cost of up to $23 billions.

30. Cf. Francis M. Bator, *The Question of Government Spending* (New York: Harper, 1960), Ch. 4.

31. One wonders why some states have not taken advantage of the Research and Demonstration grants under section 1115 of the Social Security Act to experiment with assuring some AFDC families or other "problem families" a respectable income for 3 or 4 years. The "on again-off again" experience of these welfare families must be destructive of all initiative.

32. The number of known persons with two or more jobs has fluctuated between 3 and 4 million since a survey made in 1956 and is most frequent among males

25–44 years of age. Harvey R. Hamel and Forrest A. Bogan, "Multiple Job-holders in May, 1964," *Monthly Labor Review* (March, 1965), 266–274.

33. M. Jacques Hochard, in *Aspects Economiques des Prestations Familiales,* Union Nationale de Caisses d'Allocations Familialee, Paris, 1961, was unable to run down any significant studies. My own inquiries some years ago were abortive, and I gather from demographers interested in this question that there is no reliable evidence even today.

34. For the influence on family limitation of the "culture of poverty" see Lee Rain-water, *And the Poor Get Children* (Chicago: Quadrangle Books, 1960).

35. *The Report on the Implementation and Results of the 1962 Service Amend-ments to the Public Assistance Titles,* issued by the Welfare Administration, November 25, 1964, covers action up to June, 1964. In the main, activity seems to have been in the (much-needed) staffing area. There were relatively few states who developed special services for self-care or self-support. About half the states developed joint projects with other agencies, and 40 reported some type of demonstration project. Unfortunately, analysis of results is based on comparable reports from only 50 counties in 14 states, serving some 30,500 APTD families and 9500 aged, blind, or disabled persons and no information is given about the services that were unsuccessful. It is, however, claimed that there was a total monthly reduction in assistance payments of approximately $796,600—but there is no information as to the total cost of the services rendered.

Part VI GUIDELINES FOR SOCIAL POLICY

Editors' Introduction

Preceding sections of this book have dealt with a series of specific problems —housing, segregation, citizen participation, poverty. This choice of subjects represents an effort to survey the focal points where social policy is being developed and debated in American cities today. Our aim, however, is to move beyond the realities of current experience to the development of guidelines for improved public policies, and to a better understanding of the character of social planning that is needed on a continuing basis.

The conclusions that can be drawn from recent experience are necessarily tentative. Our understanding of urban problems has improved materially in the past decade, but the programs and policies that we have fashioned are at best experimental; none can be counted an unqualified success. Social planning does not yet exist as a distinct field of professional expertise, nor do we have appropriate institutions for carrying on systematic social planning. But events in American cities are moving in both these directions. Policy-makers and administrators have become increasingly aware of the interconnections between urban problems that once seemed separate from each other. Professional concerns are gradually shifting from problem-solving in a narrow sense to broader formulations of public policy. Planning agencies are giving increasing attention to the relationships between traditional areas of concern and to the coordination of specialized planning operations with one another.

In short, the current wave of activity on urban problems has produced some important research and new understanding, as well as a variety of valuable experience in formulating and administering public programs. This research and experience can serve as a basis for further advances in social planning. The needs are twofold. First, guidelines are needed for improving the orientation and management of present programs and policies. In addition, there is a need to chart further directions for the development of a continuing process of social planning, and—perhaps most lacking in current proposals—to establish strategies for getting from here to there. Long-range concepts of social planning have been with us for some time, in utopian contexts as well as in contemporary American settings. A host of "middle-range" issues remain to be explored: the content of such planning, its institutional framework, its methods, its connection with present activities.

The articles in this section are concerned with urban policies for the reorientation of present programs as well as with the establishment of improved forms of social planning. They comment at length on three sets of issues: the governmental framework for planning and policy-making, the substantive content of social planning, and the use of new methods for planning.

The governmental setting

Efforts to attack particular social problems sooner or later run up against the complex network of government operating in urban areas. A traditional social welfare approach to poverty, for example, might start by offering individual or family services to help potential wage-earners find work. But attempts to plan more comprehensively for the elimination of poverty involve measures not only for counseling individuals but for establishing broader service programs and for dealing more directly with the social and economic causes of poverty. Existing programs are likely to consist partly of local government undertakings (adult education in the public schools, for example), partly of state services (such as employment offices), and increasingly of state and local programs financed with federal aid and subject to federal, state, and local standards. Adapting existing service programs or setting up new ones typically means dealing with the three levels of government and utilizing the resources of each in appropriate combinations. Whether the graduate of a training program will find a job depends to a great extent on the performance of the national economy (influenced by federal policy) and on the character of the local economy (shaped in part by state and local government action).

The public policies that bear on conditions such as urban poverty thus arise out of federal-state-local relationships. Social security, federal minimum wage laws, federally aided health and welfare programs, and federal and state aid to education all are important in planning for the elimination of poverty. The situation is much the same for other problems discussed in this book. Housing policies result from a maze of federal, state, and local aids and regulations: federal mortgage insurance, federal and state subsidy programs, federal aid for local urban renewal projects, state and local building controls. Patterns of segregation are influenced by many of these housing policies and more directly by federal civil rights legislation, state laws against discrimination, and local housing and school policies.

The activities of three levels of government thus converge in urban areas, where their interconnections have special relevance for issues of social policy. Intergovernmental relations have created barriers as well as opportunities for the planned use of resources at all levels to deal with problems that cut across federal, state, and local lines of responsibility. To a great extent, social planning must be an intergovernmental operation.

The intergovernmental character of social policy has come about for a number of reasons. The division of governmental authority among the federal, state, and local levels has made it possible for urban reform groups to pursue many different strategies at different times, leading to a variety of governmental arrangements. Local government within metropolitan areas has become extremely fragmented. The growth and spread of urban population has led to a great proliferation of local governments, especially in suburbia. New communities have incorporated and a host of special districts have been established to operate schools and provide such services as fire protection, water, and waste disposal. The 1962 *Census of Governments* counted more than 18,000 local governments within the 212 metropolitan areas.

Despite the overwhelming concentration of national wealth within metropolitan areas, the governments of these areas have been unable to raise enough revenue locally to cope with their problems. Population movement within metropolitan areas has given rise to sharp social and economic disparities between different local communities. Some have attracted predominantly middle- and upper-income families; others have developed concentrations of low-income and minority residents. Particularly in the large metropolitan areas, the central cities and some older outlying towns have attracted a disproportionate share of disadvantaged people while more affluent citizens have moved on to other communities. As a result, some localities have emerged with considerable concentrations of wealth, others with great service needs but only limited ability to raise revenue from local sources. The local tax base of central cities has been further depleted by the movement of taxpaying industries and retail outlets to the suburbs.

Central cities and other communities caught in a comparable tax squeeze have turned increasingly to the states and the federal government for help. The mayors found a better reception in Washington than in their state capitals, though a number of highly urbanized states have also mounted aid programs for the cities. The most striking development, however, has been the rapid growth of federal participation in urban affairs, marked by the funding of numerous aid programs. At the end of 1965, the Office of Economic Opportunity issued a "Catalog of Federal Programs for Individual and Community Improvement," which might serve as a handbook of federal aids for the social planner. The catalogue includes more than 250 federal programs, running the gamut from individual social services to aid for health and education to aid for housing and urban development. Many of these are administered by state agencies—thus preserving the three-level character of intergovernmental relations—but a growing number involve direct contracts between the cities and a federal agency.

Social planning is thus set firmly in an intergovernmental context, both because many social issues are inherently more than local in character and because federal, state, and local governments are all involved in operating social programs and setting social policies.

Metropolitan conflicts

For a number of key social issues, the metropolitan area has emerged as a logical planning unit. As urban growth has spread well beyond the central cities, metropolitan areas have come to constitute large integrated areas for living and working. People look for housing and jobs within a broad area, limited mainly by the convenience of commuting and by personal preferences, not by local government boundaries. The metropolitan character of housing and employment argues strongly for metropolitan-wide planning for low-income housing, relocation, desegregation, and the elimination of poverty. The achievement of social goals in all these areas requires making optimum use of the metropolitan market.

The functional integration of metropolitan areas, however, stands in sharp contrast to their fragmented pattern of government. Local governments guard their independence carefully and pursue a host of separate policies, often reflecting serious conflicts of interest among them. One conflict is of special significance for social planning: the competition for tax resources. Local strategies often take the form of attempting to attract middle- and upper-income groups, as well as taxpaying industry and shopping centers, while trying to exclude the poor or reduce the number of poor already within the community. This conflict, which is discussed in the article by Bernard Frieden, raises a fundamental issue of where the poor will live in metropolitan areas. Where local exclusionary policies are effective, they counter other policies aimed at improving housing conditions and promoting desegregation. One approach to this problem is to use intergovernmental relations to redistribute local tax resources and offset some of the effects of this competition. Increased federal and state aid for the central cities would permit them to provide more services for their low-income residents. Frieden's proposals aim at curbing some of the tax incentives that now shape local policies, in order to promote a freer movement of people throughout metropolitan areas.

The effects of fragmented and conflicting local policies have already become well recognized in matters of physical development: transportation, water supply and pollution controls, land-use regulations. Provincial policy-making in these areas has imposed many kinds of costs on neighboring communities and has retarded the provision of high levels of service to the entire metropolitan area. In response, there has been a notable movement to plan for services and to coordinate local programs and policies on an areawide basis. The usual mechanism for areawide planning and coordination of urban development is the metropolitan planning agency—an advisory body with a technical staff, representing the governments of the metropolitan area. By 1964, 150 of the 216 metropolitan areas had some form of official areawide planning. These planning agencies have focused on projecting population and economic growth, advising on needed public services, and preparing plans for physical development. Because of their purely advisory role and lack of authority to implement plans, their influence has been limited, but they have served as a forum for considering regional policies with the help of technical analyses and projections.

Social planning, originally practiced by a loose association of voluntary agencies, has also developed a formal regional structure in most urban areas. Social planning councils have engaged in some significant areawide planning, as in their attempts to encourage a more rational distribution of home medical care or family counseling services. The resulting proposals, however, have seldom been linked closely with official decision-making centers of the region. Relationships between such voluntary metropolitan associations and official planning bodies are still to be shaped.

A recent trend in federal policy has been to assign a greater role to official metropolitan planning agencies in the administration of federal aid programs. Urban development has become increasingly complex and difficult to manage, because of the profusion of federal programs as well as the maze of state and local agencies operating in this field. Metropolitan planning agencies are located at a critical point in the structure of government, with an overview of development activities in the metropolitan area and an orientation to overall development needs rather than parochial local policies. The federal government has begun to lodge certain coordinating responsibilities with these agencies. Federal grants to local communities for water and sewer facilities, open space, and transportation require that the proposed project must be undertaken as part of a metropolitan development plan prepared by an established metropolitan planning agency. Federal legislation enacted in 1966 now requires local proposals for federal aid under most urban development programs to be reviewed by the metropolitan planning agency. The planning agency decision is not final, but its comments are forwarded to the federal administrator of the program along with the local application for aid.

Metropolitan planning today is oriented more toward physical development than toward social policy, and the federal commitment to metropolitan plans applies so far only to programs concerned with the environment. But there are signs that official metropolitan planning arrangements may serve as the basis for developing social plans and programs. Harvey Perloff's article in this section urges social policy planning on an areawide as well as a local basis. An extension of federal policy to encompass metropolitan social issues has also been urged recently. The United States Conference of Mayors, at its meeting in June 1966, called on Congress to make federal grants for community development contingent upon an agreement by the local community to provide a reasonable share of the low- and middle-income housing in the area. The mayors also urged the use of federal funds for education as a lever to secure local agreements to accept pupils from poor districts, with the aim of reducing the social and economic differences between city and suburban schools. Whether or not social planning functions are assigned to metropolitan planning agencies, their operations so far have indicated a reasonable and promising course for social planning to follow at the metropolitan level. Metropolitan social planning would be complementary to existing metropolitan planning in many ways, as Perloff points out, and the case for joint planning is a strong one.

Involving the poor

The growing scope of governmental activities related to social policy promises eventually to bring public resources to bear more effectively on social problems. At the same time, however, it raises the possibility that governmental decisions increasingly removed from the local scene may become less sensitive to the views and needs of the ultimate clients of public programs. Social planning efforts today show two contrasting tendencies: increasing attention to intergovernmental relations and to federal and state policies, and increasing attention to involving the poor in local policy-making. In part, current social planning reflects a protest against government policies that have either been insensitive to the needs of people who were affected or have assigned low priority to the needs of disadvantaged groups while providing benefits for others.

David Grossman's review of the Community Action program discusses one type of response: the involvement of the poor in local antipoverty planning and in the operation of service programs. The effort here has been directed at bringing the views of poor people to bear on plans for the allocation of antipoverty funds, as well as in designing programs sensitive to the values of the people to be served. Harvey Perloff's proposals for social planning include a series of neighborhood improvement programs with similar objectives. The same programs that have been shaped to promote participation of the poor, however, have also served to enlarge the role of other people with an interest in social improvement. Liberal groups, socially aware leaders, and socially oriented technical staffs have also used the new programs to increase their influence on public policy. These other participants have been searching for ways to express the social requirements of the city in a form that can match the economic and physical requirements already embedded in city policies. Thus the widening of participation has raised issues of relationships among planners, political interest groups, and the poor. Martin Rein and Peter Marris, in discussing the planner's mandate, deal at length with this issue.

A somewhat different kind of concern for strengthening the influence of disadvantaged groups on public policy centers on the relations between citizens and officials responsible for administering public programs. Poor people are particularly in need of services that are now provided by government agencies: public housing, welfare, education, health care. But there has been disturbing evidence that those who need the service most do not always receive fair treatment, that benefits are compromised or withheld for administrative convenience or expediency in the face of pressure to limit spending. Many administrators have regarded the help of public agencies as a favor to the individual rather than a right. Edward Sparer, former director of the legal services unit of Mobilization for Youth in New York, has been one of the lawyers who pioneered in representing clients in their dealings with public agencies. His article presents the case for legal advocacy on behalf of the poor and reports on experience in New York. Others have urged an extension of the advocacy principle to include urban planners and other professionals who can help protect the interests of disadvantaged groups who are affected by other public policies. Bernard Frieden's article discusses advocacy planning in relation to housing and renewal policies; this approach may become a localized adjunct of broader social planning.

Bayard Rustin's article brings the movement from broad intergovernmental planning to direct local action full circle by tracing the opposite path. Rustin reminds us that the goals of grass-roots civil rights protests cannot be achieved without significant changes in social and economic conditions. Strong local participation in civil rights protests has been vital in building up momentum for change. Similarly, neighborhood advocacy planning will generate political support for social objectives. But the equality of opportunity sought by such local movements will not be meaningful without an expansion of opportunities in the society at large.

Content and methods

The interconnections between social problems furnish a theme for many of the essays in this book. Social planning must integrate many facets of urban life if it is to be effective in any major area of concern. Public policies in urban development have already begun to move into social areas. Plans undertaken under the Community Renewal Program in a number of cities include actions to improve social and economic conditions as well as the physical environment of blighted areas. Neighborhood diagnostic surveys, consisting of household interviews in urban renewal project areas, are designed to serve as a basis for planning social services as well as environmental changes. Other programs that are primarily social have also been expanding the scope of their actions well beyond traditional limits. The Community Action Program guide issued by the Office of Economic Opportunity includes a program checklist embracing many systems of services: education, employment, family welfare, health service, housing, economic development, consumer information and credit, and legal services. The Model Cities Program, established in 1966, is a deliberate attempt to mix social and environmental components across federal departmental lines in concerted programs of neighborhood improvement.

These current developments suggest that social planning in the future will move into new areas of growth. At this point, social planning implies a focus on the poor and on service programs. It is beginning to link environmental concerns with social services, reflecting collaborative efforts between urban planning, social welfare, and antipoverty programs. The future of social planning is likely to reflect wider definitions and concepts of social issues, affecting all urban residents. The urban environment, broadly defined, has implications for mental and physical health, social (and antisocial) behavior, cultural opportunities, and esthetic satisfactions. In this sense, "social" includes the values and behavior of people and constitutes a set of goals for planning cities in which people will want to live.

Our present urban and social planning has at least four major deficiencies which are the areas for future development dealt with by most of the articles in this section. These are: lack of specificity about social components; problems of forecasting future conditions so that planning will deal with the future, not the past; determining the connections between such components and environmental and economic elements; and developing adequate planning methods and trained manpower.

In this perspective, the article by Harvey Perloff does a great deal to specify the related social and physical elements more exactly. Perloff also offers a goal framework for linking specialized planning activities to deal comprehensively with issues of housing, jobs, and services. David Grossman draws on recent experience to discuss the varying content of social planning in community action programs and the problems of combining program components across agency and governmental barriers.

Robert Wood introduces the urban university as an institution addressing itself to city problems and thus becoming not only a political factor but a resource for enlarging knowledge about the urban environment and educating students in the skills needed for planning. Avner Hovne's article is an example of the projection of economic trends and the delineation of implications for one social area—education.

The social planning that is proposed and illustrated in this section involves more than the integration of separate plans and programs. It also requires the use of new planning methods, or the application of existing methods to new situations. Perloff discusses a number of innovations in planning methods, such as the development of local and metropolitan housing budgets. Janet Reiner, Everett Reimer, and Thomas Reiner present one new planning method, client analysis, in detail and indicate its application to public programs. Edward Sparer illustrates the radical adaptation of legal processes to new uses and new methods.

Finally, Avner Hovne's article itself illustrates many prospective characteristics of future social planning. Hovne describes a system of educational planning to meet the changing demands of the labor market. His system would plan for continuing education over a lifetime, with periods of education alternating with periods of work. It would involve striking departures from present methods of educational planning and illustrates a more utopian concept of social planning than the problem-oriented approach discussed earlier in this book. Yet its blend of long-range social objectives with pragmatic planning methods may well anticipate the future character of social planning.

20

Toward Equality of Urban Opportunity

BERNARD J. FRIEDEN

It is no accident that social reform movements in the United States have been preoccupied with the quality of life in the cities. Many of our national problems are not only highly visible in urban areas, but are even reinforced and made more difficult to solve by the way we build and organize our cities. Now the United States has dedicated itself to the achievement of important objectives in civil rights, education, housing, and the war on poverty. These national purposes imply parallel goals in the planning of our urban areas. Extending equal opportunities to minority groups means, among other things, making it possible for minorities to find decent housing throughout metropolitan areas. The attack on poverty also means, in part, giving disadvantaged groups access to better education and other health and welfare programs. President Johnson placed these goals in an urban context in his 1965 Message to Congress on the Cities: "We must extend the range of choices available to all our people so that all, not just the fortunate, can have access to decent homes and schools, to recreation and to culture."

The achievement of these national objectives poses a special challenge to urban planners. The purposes of urban planning are sometimes obscured in day-to-day efforts to sort out incompatible land uses, maintain reasonable environmental standards, and program public facilities. More broadly, the job of urban planning is to allocate land and living space in accord with social goals. As a first step, it is important to translate national purposes into goals that can be made operational in the planning of urban areas. This is a twofold assignment, involving not only identifying relevant goals for urban development, but also finding ways to orient public policies in support of these goals.

The social goals of urban planning have been debated ever since planning emerged as a profession. In an important recent paper on the social responsibilities of urban planners, which was received enthusiastically at a national planning conference,[1] Melvin Webber summarized three major objectives: to extend access to opportunity, to integrate urban development planning with other public and private planning for facilities and services, and to enlarge the range of choices available to individuals. Webber urged a joining of professions concerned with urban life and welfare, and looked to

From *Journal of the American Institute of Planners*, XXXI (November, 1965), 320–330. An earlier version of this article, entitled "The Legal Role in Urban Development," appeared in the *U.C.L.A. Law Review*, XII (March, 1965), 856–879, copyright by the Regents of the University of California and reproduced by permission.

this new partnership to produce "imaginative social inventions that will increase the city's riches, while distributing them to all the city's people."

These rather broad and abstract objectives can be applied to a number of specific issues of urban policy, centering mainly around questions of where the poor and minority groups are to live and what levels of public service they are to receive. These are not the only issues relevant for urban development today, but they are among the most important. Few planning programs make adequate provision for the disadvantaged. In many cases, the tools of planning are being employed in ways that restrict residential choices for the poor and deny them access to reasonable housing and services. To reverse this situation will require more than the good will and dedication of city planners: it will require legal and governmental innovation to curb specific abuses of land use controls, moderate the incentives that lead local governments to adopt socially detrimental policies, and to redirect urban development policies toward an improvement of living conditions and of opportunities for currently disadvantaged groups.

Residence and mobility

Where people live is significant in many ways. Different cities and towns in metropolitan areas have varying tax resources and provide vastly different quantities and qualities of public service. The resources available depend to a large extent upon the assessed value of taxable property, which in turn depends upon the income level of the residents and the amount and value of industrial and commercial property. The variation in expenditures can be considerable. As James B. Conant has pointed out, wealthy suburban schools may spend $1,000 per pupil in a year and provide a staff of 70 professionals per thousand students; while slum schools, where the job of education is more difficult, often spend less than half as much and provide 40 or fewer professionals per thousand students.[2] Even within a single community, public services often differ from one neighborhood to another, with favored areas receiving preferential treatment in school programs, recreation, sanitation, street maintenance, and so on. Residential location is a base for the provision of services; when the poor are restricted to certain locations, they are likely to receive inferior services.

The significance of residential location can be seen most clearly in the case of the group in American society that has been most sharply restricted in its choice of where to live: the Negroes. Within our metropolitan areas, the nonwhite population grew from some 6 million in 1940 to approximately 13 million in 1960. Most of this growth took place in the central cities, and within these cities the Negro population remained segregated in well-defined areas. One result has been de facto school segregation, arising from the fact that residential location is the usual basis for assigning children to school districts. Another result has been that Negroes made only limited gains in improving their housing conditions, at a time when conditions improved markedly for the urban population at large. Freedom of movement is a prerequisite for acquiring better housing: families must be able to enter new neighborhoods or move to other communities in order to take advantage of vacancies that they can afford. Negroes are limited in their ability to move to new locations, and hence in their ability to find good housing. Instead, they compete for housing in a restricted market where good housing is scarce and where prices are high for whatever is available.[3]

Residential location also implies certain social consequences. Many working-class people find it desirable and beneficial to live in distinct ethnic communities, among friends and relatives, with special clubs, churches, and other neighborhood institutions nearby. For many, these areas provide support in time of need and a bulwark against the different values of a middle-class world outside. Historically, such neighborhoods have served as way stations for migrant groups as they adjusted to urban life, improved their status, and moved on to new surroundings. For the family not yet ready to move, the availability of such a community can be extremely important. Many people who have been forced to leave because of urban renewal or highway construction have found it a shattering experience, with profound psychological and social after-effects comparable to the grief that one experiences at the loss of a family member.[4]

For those who aspire to a higher status but are forced to remain where they are because of barriers outside, the consequences can also be severe. Many Negroes, particularly, have been compelled to remain in social circumstances that they find incompatible with their personal aspirations. They do not approve of their neighbors' ways of life; they feel their children threatened by constant exposure to rougher patterns of behavior; they feel victimized by a society that allows them no escape from the working-class world. This enforced residence in objectionable surroundings can in turn destroy incentives for personal advancement and replace ambition with apathy. A lack of residential mobility may thus lead to a lack of social mobility. Robert C. Weaver has contrasted the situation confronting urban Negroes today with that confronting earlier migrant groups in the cities. Previous minority groups, he notes,

> moved out of the slums of yesterday into the suburbs and middle-class neighborhoods of today. This Nation offered them middle-class status when and if they evidenced adherence to the dominant culture. For them, there were and are real, tangible, and demonstrable rewards for industry, conformity, and ambition.
>
> Similar rewards are far less general for non-whites. Thus, the degree of social and economic mobility among this group is less.
>
> . . . It is both unrealistic and an evidence of the projection of one's own middle-class values to expect most of those who are denied middle-class rewards to strive for what experience has demonstrated to be unobtainable to them.[5]

The social import of residential location is thus complex and far-reaching. Other illustrations could be cited, but these few examples are sufficient to indicate that neighborhoods and communities satisfy or frustrate a great variety of human needs. Urban planning and policymaking cannot cope directly with these differing needs, except by attempting to ensure a wide variety of choices—including, wherever possible, the choice *not* to move from a community—and by removing barriers that prevent people from moving freely throughout our cities and suburbs. The additional significance of residential choices in enabling people to enter areas where they may receive improved public services, and where they may find better housing, also argues strongly for policies that will maximize freedom of movement for all, and particularly for disadvantaged groups.

Migration and intergovernmental conflict

In the 1930's, when agricultural upheavals sent migrants streaming across state borders in the movement chronicled in *The Grapes of Wrath,* national issues were posed that have not yet been adequately resolved. California and other states that poor migrants sought to enter attempted to exclude them by means of settlement laws, residence requirements for public assistance payments, and a number of extra-legal methods including border patrols. The Supreme Court in 1941 invalidated a California statute which made it a misdemeanor for a person to assist any non-resident indigent in entering the state. Justice Douglas, in a concurring opinion, reaffirmed the right of free movement and noted its significance in the light of state efforts to curtail this right:

> The conclusion that the right of free movement is a right of *national* citizenship stands on firm historical ground. . . . A state statute which obstructs or in substance prevents that movement must fall. That result necessarily follows unless perchance a State can curtail the right of free movement of those who are poor or destitute. But to allow such an exception to be engrafted on the rights of *national* citizenship would be to contravene every conception of national unity. It would also introduce a caste system utterly incompatible with the spirit of our system of government. It would permit those who were stigmatized by a State as indigents, paupers, or vagabonds to be relegated to an inferior class of citizenship. It would prevent a citizen because he was poor from seeking new horizons in other States. It might thus withhold from large segments of our people that mobility which is basic to any guarantee of freedom of opportunity. The result would be a substantial dilution to the rights of *national* citizenship, a serious impairment of the principles of equality.[6]

At about the same time, one of the country's foremost students of urbanism, Louis Wirth, saw the long-range implications of this migration and the hostile governmental responses that it engendered. His interpretation is still relevant for today's problems:

> Freedom to move is perhaps the most basic of human liberties. It is the very antithesis of bondage or slavery. For the perpetuation of our institutions, therefore, it is essential that this freedom be preserved. Without it, our national union could not long survive. If the States and localities should

be allowed to undermine this freedom by the erection of barriers, the unhappy prospect of the crystallization of separate civic bodies hostile to and
jealous of one another is not an unlikely one in this country.[7]

The intergovernmental warfare that Wirth foresaw is at the root of many
of our current problems in urban areas. The sphere of conflict is no longer
primarily at the state level. Now the cities and towns of metropolitan areas
are engaged in mutually hostile policies that restrict opportunities for the
poor. The planning tools that should be applied to translating national social goals into effective local action are instead deployed for the protection
of provincial interests. Within many of our large urban areas, the poor, the
elderly, and minority groups are concentrated mainly in central cities and a
handful of older outlying towns; within these communities, they are often
concentrated further in specific neighborhoods. The more affluent suburban
towns are eager to preserve their social status and to keep their tax rates
low: for these purposes, many are attempting to use land development controls to keep out the poor, who would contribute little to tax resources and
would require considerable public outlays for education and welfare programs. At the same time, many central cities are trying to reverse the population movements that have left them with concentrations of the poor, high
service demands, and a stagnant tax base. Their efforts to retain or win
back middle-income families often lead to development programs that eliminate areas of low-cost housing without providing reasonable alternatives
that the occupants can afford. Together, these policies threaten to victimize
those who are already disadvantaged by displacing them from their homes
in central cities and making it difficult for them to find places to live in the
suburbs.

This emerging conflict between local governments is a matter of first importance for city planners and for all professions concerned with urban
development. It arises from a context of intergovernmental relations in
which considerations of municipal finance join with social prejudices in creating incentives for public officials to prevent the poor from living within
their jurisdictions, or at least to hold their number to a minimum. A fundamental objective for all groups concerned with human welfare in urban
America must be to change the intergovernmental setting in ways that will
provide greater incentives for socially responsible policies. Until the legal
and political context of local government is changed in this direction, city
planners alone will be able to accomplish little in enlarging the choices
available to the poor or opening the gates for a freer movement of all people throughout urban areas.

Suburban policies

Before a path can be found for governmental reform, it is important to
understand the pressures that shape local development policies and the
forms that these policies take. Since World War II, the suburbs of our metro-

politan areas have struggled with the costs of rapid growth. By 1960, nearly half the people living in metropolitan areas lived outside the central cities. Today, we are not only an urban nation but a suburban one as well. The pace of this suburban growth necessitated vastly increased outlays for schools, roads, utility systems, and the operating expenses of local government. The spending of all local governments in the United States rose from $9 billion in 1946 to almost $45 billion in 1962.[8]

Rising local expenditures have been financed largely out of local property taxes. Increasing tax outlays have prompted suburban governments to take a closer look at their planning programs and land use controls—and in many cases to institute these controls for the first time. Methods of economic analysis have been developed so that the local costs and revenues resulting from each type of land use may be estimated in advance and projected for the future.[9] The accurate application of these techniques requires a detailed study of the local community and consideration of marginal rather than average service costs. Nevertheless, certain generalizations can be made about the impact of different kinds of new development. In general, inexpensive new housing tends to necessitate greater costs (for schools and public services) than the income that it yields via property taxes, resulting in an increase in the overall local property tax rate for the community. Clean suburban industry, shopping centers, and high-value housing generally have the opposite effect and tend to show a net gain in property tax terms over the service costs that they bring. Forewarned by this type of analysis, many sophisticated suburbs have responded by adopting land-use controls that limit or exclude inexpensive housing and encourage the development of varying combinations of costly housing, "desirable" industry, and retailing.

SCREENING OUT THE UNDESIRABLES

Robert C. Wood has documented this response in a part of the New York metropolitan region where it has dominated local planning:

> At least since World War I, Westchester has been stereotyped as a refuge of upper-income families from the City who settle in "quality" neighborhoods and consequently enjoy high-quality public services with relatively low "tax effort." During the same period, the county's political leadership has devoted most of its energies to public policies which support the pattern of low densities which topography originally encouraged. Though exceptions exist among its municipalities, Westchester remains, as someone has quipped, dedicated to "zoning against 'Bronxification.'" The stand against "Bronxification" consists fundamentally of policies designed to maintain reasonably low levels of density; to exclude developments of a character likely to result in more public expenditures than they return in revenue. . . . More recently, the expansion of "Westchester-type" industry has been encouraged; outsiders have been excluded from the county's well-developed park system; and considerable attention has been paid to keeping out what has been termed "the undesirable element." [10]

The New York Times has made the same point editorially about local zoning in New Jersey, which it claims is "too often . . . intended to discourage the growth of a community, in order to spare its present residents the cost of new schools and other public works for newcomers." [11] Similar approaches in other metropolitan areas have been noted by many observers, including the United States Commission on Civil Rights, the Advisory Commission on Intergovernmental Relations, the Commission on Race and Housing, and the National Housing Policy Committee of the American Institute of Planners.[12]

As Wood's account of Westchester makes clear, tax and fiscal considerations are often accompanied by an unmistakable undertone of determination to keep socially "undesirable" people out of the community. The strategy is essentially one of economic exclusion, however, and has come to be known as fiscal zoning. This approach usually takes the form of requiring large minimum lot sizes for new single-family houses and making little or no zoning provision for single-family houses on lots of less than one-half acre or for multifamily construction. (In New Jersey and a few other states, some local zoning controls even specify minimum house sizes.) In desirable suburban locations where land prices are high, restricting new home building to lots of one or two acres or more can add a few thousand dollars to the minimum cost of a new house and can effectively discourage builders of inexpensive houses from operating in the community. Large-lot zoning may thus slow the rate of population growth in a community as well as raise the sales price of whatever new housing is built.

Building codes and subdivision regulations are often used for the same effect. Building codes typically vary a great deal in different jurisdictions of a metropolitan area; stringent codes can raise the price of new housing by requiring expensive construction methods. Similarly, subdivision regulations can raise the cost of new houses by requiring the developer to invest heavily in wide streets and sidewalks built to demanding specifications even when the density of population does not call for such elaborate installations. It should be noted that these local policies are directly opposed to long-standing federal policies of promoting a high volume of new home building and increasing the supply of good low-cost housing.

Suburban governments can reinforce policies of this kind by acts of omission as well as by regulation. Abuses of zoning, building code, and subdivision controls serve to price housing beyond the reach of lower middle-income families. Even if these regulations were to be relaxed, low-income families would not be able to afford new private housing. A number of federal and state subsidy programs have been devised to enable local housing authorities to build for low-income families. These programs are optional: no locality is required to provide decent housing for the poor. The housing problems of the poor, however, are truly regional in nature. Low-income wage-earners are part of the metropolitan economy and in fact are needed for certain industries that help support the region at large. Nevertheless, the suburbs can easily avoid making a contribution to the solution of low-income housing problems by failing to utilize subsidy programs in their own communities. Most suburbs build little if any subsidized housing, and leave this responsibility to the cities where the poor are more numerous.

Policies of exclusion can be reinforced further by the practices of private businesses concerned with the development and sale of housing. Real estate brokers have their own policies for deciding which listings of houses for sale will be shown to which potential clients. Negroes and members of other minority groups may be shown listings for certain locations only, or may be shown none at all. Banks and financial institutions can exclude minority families from selected areas by declining to issue mortgages to them. Practices of this kind are not actually matters of local public policy, but they are subject to public regulation, and many states have brought them within the sphere of public action by means of laws against discrimination in housing.

The main impact of suburban exclusion policies falls upon low-income groups and lower middle-income groups at large rather than upon specific ethnic or racial minorities. Nevertheless these effects cannot be separated from today's concern for integrating Negroes more fully into our urban society. The vast majority of Negro families are part of the low-income housing market, and policies that exclude the poor will automatically exclude most Negroes. Thus, while economic exclusion may or may not be accompanied by practices designed to keep Negroes out of a community, land-use controls that limit new housing to upper middle-income groups and to the wealthy will permit no more than token integration of Negroes into the community. Fiscal zoning and related policies are therefore also significant in the light of current attempts to eliminate racial segregation.

Central city policies

Public officials in the central cities and in the older suburban towns are well aware of the effects of suburban exclusion policies. Former Mayor Frank P. Zeidler of Milwaukee once indicated how suburban development policies appear from the vantage point of City Hall downtown:

> The housing problem is in the central core of the cities. Here the people are packed in densities upwards of 10,000 persons per square mile and in many cities with densities many times that. As the houses deteriorate there is no method to move the people around and clear the sites.
>
> The cities are surrounded by suburbs with zoning restrictions that restrict residence to the upper income groups or that restrict the number of families per acre. Consequently, the pressure between the masses of people in the city seeking to go outward and the suburb exclusiveness creates a continual area of conflict.[13]

While the suburbs have been coping with their problems of growth, the central cities have had to deal with equally pressing problems of decline. In most large metropolitan areas, the movement of middle-income and more affluent families from central cities to suburbs has left striking concentrations of the elderly, racial minorities, and the poor in the central cities. The service needs of this population are great—for welfare, education, police and fire protection, and public health. At the same time, the tax resources of these central cities have failed to grow correspondingly with rising service costs: not only have the more prosperous residential taxpayers been leaving, but industries and retail businesses have also been moving to the suburbs.

The conflict that Mayor Zeidler had in mind is now very clear. The wealth of the central cities is passing to the suburbs, while service needs of these cities continue to grow. Most of the large central cities have responded with development programs designed to make them more attractive to middle-income citizens and to industry. Two major components of these programs are urban renewal—aimed at clearing or renovating old structures and attracting new taxable real restate investment—and highway construction to provide better access from intown locations to the rest of the metropolitan area. These programs to revitalize the old cities have unfortunate implications for the poor, however.

Both urban renewal and highway building destroy a good deal of low-cost housing and displace many families. In 99 cities over 100,000 in population surveyed in the summer of 1964, these two programs had displaced 24,000 families in the past year and were expected to displace an additional 76,000 families in the next two years.[14] It has been estimated independently that as the pace of operations grows, urban renewal and the federally-aided highway program together will displace more than a million families by 1972.[15] Highway construction clears housing without replacing any of it; and routes through residential areas destroy mainly low-cost housing, since highway planners try to keep land acquisition costs low. Urban renewal programs build housing as well as destroying it, but they build much less than they destroy and most of the new housing is far too expensive for the people who are displaced. The effects of these programs in destroying low-cost housing may be offset by other housing market trends that place additional vacancies at the disposal of lower-income groups. A large volume of clearance, however, always creates immediate hardship, and may slow the rate of improvement of housing conditions for the poor or may even reverse market trends and cause housing conditions to deteriorate further.

EXCHANGING THE POOR FOR THE PROSPEROUS

Unless these programs are accompanied by positive measures to provide good alternative housing for those who are displaced, the revitalization of central cities will increasingly restrict the housing choices available to the poor. They will have to leave areas where they now live, and the total supply of low-cost housing in the city will be reduced. For a number of reasons, central city policies appear to be working in this direction. Although relocation assistance is now available under the federally-aided highway program as well as under urban renewal, relocation is clearly an incidental function in the case of highways, and there is no strong motivation to extend more than a minimum of aid. Urban renewal, according to the Housing Act of 1949, had as one of its original purposes "the realization as soon as feasible of the goal of a decent home and a suitable living environment for every American family," but the goals of the program now appear to be somewhat different. Commissioner William L. Slayton of the Urban Renewal Administration, in testimony before Congress in 1963, gave assurances that relocation planning would receive careful attention, but his presentation suggested that it is seen locally mainly as a byproduct of renewal—an obstacle to be overcome —rather than a central objective. Slayton interpreted the original legislation in 1949 as an indication "that the clearance and redevelopment of blighted areas was a national objective" [16]—more so, apparently, than the improvement of living conditions for families in the blighted areas. Elsewhere in the same statement Slayton observes that "because one of the objectives of urban renewal has always been to sustain and increase the capacity of cities to meet rising needs for essential public facilities and services, the impact of urban renewal upon taxable values is particularly important." [17]

Urban renewal is an exceedingly complex program and raises many issues that cannot be examined adequately in a short article.[18] I suggest, however, that central-city renewal programs can generally be best understood as part of the conflict between central cities and suburbs, and in this intergovernmental competition lie a number of ominous implications. Highway building in the central cities is caught up in the same effort to refurbish the core areas to make them more desirable locations for taxpaying businesses and residents, but the major new highways are usually part of metropolitan and statewide road-building plans, so that they reflect other influences in addition to central-city policies. Thus the pressure to build new highways in the central cities may originate with suburbanites who want convenient auto access to their downtown offices, as well as with downtown businessmen trying to attract suburban shoppers. Highway building is less clearly a weapon of intergovernmental warfare than urban renewal, but it is often an integral part of plans to make the cities able to compete more effectively with the suburbs, and it tends to create displacement effects similar to those of renewal.

The current program of the Boston Redevelopment Authority, one of the most active and sophisticated renewal agencies in the country, illustrates with unusual candor the intention to build a development policy around the goal of attracting a more prosperous population to the central city. After reviewing recent population changes, including an increase in "population groups most dependent on public services—racial minorities, the elderly, and low-income groups generally," the General Plan states clearly:

> The Policy of the Development Program and this Plan is . . . to promote stability in the size of Boston's population while increasing the diversity of its composition, so that it more nearly reflects the composition of the Region's population as a whole. This would, of course, entail a reversal of present trends toward increasing proportions of low-income groups and non-whites in the core City.[19]

To achieve this goal an exchange of population is indicated in which some of Boston's poor are to be relocated outside the city and some present or potential middle-income suburbanites would live in new housing in the central city. The General Plan contemplates eliminating 29,000 units of presumably low-cost housing, and building 13,000 to 14,000 luxury units (for small families with incomes of $9,000 or more); 15,000 units of moderate-income housing; and 5,000 new units of low-cost public housing. The statement of relocation policy further underlines the exchange of population that is implied:

> Boston can provide a substantial amount of new housing for low and middle income families, but it cannot meet the entire need. Unless suburban cities and towns change their zoning policies to make presently vacant land outside the City available for low and middle income housing, the time required for eliminating sub-standard housing in the metropolitan area will be needlessly extended.[20]

RELOCATION: FEDERAL INNOVATION AND LOCAL NEGLECT

Central-city policies conceived in this spirit are understandable, but they do not augur well for people who will be caught in the squeeze between central-city displacement and suburban exclusion. Core cities are tempted to wage war on poverty by eliminating some of the poor from their jurisdiction —with federal aid. If the intent is to encourage the poor to leave the city, the city will have no motivation to provide them with new low-cost housing to replace what they had before. Relocation aid, for both renewal and highway programs, will consist mainly of assistance in finding vacancies in private housing and reimbursement for moving expenses, plus such innovations as the newly authorized payment of a short-term subsidy under renewal to help eligible families meet increased housing costs. Yet the Advisory Commission on Intergovernmental Relations, in its recent report on national relocation experience, concludes unequivocally: "The worst problem in relocating families and individuals is the shortage of standard housing for low income groups." [21] What is needed most is not counseling but an expansion of the supply of low-cost housing, which would have to involve either the construction of new subsidized housing or direct rent subsidies on a long-term basis to enable poor families to afford adequate private housing.

Far from assisting low-income families and enlarging their opportunities to find decent housing and satisfactory neighborhoods in which to live, the rebuilding of central cities is a threat to their welfare. Further, the incidence of hardship is not random but quite selective. The majority of families displaced by urban renewal has been nonwhite, and many of the white displacees are members of other minority groups that also suffer from special disabilities in the housing market: Puerto Ricans, people of Mexican background, large families, the very poor. A recent survey of 68 renewal areas conducted by the Urban Renewal Administration indicated that almost 29 per cent of the families had monthly incomes below $200.[22] According to usual budget allowances, a family earning $200 a month can afford to pay no more than $40 to $50 for rent. Most urban areas have little private housing in sound condition available at this rent level. Even rehabilitated housing in renewal areas assisted under the federal moderate-income ("221 (d)(3)") program involves monthly charges greater than $50.

The literature on relocation experience to date is extensive, and it is clear from many studies that the results have been a good deal less than satisfactory. It is now conceded that relocation in the 1950's often failed to improve housing conditions for the families affected and typically resulted in higher rents. Reliable evaluators of relocation experience have found good reason to question the rosy statistics compiled by local renewal agencies in their own accounts of relocation.[23] Robert C. Weaver, Administrator of the Housing and Home Finance Agency, grants that through the mid-1950's "relocation often created additional slums and brought blight into new areas" and that "relocation was often poorly done and human suffering frequently occasioned." [24] Further, he notes that the clearance of racially mixed areas was usually followed by the construction of new housing that few Negroes could afford, and that "urban renewal too often seemed to be an instrument for wiping out racially integrated living in one area at the same time that it failed to provide for an equal degree of racial integration on the site or in another section of the city." [25]

Under Dr. Weaver's leadership, federal policy has changed in the past few years and new legislation passed during the administrations of Presidents Kennedy and Johnson has made more liberal relocation assistance available. The federal response to problems of relocation has indeed been a positive one, and nowhere more so than in the case of urban renewal and public housing. Since 1962, relocation advisory assistance and payment for moving costs have also been authorized for people displaced by federally aided highways. Legislation now before Congress would equalize relocation aid under all federal programs to match the standards set by urban renewal and public housing. In addition, federal housing programs included in the Housing Act of 1965—particularly the rent subsidies for low-income families —should make it possible for larger numbers of displaced families to find decent places to live at prices they can afford.

But federal action alone does not solve the problem of relocation. Urban development programs are essentially local in nature and execution. Enlightened federal policies will not produce better results in practice if local governments continue to use these programs to attract middle-income families rather than to give fresh opportunities to the poor. Additional and current evidence of poor local performance came to light recently when the New York State Commissioner of Housing and Community Renewal disclosed that his office had rejected 28 of 38 urban renewal relocation plans submitted by New York communities in the past three years. He noted that "too many renewal agencies overlooked their social responsibility and would create new ghettos in their haste to get funds and clear slums for new housing and stores." "Every one wants to get rid of slums," he observed, "but no one wants to have the former slum dweller live down the block." [26]

An effective reshaping of local policies will call for changes closer to the local scene and for innovations that planners and their allies can help to bring about.

Strategies for urban reform

This review of urban development policies in central cities and suburbs has emphasized certain trends that have an adverse impact on disadvantaged groups and that result in part from the present pattern of local competition in urban areas. A number of approaches are worth exploring as ways to reorient development policies toward the goals of extending equal opportunities to all, enlarging the range of residential choices for the poor, and giving them access to high levels of public service. These approaches are: (1) changing the context of intergovernmental relations in which local decisions are made; (2) reforming present abuses of land-use controls; (3) improving the administration of laws against discrimination in housing; and (4) providing direct planning assistance to people adversely affected by urban development policies.

INTERGOVERNMENTAL RELATIONS

Policies of suburban exclusion and central-city displacement do not necessarily result from ill-feeling toward the poor: they result in large part from a situation in which local governments find that they can operate at lower cost by excluding the poor. If the presence of low-income families made no difference to the public treasury, it is likely that far fewer communities would use their development programs to control the kind of people who will live in the community. Social snobbery will no doubt have some effect in any case, but the removal of economic incentives would be an important step forward.

The cost of providing public services is now divided among local governments, the states, and the federal government. Most states provide significant grants-in-aid to localities for such services as welfare assistance, education, highways, and public health. The federal government also makes important contributions for public works, welfare programs, hospitals, and other facilities. The impact of this outside aid differs considerably from one place to another, depending to a great extent upon differences in the amount of aid that the state makes available to localities and, within any state, upon the aid distribution formulas that it uses. Where grants-in-aid cover a substantial part of local service costs, local governments will be able to cope with the needs of low-income residents without major increases in local taxes. State and federal grants for certain categories of public welfare assistance now go a long way toward meeting local needs, but localities must still rely heavily upon their own tax resources—primarily the property tax—to pay for school expenses and many other local services.

Increased aid from the states and federal government would of course moderate existing incentives to exclude the poor from local jurisdictions. A revision of present aid distribution practices could have a similar effect. Allocation formulas that give increased assistance to communities that have a larger number of poor families, such as the proposals in President Johnson's education program, could create new incentives counter to the present ones. More generally, a desirable distribution system would be sensitive to community needs as well as resources, and would work to equalize the burden of providing services for the poor. If the basic principle is that no community shall suffer financial penalties because it has low-income occupants, then a redistribution of tax revenue is clearly necessary, and the more affluent taxpayers will no longer be able to insulate themselves from regional problems by living in favored communities. More effective equalization of tax burdens would thus eliminate part of the motivation for suburban exclusion as well as central-city displacement.

The case for increasing state and federal grants and gearing aid distribution to measures of local needs and resources does not rest solely on the desirability of redirecting local development policies. Where a problem is regional or national in nature, state or federal assistance is appropriate to avoid penalizing particular localities and to ensure that necessary measures are taken at the local level. The federal antipoverty program recognizes national responsibility to help local government provide certain types of education for the poor. To a considerable extent, the central cities of our large metropolitan areas are attempting to cope with problems resulting from large migrations of people from other parts of the country—particularly from Southern states and Puerto Rico. Here, too, substantial federal assistance would appear to be warranted to share the costs more broadly and to provide newcomers with a high level of public services for education, health, and welfare.

Changes in the structure of intergovernmental grants-in-aid will obviously depend upon political and legislative solutions. Planners can prepare the way for such changes by analyzing local needs and resources, studying the present methods of distribution, and devising new standards for assigning financial responsibilities and allocating grants-in-aid. The needs of disadvantaged groups should receive special attention in the planning of public programs. The Advisory Commission on Intergovernmental Relations has made an impressive start in this direction,[27] but much work remains to be done at the state and local level.

REVIEWING DEVELOPMENT CONTROLS

The use of suburban development controls to exclude lower income groups has attracted increasing attention, and several eminent lawyers have suggested that the course may now be prepared to give more weight to the discriminatory nature of these controls in judicial review. Charles Haar has observed that "the relationship between planning controls and discrimination, since the Supreme Court's decision in the School Cases, has been subjected to increasing judicial scrutiny." [28] Norman Williams, noting that "zoning regulations directed against people have been increasingly important in recent years," finds an important break away from past approval of such zoning in a strong dissent by two judges in *Vickers* v. *Gloucester Township* (New Jersey) in 1962.[29]

Two paths warrant exploration in such cases. One is for planners and legal counsel to present the discrimination issues more clearly when exclusionary development controls are considered by local governments or are challenged in court. The other, as the Advisory Commission on Intergovernmental Relations has suggested, is to propose changes in enabling legislation that would require zoning authority to be exercised in a manner to permit a wide range of housing prices within each jurisdiction. A separate but related proposal of the Commission would change enabling legislation to give zoning authority in metropolitan areas only to large municipalities and to counties.

Still another approach to the problem would be to introduce metropolitan housing and planning considerations more explicitly in judicial review of local development controls. Questions of the misuse of these controls to exclude unwanted people are difficult for the courts to decide. The effects of local controls on the metropolitan housing market are usually complex and indirect, and can best be evaluated with the help of a technical planning staff. An independent review of local controls by a technically competent agency would clearly be helpful to the courts, and the growth of metropolitan planning opens up important possibilities for such review. The majority of our urban areas have metropolitan planning agencies. When these agencies have conducted metropolitan housing market studies that delineate overall housing needs, or when metropolitan plans have been prepared indicating land use allocations consistent with overall needs, this information should be brought to the attention of the courts as background for reviewing local ordinances.[30] A further step in this direction would be to develop a system of administrative review in which the metropolitan planning body itself would comment on the metropolitan impact of local controls.

Large-lot zoning is sometimes justified when topographic considerations make high densities undesirable, as in flood plains. Metropolitan studies and review could be useful in these cases, as well, since local large-lot zoning for topographic reasons should be in accord with regional studies of drainage basins or soil quality. Further, changes in enabling legislation could limit the use of large-lot zoning to instances when it is part of a regional plan based upon these or similar considerations.

In curbing local exclusionary policies, a metropolitan approach is also important to ensure that no single community bears the full brunt of development pressures by letting down the barriers while other localities still maintain them. Judicial challenges to local controls should therefore be handled so as to apply as quickly as possible to all communities practicing policies of exclusion. If local controls permit inexpensive housing in a great number of jurisdictions, it is unlikely that one or two will be overcome by sudden increases in service demands.

ANTIDISCRIMINATION LAWS

By the end of 1963, 12 states had laws prohibiting discrimination in various categories of private housing; a number of others had laws applying to public and publicly assisted housing.[31] The President's Committee on Equal Opportunity in Housing is now coordinating the work of various federal agencies concerned with carrying out President Kennedy's executive order prohibiting discrimination in federally aided housing. In addition, many private fair-housing groups are helping members of minority groups to enter previously segregated areas.

Although the number of public and private agencies in this field is growing rapidly, much remains to be done. Procedures need to be developed for coordinating the enforcement of fair housing laws by all government agencies concerned with housing, and for rapid disposition of cases of alleged discrimination. Private groups in particular need the advice of informed planners on ways of directing their efforts most effectively toward the elimination of discriminatory practices. Observers have noted a tendency among both public and private agencies to become enmeshed in individual cases rather than focusing on institutional practices that exclude minority groups from entire sections of our metropolitan areas.[32]

A continuing evaluation of experience under the various state laws and agencies is also important, so that appropriate changes can be proposed. Close observation will be necessary to probe relationships between economic exclusion and racial segregation—both in suburban development controls and central-city renewal programs—and to challenge discriminatory practices in the light of state laws.

DIRECT ASSISTANCE AND "ADVOCACY PLANNING"

It is clear that disadvantaged groups often suffer considerable hardship as a result of development programs that affect the neighborhoods where they live. These groups generally lack the political power to modify local programs so that their detrimental effects may be reduced. Programs of urban renewal and highway construction are extremely complicated, and considerable expertise is needed to register effective protests, propose reasonable alternatives, and obtain a fair hearing for the views of those who are affected.

Professionals in several different fields are currently attempting a new approach for assisting groups of people, usually on a neighborhood basis, in their dealings with local officials. A handful of urban planners, social workers, and lawyers have been working directly for neighborhood groups rather than for city-wide agencies. In Chicago, a neighborhood group hired Saul Alinsky to head a program of community organization that led to the creation of The Woodlawn Organization. Alinsky's work focused on increasing the political effectiveness of people in this neighborhood and their capacity to cope with their social and economic problems. When the community was threatened by a proposed urban renewal program, the Organization hired its own planning consultants to evaluate the city's proposals and present more acceptable alternatives. As a result, the city's original plan was modified to include the construction of low-cost housing on vacant land in the area before any existing housing is cleared.[33] A few neighborhood associations in the New York area have also hired planning consultants to prepare renewal plans in their behalf. Mobilization for Youth, an independent community agency supported primarily by federal funds, has taken a similar approach in its community organization activities for the residents of New York's Lower East Side.

These efforts have placed professional staff in a new relationship to the people of the communities for which they work. Staff members are not responsible to city governments and do not assume the function of weighing neighborhood needs against city-wide considerations. Their purpose is rather that of articulating the felt needs of people in the neighborhood and serving as professional advocates for local groups. They may advise local people on rent strikes, represent them in their dealings with local officials, propose educational and housing programs, and give aid at administrative hearings and in court. An important aspect of the philosophy underlying this advocacy function is to end the feelings of dependence and passivity that usually characterize relationships between the poor and the public agencies that provide them with various kinds of service. Efforts are made to assert the rights of the poor to receive public service; the service is not regarded as a favor.

The advocacy approach has already attracted considerable attention in legal circles. Robert F. Kennedy, while serving as attorney general, thought in these terms when he delineated the contribution that lawyers can make to the attack on poverty, in an address at the University of Chicago Law School:

> We have to begin asserting rights which the poor have always had in theory—but which they have never been able to assert on their own behalf. Unasserted, unknown, unavailable rights are no rights at all.
>
> Helplessness does not stem from the absence of theoretical rights. It can stem from an inability to assert real rights. The tenants of slums, and public housing projects, the purchasers from disreputable finance companies, the minority group member who is discriminated against—all these may have legal rights which—if we are candid—remain in the limbo of the law.
>
> We need to begin to develop new kinds of legal rights in situations that are now perceived as involving legal issues. We live in a society that has a vast bureaucracy charged with many responsibilities. When those responsibilities are not properly discharged, it is the poor and the helpless who are most likely to be hurt and to have no remedy whatsoever.
>
> We need to define those responsibilities and convert them into legal obligations. We need to create new remedies to deal with the multitude of daily injuries that persons suffer in this complex society simply because it is complex.
>
> I am not talking about persons who injure others out of selfish or evil

motives. I am talking about the injuries which result simply from administrative convenience, injuries which may be done inadvertently by those endeavoring to help—teachers and social workers and urban planners.[34]

Professional help in this spirit is needed for urban development programs as well as for other purposes. Edgar S. and Jean C. Cahn have recently presented a most significant proposal for a "neighborhood law firm" that would represent people in the community in a great variety of circumstances involving public officials, private service agencies, and businessmen.[35] It should be clear by now, however, that the regulations and programs associated with urban development—urban renewal, highway construction, housing code enforcement, public housing—can have a critical impact upon the lives of the poor, and can either frustrate or promote the goals of equal opportunity and freedom of residential choice. Neighborhood planning advisors would thus have a special role in influencing these programs by making public officials more aware of local needs, advising local citizens on presentations at public hearings, making citizens aware of their rights and opportunities under the various programs, and, where necessary, by challenging administrative findings such as those upon which federal renewal aid depends—that the area is blighted, that adequate relocation housing is available.

Finally, planners in these areas could help prepare positive plans and programs incorporating the neighborhood's own assessment of its problems and needs. Before agreeing to such plans, the city would of course evaluate them in a wider perspective and no doubt they would be modified. Nevertheless, the programs that emerge from this interplay of ideas will almost certainly reflect greater sensitivity to local needs than programs for the neighborhood formulated by city officials. Further, it is likely that growing interprofessional concern for the problems of people who now suffer from urban development policies will lead to many proposals for totally new approaches to urban problems. For example, metropolitan approaches to relocation might be investigated: perhaps a state agency with the power to subsidize rents on a long-term basis, build low-cost housing in any jurisdiction, and assist localities in providing services for low-income displacees could operate effectively in meeting the varied housing needs of displaced people throughout the metropolitan area.

The major obstacle blocking more widespread use of the advocacy approach to planning is the difficulty of paying for professional staffs. Neighborhoods of disadvantaged people are unlikely to have funds available for this purpose. Foundations, churches, and labor unions, as well as neighborhood associations, have participated in some of the current experiments. Federal funds administered by the President's Committee on Juvenile Delinquency and Youth Crime have also supported community agencies using the advocacy approach. Additional funds may well become available under the federal poverty program. The Cahns' proposal for a neighborhood law firm would have it affiliated with a university. University sponsorship may be particularly appropriate when the neighborhood agency also serves teaching and research functions or when it is part of a university-sponsored "urban extension" program.[36] In short, financing may be available from a number of sources, and the prospects at this point are by no means discouraging.

Urban development and social conflict

Within the space limitations of this article it has been possible only to sketch briefly some of the problems posed by current urban development policies and some ways in which planners can contribute to their solution. Urban planning and development controls are both concerned with the allocations of urban space among competing interests. Intergovernmental competition in our metropolitan areas has tended to sharpen certain conflicts for space: public programs in the older communities have laid claim to living space occupied by the poor and by minority groups, while development controls in many of the newer suburbs tend to exclude these groups from space available there. Conflict over living space can shade easily into social and class antagonism. Consider the following accounts of interviews with people in Washington, D.C., who were living in the path of a proposed highway:

> A white homeowner who had purchased his property a few years ago and was proud to live in an integrated neighborhood, said that he felt strongly that "changes effected thus far and those contemplated . . . have been made or considered without due regard for the interests of citizens in general, the underprivileged especially, Negroes in particular." He believes that major changes are generally made in the interests of large property owners and builders who profit from these developments.
>
> A well-informed elderly lady commented that "It just isn't just for those people out in Maryland and Virginia with such beautiful homes to expect us to give up the little we have just so they can get into the city more conveniently." She said that she hoped that she will be dead before they begin displacing people. . . .
>
> A dental student with a young family who had grown up in the area said: "You can tell whoever you are working for that I want to be relocated in Silver Spring or Takoma Park. I want to live where I want to, not where somebody says I got to. I want to live in one of those apartment buildings that's got a swimming pool and be able to get out with my white neighbors. Sure I know why they want to get that freeway through here. It's so the white folks will have a better way to get to the suburbs." [37]

The bitterness and antagonism reflected in these interviews is likely to become much more widespread as our urban areas grow and rebuild, unless we take corrective action. Urban planning can serve to ameliorate social conflict, if it is properly oriented. Planners can help establish favorable conditions for socially oriented development policies, and can give content to these policies by using their special skills to advance the interests of people who do not yet enjoy the full benefits of our urban society.

NOTES

1. Melvin M. Webber, "Comprehensive Planning and Social Responsibility: Toward an AIP Consensus on the Profession's Role and Purpose," Chapter 1, pp. 9–22, this book. This paper was originally prepared for the 1963 American Institute of Planners Government Relations and Planning-Policy Conference.
2. James B. Conant, *Slums and Suburbs* (New York: McGraw-Hill, 1961), p. 3.
3. For a general summary and analysis of research on segregation in housing and the characteristics of the nonwhite housing market, see Davis McEntire, *Residence and Race* (Berkeley: University of California Press, 1960). The extent of recent improvement in housing conditions for whites and nonwhites is discussed in Bernard J. Frieden, *The Future of Old Neighborhoods* (Cambridge: M.I.T. Press, 1964), pp. 12–30.
4. See Marc Fried, "Grieving for a Lost Home," Leonard J. Duhl (ed.), *The Urban Condition* (New York: Basic Books, 1963), pp. 151–171; and Peter Marris, "A Report on Urban Renewal in the United States," *The Urban Condition, op. cit.,* pp. 113–134.
5. Robert C. Weaver, *The Urban Complex: Human Values in Urban Life* (Garden City, N.Y.: Doubleday, 1964), pp. 264, 267.
6. *Edwards* v. *California,* 314 U.S. 160, 181 (1940).
7. Statement by Louis Wirth in U.S. Congress, House, Select Committee to Investigate the Interstate Migration of Destitute Citizens, *Hearings, Interstate Migration,* 76th Cong., 3rd Sess., 1940, p. 888.
8. U.S. Bureau of the Census, *Historical Statistics of the United States, Colonial Times to 1957* (Washington, D.C.: Government Printing Office, 1960), p. 730; U.S. Bureau of the Census, *Statistical Abstract of the United States: 1964* (Washington, D.C.: Government Printing Office, 1964), p. 417.
9. See Walter Isard and Robert E. Coughlin, *Municipal Costs and Revenues Resulting from Community Growth* (Wellesley, Mass.: Chandler-Davis, 1957); and William L. C. Wheaton and Morton J. Schussheim, *The Cost of Municipal Services in Residential Areas* (Washington, D.C.: Government Printing Office, 1957).
10. Robert C. Wood, *1400 Governments* (Cambridge: Harvard University Press, 1961), pp. 93–94.
11. "New Jersey's Future Growth" (editorial), *New York Times,* December 21, 1964, p. 28.
12. See U.S. Commission on Civil Rights 1959 Report (Washington: Government Printing Office, 1959), p. 338; U.S. Advisory Commission on Intergovernmental Relations, *Metropolitan Social and Economic Disparities: Implications for Intergovernmental Relations in Central Cities and Suburbs* (Washington, D.C.: Advisory Commission on Intergovernmental Relations, January, 1965), p. 95; Davis McEntire, *op. cit.;* and American Institute of Planners, "Report of the Planning-Policy Committee on National Housing Policy" (January, 1964). The AIP committee report states: "Present patterns of residential development in most outlying areas, under the influence of local zoning and subdivision practices and financing policies, meet the housing needs of a limited and privileged sector of the population and effectively exclude minority groups. Extension of typical suburban patterns of land use, density and housing types, with the consequent effects on the political, social, economic and physical patterns of metropolitan areas should not be supported by the planning profession. Rather, the profession should work to create diversified developments necessary to permit an expanded housing choice for all Americans." (p. 6.) See also William F. Doebele, "Key Issues in Land Development Controls," *Planning 1963,* Selected Papers from the ASPO National Planning Conference (Chicago: American Society of Planning Officials, 1963), pp. 5–14; and Norman Williams, Jr., "Planning Law and Democratic Living," *Law and Contemporary Problems,* XX (Spring 1955), 317–350.

13. Quoted in Edward C. Banfield and Morton Grodzins, *Government and Housing in Metropolitan Areas* (New York: McGraw-Hill, 1958), p. 85.
14. U.S. Advisory Commission on Intergovernmental Relations, *Relocation: Unequal Treatment of People and Businesses Displaced by Governments* (Washington, D.C.: Advisory Commission on Intergovernmental Relations, January 1965), p. 12.
15. Cited in address by Representative Clifford Davis, Chairman, House Select Sub-committee on Real Property Acquisition, reprinted in *Congressional Record,* 88th Cong., 2nd Sess., 1964, Vol. CX, No. 111, p. A2998. See also Alvin L. Schorr, *Slums and Social Insecurity* (Washington, D.C.: Government Printing Office, 1963), p. 61.
16. Statement of William L. Slayton, Commissioner, Urban Renewal Administration, in U.S. Congress, House Subcommittee on Housing of the Committee on Banking and Currency, *Hearings, Urban Renewal,* 88th Cong., 1st Sess., 1963, pp. 391–392.
17. *Ibid.,* p. 425.
18. For an informed critique and discussion of urban renewal, see Herbert J. Gans, "The Failure of Urban Renewal: A Critique and Some Proposals," *Commentary,* XXXIX (April 1965), 29–37; and a subsequent exchange of views on this article, "Urban Renewal," *Commentary,* XL (July 1965), 72–80.
19. Boston Redevelopment Authority, "1965–1975 General Plan for the City of Boston and the Regional Core" (November, 1964), p. vi–3.
20. *Ibid.,* p. vi–5.
21. U.S. Advisory Commission on Intergovernmental Relations, *Relocation, op. cit.,* p. 104.
22. William L. Slayton, *op. cit.,* p. 414.
23. For a review and analysis of relocation experience to date, see Chester Hartman, "The Housing of Relocated Families," *Journal of the American Institute of Planners,* XXX (November, 1964), 266–286. A national survey sponsored by the Housing and Home Finance Agency in 1964–65 reports greatly improved performance in relocation resulting from urban renewal. See Housing and Home Finance Agency, *The Housing of Relocated Families* (Washington: Office of the Administrator, Housing and Home Finance Agency, March, 1965). The finding that 94 per cent of displaced families were relocated in standard housing is subject to several important qualifications, however. Among the major limitations of this study are the following: the survey covered only displaced families and not displaced individuals; of the original sample of 2,842 families, 542 were "lost" and no information was secured on their rehousing; no information is given on the number of families relocated into other areas slated for clearance in the near future; data are not reported by city but on a national basis which includes many small cities outside of metropolitan areas.
24. Robert C. Weaver, *op. cit.,* pp. 53, 54.
25. *Ibid.,* p. 54. Additional discussion of the implications of urban renewal for class segregation appears in Peter H. Rossi and Robert A. Dentler, *The Politics of Urban Renewal* (New York: The Free Press of Glencoe, 1961); and James Q. Wilson, "Planning and Politics: Citizen Participation in Urban Renewal," Chapter 14, this book.
26. "State Housing Chief Denounces 'Soft Heads' Who Snag Renewal," *New York Times,* June 15, 1965, p. 35.
27. See Advisory Commission on Intergovernmental Relations, *Metropolitan Social and Economic Disparities, op. cit.* The first recommendation of the Advisory Commission in this report is of special significance to urban planning: "The Commission recommends that each local governmental unit and agency within metropolitan areas, whether central city or suburban, ascertain, analyze, and give recognition to economic and social disparities affecting its programs. Federal planning aids for urban development, including 'Section 701' urban planning assistance and comprehensive transportation planning, should specifically authorize and encourage economic and social policy planning for the community as a basic justification for physical planning" (p. 91.)
28. Charles M. Haar, "The Social Control of Urban Space," Lowdon Wingo, Jr. (ed.), *Cities and Space: The Future Use of Urban Land* (Baltimore: Johns Hopkins Press for Resources for the Future, 1963), p. 219.

29. Norman Williams, Jr., "Annual Judicial Review, Recent Decisions on Planning Law: 1962," *Journal of the American Institute of Planners,* XXIX (May 1963), 130.
30. For a fuller discussion of metropolitan planning and its relevance for housing and urban development problems, see Joint Center for Urban Studies of M.I.T. and Harvard University, *The Effectiveness of Metropolitan Planning* (Washington, D.C.: Government Printing Office, 1964), pp. 3–24, 147–148.
31. American Jewish Congress, "Summary of 1962 and 1963 State Anti-Discrimination Laws" (New York, 1964).
32. For an analysis of comparable experience in the area of fair employment practices, see Herbert Hill, "Twenty Years of State F.E.P.C.: A Critical Analysis with Recommendations," *Buffalo Law Review,* XIV (Fall, 1964), 22–69.
33. See Charles E. Silberman, "Up from Apathy: The Woodlawn Experiment," Chapter 12, this book. The philosophy and experience of Mobilization for Youth in carrying out comparable legal programs in New York are described in Charles Grosser, "Neighborhood Legal Service: A Strategy to Meet Human Need," paper presented at the Conference on the Extension of Legal Services to the Poor, Washington, D.C., November 12, 1964; Charles F. Grosser and Edward V. Sparer, "Legal Services for the Poor: Social Welfare and Social Justice," *Social Work,* XI (January 1966), 81–86; and Edward V. Sparer, "The Role of the Welfare Client's Lawyer," *U.C.L.A. Law Review,* XII (January, 1965), 361–380. The role of urban planners as advocates for disadvantaged community groups is discussed in Paul Davidoff, "The Role of the City Planner in Social Planning," American Institute of Planners, *Proceedings of the 1964 Annual Conference* (Washington, D.C.: American Institute of Planners, 1964), pp. 125–131.
34. Attorney General Robert F. Kennedy, Address on Law Day, May 1, 1964, at the University of Chicago Law School, cited in Edgar S. and Jean C. Cahn, "The War on Poverty: A Civilian Perspective," *Yale Law Journal,* LXXIII (July, 1964), 1337.
35. Edgar S. and Jean C. Cahn, *op. cit.,* pp. 1317–1352.
36. See Kirk R. Petshek, "A New Role for City Universities—Urban Extension Programs," *Journal of the American Institute of Planners,* XXX (November, 1964), 304–316.
37. Barbara Kemp, "The Social Impact of a Highway on an Urban Community," paper presented at 43rd Annual Meeting Highway Research Board, January, 1964, pp. 5, 8–9.

21

From Protest to Politics: The Future of the Civil Rights Movement

BAYARD RUSTIN

I

The decade spanned by the 1954 Supreme Court decision on school desegregation and the Civil Rights Act of 1964 will undoubtedly be recorded as the period in which the legal foundations of racism in America were destroyed. To be sure, pockets of resistance remain; but it would be hard to quarrel with the assertion that the elaborate legal structure of segregation and discrimination, particularly in relation to public accommodations, has virtually collapsed. On the other hand, without making light of the human sacrifices involved in the direct-action tactics (sit-ins, freedom rides, and the rest) that were so instrumental to this achievement, we must recognize that in desegregating public accommodations, we affected institutions which are relatively peripheral both to the American socioeconomic order and to the fundamental conditions of life of the Negro people. In a highly industrialized, twentieth-century civilization, we hit Jim Crow precisely where it was most anachronistic, dispensable, and vulnerable—in hotels, lunch counters, terminals, libraries, swimming pools, and the like. For in these forms, Jim Crow does impede the flow of commerce in the broadest sense: it is a nuisance in a society on the move (and on the make). Not surprisingly, therefore, it was the most mobility-conscious and relatively liberated groups in the Negro community—lower-middle-class college students—who launched the attack that brought down this imposing but hollow structure.

The term "classical" appears especially apt for this phase of the civil rights movement. But in the few years that have passed since the first flush of sit-ins, several developments have taken place that have complicated matters enormously. One is the shifting focus of the movement in the South, symbolized by Birmingham; another is the spread of the revolution to the North; and the third, common to the other two, is the expansion of the movement's base in the Negro community. To attempt to disentangle these three strands is to do violence to reality. David Danzig's perceptive article, "The Meaning of Negro Strategy," [1] correctly saw in the Birmingham events the victory of the concept of collective struggle over individual

Reprinted from *Commentary*, XXXIX (February, 1965), 25–31, by permission; copyright © 1965 by the American Jewish Committee.

achievement as the road to Negro freedom. And Birmingham remains the unmatched symbol of grass-roots protest involving all strata of the black community. It was also in this most industrialized of Southern cities that the single-issue demands of the movement's classical stage gave way to the "package deal." No longer were Negroes satisfied with integrating lunch counters. They now sought advances in employment, housing, school integration, police protection, and so forth.

Thus, the movement in the South began to attack areas of discrimination which were not so remote from the Northern experience as were Jim Crow lunch counters. At the same time, the interrelationship of these apparently distinct areas became increasingly evident. What is the value of winning access to public accommodations for those who lack money to use them? The minute the movement faced this question, it was compelled to expand its vision beyond race relations to economic relations, including the role of education in modern society. And what also became clear is that all these interrelated problems, by their very nature, are not soluble by private, voluntary efforts but require government action—or politics. Already Southern demonstrators had recognized that the most effective way to strike at the police brutality they suffered from was by getting rid of the local sheriff—and that meant political action, which in turn meant, and still means, political action within the Democratic party where the only meaningful primary contests in the South are fought.

And so, in Mississippi, thanks largely to the leadership of Bob Moses, a turn toward political action has been taken. More than voter registration is involved here. A conscious bid for *political power* is being made, and in the course of that effort a tactical shift is being effected: direct-action techniques are being subordinated to a strategy calling for the building of community institutions or power bases. Clearly, the implications of this shift reach far beyond Mississippi. What began as a protest movement is being challenged to translate itself into a political movement. Is this the right course? And if it is, can the transformation be accomplished?

II

The very decade which has witnessed the decline of legal Jim Crow has also seen the rise of de facto segregation in our most fundamental socioeconomic institutions. More Negroes are unemployed today than in 1954, and the unemployment gap between the races is wider. The median income of Negroes has dropped from 57 per cent to 54 per cent of that of whites. A higher percentage of Negro workers is now concentrated in jobs vulnerable to automation than was the case ten years ago. More Negroes attend de facto segregated schools today than when the Supreme Court handed down its famous decision; while school integration proceeds at a snail's pace in the South, the number of Northern schools with an excessive proportion of minority youth proliferates. And behind this is the continuing growth of racial slums, spreading over our central cities and trapping Negro youth in a milieu which, whatever its legal definition, sows an unimaginable demoralization. Again, legal niceties aside, a resident of a racial ghetto lives in segregated housing, and more Negroes fall into this category than ever before.

These are the facts of life which generate frustration in the Negro community and challenge the civil rights movement. At issue, after all, is not *civil rights,* strictly speaking, but social and economic conditions. Last summer's riots were not race riots; they were outbursts of class aggression in a society where class and color definitions are converging disastrously. How can the (perhaps misnamed) civil rights movement deal with this problem?

Before trying to answer, let me first insist that the task of the movement is vastly complicated by the failure of many whites of good will to understand the nature of our problem. There is a widespread assumption that the removal of artificial racial barriers should result in the automatic integration of the Negro into all aspects of American life. This myth is fostered by facile analogies with the experience of various ethnic immigrant groups, particularly the Jews. But the analogies with the Jews do not hold for three simple but profound reasons. First, Jews have a long history as a literate people, a resource which has afforded them opportunities to advance in the academic and professional worlds, to achieve intellectual status even in the midst of economic hardship, and to evolve sustaining value systems in the context of ghetto life. Negroes, for the greater part of their presence in this country, were forbidden by law to read or write. Second, Jews have a long history of family stability, the importance of which in terms of aspiration and self-image is obvious. The Negro family structure was totally destroyed by slavery and with it the possibility of cultural transmission (the right of Negroes to marry and rear children is barely a century old). Third, Jews are white and have the *option* of relinquishing their cultural-religious identity, intermarrying, passing, etc. Negroes, or at least the overwhelming majority of them, do not have this option. There is also a fourth, vulgar reason. If the Jewish and Negro communities are not comparable in terms of education, family structure, and color, it is also true that their respective economic roles bear little resemblance.

This matter of economic role brings us to the greater problem—the fact that we are moving into an era in which the natural functioning of the market does not by itself ensure every man with will and ambition a place in the productive process. The immigrant who came to this country during the late nineteenth and early twentieth centuries entered a society which was expanding territorially and/or economically. It was then possible to start at the bottom, as an unskilled or semi-skilled worker, and move up the ladder, acquiring new skills along the way. Especially was this true when industrial unionism was burgeoning, giving new dignity and higher wages to organized workers. Today the situation has changed. We are not expanding territorially, the Western frontier is settled, labor organizing has leveled off, our rate of economic growth has been stagnant for a decade. And we are in the midst of a technological revolution which is altering the fundamental structure of the labor force, destroying unskilled and semiskilled jobs—jobs in which Negroes are disproportionately concentrated.

Whatever the pace of this technological revolution may be, the *direction* is clear: the lower rungs of the economic ladder are being lopped off. This means that an individual will no longer be able to start at the bottom and work his way up; he will have to start in the middle or on top, and hold on tight. It will not even be enough to have certain specific skills, for many skilled jobs are also vulnerable to automation. A broad educational background, permitting vocational adaptability and flexibility, seems more imperative than ever. We live in a society where, as Secretary of Labor Willard Wirtz puts it, machines have the equivalent of a high school diploma. Yet the average educational attainment of American Negroes is 8.2 years.

Negroes, of course, are not the only people being affected by these developments. It is reported that there are now 50 per cent fewer unskilled and semiskilled jobs than there are high school dropouts. Almost one-third of the 26 million young people entering the labor market in the 1960's will be dropouts. But the percentage of Negro dropouts nationally is 57 per cent, and in New York City, among Negroes 25 years of age or over, it is 68 per cent. They are without a future.

To what extent can the kind of self-help campaign recently prescribed by Eric Hoffer in *The New York Times Magazine* cope with such a situation? I would advise those who think that self-help is the answer to familiarize themselves with the long history of such efforts in the Negro community, and to consider why so many foundered on the shoals of ghetto life. It goes without saying that any effort to combat demoralization and apathy is desirable, but we must understand that demoralization in the Negro community is largely a common-sense response to an objective reality. Negro youths have no need of statistics to perceive, fairly accurately, what their odds are in American society. Indeed, from the point of view of motivation, some of the healthiest Negro youngsters I know are juvenile delinquents: vigorously pursuing the American Dream of material acquisition and status, yet finding the conventional means of attaining it blocked off, they do not yield to defeatism but resort to illegal (and often ingenious) methods. They are not alien to American culture. They are, in Gunnar Myrdal's phrase, "exaggerated Americans." To want a Cadillac is not un-American; to push a cart in the garment center is. If Negroes are to be persuaded that the conventional path (school, work, etc.) is superior, we had better provide evidence which is now sorely lacking. It is a double cruelty to harangue Negro youth about education and training when we do not know what jobs will be available to them. When a Negro youth can reasonably foresee a future free of slums, when the prospect of gainful employment is realistic, we will see motivation and self-help in abundant enough quantities.

Meanwhile, there is an ironic similarity between the self-help advocated by many liberals and the doctrines of the Black Muslims. Professional sociologists, psychiatrists, and social workers have expressed amazement at the Muslims' success in transforming prostitutes and dope addicts into respectable citizens. But every prostitute the Muslims convert to a model of Calvinist virtue is replaced by the ghetto with two more. Dedicated as they are to maintenance of the ghetto, the Muslims are powerless to affect substantial moral reform. So too with every other group or program which is not aimed at the destruction of slums, their causes and effects. Self-help efforts, directly or indirectly, must be geared to mobilizing people into power units capable of effecting social change. That is, their goal must be genuine self-help, not merely self-improvement. Obviously, where self-improvement activities succeed in imparting to their participants a feeling of some control over their environment, those involved may find their appetites for change whetted; they may move into the political arena.

III

Let me sum up what I have thus far been trying to say: the civil rights movement is evolving from a protest movement into a full-fledged *social movement*—an evolution calling its very name into question. It is now concerned not merely with removing the barriers to full *opportunity* but with achieving the fact of *equality*. From sit-ins and freedom rides we have gone into rent strikes, boycotts, community organization, and political action. As a consequence of this natural evolution, the Negro today finds himself stymied by obstacles of far greater magnitude than the legal barriers he was attacking before: automation, urban decay, de facto school segregation. These are problems which, while conditioned by Jim Crow, do not vanish upon its demise. They are more deeply rooted in our socioeconomic order; they are the result of the total society's failure to meet not only the Negro's needs, but human needs generally.

These propositions have won increasing recognition and acceptance, but with a curious twist. They have formed the common premise of two apparently contradictory lines of thought which simultaneously nourish and antagonize each other. On the one hand, there is the reasoning of *The New York Times* moderate who says that the problems are so enormous and complicated that Negro militancy is a futile irritation, and that the need is for "intelligent moderation." Thus, during the first New York school boycott, the *Times* editorialized that Negro demands, while abstractly just, would necessitate massive reforms, the funds for which could not realistically be anticipated; therefore the just demands were also foolish demands and would only antagonize white people. Moderates of this stripe are often correct in perceiving the difficulty or impossibility of racial progress in the context of present social and economic policies. But they accept the context as fixed. They ignore (or perhaps see all too well) the potentialities inherent in linking Negro demands to broader pressures for radical revision of existing policies. They apparently see nothing strange in the fact that in the last twenty-five years we have spent nearly a trillion dollars fighting or preparing for wars, yet throw up our hands before the need for overhauling our schools, clearing the slums, and really abolishing poverty. My quarrel with these moderates is that they do not even envision radical changes; their admonitions of moderation are, for all practical purposes, admonitions to the Negro to adjust to the status quo, and are therefore immoral.

The more effectively the moderates argue their case, the more they convince Negroes that American society will not or cannot be reorganized for full racial equality. Michael Harrington has said that a successful war on poverty might well require the expenditure of $100 billion. Where, the Negro wonders, are the forces now in motion to compel such a commitment? If the voices of the moderates were raised in an insistence upon a reallocation of national resources at levels that could not be confused with tokenism (that is, if the moderates stopped being moderates), Negroes would have greater grounds for hope. Meanwhile, the Negro movement cannot escape a sense of isolation.

It is precisely this sense of isolation that gives rise to the second line of thought I want to examine—the tendency within the civil rights movement which, despite its militancy, pursues what I call a "no-win" policy. Sharing with many moderates a recognition of the magnitude of the obstacles to freedom, spokesmen for this tendency survey the American scene and find no forces prepared to move toward radical solutions. From this they conclude that the only viable strategy is shock; above all, the hypocrisy of white liberals must be exposed. These spokesmen are often described as the radicals of the movement, but they are really its moralists. They seek to change white hearts—by traumatizing them. Frequently abetted by white self-flagellants, they may gleefully applaud (though not really agreeing with) Malcolm X because, while they admit he has no program, they think he can frighten white people into doing the right thing. To believe this, of course, you must be convinced, even if unconsciously, that at the core of the white man's heart lies a buried affection for Negroes—a proposition one may be permitted to doubt. But in any case, hearts are not relevant to the issue; neither racial affinities nor racial hostilities are rooted there. It is institutions—social, political, and economic institutions—which are the ultimate molders of collective sentiments. Let these institutions be reconstructed *today,* and let the ineluctable gradualism of history govern the formation of a new psychology.

My quarrel with the "no-win" tendency in the civil rights movement (and the reason I have so designated it) parallels my quarrel with the moderates outside the movement. As the latter lack the vision or will for fundamental change, the former lack a realistic strategy for achieving it. For such a strategy they substitute militancy. But militancy is a matter of posture and volume and not of effect.

I believe that the Negro's struggle for equality in America is essentially revolutionary. While most Negroes—in their hearts—unquestionably seek only to enjoy the fruits of American society as it now exists, their quest cannot *objectively* be satisfied within the framework of existing political and economic relations. The young Negro who would demonstrate his way into the labor market may be motivated by a thoroughly bourgeois ambition and thoroughly "capitalist" considerations, but he will end up having to favor a great expansion of the public sector of the economy. At any rate, that is the position the movement will be forced to take as it looks at the number of jobs being generated by the private economy, and if it is to remain true to the masses of Negroes.

The revolutionary character of the Negro's struggle is manifest in the fact that this struggle may have done more to democratize life for whites than for Negroes. Clearly, it was the sit-in movement of young Southern Negroes which, as it galvanized white students, banished the ugliest features of McCarthyism from the American campus and resurrected political debate. It was not until Negroes assaulted de facto school segregation in the urban centers that the issue of quality education for *all* children stirred into motion. Finally, it seems reasonably clear that the civil rights movement, directly and through the resurgence of social conscience it kindled, did more to initiate the war on poverty than any other single force.

It will be—it has been—argued that these by-products of the Negro struggle are not revolutionary. But the term revolutionary, as I am using it, does not connote violence; it refers to the qualitative transformation of fundamental institutions, more or less rapidly, to the point where the social and economic structure which they comprised can no longer be said to be the same. The Negro struggle has hardly run its course; and it will not stop moving until it has been utterly defeated or won substantial equality. But I fail to see how the movement can be victorious in the absence of radical programs for full employment, abolition of slums, the reconstruction of our educational system, new definitions of work and leisure. Adding up the cost of such programs, we can only conclude that we are talking about a refashioning of our political economy. It has been estimated, for example, that the price of replacing New York City's slums with public housing would be $17 billion. Again, a multi-billion-dollar federal public-works program, dwarfing the currently proposed $2 billion program, is required to reabsorb unskilled and semiskilled workers into the labor market—and this must be done if Negro workers in these categories are to be employed. "Preferential treatment" cannot help them.

I am not trying here to delineate a total program, only to suggest the scope of economic reforms which are most immediately related to the plight of the Negro community. One could speculate on their political implications—whether, for example, they do not indicate the obsolescence of state government and the superiority of regional structures as viable units of planning. Such speculations aside, it is clear that Negro needs cannot be satisfied unless we go beyond what has so far been placed on the agenda. How are these radical objectives to be achieved? The answer is simple, deceptively so: *through political power.*

There is a strong moralistic strain in the civil rights movement which would remind us that power corrupts, forgetting that the absence of power also corrupts. But this is not the view I want to debate here, for it is waning. Our problem is posed by those who accept the need for political power but do not understand the nature of the object and therefore lack sound strategies for achieving it; they tend to confuse political institutions with lunch counters.

A handful of Negroes, acting alone, could integrate a lunch counter by strategically locating their bodies so as *directly* to interrupt the operation of the proprietor's will; their numbers were relatively unimportant. In politics, however, such a confrontation is difficult because the interests involved are merely *represented*. In the execution of a political decision a direct confrontation may ensue (as when federal marshals escorted James Meredith into the University of Mississippi—to turn from an example of non-violent coercion to one of force backed up with the threat of violence). But in arriving at a political decision, numbers and organizations are crucial, especially for the economically disenfranchised. (Needless to say, I am assuming that the forms of political democracy exist in America, however imperfectly, that they are valued, and that elitist or putschist conceptions of exercising power are beyond the pale of discussion for the civil rights movement.)

Neither that movement nor the country's 20 million black people can win political power alone. We need allies. The future of the Negro struggle depends on whether the contradictions of this society can be resolved by a coalition of progressive forces which becomes the *effective* political majority in the United States. I speak of the coalition which staged the March on Washington, passed the Civil Rights Act, and laid the basis for the Johnson landslide—Negroes, trade unionists, liberals, and religious groups.

There are those who argue that a coalition strategy would force the Negro to surrender his political independence to white liberals, that he would be neutralized, deprived of his cutting edge, absorbed into the Establishment. Some who take this position urged last year that votes be withheld from the Johnson-Humphrey ticket as a demonstration of the Negro's political power. Curiously enough, these people who sought to demonstrate power through the non-exercise of it also point to the Negro "swing vote" in crucial urban areas as the source of the Negro's independent political power. But here they are closer to being right: the urban Negro vote will grow in importance in the coming years. If there is anything positive in the spread of the ghetto, it is the potential political power base thus created, and to realize this potential is one of the most challenging and urgent tasks before the civil rights movement. If the movement can wrest leadership of the ghetto vote from the machines, it will have acquired an organized constituency such as other major groups in our society now have.

But we must also remember that the effectiveness of a swing vote depends solely on "other" votes. It derives its power from them. In that sense, it can never be "independent," but must opt for one candidate or the other, even if by default. Thus coalitions are inescapable, however tentative they may be. And this is the case in all but those few situations in which Negroes running on an independent ticket might conceivably win. "Independence," in other words, is not a value in itself. The issue is which coalition to join and how to make it responsive to your program. Necessarily there will be compromise. But the difference between expediency and morality in politics is the difference between selling out a principle and making smaller concessions to win larger ones. The leader who shrinks from this task reveals not his purity but his lack of political sense.

The task of molding a political movement out of the March on Washington coalition is not simple, but no alternatives have been advanced. We need to choose our allies on the basis of common political objectives. It has become fashionable in some no-win Negro circles to decry the white liberal as the main enemy (his hypocrisy is what sustains racism); by virtue of this reverse recitation of the reactionary's litany (liberalism leads to socialism, which leads to Communism) the Negro is left in majestic isolation, except for a tiny band of fervent white initiates. But the objective fact is that *Eastland and Goldwater* are the main enemies—they and the opponents of civil rights, of the war on poverty, of medicare, of social security, of federal aid to education, of unions, and so forth. The labor movement, despite its obvious faults, has been the largest single organized force in this country pushing for progressive social legislation. And where the Negro-labor-liberal axis is weak, as in the farm belt, it was the religious groups that were most influential in rallying support for the Civil Rights Bill.

The durability of the coalition was interestingly tested during the election. I do not believe that the Johnson landslide proved the "white backlash" to be myth. It proved, rather, that economic interests are more fundamental than prejudice: the backlashers decided that loss of social security was, after all, too high a price to pay for a slap at the Negro. This lesson was a valuable first step in re-educating such people, and it must be kept alive, for the civil rights movement will be advanced only to the degree that social and economic welfare gets to be inextricably entangled with civil rights.

The 1964 elections marked a turning point in American politics. The Democratic landslide was not merely the result of a negative reaction to Goldwaterism; it was also the expression of a majority liberal consensus. The near unanimity with which Negro voters joined in that expression was, I am convinced, a vindication of the July 25 statement by Negro leaders calling for a strategic turn toward political action and a temporary curtailment of mass demonstrations. Despite the controversy surrounding the statement, the instinctive response it met with in the community is suggested by the fact that demonstrations were down 75 per cent as compared with the same period in 1963. But should so high a percentage of Negro voters have gone to Johnson, or should they have held back to narrow his margin of victory and thus give greater visibility to our swing vote? How has our loyalty changed things? Certainly the Negro vote had higher visibility in 1960, when a switch of only 7 per cent from the Republican column of 1956 elected President Kennedy. But the slimness of Kennedy's victory —of his "mandate"—dictated a go-slow approach on civil rights, at least until the Birmingham upheaval.

Although Johnson's popular majority was so large that he could have

GUIDELINES FOR SOCIAL POLICY

won without such overwhelming Negro support, that support was important from several angles. Beyond adding to Johnson's total national margin, it was specifically responsible for his victories in Virginia, Florida, Tennessee, and Arkansas. Goldwater took only those states where fewer than 45 per cent of eligible Negroes were registered. That Johnson would have won those states had Negro voting rights been enforced is a lesson not likely to be lost on a man who would have been happy with a unanimous Electoral College. In any case, the 1.6 million Southern Negroes who voted have had a shattering impact on the Southern political party structure, as illustrated in the changed composition of the Southern congressional delegation. The "backlash" gave the Republicans five House seats in Alabama, one in Georgia, and one in Mississippi. But on the Democratic side, seven segregationists were defeated while all nine Southerners who voted for the Civil Rights Act were re-elected. It may be premature to predict a Southern Democratic party of Negroes and white moderates and a Republican Party of refugee racists and economic conservatives, but there certainly is a strong tendency toward such a realignment; and an additional 3.6 million Negroes of voting age in the eleven Southern states are still to be heard from. Even the *tendency* toward disintegration of the Democratic party's racist wing defines a new context for presidential and liberal strategy in the congressional battles ahead. Thus the Negro vote (North as well as South), while not *decisive* in the Presidential race, was enormously effective. It was a dramatic element of a historic mandate which contains vast possibilities and dangers that will fundamentally affect the future course of the civil rights movement.

The liberal congressional sweep raises hope for an assault on the seniority system, Rule Twenty-two, and other citadels of Dixiecrat-Republican power. The overwhelming of this conservative coalition should also mean progress on much bottlenecked legislation of profound interest to the movement (e.g., bills by Senators Clark and Nelson on planning, manpower, and employment). Moreover, the irrelevance of the South to Johnson's victory gives the President more freedom to act than his predecessor had and more leverage to the movement to pressure for executive action in Mississippi and other racist strongholds.

None of this *guarantees* vigorous executive or legislative action, for the other side of the Johnson landslide is that it has a Gaullist quality. Goldwater's capture of the Republican party forced into the Democratic camp many disparate elements which do not belong there, Big Business being the major example. Johnson, who wants to be President "of all people," may try to keep his new coalition together by sticking close to the political center. But if he decides to do this, it is unlikely that even his political genius will be able to hold together a coalition so inherently unstable and rife with contradictions. It must come apart. Should it do so while Johnson is pursuing a centrist course, then the mandate will have been wastefully dissipated. However, if the mandate is seized upon to set fundamental changes in motion, then the basis can be laid for a new mandate, a new coalition including hitherto inert and dispossessed strata of the population.

Here is where the cutting edge of the civil rights movement can be applied. We must see to it that the reorganization of the "consensus party" proceeds along lines which will make it an effective vehicle for social reconstruction, a role it cannot play so long as it furnishes Southern racism with its national political power. (One of Barry Goldwater's few attractive ideas was that the Dixiecrats belong with him in the same party.) And nowhere has the civil rights movement's political cutting edge been more magnificently demonstrated than at Atlantic City, where the Mississippi Freedom Democratic party not only secured recognition as a bona fide component of the national party, but in the process routed the representatives of the most rabid racists—the white Mississippi and Alabama delegations. While I still believe that the FDP made a tactical error in spurning the compromise, there is no question that they launched a political revolution whose logic is the displacement of Dixiecrat power. They launched that revolution within a major political institution and as part of a coalitional effort.

The role of the civil rights movement in the reorganization of American political life is programmatic as well as strategic. We are challenged now to broaden our social vision, to develop functional programs with concrete objectives. We need to propose alternatives to technological unemployment, urban decay, and the rest. We need to be calling for public works and training, for national economic planning, for federal aid to education, for attractive public housing—all this on a sufficiently massive scale to make a difference. We need to protest the notion that our integration into American life, so long delayed, must now proceed in an atmosphere of competitive scarcity instead of in the security of abundance which technology makes possible. We cannot claim to have answers to all the complex problems of modern society. That is too much to ask of a movement still battling barbarism in Mississippi. But we can agitate the right questions by probing at the contradictions which still stand in the way of the "Great Society." The questions having been asked, motion must begin in the larger society, for there is a limit to what Negroes can do alone.

NOTE

1. *Commentary,* February, 1964.

22

Common Goals and the Linking of Physical and Social Planning

HARVEY S. PERLOFF

The United States has embarked on a far-reaching national effort to come to grips with a number of difficult social problems, including poverty, juvenile delinquency, racial discrimination, and mental illness. In a very few years' time, important new legislation and programs have been developed. Billions of dollars of federal government money are being put into these programs.

The process of developing and carrying out the new federally assisted programs has brought an increasing appreciation that many of the hard-core social problems are essentially interrelated and that the human resources issues must be treated in a coordinated manner. Thus, for example, it has become apparent that to overcome the poverty of many urban families, not only must civil rights be more firmly established but also the disadvantaged in the minority groups must be equipped with the tools of education and provided with job opportunities appropriate to their skills.

The role of physical planning and development in achieving human resources objectives has, as yet, received relatively little attention and is essentially hanging in mid-air. More than that, in many communities in the United States the existing situation is one of tension and conflict between those interested in physical planning and development on the one side and those concerned with human resources programs on the other. The antagonism is most unfortunate, particularly because it reduces our capacity to tap fully the great new potentialities for a more effective attack on our major urban problems which recent legislation has provided. There is need for some understanding of what is behind the difficulties if a basis for collaboration and effective joint action is to be evolved.

A number of factors have a role in creating the difficulties. Important among these is the disillusion in many quarters with existing physical development programs. Thus, for example, the enthusiasm for public housing which was so apparent in the 1930's has frequently turned to disenchant-

From *Planning 1965,* selected papers from the 1965 joint planning conference of the American Society of Planning Officials and the Community Planning Association of Canada, Toronto, Canada, April 25–29, 1965 (Chicago: American Society of Planning Officials, 1965), pp. 170–184. This article was the third annual Pomeroy Memorial Lecture, commemorating Hugh Reynolds Pomeroy (1899–1961) and commissioned by ASPO for the advancement of ideas on planning, zoning, and related fields.

ment because of the many problems that have been associated with the housing projects. In some areas, serious resistance to local urban renewal programs has developed. It has centered on such considerations as the impact of slum clearance on poorer minority families, the difficulties associated with relocation, the dislocation of small merchants, and the disruption of existing communities. There has been a similar reaction to the search for exclusiveness which characterizes so much of our suburban development, through racial restrictions and large-lot zoning directed specifically at keeping lower income families out.

Not unexpectedly, physical planning has been associated with all of these features, so that those concerned with human resources programs generally see city planning and its related activities as essentially class-oriented, with little regard for the problems of disadvantaged groups. It has, in fact, been called a "plaything of the neatness-minded middle classes."

There are other reasons why physical planning and human resources programs have not been more closely integrated and attuned to each other. While quite a few can be mentioned, I will focus attention on the problem which I take to be of central importance—the lack of "integrating" concepts and goals, or, put more precisely, the lack of an adequate appreciation of their existence and potential role. By "integrating concepts" I mean concepts that can provide an intellectual and action base for effective collaboration between physical and social planning in the attack on critical urban problems. The concepts that have been used in the past by the physical planners on the one side and the social planners on the other have had more of a divisive than an integrative effect. This has been true of the strong emphasis in city planning on land-use planning and control (that is, as an organizing concept rather than merely as a technical tool). This concept has proved to be difficult to "translate" into meaningful social and human resources terms. However, equally difficult of "translation" has been the emphasis on social pathology and on problem families on the part of those directly concerned with human resources. Clearly both of these concepts have been too narrowly conceived to serve as a framework for joint planning and action.[1]

The lack of integrating objectives or goals is the other side of the same coin. For example, the social workers or educators who are trying to evolve long-range programs to help disadvantaged groups are not exactly enchanted by slum clearance as a community goal, any more than city planners can find the goal of adequate social welfare assistance particularly helpful in their efforts to create more viable and attractive communities. Again, the objectives that have been set for these two categories of activities have been too narrowly conceived to provide common ground for joint planning and action.

The importance of having "integrating" concepts and goals in achieving coordinated governmental and private policy and action can be illustrated by reference to our business cycle experience. It is well to recall that there was a tremendous amount of floundering around with bits and pieces of programs—gold manipulation, NRA, WPA, PWA, relief handouts, and the like—until the federal government in 1946 clearly accepted responsibility for "full employment" as a relatively well-defined goal and organizing concept and geared its fiscal and monetary machinery to this goal, as well as set up social security assistance for the unemployed—a logical corollary of the central organizing concept. In urban affairs we are still in the "WPA" phase —struggling with symptoms rather than the more basic elements.

It seems logical to assume that efforts to create more desirable cities would be significantly advanced if physical and social planning *could* be brought together around a set of rather basic goals common to, and meaningful for, both of these activities. The lack of clear-cut, broadly defined goals has been plaguing both sides of the planning equation. The "goals" that have received the most attention have been more instrumental than basic, more concerned with means than with broad human objectives. "Goals" like slum clearance or the avoidance of mixed land uses on the one side or "goals" like more welfare payments on the other can hardly excite the necessary public support or generate a genuine attack on fundamentals. I believe that over time a common set of far more basic urban goals will be forced by the political process (particularly the growing political strength of Negroes in the city and the growing acceptance by middle-class whites of the need to do something about the racial and poverty problems), but the professionals can contribute greatly to easing the progress and shortening the time.

It is already possible to discern some of the areas around which a workable minimum of agreement can be expected. These are areas which, like the full-employment goal in an earlier period, are the focal points of an evolving consensus, a sensing, even by consciously competing groups, that progress along these lines is important for community cohesion and to prevent disruptive tensions. This is not to suggest that a consensus is likely to encompass fully the goals discussed here. There is always going to be a certain trading off, for political and technical reasons, since there are inevitable incompatibilities.

Also, it is possible to speculate on the types of action programs and changes in the "rules of the game" which can contribute importantly to the major objectives. Such speculation permits us to see some of the areas in which physical planning and development can contribute to human resources objectives. The materials presented here will obviously be purely illustrative since the actual goals and the specific programs will have to be worked out, both nationally and within individual communities, through the political process, that is, through the resolution of conflicts of interests, the trading-off process.

Organizing concepts

In looking for potentially effective organizing concepts, it seems logical to turn to what seems like a natural integrating feature—the *bundles* of decision areas which are characteristic of the major decision units in the community: the households, businesses, and governments.

Thus, for example, when a family or household decides to move or to stay it will consider at one and the same time the interrelated aspects of jobs and income, housing, and environment (including both the physical and social environment, the latter including, for instance, the probability of acceptance or rejection by neighbors), and the public services and facilities. The latter would cover not only the quality of the schools but, for the poorer families, possibly also the generosity of the welfare assistance. Thus, the household does not see the community in physical, economic, and social compartments, but as a unified environment of a given quality and "tone."

The same is essentially true for the private enterprises. They will also consider a "bundle" of factors—the community as a good or not so good place for doing business, the relative size of the local market and the relative ease of reaching other markets, the availability of physical sites, and the ease of attracting the necessary labor force and management personnel. Thus, business is also concerned with jobs and income, housing and the environment, and the quality of the public services and facilities.

For governments, these evaluations on the part of households and businesses add up in total to a framework of political requirements, thus shaping the pattern of public services and facilities provided, as well as the types of controls over property and persons which are exerted. Here again questions of jobs and income, housing and environment, services and facilities call for decisions which usually are joint in nature. Such is the case, for example, when water and sewerage facilities are extended by a municipality to attract new businesses and additional subdivisions or when a renewal project with superior public services is pushed to attract wealthier families back to the central city.

This is not to suggest that all these decisions are always inherently joint ones. Rather, the main point is that the nature of the urban community is such that these various functions are naturally linked, so that major decisions must inevitably take account of the linkages.

Some common goals

Against such a background, it is useful to try to translate the organizing concepts which have been mentioned into the objectives around which physical and social approaches to the solution of urban problems might be brought together. Some of the most important of these objectives I would take to be:

1. A "decent home and suitable environment" for every family (the key objective established in the 1949 Housing Act).
2. Jobs for all and a minimum family income.
3. Adequacy and equality in public services and facilities.

I will discuss each of these briefly, mainly to highlight the potential areas of linkage between physical and social planning and action.

1. A decent home and suitable environment. A return to first principles on the part of physical planning and development can play a significant role in bringing together those who are interested in the human resources programs and those concerned more directly with physical development. An attack on inadequate housing at least as broadly conceived as the current attack on the poverty problem is clearly needed for its own sake; in addition, it is likely to get the enthusiastic backing of the persons interested in human resources programs, the very persons who today tend to fight slum clearance and urban renewal as currently practiced.

What this implies is largely a matter of priorities, that is, placing a very high priority on the requirement of providing homes for those most in need of better housing, without necessarily giving up other significant physical development objectives.

It is certainly clear by now that many of the arguments made in the 1930's and earlier by the groups devoted to the idea of eliminating slums were extravagant, particularly in associating such a large part of all the social evils with the mere existence of slums. We know now that many human problems are carried over into public housing units no matter how spanking new and carefully designed the homes may be; that the displacement of families from slum homes may destroy significant community values; and that an impact on many tough human problems can be made within the slums themselves if the strategy is sound and the assistance is adequate in scope.

However, it is equally important to recognize that there would be a great social loss if the original sound intuition, which called for better housing and better neighborhoods as key facets of urban improvement, were to be lost. People do react to their environment. They do long for better housing and neighborhood improvement. These must clearly be considered a significant part of a balanced program to overcome the many difficult urban problems that center on poverty, deprivation, and prejudice. As Alvin L. Schorr has pointed out, the evidence makes it clear that housing affects perception of oneself, contributes to or relieves stress, and influences health and illness. In myriad ways, housing affects the ability to improve one's circumstances.[2]

A potentially useful planning technique to advance the housing goals which suggests itself is a "housing budget" for each community and for the metropolis as a whole.[3] Such a budget could provide a comprehensive picture, first in physical terms (e.g., recording the existing standard and substandard housing and whether these are located in "suitable" or "unsuitable" environments, according to specified criteria), in human resources terms (e.g., needs, current and projected, again according to specified criteria), and, finally, in economic and financial terms (e.g., projected effective demand, and availability of financing means).

The development of such local and metropolitan housing budgets might well be a logical requirement of the federal government, given its tremendous commitment to housing through its various agencies. Whether required by the federal government or not, however, this is a tool which the planner might well use to bring the physical and human resources considerations together in a meaningful way. It would bring before the community the anticipated housing requirements, the anticipated housing supply, the quantitative and qualitative gaps, and just what it would take to overcome these gaps. It would provide a much more realistic base for working out action programs geared to high-priority needs and demands than exists at the present time.

If the objective of a decent home and suitable environment is to be achieved, however, more than improved measurement tools will have to come into play. More substantial action programs are clearly needed, and the physical and social planners might well join forces in working out the requirements and in providing evaluations of alternative possibilities, including the use of scattered small public housing sites and of rent subsidies and various means of enlarging the middle-income housing program. Especially important are measures to stimulate private construction of housing for lower-income families. Many techniques for achieving this end have been proposed, including the use of differential interest rates depending on the income class for which the housing is intended and the encouragement of uniform building codes based on performance standards to allow new technologies to be used.

Consideration might also be given by planners to the possibility of a coordinated attack on urban problems through long-term improvement programs for individual neighborhoods, particularly in neighborhoods where community action and human resources projects loom large. A beginning on such improvement programs has been made in a number of cities around the country, enough to suggest that such programs can help bring physical and human resources considerations into play in a relatively effective way.

A conceivable form would be the preparation of, say, five-year development programs for individual neighborhoods where physical structures are not beyond redemption. Such development programs would have to be evolved from community efforts broadly involving the residents of the neighborhood, but bringing to bear as well the know-how and strength of the city-wide planning and action agencies. Such programs could be prepared by technicians from the city planning agency, in cooperation with technicians from the human resources agencies, seeking ways in which the problems of the neighborhood could be overcome and the realistic aspirations of the residents achieved. Such programs would be likely to include many elements, ranging from spot redevelopment and rehabilitation of existing housing to the improvement of traffic flows for safety, the improvement of the public facilities, and the strengthening of various human resources programs such as education, health, welfare, and recreation.

Where communities have organized themselves for an improvement effort, the results, in some cases, have been quite striking. The priorities chosen may sometimes seem odd as, for example, when a poor community puts its first effort into the building of a swimming pool, but on closer inspection, such efforts often make good sense. It is impressive to see the joint impact of both the physical improvement and the community learning to work together. In the past, however, there has been a missing ingredient. The great potential of community cooperation can be and should be greatly enhanced by competent planning services provided by the city planning agency and the social planning organizations, although the difficulty of achieving a consensus on controversial projects should not be underestimated. Direct organizing work from outside might often be necessary, and, in fact, such insider-outsider coalitions might well be a key requirement for the design of effective neighborhood improvement programs.

As with housing, so neighborhood improvement programs can become effective tools only if they are backed by far-reaching action programs. Given the great difficulties in carrying through broad-scale rehabilitation and conservation, it may well be that serious consideration should be given to the possibility of employing new and more powerful institutional means. One that deserves consideration is the use of urban development corporations that can (1) provide new housing in central areas (using federal assistance such as 221 (d)(3) financing), (2) acquire private rental property and rehabilitate it, (3) provide specified public facilities as part of a neighborhood plan, (4) channel various sources of financing, and (5) in general, seek to provide balanced and attractive communities in central areas, employing those "new town" features that are feasible and desirable in terms of the people who will be living in the area. Again, considerations such as these are best handled jointly through the efforts of both the physical and social planners.

There is a converse point to be made. If the goal of a decent home and suitable environment for every American family is to be achieved even by the end of this century, homes for lower-income families will have to be built—and on a fairly large scale—in outlying areas as well as in the central cities. Planning somehow will have to encompass in the same framework both suburban construction *and* downtown rehabilitation and renewal. The full potentialities of neither public housing and urban renewal nor antipoverty and antidiscrimination programs can be realized as long as low-income and racial ghettos are permitted to grow end-on-end and minority families are bottled up in one or two limited areas of the metropolis. Segregation and isolation feed upon themselves. The greater and the more massive the segregation pattern the more difficult it is to bridge the communication barrier.

Since the end of World War II, private suburban developments have created endless series of closed enclaves tending to consist of families of one color and within a limited range of income. Even central cities have tended to become more segregated. The Advisory Commission on Intergovernmental relations has pointed out in a recent study that "population is tending to be increasingly distributed within metropolitan areas along economic and racial lines." [4] The destructive impact of such segregation on the metropolitan "sense of community" is seen at every turn, in the each-community-for-itself attitude toward the construction of needed throughways, the difficulty of launching meaningful metropolitan planning efforts, and the tension between the races in so many communities. There is strong logic to suggest that an effective way of breaking through the forces which make for this type of segregation would be to create new communities which are so attractive as an environment for the average family that very many people who now resist it would be willing to accept open occupancy and mixed communities.[5]

In the case of public housing in the central city, it becomes ever more difficult to find good sites that can receive the necessary approval by the determining political groups, so that the number of housing units that can be built is severely restricted. Urban renewal in many communities runs into a wall of resistance when relocatees come to feel that they are not getting an adequate *quid pro quo* for leaving an accustomed area. The problem we face is to be able to remove slums that are not fit for human habitation and to modernize the city in keeping with the human and new technological requirements, and yet in public policy to give top priority to the housing needs of those least able to acquire decent housing for themselves.

It is doubtful whether under present conditions this can be done without large-scale building programs, assisted through federal funds, to provide housing for lower income groups in the outlying areas of the metropolitan region, as well as concentrated efforts to achieve open occupancy. To an important extent, these two are interrelated. The elimination of racial segregation in housing may take a heartbreakingly long period of time unless suburban communities are built under conditions which make open occupancy a key requirement. And open occupancy may well be only an empty gesture unless suburbs are developed to embrace housing across a wide range of prices.[6]

The private land development and building industry has produced many attractive and satisfying suburban developments, with fine homes, good services, and good transportation, and should be encouraged in every way possible to continue to do so. However, new measures are needed to extend to the largest possible group of potential home owners and apartment house tenants, including those in lower income groups, many of the advantages today achieved only by those who acquire houses in the relatively few well-planned, privately built, large-scale communities.

One of the most promising of the new approaches that has been proposed, based on successful practice in Scandinavian countries, would encourage public sponsorship of new communities as well as extensions of existing suburban communities. As provided in recent legislative proposals, this could take the form either of FHA insurance of loans for private land development for new towns or of assistance to state and local public agencies to plan and develop new communities on predominantly open land. The latter would call for federal grants and loans to such agencies following a process similar to that now employed in urban redevelopment. These would seem to be sensible types of experiments (and they clearly should be carried out as experiments) in the search for a more effective public framework within which private enterprise can furnish needed housing for a variety of income classes. An attractive feature would be the requirement of a plan of development which considered equally the physical and human resources elements in the situation. This, in fact, is one of the major reasons for considering a broader role for government in urban development.

The introduction of such considerations is only the beginning of the task for physical and social planners. Large and troublesome issues will have to be worried through. How much subsidy will be needed—and justifiable—to achieve combined better housing and "neighborhood-inclusiveness" goals? What types of racial integration patterns will be accepted and rejected by different groups in the community and what kinds of public pressure for neighborhood inclusiveness will be both feasible and effective? The problems are many. At a minimum, the physical and social planners must join forces not only to probe these issues but also to make the general community aware of their relationship to its major goals.

2. A job for everyone willing and able to work and a minimum family income. Jobs and minimum income are at the very center of the concern of the new anti-poverty programs. These goals immediately bring to the forefront the question of the strength and viability of the local economy, and it should be evident that this is a core issue not only for human resources planning but for physical planning as well.[7]

Clearly, physical city planning has a major contribution to make to the realization of the goal of jobs and minimum family income. Not only is this true at the region-wide scale—in the planning of industrial location, transportation, water facilities, and the like (the macro-scale), but at the micro-scale as well. Municipal and neighborhood planning must be carried out with a sensitivity to the special problems of each group and each section of the community. For example, recent experience in poverty areas has shown that the poorer and more disadvantaged the group, the more important is the availability of jobs in *nearby* areas. The availability of nearby part-time jobs is particularly important to keep the youths in school.

On the other side of the same coin, it has been found in a number of studies that an important source of strength of the more stable poor communities is the existence of a large number of small businesses. In a study of a northeast area of Washington, D.C., for example, it was found that local businessmen contribute significantly to the stability and cohesiveness of the community in several ways: a good proportion of the money earned by the local residents circulates within the area; the enterprises provide jobs; and the businessmen provide active leadership in the community because they have a personal and financial stake in it. These types of findings have important implications for the design of sensible physical development, including urban renewal, programs. Physical planning can play a large role in seeing to it that small businesses are maintained in redevelopment areas and in general seek to contribute to the provision of jobs near the areas where the poor and disadvantaged live.

In the same light, a strong case can be made for the use of urban renewal in blighted central city areas to bring industry back into the city and to provide the sites and facilities to encourage the expansion of a wide variety of trade, governmental, institutional, and service industries. We have become so enamored of the industrial estate and the value of attracting nice clean "research and development" industries that we have tended to overlook the great importance, for a high percentage of the people within the city, of jobs calling for relatively little skill. Redevelopment that provides sites for labor-intensive industries and for a great variety of services can play an important role in helping to bring jobs close to the poor and the less skilled, thus making a great contribution to the goals of our human resources programs.

There are other contributions that physical planning and development can make to the goal of jobs and income, for example, seeing to it that in central city areas the housing of the poor can remain close to transportation hubs, or at least not very far away, and that as new factories are built in the outlying areas appropriate housing for the lower income groups is provided nearby. When the urban scene is viewed in this light, one cannot help but question the traditional view that finds the mixing of employment places and homes an unmitigated evil to be prevented by zoning or stamped out by redevelopment where it exists. Concern for the human resources goals suggests that this may well be a questionable objective and that we should look to industrial standards to maintain pleasant environments rather than to flat prohibitions against such mixing. It doesn't take very much imagination merely to prohibit the mixing of employment places and homes; the real challenge is to make nearby work places compatible with residences.

Certainly, here is an area where physical and social planning not only *can* work fruitfully together, but where the goals can be achieved *only if* physical and social considerations are handled in a joint fashion—and with some imagination.

3. The goal of adequacy and equality in public services and facilities. We know that the quantity and quality of public services and facilities in a community play an important role in its capacity to advance all the other major community goals, but I believe we are falling far short of achieving what is possible because we are not bringing the physical and human resources considerations to bear in an optimum fashion.

Transportation planning in our metropolitan regions has rarely been closely related to the various community economic development programs —the programs seeking to attract new industries—nor has it provided continuing interplay between the locational and transportation decisions. Even rarer are attempts to link transportation decisions to considerations arising from anti-poverty programs, even though transportation is obviously an important element in any effort to minimize unemployment and poverty.

Public facilities are often hopelessly out of date because their planning is not related to a continuous and deep probing of group needs and demands, as when the emphasis in recreation is placed on parks at a time when young people clearly show a preference for vigorous water sports, for swimming pools, and for drag strips or their equivalent.[8]

Adequacy and equality in public services and facilities are of course changing concepts, but that does not in any way reduce their importance in planning. The attempt to clarify and to give such concepts substance is itself of significance in both physical and social planning.

The "adequacy and equality" goal is of special significance for the poorer areas of the city. The almost uniformly poor quality of public services and facilities in the areas where the disadvantaged families live is one of the most shameful features of United States urban communities today. Only now is the nation really beginning to be actively concerned about the quality of education and of other services on which the poor have to rely. And the question is being asked whether equality can be achieved by uniformity or whether in some case superior services are not called for in the poorer areas to make up for some of the deprivation of the past and for the many built-in disadvantages, that is, equality somewhat in the nature of a handicap race.

There is a great deal to be done to create public facilities that serve the poor more effectively than the present ones. New types of educational recreational complexes may well be called for, as well as other kinds of facilities that can provide for a variety of needs, including health, day care, informational centers, and the like. While the quality of the services themselves might be the critical question, there is no doubt that imagination in design of facilities and their general excellence can contribute enormously to the objectives of the human resources programs. Among other things, they can help to create a new total environment which not only influences the outlook and motivation of the residents, but serves to spark physical improvements throughout the whole community.

Publicly provided recreational and cultural services and facilities have a large role to play. If we are serious about our anti-poverty and anti-discrimination goals, then we must recognize that voluntary efforts have their limits and that the public should accept the responsibility of providing good recreational and cultural services and facilities which can enrich the lives of the poor and disadvantaged. Also, as some of the more imaginative anti-poverty programs are showing, the provision of such services can be an important source of jobs for the people in these areas. It is extremely satisfying to note how quickly troubled young people can become excellent workers in the recreational and cultural fields with some help from outside.

Plans for the public services and facilities would need to play a key role in any neighborhood improvement program and, here again, we have an essential point of cooperation between the social and physical planners.

The broader considerations[9]

A look at some of the major common goals seems worth while because it is suggestive, in a relatively specific way, of logical points of contact between physical planning and development on the one side and social planning and human resources programs on the other. However, if we accept the notion that the most useful central organizing concept for both of these concerns itself with the *bundles* of decision areas which are particularly meaningful for households, businesses, and governmental units, then it is certainly important to look through the other end of the telescope—the search in urban planning for a sense of comprehensiveness and for a workable overview of the total community. Thus, for example, it seems evident that the planning apparatus of the community as a whole should aim at bringing together the individual functional programs into sensible total neighborhood programs as well as into effective over-all municipal programs—and even into relatively integrated metropolitan programs. Processes have to be available for the balancing of the different individual goals and the trade-offs among them, as well as of the different, and often conflicting, claims of the individual neighborhoods, trying always to see the requirements and potentialities of the community as a whole.

Unfortunately, the achievement of such a view, which clearly calls for an intimate linking of physical and social planning, involves a number of severe practical difficulties aside from the ones which I have already discussed. Particularly bothersome is the different time horizons of the social and physical planners. The former tend to focus their attention on relatively short-term programs, characterized in large part by items covered typically in an annual operating budget. The physical planner has a much longer time horizon (to the point where he is sometimes accused of being a dreamer and unrealistic), so that, by contrast, even the five-year capital budget cannot really incorporate the main physical planning features. It will take a great deal of inventiveness to work out techniques for combining the shorter and longer range concerns into workable over-all strategies of development, but that is precisely what must be done. Thus, for example, it will obviously be necessary to fit plans for housing construction and for the development of new communities and renewal of run-down communities to the changing housing market, in keeping with the hoped-for increases in employment and income and the anticipated extent of desegregation following upon the human resources programs.

The linking of physical and social planning clearly calls not only for better merging of time horizons but also for geographic or areal horizons as well. The social planners have traditionally been largely concerned with individual neighborhoods, and particularly the neighborhoods in which the poor are residing; the physical planners have tended to focus major attention on the larger areal scene. The requirements are clearly for a deepening and broadening of viewpoints on both sides, so that coherent programs can be worked out which relate neighborhood considerations and metropolitan-wide considerations to the same set of goals and strategies. I have already touched on the importance of extending the physical view to encompass specific neighborhood needs and possibilities; it is equally important that the social view begin to encompass the total metropolis, and even beyond. For, as suggested earlier, to achieve our major common goals, it will be necessary to consider *at one and the same time* the possibilities of very large redevelopment projects aimed quite specifically at strengthening the viability of the central city and of the total region by bringing wealthier people and business back into the central city, while simultaneously providing for the housing and other needs of the disadvantaged and poor families in various parts of the metropolis. This type of planning would provide a meaningful kind of "comprehensiveness," with adequate consideration of all the important groups in the community and their many needs, and not just a one-project-and-one-objective-at-a-time approach.

If all this makes sense, then we should be considering seriously how we might go about the linking process to achieve a more effective and meaningful type of urban planning. The cities that have already begun to use the Community Renewal Program (CRP) to bring social and physical planners together have a leg up on this. As an openly experimental program and approach, CRP offers significant opportunities for joint efforts. Either beyond CRP, or under its auspices, much can undoubtedly be accomplished by the establishment of joint research programs which can highlight the interrelationships among key physical, political, economic, social, and behavioral, aspects or urban change. Effective linkages can only be evolved on the basis of deep understanding of the major forces that we have to cope with. Attempts to overcome the extreme *organizational* separation and compartmentalization between physical and social planning will also have to be made. Both sides have been functioning essentially in worlds of their own, and that, somehow, must be corrected. Even more important than the purely organizational arrangements is the need to bring both physical and social planning into effective ties with the political order. In the past, in far too many cases, both sides have sought isolation from the political forces. The search for political purity may have had certain advantages, but it has also meant giving up the compromising, allocating—and integrating—force of politics. The difficulties that have arisen in urban renewal and public housing should have made this clear to everyone. We need the compromising capacity of politics to achieve a set of broad and complicated urban goals.

There are, obviously, other requirements to achieve an effective linking of physical and social planning, but that by itself is a subject worthy of a paper. I am satisfied here merely to underline the need for such linking and its potentialities in the context of the important common urban goals that we have been evolving.

NOTES

1. This question is discussed in some detail in my article "New Directions in Social Planning," prepared for the 1964 International Conference on Social Work, and published in *Journal of the American Institute of Planners,* XXXI (November, 1965), 297–304.
2. Alvin L. Schorr, *Slums and Social Security* (Washington, D.C.: Government Printing Office), p. 3.
3. The metropolitan view is needed to arrive at a realistic picture of *where* the new housing needs can be met. It is not enough to look at the central city alone.
4. *Government Structure, Organization, and Planning in Metropolitan Areas* (Washington, D.C.: Government Printing Office, 1961), p. 7.
5. The problem of racial discrimination and its implications for city planning is treated with clarity and insight by Robert C. Weaver in *The Urban Complex* (New York: Doubleday, 1964).
6. Beyond the "social" reasons for publicly sponsored new construction in the suburbs, there are powerful "developmental" reasons for extension of public concern to the outlying areas of the metropolitan regions. There can be deemed to be a general, long-range interest in avoiding the development of suburbs or new towns that are poorly built, candidates for early blighting, without adequate public services (lacking the necessary revenue base for such services), and involving the loss of strategically located open space so that development begins to take on an undifferentiated look without relief and without adequate room for nearby outdoor recreation. For a valuable discussion of this point see Dennis O'Harrow's "Proposals for New Techniques for Shaping Urban Expansion," in *Urban Expansion—Problems and Needs,* papers presented at the Administrator's Spring Conference (Washington, D.C.: Housing and Home Finance Agency, 1963).
7. See Wilbur Thompson, *A Preface to Urban Economics* (Baltimore: The Johns Hopkins Press, 1965). Thompson provides a thoughtful discussion of the economic problems of our metropolitan regions.
8. On this point, see Harvey S. Perloff and Lowdon Wingo, Jr., "Urban Growth and the Planning of Outdoor Recreation," in *Trends in American Living and Outdoor Recreation,* Report No. 22 of the Outdoor Recreation Resources Review Commission (Washington, D.C., 1962), pp. 81–100. See also the articles by Mead, Goode, Gans, and others in that volume.
9. A number of the issues which have been touched on in the previous sections are discussed in some details in various papers included in Leonard J. Duhl (ed.), *The Urban Condition* (New York: Basic Books, 1963).

23

The New Public Law: The Relation of Indigents to State Administration

EDWARD V. SPARER

A phenomenon of extraordinary importance to any serious effort to cope with the legal problems of the poor has taken place within the last thirty years. Government ceased its passive role in the lives of our citizens and undertook its affirmative obligations. It became a mediator and regulator, a dispenser of services, and the source of what Reich has labeled the "new property." [1] Government undertook these roles for all our citizens, including the poor; and, in addition, for the poor, government undertook particular efforts—in public housing, unemployment, and other social insurance, juvenile court reform, and youth rehabilitation, a variety of public welfare programs, private housing codes, and mandatory repair laws, various educational programs, minimum labor, health and safety standards and other laws—designed to relieve the harsh conditions of poverty and promote the common good.

With the change in the role of government, both national and local, has come a profound though insufficiently noticed change in the legal relationship of the poor. No longer is the primary contact of the poor man with the law in the ordinary courtroom (criminal or otherwise), but in the anteroom of a city, state, or federal agency as he awaits a determination of vital significance to him and his family.

The better part of the public—including the relevant professionals in social work, law, and agency administration—did not and still do not infer, from the relationship the poor have with the legal power of government agencies, that the poor need legal assistance and advocacy in dealing with the agencies. Three rationales have been implicit in this situation. First, it is widely thought that there is generally *no right* to governmental intervention and assistance. Second, governmental agencies dealing with the poor are created to *help* the poor and not exploit the poor; therefore, legal help is hardly needed to contend with such agencies. Third, governmental agencies dealing with the poor often base their judgments on *expert social evaluations* of what's best for any given poor person or family; to interject the rigidity and contentiousness of lawyers advocating against the position of

From U.S. Department of Health, Education, and Welfare, Office of Juvenile Delinquency and Youth Development, *Conference Proceedings: The Extension of Legal Services to the Poor*, November 12–14, 1964 (Washington, D.C.: Government Printing Office, 1964), pp. 23–40.

the agency is, in result, to militate against the best interests of the poor themselves.[2]

The hard test of any position, however, is concrete analysis of the experiences which flow from it. The closer we move toward grasping the concrete experiences of the impoverished, the more disturbing are the questions raised for analysis. Is there a need demonstrated for the lawyer's counsel and possibly his militant advocacy when a deserted mother and her children are suspended from a welfare program because of anonymous complaints that she occasionally sleeps with a man? When a slum tenant daily observes the failure of the local housing agency to enforce codes requiring heat in the winter, elimination of rats, and plastering of holes? When a tenant living in a public housing project is evicted with his wife and five children because a sixth offspring has been imprisoned? When an imminent school suspension hearing may leave a child on the streets and out of school for several months? When an unemployment insurance referee determines that a worker had "provoked" his own firing and is, therefore, ineligible for such insurance? When there is a breakdown in communications between the poor man and any one of a number of vital governmental or quasi-governmental agencies, even including, perhaps, the local arm of the antipoverty program?

This essay will attempt to examine three related aspects of the relationship of state administration to the legal problems of the poor:

1. The scope of the new legal problems involved as may be indicated by an analysis of those raised by one major area—welfare administration.

2. Decision making in local governmental agencies and the role of the lawyer: the history of an issue.

3. Legal needs of the poor in relation to other governmental agencies interested in representation for the poor.

This essay sets forth the thesis that the new public law,[3] dealing with the legal relationship of administrative agencies to the poor, requires the vigorous participation of lawyers representing the poor for its own proper development as well as for the protection of the particular interest of any given poor person. An effort at such representation in turn requires renewed examination of an old problem: Can lawyers paid from government monies effectively contend against government decisions?

The scope of the legal problems at issue: welfare administration

We choose welfare administration for an exposition of some of the many outstanding and unattended legal problems for two reasons. One is that the welfare program is enormously important: welfare is a matter of life or death to more Americans than any other single government antipoverty program. (In the city of New York alone, nearly 450.000 people receive public aid under the several welfare programs; 320,000 are assisted under the Aid to Dependent Children program alone.[4] In the same city, by esti-

mate of Welfare Commissioner Dumpson, a millon people are "poverty-stricken"—belonging to families whose total income is less than $2,000 per year and individuals [unattached] who earn less than $1,500 per year.[5])
The second reason is that no other long-range governmental program for the poor has been torn by as much dispute and doubt on that which is a matter of legal "right" and that which is a matter of charitable "privilege."

What kinds of legal issues of significance to proper welfare administration have come to light in various parts of our country? In Washington, D.C., a court of general sessions enjoined the local welfare department from enforcing a policy of prohibiting a father, separated by agreement from his wife, from visiting the home "too frequently" in violation of the "man in the house" rule. The department has appealed (*Simmons* v. *Simmons,* D.C. Gen. Sess. D–2545–61, June 12, 1964).

In St. Lawrence County, New York, a criminal indictment was returned against six men who refused to engage in a work relief project requiring them to cut brush in knee deep snow in 12-degree weather. The trial court found them guilty of interfering with the proper administration of welfare. An appellate court reversed, upon an appeal brought by the American Civil Liberties Union (*People* v. *LaFountain,* 21 AD 2d 719 (Third Dept., 1964).

In *Collins* v. *State Board of Social Welfare,* a 1957 Iowa district court decision, a state law setting a maximum level to grants regardless of family size was held unconstitutional.

In Alameda County, California, and numerous other places throughout the country, sharp constitutional challenge has been raised against the practice of "midnight raids" without search warrants by welfare workers seeking evidence of fraud.[6]

The list of problems and issues around the country, ranging from the notorious Newburgh, New York, "Thirteen Point Plan" of 1961 to the "suitable home" issues raised in New Orleans in recent years, is endless.[7]

I would like to specify some of the issues existing in one corner of one city, the Lower East Side of New York, where I work and have some experience. Each of the problems noted below is based upon actual cases.

Does a family suspended from welfare assistance on the ground of some kind of wrongdoing or fraud have a right to know the precise nature and basis of the ground for suspension? At times, clients—even aided by private social workers—cannot obtain such information. How is the client to disprove the charge? May the client know who his accusers are? If not, can he effectively disprove the charge despite his contention that it is false? Are not these legal issues requiring legal assistance in the face of negative agency determinations?

May a local welfare department refuse assistance to a New York State resident and her baby (born in New York and living in New York for over a year) on the grounds that it is more "socially valid" for the resident to live in another part of the country where her stepmother has allegedly offered a "resource," home shelter, even though she is not eligible for welfare aid in the other state because of her New York State residence? Are there constitutional issues in this case which only a lawyer could raise? Consider *Edwards* v. *California,* 314 U.S. 160 (1941), and *Sherbert* v. *Verner,* 374 U.S. 398 (1964), in relation to this issue.

If the woman in the above case challenges the factual allegations made by the welfare department, e.g., that her stepmother in the other part of the country really did offer to give her shelter (though nothing else), who can better help her establish her challenge to the factual allegations at a hearing than a lawyer?

If a client needs some beds for the children to sleep on—or a motorized wheelchair for her paralyzed body—or a bigger rent allotment than that given as the result of a caseworker's mistake—is there a time limit to how long the bureaucratic process may take in resolving the family's request for help? Or can the rent checks go unadjusted for over half a year and the wheelchair ungranted for more than a whole year (despite clear need and private social worker's help in presenting the requests)? Is there a remedy in law to force a reasonably prompt determination and grant? Under New York law there is, but how is it to be obtained without a lawyer's help?

If the head of a family on relief defrauds the welfare department by earning a hundred dollars selling dresses and not reporting that income, may the welfare department suspend aid to the three children of the client, all under the age of 4 years, and thereby create a danger of starvation? Is this an issue of the intent of the social welfare law? If the welfare department may suspend aid—for how long may they suspend aid? Can the babies be indefinitely punished for the mother's sin?

Can they be so punished for one year or for six months? Is this an issue which needs a lawyer's assistance?

In a state which bars welfare aid to those who came for the purpose of obtaining such aid, what facts are relevant to the determination of purpose? Does the very need for aid give rise to a presumption of purpose? If a young mother of six children, abandoned by her husband, comes to New York with her children to be near her relatives, including her own mother and father, but needs welfare assistance, can she be found as having come here for the purpose of obtaining welfare aid? Are not these issues matters on which legal assistance is warranted for the client?

If a family is in need, but is under investigation for some kind of alleged failure to cooperate, shall the children get emergency assistance pending the investigation's final result? New York law is clear that they "shall" receive emergency aid. When they do not, as will happen—and a social worker's effort to help fails—do they have an effective remedy in law? The writer believes so, but surely it would require a lawyer to effect the remedy.

One could go on with the issues. For example, New York has its own variant of the "midnight raid" and "man in the house" rule. One case sent to our office dealt with an abandoned mother who was the subject of anonymous complaints that a certain man slept with her. The theory of the welfare department apparently is that if a male sleeps with the client, he is presumably a source of income. If he is a source of income, then suspension will result if the client failed to report the income. The woman's home was "raided" by a special investigator and a uniformed policeman at 6:30 A.M., without a warrant. A man was found in the apartment.

Is the presumption of support reasonable? Is the alleged though disputed consent obtained to the search sufficient in law? Is this method of obtaining evidence legal? Failure to report income is also a criminal offense. Should the welfare mother be entitled to the same legal protections as the suspected ordinary criminal? *Time* magazine has recently described New York's version of the midnight raid as: "The Early Morning Visit, in which investigators charge into a woman's flat at 5 A.M. like gangbusters, and if a man is present, try to find out whether he is filching welfare money or dodging child support. Not surprisingly, some welfare workers object to the technique." [8]

How pervasive are some of the other problems mentioned above? The most frequent problem encountered by persons already on the welfare rolls appears to be that dealing with unreasonable delay in the granting of needed items of aid. The "welfare abuse" problem referred to above, that is the case dealing with alleged purpose in coming to New York, has been an extensive problem and is discussed in detail below. Another problem discussed above, the case of the lady who originally came from another state, appears quite similar to the problems of the group of people described in the 1962 Annual Report of the New York State Department of Social Welfare as numbering 1,347 in the 20-month period preceding the report.[9]

One of the cases cited above deals with the Kafka-like situation one family head found himself in when aid was suspended to his family and he was unable to find out why. In fact, it was not until a lawyer appealed his case that reasons were forthcoming. Shortly after the appeal, before a hearing was held, the welfare aid was reinstated. How often are people suspended from Welfare without even knowing the reason—no less the particular information necessary to answer any charges? The Moreland Commission Report on Public Welfare in the State of New York (1963) stated (p. 68): "Similarly, when cases are closed, are reasons given? Again—not always. In one county, for example, 35.7 per cent of those interviewed claimed they were not told why assistance was cut off, and the case records failed to indicate that the former recipient had been given a reason."

Several of the particular cases referred to above go to the question of initial eligibility rather than administration after eligibility is determined. Does this reflect too much of a concern for eligibility issues on the author's part? In 1961, more than a quarter of a million applications for public assistance were made in New York. Thirty-nine per cent of these were rejected.[10] Consider this rejection rate against the background of Commissioner Dumpson's estimate, cited earlier, that a million persons in New York City are poverty-stricken, below the margin of adequate subsistence, while at the same time less than half that number actually receive public aid. In Westchester County, just north of New York City, the President of the Westchester Council of Social Agencies two weeks ago released the findings of a study of persons living there in "abject poverty" (defined as an income of less than $3,000 a year for an urban family of four or more). She stated: "The most startling fact is that more than five times as many people are living in abject poverty as are receiving aid from the Westchester County Department of Public Welfare." [11]

Many of the 39 per cent rejected for welfare aid are undoubtedly among the great numbers of New Yorkers who live in "abject poverty." Is the great concern of welfare workers for rooting out the supposedly ineligible—reported by the Moreland Commission as a primary preoccupation of welfare workers—a matter to be carefully scrutinized by an advocate for the supposedly ineligible? We know that one major consequence of the effort to root out "ineligibles" is that less time and effort are given toward actual help and rehabilitation efforts with the families.[12] Commenting on this emphasis on eligibility, Greenleigh Associates, the research organization for the Moreland Commission, declared:

> An applicant becomes eligible for assistance when he exhausts his money, gives a lien of his property to the welfare department, turns in the license plates of his car and takes legal action against his legally responsible relatives. When he is stripped of all material resources, when he "proves" his dependency, then and then only is he eligible. Welfare policies tend to cast the recipient in the role of the property-less shiftless pauper. This implies he is incompetent and inadequate to meet the demands of competitive life. He is then regarded as if he had little or no feelings, aspirations, or normal sensibilities. This process of proving and maintaining eligibility in combination with the literal adherence to regulations and procedures tends to produce a self-perpetuating system of dependency and dehumanization.[13]

If needy people are to be rejected because of a caseworker's "literal" interpretation of a regulation, is it possible that a lawyer's advocacy on the proper interpretation might be desirable? If the result of present policies tends to dehumanize welfare clients by treating them as devoid of feelings and sensibilities, is it possible that a lawyer's dedicated representation can contribute not only to the client's financing, but to his or her self-recognized status as a man, a woman, an equal American citizen? Indeed, is it possible that representation of clients by lawyers can improve the humane administrator's ability to effect better policies? We turn to the latter question next.

Decision making in local governmental agencies and the role of the lawyer: the history of an issue

Most of us are inclined to place a great deal of faith in the "good guy" versus the "bad guy" theory of government. If there are problems in the legality of various agency practices—put in a "good guy" to head the agency. If the agency ineffectively carries out its enforcement duties, it must be because the agency is led by some sort of "bad guy"—throw him out and replace him with a "good guy." Good guys, after all, will see to it that good policies are effectively carried out and fairly applied.

Unfortunately, the functioning of government becomes somewhat more complicated for those who are its agents; this is particularly true on a municipal or otherwise local agency level. The life of the agency head, no matter how dedicated and competent he may be on his professional level, consists of a highly politicized effort to maintain his own survival and the survival of the agency, while he accepts a compromise here to win a professional gain there. Sayre and Kaufman, in a brilliant analysis of the administration of the line agencies in New York City, summed up the administrators' problems this way:

> The strategies of the line administrator—winning internal control of his agencies, and manipulating his environment—require, as we have seen, accommodations with all the participants in the contest for the stakes of politics who are concerned with the agency decisions. To render himself less vulnerable to all the conflicting and contradictory demands and instructions, and to all the forms of resistance and opposition to his will, the agency head has to muster the support of all the friends he can find and strike bargains with everyone around him. To preserve his discretion in some areas of his jurisdiction, he must surrender in others. He has to placate his allies to keep them on his side and pacify those who are rarely active in his aid lest they use their influence to injure him and his agency. He has to balance a welter of factors to survive, let alone to progress, for virtually everyone he deals with has an independent source of power.[14]

The line administrator then, no matter what his personal excellence, almost invariably has to bargain and compromise. He does not and cannot call his own shots, developing his own policies in the manner that his best professional instincts may cry out for him to do. This is as true, or truer, in welfare administration as in that of any other local government administration.

Among the many extraordinary pressures which welfare administrators in most large cities must contend with are: the ordinary pressures for economy; the extraordinary pressures for economy that continually arise; the organized and strident anti-welfare demagogues who constantly seek material to exploit for their claims that the lazy and fraudulent and the welfare client are synonymous; the constant internal pressure from an overworked, underpaid, and ever-changing staff; internal maneuvering from a would-be successor; external relations with a state agency which may be led by an administration of the other political party.

Additionally, as noted by Dean Rostow, the administrator, in the face of such pressures, must work with statutes which are often purposely made ambiguous so as to allow room for shifting compromises resulting from a lack of any effective political consensus on what should be done.[15] Moreover, though the pressures are many, one of the weakest pressures of all—indeed it is virtually nonexistent—is that which comes from the welfare clients themselves.

In the context of the problems and politics of agency administration, the lawyer who represents the impoverished client introduces a new element. By fighting for his client, by engaging the issue involved in his client's cause with the judicial or quasi-judicial process, the lawyer not only creates the possibility of reversing an improper interpretation of law which affects many others in addition to his client, the lawyer increases the administrator's potential for effecting humane policy and the clientele's rightful entitlements.

It is helpful at this point to examine in some detail the history of one major issue in New York welfare administration and the lawyer's contribution to its solution.

THE HISTORY OF AN ISSUE: THE "WELFARE ABUSES" LAW OF NEW YORK

New York has never had a residence law which required a person to live in the state for a certain period of time before he became eligible for welfare. In 1960 and 1961, however, certain groups in the state, disturbed by recent migrations, undertook a strong campaign to effect such a law. A hue and cry was raised, fed by the antics of Manager Mitchell in Newburgh,[16] alleging that undesirable newcomers were flooding the state relief rolls. Though less than 2 per cent of public assistance furnished by the state went to persons in the state for less than a year, in 1960 the legislature passed a bill restricting aid to residents. It was vetoed by the Governor.[17]

In 1961, the effort for a residence restriction law was again underway. Commissioner Dumpson of New York City, vigorously opposing a residence law, answered the argument that newcomers come to the state for the purpose of obtaining relief. He stated:

> . . . In recent years, due to the restricted immigration laws, immigration to New York has come largely from Puerto Rico and from the southern states. Our experience in the Department of Welfare clearly indicates that people migrate to New York City in search of a "better life." They are seeking employment opportunities, a better employment experience, better housing, better educational opportunities for their children, for health reasons, and to join friends and relatives. These are the reasons for which five million Americans move within the nation every year. They are the reasons which prompted migration to the United States from the beginning of our history. People do not move to New York in order to receive public assistance. People come to New York City in response to the lure of many of our industries. Indeed, our State and local economy, in large part, is dependent on this in-migration of workers. In simple justice, we cannot enjoy the benefits of our health and welfare services when need arises . . . .[18]

In the spring session of the state legislature, the pro- and anti-residence law forces seemed deadlocked. Finally, a "compromise" appeared: a proposed bill to deny welfare aid to those who came to New York for the *purpose* of obtaining welfare aid but to grant it to other newcomers. The bill, in an effort to please the humanitarian groupings, also provided that temporary emergency assistance shall be given to those who are in immediate need, regardless of their purpose in coming to New York. The pro-residence law forces accepted the compromise. They could say that the law now barred aid to the "freeloaders." Some of the anti-residence law forces accepted the compromise.[19] They knew that hardly anyone really came to New York for such a purpose; no one would suffer.[20]

The bill, then, was a compromise between varying political factions. Each faction anticipated a different result. It was passed into law, and labeled the "welfare abuses" law. The legislative contentions were over. It was time for the varying pressures directed toward the administration of the law to begin.

In the first ten months of the law's existence, 2,730 people were denied aid on the ground that their purpose in coming to New York was to receive aid. Of these 2,730 persons, only 387 were given emergency aid.[21] The total number rejected was, to say the least, surprising in the light of the firm conviction of social workers and others, including the New York City Commissioner of Welfare, that people simply do not migrate for the purpose of receiving welfare aid. The minuscule number who received emergency aid —about one out of every nine rejected—seems even more surprising. If the 2,730 were rejected because of their purpose in coming to New York and not because of their lack of pressing need, would not more than one out of nine need temporary assistance?

Two years went by. The numbers of rejectees continued to mount. The numbers denied emergency aid grew. In 1964, a lawyer interviewed the heads of several families who had been denied aid—emergency or otherwise. We spare the reader the "details" of their stories: pain and suffering, the edge of starvation, a dank basement room for six children with no electricity—cooking facilities—or toilet, the odor of death. We note only that to both the rejected applicants for aid and the lawyer it seemed clear that their purpose in coming to New York was *not* to obtain welfare aid, though they desperately needed welfare aid, but for a variety of other perfectly legitimate reasons. It also seemed clear that a terrible need for emergency aid in each case existed.

As the lawyer interviewed clients, a pattern seemed to emerge. The same two erroneous presumptions by welfare workers appeared regularly. These were:

1. A person who comes to New York without an adequate plan of support, and possibly knowing that she will need welfare help, therefore comes for the *purpose* of obtaining welfare help. (Clearly, the actual purpose of such a person who comes to New York could be for a variety of other reasons; e.g., family reasons.)

2. The presumption that emergency aid under the welfare abuses law should only be given to those who agree to leave the state. (The regulations and procedures adopted under the statutes are explicit in not limiting emergency aid to such persons.)[22]

What pressures underlay the growth of two such presumptions—presumptions inconsistent with the law that was actually passed? In part, it was the pressure of understaffed and undertrained caseworkers whose "social evaluation" plays an enormous role in any such case. Partly, also, it was a variety of "political" forces which pressured for and gradually enforced the interpretations we write of. In any event, a liberal commissioner of welfare had been rendered largely powerless to reverse the process. Indeed, by the time of the hearing of a test case on the welfare abuses law, the welfare department's lawyer argued in his brief that if the claimant's arguments were accepted

> . . . then we can no longer deny public assistance to anyone seeking better education, better hospitals, better health facilities, better municipal concern for the downtrodden and the underprivileged. This City and State could then become the Mecca for all disadvantaged persons, regardless of their origins; and the taxpayers of this State would be required to assume the burden for all who come or are induced to come here.

Nevertheless, the hearing process, the briefing of the case and reply briefs, the readiness for further court appeal if necessary, the light of rationality and quasi-judicial and judicial decision-making power, also had its effect. The false presumptions were declared the errors that they were and the determination of ineligibility was reversed. Every other case in this area also brought to the lawyer's attention was reversed and aid granted—each was based on similar error.

It is the writer's serious speculation that, of the 2,730 cases denied in the first ten months of the welfare abuse law's existence, 2,700 could have been reversed on appeal to the state board of social welfare—or the courts—if the claimants had the vigorous advocacy of a lawyer (for the truth is, people do *not* emigrate for reasons of obtaining welfare aid). How many others since the first ten months—or even today, due to lack of sufficient uniform application of the law—needed and need such advocacy?

In any event, the contribution of legal representation on this issue was to establish the *right* to entitlement, puncture slipshod social evaluations, and make more possible the humane policy urged from the first by the administrator of the agency in question.[23]

Other areas of legal need involving governmental agencies—and a problem of ethics for lawyers and governmental agencies interested in the legal representation of the poor

This essay began by suggesting that there was a need for legal counsel—and at times militant advocacy—for the poor in their dealings with virtually all agencies charged with the administration of the new public law. We have chosen to concentrate on the legal needs arising in connection with one agency, welfare administration, only to illustrate the more general point. Perhaps a limited discussion of some issues from other significant agencies is here appropriate. We consider two other agencies, the public housing authority and the local board of education.

PUBLIC HOUSING

The New York City Housing Authority, established in 1934 to provide homes for families of low income and to clear slums, is today the city's biggest landlord (housing several hundred thousand persons).[24] A low-income family in New York City today, seeking decent apartment quarters, will either be fortunate enough to obtain public housing or will probably have to suffer the consequences of living in a substandard slum home.[25] The authority receives approximately 85,000 applications per year; there is room for only a fraction of that number.[26] Obviously, the grounds used to reject an application—and the grounds used to evict a family already admitted—are of fundamental importance to the poor.

The public landlord is concerned, quite properly, with tenants who will not pay rent, who will destroy the landlord's property, who will spoil the possibilities for good relationships among the other tenants. So, too, is the responsible private landlord concerned with these things. Nevertheless, even the most pro-landlord lease designed by a local real estate board will usually prohibit a landlord from arbitrarily terminating that lease. If the landlord does so act, the tenant will have remedy either in court or in an arbitration proceeding.

But the typical public landlord offers his tenants no such protection. Upon the recommendation of the Federal Housing and Home Finance Agency, the typical public housing lease is drawn on "a month-to-month basis whenever possible." Is this a recommendation designed to protect the tenant? Hardly. The Agency states as the reason for its recommendation: This would permit any necessary evictions to be accomplished with a minimum of delay and expense on the giving of a statutory Notice to Quit *without stating the reasons for such Notice.*[27]

However, where housing authorities choose to assert an arbitrary ground for denying admission or terminating a tenancy, such authorities have exceeded their legal power. Said one court: The government is under no duty to provide bounties in the form of low-rent housing accommodations for its citizens. If it elects to do so, however, it cannot arbitrarily prevent any of its citizens from enjoying these statutorily created privileges. . . .[28]

Is it not time for lawyers—representing public housing tenants—to seriously review the statutes and other decisional material to determine whether the quiet refusal of a housing manager to state reasons for termination is consistent with law?

In New York City, in the late 1950's, hundreds of tenants were evicted from city housing projects on loosely stated charges of "undesirability," without opportunity for fair review. Citizens groups publicly stated their "outrage" at such "unjust evictions." [29] Wide-scale demand for a change was made and a change was indeed instituted. A tenant review board (composed of authority representatives) was created to review and make a final determination of all proposed evictions regarding nondesirability. An opportunity is given to the tenant to appear and hear the charges against him, make a statement, and present his own witnesses.[30]

But the tenant is not allowed to cross-examine those who made the charges against him; he cannot even learn who they are; he cannot have a record of the hearing. No official notes are even kept of the hearing which he may see. If one of his sons has been imprisoned, that is a ground for his eviction; if another younger son has played on the grass, that fact is recited —to show "the whole family pattern." The loosest sort of hearsay statements are quoted against the family—and if a tenant questions the source, he is told it is from a trusted employee of the project. If a tenant's lawyer then questions whether the statement was made by the trusted employee because he was a witness or whether the employee is merely repeating what another person told him, the lawyer is met, in some instances, with a blank stare on the part of review board members. In other instances, the lawyer is asked, "What do you want, a regular trial of all these incidents?"

There is enormous need for lawyers to test the standards and procedures of eviction procedures in public housing. Such tests will have the further desirable effect of clarifying some of the admission standards which affect even greater numbers of persons.

EDUCATION

Some of the most subtle and yet important issues for lawyers to be devoting attention, and perhaps representation, are in connection with public education. There is at least general familiarity with the difficult legal issues relating to de facto segregation and integration in the public schools. How about the ordinary school suspension hearing, however? Are the factual issues which must form the basis for the disposition reached by such hearings adequately attended to? The consequences to the life of the child in question may be far more severe than a minor criminal charge in later years.

The hearings that I have been informed about do not deal with trivial matters—as they should not if a suspension is involved. They deal with alleged assaults, thefts, indecent exposure, extortion, and the various conduct patterns which often appear in a juvenile court proceeding. Lawyers— if they have any virtues—are presumed to be experts in the methods of determining facts. Nevertheless, I know of no effort anywhere—even on a study basis—to analyze factfinding in suspension hearings with a lawyer's eyes and skills.

Equal in importance to the factfinding at such hearings is the disposition of suspension cases. Yet it is not infrequent, at least in my city, for suspended children to be left without any plan whatsoever for months (or longer) at a time, while their case records churn through the bureaucratic procedures or are left to rest in untouched files. Such results can be more than unfortunate to the well-protected middle class child. To the slum child, it can mean personal disaster of the worst sort.

Statute, at least in New York,[31] requires the board of education to take "immediate steps" to institute an alternative plan of education for a suspended child. When a suspended child is ignored for months, has there been a failure in legal obligation? Does the legal obligation itself imply that the parent can take legal steps to require the board to perform its legal duty? Would not such an action force a revision and improved procedure generally? Questions, not answers, are here being posed. But they are questions which require the involvement, the time, and the dedication of lawyers. To those who would argue that these are matters for educators and social workers, the writer contends that a lawyer's role may at times be that of impelling educators and social workers to do their duty.

A problem of ethics for lawyers and for governmental agencies interested in the representation of the poor

There is a peculiar aspect of striving for legal representation of the poor in their dealings with government agencies which requires one to speak of the reaction of the government agencies when the representation occurs. The rich pay for their own counsel; the antagonism of their opposite parties customarily has little effect on the dedicated nature of the legal representation. The impoverished cannot pay for their own counsel. With regard to the legal needs we have been speaking of, it is the same government with which the poor are contending that must pay the bill or develop and fund the institutional entity that employs the lawyer.[32] That is why the reaction of the government agencies to representation of the poor is a subject to be considered.

The subject becomes a particularly pressing one when the board of directors of the institutional entity that employs the lawyer is the "microcosm of the total community"[33] that is typical of antipoverty or antidelinquency projects. Such an institutional entity includes on its board of directors leading representatives of each of the local agencies with which the lawyer must contend.

There is, of course, no uniform reaction on the part of agency representatives to the results of legal service for poor persons in contention with the agency. Particularly with agencies which, for varying reasons, are not unused to the lawyer's role, problems caused by reaction to advocacy are minimal.[34] With others, the reaction can be sharply different. Still elsewhere, the worst of the matter might result from anticipation of reaction on the part of the project's friends in local government who are interested—quite legitimately—in the maintenance of good relations between the project and the local government.

Neither is there a uniform reaction based on the nature of the issue which has become the source of legal contention. Earlier we spoke of legal advocacy for claimants which makes it more possible for humane administrators to effect policies they endorse. Yet, legal action may produce strains, irritations, and a sense of being threatened which clouds all else. Who, after all, readily accepts the notion that additional pressure of a compelling sort is something to be directed at oneself? When the nature of the issue involved produces direct conflict with policies the administrator favors—or flouts the professional pride of a specialized group—the reaction may be even sharper.

The lawyer who represents the poor in contention with government, while paid with government money in an institution partly directed by government personnel, may quickly find that his position is not fundamentally different from that of the line administrator as described by Sayre and Kaufman. He is soon involved in a highly politicalized effort to maintain his own survival and the survival of his agency—while he accepts a compromise here to win a professional gain there. To preserve his discretion in some areas, he may surrender in others. Accommodation with those who are concerned with his agency's decisions is often needed to render himself less vulnerable to all the conflicting demands of others who may affect his agency's future.

How does pressure make itself felt? If the lawyer writes to a local board of education for a copy of its suspension rules, he may find that his letter has been brought to the attention of others in the project. If he takes his client through a state welfare department hearing, he may learn to his surprise that a complaint has been lodged with the referee of the hearing charging him and his organization with "the unauthorized practice of law." [35] If the lawyer is too persistent and too militant in his advocacy with certain agencies, he may find that a high official writes to his organization's director to state that the lawyer's activity on behalf of his client "raises a serious situation in our inter-agency relationship." [36] At another time, a well-connected and highly placed person will tell the lawyer that he must not "threaten" litigation on behalf of certain clients already retained; perhaps a "study project" will provide the best solution.

The lawyer may go to his organization's director and find that he is fortunately situated with a decent and dedicated man who supports the lawyer's work. The lawyer may go to his university faculty advisors and find extra sources of strength. In the end, as with all of us, he must look toward himself.

There is a lawyer's ethic requiring him not to betray his client—observing that ethic is both his duty and his greatest source of strength. Meanwhile, he will slowly learn that open and frank discussion of the pressures and problems he meets is, in the long run—though perhaps not immediately—the very best contribution he can make toward the provision of adequate legal services for the poor in their dealings with governmental agencies.

The lawyer's ethic in serving his client, poor or rich, is a well-established one. That ethic applies, however, only to a lawyer-client relationship already established. It does not and cannot serve to prevent a policy decision preventing him from establishing a lawyer-client relationship on certain matters or in relation to certain agencies. It is in this connection that government, if it is truly interested in making counsel available for the poor with whom it deals, must establish its own ethic: it will make lawyers available without any conditions or limitations other than those imposed by the lawyers' own legal judgment and sense of duty.[37]

The government's obligation to establish legal recourse for the poor in their dealings with governmental agencies is today merely in the argument stage. It is an obligation, however, which should be assumed, particularly in the war against poverty, partly because the poor themselves need representation; partly because the law is best developed with representation; partly because the war against poverty needs that "civilian perspective . . . of dissent, of critical scrutiny, of advocacy, and of impatience" [38] which lawyers for the poor can bring to it.

The assumption of such an obligation on the part of government will mark the beginning of a new blossoming of civilized and dignified human relationships within our country. Assumed without conditions attached, it will establish a new and higher ethic for government. Surely this should be done.

NOTES

1. Charles R. Reich, "The New Property," *Yale Law Journal,* LXIII (1964), 731.
2. Nowhere is the philosophy underlying state social agencies' concern for the client's best interests rather than his procedural or substantive "rights" more highly articulated than in the literature dealing with the juvenile court reform movement. An early but unusually clear exposition is by Miriam Van Waters, "The Socialization of Juvenile Court Theory," *Journal of Criminal Law and Criminology,* XIII, 61. Among the recent expositions arguing in favor of the "best interest" judgment of the agency in lieu of a "rights" concept, is that delivered by Philip Sokol, on April 18, 1964, to a Columbia School of Social Work Alumni Conference. Mr. Sokol is Deputy Commissioner and Chief Legal Officer of the Welfare Department of New York City. However, at the September 11, 1964, Northeast Regional Conference of the American Public Welfare Association, the same speaker modified his position and emphasized the legal entitlements of welfare clients in a context of obligations.
3. The author confesses some uncertainty about the appropriate label for the ill-defined areas of law here discussed. Generally, the law involved is "public" in that it flows from government grant or regulation. It is "new" in that it is primarily a product of the last thirty years and deals with aid to the poor rather than the subject matter of other "public law." Some writers have preferred the term "urban law" in dealing with similar subjects. See, e.g., the excellent work of Edgar C. and Jean Cahn, "The War on Poverty: A Civilian Perspective," *Yale Law Journal,* LXXIII, 1317, 1341. The difficulty with the term "urban law" is that some of the problems dealt with—e.g., welfare, social insurance, etc.— are as relevant to the rural poor as to the urban poor.
4. The figures are taken from *Social Statistics: A Monthly Summary,* issued by the New York State Department of Social Welfare for the month of June, 1964.
5. *The New York Times,* January 11, 1964.
6. See Charles A. Reich, "Midnight Welfare Searches and the Social Security Act," *Yale Law Journal,* LXXII (June, 1963), 1347.
7. See Lukas, "The Rights of the Poor—In What Ways Are Civil Rights of the Poor Safeguarded or Infringed on by Social Work Practices," paper presented at the Alumni Conference of the Columbia School of Social Work, April 18, 1964, for a general summary of some national items.

8. *Time,* July 31, 1964, p. 17. William Stringfellow, a deeply religious young lawyer who spent seven years in East Harlem practicing law for poor people, reports in his book, *My People Is the Enemy* (New York: Holt, Rinehart and Winston, 1964), "I had one case in which an investigator climbed a tree at 2 o'clock in the morning in order to perch there and spy into the window of a project apartment of a welfare family waiting to see or hear something that could be used against the family to disqualify them for further assistance" (p. 75).

9. *Public Welfare in New York State in 1961,* Annual Report of the New York State Department of Social Welfare, issued February 15, 1962, p. 25. The 20-month period immediately preceded August 31, 1961. The persons in the category described were referred to as residents of other states. Initially, at the hearing of the case referred to in the text, the welfare department referred to her as the resident of another state. When it was established that the claimant was in fact a New York resident, the department contended that that fact was irrelevant since the claimant "belonged" in the other state despite the acquisition of residency here.

10. *Ibid.,* p. 32.

11. *The New York Times,* October 29, 1964, p. 37.

12. Moreland Commission Report (1963), p. 27.

13. Greenleigh Associates, Inc., "Report to the Moreland Commission on Welfare of Findings of the Study of the Public Assistance Program and Operations of the State of New York" (November, 1962), p. 78.

14. Wallace Sayre and Herbert Kaufman, *Governing New York City* (New York: Russell Sage Foundation, 1960).

15. Eugene V. and Edna G. Rostow, "Law, City Planning and Social Action," in Leonard J. Duhl (ed.), *The Urban Condition* (New York: Basic Books, 1963).

16. Mitchell promulgated his infamous 13-point plan in 1961. Upon motion of the State Department of Social Welfare the New York Supreme Court enjoined the city of Newburgh from effecting the plan. *State Bd.* v. *Newburgh,* 28M 2d 539 (1961). The plan, designed to drive people from the welfare rolls in a variety of ways, was in part based on the charge that great numbers of "undesirables" go to Newburgh to get public assistance. In point of fact, only $205 was spent by that city for home relief in 1960, and that sum was fully reimbursed by the State. Nothing was spent on ADC for nonresidents in 1960. *Public Welfare . . . , op. cit.,* p. 6.

17. See Governor Rockfeller's veto message of March 22, 1960. The "less than 2 per cent" figure is taken from that message.

18. "Statement on the Proposal to Enact a Residence Law for Public Assistance," by James R. Dumpson, Commissioner of Welfare, New York City, reproduced in *Here It Comes Again* (New York: State Charities Aid Association, 1960).

19. See the "Legislation Information Bureau Report" of the State Charities Aid Association, March 28, 1961.

20. The Governor, in approving the law, noted that only those who came for the "sole purpose" of receiving public assistance were ineligible under the law. See 1961 New York Legislative Annual Report, pp. 446–447.

21. Moreland Commission Report (1963).

22. See, e.g., Procedure No. 61–61, New York City Department of Welfare.

23. The history of this issue is not yet complete. In welfare administrative generally, hearing decisions do not have the precedent effect they should. Indeed the decisions are often unknown from department to department or area to area. Social agencies have not, generally, carried out the informational campaign that they should as they are largely unattuned to the legal process in welfare administration.

24. *Tenants' Handbook,* New York City Housing Authority, p. 2.

25. *1962 Annual Report,* New York City Housing Authority.

26. In 1962, 10,000 families moved into public housing apartments (*ibid.*).

27. *Local Housing Authority Management Handbook,* The Public Housing Administration—Housing and Home Finance Agency, pt. IV, sec. 1, No. 6(d).

28. *Peters* v. *N.Y.C.H.A.,* 128 N.Y. 2d 224, 236, *aff'd* and *modified,* 283 App. Div. 801, *rev'd on other grounds,* 307 N.Y. 519 (1954). See also, *Chicago Housing Authority* v. *Blackman,* 4 Ill. 2d 319 (1954); *Housing Authority of Los Angeles* v. *Cordova,* 279 P. 2d 251 (1955); *Lawson* v. *Housing Authority of Milwaukee,*

270 Wisc. 269 (1955). These cases deal with efforts to impose loyalty oaths as a standard of eligibility for public housing. Few cases treat the adequacy of eviction standards and procedures on "nondesirability" issues. See, e.g., the dissent of J. Hofstader in *Watson* v. *N.Y.C.H.A.,* 27 M. 2d 618 (1960).

29. *The New York Times,* March 29, 1958.
30. New York City Housing Authority, Resolution Relating to Desirability as a Ground for Eligibility, Res. 62–9–683, September 12, 1962.
31. Education Law, Sec. 3214(6)(b).
32. Of course, some legal aid societies are voluntarily financed. To expand the work of such societies in such a manner as to allow comprehensive coverage of legal need relating to governmental agencies would, in all probability, be well beyond the capacities of voluntary financing.
33. For a description of the varying forces that constitute the Board of Mobilization for Youth, Inc., in New York City, see Charles Grosser, "Neighborhood Legal Service: A Strategy to Meet Human Need," presented at the Conference on the Extension of Legal Services to the Poor, November 12, 1964, Washington, D.C., pp. 9–11.
34. For example, there has been no hostile reaction experienced whatsoever on the part of MFY Legal Services Unit with Housing Authority representatives, though the unit is presently engaged in court challenge of existing practices.
35. Fortunately, however, the lawyer will be able to explain that his organization has been authorized to practice law by the appropriate court and that he is a member of the bar; he will also note that state welfare department rules make clear that a representative of a social agency (which lacks authorization to practice law) is entitled to represent claimants in state board hearings. The referee will be satisfied and the lawyer will wonder who could have made the complaint.
36. The letter will also note that "we agreed to work cooperatively in the use of your legal services unit." The lawyer will wonder who agreed to what. He will speculate on how such formulations affect the duties he owes exclusively to his client—and not to his employing organization or to local agencies before which he represents his clients.
37. For an excellent paper urging legal services for the poor, including services before crucial governmental agencies, see Alanson W. Wilcox, "Enlisting Legal Services in the War on Poverty," given before the Virginia State Bar Association, on July 4, 1964.
38. Edgar S. and Jean C. Cahn, "The War on Poverty: A Civilian Perspective," *Yale Law Journal,* LXXIII, 1317, 1318.

24

Client Analysis and the Planning of Public Programs

JANET S. REINER, EVERETT REIMER, AND THOMAS A. REINER

The framework

A city or regional plan, only slightly less than a national plan, must recognize diversity of aims and conflicting values among population groups. The marketplace registers preferences and allocates resources for many wants. And planners, too, recognize that people with different incomes show different expectations, preferences, and behavior patterns—when they are spending their own money. Plans reflect this diversity: in providing for a variety of residential densities and a range of shopping-center standards. But, in the realm of public facilities and services—perhaps from a well-meaning, reform-based, and possibly naïve democratic credo—there is commonly a failure to recognize that people differ in what they want, and what in fact they do get. All too often, objectives to be served by public institutions are stated by planners only in terms of the equality due to all [1] —in the face of the self-evident fact that any geographic and administrative-political area is peopled by many social groups, some conscious of their common interests, others not. Such groups do not agree on how the community's public resources should be allocated. It is true that community of interest—and community interest—may be observed or inferred in certain restricted spheres. It is also true that common paths may lead to distinct ends—politics do make strange bedfellows.[2] But in the realm of most of today's significant issues, contemporary society—developing or developed —is pluralistic and is an arena for the pursuit of plural goals held and expressed by variously endowed segments of the society.

In the face of inequality, disparity, and conflict, effective plans must express at one and the same time various, and to some degree inconsistent, conceptions of the public interest. The planner must make, of the totality of interests of disparate groups, an amalgam rather than a true compound. An effective plan may, over the long run, produce a community characterized by a harmony of interests, but even the production of such harmony depends upon the recognition of the disparities, inequalities, and conflicts which will exist at all times prior to the achievement of the ideal.

From *Journal of the American Institute of Planners*, XXIX (November, 1963), 270–282.

We take as a starting point for our analysis the fact that inequality along the many dimensions in which welfare is measured will characterize the planner's population—in every jurisdiction but heaven. This is not merely to maintain that the rich and poor have different demands and needs, and likewise the well and sick, strong and weak, old-timers and new comers, young and old. It is also to claim that the individual's reliance upon or rejection of public or other institutional services is related, in part, to his relative ability to satisfy his own needs and serve his own objectives by recourse to his own wherewithal. Given these diverse aims, unequal resources, and the consequently different demands on public and other institutional resources, we believe conflicts can best be resolved and allocation decisions most rationally made by bringing tacit disagreements into the open, making them explicit and thus subject to public scrutiny and debate. Analysis of the current and future demands for and supplies of facilities such as schools and recreation centers, of services such as health and welfare, of public and private housing—all must be studied within a framework keyed to diversity if the planner's contribution is to be valid, valued, and realistic.

Recognition of conflicting interests, rather than belief in a community interest, forces the planner to relate the range of public activities to the diverse groups of the population with distinct preferences and aims. Such preferences and aims can be expressed and analyzed in many different ways. We work with behavior as an evident and measurable social fact (à la Durkheim)—that is, behavior of individuals aggregated by characteristics. While knowledge of preferences, attitudes, and goals is the requisite of intelligent planning (whether the planner views his task as goal-oriented or as "adaptive") it is not readily measurable. An index to these preferences, attitudes, and goals will be found in the behavior of individuals making real choices—individuals as lawmakers, as program administrators, and as users (and rejectors) of facilities and services. We maintain that information on behavior is reliable, readily available, and directly applicable to planning tasks.

We propose here to describe and illustrate a particular method of analysis which appears to be fruitful. Client analysis, as a first step, examines public programs in being and deduces the goal positions of sectors of the community from the behavior of members of the community confronting and possibly participating in these programs. Client analysis, with minor modifications of the method described in this article, could be applied to any situation in which members of a public are served by institutions, whether public, semi-public, or private.[3] The goals and objectives thus deduced provide a further basis for planning and programming. An appraisal of the effectiveness of agency operations, in relation to avowed objectives, is an important by-product of the analysis. The basic units in client analysis are government programs, on the one hand, and affected population groups, on the other.

Client analysis is used to indicate the changing size of the social tasks which government has undertaken, the progress which has been achieved with present programs, the distribution of benefits resulting from these programs, some of the significant growing social problems and opportunities, and the amounts of resources which are committed to existing programs. An estimate of the resources committed to existing programs also makes it possible to estimate the resources which remain available for the extension of public programs: either to serve additional people, or for increases in the per capita benefits of present programs, or for new programs directed toward newly recognized needs.

An exposition of any new analytic method necessarily raises questions about its relationship to established techniques. Relationships of client analysis and benefit-cost analysis are particularly important to note. Essentially, the two methods are complementary. Benefit-cost analysis is predominantly made in dollar terms with monetary assessment of opportunity gains and losses where possible; it is a device for the uniform treatment of each of a set of projects, under certain restrictive assumptions. Client analysis may be regarded as a device for the consistent study of a set of programs over a time span. It is a way to evaluate the range of a government's commitments, in the present and as these are carried into the future. Since the findings of client analysis focus on the people served by programs, they provide a broader framework for decisions than do the conclusions of benefit-cost analysis with their monetary and project basis.[4] Client analysis, furthermore, is particularly well suited for use in continuous surveys and forecasting; it may, therefore, become a useful tool for the periodic evaluation of public programs.

The method

Client analysis is a technique for investigating relationships between people's wants, the recognition of these wants as needs (by other people), eligibility to receive goods or services in satisfaction of these recognized needs, actual receipt of service, and benefits, if any, from such service. Most of the traditional schemes of social analysis begin with an attempt to define social needs and then proceed to consider alternative means of satisfying these needs. The philosophic difficulties of coming to grips with needs and benefits are too well known to be repeated here. We assume that these difficulties are basic but that the concepts of need and benefit nevertheless remain indispensable. Our thesis is that specific categories of needs and benefits can be rendered progressively, although never perfectly, clear and objective if approached through such concepts as provision of, eligibility for, and actual receipt of, institutional services.

1. In the case of public programs, the analysis begins with a review of what the law establishing a given program commits the government to do, and, in certain cases, restrains the government from doing. Specifically, the analyst will interpret this legislative intent in terms of "what," and "for whom"; that is, (a) the benefits and services to be provided under the pro-

gram; and, (b) the identification of that sector of the population which it is intended to benefit or serve with the particular program. Analysis begins with an examination of the authorizing legislation and the legislative record.

Although enabling laws generally specify quite clearly the need for programs, they are not usually formulated in a way which embodies an explicit quantification of this concern. The analyst must establish criteria which can be used to identify the proposed program benefits and beneficiaries with precision. Any criterion not explicitly stated in the law can, of course, be contested, but once explicitly stated it is also subject to reasoned challenge.[5] In establishing eligibility criteria, the analyst should use relevant expert studies which contain estimates independent of those which have been established administratively. Studies of other jurisdictions can be used with appropriate adjustment for relevant differences. For example, if a city is in a state which has prepared a master plan to avail itself of Hill-Burton hospital construction funds, such a plan might include working definitions of indigence, and also of medical indigence,[6] which define two parts of the population group the enabling act is designed to serve with hospitalization. For a particular city, the state-wide figures would require adjustment for differences from state-wide levels of public health, education, and welfare services, and particularly for differences between urban and rural areas.

Further refinements may be made in the analysis of enabling legislation. Depending on the time and resources available, the study could be extended to include investigation of legislative hearings, judicial decisions, and general legislation bearing on eligibility for a broader range of public services.

2. The next step is a calculation of the size of the legally eligible population, over the time span from passage of the legislation to the present. This involves no more than traditional demographic analysis, although exact statistical counterparts of the legislatively designated groups are often hard to find, and ad hoc adjustments and estimates must perforce be made. We label that portion of the population legally eligible for a specific public service the *client population* of the program. For most programs, once criteria have been established, the client population can be quantified by use of familiar census data.[7] Some unpublished cross tabulations may have to be purchased from the Census Bureau, as for example where certain age-income classes are entitled to benefits.[8]

3. To turn, so to speak, to flesh and blood, an estimate is next made of the number of people who have actually used the services provided by each program. Distinctions are made within the population group by the kinds and amounts of services received, where this is relevant and possible (for example, days of service rendered, dollars of aid provided). Agency records, organization and management studies, budget bureau analyses, and citizen agency investigations should yield this information. Again, the time span of the analysis is over the period from passage of the enabling legislation to the present. The program-participating members of the client population are labelled *clients* of the program.

4. The next stage in the analysis is a comparison between client popula-

tion and clients. The comparison will, of course, take note of the size of the respective groups, but this will be only part of the story. More significant analytic conclusions can usually be drawn from comparison of specific characteristics of the client population and clients. It would be logical to make comparisons of such characteristics as income, education, urban vs. rural residence—any characteristic or attribute which competent observers have hypothesized might differentiate between client population and clients.

5. In order to reach a better understanding of the reasons for the differences between client population and clients, in number and in characteristics, the analysis proceeds to a study of the conditions under which services and benefits of each program are offered and received. Not only the enabling legislation and subsequent laws, but also the stated administrative policies and actual operations of the agency administering the program are investigated, in order to gain a detailed understanding of the manner by which the number of people eligible to use a service is, ordinarily, restricted to some fraction of the client population. In general, the ratio of clients to client population, for any program, depends in large measure upon the *selection standards,* which govern access to the program, and the *standards of service,* which govern acceptance of the program.

a. Administrative selection standards are those requirements and procedures of the agency administering the program which explicitly eliminate a portion of the legally eligible client population. The remaining portion of the client population may be labelled the "effectively eligible" sector. For example, in some municipalities, inability on the part of the household head to produce a birth certificate renders the family ineligible for public housing. This may reduce the number of clients significantly in localities experiencing heavy in-migration from rural areas. Another example of a type of selection standard which is limited to a single program is the exclusion from public housing of fatherless families, where it has been established that a child below a stipulated age is illegitimate. The minimum effect of this particular selection standard in reducing the effectively eligible population could be estimated from data of the federally subsidized aid-to-dependent-children program of the local welfare department.[9]

b. Standards of service for any program include, in addition to the quantity and quality of supposed benefits, any consciously determined (or implicitly followed) features such as cost to client, if any, location of facility, nature of the service staff, and various convenience considerations. None of these are items which directly say: person X is eligible, person Y is not. Nominally, the prospective client decides whether the service standards make it possible and worthwhile for him to become a client. Actually, the values, capacities, and knowledge or awareness of the effectively eligible client population determine how many people become clients. For example, women in certain ethnic ghettos may find it impossible to participate in programs where they feel their modesty challenged. Or, in programs that involve considerable paper work, functional illiterates may be effectively excluded from participation. Or the individual who works at an "eight-to-five" Monday-to-Friday job may be unable to get program information from a municipal office keeping similar hours: effectively, he remains as much a greenhorn as the newly arrived migrant, and is as effectively barred from becoming a client as one who has not yet met residence requirements. All the foregoing are examples of standards of service which restrict clientele and, for purposes of client analysis, should be treated as such, on the assumption that the program was intended by the enabling legislation—unless there is specific evidence to the contrary—to be oriented to all of the client population. This assumption, it should be noted, runs counter to the usual practice of limiting program evaluation to criteria established by the agencies supplying the public service.[10]

Where study of the characteristics of the client population and the clients shows that these are different, it is evident that further investigation is necessary. The analysis of such a gap cannot rest solely on census data, the records of operating agencies, or similar sources. Field observations, interviews, and sociological and anthropological research all have a part to play and may reap rich rewards, not only in improvement of program operations but in the formulation of social policy and the advance of social science.

The amount of emphasis given to this portion of the analysis would depend on how much the demographic characteristics of the actual clients differ from those of the client population. If clients are only 10 per cent of the client population, but show the same income, age, occupation, and ethnic distribution as does the client population, then it is not too heroic an assumption to assert that greater resources allocated to a given program would contribute to achieving program goals. If, on the other hand, client population and clients differ (say with regard to family size, race, or location of employment), then it can safely be claimed that some selection standards or standards of service are explicitly or implicitly employed. These standards must be identified and carefully analyzed to anticipate and meet the contention that the effect of such standards is to divert the program from its avowed objectives. The extent of the disparity between client population and client groups would normally determine the effort made to discover the significance of the standards of selection and service.[11]

6. Description and evaluation of programs requires one further step. The analyst must determine the proportion of clients who benefit from the program. Since this is seldom an "all or nothing" proposition, it must be restated as the determination of how many benefit, and how much. This portion of the client population may be called the "effectively benefited." There are, of course, programs where the condition of being a client is virtually equivalent (at least at the first level of analysis) to being a beneficiary: for example, passing the turnstile into the municipal zoo. Many programs would seem to imply this kind of equivalence; but for most programs, it is patently wrong to maintain that there are as many benefited as there are clients.

Many education programs measure achievement in terms of clients, as if the number in attendance indicated the number educated. Clearly some of the clients of many school systems do not benefit in terms of even such a minimum index as the achievement of functional literacy at the end of grade school. Their benefit may be limited to no more than custodial care (which may, of course, be more than an insignificant gain to the working parent). Vocational education in trades which are effectively closed to the trainees, on grounds of race, for example, or in which the skills required are shifting, are other examples where there is a difference between clients and beneficiaries.

Assuming that a desired statistic, such as the proportion of illiterates in graduating grade school classes, is not available, a surrogate ratio could be constructed from literacy studies in other cities, or from a combination of the figures on dropouts (studies have been made which give reliable estimates of illiteracy among dropouts) and enrollment in "general programs" in high school. The information sought might be obtained from a study of unpublished agency records; it should be in the interest of educational agencies to open their files as part of a cooperative study.

Program accomplishments can be measured: (a) in terms of the proportion of the client population which is served at least at minimum standards; (b) in terms of the levels of service actually achieved in relation to minimum standards; and (c) in terms of the proportion of clients who receive actual benefits.

At this point, the client-analysis practitioner possesses a far richer knowledge of program operation than is usually available, organized in a far more useful fashion than the traditional data. Disparities are highlighted, and, to a certain extent, this in itself may result in remedial measures: more funds allocated, standards of service changed, or a more realistic set of laws, cognizant of resource or client limitations, put into effect. It is clear that the technician has in hand a potent political document as well as a useful piece of analysis. Yet, in terms of planning, still more can be done by proceeding further along the path on which we have set out. Our further objective is to see how the declared intent and desire of a society to supply future benefits and services—by means of existing programs—can be matched with the willingness and ability of members of the society, in their dual roles as producers and consumers of services, not only to supply but also to utilize the services implied in present programs.

Four more client analysis steps are therefore suggested.

7. The size of the client population is estimated for some selected future date, on the assumption that there will be no change in legislation defining benefits and beneficiaries. Even where such an assumption appears unrealistic, it has certain advantages. For one thing, it places various claims for improved or additional benefits and services on an equal footing. For making projections of client populations, it is assumed that the planner has access to basic demographic and economic projections, and that these are so formulated as to allow estimates to be made of the future client populations of various programs.

8. Similarly, for the same future date, an estimate is calculated of the

most probable number of actual clients of the program. The additional assumptions required for such an estimate are that: (a) selection standards and service standards will remain constant, and (b) funds will be provided to serve the number of clients consonant with the intent of law and these selection and service standards. Since the society is presumed to be changing, even though the standards in question are not,[12] the significance of being or not being a client is subject to change. The value placed upon constant benefits, from many types of programs, would be likely to decline in a developing economy and to increase in a declining economy. Thus, public housing would appear progressively more valuable in a housing shortage of increasing severity.

Where the total amount of service rendered by an authorized public program does not meet the demands of the client population, client analysis assumes a government commitment to increase allocations to the program until, at the selected target date, the anticipated demand of the estimated client population of that date will be met. Where administrative standards of selection make part of the client population effectively ineligible, and where standards of service are below the minimum standards implied in the enabling legislation, government is assumed to be committed, by the target date, to rectify these standards of selection and to raise the actual standards of service to the appropriate minimum level. Government is not assumed, in client analysis, to be committed to raise criteria above the presently accepted minima (as established in or interpreted from the law), nor to relax those eligibility provisions stated or implied in law.

9. Despite, or in some cases because of, the preceding assumptions, the number of future beneficiaries, as a proportion of client population or clients, will shift up or down, depending on the course of outside events. For example, if we assume that the children of educated parents are more likely to benefit from present types of schools (those who remain functionally illiterate after years of grade school tend to come from uneducated families), and that the proportion of educated parents increases over time, it is plausible to expect that, over time, a larger proportion of graduates from grade school will be functionally literate—that is, will be beneficiaries as well as clients of the elementary education program.

10. The final step is a comparison of the estimated numbers and proportions of future client population, clients, and beneficiaries. This step permits an identification of possible inability to meet demand, or of possibly underutilized services. Questions which might be asked are, among others, "Is less than full utilization of program allocations likely to be temporary, or permanent?" Thus, calculation of the classrooms needed to satisfy the client population will, in developing countries, or in cities of high in-migration from rural areas, show an unusually severe but very transitory peaking after infant mortality has been successfully combated but before the anticipated decline in the birth rate takes hold. Other questions which might be answered by client analysis projections are: "How will the characteristics of future clients differ from those of the client population?" or: "Does a

projected growing gap between clients and client population reflect, in the main, selection standards, service standards, or demographic features?" Finally, one could profitably ask, "How amenable are predicted program gaps to manipulation—manipulation of the law, the agency, or the client population?"

A hypothetical example

The foregoing exposition can be rendered more meaningful by partially carrying through a sample client analysis study, showing each step for a specific program in a given city. In order to focus on the method rather than on the particulars of an existing program or locality, we have constructed a hypothetical housing program in a core city, typical of the larger metropolitan areas of the United States.

We assume the city had, in 1960, a population of 700,000. Forecasts have been made for 1965 and 1970. Considerable economic growth is predicted for the metropolitan area; this is associated with significant changes in the population. Though many demographic indices should shift over the decade, the total population of this core city is expected to remain stable at 700,000.

The city has been party to a number of housing programs, including the full complement of federally aided activities; Community Renewal Program studies are now under way closely linked to review of the capital budget.

The planning commission has found that despite a high volume of private and public residential construction since the end of World War II, and a good deal of demolition of substandard units as part of urban renewal, only small inroads have been made in supplying "standard" housing for the very poor. The 1960 Census showed that 30 per cent of the dwelling units were substandard; these were 95 per cent occupied, though the city-wide vacancy rate was 10 per cent.

Almost a decade ago, as a result of findings from an application of the client analysis method to then existing low-income housing programs, the "Free Housing Program" (FHP) was instituted to confront this problem. It is this program which we now study by means of client analysis.

The law

The FHP was introduced as a municipal program in 1953. Its intent was to extend the welfare function of government to housing—the function of providing a minimum subsistence level. The law established that free housing was to be made available to certain occupants of substandard housing: (1) families with incomes so low that even the minimum public housing rentals could not be paid without ill effects on such essentials as minimum diet; and (2) low-income single-person households which had been excluded from the federal and state subsidized programs.

Client population

In order to define the population made eligible by legislation for free housing, some interpretation had to be made of the law's use of "lowest income families," "low income single person households," and "substandard housing." All three of these terms are relative. The analyst might determine a schedule of lowest-income families and low-income single-person households by pinpointing one poverty threshold, such as income below $2,000 annually.[13]

The numbers of households in these low-income categories are shown in Table 24–1. Data for 1960 were obtained directly from the 1960 *Census of Population*. Projections for 1965 and 1970 were derived from an application to Case City of a set of national high economic growth estimates.[14] The number of households which occupied "standard" dwelling units[15] was subtracted from the figures of Table 24–1 to give Table 24–2: the client population.

Addition of each of the relevant elements of Table 24–2 yields, for 1960, a client population of almost 25,000 households. The client population may be expected to decrease significantly in the next decade.[16] This decrease is expected to result mainly from an over-all economic upgrading of the city, with its direct decrease of the potential eligibles, and from the less direct increase in the stock of standard housing. If economic development continues after 1970,[17] however, the free housing built by the municipality during the 1960's would soon become a drug on the market. There would be a call to upgrade these units—in size and amenities, for example, or to adapt them to other programs or functions.

Table 24–1. Case City—Number of Households by Income and Household Size: 1960, 1965, and 1970

Year	Household Size	Income* $0–999	1,000–1,999	2,000+	Total
1960	1 person	5,600	6,900	21,600	34,000
	2 or more persons	3,600	8,400	154,000	166,000
	Total households	9,200	15,300	175,600	200,000
1965	1 person	2,000	4,900	30,100	37,000
	2 or more persons	300	1,500	167,200	169,000
	Total households	2,300	6,400	197,300	206,000
1970	1 person	500	1,500	40,000	42,000
	2 or more persons	†	200	169,800	170,000
	Total households	500	1,700	209,800	212,000

* Income in constant 1960 dollars.
† Less than 50 households.

Source: 1960: U.S. Census data. 1965 and 1970: Estimates, based on projections and targets indicated in comprehensive plan.

Table 24–2. Case City—Client Population* for Free Housing Program by Income and Household Size: 1960, 1965, and 1970.

Year	Household Size	Income †		Total
		$0–999	*1,000–1,999*	
1960	1 person	6,432	6,555	12,987
	2 or more persons	3,492	7,980	11,472
	Total households	9,924	14,535	24,459
1965	1 person	1,900	4,165	6,065
	2 or more persons	285	1,275	1,560
	Total households	2,185	5,440	7,625
1970	1 person	500	1,500	2,000
	2 or more persons	‡	200	200
	Total households	500	1,700	2,200

* The unit of client population and clients for this program is presented in terms of number of households. Number of individuals may be calculated from average household size, which is 3.5 persons for the entire population and 3.9 persons for households of 2 or more persons.
† Income in constant 1960 dollars.
‡ Less than 50 households.

Source: Figures from Table 23–1, less the number of households residing in standard housing. The latter was calculated for 1960 from U.S. Census data, and for 1965 and 1970 estimated from the same source as noted in Table 24–1.

CLIENTS

Calculation of the number of clients in this case utilizes the annual report of the agency. It begins with the number of dwelling units extant. As of 1960 there are, in this hypothetical program, 750 units.

This does not tell the whole story, however. As is well known, turnover and vacancy will affect the number of client households.[18] Only certain forms of moving out from free housing may properly be termed positive turnover. "Positive turnover" effects a move from the FHP to standard housing, either a subsidized unit or one found on the free market. "Negative turnover" is based on a move out of free housing into a substandard unit;[19] it does not indicate a reduction in need for free housing, nor an upgrading of the housing stock, nor an increase in value of housing to the client. Thus, given the objective of the FHP to provide long-term standard housing for those in extreme poverty,[20] it is established that negative turnover cases, despite part-year occupancy, are counted as part of the client population and not as clients. See Table 24–3.

There were in 1960, then, 792 clients, or only 3 per cent of the client population. However, reference to agency data discloses that the waiting list of "approved" potential clients includes another 18 per cent of the client population.

Data in Tables 24–2 and 24–3 show that the clients as a proportion of the client population will change from 3 per cent to 22 per cent and 100 per cent in 1965 and 1970. But this is primarily the result of a decrease

Table 24–3. Case City—Clients of Free Housing Program and Number of Units Extant: 1960, 1965, and 1970

| Year | Units Extant † | Clients* | | Total |
		Whole Year	Part-of-Year	
1960	750	576	216	792
1965	1,500	1,152	432	1,584
1970	2,250	1,648	648	2,296

* The client unit for this program is the household. Refer to * of Table 24–2 for indices of conversion to individuals.

† Only dwelling units ready for occupancy January 1 of the year of count are included.

Source: Based on a study of turnover in free housing from 1953–1960; estimates were prepared of the average occupancy rate (96 per cent) and the average turnover rate (20 per cent) as well as the "positive-negative" distribution of turnover (50–50) noted above.

1965 and 1970: estimates of construction of free housing units were based on continued commitments of 150 units per year. Estimates of vacancy and turnover rates were based on an assumption that rates do not change.

projected for the client population; construction of FHP units at the current annual rate is a minor contributory cause. Maintenance of current commitments will apparently lead, by 1970, to an excess in the supply of FHP housing,[21] even where standards of selection and of service have been changed to accommodate all subgroups of the client population. Two intelligent courses of action are opened by client analysis. Either the rate of construction should be sharply curtailed, or the program intent and criteria should be adjusted to embrace a new client population (for example, income ceiling raised or definition or substandard amended). However, those who are at the very bottom of the income ladder will avail themselves of the FHP only if the program, within its legally defined limits, continues to reach out for those not yet served.

STANDARDS OF SELECTION

Why the difference between the client population and the number of clients? Study of the program's operating manual discloses certain practices which explicitly exclude portions of the client population: (a) households composed of eight or more persons; (b) households where the primary wage earner is self-employed; (c) households where the head is unable to present a birth certificate.

Estimates of the impact of standards (a) and (b) can be prepared from published census materials; standard (c) requires a small special study. Three hundred households in the client population are affected by the household size limitation; 120 primary wage earners in the client population (and resident in substandard housing) are self-employed—20 of these households, however, have already been disqualified for reasons of size. The sample survey discloses that another 200 in the client population are disqualified by application of standard (c). Thus, in 1960, the "effectively eligible" and not yet served constitute 23,067 households, or 94 per cent of the client population.

STANDARDS OF SERVICE

If those households which are eliminated by selection standards are added to those which already are clients and those on FHP waiting lists, 76 per cent of the client population still remains to be accounted for. Numerous standards of service must be searched out.

The occupational and age distributions of the clients in 1960 differed significantly from those of the client population. For example, a larger proportion of the unemployed was among the clients (and on waiting lists). This statistic disclosed that no full time "eight-to-five" employee could afford the several visits to housing authority offices which kept nine-to-five hours. The programming implication is obvious: change office hours. But why were there also relatively few old people among the clients? These projects are located on hitherto undeveloped land along Case City's periphery. It was found that the elderly are loath to leave locations with family or institutional ties. A special study had been undertaken to establish this, and to quantify the strength of the relationship. Finally, on the basis of knowledge of program operation elsewhere, it was held likely that misinformation of the program's aims and operation was rife. Many in the client population failed to apply for admission.[22]

Obviously a program as new as the FHP is very far, in 1960, from serving all who would benefit by its services and facilities. However, planning involves not only choices among objectives, but, equally, decisions as to how far objectives should exceed current capacities. It is unlikely that Case City could immediately satisfy a substantial part of the need for free housing while meeting its other obligations. Only the first steps in this client analysis have been presented. When the analysis, as outlined in the previous section, is completed, the responsible decision maker can determine more rationally the rate at which the city might meet its specific obligations.

The implications

Once client analysis has been carried out for a group of programs, it becomes possible to compare these programs on a number of major dimensions. First, they can be evaluated as to the scope and depth of the social commitments they are designed to carry out. The scope of the social responsibilities represented by these programs is reflected in the kind and number of persons who are in the client population. The depth of these responsibilities is reflected in the minimum standards of service which the programs are committed to provide. Once comparative measures of the scope and depth of commitments have been established, the programs can also be compared as to accomplishments. Program accomplishments can be measured in the proportion of the client population served, in the levels of service actually provided in relation to the minimum standards, and in the rates of progress toward serving the entire client population at minimum standards. Finally, when comparisons of program commitments and accomplishments are available, cost comparisons between programs also become meaningful.

Neither the concepts nor the numbers which are used to make the comparisons are, of course, capable of reducing the most significant aspects of food, clothing, education, health, housing, or public utilities to a common denominator. Thus, the elements of subjective judgment cannot be removed from decisions which have to be made among different programs. But such decisions can be made less subject to errors of ignorance, more communicable, and, therefore, open to wider participation by people who have a stake in them.

It is important that the concept of client analysis be used to expose rather than cover up differences between programs. In terms of the letter of the law, eligibility for public education in a given jurisdiction is likely to be far broader than eligibility for hospitalization, housing, or public assistance. But even where everyone is eligible for public schooling, custom usually decrees that schooling is for the young. Thus, the legal income restrictions on eligibility for other programs have a parallel, of a sort, in the practical age restriction on eligibility for schooling. In addition, eligibility for schooling must be maintained by successful performance within the school system.

The law defining eligibility for public hospital care may well refer to the "medically indigent"; the public assistance law to the "needy"; and the housing law to "persons of low income." But "low income" as used in the housing law may have been administratively defined to mean $4,000 per family, while "needy" as used in the welfare law may have been defined to mean an income of $1,500 or less, for a family of five. "Medical indigence," as formally defined by the health department, may mean annual family income of less than $1,000, and yet depend, in fact, on length of hospital stay and, in practice, be very flexibly defined.

Suprabeneficiaries and deprived groups can be spotted by client analysis comparisons. They can be identified by focusing on minimum standards and on program accomplishments in terms of clients, money, and time. Only at this level of comparison is it possible to be precise about the progress governments are making in fulfilling their stated goals.

One of the happy conclusions, on the single occasion where client analysis was put to practical use,[23] was that governmental responsibilities do decline, at least in certain aspects. If this were not so, the inevitable trend would be toward government monopoly of all public activities. On the other hand, client analysis will also serve to discover areas of human endeavor where public responsibilities can scarcely help but grow.

Recommendations

The purpose of this essay is to present a method by which decisions on social policy may be enlightened. It is an implicit premise of this approach that the appropriate decision makers are the members of society, acting directly and through their representatives. A corollary is that planners, as such, have no special competence for the making or guidance of social policy, but only for enlightenment of the process by which it is made. Enlightenment may, of course, be achieved in many ways: by intuitive insight, by scientific discovery, by systematic and orderly arrangement of data, by quantification, by criticism, and so forth. What all these ways have in common is that none endows the planner with any special responsibility for determining social policy or with any special wisdom for guiding it. A planner may be wise, but as a person and not as a planner.[24]

It follows from the above that this essay can have but one recommendation: namely, that its method be adopted, elaborated, and used. Nevertheless, this recommendation may be made more explicit by discussion and breakdown into a number of component suggestions.

Client analysis requires something of a tour de force, in that the data on which a demonstration of its value must be based have, in the first instance, to be constructed in order to show how useful such data can be. Some elements of the data needed for client analysis do exist, but in general the appropriate data are not available, at least not in a reliable or convenient form.

Four kinds of data are required: data on needs, on eligibility, on service rendered to clients, and on the need satisfaction or benefit resulting from the service rendered. (It is assumed that the planning process has produced social and economic targets, projections, and profiles as part of a comprehensive plan.) There are two major sources of data: the general population, and the agencies rendering service. Some specific recommendations for obtaining data follow.

Recommendation 1. A general, all-purpose population survey should be established to obtain, on a continuing basis, data on social needs, eligibility for various public services, client status, benefits derived, etc. Family characteristics such as income, family size, types of interdependence of family members, and group memberships of the family and individuals, would be obtained along with the more traditional types of data on individual family members.[25]

Recommendation 2. Certain uniform requirements for record keeping, data processing, and cost accounting should be placed on all government agencies, so as to yield:

(a) for each person receiving or applying for any service of the agency, data on:

    i. type of service applied for and given, refused, or rejected;

    ii. whether the service was given, refused, or rejected;

    iii. characteristics of the applicant or client and of his family;

(b) costs of the various services rendered the clients, including a properly weighted share of administrative and other general costs.

In addition to the data indicated, application of the method of analysis described in this article would require a considerable elaboration of definitions and analytic procedures. Very specific definitions of need, eligibility, standards, and so forth, involve unique problems in each type of program, and yet each definition must be made as nearly consistent with all others as is possible. Much of the analysis could take place within the agencies responsible for programs, but central technical direction would be needed.

Recommendation 3. The client analysis method is useful not only for comparison and study of major programs, at the central government level of the nation, region, or locality, but also for comparison of sub-programs at the agency level. Therefore, a planning or analysis unit should be designated in each operating agency and assigned the responsibility for developing the definitions and procedures required to carry out, for all agency programs, the method of analysis described here.

Recommendation 4. Units within central management or planning agencies should be assigned the responsibility for giving technical guidance to the operating agency planning units, for supervising the surveys outlined in recommendation 1, and for preparing government-wide analyses following the client analysis model.

Recommendation 5. Procedures should be established for a regular review of government programs—utilizing the analyses outlined above—by elected officials at the several levels of government, and for making these analyses available, in appropriate form, to the various electorates; that is, for the publication of such analyses, and for securing and appraising public response to what has been done, and what ought to be done, by the government, in relation to the needs of the society.

NOTES

1. Philadelphia City Planning Commission, *Comprehensive Plan; The Physical Development Plan for the City of Philadelphia* (Philadelphia, 1960), Ch. 8, pp. 57–69.

    Patrick Abercrombie, *Greater London Plan 1944* (London: HMSO, 1945), Ch. 8, pp. 116–118.

2. The importance of this commonplace for city planners is lucidly illustrated in Paul Ylvisaker, "Diversity and the Public Interest: Two Cases in Metropolitan Decision Making," *Journal of the American Institute of Planners,* XXVII (May 1961), 107–117.

3. Some aspects of client analysis, but by no means all, have counterparts in market analysis.

4. Knowledge of the costs and benefits, or of the beneficiaries, of a hospital as

compared to a school, does not provide the basis for a definitive comparison of their relative value; nor does it allow determination of the worth of a life saved in terms of education foregone. There are many comparisons of this sort which lie beyond the scope of analytic techniques available today.

5. On the significance of explicitness in the social sciences and their policy formulations see Robert K. Merton, "The Role of Applied Social Science in the Formation of Policy," *Philosophy of Science,* XVI (July 1949), 161–181; and Gunnar Myrdal, *Value in Social Theory* (New York: Harper, 1958), especially Ch. 2.

6. Low-income indigence for hospital planning purposes obviously need not be set at the same threshold as, for example, that for standard housing in the private market. Some discussion of "medical indigence" will be found in Nora Piore, "Metropolitan Areas and Public Medical Care," paper delivered at the Conference on the Economics of Health and Medical Care, University of Michigan, Ann Arbor, sponsored by U.S. Department of Health, Education, and Welfare, Public Health Service, National Institutes of Health, May 10–12, 1962.

7. On the use of census data for local and regional planning purposes, see Leo F. Schnore, "A Planner's Guide to the 1960 Census of Population," *Journal of the American Institute of Planners,* XXIX (February 1963), 29–39.

8. Census data will not always provide the answer. The identification of the medically indigent, as part of the study of hospital services, would require a special morbidity study which could not be based on census information. It might require analysis of research conducted elsewhere: see, for example, "Meeting Health Needs by Social Action," *Annals of the American Academy of Political and Social Science,* CCCVII (September, 1961), and references cited therein.

9. One procedure would be to match cases where the youngest child has been born after aid has begun (ADC, by definition, is given only where the family lacks a male head). This can serve as a minimum figure, for there are, of course, other low-income families with illegitimate children who do not avail themselves of ADC. Low income, as defined by the welfare agency, is generally much lower than the low-income ceiling for public housing eligibility.

10. It is fruitful to think of agencies as producers and suppliers of services, with agencies' goals differing from those of the clients. A critique, based on such framework, of the traditional evaluation of the programs provided by operating agencies will be found in John W. Dyckman, "Standards and Requirements in Community Planning, the Case of Public School Facilities" (Ph.D. dissertation, University of Chicago, 1957); and Herbert J. Gans, "Recreation Planning for Leisure Behavior" (Ph.D. dissertation, University of Pennsylvania, 1957).

11. Since successive samples drawn from a parent population can be expected to differ somewhat, due to the working of chance factors, the significance of any difference between client populations and clients should be evaluated by standard statistical testing.

12. It is to be expected, however, that client population levels for given programs will change, owing to projected shifts in age composition, and to other demographic and economic factors.

13. As an alternate method, it would be feasible to set different poverty thresholds for different family sizes, and then to estimate the number of people forming the client population for the FHP by relating the families of different sizes to these different income levels. However, net results from this more complicated method might differ but little: "it appears that poverty is fairly evenly distributed among families of various sizes because the smaller families have lower incomes on the average than the larger families." Conference on Economic Progress, *Poverty and Deprivation in the U.S.* (Washington, D.C., 1962), p. 14.

If the analyst, however, wishes to avoid overlap with existing subsidized programs, he is forced to use their minimum income requirements as the level which determines maximum income for the FHP. These minimum income levels are usually based on family size.

If single-person households had not been excluded from federally aided public housing, a double standard might have been realistic. The previously cited work used, as a poverty threshold, $2,000 for single persons and $4,000 for families regardless of size.

14. Projections for 1965 and 1970 are based on "Goals for Family Income, 1965 and

1970 Consistent with High Economic Growth," and like goals for "Individuals" (*ibid.,* pp. 75–92). These projections of improved living standards provide a framework for a significant portion of the population profile of 1965 and 1970. The impact of such a profile on public services is rarely recognized in comprehensive plans. For plan-related projections of this type, see Puerto Rico Planning Board, *Economic Report to the Governor, Part Two, 1960, The Economic Picture for the Decade 1960–1970* (San Juan, 1960).

15. In order to obtain these figures, a special runoff of 1960 Housing and Population Census data had to be obtained. When such a cross tabulation of housing quality with income of household is made, the figure automatically includes the small number of very poor households now clients of the federal public housing program and those already clients of the FHP. A determination had been made to include clients of a given program among the client population of that program. Therefore, to avoid double-counting, clients of the FHP were subtracted from the number known to be living in standard housing.

Estimates of standard housing occupied by low-income families in 1965 and 1970 include consideration of further expected construction under the FHP and other federally subsidized housing. The proportion of low-income households living in standard housing (and, to a lesser extent, the number) is expected to grow by 1970.

16. An early program plan, based on economic and demographic projections and objectives, will be found in Commonwealth of Puerto Rico, Committee on Human Resources (Everett Reimer, Executive Secretary), *Puerto Rico's Manpower Needs and Supply* (San Juan, 1957). The conclusions of this study (which focuses on education needs in relation to labor force requirements) parallel the hypothetical findings presented here.

17. A further adjustment of this forecast might be called for if further studies were to show that despite the projected development, or because of it, the least educated or skilled sector of society becomes worse off than it is now.

18. The number of client households will also be affected by the fact of clandestine multi-family, or extended family, occupancy of program dwelling units. The number of clandestine clients cannot be known without a special study, since such occupancy is cause for eviction.

19. Negative turnover has been classified into two types: *push* and *pull.* "The former stems from dissatisfactions rooted in the public housing system itself. These are controllable . . . and the financial costs caused by unnecessary frictions [may thus be] decreased. Pull motivations, however, are not controllable in the narrow sense. [They] are influenced by the entire range of environmental considerations, affecting economic requirements and personal preferences." Chester Hartman, *Family Turnover in Public Housing* (San Juan: Puerto Rico Urban Renewal and Housing Administration [1960]), pp. i–ii.

20. The FHP program was developed some time after Case City instituted an emergency shelter program designed for high turnover, hardship cases.

21. Allowing for the small, even if diminishing, number of standard free market units available to this lowest income sector would advance the date of program target fulfillment.

22. For example, studies for Baltimore and from Puerto Rico are relevant: Baltimore City Housing Authority, *A Study of the Attitudes of Potential Applicants Toward Public Housing* (1954); and Kurt W. Back, *Slums, Projects and People* (Durham: Duke University Press, 1962). Both indicate that over one-half the residents of substandard housing could not, when questioned, give criteria used for public housing selection. Back further shows that the overwhelming majority (72 per cent to 90 per cent) believed that purchase of cars, refrigerators, or radios would result in higher rent in the public housing projects. It was also found that many interviewees who were in the client population for public housing and living in substandard housing feared what they understood of project life, and thus rejected public housing. Among these "regulations" were prohibitions of pets and of overnight visitors. The former is indeed a program prohibition; the latter is a fiction.

23. The method outlined here has been applied, in the Puerto Rico Planning Board, to the major social programs of the government of Puerto Rico. In the case of every program, under the assumptions outlined above, government responsibilities

were predicted to decrease. It is important to stress that this conclusion followed from three major assumptions: *one,* eligibility not extended; *two,* standards not raised; and *three,* family incomes rising rapidly under the continued impact of industrialization, and shifts in population composition and numbers. The practical value of these assumptions is that they permit an estimate of the uncommitted resources the Puerto Rican government will have and an unbiased comparison of various claims upon these resources.

These studies are noted in: Alvin Mayne, "Designing and Administering a Regional Economic Development Plan," Ch. 7 in Walter Isard and John H. Cumberland (eds.), *Regional Economic Planning* (Paris: O.E.E.C., 1961), pp. 158–159.

24. One elaboration of these comments, and of their underlying assumptions, will be found in: Paul Davidoff and Thomas A. Reiner, "A Choice Theory of Planning," *Journal of the American Institute of Planners,* XXVIII (May 1962), 103–116.

25. This recommendation is made with full recognition that we have a surfeit of highly elaborated data systems at the federal, state, and municipal levels. However, while these systems provide a great deal of information, they do not permit statistics about the same person, family, or subgroup to be related to each other. They do not, for example, permit data on the health of a family to be related to data on its education and employment. They do not, in general, permit information about an individual to be associated with knowledge of that individual's family or subgroup relationships. The elaboration of present data systems, far from solving these problems, aggravates them, particularly in terms of the current employment of sampling procedures for securing statistics about bits and pieces of the society. In general what present data systems do not give us is the relative position of an individual, family, or subgroup upon a sufficient number of value scales. Such relationships obviously lie at the heart of significant social analysis.

Recognition of this point, and of the economies of an integrated system using modern sampling techniques, is seen in the national data system of India, the characteristics of which are described in *Sankhyā,* Journal of the Indian Statistical Institute, "National Sample Survey, General Report No. 1," XIII, parts 1 and 2 (1953), pp. 47–214, and subsequent reports in other issues.

A start has been made in initiating and operating such a data system in Puerto Rico: see Puerto Rico, Department of Health and Welfare (Office of Research, Planning and Evaluation), "A Continuing Master Sample Survey for Puerto Rico as a Community Health Service Project" (San Juan, 1962; mimeographed). Somewhat further along is comparable work for a subarea of New York City: see Jack Ellinson, *Washington Heights Master Sample Survey,* paper delivered at a meeting of the New York City Chapter, American Statistical Association, April 1960.

25

The New Metropolis and the
New University

ROBERT C. WOOD

The task of bringing the perspectives of several diverse groups to bear on our common problem—the future of the American city—involves both strengths and weaknesses. The strengths stem from a united front in the determination to master the perplexities of the new metropolitan communities and to make sure that their great educational institutions play a full part in the endeavor. The weaknesses are principally those of communication among faculty members, academic administrators, civic leaders, and public officials and the concomitant failure of each group to appreciate properly the others' goals and obligations.

When one talks on urban affairs to academics, one mentions their wisdom and foresight and decries the fact that politicians and businessmen ignore their counsel. Addressing civic leaders, the message is that *they* are the true city builders. If their energy and judgment could only be liberated from the red tape of City Hall and the fuzzy thinking of the theorists, a new and splendid metropolis would emerge overnight.

There are two approaches to use in talking to politicians. The first expresses sympathy that public officials are so misunderstood by the public at large; while the middle class and industry flee to the suburbs, the politicians hold the city together by sheer will power and unparalleled devotion. The politician thus emerges as the unsung hero of our urban culture. The alternative approach is to admit that things are pretty bad, but point out that they are much worse in Boston.

Taken one at a time, such arguments usually get good receptions. But combining them is a difficult assignment. Let me begin by outlining our common ground—the facts of urban life commonly accepted by knowledgeable and experienced people. Most readers would agree that the physical form of contemporary urban America is irreversibly that of the Spread City. To be sure, the core city has a vital and continuing role to play in the new metropolitan region. But the center cannot and will not recapture the people, industry, and land uses it once possessed. To believe that it will recapture its former glory is a flight of fancy. The task of the great American city today is to determine realistically its new mission in a greater complex. Its renaissance is necessary for a viable urban community, but it is not

From *Educational Record* (Summer, 1965), pp. 306–311.

sufficient. To concentrate solely on the central city is to understate and mistake the character of our urban problem.

As a corollary, I think we will all admit that the suburbs are here to stay. Our colleague, James A. Norton, pointed to this reality some years ago when he emphasized that any observer had to take the suburbs as "givens" —constant elements in the urban equation that would not change. Today's garrison suburb, practicing station-wagon socialism, planning, scheming, and zoning to bring in the right people and industry and exclude the wrong people and the wrong industry, is no isolated occurrence. To the barricades, the citizens of suburbia rush at the first threat of invasion. They are impelled by deep, strong, psychic and social motivations and reinforced by a powerful grass-roots ideology. Their attitudes will not easily be changed nor their mood made repentant. And we must learn to live with them.

Third, I think most of us agree that not every metropolitan area has a future. Especially in the Continental heartland of the United States, and especially in the areas with less than 250,000 people, urban regions are in trouble. As one sifts through the figures of the 1950 and 1960 censuses, a critical mass of one-half million residents emerges as a prerequisite for the "take-off" for future development. At least during the 1950–1960 decade, regions got bigger, with growth especially around the rims of the country. One does not talk carelessly of growth and expansion at conferences in Iowa or Kansas, Nebraska, or parts of Pennsylvania these days. One does not predict that Savannah, Georgia, for example, is guaranteed a bright and rosy future. So our analysis of urban problems and our policy proposals must be discriminating. We cannot use one model to fit all circumstances; we cannot peddle patent medicines.

Fourth, most of us acknowledge that metropolitan government in the sense of a comprehensive restructuring of our local political institutions is not just around the corner. Indeed, it is not even far down the road. In all likelihood we will live out our lives in metropolitan regions that do not possess neat and tidy structures of government. We will live in an urban world characterized by many centers of political power, by diffused influence structures. We will see decisions painfully arrived at by the interaction of many groups, often on the basis of the lowest common denominator. Occasionally, a superstructure of civic leaders may be visible, persisting in the belief that they are in charge. But these elites will in the end find themselves capable of settling only the budget of the annual community chest drive.

Finally, there may be consensus among us that the characterization of American society so often depicted by many of the commentators of the 1950's as monolithic, conformist, and overorganized is untrue. Instead, with the perspective of the 1960's, our culture seems increasingly pluralistic, diversified, and racked with major controversy that cannot be settled by authoritative fiat. Big Brother is not looking over our shoulder; neighbors do not invade our privacy through the cracked picture window. As the evidence from serious social science research continues to come in, increasingly America appears as a society of awesome loneliness, unsupported by familial or neighborly ties that exist in other cultures, forcing the individual personality to cope unassisted with the pressure of the outside world. Our citizens often seem quick to forget the problems of others. At any rate, as a nation we tolerate levels of social services and urban amenities that lag behind those provided in the rest of the Western world.

This knowledge, common to us all, drives home the intractability of many aspects of our urban condition, deprives us of simplistic solutions, highlights painful dilemmas. But it also identifies opportunities. Let me suggest three inferences to be drawn from the data, and one conclusion of specific relevance to universities.

First, contrary to the alarms of the Sunday supplements, we do not face a crisis of an exploding metropolis that threatens orderly community existence. That is, the disappearance of the compact, congested Victorian city does not herald the loss of a viable, vigorous, attractive way of life. Even less can a moral decline in the American character be detected that makes us less aggressive and more evil than our forefathers.

We do have a new and complex process of urban development to guide, and there are problems in this process. But they are essentially problems of growth opportunity—of the effective use of our potential. They are not problems of a civilization hell-bent on a reckless spree, and dangerously close to spinning out of control. To repeat, those who have argued that this nation should be interpreted as overorganized, conformist, and morally bankrupt have not made their case in other than emotional, impressionistic, and essentially erroneous terms. Study, planning, and thinking are required in our present situation, but not a crusade.

The second inference follows from the first. As we reject the alarmist view of urban America, and continue our research, the process of the urban development becomes explicable. The mystery of the sprawling, sick megalopolis disappears.

To be sure, we still lag far behind our colleagues in the physical sciences and engineering in their explanatory powers. But, it is now possible to be empirical as well as plausible in our explanations about what is happening to urban America.

We can demonstrate now that the changing form of our cities is triggered increasingly by the flood of technological innovation that shape land use. Science-based industry and technically trained labor force now emerge as key determinants of city growth, supplementing if not replacing the influence of natural resources, transportation, market and semiskilled labor advantage. Not only is the sheer thrust of science and technology important to regional growth, but the new public managers of research and development are a special factor to take into account. The present dispenser of community comfort and joy is not Santa Claus, nor private enterprise, so much as it may be the National Aeronautics and Space Administration.

Thus, Richard Meier has argued provocatively that the existence or nonexistence of public amenities of urban life, the career preferences of young scientists and engineers, the new dependence of the technically oriented industry upon the university and the technological library, are key new variables to be examined. Cities may flourish to the degree they can provide the amenities of culture and civilization that attract the frontier professions and the frontier industries.

But if the new community is both fathomable in its growth process and capable of some direction, the task of management remains difficult. So the third inference is that a sound process of urban development depends more on the way information flows among a diverse group of leaders in many areas of community life than it does on institutions and laws. If one views the pattern of metropolitan decision making as one in which many power centers collaborate in shifting and volatile alliances, then the information they possess and options they perceive are of central importance. For what rules the metropolitan region is not a political structure but a political *system*—informal coalitions of local officials, civic leaders, church and university people that form and re-form on every issue.

This embryonic political system, painfully beginning to make decisions, has its problems. But it has its promises, and one of these is the university. For as monolithic political machines and cliques of economic notables have disappeared, the university has risen as an increasingly important focal point for bringing coherence and reason to metropolitan affairs.

There are a number of reasons why the university's role is now central in the new arena of urban parapolitics. First, its size, its resources, and its personnel have magnified so rapidly in recent years that compared to any other organization on the current scene it is an entity of consequence. With faculties and students roughly doubling in absolute number within the last ten years, totaling well over 300,000 academic personnel and 4 million students; with university enrollment growing twice as rapidly as our population with public expenditures for higher education rising from one to five billion dollars in a decade; higher education in this nation is inescapably both a big industry and a growth industry. In and of themselves, these are formidable orders of magnitude.

Second, as Clark Kerr has pointed out, universities are now objects of high value in our society. For all their diversity, their products are useful not just to a few, not just to the intellectually curious or the intelligentsia concerned with the preservation of culture. Today, the universities have value for almost every walk of life. Their faculties in the natural and social sciences have completed the transition from a role of being intellectuals to that of becoming scholars. As David Bell suggests, the chief concern of the scholar—as distinct from the intellectual—is to make cumulative contributions within disciplined and bounded fields of knowledge. It is the state of one's chosen art or science, rather than the attention paid to one's personal opinion and judgment, that yields satisfaction.

As a consequence of this change in style and advance of knowledge, output is up. Our common efforts to understand, to explore, to demonstrate, grow exponentially, as attested by spiraling university research and development budgets of one and one-half billion dollars, up a hundredfold in this generation. And the number of professionals engaged exclusively in campus research has increased during the last ten years by 29 per cent, in contrast to a 15 per cent rise in ranks of the teaching faculty. Research activity producing knowledge required to meet public and private needs now engages the attention of 13 per cent of all professionals on campuses today. Knowledge, as Kerr says, has become a central mainstay of the society, for it is knowledge "for everybody's sake."

To be big and to be useful are two reliable signs of power.

Finally (and concomitantly with growth in size and value), the prestige of the academic community has risen. We have, despite the convictions of our wives, achieved a living wage. The public now knows that there are physicists, even if it does not know what they do. Politicians across the country now have brain trusts for window dressing if not for advice. And even some of the practical power of politics is now vested in academic hands. As not a few practicing politicians have discovered, the true coins of the political realm are no longer Christmas baskets, buckets of coal, and jobs in the state highway departments. Admission of one's children to college becomes a greater concern to more and more voters.

In short, the university has a peculiar "fit" in the new urban world of urban systems, the expanding sets of human behavior that have replaced institutions, structures, visible manifestations of order and authority. If our society cannot be properly described as the Mass Society or the Organization Society, perhaps it can be viewed as a Persuasive Society. That is, it is community life organized and made cohesive by the capacity of men to enlist or co-opt the support of others, to change attitudes by education or communication, to exercise influence increasingly by "the word."

In a Persuasive Society the university is a critical component. For affairs progress not by fiat or authoritative decree: progress depends on popular understanding and support, and most of all on the voluntary acceptance of responsibility by men and women in professional roles in industry, labor, politics, and education. As control mechanisms and oversight decline, individual self-discipline rises in importance, if our skills, resources, and capabilities are to be put to use. So does the pressure on individual personality structures, the need to develop professional standards and largely self-regulating ethics.

Now the direction of this society can be hopeful or dangerous, depending on whether understanding and consent is arrived at through honest transfer of information or by more cynical manipulation of symbols and critical emotions. The university's role becomes increasingly important; because the Academy has always been a Great Persuader, and basically an honest one. If the Academy plays its part, the new society can be both vigorous and free, far removed from the stereotypes of mass culture.

Three specific university obligations seem clear. First, the university must direct more research capabilities to analyzing and understanding the facts of urban life. One possibility that has long been a personal favorite is the establishment of a network of urban observatories patterned after the agricultural experimental stations created for rural America. In such a network, the small college could join hands with the larger universities in common endeavors. The young scholar, wherever he was located, could participate in more comprehensive and meaningful research endeavors, could indulge in empirical research rather than occasional commentary. And cumulative comparative information would be the result—with promise for better social science and better public policy.

If we had had, for example, a common research design for both the New York and Upper Midwest economic studies, urban economics would now be a far more advanced field of knowledge. If we had made common "capture and record" arrangements to analyze the efforts for governmental reform in Cleveland, Atlanta, Houston, and Miami, political science might have a higher batting average in its experiments in social engineering. In short, not only do we need more university research in urban matters, but we need to pursue it on a scale and under collaborative arrangements similar to those which made possible the spectacular breakthrough of natural sciences.

Second, I join Father Joyce of Boston College in his advocacy of corporate citizenship when the university as an organization impinges directly on urban development. The involvement of university people in large civic ventures is already a fact of life in many metropolitan areas. But we need more contact and working relations with city fathers and business and labor groups as we go about university affairs. Moreover, we need to be more aware of their practical policy problems and more sympathetic in assisting in the search for solutions to the immediate crises of the day.

This does not mean that the university and the city government will always agree, especially as university land needs grow and insofar as their land is tax-exempt. But it is important that responsible lines of communication are opened and that direct encounters and confrontations occur on matters of common practical concern.

Finally, the universities and their faculties have an obligation to take stands on larger public issues of urban areas not immediately related to the organizational interests of the campus. This open participation in urban politics has its dangers, especially when outspoken faculty members oppose influential alumni. But it also brings a new voice into the public arena, sometimes with a more rational point of view.

And the obligation is, at rock bottom, inescapable. We cannot teach and preach to our students, carry out our function of socialization of the young without some evidence that we practice as well as talk.

In the end, these observations and opinions combine into two simple conclusions. First, the battleground of the United States today—the place where we will shape the quality and character of our new society—is inevitably the urban arena. Second, the citadel of reason and good will within that arena is and must be the university.

In a Persuasive Society, the critical question is always whether or not information will be available, choices determined, and attitudes shaped on the basis of wide access to facts, reasonable analysis, and reasoned debate. So, in great measure, the process of resolving our burning issues of civil rights, the ordering of urban space, the control of violence, the building of new communities, will turn on the vigor and excellence of university participation.

It is my personal conviction that this participation is a matter of some urgency: We are painfully forced to re-examine the proposition that this is a civilized nation. We test that proposition that ours is a healthy society each day. We test it in the Kew Gardens of New York with its helpless victim, sick offender, and its immobilized spectators. We test it in our stumbling, clumsy first efforts to bring real help to the marginal man of society. Certainly, in the poverty programs, we will need all the academic skill we can muster to devise effective techniques by which we bring a fifth of our population back into the American mainstream of well-being. We test it in our capability to manage the backlash of the drive for civil rights. Here, the university has a special responsibility; for the semi-educated suburbanite, now so vociferous a critic of that drive, is more often than not one of our graduates.

All these issues are urban issues. The search for a workable solution to civil rights will take place in our new urban areas. So will the effort to find real answers to poverty and to better planning for space for healthier and more attractive communities. Headlines to the contrary, the future of the United States will not be settled in the ignorant, defensive backwaters and bayous of our society. It will be settled where the people are.

In these circumstances a university that does not serve its community is not a university. The advocates of the reasonable and the rational have a special duty to speak out.

Clinton Rossiter, our distinguished colleague from Cornell, summed up the challenge as well as anyone in his chapter in *Goals for Americans*. You recall after he traced the inadequacies of our governmental process, and institutions in the modern world, he did not despair. Instead, he wrote:

> In the end, of course, the fate of American democracy rests in the minds and hearts of men rather than in political machinery or social conditions. If enough minds in this country were to work rationally and enough hearts to beat kindly, the machinery of freedom could be far more rusty and conditions far less propitious than they are today—and still America would face the world as a proud, secure, confident democracy.[1]

Working minds and kindly hearts do indeed seem to be secrets for success in our new kind of society. And working minds and kindly hearts—of trained intelligence, and the inculcation of human values, if you prefer—are the hallmark of the educated man. I scarcely need add that the production of these necessities of modern life is the chief business of the universities. And the pursuit, the active, responsible, unflagging pursuit of knowledge and love, not the idle and passive contemplation of these objects, is the business of their faculties.

NOTE

1. Clinton Rossiter, "The Democratic Process," in *Goals for Americans,* U.S. President's Commission on National Goals (Englewood Cliffs, N.J.: Prentice-Hall, 1960), p. 75.

26

Manpower Planning and
the Restructuring of Education

AVNER HOVNE

The past few years have brought a surge of interest in manpower planning. In the developed countries it is hoped that planning will avert future shortages of highly trained manpower. In the developing countries such shortages are already felt and are feared for the future; and these countries also have additional and sometimes more urgent problems. How should the limited funds, talent, and time available for education be allocated, when nearly every kind of education is needed? How can a modern farming population be created, quickly, from among the illiterate and tradition-bound? How is one to meet the future needs for teachers, workers, technicians, and managers at all levels, not only the highest?

Manpower planning must take account of many different considerations: diet, hygiene,[1] land tenure, administrative traditions, education, and much else. Among these, education is extremely important, and in this article only the educational aspects of manpower planning are discussed. The term "education" is used in a broad sense to include professional and occupational training of all kinds.

How far should a person who is not an educator, who is interested in education primarily as an instrument of economic growth, interfere in the planning of education? Obviously, education is much more than preparing people for work. The responsibility of education to form manpower must be integrated with its broader and primary responsibility to form civilized human beings and good citizens. Some educational leaders take the position that manpower planners should tell them how many graduates they will need, and from which levels of school, and should help to obtain the funds; but that they should not meddle in so complex a professional field.

This point of view is rejected by many who have thought about manpower problems,[2] and it is rejected here too. In fact, for the sake of simplicity in the discussion, education is treated here as if it were simply an instrument of manpower policy. It may turn out that the kind of education that is best for manpower formation is also best for handing on and developing our culture as a whole, but that is not what is argued here. What is argued is that, to enable developed countries to meet shortages, and developing countries to deal effectively with their many manpower problems, basic changes in the conventional structure of education may be needed.

From *International Labour Review*, LXXXIX (June, 1964), 529–550.

The planning of manpower today

Let us define, at the start, what is meant in this essay by the conventional structure of education and indicate broadly the kind of basic changes we shall later be discussing. By the conventional structure of education is meant two things: first, the interrelated structure of primary or elementary school, secondary school (which may be general or vocational), and higher learning; and, secondly, the progress of pupils through this system—or a part of it—in full-time study and uninterrupted time sequence. The kind of basic changes on which this essay focuses have to do with the second aspect, with changes in what we shall call the *time structure,* that is, the custom of full-time study and uninterrupted progression.

Many who deal with manpower planning (or assessment or forecasting —the distinctions are ignored here) assume there is no need for any change whatever in the conventional structure and limit their problem (which is, in all conscience, complicated even so) to determining the desirable rate of expansion of the different parts of that structure.[3] But even persons who call for change in it do not pay much attention to the *time structure*. Their proposed changes range wide but elsewhere, dealing with the training of teachers, the selection of pupils, teaching techniques, the need for more technological subject matter, and much else. If there have been proposals for a general revision of the customary time structure, I have not seen them.

A good example of a discussion of the qualitative aspects of education for work is the recent article by Professor Harbison in this journal.[4] Among his major recommendations is the shifting of responsibility for specialized occupational training from the conventional educational system to employers. This indeed redefines the role of conventional education as carried on in some places, but it seems to assume that its present time structure will remain unchanged.

The present time structure of education fits in, broadly speaking, with the present method of estimating the rates of educational expansion required for future manpower needs. Manpower planning methods today can be looked upon as having a five-stage program:

Stage 1: The manpower planner is given, or himself makes up, a target or forecast of the Gross National Product in the future.

Stage 2: From this is derived the number of persons who will have to be employed in each economic branch.

Stage 3: From this is derived their distribution by occupation.

Stage 4: From this is derived the number of persons in the population who, at given future dates, must have completed specific types and levels of education.

Stage 5: From this are derived four schedules of the activities required to expand educational flows. The schedules deal with (a) building construction, (b) teacher training, (c) student enrollment, and (d) budgets.

This is, admittedly, a very simplified summary; existing differences and nuances are many. For example, the first stage may begin earlier and be a forecast of future population and labor force, from which the Gross National Product is derived; or the Gross National Product may even be left out of the calculations and future educational needs derived directly from the anticipated population figure. Or, although the start may be made at stage 1, there may be a direct jump from it to stage 4. And the process is often hedged in with many qualifications and tests of feasibility not mentioned above. However, these differences do not bear directly on the present argument.

Whatever the modifications, such a method of planning educational expansion makes it unavoidable that the plans must span considerable periods of time, or in planning jargon, require a considerable "lead time." This may be as much as ten years in the case of assistant maintenance technicians for example, and considerably more for occupations requiring higher levels of study, such as mathematicians, engineers, or top managers. Indeed, there is general agreement among manpower planners that ten years' lead time is minimal and twenty years not unreasonable.[5]

There are two fundamental objections to such long-run planning. First, it is sometimes impossible to wait so long. Second, it is difficult to believe in the reliability of such distant forecasts.[6]

Manpower planners are keenly aware of these difficulties, and they have responded to them in a variety of ways.

One response is to seek means by which manpower may be planned with a minimal use of—and dependence on—the planning of educational outflow. The techniques proposed for this purpose usually seek to improve the free functioning of the labor market. It is argued that if wages are allowed to respond to the supply of and demand for manpower, there will be fewer shortages[7] and so less planning will be needed.

Another technique seeks to reduce the burden of central planning by transferring to employers more responsibility for manpower formation. Furthermore, there are impediments to the full utilization of manpower, such as ignorance of educational and work opportunities; prejudices on account of sex, age, race, or religion; and economic and social obstacles to free movement. The reduction of such hindrances will, it is hoped, diminish the need for planned educational activities.

A different response is to try to improve the planning technique. A general secondary education or a university education may be considered a basic educational qualification, because it prepares for very many different occupations. The risk of error is much less in scheduling the expansion of education for such basic educational qualifications than in scheduling for a larger number of more specialized certificates and degrees. It is therefore proposed to restrict planning to the basic educational qualifications and also to subject the whole five-stage program to periodic review in order to adjust the schedules, so far as possible, before irrevocable commitments have been made.

Research is also called for to improve the reliability of the plans. Each stage in the program provides an area for useful investigation into the past and the present, and much of this information is still to be gathered. The trends and patterns it reveals can easily be misread, and serious thinking is needed to learn how to identify the important and dependable causes, to which they usually give very blurred expression.[8]

Some experts, having carefully weighed the matter, have concluded that it is practically hopeless to attempt quantitative forecasts or plans for education.[9] No matter how simplified the answers which are asked for and how sophisticated the techniques for obtaining them, they feel that there cannot be available at any given time the essential information needed to make worthwhile estimates or plans in this highly complex and dynamic field for a period ten years or more ahead.

On the other hand, most—I think—of those who have pondered the subject conclude that these quantitative plans and forecasts, for all their limitations, provide useful guides for decisions which would otherwise be made by even more faulty, impressionistic methods. As a complement to this position it has been suggested that for the short run, for which the general planning is inappropriate, stop-gap measures should be organized: intensive courses outside the framework of conventional education; large-scale use of expatriate manpower; or an adaptation of the organization of work to the kinds of manpower actually available.[10]

In this article the position is adopted that it is worthwhile to attempt quantitative planning. Some who hold this view feel that more ought to be done to respond to the fundamental objections against long-run planning.[11] Consequently, an effort is made here to carry the thinking along these lines one step further.

Several of the proposals that have just been reviewed touch on the assumption that the conventional time structure of education will continue; they bump against it, so to speak, though they do not pierce it. This applies to the proposal to increase management's responsibilities, the suggestion to limit planning to basic educational qualifications, and the idea of planning intensive training courses outside conventional education as a stop-gap measure. Our next step is to develop an alternative assumption concerning the future structure of education, an assumption which embraces the above proposals, and perhaps others, in a more systematic manner.

Recent trends in education

Two forces which have been responsible for great changes in education during the past half-century are the democratization of education and the requirements of an increasingly technological society. These forces created serious problems at all levels of education, but at the primary and at the higher levels they did not call for structural changes as far-reaching as at the intermediate or secondary level. By secondary level we mean education for boys and girls, from the age of 11–12 to 17–18, who have had some primary education.

In the older European tradition the class origin of an adolescent dictated, with rare exceptions, what kind of education was to be available to him. Secondary education for the lower classes was directly vocational, and highly specialized; for the upper classes it was general and humanistic. The growing twentieth-century tradition seeks, instead, equal educational opportunities for all children, regardless of the circumstances of their birth. It also seeks to meet the technological requirements of society by the provision of effective vocational preparation for all, the occupational goal of the child being determined by his natural endowments and personal tastes.

The various expressions of this growing tradition differ from country to country, and it seems that in none has one been found that is completely satisfying. However, many countries exhibit similar general trends in the organization and content of secondary education. One such trend is to regard secondary education as a direct continuation of primary education, or even to treat primary and secondary education as a single unit, as in Denmark, Sweden, and the Soviet Union. Another trend is to integrate cultural and vocational elements in the curriculum. Related to this latter and of particular importance in the context of this article is the trend to postpone narrow vocational specialization.[12]

Let us now attempt to interpret these trends as they impinge on the boundaries of the conventional time structure.

EDUCATION FOR ALL AGES

The demand for enlarged educational opportunity has been raised in many countries, not only for children formerly discriminated against because of their class origin but also for persons formerly discriminated against because they were no longer children. Only in exceptional cases does the demand go so far as to claim disregard of age in admitting students to courses intended for the young, such as the provision made in some countries for ex-soldiers or the elimination of the traditional upper age limits for admittance to apprenticeship. Broadly speaking, adult education has grown in special adult forms.

Some of these special forms of study lead to conventional certificates and degrees, and the study is done not full time and continuously, but occasionally, or part time, or by correspondence, radio, or television. Other forms of study for adults have no such formal relation to conventional education and consist of *ad hoc* courses for vocational, recreational, humanistic, or scientific purposes.

WORK AND STUDY INTEGRATED

The trend toward integration of cultural and vocational elements in education has already been mentioned. The vocational elements in secondary schools are often centered on the classroom and taught within the school building: there are only occasional visits to workplaces, at best only the use by a whole class of a workshop located in a plant. The kind of integration of work and study that we shall now consider is a very different matter: it involves regular work experience by an individual in a workplace, arranged as an integrated part of a course of study.

In a number of countries a "sandwich" plan has been tried, in which students alternate, each quarter- or half-year, between full-time study and full-time work. The practice is widely developed in the United Kingdom and other countries of Western Europe. Another manner of integrating work with study is to require, as is done in Hungary, that students spend half their summer vacations in some employment related to their studies. In a number of technical colleges in several countries, a three-year course is broken by a half-year or more of work in industry. In the Soviet Union a student is required to work for two full years before being admitted to an institution of higher learning.

Underlying these variations on a pattern are pedagogical considerations concerning the interrelation of learning and doing. Particularly in Eastern Europe they also reflect a desire to avoid the divorce of study from life and the formation of a class or caste of the educated who consider themselves superior to hard or even ordinary work.

While secondary school tends to assimilate work experience, apprenticeship in Western Europe tends to assimilate formal schooling. In some countries apprentices are required by law to devote a full day or even two days each week to study. Their theoretical studies are supervised by the national education authority, and to complete their apprenticeship they must not only demonstrate their skill in the trade but also pass an examination set by that authority. Certain countries prefer a shorter period of apprenticeship and an increased theoretical content. In some cases apprenticeship may be initiated by a year of full-time study. Thus the system of apprenticeship shows many characteristics of a special kind of sandwich plan.

A different form of integration of work and study is represented by the growing practice of enabling employees at all levels of the occupational hierarchy to be released from work for periods of full-time study. Seminars for top-level management are an important recent development.

RECURRENT SPECIALIZED TRAINING

A particularly important way in which work and study are being increasingly interrelated is represented by accelerated courses. These provide intensive training in one skill, such as arc welding, for persons who do not necessarily have much general education or technical experience. Accelerated courses enable people to make a rapid transition to a new kind of work from a different kind or none at all.

Modern technology generally requires that a newly employed person must have special training. At the same time modern conditions create a constant, large-scale shift from one workplace to another. Among the reasons for this are: rapid reductions in employment in particular industries and places; the rise of new industries such as plastics and electronics, and of new techniques of work; and the introduction of modern production and services to places where they were formerly unknown. It is increasingly true that an occasional period of intensive study must be undertaken by the worker as a condition of remaining in the labor force.

Recurrent specialized training is also needed by highly trained workers solely in order to keep up with the changes in their own fields.

NON-CONVENTIONAL EDUCATION SYSTEMATIZED

From what has been said above it is clear, then, that events are laying the basis for a new, larger unity of education—not just the continuity of the primary and secondary schools, but the continuity of a whole lifetime of education.

The ideas underlying the integration of cultural and vocational elements in the secondary school are being extended. Work and study tend no longer to be quite separate experiences but may be interrelated in a variety of ways over a whole lifetime. While narrow vocational education is more and more postponed for the child, the need for it is increasingly likely to recur throughout the life of the adult.

Non-conventional forms of education are gaining a status comparable to the conventional forms, by virtue of being systematized in nation-wide (and supranational) frameworks.

The ultimate development: a lifetime of work and study

Let us now make two assumptions: that the forces which underlie the recent trends in education will continue in strength, and that an adequate response to them will be developed in a large number of countries. That is, we are assuming that the day will come—before the year 2000—when there will be a reasonable opportunity for everyone in these countries to obtain all the education he wants for himself and his children; when the high requirements in theoretical knowledge posed by the economy will be adequately met; when there will be little ground for concern over a divorce between study and working life; and when the rapid shifts in employment requirements which will occur will cause relatively little personal and public dislocation. On that day, what will the shape of education be?

I believe that the overwhelming majority of the whole population will be engaged in a career combining work and study. At any given moment perhaps half of all the adults will be currently studying during the day. Wages, salaries, and profits will be based on the assumption that an acceptable standard of annual income will be earned by people who spend as much time—or nearly as much—studying as working. In many countries the need for work time will have been greatly reduced by automation,[13] and employment will be so organized as to make study an interlude to work. Some industries will be operated on the basis of a two-man job; one will be full time on the job, the other will be full time at school. In countries not yet so fully automated it will be recognized that most people need recurrent study, even at the expense of production, and expenditure on this account will be included in the budget for development.

Mental inertia, or a simple preference for either more leisure or more work in place of study, will lead many adults to opt out of study. It must be remembered, however, that study will be far more attractive, as well as more effective, than it usually is today. Mechanical aids—such as television, teaching machines, and others still unknown—will help; and methods of teaching person-to-person, individually, and in small groups will be greatly improved and widely used.

The educational system will be far more unified, but also far more complex, than it is today. There will be a greater array of conventional and nonconventional forms of study, but most of these will be related to a single system of certificates and degrees.[14] The span of study from one level of certificate or degree to the next will be much smaller. For example, if we call the completion of primary school, at about 14 years of age, level 1, there will also be at least level 2, junior secondary; level 3, senior secondary; level 4, junior higher; and level 5, senior higher. Each level will require about two years of intensive, or about four years of extensive, study. Level 2 will provide a meaningful goal for students who have no taste for abstraction, or who for any other reason will go no higher but may thereafter earn additional level 2 certificates in various specialized subjects.

In certain countries today technicians of various kinds—nurses, teachers, social workers, and others—qualify for their work by virtue of certificates which are not related to the general hierarchy. These will be assimilated to levels 3, 4, or 5, thus encouraging flexibility both in individual careers and in development of the different professions. For example, if the nurses' certificate should be set at level 3, a degree may be added, if needed, at level 4 in some specialized aspect of nursing.

There will be sufficient standardization of certificates and degrees among most countries of the world to make convenient the pursuit of a study career, or one combining work and study, without the student being limited to the facilities of his own country.

When a boy or girl leaves full-time school—at whatever age that may be—he or she will start not a lifetime of work but a lifetime of work and study. A person who ceases intensive education at 14 may obtain a level 5 degree, such as B.Sc. or B.A., at about 30; or he may take longer, having added one or more specialized certificates along the way. Some may take less time, having devoted one or more periods of a few years each to intensive study. Most boys and girls, however, may not have the wish or the need to obtain a level 5 degree, and may find it more useful and interesting to take a succession of certificates in different subjects at lower levels. For boys and girls who, for any reason, have missed early intensive schooling, there will be opportunities to cover level 1 as adults.

EFFECTS ON OCCUPATIONAL STRUCTURE

Today the labor force is divided for many analytical purposes into agricultural and non-agricultural. In the future, agriculture will occupy an ever smaller ratio of the total number of workers (and those employed in it will be assimilated to the conditions of work in industry), while teaching will grow to such great proportions and be so crucial for development that the major division of the labor force will be between teaching and non-teaching.[15] The teachers' ratio will be a key indicator of economic development.

More teachers will be giving instruction in the extensive forms of education (that is, today's non-conventional forms) than in the intensive; there will, however, be uniform standards and effective supervision of all. Many more teachers will be qualified than will be actively engaged in the profession at any one time, because teachers too will have alternate periods of work and study, giving more time to study (and in many cases to work other than teaching) than is common today.[16] Training to teach will be incorporated in the curricula leading to many certificates and degrees from an early level. Teaching will be able to provide alternative employment for most of the better-educated persons in the labor force. For teenagers, educational work with pre-school children—under close supervision—will be a common form of work experience.

Compared with today, there will be a great multiplication in the numbers of persons engaged in educational administration, the training of teachers and educational research. And, of course, there will also be a great increase in the number of teachers and the variety of their specialities.

THE ROLE OF MANAGEMENT AND LABOR

Management will be deeply involved in educational activities. The training departments of large enterprises will have broader responsibilities, and small enterprises will make use of external or cooperative training services. The training departments and services will conduct on-the-job training, in-service training courses, and apprentice training. They will help to coordinate the requirements of current operation with, on the one hand, the employment of students from various "sandwich" courses and, on the other, the extensive practice of releasing regular employees for educational purposes. They will represent the needs of their own operation and contribute by their experience to the local and national planning of education. At the same time they will see to it that the operations of their enterprises are effectively aligned to current and future manpower supply. This means that their hiring plans will be attuned not only to the system of certificates and degrees but also to the number of applicants for employment that may reasonably be expected. Of course hiring will not be based solely on these considerations; then, as now, experience and personal adaptability will be the major qualifications for some occupations.

Organized labor will also be deeply involved. In some countries today trade unions conduct important educational activities; these will be increased in scope.[17] A major change from the present situation will be the important place given in collective bargaining to conditions of education. In some countries the demands of organized labor may be the major force in restructuring education.[18] Workers' representatives in local and national educational planning bodies will protect trade union interests and contribute from union experience. Labor spokesmen will make publicly known, and give leadership to the formation of, the workers' attitude toward study.

GOVERNMENT'S ROLE

The task of coordinating the complex and large-scale educational activities of the future will fall mainly on government, which will be engaged in manpower planning, within which educational plans will play a central role. The technique of manpower planning will be different from that which was described earlier, and I shall come back shortly to describe it in a little detail. Here it is sufficient merely to indicate the broad types of activities in which manpower planning will involve government.

Government will be kept currently and effectively informed[19] about economic trends and plans; about changing techniques in producing goods and services; about trends and plans related to education; and about manpower resources abroad. It will be able to make use of tried channels of consultation with educational authorities, management, and labor and to take decisions concerning education and put them into effect.

The instruments for putting decisions into effect will cover a wide range.[20] Policy will be expressed in public statements and in specific information and guidance given to all involved in educational activities. The state budget will constitute a decisive instrument, determining the character of the educational activities under direct government control and providing supplements and subsidies for educational activities of selected types, for teachers whose temporary services are urgently required, and for students who follow needed courses of study.[21] Another important instrument will be the conditions of government employment, which can influence students and educational authorities to prefer one path of study or another.[22]

This, then, is my guess at the ultimate development of recent trends in education. It amounts to a radical restructuring of education. It may be said to start from the assumption that there will be a large section of the population whose whole life will be devoted to work and study.[23] It also assumes a modification of one of the aims of modern education, which the *World Survey of Education* says is "to provide both a humane general education and a specialized training for all, according to their natural endowments and personal interests." [24] The modification consists in doing this in the light of the over-all needs of the economy, as expressed in a planned system of opportunities and incentives. From these assumptions there follow broad changes in the relations between different kinds of educational activity and in the nature of the teaching sector, and new degrees of involvement in education on the part of management, labor, and government.

SOURCES OF RESISTANCE TO CHANGE

How likely is it that so far-reaching a restructuring will actually be realized? It is hard to think up good reasons why the underlying forces might possibly not continue to exercise influence, but easy to imagine circumstances under which the responses to these forces might fail.

One has already been mentioned: the possibility that not enough people will be able or willing to study. However, it may prove even harder to get work out of those who expected only to study, particularly where study carries high status and the work to be done carries a low one.[25] In many cases the well-off sections of the population will be asked to bear a considerable share of the cost of expanding educational activities—an expansion along channels that will not necessarily enable their own children to obtain a higher education by continuous study.

The establishment of new levels at which school life can be terminated, such as levels 2 and 4 referred to earlier, may be opposed by many people. Today, a person who obtains a diploma in draftsmanship can, with a little more effort, pass on to a degree in architecture, which carries far more prestige in some countries. As a result, though draftsmen may be needed more than architects, students do not become draftsmen, and the technical colleges revise their functions so as to produce architects.[26] Opposition to the rationalization of educational levels may also come from tradition-bound management or trade unions.

It has been claimed that the M.D. degree requires training much higher than that really necessary for many of the actual functions of the general practitioner.[27] Even if this were proved irrefutably to be true, many physicians would doubtless still oppose the institution of a very long work-and-study career, leading by non-conventional paths and through several professional levels, at one or another of which most practitioners would stop, to the M.D. degree. Professional traditionalism could be expected in other occupations also.

In some countries a practical problem raised by the restructuring of education may be how to find all the teachers needed. In many developed countries, however, a prompt and massive opening of attractive jobs in the field of education could constitute a major weapon against the threat of chronic unemployment following the spread of automation. In the developing countries, if candidates are promised the status and salary they deserve as teachers, they are not likely to be in short supply, given time.

Another practical problem—*the* practical problem in the future of education in general—is cost. Although in this article there is no discussion of the problem in general, the question of comparative costs will be briefly explored later: the cost of an expanding educational system based on the conventional structure will be compared with that based on the new structure under consideration.

Resistance to the restructuring of education may be anticipated from persons among both management and labor who will not be eager to take on themselves the new responsibilities outlined above. Workers will need to have complete ease in moving between employment and study and between different places and different kinds of employment. All important obstacles to free movement of this kind must be eliminated; and attempts to eliminate certain obstacles will encounter strong resistance. For example, in many countries the workers' right to a pension and other benefits are dependent on their continuous employment by one firm. It will be necessary to change this practice and to ensure full pension and other rights for workers who follow a career of flexibly alternating work and study. Many of those who control the extremely rich pension funds will probably object strongly to such changes.

Serious practical difficulties may be encountered when governments attempt to fill the roles assigned to them in the new structure. Interagency jealousy, bureaucratic rigidity and inertia, and lack of competent staff may doom such attempts at the start. A far-reaching revision of current priorities will usually be needed in order to ensure that appropriate powers, adequate budgets, and effective leadership are assigned to this task.

In addition to dealing with practical difficulties and with the opposition of groups who have special interests, efforts to restructure education must also face up to the fact that important values of recognized worth may be threatened. In education as now organized there are embedded in many countries cultural and human achievements which could be lost in a ruthless restructuring. One of these is academic freedom. I think that such values can be not only preserved but perhaps strengthened, but I think also that this will require vigilance and effort.

Whether or not a restructuring of education will actually take place will depend mainly on the social values of the dominant groups in the nation. It would need great determination for a government to employ the instruments described above for giving effect to its coordinating decisions, especially the decisive instruments of the state budget and the adjustment of the conditions of government employment. To do so in the face of all the resistances and difficulties would require a moral revolution in some countries. No government is likely to take this path unless it has adopted as its own guiding values the maximum democratization of educational opportunities, the marriage of study and work, and the full exploitation for society of the potentialities of technology. In short: Only where there is abiding enthusiasm for the underlying forces which call for a restructuring of education is that restructuring likely to be realized.

Manpower planning revised

Let us review how far we have come in the argument. Manpower planning today assumes an indefinite continuation of the conventional organization of education. On this assumption the planning of education for skilled and high-level manpower requires a long lead time; which is not satisfactory. The structure of education is already changing, however, in response to powerful modern forces, and a thoroughgoing restructuring may be experienced in countries where those forces are highly valued.

A revised form of manpower planning has been mentioned as one element in a restructured educational system. This revised form obviously would not assume an indefinite continuation of the conventional organization of education but the possibility—or rather the desirability—of a new structure for education, such as has been outlined. What, then, might this manpower planning be like?

A SHORT LEAD-TIME

For the purposes of this article the most important difference between manpower planning today and manpower planning geared to a restructuring of education lies in the added possibility of creating conditions under which the education of skilled and high-level manpower could be planned with a short lead-time.

There are four conditions:

1. As the reader will recall, under manpower planning today, one technique for reducing error is to give large numbers of students basic educational qualifications. Under revised manpower planning, reserves of students are prepared for the most important of these basic educational qualifications.

2. Reserves of teachers and of facilities are also prepared; not for the basic educational qualifications but for specialized training which may have to be expanded at short notice.

3. People must be accustomed to alternating between work and study, and the authorities must be able to start new specialized training easily.

4. Specialized courses must be of short duration.

The notions of specialized courses of short duration and of easy mobility of students between different forms of education are a part of restructured education, and have been discussed earlier. The new notion here is that of reserves. Now, it is precisely because they are aware of manpower shortages that most countries are interested at all in manpower planning. To talk of the accumulation of educational reserves as a planning method is a little like talking about savings to a man who is hungry. However, in a society where there is a great hunger but where also the existing opportunities for savings are not being realized, there is point in talking about savings. Similarly, in a society with great current and imminent manpower shortages, there is point in talking about managing its educational resources (whatever they may be) so as to create educational reserves.

COMPARATIVE COSTS

This brings us to the question of the comparative costs of conventional and of restructured education. Certain non-conventional forms of education are, from one point of view, more costly than conventional forms. For example, the sandwich plan requires greater outlays on administration and supervision because it must embrace the workplace as well as the school.[28] Some non-conventional forms may cost less. However, for the sake of simplicity let us assume that, generally, the cost per unit of study per person will be greater in the restructured than in the conventional system.

But if we take as our measure the aggregate costs of meeting the social and economic requirements which education must fulfill today, then the restructured system comes out better. These requirements I take to be twofold: reasonable satisfaction of the demands of the people for expanded educational opportunities; and the effective preparation of urgently needed manpower. And if we take as our measure the cost per person served per year, then extensive education costs less than intensive education and, for a given annual expenditure on education, can serve more people who want new educational opportunities. Furthermore, a longer time is needed in work-and-study programs than in full-time, uninterrupted study for a person to complete a given level of education. The result is that a longer time elapses before the need is felt to move on to a higher level.

It follows that, if the resources available for education are limited, it is generally wise to expand educational opportunities through combined work and study and concentrate opportunities for intensive study on those subjects and levels which are urgently needed either to meet current manpower shortages or to create educational reserves.

The question may be raised: How can students, teachers, and educational facilities be held in reserve? So far as students and teachers are concerned, the new structure of education which is envisaged would make this far more practicable than it would be today.[29] The reserve students and teachers would not be unemployed but would be active members of the work-and-study population, who have, at a given moment, the educational qualifications enabling them to meet a special need. The organization of reserve physical facilities would be a new, added task of manpower planning. Most often use would be made of an industrial, commercial, or service site suitable for the purpose. In addition, educational authorities might devise mobile classrooms and laboratories which were convertible to different subjects. As in past (wartime) emergencies, cinemas, churches, union halls, and other community premises might, if necessary, be used for short courses.

The proposed new time structure of education thus calls for the integration in a single system of intensive education and an increased measure of extensive education. A systematic differentiation between the two forms of education would permit the establishment of educational reserves and thus make it possible to plan the education of skilled and high-level manpower with only a short lead-time.

PLANNING METHOD

It has been suggested above that manpower planning today, insofar as it deals with the future supply of persons with particular educational qualifications, is generally carried on within a simple framework: a five-stage program for translating Gross National Product into schedules for the expansion of education.

The revised planning, which makes the structure of education a variable instead of a constant factor, requires a more complicated framework. It has three parts: (1) a plan of the educational structure; (2) a long-term manpower plan; and (3) short-term coordination of manpower activities. It is in the third part that effective decisions are made; the first and second parts together form a perspective or background plan.

1. The purpose of the plan of the educational structure is to describe, for periods ranging from one to twenty years ahead, the kinds of educational activities which will be carried on. In each period these activities will have to be consistent with the presumed state of technology, the long-run goals of restructured education, and the changes in the educational structure from period to period; moreover, they must be consistent among themselves as regards subjects, levels, modes of study, and educational progression. This plan will be qualitative. It will summarize the best current knowledge about the general relations between economic activity and educational activity. But it will not be concerned with costs or feasibility, except pedagogic feasibility.

2. Numbers, costs, and physical feasibility are the province of the long-term manpower plan. Like manpower planning today, it will rest on a five-stage program and will work with a lead-time of from five to twenty years. As has been mentioned above, manpower planning today is often highly aggregative; the long-term manpower plan under the revised approach is, if anything, more aggregative and simple. The reason is that there is built into the system the means of dealing directly with details, errors, and unpredicted events.

If we compare the five-stage program under the revised approach with that of manpower planning today, the major differences are seen to be at stages 4 and 5.

At stage 4—where the focus is the number of persons to be educated, by types and levels of education—the framework of the numerical calculation is not the conventional structure of education but the plan of the educational structure—part 1 above.

At stage 5 (the four schedules of educational expansion) account is taken not only of requirements as derived from expected economic developments, but also of the planned educational reserves. At this stage, when the scheduled expansion has to be modified for feasibility, a major method of coping with otherwise inadequate resources is to differentiate systematically between extensive and intensive education.

3. The short-term coordination of manpower activities also deals with numbers, costs, and physical feasibility. Here, where the effective decisions are made, matters are considered in full detail. It is in this framework that specialized courses of intensive study are opened and closed as required, thus regulating the final stage of supply of educated manpower, up to the very highest levels. Here, too, practical steps are taken to expand the whole

educational system, as determined by the long-run manpower plan and modified by current information. Similarly, general policy concerning relations with the outside world are here interpreted and implemented in the light of current needs.

Although it rests on the broad-ranging intellectual considerations embodied in the plan of the educational structure and the long-term manpower plan, the short-run coordination of manpower activities is primarily administrative in character.

Considerable means are necessary for gathering current information, making informed decisions and putting them into effect. These have already been mentioned in the discussion of the ultimate development of recent trends in education. The reader will recall that the means differ between centrally controlled and other societies, and that it was suggested that difficulty in obtaining such means was one of the major barriers to the restructuring of education in general.

Concluding remarks

The significance of the revised approach to manpower planning may differ greatly between countries in different stages of educational development. In some countries the emergence of restructured education is well advanced and many aspects of what has been described here as revised manpower planning are established practice. If the analysis offered here is right, there will be further gradual development along the lines indicated.

For a country with few educational facilities a revised approach to manpower planning would mean something quite different. It is natural for people in many developing countries to take as their guides not only the production techniques and living standards of the developed countries, but also many of their forms and traditions, including those concerning education. I have tried to suggest that the present time structure of conventional education will soon be outmoded in the developed countries; for the developing countries to base long-run and expensive educational expansion on this time structure may be very imprudent.

Mention has already been made of resistance to the restructuring of education; the adoption of the kind of manpower planning which aims at making such changes in education would—if it is recognized for what it is—also probably be strongly resisted. To a manpower plan which leads to a simple statement of the expansion needed in conventional educational institutions, the response may be "Yes, we will somehow do it," or "It's too cautious; we'll do more," or "Fine, but it's beyond us." Planning which deals with changes in the way people's lives are organized for study and for work, and which places new kinds of responsibilities on many groups, cannot be responded to so simply. It can be undertaken only after very serious consideration.

However, if the analysis made here is correct, some countries will certainly try. Recalling that it was the United States and the Soviet Union—

both countries relatively unburdened by class traditions in education—which pioneered the reform of secondary education, I close with a final speculation: that it may well be a newly rising state of today that, able to free itself of time traditions in education, will pioneer in the creation of a life-long, flexible pattern of work and study for a whole people.

NOTES

1. The simultaneous effects of poor nutrition and poor health have been estimated to reduce working capacity by up to one-half in some countries (such as Ecuador and Mexico) and by up to one-third in many others. See Hector Correa, *The Economics of Human Resources* (Rotterdam: Netherlands Economic Institute, 1962).

2. See the Report of the Conference Secretary-General on "Human Resources" (E/Conf. 39/GR. 2(B)), presented to the United Nations Conference on the Application of Science and Technology for the Benefit of the Less Developed Areas (hereafter referred to as UNCSAT), which was held in Geneva in February 1963. The report calls for "training programmes new in structure, methods and means of application . . . comprehensive, dynamic and imaginative." A paper prepared for this conference by Frederick H. Harbison, on "High Level Manpower Development" (E/Conf. 39/B/55) states: "Education policy should not be left exclusively in the hands of educators or education ministries. It must be influenced at strategic points by those who are concerned with the general problems of economic growth."

3. See, for example, the reports on Sweden, France, and the Netherlands in OECD, *Employment Forecasting, International Seminar on Employment Forecasting Techniques, Brussels 1962, Final Report* (Paris, 1963). In the report in the same volume by the Rapporteur-General, Jan Tinbergen, non-conventional education is, however, given considerable attention.

4. Frederick H. Harbison, "Human Resources Development Planning in Modernising Economies," *International Labour Review*, LXXXV, No. 5 (May, 1962), 435–458.

5. If the target date is defined as that on which there will be available qualified practitioners of, not merely qualified candidates for, the occupation, several more years of lead-time must be added to cover the gaining of experience.

6. France is the only country with a number of years' experience in manpower planning concerning which I have seen published figures showing the disparities between plans and reality. The figures related only to four-year planning periods and deal only with stage 2 of our scheme (employment by branch). The disparities are considerable. See Jean Fourastié, "Employment Forecasting in France," in *Employment Forecasting, op. cit.*

7. Not—as commonly argued—because low wages do not attract candidates, but because when high-level skills are underpaid they are likely to be employed wastefully. See John Vaizey, "The Labour Market and the Manpower Forecaster —Some Problems," *International Labour Review*, LXXXIX, No. 4 (April 1964), 353–370 (paper originally submitted to the Meeting of Experts on the Assessment of Manpower and Training Requirements for Economic Development, hereafter referred to as the Meeting of Experts, held by the International Labour Office in Geneva, October 1–12, 1962).

8. For example, how can we decide to what extent graduate civil engineers may have been employed in a given country at a given date because they were specifically needed for the work which had to be done, and to what extent they were employed because they were available and could be adapted to the work which had to be done? See R. J. Hollister, "The Economics of Manpower Forecasting," *op. cit.*, pp. 371–397.

9. See the statement of the Danish spokesman, M. Eric Ib Schmidt, "Economic

Growth and the Manpower Sector," in OEEC, *Forecasting Manpower Needs for the Age of Science* (Paris, September, 1960), p. 15.

10. This summary of the position follows Jan Tinbergen, "Employment Forecasting and Planning," in *Employment Forecasting, op. cit.*

11. An example of the general dissatisfaction with the state of forecasting methods is to be found in Jef Rens, "Reflections on the Melbourne Conference," in *International Labour Review*, LXXXVII, No. 4 (April, 1963), 315–327. Basing himself, in part, on the findings of the Meeting of Experts, he wrote: "The techniques of assessing supply of and demand for human resources (in terms of quantity as well as quality) are still being worked out and consequently are far from satisfactory."

12. This summary relies heavily on UNESCO, *World Survey of Education. III: Secondary Education* (Paris, 1961).

13. However, I do not think that everything will have been fully automated and the labor force divided between two broad occupations: system planners and system tenders. Rather, I think there will be many degrees of automation, much physical production, and many services, not at all automated, and a wide variety of personal attributes and of specialized educational qualifications still in demand.

14. It is not suggested that on-the-job training or highly specific in-training courses can be related to the general system of education. However, many in-training courses *can* be, whether carried on by a single plant or in an outside school or training center.

15. In the United States the number of teachers is already nearly as great as the number of farmers.

16. In a report to UNCSAT (E/Conf. 39/K/53), Herta Haas of Yugoslavia stated: "The work of engineers and other qualified experts from the production field, as part-time teachers, has given excellent results."

17. As called for by Jef Rens, *op. cit.*, p. 322.

18. In the United States, where organized labor played a major role in the nineteenth century in obtaining compulsory universal primary education, the steelworkers' union recently obtained—for the half of the wage earners (in each of the 11 major basic iron and steel companies) with the greatest seniority—13 weeks' vacation with pay every fifth year. (In the intervening years, they will have their usual three of four weeks' vacation.) See "Developments in Industrial Relations," *Monthly Labor Review* (Washington), LXXXVI, No. 8 (August, 1963), 659. The purpose is to spread employment in the face of automation; but the next step could be for management and union to provide campuses for study in accredited courses, alongside recreation for workers and their families during regular sabbatical leaves.

19. It is not necessary to be fully informed, only effectively informed. "In emerging nations . . . it is often possible to identify one or two major elements in manpower planning which are of crucial importance to later development and thus to limit the initial attack upon the problems" (J. L. Thurston, *Human Resources and Manpower Planning in Tanganyika* [New York: Ford Foundation, 1960]).

20. In countries which practice both central planning and control, the methods will differ greatly even in comparison with countries which practice central planning only. Compare in this respect Hungary, as described by János Timar in a paper presented to UNCSAT, "The Problems of Planning and Recruiting Qualified Personnel" (E/Conf. 39/K/26), and France, as described by Jean Fourastié, "Employment Forecasting in France," *loc. cit.*

21. An example of how this is currently being done in Ghana is given in a paper presented to UNCSAT by Robert D. Loken: "Forecasting the Requirements and Priorities of Numbers and Types of Scientists and Technologists: Allocation of Students" (E/Conf. 39/K/1).

22. As called for by Frederick H. Harbison in "Human Resources Development Planning in Modernising Economies," *op. cit.*

23. This idea has been broadly endorsed in recent years. As the Report of the Meeting of Experts (para. 81) states: "Education must be considered as a permanent process in a developing society, but much progress has still to be made in translating this idea into reality."

24. *World Survey of Education. III: Secondary Education, op. cit.*, p. 148.

25. See, for example, Adam Curle, *Educational Strategy for Developing Societies* (London: Tavistock, 1963), pp. 81–93.

26. An actual example given by Curle, *op. cit.,* p. 60.

27. Frederick H. Harbison, "Human Resources Development Planning in Modernising Economies," *op. cit.,* p. 437. The same claim has been made concerning engineers, teachers, and nurses.

28. Sandwich courses for secondary vocational schools were tried in Israel and were found highly effective, but were abandoned because they demanded more budget for inspection and supervision than could be made available. See P. F. Harburger, "Experiments in Vocational Education in a Developing Country," *International Labour Review,* LXXXIX, No. 1 (January, 1964), 37–38.

29. The paper prepared for UNCSAT by the ILO, "Methodology of Manpower Forecasting" (E/Conf. 39/B/26), states: "Obviously skilled manpower resources cannot to any significant extent be stockpiled awaiting the development of forecast requirements" (para. 36). That statement is true; what is proposed here is not stockpiling but planning for reserve capacities of employed persons.

27

Poverty and the Community Planner's Mandate

MARTIN REIN AND PETER MARRIS

This essay examines some of the dilemmas of planning in a democratic society. The issues we present arose from our study of planning, conducted on some of the most imaginative and ambitious attempts to manipulate deliberate social change between 1960 and 1964.[1] These projects were promoted and largely financed by the Ford Foundation and the Juvenile Delinquency and Youth Offenses Control Act of 1961, absorbed into the poverty program, and diffused as a national strategy. They have come to be known as community action projects—local agencies which, drawing on federal funds, concert the resources of a community in a democratic, coherent attack upon the handicaps of the poor.

The problem of redistribution

The poor are found in all sections of the nation, and the causes of their poverty are a mixture of national, local, and personal circumstances. Locally, the poor tend to concentrate in certain sections of the metropolitan area and to be separated, by some distance, from their more fortunate fellow citizens, who live in other political jurisdictions. This separation by income often means a separation between local needs of the poor and local resources for their relief.

The poor urgently need much more public money spent on their education and training, their housing, their health, and the welfare benefits which sustain mothers, old people, unemployed. They need better protection under social insurance and minimum wage laws. And they need jobs which even an expanding economy is not likely to provide soon enough, often enough, nor in the right place. At least for the time being, the full employment of young people from the slums in worthwhile careers depends upon the deliberate creation of opportunities where their talents can be used. They can be absorbed in the improvement of education and social services, in building new houses, in any of the undermanned, underdeveloped services where the highly trained skill of scarce professionals could be more efficiently exploited with the help of aides. But the jobs must be paid for, chiefly from public funds. And no one, naturally enough, enjoys higher taxation, especially when the benefit goes to someone else.

Collectively, society may recognize that poverty is intolerable to their sense of justice, dangerous and expensive, and that at length the palliation of its ugly symptoms is less sufficient and economical than a radical cure. But the immediate, individual interest is less far-seeing. Negro families should be decently housed, but not in my neighborhood; jobs should be found, but not if it threatens my professional status, or requires me to employ an insecure, temperamental human being where a steady, uncomplaining machine would cost no more. Hopefully, someone else, who can better afford it, will make the sacrifice. The cost-benefit analysis of social policy reads very differently from a short-term, personal standpoint than a long-term, collective one. And the collective interest is harder to sustain in America than in most prosperous democratic societies, because social services here are by tradition a local responsibility, and the fragmentation of government narrows this responsibility to increasingly homogeneous communities.

Thus whenever the need is greatest, the resources tend to be least adequate, and any attempt to redistribute wealth only drives that wealth elsewhere. City and suburb divide into poor and prosperous, each with its independently run, and largely independently financed, institutions. The inner city, with the most need, can raise proportionately less money, and the higher its taxes, the more it hurries the well-to-do across its boundaries into a less exacting jurisdiction. But the poor, unable to afford suburban housing, cannot follow. To restore its fortunes, the city can only try to bring the wealthy back, and this leads to the dilemma most evident in urban renewal. To provide good schools for the poor, you must have citizens who can pay for them; but to attract these citizens, you must first dispossess the poor, crowding them ever more uncomfortably within the city limits, and so driving out more of the taxable residents from the margins of slum neighborhoods. In the same way, to redistribute school children by bus throughout the city, in search of a more integrated, homogeneous standard of education, may only provoke the better-off to make their escape across the border. Within such constricted jurisdictions, the pursuit of equality is self-defeating.

The same discontinuity acts on a larger scale: communities, even regions, are ruined by technological changes which spread their benefits elsewhere. Poor states can only attract new industries by promising not to exploit them in the interests of social justice; sites are subsidized, taxes waived, and the cheapness and docility of local labor frankly put forward as a further inducement. Since every community and every region is competing for wealth, each undercuts the others, imposing fewer and fewer claims for fear of being left with no one to claim from.

Hence, only the federal government has a jurisdiction wide enough to ensure redistribution.[2] But if it intervenes directly in the allocation of social services, it affronts two vigorous traditions: that this is a community, and preferably not even a governmental, responsibility. To open the way to federal control of municipal decision making or of social planning councils is doubly shocking. And since social policy is inseparable from the problems of segregation, those states which stand to gain most from federal intervention to promote social development are the first to block it because of the implicit erosion of segregated living to which they are accustomed. So the one level of government with the means to redistribute social services more equitably has never secured a firm mandate to undertake it.

Community action as a redistributive mechanism

Poverty is therefore both a national problem in the distribution of resources and a local problem of their management. In the past few years, a new kind of structure has been evolving, which can be seen as an attempt to plan the revision of services to the poor within this context. The community action agencies promoted by the Economic Opportunities Act—and pioneered by the Ford Foundation and the President's Committee on Juvenile Delinquency—derive their funds mostly from the federal government, but draw on the tradition of local initiative and responsibility. By putting the programs under the control of an independent agency with its own local board, community action characteristically tries to create a means of distributing federal funds detached from the politics of city hall or any sectional interest, yet responsive to them all. At the same time, the agency acts within the framework of principles laid down by its source of funds. As the instrument of a national concern with poverty, community action attempts to reconcile the inevitability of tackling redistribution at a federal level with respect for the variety of local circumstances and the autonomy of community self-government. It is to recruit new resources, and divert them where they are most needed.

This is not the only interpretation of community action. It can be used instead to enable the poor to protect their rights more effectively, through legal services, advice, and organization; to create new community services which the people of poor neighborhoods will themselves control and largely staff; or to extend city hall's responsibility for social policy.[3] Experience suggests, too, that community action agencies can sometimes evolve toward executive planning, detached from any one political jurisdiction, where a coalition of community leadership powerful enough to back them across a wide range of jurisdictions has already been created. Without this support, the competition between agencies and governments to secure their funds and dominate their decisions has usually frustrated such attempts. The agency cannot hope to represent more than the desire, among a range of interests already in alliance, to submit their interaction to a more professionally informed and far-sighted process. Where power is as widely diffused as in America, and reform depends so much on the competitive assertion of diverse interests and values, planning itself cannot attempt to reconstruct the social order. But it can be a way for the competing claims to come to terms more rationally. Within the scope of their limited funds and ambiguous authority, some community action agencies are, then, pioneering a new form of planning.

Their originality lies in the way they straddle or bypass political jurisdictions. If they were simply the agents of the federal departments from which they draw their funds, they would rebuff local initiative, affront the traditions of decentralized democracy, and adapt very clumsily to local circumstances. If they were controlled by city or county, they might not be able to defend the minority interests uncertainly protected by elected government, nor act across jurisdictional boundaries. Their purposes could be served as well by direct federal subsidy to local governments. And they have bypassed state government almost entirely. As James Reston has remarked of community action in the Midwest:

> Washington is now so directly involved in the new Federal social programs in the cities and towns that the Governors here in the Middle West not only have little control over them but in some states don't even know what the Feds are doing within their boundaries. . . . The Middle Western Governors have been complaining about "the centralization of power in Washington," but actually this phrase is slightly out of date. . . . The Federal Government of course retains the right to approve these local plans in the war on poverty, but, instead of centralizing its power, it is actually creating new centers of political power and a whole new class of political managers and educators. . . . In the upper peninsula [of Michigan] an organization has been set up to administer the programs in fifteen poor counties, and this is just one other example of the new breed of public servants coming into American political life today. . . . A new political structure is being created in America.[4]

The problem of legitimacy

If community action agencies are to function in this way, they must be free to arbitrate between national and local demands, pursuing the long-term need through the tangle of immediate pressures. The search for a less political planning may depend on whether the community's leaders recognize the need, and are united enough to give it scope for the sake of the federal money it attracts; but the planners themselves cannot be identified with any single government or lobby. The planner's ability to negotiate the political issues itself depends upon a professional neutrality which can alone earn the trust of all parties. Although a planner must ultimately answer to government, he tests the political will against his own judgment, without taking elected representatives as the only spokesmen to whom he need pay attention. As the determination of policy becomes more and more complex, disinterested professional understanding begins to seem more relevant than the presumable views of an inadequately informed electorate, which expresses through its choice of leaders only a vague consensus. To protect the long-term interests of society from the capricious interpretation of the majority vote, the planner must of necessity be free to pursue long-term goals which have been sanctioned by society despite the short-term contradictions of the traditional democratic apparatus of elected government and its subordinate bureaucracy.

But this aloofness is also suspect, since it seems to put the planner's decisions beyond the control of democracy. The authority of community action depends not only on disinterested social analysis, but on its political sensitivity. If it alienates powerful interests, the delicate balance between federal and local participation is upset. The institutions on which the implementation of programs depend will set themselves to outmaneuver policies they resent, and by this battle of wits the whole endeavor can be fatally disrupted, since the only weapons are the withdrawal or refusal of funds. Community action must, then, be dispassionate enough to arbitrate convincingly the claims of different interests, using its federal backing to bargain for far-sighted reconciliation.

In the pursuit of goals the community action agency cannot be a single-minded lobby for the poor. Its own position as an agent of social justice will be much stronger if the poor are organized to press their demands. But if it undertakes this organization itself, it must either enfeeble the organization of the poor, or undermine the claim of community action to represent the best interests of the community as a whole. Nor can it be mainly a research outfit. True, it needs to adjust its work continually in the light of carefully collected information fed back from its programs, and to review from time to time its general direction. But its success depends on a flexibility incompatible with controlled experimentation. New techniques must be first proved apart from the world of action, where an exactly determined failure can be accepted as more useful than imperfectly analyzable success.

If, then, planning does not represent unambiguously any one legitimate interest, or the expertise of social science, how are its decisions justified? Given that the federal government, the state, and the community's leaders are willing for the sake of more coherent, adaptable, and far-reaching policies to surrender some part of their prerogative, how does the planning agency interpret the freedom it has been granted? Unless the planner's role can be reconciled with the principles of representative government, he may well be repudiated as soon as the issue comes into the open.

This difficulty seems to have been obscured by the slogan of a "war on poverty." A war implies an enemy, and the military metaphor breaks down as soon as you seek to give this enemy an identifiable persona. Who defends poverty? The only recognizable villains are a rabble of racketeers—camp followers who surely could not challenge the will of a nation. Poverty cannot be projected as an external evil, but arises out of the structure of society itself. If war at all, the attack on poverty is a civil war against narrow self-interest, where the generals who lead the campaign are themselves confused by doubtful loyalties. So the image of community action mobilizing resources against a common enemy disguises the conflicts of interest it must somehow master. If it is to defend its decisions, it may need to formulate and establish the principles on which its legitimacy rests. And this raises issues which are hard to resolve within a democratic ideology.

The legitimation of planning

The planner's right to take decisions seems to lie in the understanding that he is concerned with means, not ends—a technician computing the best solution to a given problem. So long as the problem is defined for him by some democratic process, he usurps no political prerogative. This is all very well, provided that the best solution looks the same from every legitimate point of view, and that the advantages and disadvantages of alternative choices can be objectively estimated in comparable terms. Unfortunately, such is rarely the case in any social planning. Take, for instance, the relatively limited question of highway layout. If the planner's only problem were to maximize the flow of traffic, the choices might be manageable according to a technical analysis. But since roads also destroy amenities, divert customers, and influence the development of housing, the decisions will have different consequences for different people, and what they gain or lose cannot be measured on a single yardstick. How much is unspoiled countryside worth compared with so much faster traffic? How does the noise and danger to a neighborhood weigh against the convenience of commuters? The planner's choices lie between various kinds of benefit which distribute unequally to different interests. But it is just such complex problems which most need rational assessment.

Faced with the intrinsic difficulty of submitting social decisions to impartial cost-benefit analysis, the attempt can be abandoned altogether, in favor of the more anarchic resolution of competing interests. If everyone campaigns for his own choice, a tolerable compromise should work itself out.[5] But in practice, the outcome is characteristically much less constructive. Either the conflict ends in stalemate, or the compromise is scarcely rational from any point of view. Communities can be led into "neurotic" solutions, where the balance of power comes to rest in an organization that cannot function, but serves to disguise the unresolved issues.

A rough analogy may help to make this clearer. Suppose that football has lost its vitality, because the defensive skills of the teams are too evenly matched. Neither side can win, or even bring off an exciting play, so efficient are its opponent's blocking tactics. This deadlock is frustrating to players and spectators alike. The game stultifies in abortive maneuvers, and everyone would prefer a liberating change in its rules or strategies. But the players cannot agree on any plan of reform, since each will naturally put forward suggestions which enhance his own position in the team or his team's chance of winning. As interested parties, they agree upon the ultimate purpose, but each will seek to reconcile it with his own immediate advantage. The proposed reform waits upon interminable wrangles. Any viable solution depends upon the intervention of a disinterested arbitrator.

The civil rights conflict is in danger of reaching such a stalemate again. The relatively impartial Supreme Court set in motion recent governmental action to reduce segregation in schools. Certain changes resulted, and then a backlash of opposition set in. Locally, political pressures forced these developments to a halt, or at least slowed them down. The federal government and certain voluntary groups, such as the churches, are seeking ways to break off the seeming stalemate. For a time, confusion and uncertainty dominate the scene.

In such a situation no party in power can itself altogether fulfill the arbitrator's function, since, in a democracy, it cannot easily escape the calculation of its own immediate electoral advantage. It needs to put policy beyond the reach of short-sighted intervention, by submitting its mandate to the control of another kind of authority. Whatever decisions government takes must also be rational: and the rationality of alternative choices can only be convincingly analyzed in detachment from political pressure. Therefore at some stage, and to some degree, decisions must be taken out of the political context and handed over to the planner. The more complex the problems, and the longer the perspective in which they need to be examined, the more decisive is the planner's influence likely to become. So the crucial dilemma of planning cannot be avoided: the problems can only be solved by dispassionate analysis, but the costs and benefits to be analyzed do not easily lend themselves to objective assessment.

American planners confront this dilemma more directly than in European democracies, where government is more centralized, and more elitist, and where the impulse to plan has arisen from economic rather than social problems. At least in theory, an economic plan deals in alternatives with a measurable outcome—the maximizing of national wealth. But what is the desired outcome of a social plan? If it is defined in utilitarian terms as the greatest happiness of the greatest number, how is a unit of happiness to be determined?

Here again one can seek to avoid the difficulty by treating the planner as an advocate for a particular point of view. Given that the complexity of social problems calls for expert analysis, why should not every interest promote its own plan? Even though they are not measurable, the costs and benefits of alternative decisions can then be evaluated in terms of the client's interest. The political conflict is now engaged between policies which are, at least, rational solutions from some standpoint. But since the outcome of political conflict is usually compromise, the fundamental difficulty only reappears at another level. If the compromise between the plans of interested parties is itself to be rational, it too must be planned. Advocacy requires adjudication. Thus the planner as advocate implies another planner as judge, who can interpret the arguments to the jury. And we are still left with the question: by what body of law does the arbitrator of social plans justify his recommendations?

In practice, the consensus of values which seems to inform society offers a planner the only frame of reference for his arguments. He can exploit a common set of principles much as a judge exploits common law, or the notion of natural justice. The principles are certainly very general, and can easily be pursued into mutual contradiction. But however controversial their interpretation, at least they provide a context in which an analysis of problems can be disinterestedly presented. And this suggests how planning relates to politics in a democratic society.

As the determination of policy devolves upon the planner, the politician becomes correspondingly more concerned to maintain the consensus on which it ultimately rests. Planning is pragmatically legitimized by political sleight of hand. The successful politician cultivates every interest, and having gained its confidence, interprets it in the most general and noncommittal terms, as if all were aspects of a united purpose. By asserting the consensus, by tirelessly presenting the needs of each as the needs of all, by more intimate bargaining, he upholds a sense of priorities loose enough to accommodate divergent claims, but from which a rough evaluation of costs and benefits can be derived. Thus political leadership becomes less concerned with deciding policy issues than with promoting a language in which the issues can be argued. That is, its principal function is to legitimize planning, not so much by endorsing the specific outcome as by establishing the assumptions from which an objective analysis of problems can take its departure.

If it is once accepted that the interaction of immediate interests need not result in a sensible policy from any point of view, the rest seems to follow. Some form of planning, authoritative enough to override these interests, must intervene. But in a democratic society, governments at every level remain highly sensitive to the impulses of the electorate: their lives are short, and too austere a preoccupation with long-term needs soon robs them of a mandate to attempt anything at all. Nor are all sections of the electorate equally able to apply political sanctions. Planning, therefore, has to be withdrawn from close political control. But since its only independent authority lies in the rationality of its analysis, it cannot function without a generally accepted basis of argument. Since social planning deals in costs and benefits which can only be subjectively assessed, it must appeal to a common system of values. And this only political leadership can provide. The electoral process which, as a way of deciding issues, seems both crude and illogical, works much more ably to define a consensus. The plausible ingratiation, windy slogans, and vague promises which characterize most political campaigns do not merely manipulate votes in the service of personal ambition. They assimilate very diverse desires to a single conception of social purposes that is only partly spurious. But the trick would hardly come off unless, beneath the manifest conflicts, the consensus had some foundation.

No society could even try to submit its decisions to rational calculation, if the rationalization rested on wholly hypocritical assumptions. Planning implies an underlying utilitarian philosophy, from which the manipulation of public opinion derives an honorable logic. Except in the vaguest terms, this philosophy is never made explicit: political leaders often assert the national interest, but wisely do not try to explain just how they have worked it out from all the competing interests which make up the nation. But even if personal moral choices can never be excluded altogether from the weighing of alternatives, there lies behind the concept of planning something more than an illusion of a coherent system of thought; there exists a hard core of reality in which conflicting interests find satisfaction in newly discovered patterns of action.

Though an argument of this kind can in theory confirm the planner's intellectual authority, by clarifying the logical connection between his specific proposals and the shared values on which they ultimately rest, it helps him only where these values and their interpretation are indeed both shared and honored. In the last resort, moral values can only be asserted, and the humanity of social policy depends upon the courage, the imagination, the persistence, and the success with which the ideals of social justice are promoted. The community planner, whose role we have tried to analyze, can only work within the context of a prevailing sense of the common interest. His authority is technical, not moral. He cannot displace the radical reformer whose sense of what ought to be refuses to compromise with what is, any more than the radical can dismiss the social engineer whose patient maneuvers he scorns. But within these limits, community action could provide a setting in which a politically sensitive planner, by channelling federal resources expertly to meet the variety of local needs, could substantially advance the liberties of those who are poorest—and in doing so, make the towns and cities of America better places for anyone to live.

NOTES

1. The evidence on which the authors' conclusions are based consists of interviews with local planners and officials in the study city. Details of the study are contained in Martin Rein and Peter Marris, *Dilemmas of Social Reform: Poverty and Community Action in the United States* (New York: Atherton Press, 1967).
2. The term "redistribution" is used here to mean the distribution of federal tax funds to support local functions, and to move them in one direction or another. This may have an economic redistributive function but only in the most general sense.
3. The community action agencies have, among other steps, organized the poor and the segregated to protest their neglect more effectively, through tenant and citizen associations; they have financed low-cost legal services with which the poor can attack inequities in the administration of public services; they have placed municipal authorities behind the effort to equalize the quality of education for residents of segregated districts; they have organized self-help cooperatives and special training programs for the socially inept or unskilled.
4. James Reston, "Detroit: Power and the Governors," *The New York Times,* June 24, 1966, p. 36.
5. Charles E. Lindblom, for instance, points out, in *The Intelligence of Democracy: Decision Making Through Mutual Adjustment* (New York: The Free Press of Glencoe, 1965), p. 296: "One of the merits of partisan mutual adjustment is that it is adapted to situations in which there are no criteria adequate for resolution of a policy problem by a central decision maker." He argues that this mutual adjustment involves a rational assessment of alternatives. But though each individual decision-maker may be calculating rationally, it does not follow that the collective outcome will be rational.

28

The Community Action Program: A New Function for Local Government

DAVID A. GROSSMAN

The Economic Opportunity Act of 1964 added many activities to the federal government's efforts to aid low-income families and individuals. One of these new features, the community action program,[1] represents a major new function for local government. While it may still be too early, after only two years of operation, to assess the community action program's full potential and significance, it is possible to sketch the major ideas and issues involved in this new endeavor, in an effort to place the community action program in the broader context of urban social change with which it was designed to cope.

Origins of the program

The community action program was initially developed as one of a series of competitive proposals put forward in response to President Lyndon B. Johnson's announcement of a war on poverty, a major feature of his first State of the Union Message in January, 1964. The presidential declaration appears to have had its origins in the "new economics" of the Kennedy administration, when the Council of Economic Advisers, relying on neo-Keynesian analyses, advised the President of the potential rise in Gross National Product possible in an expanding peacetime economy. Rising GNP, they reasoned, would be accompanied by rising federal revenues. These, in turn, offered an opportunity to expand the economy further by correcting the maldistribution of personal income that saw a fifth of the nation's population living on submarginal incomes. This analytic insight was undoubtedly spurred on by influences such as Michael Harrington's penetrating analysis of American poverty—and by Dwight McDonald's even more widely read review of Harrington's book in the *New Yorker*. Yet another major factor influencing the decision was President Johnson's own clear recollection of Franklin D. Roosevelt's New Deal to which the generation of his youth had dedicated itself, and his deep desire to get on with what he saw as America's unfinished business.

The State of the Union Message announced that there would be a national war on poverty, but it did not set forth in any detail the way in which the war was to be fought. To this question, federal domestic agencies, as well as other interested national interest groups and organizations, promptly addressed themselves. The conflicting proposals of these agencies and organizations, and their vigorous attempts to win for themselves and their policies the key role in the war on poverty, culminated in the President's designation of Sargent Shriver, then director of the Peace Corps, as the coordinator of federal planning for the war on poverty. A Presidential Task Force led by Mr. Shriver assembled talent and ideas to develop what became the Economic Opportunity Act of 1964.

The principal features of the Act were, first, the creation of a new branch of the Executive Office of the President—the Office of Economic Opportunity—as the focal point of the new program and, second, the creation of a wide range of new or modified federal programs as the initial basis of the war on poverty. To some degree, nearly all the major ideas proposed by competing federal agencies were adopted by the Shriver-led task force. Included were a residential program of vocational training camps for youth; a community-based program of publicly financed jobs for unemployed young people; work and earning opportunities for college-bound youth from low-income families; adult literacy programs; rural loans and grants for poor farmers; aid for migrants and loans for small businessmen; a Domestic Peace Corps; work training for welfare recipients; and others. Few, if any, of these programs were wholly new. Most had their origins in predecessor programs or in ideas that had been discussed for years. And each could lay claim to being based on an analysis of American poverty: for example, unemployment was devastatingly high among teenage youth; minority businessmen faced oppressive problems in obtaining capital; poverty was at its most degrading level in rural areas and among migrants. Still, the collection of programs that was proposed left large portions of the poverty population untouched, whether measured in terms of age spectrum, geographic distribution, or other dimensions of poverty.

To fill this gap, or at least to reduce it, since it was early recognized that America's problem of poverty was too large and complex to yield readily even to an ambitious set of new programs, the community action program was included as a major feature of the Economic Opportunity Act.

Community action, too, had predecessors. It, too, was based on an analysis of poverty. But the predecessor programs were relatively recent in origin and the analysis was a novel one.

The direct predecessors of the community action program included a series of Ford Foundation-financed "gray area" projects and the program of the President's Commission on Juvenile Delinquency. The Ford projects and the federal antidelinquency activities proceeded from a common agreement that the serious social problems of urban America demanded new and vigorous efforts to change existing institutions and to create new, more effective ways to combat deprivation and delinquency. These initial attempts were research- and planning-oriented and, to a significant degree, focused on the problems of delinquent youth. Many of them shared an intellectual base in the analyses of gang behavior made by Richard Cloward and Lloyd Ohlin in their book *Delinquency and Opportunity*. In drastically simplified form, the Cloward-Ohlin analysis said: youth from low-income families adapt to the lack of opportunity for acceptable forms of advancement (education, work, stable family life) by antisocial behavior, designed to obtain prestige, money, excitement, and other desirable objects. For them, delinquency is an all-too-normal response to an abnormal society and to inadequate opportunity for more acceptable behavior. To cope with delinquency, or the related problems associated with poverty, it is necessary to change the society that creates delinquency, or at least to change the institutions that fail to offer acceptable, legitimate opportunities.

This analysis of the need for institutional change was persuasive to many people, and the more closely they looked at the glaring inadequacies of the schools, job training, and public services supposedly serving the slums, the more acceptable the thesis appeared. But analysis alone was insufficient. A proposed solution to the problem of inadequate institutions was needed. This came in the form of opportunity-creating projects, designed to change and adapt slum-serving institutions to the needs, abilities, aspirations, and life styles of the poor.

The Ford Foundation made grants to a number of urban communities for neighborhood-scale, evaluation-oriented training and remedial education projects designed to attack the social problems of urban slums. For the most part, the Ford grants were made to new locally created nonprofit corporations directed by imaginative local leadership and including, wherever feasible, public officials from the city government and schools, as well as members of the voluntary agency establishment. There was a deliberate effort to establish in the organizations selected to operate "gray area" projects a spirit of seeking change in the established ways of community institutions.

The Ford Foundation's activities were soon paralleled by those of a new federal agency, the President's Commission on Juvenile Delinquency and Youth Crime. This interagency effort was established by the Juvenile Delinquency and Youth Offenses Control Act of 1961. The President's Commission was directed by then Attorney-General Robert F. Kennedy, and included representatives of the Departments of Labor and Health, Education, and Welfare, as well as the Justice Department. The juvenile delinquency program, from its inception, worked toward a comprehensive and coordinated approach to the underlying social problems that it believed were the causes of juvenile delinquency. With a relatively small initial budget, the juvenile delinquency program stimulated applicant communities to plan comprehensive programs and then to utilize other, available federal funds to help finance their operations. In many cases, it worked with the same local organization as had the Ford Foundation. Among the cities that were financed from both sources were New Haven, Boston, Washington, and Philadelphia.

The Ford Foundation and the juvenile delinquency projects sought to construct comprehensive programs that could overcome the inadequacy of existing social institutions serving low-income populations. A comprehensive approach, rather than concentration on a single function such as education, was seen as essential because of the need to change the entire environment that denied opportunity, fostered delinquency, and maintained poverty. The comprehensive program was seen as involving changes in elementary and secondary education, in prevocational and vocational training, in health services, and in such areas as housing improvement and the provision of legal services to help the poor obtain fair treatment under the law. Few projects developed the full range of possible activities. Perhaps the most successful in this regard were Mobilization for Youth in New York City's Lower East Side and New Haven's Community Progress, Inc., which concentrated its attention on that city's urban renewal areas. Some of the pioneering projects failed to get off the ground at all, caught in the bitter competition among local public and private social welfare and education agencies, whose desire for additional funds was not always paralleled by a willingness to accommodate themselves to institutional change.

The Ford juvenile delinquency experiments had many novel features. But perhaps their single most valuable contribution was their dedication to a comprehensive approach to social problem-solving. They were firmly devoted to an interdisciplinary approach to attacking social problems that wedded traditional public agency concerns (such as education, public assistance, manpower training, urban renewal, and housing) to the traditional concerns of private voluntary agencies (such as those of health and welfare councils, family service agencies, and legal aid societies).

Sargent Shriver's Presidential Task Force on the war against poverty drew heavily on the concepts and experience of the Ford and juvenile delinquency efforts in developing the ideas that became the programmatic and legislative basis for the Community Action Program. To these ideas some new approaches were added.

Legislation and organization

The community action program took its initial shape in administration drafts of the proposed legislation, but it was hammered into final form by Congress, both during initial consideration of the Act in 1964 and subsequently in 1965 and 1966. The central features of the legislation, as ultimately enacted and as modified by subsequent amendments and policy decisions, are:

1. The federal government offers grants-in-aid to pay most of the cost of local anti-poverty efforts.[2] The local share can be provided either in cash or by contributions in local facilities or locally paid personnel. This generous federal support level has undoubtedly been a major stimulus to rapid program growth.

2. Community action programs are operated by community-based rather than state-wide organizations. The initial Republican-backed counterproposal to the administration's community action program concept would have employed the technique of funding localities through state government, rather than directly by a federal agency, in the pattern common to

many HEW programs. This was not adopted, but to reassure state governments a compromise was worked out which gave the governors a veto power over federal grants to most local programs. (This compromise was later revised to allow the Director of OEO to "unveto" governors' vetoes.)

While the gubernatorial veto was much discussed and argued over in the early days of the program, it seems clear by now that it has had relatively little direct effect on the operation of the community action program. The veto has been rarely used—less than a dozen times altogether—and while the threat of its use may have affected the design or operation of some local projects, its overall impact appears to have been small.

3. A single community-wide agency, which has become known as an "umbrella" agency in the technical jargon of the war on poverty, is the preferred vehicle to receive all federal antipoverty funds and to coordinate the local antipoverty program. This decision received the brunt of congressional attention both in 1964 and subsequently. Congress weakened the original Administration proposal, which would have staked out a near-monopoly for umbrella agencies covering an entire political jurisdiction. Despite this, the "umbrella" pattern of a single coordinating agency spread to most communities that started community action projects. To emphasize its continuing concern, Congress adopted in 1966 a requirement that OEO bypass its favored community-wide agencies by granting at least 5 per cent of Title II-A funds to independent local agencies that were not part of the umbrella organization. Despite congressional worries, a clearly predominant role was marked out for community-wide agencies because of the acceptability of the umbrella idea to most localities. Mayors and other local leaders recoiled against the idea of a multiplicity of uncoordinated local agencies receiving federal funds to war on poverty and insisted on a single central local agency. To reduce the level of conflict over this issue, OEO has taken two steps. First, it has made grants to independent or "single-purpose" agencies, especially in localities where no coordinating umbrella or community action agency had yet been created. In addition, another device went far to reduce both congressional and local friction over the monopoly issue: OEO allowed and encouraged community action agencies to contract with other public and private nonprofit agencies to conduct component projects of a community action program. Thus, each single community-wide agency tends to have many operating "delegate" agencies carrying out parts of its program. In Chicago, for example, more than twenty-five different public and private agencies carry out projects under contract to the Chicago Committee on Urban Opportunity, the city-wide community action agency.

4. Both public and private nonprofit agencies are eligible recipients of federal funds. Lobbying efforts made on behalf of local government to restrict eligible grant recipients to public agencies were defeated in favor of allowing eligibility to private nonprofit organizations to be eligible. Congressional fear of domination of the program by mayors, and the self-protective instincts of private voluntary agencies, played major parts in this decision.

In practice, most community action agencies (about three-quarters of the total) have been organized as private nonprofit corporations. But the uniform presence of public officials on their governing bodies, and the role of public officials in creating many of them, has given to these private organizations a considerable measure of "quasi-public" character.

5. The range of eligible community action activities is broad enough to create a comprehensive program. A virtually unparalleled flexibility in the original legislation has allowed community action programs to include a broad array of activities in the fields of health, welfare, vocational training, housing, and the many other social services which low-income families need. Virtually the only major legislative restriction that has been placed on program breadth is in the field of education, where OEO funding is restricted to "remedial and non-curricular" activities.[3]

6. The community action program is intended to play a concerting or coordinating role with regard to other federal programs. The inclusion of legislative language providing that all federal administrators shall give "preference" to requests for aid that will constitute a "component" of community action program clearly established this objective.[4] Steps to achieve the statutory preferential treatment were slow in developing, in part because it was first necessary for OEO to create a network of local community action agencies capable of exercising a coordinating effect, and in part because of the inherent difficulties of coordination of federal agency activities. A significant step in this direction has been the promulgation of agreements between OEO and other federal agencies on a "checkpoint" procedure for advance coordination of local applications for funds between community action agencies and other local applicants for federal funds. These agreements are now operative for Title I of the Elementary and Secondary Education Act, the Neighborhood Youth Corps, the welfare work-experience program, and the Department of Housing and Urban Development's neighborhood facilities and leased housing programs. Other coordinating efforts have included joint funding by OEO and other federal agencies of manpower, pre-school education, and comprehensive health programs operated by community action agencies.

7. The definition of a community action program states that such a program is one which is developed, conducted, and administered with the "maximum feasible participation of the residents of the areas and members of the groups to be served." There are few, if any, known precedents for this requirement and it seems clear, in retrospect, that the phrase took on a meaning, perhaps latent, but presumably not overt in the minds of most participants in the legislative process. To the extent that there were precedents for the participation concept, they were to be found primarily in the employment of poor persons in Ford and juvenile delinquency projects in nonprofessional roles such as aides and "bridge persons" to work in the local community and to gain on-the-job experience in the social services fields. The question of resident participation was barely discussed at all during the extensive 1964 congressional hearings on the Economic Op-

portunity Act. The considerable impact of the "maximum feasible participation" phrase, and the ways in which its meaning has developed in practice and through post-1964 legislative history, are discussed later in this essay.

The seven features of the community action program noted above do not, of course, constitute a full and exhaustive description of the important issues in the legislation. Nor do they fully account for the many controversies over the program which have made daily reading in the newspapers of the nation for the last two years. Such issues as the role of the states in providing technical assistance and aid (and occasionally obstructions as well) to local antipoverty programs, the publicity given to supposedly high salaries of community action agency employees and their feared participation in local politics, the role of mayors and private voluntary agencies, the funding levels and formulas for distribution of community action grants, and many others are worthy of more exploration and analysis than is possible within the scope of the present article. This process has begun in such publications as a recent report of the Advisory Commission on Intergovernmental Relations on intergovernmental aspects of the program,[5] but there is ample material yet untouched to fuel many dozens of articles, books, and dissertations.

Principal elements of community action

The preceding brief survey of the major features of the community action program provides a setting for an examination of its two dominant elements —the effort to develop comprehensive service programs to attack poverty and the involvement of the poor themselves as active participants in this process. These two elements are consistent with each other in terms of an analysis of poverty as a problem of inadequate institutional response; but they have called forth very different programmatic responses. Their interplay has done much to shape the character of the community action program in its first two years.

The first of these elements—the approach to institutional inadequacy through the construction of a more effective, comprehensive framework of social services—involves the creation of new service arrangements. Prominent among these arrangements has been creation of the broadly based, coordinating community action agency and of its net of contractual relationships with the public and private organizations to which it delegates responsibility for operation of many of its action projects. A second, equally important aspect has been the role of the community action agency in filling gaps in the existing social services system with opportunity-offering projects. In the comprehensive approach, the services needed by the low-income population are seen as units of an overall community service system with such major subsystems as the following:

1. The educational system, made up of public and private schools, libraries, and other local and state agencies providing educational services. Com-

munity action programs have placed major emphasis in their own activities on pre-school education to prepare the children of poverty for their subsequent experience with the public school, and remedial education, and tutorial programs to bring personal attention to the child locked into a rigid and depersonalized school system.

2. The employment system, including the state-federal employment security system, apprenticeship agencies, private and public employers, labor unions, educational agencies that train and retrain workers for specific occupations, and vocational rehabilitation agencies. Community action agencies have increasingly devoted attention to manpower training and development, and in a number of notable instances have fostered establishment of comprehensive manpower units that cover the full gamut of outreach, recruitment, assessment, basic education, prevocational and vocational training, placement, and follow-up. Emphasis has been placed, too, on the roles that poor and uneducated persons can play as nonprofessional workers in such jobs as teacher's aides, health aides, and multipurpose and outreach workers.

3. The family welfare system, including the public assistance agency and private family welfare agencies that provide services such as casework and counseling. Community action agencies have not themselves provided any direct welfare assistance to the poor, but they have expanded homemaking, home management, counseling, and related welfare services available to the poor.

Community action agencies have also sought to work with, and to supplement, the activities of local agencies in the other service systems devoted to health, housing, economic development, consumer information and credit, and legal services.

An idea of the range of social services that have been provided by community action programs can be seen in the following table, which lists the categories of service that have been included in community action programs funded by OEO through October, 1966.

Constructing a new, tighter, more effective network of arrangements among the social services provided to the poor is a challenging and difficult task to which the knowledge and negotiating ability of local administrators have not always proven adequate. In only a few communities, with New Haven, Connecticut, as the often-cited example, has there been the combination of political skill and administrative competence needed to attract sizable amounts of federal, state, and local funds and to knit them together into an effective whole. Other urban communities whose performance approaches New Haven's (though none yet comes close to surpassing it) include Detroit and St. Louis. In each case effective local leadership, in both the public and private spheres, has been combined with good staff and good program ideas. The progress made in these communities provides a goal for the 1,000 other urban and rural jurisdictions that have established community action agencies and have set out to establish comprehensive antipoverty programs.

Table 28–1. Funds Obligated by OEO for Community Action Programs, by Category of Service, from November, 1964, through October, 1966.

Category of Service	Amount in Millions
Housing and home management	$18
Health	31
Employment opportunity	31
Job and vocational education and training	30
Financial assistance	3
Legal services	27
Multi-purpose neighborhood centers	80
Special welfare services	10
Summer Head Start	193
Full-year Head Start, nursery, and day care	163
Education	123
Educational services	15
Physical facilities	16
Social programs	63
Small business development	9
Program development, administration, staff training, and evaluation	165
Total, All Categories	$977

Source: Office of Economic Opportunity.

The fact that only a few communities have realized this objective is clear evidence that it is a difficult one. The techniques of program planning, coordination, operation, and evaluation needed to complete the task are as yet in their infancy. The fact is, though, that the crucial first steps have been taken: the task has been recognized, the mobilization of community resources has begun, the work is under way.

"Maximum feasible participation"

Paralleling this nationwide beginning toward the building of new patterns of social services has been progress toward the second element of community action, the participation of the poor. The origins of this idea are less clear than is the pattern of experimental projects that led to the idea of a comprehensive program of antipoverty services. Few, if any, parallels to the concept of participation of the poor, at least in the form in which it has now become a subject of wide discussion, can be found in the Ford Foundation or juvenile delinquency projects. True, many of them did include an emphasis on creating new job roles for the poor in such capacities as aides to social workers and teachers. Some included a few area residents on one or another of their advisory boards. Some engaged in community organization efforts to establish local groups to discuss the problems of welfare clients and the worries of neighborhood residents over plans for urban renewal. But the theme of participation, where it was present, elicited little comment and was rarely cited as a major program feature.

The inclusion of the requirement for "maximum feasible participation" of the poor in the administration proposals for the text of the Economic Opportunity Act aroused little attention from Congress during the extensive pre-enactment hearings of 1964. And except for a brief statement on the subject by Attorney-General Kennedy, administration spokesmen were either silent or, when questioned, referred to potential roles for nonprofessional workers and to possible appointment of local advisory groups. Neither the House nor the Senate committees that held hearings on the Economic Opportunity Act in 1964 referred to "maximum feasible participation" in more than cursory fashion in their reports. The initial policy publication of the Office of Economic Opportunity[6] placed emphasis on "resident participation" and suggested—but did not specifically require—alternative means by which it might be achieved. One of the suggestions was employment of nonprofessional workers chosen from the ranks of the poor, another was the use of neighborhood councils as advisors, a third was the inclusion of representatives of low-income neighborhoods on the policy-making body of a community action agency. What happened to cause this little-discussed subject to become a matter of national concern, vigorously debated in the halls of Congress, in city halls, indeed wherever the war on poverty was discussed?

The year 1964 was notable for more than passage of the Economic Opportunity Act. Another measure of at least equal historical significance was adopted in the same year: the Civil Rights Act of 1964. These two new laws were seen as intimately related, particularly by the leaders of the civil rights movement, which itself expressed overtones of a participatory democracy that had been dormant in American life for decades. The Civil Rights Act was to open up opportunities for Negroes and other minorities to claim long-overdue rights; the Economic Opportunity Act was to make the exercise of these rights more than a theoretical possibility for the vast proportion of these minorities who were trapped in poverty. This legislative combination clearly had much to do with the way the "maximum feasible participation" phase was interpreted by Negroes, and to a lesser extent by Puerto Rican, Mexican-American, and other minority groups awakening to a consciousness of their rightful role in American society.

Across the nation, the local meetings at which community action agencies were organized in 1964 and 1965 began to consider the meaning of the "maximum feasible participation" phrase. OEO, too, re-examined its initial policy stance on the role of the poor in community action programs. The second issue of the agency's basic policy document[7] included a mandatory requirement that the residents of each of the low-income "target" areas to be served by a community action program must be represented on the policy-making body of each grantee agency.

While OEO's requirements on what constituted an adequate local response to providing participation for the poor remained flexible, a developing consensus, both within the agency and in the Congress, settled on a pattern by which at least one-third of the seats on a community action agency's governing body were to be held by directly selected representatives of the poor. In some communities, such as San Francisco, representatives of the poor held more than half of such positions. In others, such as Chicago, few identifiable members of the community action agency's governing body could be considered to have been selected by the poor.

It took time for the consensus on representation of the poor to harden into law. OEO's general position on the meaning of "maximum feasible participation" was extensively discussed and considered by both houses of Congress during 1965. The result of these discussions, which generated considerable heat at times, was a reaffirmation of the section of the Act that specified "maximum feasible participation" with widespread evidence of general approval by the Congress of the flexible position taken by OEO. But during the 1966 congressional session, a Republican proposal to set as a minimum requirement that one-third of the members of every community action agency governing body be representatives of the poor and that these representatives must actually be selected by the poor was accepted by the administration and was adopted with little debate. Thus, a little-heralded development which has been seen by many social scientists as having near-revolutionary implications for the operation of social service programs was quietly and inauspiciously written into federal law.

These two different themes, the comprehensive approach and participation of the poor, have been of fundamental importance in shaping the community action program. Their influences have, at times, appeared to conflict; at other times they clearly reinforce one another. Conflict may arise, for example, when the opinions of neighborhood residents, expressed through effective and powerful neighborhood councils, differ with the conclusions reached by the central administrative structure of a community action agency over priorities, need, and acceptability of particular projects or activities. Such differences may serve as a challenge to the program administrators to educate residents as to why a proposed activity is more feasible or desirable than another alternative, or they may even—wonder of wonders —cause the administrators to reconsider their course of action. Surely differences between planners and policy-makers are not new; need the fact that the policy-makers speak in the accents of poverty and from a basis of urgency and past disappointment make this a unique, unsolvable arrangement?

At times, the potential for conflict between the comprehensive and participatory approaches has even been raised to the level of doctrine. The comprehensive approach is seen as a "consensus" model in which differences are to be adjudicated and compromised out. The "umbrella" community action agency, dominated by the public and private welfare establishment, is seen as the natural habitat for reaching this consensus. In contrast, the participatory approach, raised to an extreme, has been seen as a "conflict" model that mounts an attack on the establishment as its natural course, and builds the self-confidence of the poor as it unveils the hypocrisy of the establishment. The "conflict" model has had its most outspoken advocate in Saul Alinsky; among OEO-funded projects, its most prominent exponent has been the community development project in Syracuse, an effort to organize the poor around the focus of their problems. OEO's acceptance of both themes in its general policy, and the impure way in which the themes have worked out in practice in most communities, have confused clear theory. Alinsky-influenced groups—such as The Woodlawn Organization of Chicago and other neighborhood-based participatory organizations, among them the Westminster Association of Los Angeles and the Blazer Youth Council of Newark—work under the umbrella, as delegates of their local community action agencies. In other communities, the umbrella agencies themselves are dominated by neighborhood representatives, as in San Francisco. And nearly everywhere, OEO's insistence that neighborhood representatives have a significant degree of policy-making power, together with a rapidly expanding pattern of neighborhood councils with the power to initiate and to veto program proposals, has meant that most community action agencies combine the participatory with the comprehensive approach.

A good example of how the two themes of community action interact and reinforce one another can be seen in the case of the neighborhood multi-service center which has become an important feature of nearly every urban community action program. The multi-service center is in itself a microcosm of the community action program. It seeks to bring a comprehensive range of social services physically closer to the poor by its location and psychologically closer by associating them in a single facility. It is ideally suited to participation by local residents on its advisory or policy-making board and as a locus for employment of local, nonprofessional residents in policy-influencing jobs as community organizers, aides, and outreach workers. Within the multi-service center, too, the tensions between the two themes can be seen. A recent conference sponsored by OEO on the subject of the neighborhood center, attended by community action agency and center directors and board members from a dozen cities where the neighborhood center system is most firmly established, spent much of its time discussing alternate concepts of center emphasis. One school of thought, with the Syracuse and Washington, D.C., representatives as its most ardent advocates, stressed the participatory role of the neighborhood center. It should serve, they argued, primarily as a focal point for organizing and vitalizing the neighborhood, leaving the mere provision of services to established agencies to whose inadequacies center-created groups could address their vigorous attention. Others from Chicago, Atlanta, and Oakland argued for the center as a locus of improved services which otherwise would never reach the poor or would run them through the rat race of referral. Cincinnati, St. Louis, and Cleveland took a middle course, attempting to merge the functions so that each could reinforce the other. A quick review of the more than 200 OEO-funded neighborhood center systems (operating a total of about 800 centers) suggests that the middle way may be dominant nationally in this as in other respects.

The rise of national emphasis programs

A factor that was not clearly contemplated in the original thinking that gave rise to the community action program also raises questions about the degree to which the comprehensive and participatory themes can continue to operate in tandem. This is the increasing prominence being given to national emphasis programs fostered by the federal government and "sold" to local communities. The earliest and most successful of these is Head Start, which began in the summer of 1965 as a crash effort to provide pre-school experience to poor children about to enter school. Enriched with medical examination and treatment, nutrition programs, and social, psychological, and parent-education elements, Head Start won instant approval from thousands of localities. Further "packaged" programs followed, as OEO responded to the difficulties of community action agencies in designing effective projects of their own by offering such activities as the Upward Bound program for pre-college students, Legal Services programs designed to help counter the fact that the legal profession was failing to meet the needs of poor persons with legal problems, the Foster Grandparents program to employ the aged to provide personal attention to institutionalized children, Medicare Alert to recruit potential beneficiaries for Medicare, and others.

Congressional attention was given to the national emphasis idea during the 1966 legislative session, and the merits of a locally conceived, locally planned community action program were argued in opposition to the idea of clearly designated program components to which nation-wide emphasis would be given. The latter won, to a very considerable degree, and the discretion available to OEO to allow local communities to set their own priorities was considerably whittled down by the "earmarking" of much of the community action funds. Nearly two-thirds of all available funds under Title II-A were set aside for such national emphasis programs as Head Start, Legal Services, Comprehensive Health Centers, Adult Basic Education, Work-Training for the unemployed, aid to narcotics addicts, and small loans to needy families. The portion of funds left in the "versatile" category, which communities could devote to purposes their own policy-makers feel are most important, was whittled down to the point where it can do little more than refund existing community action projects.

Paralleling the congressional designation of national emphasis programs has been the advancement of OEO's own planning efforts, based on continuing analyses of the characteristics of poverty and the relative effectiveness of alternative solutions. While in general this planning has reaffirmed the soundness of much of the original community action concept, it has given rise to some tendency to substitute a national judgment of priorities among functional activities for the local initiative that has been an important asset in the successful marriage between the comprehensive and participatory themes. This is not to say that national appraisals of program effectiveness and emphasis will necessarily deny local initiative; they do, however, raise new issues to which the mechanisms of a locally based community action effort must adapt.

The role of local planning

If a national decision on program emphasis were to reflect a very different assessment of needs from that seen by the local community, and especially by the poverty population, new conflicts could arise between the comprehensive and participatory approaches to community action. At least one way out of this possible conflict can be found in a more effective local planning process that would have its impact on national plans, just as the latter do on local choices. OEO has already begun to finance such local planning efforts in cities whose community action programs have reached the degree of sophistication where program priorities can be assigned on a more rational basis than the approval of whatever local agency idea is well enough detailed to warrant submission to OEO. Further, plans are well advanced to require comprehensive antipoverty planning by every community action agency, in an effort to get these agencies to recognize the need to make choices among alternative uses of OEO funds and to plan for the use of other available federal funds at the same time.

To be successful, human resources planning will have to cope with the two themes of community action. With regard to planning for the comprehensive approach, the "state of the art" must be considerably advanced, so that adequate appraisals can be made of the necessary and desirable linkages among different activites designed to aid the poor. Also, a far greater capacity will be needed than now exists to calculate the relative costs and benefits of alternative actions. Some signs that this is feasible are apparent. For example, on a cost-effectiveness basis with an absolute reduction in the number of poor persons as the principal value, family planning or birth-control activities can be clearly seen to have a very high pay-off. For another instance, while such an essential question as the relative merit of a summer Head Start experience (at less than $200 per child) versus a year-long exposure to pre-school (at about $1,000 per child) cannot be answered with great assurance, a growing body of evaluative evidence suggests that the short-term experience may have little or no lasting value, but that the benefits of the long-term project do last.

The aspect of local antipoverty planning that is most closely linked to the participatory theme is the process of making decisions, or choosing among alternate courses of action. The involvement of the poor in this process raises some new questions, especially for planners accustomed to dealing with a small number of sophisticated decision-makers whose life styles and value systems closely resemble those of the planners. Techniques of client analysis may be of value in this process, but so will the real-life experience the planners can gain if they enter the arena of vigorous neighborhood participation that characterizes the most effective community action projects.

There is room within this framework for the development of the art of planning as advocacy, in the fashion best described by Paul Davidoff of Hunter College,[8] as well as for the more familiar role of the planner as a technician serving local government.

The future of community action

It is not at all clear, after only two years of operation, what the long-run impact of the community action program will be, either on the level of poverty that afflicts America, or on the many public and private institutions that have addressed themselves to the needs of the poor. Among the factors that cloud the future are the doubtful availability of sufficient funds to allow community action agencies to operate at levels that will get to the roots of poverty. In its first year, OEO was hard pressed to expend $240 million on the community action program, because of the problems encountered in the creation of a new institution, the community action agency. But by 1966, when the local agency structure had been established and the time was ripe to begin making an investment in America's neglected human resources at the levels initially contemplated by the Council of Economic Advisers, the Vietnam war had pre-empted virtually all surplus federal revenues.

Other factors that raise doubts about the future include the stormy political career of OEO as an independent agency vis-à-vis the older, entrenched federal departments who see education, manpower, health, housing, and welfare as coming within their own jurisdictions.

These and other questions about the future course of the community action program are likely to do little more than delay, rather than prevent, the further development of the initiatives it has activated. The participation of the poor in programs designed to serve them and the comprehensive approach to solving human resource problems are ideas that cannot be suppressed, if for no other reason than that there now exist local agencies dedicated to these ideas in 1,000 American communities. Their impact will be felt in the years to come.

Perhaps the most notable contribution of the community action program to ways of thinking about government, as well as about ways to serve the poor, is the very great flexibility that has characterized it. The very fact that the two distinct themes of comprehensiveness and participation could develop simultaneously, and to their mutual benefit, is a welcome innovation in government. This may, indeed, be the most meaningful impact that the program has had and may, in the long run, exceed the other values with which it has been associated: the casting out of shibboleths about what the poor can and can't do for themselves and for the community and the degree to which steadfast and hardened local institutions can respond to a new, more flexible source of funds. The principal lesson of the first two years of the community action program may well turn out to be an enhanced understanding that change can occur, and that the institutional rigidities of American life are less firmly emplaced than we had thought.

NOTES

1. The Community Action Program was authorized in Title II, Part A, of the Economic Opportunity Act of 1964.
2. Ninety per cent for the first three years of the program, declining to 80 per cent after June 30, 1967.
3. This restriction arose as part of a compromise in 1964 that allowed private and religious schools to receive funds on a basis essentially equal to that of public schools. This decision represented a major change in the *status quo ante* of the church-state issue that has arisen with regard to any federal program involving aid to education.
4. This requirement is contained in Sections 211 and 612 of the Economic Opportunity Act. Parallel requirements encouraging coordination by community action agencies is contained in other federal legislation, such as the Elementary and Secondary Education Act of 1965, the Housing and Urban Development Act of 1965, and the Economic Development Act of 1965.
5. U.S. Advisory Commission on Intergovernmental Relations, *Intergovernmental Relations in the Poverty Program* (Washington, D.C., 1966).
6. "Guide to Community Action Program Grants" (Office of Economic Opportunity, November, 1964; mimeographed, labeled "Draft for Discussion Purposes Only").
7. Office of Economic Opportunity, *Community Action Program Guide,* Volume I (Washington, D.C., October 1965).
8. "Advocacy and Pluralism in Planning," *Journal of the American Institute of Planners,* XXXI (November, 1965), 331–338.

Index

Abrams, Charles, quoted, 138
Action for Community Development (Boston), 32, 220
Addams, Jane, 39, 60
Adrian, Charles, 225 *n.*
Adult Basic Education program, 444
Advisory Commission on Intergovernmental Relations, 7, 319, 323, 326, 327, 353, 438
advocacy planning, 311, 328–331
aged, the, payment of demogrant minimum to, 296–297
Aid to Families with Dependent Children (AFDC), 116, 288, 289, 290, 291, 293, 299, 361
Alabama, 344, 345
Alameda County, California, welfare administration in, 362
alcoholism, 45, 75, 259
alienation, from urban political process, 222
Alinsky, Saul D., 180, 187–193 *passim*, 203, 204, 206, 207, 219, 262, 328, 442; quoted, 187, 188, 192, 195, 206
American Civil Liberties Union, 362
American Friends Service Committee, 144
American Institute of Planners, 39 *n.*, 319
American Institute of Public Opinion, 149
Anti-Defamation League of B'nai B'rith, 144
Appalachia program, 287
Area Redevelopment, 287
Arkansas, 344
Aronovitz, Stanley, quoted, 207
Atlanta, 401, 443
Atlantic City, 345
Auden, W. H., 110; quoted, 111
Australia, 298
automation, 13, 52, 246, 247, 248, 269, 274, 275, 276, 338; *see also* technology

Baltimore, Negro population in, 125
Banfield, Edward C., 34, 36, 149, 217; quoted, 149

Bauer, Catherine, 112
Bell, Daniel, quoted, 34
Bell, David, 399
Bellin, Seymour S., 261
benefit-cost analysis, *see* cost-benefit analysis
Berkeley, California, school desegregation in, 164
Birmingham, Alabama, 335, 336, 343
birth control, 300
Black Muslims, 338–339
blockbusting, *modus operandi* of, 130–131
B'nai B'rith Anti-Defamation League, 144
Boston, 219 222, 279, 434; Action for Community Development in, 32, 220; Charlestown area in, 215, 220; North Harvard-Allston area in, 220; playgrounds in, 39; Redevelopment Authority in, 219–220, 322–323; slums of, 63, 64, 70; Washington Park-Roxbury area in, 220; West End redevelopment project in, 215
Bremner, Robert H., 210
Britain, *see* Great Britain
Buffalo, church social service activities in, 199
building codes, 319
Burns, Eveline M., 249, 250, 287–300

Cahn, Edgar S., 330
Cahn, Jean C., 330
California, 316; integration of executive departments in, 35; southern, expansion of population in, 28
Cambridge, Massachusetts, 222
Canada, 293, 299
Caples, William G., 190
Caplovitz, David, 91
Catholic Church, 193, 202, 203
Census, 1960, 127, 139
Census of Governments (1962), 307
Charity Organization Society, 23
Chicago, 189, 203, 204, 207, 209, 442, 443; Association of Community Coun-